Prof. Dr. Gerhard Robbers (ed.)

State and Church in the European Union

Second Edition

In conjunction with the European Consortium for State and Church Research

 Nomos

Die Deutsche Bibliothek – CIP-Einheitsaufnahme

Die Deutsche Bibliothek verzeichnet diese Publikation in
der Deutschen Nationalbibliografie; detaillierte bibliografische
Daten sind im Internet über http://dnb.ddb.de abrufbar.

Die Deutsche Bibliothek – CIP Cataloguing-in-Publication-Data

Die Deutsche Bibliothek lists this publication in the Deutsche
Nationalbibliografie; detailed bibliographic data is available
in the Internet at http://dnb.ddb.de.

ISBN 3-8329-1311-4

2. Auflage 2005
© Nomos Verlagsgesellschaft, Baden-Baden 2005. Printed in Germany. Alle Rechte, auch die des Nachdrucks von Auszügen, der fotomechanischen Wiedergabe und der Übersetzung, vorbehalten. Gedruckt auf alterungsbeständigem Papier.

This work is subject to copyright. All rights are reserved, whether the whole or part of the material is concerned, specifically those of translation, reprinting, re-use of illustrations, broadcasting, reproduction by photocopying machine or similar means, and storage in data banks. Under § 54 of the German Copyright Law where copies are made for other than private use a fee is payable to »Verwertungsgesellschaft Wort«, Munich.

Preface

In its Constitution for Europe the European Union promises to guarantee religious freedom and non-discrimination, to respect religious diversity and to maintain a dialogue with churches, religious communities and non-confessional organisations. At the same time the Union will respect the status of these churches and organisations under Member State's law. The European Union has become aware of the importance of religion. The Union draws inspiration from the religious inheritance of Europe.

With the accession of several new Member States to the European Union, the Union is enriched by new experiences and different needs concerning religion. This is reflected in the progressive development of the civil ecclesiastical law of Member States.

The second edition of this book responds to these developments. It gives an account of the civil ecclesiastical law in all the Member States and in the European Union itself. The contributions follow a similar structure in order to facilitate the comparison between the various systems.

All translations of the reports into English have been revised by Professor David McClean of Sheffield and Penny Granger of Cambridge. All contributions to the first edition have been updated. The updates of the report on Portugal have been translated into English by Mr. Florian Decker. The report on Poland and Spain and all other updates have been translated by myself.

I do thank all those who have contributed to make this book possible, especially Ms. Scholzen-Wiedmann, Ms. Claudia Lehnen, Ms. Christine Mertesdorf and Mr. Michael Rahe.

Trier, Spring 2005   *Gerhard Robbers*

Table of Contents

Rik Torfs
State and Church in Belgium 9

Jiří Rajmund Tretera
State and Church in the Czech Republic 35

Inger Dübeck
State and Church in Denmark 55

Gerhard Robbers
State and Church in Germany 77

Merilin Kiviorg
State and Church in Estonia 95

Charalambos Papastathis
State and Church in Greece 115

Iván C. Ibán
State and Church in Spain 139

Brigitte Basdevant-Gaudemet
State and Church in France 157

James Casey
State and Church in Ireland 187

Silvio Ferrari
State and Church in Italy 209

Achilles Emilianides
State and Church in Cyprus 231

Ringolds Balodis
State and Church in Latvia 253

Jolanta Kuznecoviene
State and Church in Lithuania 283

Alexis Pauly
State and Church in Luxembourg 305

Balázs Schanda
State and Church in Hungary 323

Ugo Mifsud Bonnici
State and Church in Malta 347

Table of Contents

Sophie C. van Bijsterveld
State and Church in the Netherlands 367

Richard Potz
State and Church in Austria 391

Michał Rynkowski
State and Church in Poland 419

Vitalino Canas
State and Church in Portugal 439

Lovro Šturm
State and Church in Slovenia 469

Michaela Moravčíková
State and Church in the Slovak Republic 491

Markku Heikkilä, Jyrki Knuutila, Martin Scheinin
State and Church in Finland 519

Lars Friedner
State and Church in Sweden 537

David McClean
State and Church in the United Kingdom 553

Gerhard Robbers
State and Church in the European Union 577

Rik Torfs
State and Church in Belgium

I. Social Facts

An exact overview of religious adherence in Belgium is difficult. There is no longer a National Census, but even when there was, questions about religion were perceived as incompatible with religious freedom.
However, some statistics do exist. Today the total population of Belgium stands at slightly more than 10 million. Approximately 70 % of the population belongs to the Roman Catholic Church; this is 10 % less than twenty years ago.
The number of Protestants is estimated at between 70,000 and 100,000: less than 1 % of the population.
Muslims, present in Belgium only since the 1960s, represent approximately 4 % of the population.
All the other religious groups are much smaller. There are some 21,000 Anglicans, 40,000 Jews, and more than 60,000 Orthodox.
With regard to the non-believers, numbers are a matter of some debate. Representatives of official movements of non-believers estimate their number at 1.5 million, or 15 % of the population.[1] According to the government, there are only 350,000.[2] The difference may be explained by the fact that although many people do not believe or have agnostic convictions, they do not want to be part of an official and well structured group of non-believers.
In practice, Belgium is characterised by a wide degree of secularisation, which is, according to various experts, more widespread than in countries such as the Netherlands and Germany. But in spite of all this, religion remains an extremely important social phenomenon. As a result of the prominent presence of Islam and the integration process of "new Belgians" in the current society, religion is more than ever before an issue on the political agenda.

---

1 Cf. *Questions and Answers*, Chamber of Representatives, 2000-2001, 13 August 2001, 1003 (Question nr. 373 Van Den Eynde).
2 See www.state.gov/g/drl/rls/inf/2001.

II. Historical Background

The basis for the legal relationship between State and Church is to be found in the Belgian Constitution of 1831. Since that date, there have been amendments to the Constitution on several occasions, yet the main principles governing State and Church have remained in place. The pervading mood of 1830, the year Belgium became independent, can still be felt. It was a time when bright young liberal politicians not only wanted to propagate the modern freedoms, but also wanted to protect them constitutionally. Equally, it was a time when what was a rather progressive Belgian Church was prepared to step forward and to be an ambitious partner in the negotiation of the Constitution. The letter from the Prince de Méan, Archbishop of Mechelen, which was read out before those gathered during the meeting of the National Congress on 17 December 1830, undoubtedly had a major influence on the final form of Articles 14, 15, 16 and 117 of the 1831 Constitution, in which the basis for the relationship between Church and State was to be laid down.[3] After many reforms beginning in the 1970s, the numerical order of the Articles making up the Belgian Constitution was modified. So, since February 1994, the relationship between State and Church has been laid down in Articles 19, 20, 21 and 181.

The Constitution is an historic compromise between Catholics and Liberals. The anti-clerical liberals in the Constituent Assembly abandoned their attempt to exercise absolute governmental supervision over the Church. Meanwhile, Catholic politicians no longer upheld the once privileged position of the Roman Catholic Church.

III. Legal Sources

Church and State relationships in Belgium are largely governed by the Constitution of 1831. Constitutional rights and liberties also apply to various religious matters, for example freedom of education (Art. 24) or freedom of the press (Art. 25). But the Constitution also

---

3 E. *Huyttens*, Discussions du Congrès national de Belgique, I, Brussels, Société typographique belge, 1844, p. 525.

specifically provides for the freedom of religion as such. Four specific Articles are devoted to this topic.

Freedom of worship and its free and public practice are guaranteed under Article 19 of the Constitution, with an exception allowing the punishment of criminal offences committed in the exercise of these freedoms. Article 20 is the negative counterpart of Article 19: no person may be forced to participate in any way in the acts of worship or rites of any religion or to respect its days of rest. Article 21 stresses that the State has no right to interfere with the appointment or induction of the ministers of any religion, to forbid them to correspond with their Church authorities or to publish the latter's Acts, subject to the ordinary rules of liability concerning the use of the press and publications. This Article is generally interpreted as an affirmation of the freedom of internal ecclesiastical organisation. It contains at the same time an exception to this principle by providing that civil marriage must always precede a religious marriage ceremony, except in specific cases established by law.

Finally, Article 181 says that the salaries and pensions of the ministers of a religion should be borne by the State budget.

Recently, the gradual regionalisation of Belgium has had consequences in the relationship between State and Church.[4]

This influence is both *direct* and *indirect*.

Indirectly, the regionalisation of areas such as culture and education has consequences touching the legal position of religion. For instance, the place of religion on radio and television is a regional matter. And although religious education is compulsory according to the Constitution, the interlocutors of churches and religious bodies are chosen at regional level.

Directly, regionalisation has affected religion since the coming into effect of the Law of 13 July 2001. From that time, the regions (and not the federal state) have been responsible for the material organisation of the recognised religions.[5]

Gradually the legal position of religion is becoming a mixed matter. Although the main elements, including the four relevant Articles of the Constitution, remain federal, the influence and competence of the regions is slowly increasing.

There are also ordinary laws or stipulations and statutory provisions concerned with the legal relationship between Church and State.

---

4 J. *Dujardin/E. Vandenbossche*, "De regionalisering van de bestuursinstellingen van de erkende erediensten", Tijdschrift voor Bestuurswetenschappen en Publiek Recht, 2002, p. 447 e.v.
5 Article 4 of the Law of 13 July 2001, Moniteur belge, 3 August 2001.

Here are some examples. Under Article 268 of the Code of Penal Law religious ministers who make direct attacks on the authorities during gatherings held in public are to be punished with a fine and a prison sentence; Articles 143 and 144 of the Code of Penal Law lay down penalties for disturbance, disorder and taunts which stem from worship; Articles 145 and 146 cover the defamation of and assaults upon a minister; Article 228 protects official robes; and Article 267 makes it an offence for ministers to bless marriages before a civil marriage service has been held.

IV. Basic Categories of the System

It is not unusual for the term 'separation of Church and State' to be used as a description to sum up the relationship between the two bodies. This is arguably a somewhat unfortunate choice of terminology.[6] Much depends, of course, on what exactly is understood by 'separation'.[7] If this term gives the impression that Church and State have absolutely nothing to do with each other, then it is an inadequate one. Separation in such a sense cannot be reconciled with Article 181 of the Constitution, in which it is stated that the payment of wages and pensions to ministers of a religion is to be met by the State. Nonetheless, the question is raised as to whether 'separation' necessarily entails an absence of all contact between the two parties.
There is another term, however, which probably brings more clarity to the issue: a number of writers speak of the mutual independence of Church and State.[8] This term emphasises not only the freedom which exists, but also the mutual consideration which, of course, demands at the very least the notion of accepting each other's existence. This all continues to be a delicate affair. Both the independence of Church and State and the prevalence of pluralism in Belgium compel the

---

6 Cf. on this topic *H. Wagnon*, "Le Congrès national belge a-t-il établi la separation de l'Église et de l'État?", in: Études d'histoire du droit canonique dédiées à Gabriel Le Bras, Paris, Sirey, 1965, I, p. 753-781.
7 The notion *separation* was used by eminent older authors, e.g. *A. Giron*, Le droit public de la Belgique, Brussels, A. Manceaux, 1884, p. 342.
8 Cf. *P. Errera*, Traité de droit public belge, Paris, Giard et Brière, 1918, p. 87: "indépendence mutuelle"; *F. Laurent*, L'Église et l'État en Belgique, Brussels/Leipzig, Lacroix Verbroeckhoven, 1862, p. 351.

State to take up a neutral position.⁹ This does not imply that it needs to be seen to be agnostic in the face of the phenomenon of religion. The government bestows support and protection to churches and non-confessional organisations. Indeed, that only serves to show their importance to society. The State positively promotes the free development of religious and institutional activities without interfering with their independence. In that sense, one might call this positive neutrality.¹⁰

V. The Legal Status of Religious Communities

Although Belgian law recognises a theoretical equality between all religions,¹¹ one cannot deny that some receive different treatment from others. Several religions have obtained official recognition by, or by virtue of, a law. The main basis for such a recognition is the social value of the religion as a service to the population.¹² Currently, six denominations enjoy this status: Catholicism, Protestantism, Judaism, Anglicanism (Law of 4 March 1870 on the organisation of the temporal needs of religions),¹³ Islam (Law of 19 July 1974 amending

---

9   Comp. *Ph. Braud*, La notion de liberté publique en droit français, Paris, L.G.D.J., 1968, 383. The principle was restated by the Deputy Prime Minister, who is also Minister of Justice, at a meeting with religious leaders in 2004, following the French decision to ban Muslim headscarves. They were reminded that Belgium is a neutral, not secular, country, and that religious discrimination must not become an issue.
10 *J. De Groof*, "De bescherming van de ideologische en filosofische strekkingen. Een inleiding", in: *A. Alen/L.P. Suetens* (ed.), Zeven knelpunten na zeven jaar staatshervorming, Brussels, Story-Scientia, 1988, p. 312. *H. Wagnon* uses the notion *protected liberty, liberté protégée*. Cf. *H. Wagnon*, "La condition juridique de l'Église catholique en Belgique", *Annales de droit et de sciences politiques*, 1964, p. 70.
11 *C. De Brouckère/F. Tielemans*, Répertoire de l'administration et du droit administratif, V, Brussels, Weissenbruch, 1838, p. 485 (Culte).
12 For the concrete criteria with regard to recognition, see *Questions and Answers*, Chamber, 1999-2000, 4 September 2000, 5120, (Question nr. 44, Borginon); *Questions and Answers*, Chamber, 1996-1997, 4 July 1997, 12970 (Question nr. 631, Borginon). The religious group should be (a) considerably large; (b) well structured; (c) present in the country for some decades; (d) socially important; (e) free of any action threatening social order.
13 This law is not the only source. The recognition of Catholicism is a direct result of the Concordat of 1801, confirmed by the law of 18th Germinal X (8 April 1802). Protestantism also obtained recognition as a result of the law of 18th Germinal X, whereas Judaism found its recognition through the decrees of 17 March 1808. Finally, Anglicanism obtained recognition through the decrees of 18 and 24 April 1835. All this was confirmed by the law of 4 March 1870.

13

the law of 1870) and the (Greek and Russian) Orthodox Church (Law of 17 April 1985 amending the same law of 1870).

A change to the Constitution on 5 June 1993[14] added groups of non-believing humanists[15] to the financial responsibilities of the State.[16]

Apart from the modest stipends (Art. 181 of the Constitution) for the ministers of religion of a government-approved parish or bishopric[17] provided for in the State budget, recognition also entails a few other benefits for the religions concerned.

Legal personality is attributed to the ecclesiastical administrations responsible for the temporal needs of the Church.[18] The Church and Church structures themselves do not enjoy any legal personality. Attention must also be drawn to the fact that deficits incurred by ecclesiastical administrations for temporal goods must be paid by the municipalities. This possibility for escape does not always encourage proper responsibility on the part of the administration.[19] Another advantage for the Church is State subsidies for the construction or renovation of church buildings.[20]

Pastors and bishops must be given appropriate[21] housing and any expenditure for this purpose is chargeable to the municipalities or provinces.

Furthermore, recognised religions are entitled to free public radio and television broadcasting time.[22]

---

14 For an overview of the developments leading to the change of the Constitution, see *J.-P. Martin*, "La Belgique: de l'affrontement laïques-confessionnels au pluralisme institutionnel", in *J. Bauberot* (ed.), Religions et laïcité dans l'Europe des Douze, Paris, Syros, 1994, p. 29-39.
15 Their representative bodies are the Centrale Vrijzinnige Raad/Conseil Central Laïque.
16 For an overview of all the financial consequences, see *P. De Pooter*, De rechtspositie van erkende erediensten en levensbeschouwingen in Staat en maatschappij, Brussels, Larcier, 2003, p. 207-214.
17 Around 1,000 euro a month for a Catholic priest.
18 The legal basis for these "kerkfabrieken" "fabriques d'églises" was for a long time the Imperial Decree of 20 December 1809 and by the Law of 4 March 1870, Moniteur belge, 8 March 1870. Following the regionalisation of this area, a new Flemish decree is expected soon. For possible future developments, see *F. Amez*, "Un aspect oublié de la réforme de l'État: le régime des cultes", *Journal des Tribunaux*, 2002, p. 509-537.
19 In Wallonia, the municipalities spend 1.2 % of their average expenses on religion, cf. *R. Collinet*, "À propos des fabriques d'églises, des secours communaux et de quelques subsides", in: Le Semeur sortit pour semer. Grand Séminaire de Liège 1592-1992, Liège-Bressoux, Éditions Dricot, 1992, p. 407.
20 The legal sources are: Art. 92(3) of the Imperial Decree of 30 December 1809; the Law of 4 March 1870 (Moniteur belge, 9 March 1870) and the Law of 7 August 1931 (Moniteur belge, 5 September 1931), as well as the Royal Decree of 2 July 1949 and 1 July 1952.
21 "Appropriate" means: in accordance with his social status. See e.g. *Council of State*, 2 April 1953, Rechtskundig Weekblad, 1952-1953, p. 1691.

Finally, religions may appoint army and prison chaplains, whose salaries are carried by the State budget.[23]

Of the six recognised religions, Roman Catholicism is the most important. The figures provide indisputable proof of this. It has not resulted in it having a privileged position, *de iure*. However, that is not entirely true *de facto*. First of all, one cannot escape the conclusion that the legal status of religions in Belgian law really finds its source of inspiration in the structure and functioning of the Roman Catholic Church. Here is an example of this: to be able to make an actual claim for State payment of religious ministers, a clearly hierarchically structured religious community is necessary, as is one which works on a territorial basis. For the Catholic Church this is not such a big problem, but the Islamic faith fares differently. Islamic religious ministers are still not paid by the State.

In addition to this, the Roman Catholic Church plays a bigger role than other religions when it comes to public expressions of faith. This is seen when the military services salute as *Te Deum* is played during the National Day celebrations.[24] The Catholic Church also had a prominent role at the funeral of King Baudouin on 7 August 1993.

In summary, it may be said that there are six recognised religions, among which Catholicism is *'primus inter pares'*.

As well as the six recognised religions, there is a whole range of unrecognised ones. In terms of numbers, Jehovah's Witnesses are in the lead with around 20,000 members, followed by the Mormons who have something like 3,000 believers. Numerous other groups have memberships approaching or well into the hundreds.

These movements do not always have a legal status which could be said to be enviable. Not only do they not enjoy the advantages the recognised religions can lay claim to, but they are sometimes not even regarded as religions, pure and simple. There is no legal definition of the term "religion". Therefore the decision is left to the courts of law. In view of the freedom of religion and the relationship between Church and State as exists in Belgium, when a judge has to determine whether a movement is a religion, he or she is not nor-

---

22 See *E. Henau*, God op de buis. Over religieuze uitzendingen in de openbare omroep, Louvain, Davidsfonds, 1993, p. 112.
23 *Pandectes belges*, Aumônerie, Aumôniers, nr. 1-16.
24 According to Cass., 18 June 1923, *Pasicrisie*, 1923, I, p. 375 this was not contrary to Art. 15 of the Constitution and the negative religious freedom expressed by this Article. However, recently, the *Te Deum* lost ground. Although it remains part of the official ceremonies on 21 July (National Day), it is no longer officially programmed on 15 November (Dynasty Day).

mally allowed to fall back on arguments concerning their content.[25] For a judge who, for example, looks at the criminal law or tax exemption files to establish whether this is indeed a religion,[26] this entails having to work out whether the society concerned looks as though it is serious and in all reasonableness may be called a "religion".[27] When doing so, in the first place the judgment should be based on external aspects such as the existence of temples, prayer texts, or ritual acts. Sometimes, however, even this does not yield sufficient clarity and a certain amount of analysis of what is contained within the movement is still necessary. Jurisprudence takes the view that for it to be regarded as a religion, there needs to be the cult of a deity.[28]

Non-recognised religions or religious groups are more likely to disagree with concepts such as public order and good practices within the State order. Up until the abolition of compulsory military service, the problems that Jehovah's Witnesses encountered were very well known. They refused to do not only military service, but also the alternative to it – civic service. On the basis of Article 46 of the military penal statute book, a person concerned was classed as a deserter, and this generally led to a two-year prison sentence.[29]

To put it briefly, having taken everything into consideration, three categories of religion may be differentiated:
(a) the legally recognised and, in real terms, the major, Roman Catholic church;
(b) the five other legally recognised but, in real terms, minor religions as well as the non-believing humanists;
(c) the unrecognised movements, whether or not they fulfil the requirements which the law lays down on the concept of religion.

---

25 See *G. Van Haegendoren*, "Sekte of kerk: de niet-erkende erediensten in België", Tijdschrift voor Bestuurswetenschappen en Publiek Recht, 1986, p. 390.
26 See e.g. the example of Stévinisme, Court of Appeal Gent, 14 January 1885, Pasicrisie, 1885, II, p. 121; of Salvation Army, Corr. Tribunal of Gent, 4 December 1890, Pasicrisie, 1891, III, p. 117 and Corr. Tribunal of Brussels, 6 February 1891, Journal des Tribunaux, 1891, p. 204; of Baha'i, Court of Appeal of Brussels, 12 October 1960, quoted by Commentaar W.I.B., 157/28; and of Jehovah's Witnesses, Court of Appeal of Brussels, 24 January 1962, quoted by Commentaar W.I.B., 157/29.
27 See the jurisprudence quoted by *P. Mahillon/S. Fredericq*, "Het regime van de minoritaire erediensten", Rechtskundig Weekblad, 1961, 62, p. 2376.
28 Cf. Court of Appeal of Liège, 21 November 1949, Pasicrisie, 1950, II, 57. Antoinism is a cult limited to its members themselves. Consequently it was considered by the authorities to be an "oeuvre philantropique", without the quality of a religion.
29 Cf. *R. Torfs*, "L'objection de conscience en Belgique", in: *European Consortium for Church-State Research* (ed.), Conscientious Objection in the E.C. Countries, Milan, Giuffrè, 1992, p. 217 e.s.

In more recent years, Belgium has been among the countries that were strongly worried by so-called harmful sectarian organisations.[30] A parliamentary report on this issue was submitted to the Chamber of Representatives on 28 April 1997. This report contained an additional list, a kind of "synoptical table" setting out the names of organisations. The publication of this list occasioned a great deal of commotion. So the parliamentary commission that issued the report, including the synoptical table, quickly stated that the presence of a certain movement on the list did not mean that the group was a sect and, *a fortiori*, that it was dangerous.[31]

After examination of the report, a so-called information and advice centre was established by a law of 2 June 1998.[32] The Centre and its functions led to some questions, both in Belgium and abroad. In 2000, the Court of Arbitration stated that the Centre cannot forbid the expression of an opinion by a philosophical or a religious minority. The Centre may only inform the public with regard to activities of certain associations, so that people can more accurately evaluate opinions which could be dangerous.[33]

Article 21 of the Constitution has always been considered as a solid juridical basis for the self-government of religious communities. The State may not supervise the Church and the latter is free to choose its own internal structure. Does this mean that the State has absolutely no possibility of controlling churches and their activities? That would be an over-statement.

Traditionally, the control exercised by secular courts remained exclusively formal, which means that the civil judge only had the right to determine whether a challenged decision was taken by the competent ecclesiastical authority. This approach was dominant throughout the nineteenth century.[34]

With two decisions by the Belgian supreme court, the Cour de Cassation, in 1994 and 1999,[35] some development unmistakably took

---

30 Cf. *L.-L. Christians*, "Vers un principe de précaution religieuse en Europe? Risque sectaire et conflit de norms", *Il Diritto Ecclesiastico*, 2001, p. 173-213; *R. Torfs*, "Sekten en recht", *Collationes*, 1998, p. 385-406; *R. Torfs*, "Sekten, godsdienstvrijheid en de staat", Ethiek en Maatschappij, 2002, nr. 1, p. 69-81.
31 Parliamentary Documents, Chamber, 1995-96, 313/8, p. 227.
32 Moniteur belge, 25 November 1998. The internal statutes can be found in the Parliamentary Documents, Chamber, 1999-2000, nr. 231/001, p. 269. For more information: *L. Vervliet*, "Bestrijding van schadelijke sektarische organisaties", Intercontact, 1999, p. 30-33.
33 Court of Arbitration, nr. 31/2000, 21 March 2000, Moniteur belge, 22 April 2000.
34 Cf. for instance Tribunal de Liège, 29 July 1848, Belgique Judiciaire, 1848, p. 1078; Court of Appeal of Liège, 22 March 1883, Pasicrisie, 1883, II, p. 157.
35 Cour de Cassation, 20 October 1994, Arresten van het Hof van Cassatie, 1994, 861, Rechtskundig Weekblad, 1994-1995, p. 1082 and Recente Arresten van het Hof van Cassatie,

place. The Cour de Cassation clearly remembered the principle of autonomy as formulated in Article 21 of the Constitution. It also rejected the decision by two Courts of Appeal, stating that religious groups should not only correctly observe internal procedures as prescribed internally, but should also respect the right of defence as well as all other principles formulated by Article 6(1) of the European Convention on Human Rights.[36] The Cour de Cassation did not support this rather revolutionary viewpoint, but then again it seemed to accept the key principle admitting that religious groups have to act "within the norms of the concerned religion".

By taking this position, the Cour de Cassation went further than the traditional position, without, however, following the radical option taken by the two Courts of Appeal.

This could be summarised in a diagram distinguishing three levels:

A	Traditional Position	Did the competent religious authority take the challenged decision?
B	Current Supreme Court Position	Did the competent religious authority take the challenged decision complying with the procedural norms of the concerned religion?
C	Rejected Radical Position	Did the competent religious authority take the challenged decision complying with the procedural norms of the concerned religion? And do these norms respect the right of defence as well as the other principles formulated by article 6(1) of the European Convention on Human Rights?

1995, p. 57; Cour de Cassation, 3 June 1999 (United Chambers), Chroniques de droit public. Publiekrechtelijke kronieken, 2000, p. 214 and Jaarboek Mensenrechten 1998/2000, p. 253-255; K. Martens, "Het Hof van Cassatie en de interpretatie van artikel 21 G.W.: de verhouding tussen Kerk en Staat dan toch niet op nieuwe wegen?", (note under Cass. 3 June 1999), Chroniques de droit public. Publiekrechtelijke kronieken, 2000, p. 215-218; R. Torfs, "Religieuze gemeenschappen en interne autonomie. Fluwelen evolutie?", Jaarboek Mensenrechten 1998/2000, p. 256-264.

36 Court of Appeal of Mons, 7 January 1993, Jurisprudence de Liège, Mons et Bruxelles, 1993, p. 242, note L.-L. Christians and Revue de droit social, 1993, p. 69, note R. Torfs; Court of Appeal of Liège, Jurisprudence de Liège, Mons et Bruxelles, 1998, p. 680, note M. Westrade.

In addition to this question of principle, there is still the problem of stating the range of Church activities which enjoy protection. On this point, it can be said that it is only the Church organisation in the strictest sense that fully enjoys the autonomy outlined by Article 21 of the Constitution.

Churches desiring to organise activities in other fields, such as health care and education, are bound by the civil legislation relating to that field. In order to participate properly in those areas, Church representatives need to constitute a legal person according to Belgian law, usually a V.Z.W./A.S.B.L. (Vereniging Zonder Winstoogmerk / Association Sans But Lucratif).[37] This is necessary for two reasons. Firstly the churches themselves, and also dioceses, parishes and other church structures, do not possess legal personality according to Belgian law. And secondly, the V.Z.W. structure is needed in various areas for the simple reason of mere survival, as it is quite often required in order to receive financial support from the State.

Every policy on Church activities within the context of charity must start from this reality. Civil structures are indispensable. One has to accept them as a starting point: Canon Law requirements and aspirations assumed by the Church authorities have to be integrated within this mandatory framework.[38]

VI. Churches and Religious Communities within the Political System

The relationship between politics and religion in Belgium has always been informal but important. For many years, the Catholic or Christian Democratic Party has played a key role in Belgian politics. After World War II, it was continuously in power, in various coalition governments, except during the period 1954-8. In the late 1960s, the Christian-Democrat Party split into two: a Dutch-speaking party (CVP) and a French-speaking one (PSC). This was by no means an isolated phenomenon, as the same happened to the two other main political families, the socialists and the liberals. Until 1999, the

---

37 Law of 27 June 1921, Moniteur belge, 1 July 1921.
38 This was also my own starting point in a study on future structures for Catholic health care institutions: *Torfs, R.*, Congregationele gezondheidsinstellingen. Toekomstige structuren naar profaan en kerkelijk recht, Leuven, Peeters, 1992, XX+336p.

Christian Democrats remained in the government, but then they lost the elections and became, for the first time in more than forty years, opposition parties. The latter is still the case in the federal government, after the 2003 elections. However, after having obtained good results in the 2004 regional elections, they re-emerged in regional government. As coalitions are traditionally the same at both regional and federal levels, a return to power of the Christian Democrats at federal level would not be a complete surprise.

In the meantime, the link between the Catholic Church and the Christian Democrats has gradually weakened. The influence of church leaders has become less outspoken, and is today no more than marginal. The Belgian abortion law, approved by Parliament in 1993, was not supported by the Christian Democrats, but although they were in government they left the matter to a free vote in Parliament.[39] The Christian Democrats were in opposition when the very liberal euthanasia law was passed in 2002, but their resistance focused merely on technical points and was far from fierce.[40] Finally, in 2003, homosexual marriage was approved, without Christian Democratic opposition at the level of principle.[41]

To sum up: although Christian Democratic parties are still prominent in Belgium, their link with the church is considerably weakened. Today, the Christian Democratic parties are also open to non-believers.

VII. Culture

The Churches, especially the Catholic Church, play an important role in Belgian cultural life.

In the area of education, in terms of numbers, Catholic education outstrips State education.[42] 60 % of Belgian pupils in secondary education go to schools within the Catholic network. This figure reaches 75 % in Flanders, a percentage which is the highest in Western Europe.[43]

---

39 Law of 3 April 1990, Moniteur Belge, 4 April 1990.
40 Law of 28 May 2002, Moniteur Belge, 22 June 2002.
41 Law of 13 February 2003, Moniteur Belge, 28 February 2003.
42 Cf. *D. Grootaers*, Histoire de l'enseignement en Belgique, Louvain-la-Neuve, CRISP, 1998, p. 615.
43 See *J. Bulckens*, "L'enseignement de la religion dans les écoles secondaires catholiques en Flandre", in: *J. Bulckens/H. Lombaerts* (ed.), L'enseignement de la religion catholique à

Other religions also organise education.[44] The Jewish faith, for example, has a long tradition in this area. In September 1989 the first Islamic school in Belgium, the Al-Ghazi school in Brussels, opened its doors. For different reasons, various politicians have expressed their concerns about it.[45]

Alongside the free school network is the "official" one, which appears to the outsider to have a very complicated structure. Since the constitutional revision of 15 July 1988, education in Belgium has been totally reorganised along community lines.[46] That date marked an important stage in an evolution, which was already under way by 1970. From 15 July 1988, the Dutch, French and German-language communities have been organising their own education. This has meant that they are all able to put their policies into action by means of their own legislation. The only point that binds them is Article 24 of the Constitution, which in the field of education ensures protection for all ideological options. That is particularly apparent from the first section of the Article, stating that the community guarantees the parents' freedom of choice and organises neutral educational instruction (not bound by any specific ideology). This implies respect for the philosophical, ideological or religious opinions of parents and pupils. Schools organised by public authorities offer, for the duration of compulsory education, a choice between instruction in one of the recognised religions and instruction in non-religious ethics. And, as Article 24(3) adds, all students of compulsory education age have the right to a moral or religious education at the community's expense.

This legal settlement, in fact a result of the political settlement embodied in the so-called School Pact and in the School Pact Act of 29 May 1959,[47] causes two different kinds of problems.

The first problem concerns the content of the non-religious ethics course, which must be followed if the religious education option has not been chosen. The Council of State decided in the Sluijs case in 1985 that no one can be forced to take ethics courses which manifestly define themselves as non-confessional and which expressly

---

l'école secondaire. Enjeux pour la nouvelle Europe, Leuvain, University Press/Peeters, 1993, p. 143.

44 *A. Overbeeke*, "De uitwerking van het recht op onderwijs door levensbeschouwelijke minderheden", Tijdschrift voor Onderwijsrecht en Beleid, 1994-1995, p. 295 e.v.

45 *J. Leman/M. Renaerts/D. Van den Bulck*, "Islam en islamitisch recht in België", in: Recht van de Islam 10, Maastricht, Rimo, 1992, p. 53-54.

46 Law of 15 July 1988, Moniteur belge, 19 July 1988. Cf. *M. Leroy*, "La communautarisation de l'enseignement", Journal des Tribunaux, 1989, p. 71-74.

47 Law of 29 May 1959, Moniteur belge, 19 June 1959.

promote ideas which can be labelled as "free thinking".[48] After education was drawn up along community lines, one such judgment was pronounced in the case of the Jehovah's Witness, Vermeersch, who did not want to opt for religious classes in any of the six recognised religions. According to the Council of State, no one could be forced to make such a choice against his or her own convictions.[49]

Gradually this led to an increasing number of requests for exemption from both religious education and non-religious ethics. The main driving force behind all of this was not philosophy, nor a moral dilemma, but actually indifference. It may be said that the government has been increasingly ready to accept total exemption. For example, since a circular of 8 July 1992, in schools in Flanders, exemption has no longer to be granted by the minister, and has been left up to the boards of governors of the individual school; inevitably this has resulted in a relaxation of practice.

At university level, there is no interconnection between State universities and the teaching of or research into theology. The Faculté universitaire pour la théologie protestante was founded in 1950. It was recognised as an institute at university level in 1963.[50]

The Instituut voor Hoger Joodse Studies / Institut de Hautes Études Juives was started in 1959. Ii was connected with the Institute of Sociology of the Université Libre de Bruxelles (ULB). From the academic year 2000-2001, the Dutch speaking part of the Institute was taken over by a new Instituut Joodse Studies of the University of Antwerp. This new Institute receives financial support from the Flemish community.

Obviously, the position of Catholic theology is more important and more developed. There are six Catholic universities in Belgium.[51]

---

48 Council of State, 14 May 1985, n° 25.326, decision Sluijs.
49 Council of State, 10 July 1990, n° 35.442, decision Vermeersch.
50 The Protestant Faculty of Theology has historical roots and was re-established between 1942 and 1944. It had a new start in 1950, with the foundation of the Faculté universitaire pour la théologie protestante. 1954 was the first year of the Dutch speaking Universitaire faculteit voor protestantse godgeleerdheid. The two faculties still have a common board of governors. In 1963 they were recognised as institutions for higher education. The costs of these faculties are partly covered (60 %) by public authorities. There is a clear contrast with the theology faculties at the Katholieke Universiteit Leuven and Université Catholique de Louvain, where the authorities meet all the costs. There is also an evangelical theological faculty in Heverlee. It is entitled to deliver the same awards as the Protestant faculty, but without any government financing, cf. *Questions and Answers*, Flemish Parliament, 1998-99, 3 December 1998, p. 1101 (Question nr. 46 Lauwers). For more details, see *P. De Pooter*, o.c., 443.
51 The six universities are: Katholieke Universiteit Leuven, Katholieke Universiteit Brussel, Université Catholique de Louvain, Facultés Universitaires Saint-Louis (Bruxelles), Fa-

"Catholic" is more a sociological than an ideological notion, as many students and staff members are non-believers. Catholic theology is taught only at the Katholieke Universiteit Leuven (in Dutch and English) and the Université Catholique de Louvain (in French). Canon Law is taught only at the Katholieke Universiteit Leuven, in both English and Dutch.

As far as religious broadcasting on radio and TV is concerned, Belgium has a system called le droit à l'antenne. This is the right for private associations, representing socio-economic, as well as philosophical and religious groups, to broadcast via the public media in the interests of their members as well as of the general public.

This principle was first worked out in a Royal Decree of 2 July 1964.[52] Today, radio and television are regional matters. In Flanders, the Decree of 29 April 1997 is the current legal basis for the broadcasting of religious programmes.[53] In the French and German community, similar rules have been promulgated.[54]

Not everyone is satisfied with the existing system. As there are already specific broadcasts with generally low viewing figures, the public service broadcasters feel they no longer need to devote much attention to religious news. But many feel that it is preferable that the presence of the Church in the media is realised through public broadcasting facilities.

In the written press, the role of the Church is more indirect. A large number of the daily newspapers were historically of a Catholic persuasion, as epitomised by *De Standaard* and *La Libre Belgique*, though the Church authorities did not have editorial control. Many newspapers which began as Catholic have moved towards pluralism, sometimes even with sometimes negative feelings towards the Roman Catholic Church. Today, no important daily newspaper is completely Catholic. In Flanders, in response to this new situation, the Church together with external sponsors started a new weekly, *Tertio*, with a limited number of readers but a very outspoken Catholic stance. The weeklies *Kerk en Leven* and *Dimanche* are also Catholic; they have considerably more readers but fewer intellectual ambitions.

In a country in which religious, State, and linguistic differences are as ingrained as they are in Belgium, the composition of official bod-

---

cultés Universitaires Notre Dame de la Paix (FUNDP – Namur), Facultés Universitaires Catholiques de Mons (FUCaM).
52 Moniteur Belge, 21 November 1964.
53 Moniteur Belge, 1 May 1997, err. Moniteur Belge, 17 May 1997.
54 See *P. De Pooter*, o.c., 180 e.s.

ies (from the Court of Arbitration to the board of governors of public service television; from university councils to committees responsible for cultural policy) always takes political and ideological balance into account. This does not, however, necessarily lead to direct church involvement. Up until the 1960s it was the custom of the Christian People's party to co-opt a priest – as a trusted representative of the church – as senator. Since then, this custom has fallen into disuse. At present some priests have seats in Parliament, though they are not in the Christian Democratic Party; however, a retired religious sister was recently returned to the Flemish Parliament.

VIII. Labour Law within the Religious Communities

An important development has been taking place in the relationship between employment law and the Church.[55] A distinction needs to be made between professed religious on the one hand and ordinary lay people on the other. As far as religious are concerned, it is possible to break it down into three stages.

The first stage saw the religious element dominate the relationship of monks and nuns with their churches. Accordingly, there could not be said to be an employment contract in force, and that is how those involved wanted it. One reason was that it meant that no social security contributions needed to be paid. The reverse side of the coin was that the religious were not entitled to a retirement pension.

The balance was disturbed when a number of religious did submit a request for entitlement to a pension. To settle this matter, there needed to be verification of whether an employment contract was in force, and it was this that started the second stage.

A 'presumption' exists in the second stage that the religious relationship dominates the entire working situation and that there is no employment contract. The special nature of religious life entails for those involved, in view of their vows, that they are no longer regarded as employees or self employed. So the notion of belonging to a religious community was given a very wide significance and

---

55 See *R., Torfs,* "Les églises et le droit du travail", in: *European Consortium for Church-State Research* (ed.), Churches and Labour Law in the E.C. Countries, Milano/Madrid, Giuffrè/Facultad de Derecho, 1993, p. 35-59.

pre-empted all the later issues in labour relations.⁵⁶ This position was slowly refined. After some time, case-law rejected the false opposition between the relationship the religious had with his or her order and the employment contract.⁵⁷ This, however, did not mean that the Cour de Cassation found recognition of an employment contract easy. Besides the traditional elements associated with employment contracts (authority, management, supervision and remuneration), effective proof of the existence of an employment contract was demanded.⁵⁸ This created an additional condition to be met before the employment contract could be recognised: in practice this was a condition that was difficult to satisfy.⁵⁹

In the third, current, stage, this presumption in favour of the religious relationship has been dropped. After being given the initial impetus by the Labour Courts of Appeal at Brussels and Antwerp,⁶⁰ the Cour de Cassation also changed its mind in a judgment of 25 January 1982.⁶¹ This u-turn in the law's position, based on the presumption of tacit consent for there to be an employment contract – at least when the employer itself is not the religious order – had become unavoidable. This is because society no longer considers labour in a religious context as manifestly different from other work.⁶²

The three-stage evolution sketched here came into being as a result of the pension files of religious. But the question of the position in employment law of secular clergy was being raised more and more often. Although generally speaking it is possible to follow the theory

---

56 See e.g. Conseil d'Etat, 25 October 1961, n° 8.883, decision Closset and R. Verstegen, "Arbeidsovereenkomsten voor geestelijken: een beslissende stap", Tijdschrift voor Sociaal Recht, 1983, p. 4.
57 See e.g. Labour Tribunal of Brussel, 7 December 1971; Labour Tribunal of Tournai, 13 February 1973; Labour Tribunal of Gent, 16 January 1976, all quoted by *R. Verstegen*, Geestelijken naar Belgisch Recht. Oude en nieuwe vragen, Berchem-Antwerpen/Amsterdam, Maarten Kluwer, 1977, p. 37-39.
58 See Cour de Cassation, 21 November 1977, Pasicrisie, 1978, I, p. 317; Arresten van het Hof van Cassatie, 1978, p. 331; Tijdschrift voor Sociaal Recht, 1977, p. 479, observation H. Demeester. A similar scepticism characterises other decisions by the same supreme court, Cour de Cassation, 7 February 1973, Pasicrisie, 1973, I, p. 541; Arresten van het Hof van Cassatie, 1973, p. 568; Cour de Cassation, 5 January 1977, Pasicrisie, 1977, I, p. 485; Cour de Cassation, 21 November 1977 (another decision than the one quoted above), Pasicrisie, 1978, I, p. 316; Arresten van het Hof van Cassatie, 1978, p. 330; Cour de Cassation, 23 February 1981, Rechtskundig Weekblad, 1981-1982, p. 2152.
59 *H. Demeester*, observation on Cour de Cassation, 21 November 1977, Tijdschrift voor Sociaal Recht, 1977, p. 485.
60 Labour Court of Appeal of Brussel, 23 March 1978, Tijdschrift voor Sociaal Recht, 1978, p. 521; Labour Court of Appeal of Antwerpen, 19 November 1980, Tijdschrift voor Sociaal Recht, 1983, p. 95.
61 Cour de Cassation, 25 January 1982, Tijdschrift voor Sociaal Recht, 1983, p. 85.
62 *R. Verstegen*, "Arbeidsovereenkomsten...", Tijdschrift voor Sociaal Recht, 1983, p. 79-80.

developed for religious here also,[63] there are a few important differences.

For the present there are the clergy active as church ministers in the manner which Article 181 of the Constitution sets out, and who receive State stipends for their work. The relationship between these clergy and the Church authorities is controlled exclusively by the internal laws of the religion involved. As far as the Catholic Church is concerned, the incardination principle of the Canons 265 and following may be referred to in particular, as well as canon law in general.

When the church authorities give clergy a different function, such as a teaching job in a school, it was clearly stated by the Cour de Cassation in a judgment of 13 January 1992 – after an initial jurisprudential trend in favour of the church[64] – that if the objective characteristics of an employment contract are present, it does indeed exist.[65] Neither Article 21 of the Constitution nor the fact that a bishop can withdraw his licence (*missio*) with regard to the teaching to be given have led to a secular priest being unable to perform the job with which he has been entrusted within the scope of an employment contract.

The Cour de Cassation judgment of 13 January 1992 has had far-reaching consequences. From that date onwards, a clear distinction has existed between clergy with a pure relationship to the Church and clergy who are sent to work elsewhere by Church authorities and who may subsequently come to be working under the conditions of an employment contract.

Together with religious and clergy, increasing numbers of lay people work for the Church. Some of them do so as a minister of religion financed by the State as a consequence of Article 181 of the Constitution. The possibility of having lay people qualified as ministers of religion has existed since 1997, as a result of a "gentlemen's agreement" between the Belgian bishops and the Ministry of Justice.[66] The notion of 'ministre du culte' has never been defined, and before 1997

---

63 Labour Tribunal of Tournai, 13 December 1985, Journal des Tribunaux du Travail, 1987, p. 37.
64 E.g. Labour Tribunal of Tournai, 13 December 1985, Journal des Tribunaux du Travail, 1987, p. 37; Labour Court of Appeal of Liège, 26 November 1986, Journal des Tribunaux du Travail, 1987, p. 411.
65 Cour de Cassation, 13 January 1992, Journal des Tribunaux du Travail, 1992, p. 225; Rechtskundig Weekblad, 1992-1993, p. 121.
66 For a detailed analysis see R. Torfs (ed.), *Parochie-assistenten. Leken als bedienaar van de eredienst?*, Peeters, 1998, X+142 p.

lay people were supposed not to qualify, a situation which, although to a limited extent, changed in 1997.
The main question with regard to the legal position of lay ministres du culte is whether or not they work under a labour contract. The alternative is the mere existence of a *sui generis* position, under the control of the Church authorities and without any effect in the field of labour law. That is exactly the position clerics who are ministre du culte do enjoy.
A clear answer to the question with regard to the presence of a labour contract can not yet be given. Case law will offer the answer one day. However, several arguments plead in favour of a labour contract.[67] Firstly, lay people work in a relationship of subordination and receive a wage. Objectively speaking, they fulfil the conditions of a labour contract. Secondly, unlike clergy, lay people are not incardinated in a diocese, which means that there is no underlying relationship with the bishop offering them any material guarantee once their function as ministre du culte comes to an end.

IX. *Financing of Churches*

As already mentioned, Article 181 of the Constitution clearly affirms that the salaries and pensions of the ministers of religion are chargeable to the State. It also states that the sums necessary for this purpose are to be included in the annual State budget.
On 5th April 1993, a second clause was added to Article 181 of the Constitution: "The wages and pensions of representatives of organisations recognised by law who extend moral services, on the basis of non-confessional philosophy of life, are to be paid by the State; the sums required for this purpose are to be drawn out of the National Budget on an annual basis."
A global evaluation of the financial system shows us that religions are almost exempt from setting their own budget policy: the personnel is almost completely paid by the State; deficits for material administration are taken care of by others; while various indirect advantages make life easier. This "automatic" finance system is topped

---

67 C. Engels, "De parochie-assistent en het Belgische arbeidsrecht, zoals vuur en water?", in: R. Torfs (ed.), Parochie-assistenten. Leken als bedienaar van de eredienst?, Peeters, 1998, p. 23-39.

up by income out of Church-owned property. The property of religious congregations sometimes turns out to be considerable value. However since the French Revolution, dioceses have no longer been significant land- or property-owners. Finally, there is the phenomenon of fund-raising. Unlike the Netherlands, for instance, Belgium has almost no tradition in this area. This lack of financial support by the faithful is largely due to State funding and the notion that people have that they are already indirectly contributing to Church finances by paying their taxes.

The current Belgian system is fairly well accepted by the population. Nobody can deny that it functions rather well. From time to time however, some criticism is voiced. In 1992 the "official" secular movement *Humanistisch Verbond* published a pamphlet arguing that the financial support given especially to the Catholic Church was too large.[68] The authors suggested two possible options for the future, the first being a system of complete separation with an entirely neutral State: a nineteenth century dream! The second possibility consists of continuing State funding of religious and secular movements, but on a basis of strict equality, with three conditions, namely that (a) the basis of the relevant organisation is taken into consideration, (b) a minimum number of members is required and (c) the acceptance of a contemporary pluralist democracy by the State financed institute is a *conditio sine qua non*.[69]

In spite of this and other publications, the current system is functioning well and is not likely to be open to change in the near future.

The existing system also offers tax benefits, i.e. the exemption from taxation on income derived from property ownership for buildings (or the part of the building) in which the worship is practised.

The system also includes other advantages. For instance, the town in which a parish is situated has to provide for the housing (or an equivalent allowance) of the pastor.[70] The local town is also bound by several other financial obligations.[71]

---

68 W. Calewaert/L. De Droogh, Voor meer gelijkheid in onze democratie. Een pamflet, Antwerpen, Humanistisch Verbond, 1992, p. 72.
69 W. Calewaert/L. De Droogh, o.c., p. 70-71.
70 Imperial decree of 30 December 1809, article 92(2).
71 See M. Coppens, "Les différents cultes reconnus en Belgique et les obligations communales à leur égard", in: Les relations entre la commune et les établissements du culte, Louvain-la-Neuve, U.C.L., 1993, p. 44.

X. Access of Religious Communities to Public Institutions

Recognised religions may designate chaplains in prisons and in the army. Their salaries are paid by the State.
Spiritual support in prisons may be traced back to the Royal Decree of 21 May 1965.[72] It offers the prisoner great scope in being able to receive support in the religion of his choice. Catholic worship enjoys a few slight advantages. The Catholic priest is the only one allowed to organise day retreats, and he also receives greater material concessions.[73]
In 2001, the existing separate service for chaplains and moral counsellors was abolished, as they were seen as not essentially different from other agencies offering assistance.[74]
The number of chaplains and counsellors is an issue of constant concern. The collaboration between counsellors coming from various religious groups continuously increases.[75]
The legal basis for the spiritual support in the Army can be found in the Royal Decree of 17th August 1927.[76] Historically the Catholic, Protestant and Jewish religions have made effective use of this right.[77] Army chaplains are nominated by the State at the suggestion of the religious authorities, but they are not classed as government officials.[78] Recently there has been a reduction in the number of army chaplains on State pay. As a result of the abolition of compulsory military service, the number of troops in the army is decreasing.[79]
For public hospitals only a limited arrangement exists and it is not State-funded. A Royal Decree of 23 October 1964 says that only Church ministers and lay counsellors who have been requested by a

---

[72] Royal Decree of 21 May 1965, Moniteur Belge, 25 May 1965. The relevant articles are 16, 36 bis and 55. The Royal Decree was amended several times between 28 April 1970 and 4 December 1990, by other Royal Decrees.
[73] Art. 50 bis and 52 of the Royal Decree of 21 May 1965.
[74] Royal Decree of 23 March 2001, Moniteur Belge, 3 April 2001. See *P. De Pooter*, o.c., 186.
[75] Cf. "Dossier Interreligieuze samenwerking binnen de gevangenis. Samenwerking met islamconsulenten en werken met moslimgedetineerden", Metanoia, 2002, p. 138.
[76] Royal Decree of 17 August 1927, Moniteur Belge, 1 September 1927. The Royal Decree was amended many times between 1 September 1927 and 2 April 1996.
[77] As a result of a law of 18 February 1991, Moniteur Belge, 7 March 1991, non-confessional moral counsellors are also admitted. A demand formulated by the Orthodox Church has always been refused, a request by the Muslims is still under consideration. See *P. De Pooter*, o.c., 191.
[78] Cour de Cassation, 23 November 1957, Pasicrisie, 1958, I, p. 983.
[79] Cf. De Standaard, 15 January 2003, 3. the new framework for moral counsellors in the army is: 10 Catholics, 1 Protestant, 1 Jew, 1 Orthodox, 6 non-confessionals.

patient have to be allowed open access to the hospital. It is to be wondered if this is also the case for a number of ministers from non-recognised churches. They could even be kept out of the hospital if the religious support they provide includes faith healing and alternative medicine.[80]

XI. Legal Status of Priests and Members of Religious Orders

In principle, the legal position of priests and religious is no different from that of other citizens. There are, however, a few exceptions.
According to article 224(6) of the Code of Civil Procedure, a church minister is exempted from having to serve on the jury of a Court of Assizes which deals with serious crimes.
There is also a number of incompatibilities which may give rise to questions. Article 36 of the Constitution demonstrates the incompatibility of being both an official paid by the State and a Member of Parliament. This means that ministers of religion in the sense of Article 181 of the Constitution are in this situation and thus cannot be Members of Parliament. Positions on committees or in bodies other than the National Parliament, in the provincial or local councils, for example, are still possible.
There is also a whole series of other positions incompatible with being a minister, such as serving as a State councillor, a member of an auditing body, a number of functions in the court of arbitration, judge, registrar, provincial governor, provincial registrar, district commissioner and member of a board of aldermen.[81]
A priest, not paid by the State as a church minister, who was hoping to become a judge was not accepted as a candidate by the Minister of Justice on the basis of his belonging to the clergy (in fact an even more obscure term, *geestelijke stand* is used). He eventually took his case to the European Commission for Human Rights where the Commission ruled against him. The Commission saw in Article 293 of the Code of Civil Procedure – on which the minister was basing

---

80 G. Van Haegendoren, "Sekte of kerk. De niet-erkende erediensten in België", Tijdschrift voor Bestuurswetenschappen en Publiek Recht, 1986, p. 390.
81 See e.g. Law of 12 January 1973, art. 107, 1°; Law of 28 June 1983, article 35(1); Code of Civil Procedure, art. 293(1).

his case – no violation of religious freedom, as is delineated by Article 9 of the ECHR.[82]

XII. Matrimonial and Family Law

As mentioned, Article 21 of the Constitution provides that a civil marriage must always precede a religious marriage ceremony, with the exception of specific cases established by law. The Code of Penal Law specifies (Art. 267) penalties for the minister of religion who notwithstanding the constitutional prohibition celebrates such a marriage, unless one of the partners stands in peril of death.
It is clear that the second paragraph of Article 21 forms an exception to the first, which confirms the freedom of the internal organisation of religions. Historic reasons, above all, lie at the root of this restriction. In the nineteenth century, in accordance with long tradition, many people were married only in Church and did so despite the fact that the bishops encouraged them also to have a civil marriage ceremony. Such a systematic practice was, of course, particularly harmful for the efficient running of the civil side of the situation. With the view of bringing an end to this, and in a spirit of reconciliation, the Catholic majority of the National Congress approved the second paragraph of the current Article 21 of the Constitution.[83]
Since then, the practice of having a civil marriage, and then only afterwards a wedding ceremony in Church, has become a fundamental part of Belgian society. A new problem is, however, raising its head.[84] Many people still wish to get married but are not prepared to suffer certain disadvantages in terms of tax and social security contributions as a result. So they then choose to have only a Church wedding, so that they ease their consciences, but do not have to forsake the financial rewards of cohabitation. The existing constitu-

---

[82] European Commission for Human Rights, H. Demeester vs. Belgium, Journal des Tribunaux, 1982, p. 524; Jura Falconis, 1981-1982, p. 449 with a critical observation by R. Torfs.
[83] *E. Huyttens*, o.c., II, p. 468.
[84] Other issues than those discussed in this brief contribution also occur, e.g. Belgium's attitude towards polygamy. Polygamous marriages is forbidden in Belgium, but there is a certain tolerance concerning the civil effects of polygamous marriages contracted elsewhere. See *R. Torfs*, "Le mariage religieux et son efficacité civile en Belgique", in: *European Consortium for Church-State Research* (ed.), Marriage and Religion in Europe, Milano, Giuffrè, 1993, p. 221-251.

tional arrangement, however, makes this option fundamentally impossible. Such a situation raises questions. On the one hand, the motives which led to the drawing up of Article 21(2) of the Constitution are less prevalent today, on the other hand, living together is viewed by broad sections of the population more and more as a viable alternative to marriage. This situation occasionally leads to the comment being made that marriage in Church is the only form of living in sin that is illegal.

This idea has even been strengthened since, in 2001, Belgium recognised homosexual marriage on an equal footing with heterosexual marriage; an exception was made for adoption, which is possible only by a heterosexual couple.

XIII. Conclusion

Church and State relationships in Belgium may be summarised as follows:
1. The system, quite favourable to religion, is more a system establishing mutual independence than separation in a strict sense.
2. Although all religions enjoy the same rights in theory, there is an important juridical difference between recognised and non-recognised religious groups. At the same time, practice shows the Catholic religion as the *primus inter pares* among the recognised groups.
3. Gradually secularisation is colouring the Belgian Church and State system. This secularisation is characterised not by a frontal attack on religion, but by a gradual loss of full autonomy of the churches in various fields. A striking example is the ongoing influence of labour law in Church life as well as recent tendencies favourable to (moderate) State control of internal church procedures.

XIV. Bibliography

Pandectes belges, V° Église et État; Églises protestante et israélite; Fabrique d'église; Puissance ecclésiastique; Traitement du clergé.

P. De Pooter, De rechtspositie van erkende erediensten en levensbeschouwingen in Staat en maatschappij, Brussels, Larcier, 2003, XXIX + 575p.

R. Georges, "La nature juridique des traitements du clergé catholique", Annales de droit et de sciences politiques, 1962, p. 85-122.

R. Torfs, Congregationele gezondheidsinstellingen. Toekomstige structuur naar profaan en kerkelijk recht, Louvain, Peeters, 1992, XX + 336p.

Jiří Rajmund Tretera
State and Church in the Czech Republic

I. Social Facts

The membership of Churches and religious societies[1] ('religious communities') is governed by their statutes. There is no State provision for the registration of church members. The Census includes a question about membership of religious communities, but individual responses are not made available to those religious communities.

According to the 1991 Census the total population of the Czech Republic (CR in the table below) was 10,302,215 of whom 44.8 % claimed membership of some religious community, 39.9 % declared themselves to be non-denominational and 16.2 % exercised their right to give no response. 89.5 % of those who claimed membership of a Church were Roman Catholics. Others included the Evangelical Church of Czech Brethren,[2] the Czechoslovak Hussite Church,[3] the Silesian Evangelical Church of the Augsburg Confession (AC), the Eastern Orthodox Church and Jehovah's Witnesses.

The next Census was taken in March 2001. The proportion of those regarding themselves as non-denominational had risen to 58.3 %, while both the total membership of religious communities (31.7 %) and the number of non-respondents (10.1 %) had fallen. A decline in the number of members is typical of the larger Churches. On the other hand, most of the smaller religious communities had increased their membership: not only the "new religious movements", but also

---

1 There is no legal distinction between the terms "Churches" and "religious societies". Usage is a matter of choice.
2 This was the first unified Church in Central Europe. It was founded in December 1918 by the amalgamation of the Czech congregations of the Evangelical Churches of the Helvetic and Augsburg Confessions. Calvinist influence prevails. Legal order is presbyterian. The Church is a member of the World Reformed Alliance.
3 The Czechoslovak Church developed from Catholic modernism. It unites both Catholic and Protestant aspects of worship and teaching with the former Hussite tradition. It was founded as a new Church in January 1920 and recognised by the State in September 1920, though not as a State religion. This Church has used the name 'The Czechoslovak Hussite Church' since 1971.

traditional Churches with an evangelical ethos (e.g. Brethren and Baptists).
The table below gives a comparison of data from these statistics with regard to religion:

	3.3.1991	1.3.2001
Non-denominational	4,112,864	6,039,991
Roman Catholic Church	4,021,385	2,740,780
Evangelical Church of Czech Brethren	203,996	117,212
Czechoslovak Hussite Church	178,036	99,103
Silesian Evangelical Church AC	33,130	14,020
Lutheran Evangelical Church AC in the CR (registered 1995)	0	5,412
Evangelical Church AC in the CR (in 1991: Slovak Evangelical Church AC)	4,151	14,885
Eastern Orthodox Church	19,354	22,968
Religious Society of Jehovah's Witnesses (registered 1993)	14,575	23,162
Church of the Seventh-Day Adventists	7,674	9,757
Greek Catholics	7,030	7,675
Christian Congregations	3,017	6,927
Methodist Evangelical Church	2,855	2,694
Church of Brethren (Congregationalists)	2,759	9,931
Old Catholic Church	2,725	1,605
Union of Baptists	2,544	3,622
Unity of Brethren (Moravian Brethren)	2,269	3,426
Apostolic Church (Pentecostal Church)	1,485	4,565
Federation of Jewish Communities in the CR	1,292	1,515
New Apostolic Church	427	449
Religious Society of Unitarians	365	302
Church of Jesus Christ of the Latter-Day Saints (recognised 1990)	among "others"	1,366
Others and imprecise responses	8,182	196,712
No response	1,665,617	901,981

However, the data from the 2001 statistics must be treated with caution. Reasons for this are not unconnected with the design of the questionnaire. For example, the non-denominational option was at the top of the form: easy to see and fill in. The column for membership of a religious community came second, but with too small a space for writing in the full official name of a religious community. So the number of those who gave their religious affiliation imprecisely, i.e. did not use the official name of their religious community, was extremely high, totalling almost 6 % of all members of religious communities. There is also evidence that membership numbers of the three Churches of Augsburg Confession (AC in the table) are confused, as their names are very similar.

In spite of the unreliability of the statistics we may claim a common tendency for a decline in official membership of larger Churches. What is the reason for this tendency?

The period of atheisation during the communist regime in Czechoslovakia lasted for a long time (1948-1989) and the persecution of religious communities was stronger in Czechoslovakia than in neighbouring communist States. Schools were an important instrument for atheisation. Teachers played the role of "priests of atheism". Believers were not normally allowed to train as teachers. The relatively high number of inhabitants declaring a membership of a Church in the 1991 Census was therefore a surprise. The decline of this number 10 years on is explained by:

1. the continued influence of teachers, most of whom were educated in the Marxist spirit;
2. the mortality of older inhabitants, who had received religious education in the pre-communist era; and
3. the growth of a consumer society.

Church members belong to the poorer classes of inhabitants of the Czech Republic. The richer people, especially these who were members of the former totalitarian regime's establishment, have shown no sign of changing their mostly negative attitude towards religious communities and supporting them. Any repentance, or admission of collective or individual guilt, is an unknown moral principle for these people.

II. Historical Background

A West-Slavonic settlement in the territory of the present Czech lands accepted Christianity under the influence of the Irish, Frankish and Greek-Slavonic mission during the 9th century in the Great Moravian Empire. The later Czech (Bohemian) Kingdom entered into a free union with the Holy Roman Empire. The Kingdom was, of course, a Roman Catholic State. But from the Hussite Reformation at the beginning of the 15th century there were two recognised denominations in the Kingdom: the Catholic minority and the Utraquist (Calixtin) majority. During the 16th century the Utraquist Church came under Lutheran Protestant influence.

Re-catholicisation after the Battle of White Mountain (1620) and the end of the Thirty Years War (1648) was connected with the victorious House of Habsburg. Protestantism was forbidden. The unification of the Czech lands with the Austrian and other hereditary Habsburg lands followed. The sovereign of this union appropriated the *iura maiestica circa sacra*. In this way the Catholic Church lost an essential part of its autonomy.

Josef II published his Letter of Tolerance for his hereditary lands in 1781. 2 % of the inhabitants of the Czech countries professed Protestantism: either the Helvetic Confession (the majority) or the Augsburg Confession.

A process of emancipation of the Churches from the State started in 1848. In December 1867 a new liberal Constitution came into being for the Cisleithan Regions of the new Austrian-Hungarian Empire. The basis of this Constitution was a secularised State, based on the principle of co-operation with Churches and religious societies, and on their parity. The right to be recognised by the State was given to all religious communities which respected its legal demands (1874). The newly recognised religious communities[4] could join in teaching religion in public schools and taking religious services in the army. The stipends of priests, pastors and rabbis were financed partly by the religious communities and partly by the State (*congrua* or subsidies). The acknowledged religious communities were supported by the State in proportion to the number of official declarations of religious affiliation made to the municipalities.

---

4 E.g.: the Old Catholic Church (1877), and the Evangelical Church of Herrnhut – Moravian Brethren (1880).

The Republic of Czechoslovakia, founded in 1918 with the dissolution of the Austrian-Hungarian Empire, adopted the legislation of the Habsburg monarchy. From 1920 the Constitution declared the freedom of religion to individuals. Children who belonged to religious communities were obliged to attend lessons in religious education in public schools.

Because the Catholic Church was accused of having too close a relationship with the Habsburg dynasty, more than 20 % of the Czech people gave up their membership of the Catholic Church. Approximately 10 % of these became non-denominational, 10 % founded the Czechoslovak Church. 1.3 % Catholics converted to Protestantism increasing the number of Protestants among Czechs to almost 4 %. 0.2 % Catholics converted to the newly founded Eastern Orthodox Church.[5] A total of 75 % of the Czech people stayed in the Catholic Church.

In 1927 a *Modus Vivendi* was concluded between the representatives of the Czechoslovak Government and the Apostolic See. It concerned all the processes in the appointment of diocesan bishops in Czechoslovakia.

During the Nazi occupation of 1939-1945, Catholics in the Czech lands actively participated in the resistance against the Nazis and being persecuted by them justified them in the minds of Czech people. After World War II, during the time of "limited" democracy between 1945 and 1948, all Churches became popular in Czech society, and religious freedoms were as they had been before 1939.

A radical change came after the Communist *coup d'état* in February 1948. All spheres of public life had to accept the "scientific", i.e. the Marxist, ideology including atheism. In the years 1948-1989, atheism played the role of a State "religion".

Religious communities became the only alternative thinking institutions whose existence was tolerated, albeit with many limitations.[6] The ultimate aim of the regime was, of course, the entire liquidation of religious communities.

All the land belonging to religious communities (forests and fields), an important source of their economic viability, was taken over by the State during 1948.

---

5   The Eastern Orthodox Church was recognized by the Letter of Tolerance in 1781 but the first Czech parish congregation of this Church was founded in 1922.
6   The communists took this attitude towards the Churches, because religiosity is deeply established in the souls of the Czech people and because a total prohibition of Church activities would be "dangerous" for their regime because of a consequent loss of control.

New Acts establishing State control over the Churches came into force on November 1, 1949. That legislation brought obligatory but very low stipends for clergy, paid by the State regardless of the wishes of the religious communities. Any religious activity of clergy or lay preachers needed State permission, which was granted only for a geographically limited territory. This State permission could be revoked without explanation. Offences under this Act were punishable with imprisonment according to the provisions of the Penal Codes of 1950 and 1961.

Obligatory civil marriage was established in January 1950 for the first time in the history of the Czech lands.

In April 1950 all the monasteries were seized and the brothers interned without legal justification for several months. Later they were sent to forced labour units for three or four years and then dispersed as workers. From August 1950 convents of sisters were sent to camps in the remote border regions; they were not allowed to admit novices, and were obliged to work in factories. This state of affairs lasted until 1989.

Also during 1950 all Church schools and seminaries were abolished. The training of clergy was provided at only three State theological faculties (one for Catholics, one for Protestants, one for the Czechoslovak Church) and with a limited number of admissions.

Almost all the Catholic bishops were imprisoned or interned and the situation did not change until the end of the communist regime in 1989. The dictatorship did not use the *Modus Vivendi* of 1927.

Until 1953 religious education in school was an obligatory subject for all child-members of religious communities. Since that year it has been permitted only as a voluntary subject; there was a move to have it removed from schools altogether, and children attending religious education lessons were discriminated against.

Only at the time of "the Prague Spring 1968" and the short time of "liberalisation" under the first years of the ensuing Soviet occupation (1968-1970) could the religious sisters in the border camps admit a number of novices. Numbers of children attending the voluntary religious education classes increased, and their presence there did not attract adverse consequences for them. Monks began to work underground.

However, from 1971 the persecution of religious communities was revived. All religious communities, especially the Catholic Church, became symbols of resistance during the communist regime. They were supported by all dissidents.

On 17th November 1989, the 50th anniversary of the closure of the Czech universities by the Nazis, communist police brutally interrupted the students' commemorative procession in Prague. The events, later called "the Velvet Revolution", were followed by the whole of Czechoslovakia. 10th December 1989 may be called a day of upheaval. On that day the last Communist president appointed a non-communist government. The following day he resigned. The Government voted for a policy of legal continuity and of value discontinuity between the new and old regimes.

Parliament repealed the legal enactments that were contrary to human rights. The Act of 13th December 1989 repealed the anti-Church enactments of the Penal Code.

In the following week delegates of the Government assured themselves during their visit to the Apostolic See that the *modus vivendi* of 1927 was now considered obsolete and void. In January 1990 the legal provision allowing State interference in the appointment of clergy, preachers and all Churches' employees was repealed.[7]

The Charter of Fundamental Rights and Liberties, passed by the Parliament of the Czech and Slovak Federal Republic (CSFR) on 9th January 1991, confirmed this principle. On its foundations was built the Federal Act No. 308/1991 Sb. dealing with the freedom of religion and the status of Churches and religious societies. The time of its validity in the Czech territory (1991-2002) may be considered as the foremost period of religious freedom in history. The legal order of the Czech Republic, founded on 1st January 1993 as an independent State, has incorporated the principles of the state ecclesiastical law of the CSFR. But new legislation, passed in January 2002, has limited some of the rights of religious communities.

III. Basic Structure

1. Legal Sources

The Czech legal system, as it concerns the Churches, has four layers: constitutional law; international agreements; internal State law; and Church-State Agreements.

---

7 By the Federal Act No. 23/1990 Sb. (Sb. = Collection of Laws of Czechoslovakia or of the Czech Republic).

1. Czech constitutional law consists of the Constitution of the Czech Republic (Act No. 1/1993 Sb.), the Charter of Fundamental Rights and Liberties (Federal Act No. 23/1991 Sb., republished under No. 2/1993 Sb.), and other constitutional laws. The Charter of Fundamental Rights and Liberties contains, especially in Articles 15 and 16, the most important constitutional provisions in Czech State ecclesiastical law.
2. According to Article 10 of the Constitution international agreements, the ratification of which has been approved by Parliament and which are binding on the Czech Republic, constitute a part of the Czech legal order; should an international agreement make a provision contrary to Czech law, the international agreement is to be applied.

    An important international treaty, which is a source of Czech State ecclesiastical law, is the International Covenant on Civil and Political Rights of 19th December 1966, which was ratified by the Czechoslovak Socialist Republic in November 1975.

    Other treaties include the Convention on the Rights of the Child of November 1989, accepted by CSFR in September 1990, and the European Convention on Human Rights (ECHR) of 1950, accepted by CSFR in 1992.

    Between 2000 and 2002 representatives of the Czech Republic and the Apostolic See prepared an international agreement which was signed by them in July 2002. But the House of Deputies of Parliament voted by 110 votes to 90 not to recommend its ratification. The proposal for such a recommendation may be resubmitted at a more favourable time.
3. The third part of the Czech legal hierarchy consists of laws under the control of the Constitutional Court.

    The regulatory framework of Czech ecclesiastical law based on Act No. 308/1991 Sb. was replaced by Act No. 3/2002 Sb. of 7th January 2002 on Freedom of Religious Expressions and the Position of Churches and Religious Societies (Act on Churches and Religious Societies). The Act was subject to a reference to the Czech Constitutional Court. The Court's Opinion published under the No. 4/2003 Sb. repealed some provisions of the Act (concerning in particular the registration of charities and other ecclesiastical bodies).

    The communist Act on the Economic Assurance of Churches by the State No. 218/1949 Sb., is still in force, amended by Act

No. 23/1990 Sb. by which the provision requiring State approval for the performance of pastoral service was abolished.
The remaining part of Czech ecclesiastical law is dispersed in various laws, decrees and administrative regulations on specialised matters relating to religious communities.
4. There are also several State-Church Treaties at an internal level in present Czech law:
   a. The Agreement on co-operation between the Ministry of Defence of the Czech Republic, the Ecumenical Council of Churches in the Czech Republic, and the Czech Bishops' Conference (1998).
   b. The Agreement on pastoral service in prisons between the Prison Administration of the Czech Republic, the Ecumenical Council of Churches in the Czech Republic, and the Czech Bishops' Conference (1999), which replaced that of 1994.
   c. The Agreement on co-operation between Czech Radio,[8] the Czech Bishops' Conference, and the Ecumenical Council of Churches in the Czech Republic (1999).

2. *Categories of System Approach*

A regime of complete (strict) separation between Church and State has never been found in the Czech territory. Nowadays the State applies the principle of non-identification with any Church and the principle of parity and autonomy of Churches, but it collaborates with them in many areas. We may describe it as a co-operative model.
The Charter of Fundamental Rights and Liberties (Czech Charter of Human Rights) declares that the Czech State is based on democratic values and should not bind itself to a single ideology or religion (Art. 2(1)).
Religious freedom is protected expressly by Articles 15 and 16 of the Czech Charter.
Article 15(1) states explicitly that everybody has the right to change his or her religion or faith, or to have no religious beliefs.
Article 16(1) concerns the right to profess freely a personal religion or faith, alone or jointly with others, through religious services, instruction, religious acts, or religious rituals. Religious freedom is

---

8   The public radio station.

guaranteed to everyone, not only to members of recognised religious communities.

Article 16(2) of the Charter refers to the collective dimension of religious freedom. It covers the freedom of religious communities to administer their own affairs: in particular to constitute their organisations, appoint their clergy, and establish religious orders and other church institutions independently of the institutions of the State.

The limitations of fundamental freedoms under the provisions of Article 16(4) are very similar to those under the Article 9(2) of the European Convention on Human Rights. Such limitations provided by law are justified if they are necessary in a democratic society for the protection of public security and order, health, and morality, or other rights and freedoms of others. In applying statutory limits, the substance and purpose of people's respective rights must be respected (Charter, Art. 4(4)).

In addition, Article 17 dealing with freedom of expression, Article 19 (the right to assemble) or Article 20 (the right to associate) may also be mentioned as implicitly protecting religious freedoms.

Similar provisions protecting religious freedoms are contained in Article 9 of the European Convention on Human Rights and Article 18 of the International Covenant on Civil and Political Rights.

According to Article 15(3) of the Czech Charter, nobody may be forced to perform military service against his or her conscience or religious belief. Detailed regulation of this is set out in Act No. 18/1992 Sb., on alternative military service. Alternative military service is performed for 18 months (compared with 12 months for basic military service); this will be lifted in the near future, since from 2004/5 the Czech Army is to become wholly professional.

IV. Legal Status of Religious Bodies

Before 1991 religious communities within the territory of the Czech Republic needed the recognition of State authorities for their legal existence. It was given by law or treaty (the Roman Catholic Church and Jewish Communities from long ago, the Evangelical Church from 1781); or by an administrative Act based on a law (1874-1949); or by praeter legem (1949-1991).

In the period 1880-1949 some religious communities opted to work on a civic basis.[9] In 1991 this freedom of choice was not renewed.
Act No. 308/1991 Sb. defined the term "Churches and religious societies", replaced the term "recognition" by "registration", and determined its conditions. Both these types of religious communities were considered to be voluntary organisations of people who share the same religion in a corporation with its own structure, its own organisations, and its own internal provisions and ceremonies (Section 4). Registration under this Act was the conditio sine qua non for their activities as religious communities within the territory of the State. According to Section 22 of the Act all the religious communities that had been recognised under the former law, and were mentioned in the Schedule to the Act, were considered to be registered Churches; 19 religious communities came under this provision of the Act.
The condition for registration under the following Act No. 161/1992 Sb. was 10,000 members domiciled within the territory of the Czech Republic, or 500 members in the case of members of the World Council of Churches.
The registration of the religious communities was to be carried out by the competent body of the State administration – in this case the Ministry of Culture of the Czech Republic. Two religious communities were registered in the years 1993 and 1995: the Religious Society of Jehovah's Witnesses and the Lutheran Evangelical Church (Augsburg Confession) in the Czech Republic respectively. No church has yet been registered on the basis of its membership of the World Council of Churches.[10]
Act No. 3/2002 Sb. defined Churches and religious societies in a narrower sense than did the previous Act. They are institutions whose aim is to spread religion and to practise worship. The new Act does not mention charitable activities. Individual Church bodies with legal personality had to register at the Ministry of Culture within one year under sanction of losing their status. In this way the existence of the Church charitable organisations became endangered, and a group of 21 Senators then submitted a proposal for the revision of the Act by the Constitutional Court in Brno. In November 2002 it repealed Sec-

---

9 In the Czech lands this route was deliberately taken by the Baptists, Congregationalists (the Church of Brethren), the Church of the Seventh-Day Adventists and others. The Communist regime had forced them to assume the status of a Church.
10 The Anglican Congregation, founded in Prague at the Evangelical St. Kliment's parish church in Prague after 1990, enjoys the rights of a registered Church as an autonomous part of the Old Catholic Church in the Czech Republic.

tion 6(2) of the Act on the limitation of activities of religious communities to worship and evangelisation. This finding was published under Act No. 4/2003 Sb.

Act No. 3/2002 Sb. made it possible for a much wider range of religious communities to gain registration by a reduction of the condition as to size from 10,000 believers to 300 believers. Newly registered religious communities[11] acquire only a basic legal personality. Almost all the rights of pre-existing religious communities were put into a new category of "special rights". New religious communities may obtain them only after 10 years from the date of registration; if the number of their members reaches 0.1 % of inhabitants (i.e. more than 10,000); if they publish annual accounts, and so on. Religious communities registered under the former Act of 1991 and listed in the Schedule to Act 3/2002 Sb. automatically enjoy these "special rights", but under some conditions the State may withdraw them.

"Special" rights are: teaching religion in schools, founding schools, pastoral care in prisons and the army, gaining State subsidies. A "special right" to maintain confessional confidentiality is to be granted only if the religious community proves that such confidentiality has been practised for at least fifty years.

The status of religious communities as corporations under public law is questionable, because of the lack of a legal definition of such a corporation. They can found charities, hospitals, schools, and use the income from them.

Religious communities and their internal bodies have a legal personality. Internal bodies, including charities, have to be entered into the register of legal persons derived from religious communities which is administered by the Ministry of Culture. Other ministries register church schools and hospitals.

Members of religious communities have the same rights as other citizens. These can be limited only by their internal rules, which are not enforceable by the State.

---

[11] During 2002 four religious communities obtained registration without "special rights": the Czech Buddhist Society, the Religious Society Hare Krishna, Christian Communities, and the Community of Christians (Theosophy).

V. Churches and Culture

1. Church Public and Private Schools: Organization

It is possible to divide Czech primary and secondary schools into three categories:
1. public schools: the majority of all schools, established by municipalities and regional authorities or exceptionally by the State (Ministry of Education),
2. schools established by a religious community (Church national centres, dioceses, orders, parishes),
3. schools established by an individual or by a legal entity of private law (private schools).

All schools must be registered by the Ministry of Education.
Church schools were abolished in 1950; in June 1990 permission to found new church schools was reinstated.
Church schools are not the same as private schools. Church school costs are mostly met by the State; their Church founder normally gives a building and appoints the director of the school. As far as the students are concerned, they are admitted on the results of admission tests, not by reference to their confession. Teachers can be non-denominational or be members of another religious community, although a basic loyalty to the Church that founded the school is presumed. This arrangement is considered to be suitable for the deeply secularised Czech people: Church schools enjoy great popularity in Czech society.[12]
Private schools have a duty to fulfil the State curriculum, and their certificates have public validity. Their costs are only partly met by the State; the schools pay the rest – this part derives, for example, from school fees. These schools are not precluded from having their own specific worldview, even based on a religion. They may also choose students according to their own criteria. The founders of such schools may also be Church bodies. But Churches rarely use this opportunity: their members are usually poor and have no money for school fees.

---

12 In the communist period the faithful had no access to pedagogic education. Therefore the relatively high number of Church schools in the Czech Republic is a great success. Now there are 88 Catholic, 22 Protestant, 2 Jewish and 2 Eastern Orthodox Church schools, and 2 schools of the Czechoslovak Hussite Church in the Czech Republic.

2. *Church Higher Schools*

Religious communities have founded several higher schools[13] providing theological and other special education. These schools accept as students those who have passed the school leaving examination at Czech grammar schools. Thus, their character is near to that of universities but their students do not obtain academic degrees. These schools prepare students for the teaching of religion, for social work, for pastoral assistance and for jobs in journalism.

3. *Religious Education*

Churches have the right to organise religious classes as a non-obligatory subject at all public schools. Teachers need to be authorised by the Church but the school pays them. All students may attend religious education classes, even if they are not members of that Church. Religious communities support this practice because of ecumenical co-operation and common need. Non-denominational students may also take religious education.

The disadvantage of this system is that in public schools there is no alternative subject and therefore religious education is taught on the only free half-day in a week, usually Wednesday afternoons.

Religious education is usually voluntary at Church schools, too, but an alternative subject – ethics – is provided. This seems to be a better model and should be adopted by public schools.

Private schools have an absolutely free choice to provide obligatory or voluntary religious education in one or more confessions. They may even exclude religious education entirely.

4. *Theological Faculties at Public Universities*

Contemporary Czech law considers universities to be autonomous institutions. They may be founded by State or private bodies. Religious communities are permitted to establish only private universities. They have not yet used this right.

There are currently five theological faculties in the Czech Republic within public universities: three at the Charles University in Prague

---

[13] The Catholic Church has founded five and Protestant Churches six higher schools in the Czech Republic.

(Catholic, Protestant and Hussite), and two Catholic theological faculties at other universities.

5. *Broadcasting*

The participation of the Churches in the broadcasting of the public Czech Radio is provided under the 1999 Agreement mentioned above. *Proglas*, a private radio station with a Catholic priest as director, is very popular. The Church of the Seventh-Day Adventists has established a private radio station, *The Voice of Hope*.
Czech public television has created a special board for religious broadcasting including representatives of the Catholic and Protestant Churches. It operates without the agreement of the religious communities, but is trouble-free. No public TV programmes may be interrupted by commercials. They can go out only between programmes.
Private TV stations have no regular religious broadcasting. All programmes there may be interrupted by commercial breaks.
Churches have not yet obtained the right to participate, through their own delegates, in the controlling councils for radio and television broadcasting.

VI. Labour Law within the Religious Communities

A decision of the Constitutional Court of the Czech Republic of 26th March 1997 rejected the jurisdiction of secular courts in disputes concerning the termination of a service relationship involving members of the clergy. In 2001 the European Court for Human Rights in Strasbourg confirmed this decision.
The employment of clergy and other pastoral employees of religious communities (even "lay" pastoral assistants) is ruled by their internal law (Church law, canon law); conflicts are dealt with by their own courts and other authorities. If there is no rule of a religious community available, it is necessary to use State rules as a subsidiary source of law.
The employment of non-pastoral employees is ruled by secular law, namely the Labour Code (1964).

VII. Matrimonial and Family Law

The Czechoslovak Family Act of 1963, which is still in force, was amended by Federal Act No. 234/1992 Sb., restoring the legality of marriages in church from 1st July 1992. Nowadays there is a free choice between the religious and civil forms of marriage in the Czech Republic. But decisions of the Church courts on nullity are not recognised by the State.

Act No. 91/1998 Sb. amended the former provisions in such way that those intending to marry now have the duty to submit within the 3 months before marriage the certificate issued by the State register office which confirms that there are no impediments in Czech civil law to their marriage. Before this Act was passed, the clergy had to inquire as to these facts.

Membership of a religious community, as far as adolescents are concerned, depends on the wishes of their parents (or legal guardians) and their own choice. Czech ecclesiastical law follows in this respect the provisions of the Convention of the Rights of the Child. The attendance of children at religious education in schools has been resolved in the same way.

VIII. Finances of the Churches

After the decline of the communist regime, the religious communities in the Czech lands owned most of the churches and parsonages including parish gardens, and the proceeds of collections and savings.[14] Until the end of 1990 the State continued to pay clergy stipends, as well as part of the costs of the Church head offices and of repairs to Church buildings. Religious communities paid from collections the salaries of vergers and of other lay employees and the regular expenses of Church buildings.

The Restitution Act, under which the property expropriated by the communist regime was given back to its former owners, does not relate on the whole to religious entities. But it turned out to be necessary to give some religious houses back to religious institutions so

---

14 At the end of the communist regime convents of religious sisters living in camps saved money from their wages.

that they could create communities, open noviciates and restore their activities. Acts No. 298/1990 Sb. and 338/1991 Sb. restored the property rights of male and female religious orders in 170 religious houses (86 male and 84 female) within the territory of the Czech Republic. Church schools and children's homes, Church social institutions, and hospitals were established in several of these buildings.

In the case of the buildings that were not assigned to the State in the estate register, some were given back by administrative or judicial routes. At the time of writing, the forest and agricultural land that was part of the property of benefices, parish churches and monasteries has not been restored to the Catholic Church. Rented houses, several fields and other nationalized property have not been restored to the Protestant Churches. Only with Act No. 212/2000 Sb. did the restitution of property to the Jewish communities begin.

The return of Church financial property is still considered to be an open question. A special statutory provision (1991) prevents the transfer of this property to another person. Part of the money had been transferred to municipalities before the promulgation of this enactment, and thus the possibility of its return was precluded. The Churches are asking for financial compensation but there is no strong political will for this.

The State continues to pay stipend subsidies to religious communities. Some political representatives support the resolution of the restitution question as a precondition for abolishing these subsidies. Most religious communities have given their consent to the move.

The main sources of income for religious communities are collections and donations. Current Church property serves as a supplementary financial source to a small extent.

The State and municipalities help to meet the cost of repairs to some historic Church buildings. Religious communities have an enormous problem in maintaining not only their historic buildings, but also non-historical and modern buildings, for lack of money.

Church schools, teachers of religion in public schools, and military chaplains are paid by the State. Pastoral service in prisons is only partly met by the State, and in other public institutions there is no State support.

IX. Religious Assistance in Public Institutions

From 1994 onwards, the Churches have provided a pastoral service in prisons according to the Agreement between the Prison Administration of the Czech Republic, the Ecumenical Council of Churches in the Czech Republic, and the Czech Bishops' Conference. A new Agreement was made in 1999. Only from June 2002 have prison chaplains from some religious communities been paid by the State. They often work in the same prisons in which they themselves were imprisoned before 1989. A large number of volunteers – members of a special civic ecumenical organisation – shares in this pastoral service.
The status of military chaplains is ruled by the Agreement on co-operation between the Ministry of Defence of the Czech Republic, the Ecumenical Council of Churches in the Czech Republic, and the Czech Bishops' Conference of 3rd June 1998. Military chaplains are officers. They are appointed on the basis of the collective proposal of all the Churches that are parties to the agreement. The position of military chaplains in the structure of their Church is irrelevant. Conditions for the appointment of military chaplains are stated in the Agreement between the Ecumenical Council of Churches in the Czech Republic and the Czech Bishops' Conference of 10th June 1998: an example of outstanding ecumenical co-operation in the Czech Republic.
Religious assistance in hospitals and social institutions is not regulated by law nor by any Agreement. It is based only on constitutional principles and depends in reality on the goodwill of the governing body of such institutions.

X. Criminal Law and Religion

According to the Czech Penal Code the use of offensive language against people for their beliefs is a criminal offence (Section 198). There is no legal provision for the punishment of blasphemy in this Code.
In Act No. 308/1991 Sb. the State recognised the right to maintain the confessional confidentiality of all persons entrusted with pastoral

care in registered religious communities (Section 8). However, Act No. 3/2002 Sb. respects that right as only one of the "special rights" granted to registered religious communities under specified legal conditions. In addition to these conditions, the grant of a special right to maintain confessional confidentiality depends on it having been a traditional practice of that religious community for at least fifty years.

XI. Legal Status of Clergy and Members of Religious Orders

The legal status of clergy and those in religious orders does not differ from the legal status of other citizens, including the right to vote. The duty of the State to recognise religious names was not put into force and so the entry of these names into personal documents is made only through goodwill. In July 2001 the Act according to which citizens can enter two first names in their personal documents came into force, so the question of religious names may be resolved by this method.
As far as the right of succession is concerned, clergy and religious have the same testamentary freedom as other citizens.
As to the duty of military service, members of religious orders often serve in the Humanitarian Service of the Army of the Czech Republic. Clergy are given certain privileges, and may work in the Pastoral Service of the Army of the Czech Republic.

XII. Bibliography

Jiří Rajmund Tretera, Rechtliche und wirtschaftliche Grundlagen für den Dienst der Kirchen, in: Gemeinsame Wege – getrennte Wege, Die Zukunft der Beziehungen zwischen Staat und Kirchen, Prag, Konrad-Adenauer-Stiftung, 1996, p. 75-85.

Jiří Rajmund Tretera, Finansowanie Kościołów w Republice Czeskiej, in: Systemy finansowania instytucji kościelnych w Europie, Towarzystwo Naukowe KUL, Lublin, 2000, p. 109-121.

Jiří Rajmund Tretera, Church and State in the Czech Republic, in: European Journal for Church and State Research, Peeters, Leuven, volume 7, 2000, p. 299-315, volume 8, 2001, p. 287-294.

Jiří Rajmund Tretera, Church Autonomy in the Czech Republic, in: *Robbers, Gerhard* (ed.), Church Autonomy, A Comparative Survey, Frankfurt a/M., 2001, p. 633-644.

Jiří Rajmund Tretera, Systems of Relations between the State and Churches in general and their Occurrence in the Czech Lands in particular, in: Many Cultures, Many Faces, Monsignor W. Onclin Chair, Katholieke Universiteit Leuven, 2002, p. 31-56.

Jiří Rajmund Tretera, Stát a církve v České republice, Karmelitánské nakladatelství, Kostelní Vydří, 2002, 156 p.

Jiří Rajmund Tretera, Die jüngsten Rechtsfragen des tschechischen Religionsrechts, Teil 1, in: Österreichisches Archiv für Recht und Religion, Heft 2, Wien, 2002, p. 230-238.

Periodicals:
Revue církevního práva/Church Law Review, Společnost pro církevní právo, Praha.
European Journal for Church and State Research, Peeters, Leuven.

Inger Dübeck
State and Church in Denmark

I. Social Facts

The Evangelical-Lutheran Church is the Danish National Church, Folkekirken or the Folk Church. In 1991 88 % of the Danish population were members of the Folk Church. In 2002 only 84 % were members. In pure numbers, membership has decreased, which could be a sign of a decreasing religiosity in the population. Denmark has a growing number of different religious denominations or communities. It is no longer possible to obtain statistical informations about the number of members, because it is illegal to register information about religious conviction in public or private registers of persons. The total population figures have increased because of the many immigrants, and many of the immigrants are members of religious communities other than the Folk Church. Presumably this has increased the level of religious activity in the population. It is obvious that questions about religion, philosophy of life and spiritual activities are more prominent in the different forms of media.

II. Historical Background

Christianity was declared the religion of Denmark by king Harold Bluetooth when he let himself be baptized in the year 960 A.D. But Frisian missionaries came to Denmark as early as about 700, and with the missionary Ansgar (801-865) Christianity was spreading in the southern part of Jutland. From around 1000 the Danish Church became strongly influenced by English church life in the Anglo-Danish empire. The Danish Church was part of the Roman Catholic Church until 1536. During the 15th century ideas of a national and state church were developing and made the country more open for the ideas of the Reformation in the 16th century. A sort of revolution or civil war took place in the years 1534-36. The result was that Christian III (1536-1559) and the gentry won control of the realm. He was crowned in 1536 as a Lutheran king. The Reformation became one of the political consequences of his victory. He dismissed all the bishops and confiscated all the Episcopal landed estates.

The reformer Johannes Bugenhagen wrote the new Church Ordinance, which was sanctioned by Martin Luther, and inducted all new Lutheran superintendents or bishops as they were soon once more called. The Danish bishops so did not obtain the apostolic succession. The church became formally a state church for which the king and his council had the power to legislate in all matters. The Absolutist Constitution, the Lex Regia, from 1665, obliged the king to follow the Augsburgian Confession of 1530 and to keep all inhabitants to the same creed and to protect all his realm against heretics, fanatics and blasphemers. Article 6 of the Constitution also gave the king all legislative and executive power in relation to the entire church administration and clergy. The Danish Codebook, "Danske Lov", from 1683 gave in Book II about religion and clergy a sort of legal definition of the accepted Christianity as a public matter.

Compulsory church membership for all citizens was replaced in the new democratic constitution of 1849 by the freedom to join religious communities according to one's own conviction. No one could be forced to belong to a certain religious community with the exception of the king or queen regnant, who according to article 6 "must belong to the Evangelical-Lutheran Church". This does not mean that the king or queen must be a member of the Folk Church, but membership of another Evangelical-Lutheran church would be sufficient.

The Danish Church became a Folk Church, "Folkekirke", which means a People's Church, and stopped being a State Church in a strict sense, although the connections between the state and the church remained close. A public debate about this relationship has developed during recent years. Some people, including some within the church, want a separation of State and Church, but most of the population are against such separation.

The Constitution formalised freedom of religion, but did not institute equality of religions. During the nearly 190 years of Absolutism (1660-1849) the state became more friendly towards foreigners of other religious denominations, so that freedom of religion was obtained in practice at the beginning of the 19th century and before the Constitution of 1849.

Denmark has today 12 dioceses of which 3 have female bishops. Until 1990 the Faroes were part of the diocese of Copenhagen, but now constitute a normal diocese, and the same holds good for Greenland, which in 1993 acquired the same status as the Faroes and in 1994 got its own bishop.

III. Basic Structure

1. Legal Sources

The ecclesiastical law comprises all valid legal sources for all Christian churches and for all religious groups or communities in Denmark. But the legal sources for the Folk Church are constitutional and general laws, statutes, governmental notices, and decided cases especially from the Supreme Court and the new special clerical Court for Doctrinal Cases. The statute laws concern issues connected with the economy of the church, church buildings and the churchyards. Other laws concern membership of the church, its employees, bishops, education, personal registration, baptism, confirmation, burial and a rather large body of rules about the parishes and parish councils. A contractual form or agreement between state and Folk Church has not been applied in the Danish legal system.
The Danish Constitution, "Danmarks Riges Grundlov", article 4, which made it a duty for the State to subsidise the Evangelical-Lutheran Church, is a sort of general clause concerning the legal position of the Folk Church. It says: "The Evangelical-Lutheran Church is the Folk Church and as such is to be supported by the State". The term "Folk Church" goes back to the first Constitution of 1849 and is unchanged in the following Constitutions from 1866, 1915, 1920 and 1953. It presupposes that most of the Danish people belong to that church. If this should change, it will not cease to exist, but article 4 would be without meaning. The support of the state concerns economic, legal and political relations. A separation between the Folk Church and the State is formally not possible without changing the Constitution, which is difficult because of the special procedural requirements for constitutional changes.
The duty of the state to support the Folk Church does not mean that other religious communities or denominations cannot be supported.

In practice some of them receive different forms of subsidies, e.g. to use certain buildings without payment or for the education of children. Article 4 does not make it a duty for municipalities to support the Folk Church, but they are free to do so, if it is in accordance with municipal legislation.

Under Article 66 the Folk Church should have its own synodical constitution, which should give it autonomy to take decisions in all ecclesiastical matters and freedom in relation to the civil authorities of the state by establishing a central church council, which could speak on behalf of the church. But this promise have still not been fulfilled. Several commissions were set up during the second half of the 19th century to work out a system of church government but without a positive result. The topic is of some current interest, because of certain political decisions taken by the Minister of Ecclesiastical Affairs, which attracted extensive criticism both from within the clergy and from outside. Many pointed to the Swedish model with separation between State and Church as desirable. In practice article 66 has been interpreted as if it only provided that "the conditions of the Folk Church shall be regulated by law".

Many particular statute laws have in the meantime decided questions concerning church matters. In 1855 the obligation to avail oneself exclusively of the services of the incumbent of the parish was removed and in 1868 the freedom and right to prefer to belong to a distinct parish was given. In 1903 an Act on free Parish Councils entitled all members of the Folk Church over 18 years to vote and to be eligible for election to the parochial church. The parishes, approximately 2,200 in number, are the fundamental democratic unit of the Folk Church. New legislation concerning international and inter-church co-operation has come into force in the 1980s and 1990s.

Though the principle of religious freedom was accepted in practice before 1849, the principle was explicitly stated in the Constitution of 1849 and in all later constitutions, now as article 67, under which "the citizens have the right to unite in communities in order to worship God in the way which corresponds to their conviction, unless the communities teach or act contrary to morality or public order".

Under Article 68, no person is obliged to support the worship of any God other than his own with personal financial contributions. Non-members of the Folk Church do not have to pay church taxes, but normal taxes, e.g. land taxes which must be paid by all owners of real property, must be paid by other religious communities and their members.

Article 69 states that "religious communities or denominations other than the Folk Church shall be regulated by a special act dealing with the legal position of dissenters". No such Act has ever been passed, but different rules in the Penal Code and in administrative legislation concerning non-discrimination on the ground of religion give a certain guarantee for such communities.

Article 70 is a non-discrimination rule. "No one can be deprived of his right to the complete enjoyment of civil and political rights on the ground of his belief or origin. And no one can refrain from the fulfilment of his civil duties on such grounds." Article 70 also gives protection for persons living abroad but having property in Denmark, and for persons with any type of religious conviction. The Act on Prohibition of Discrimination in the Labour Market (459/1996) has been used in two cases about the wearing of head-scarves for religious reasons. In the first case (U 2000. 2350) the High Court found that it was indirect discrimination to dismiss a person for wearing a scarf, and that the firm had neglected its duty to have clear instructions on the clothing question. The second case was first decided in the High Court 2001, but then appealed to the Supreme Court, where it was affirmed. The High Court found in its sentence that the firm had an objective interest in forbidding the use of a head-scarf, because it was a producer of foodstuffs and so it was a question of a necessary requirement of hygiene.

Article 71 states that "no Danish citizen can be committed to prison on account of his religious conviction". It covers every kind of compulsory imprisonment, also hospitalisation. The rule concerns only Danish citizens and may be looked upon as discriminatory. The ECHR article 14 has a general prohibition against such discrimination for political, religious or ethnical reasons, which probably must have altered article 71 in practice, though not formally. With the incorporation in 1992 of the European Convention of Human Rights as part of Danish Law the principle of religious freedom in article 9 applies generally, and serves to strengthen the formal guarantee in article 67.

2. *Categories of System Approach*

The Folk Church represents a dualism, being simultaneously a state church with a public duty to ensure the availability of the services and religious functions of the Evangelical-Lutheran Faith and a democratic institution for the great majority of the Danish people with representative local self government. It is supported by the State, but it is not a state agency in the normal sense of the word. Although it is a religious denomination, it is not a private association like the acknowledged, the recognized or the non-recognized religious communities. The Folk Church stands under Parliament, the "Folketinget", and the Minister of Ecclesiastical Affairs. There has been legal debate on the question whether the Folk Church is a religious community. Some of the church-related legislation treats the Folk Church as such a community, although it has no autonomy and all legal decisions must be taken by Parliament or the Government (the Minster of Ecclesiastical Affairs). But Parliament and Government are obliged to respect the status of the Evangelical-Lutheran Church and its doctrine.

The Folk Church has a status similar to state agencies and its legal regulations are part of public law, while the legal status of other religious communities is that of private associations and their legal regulations are part of the general legal system and may be part of private or of public law. But the legal structure of other churches and denominations will to a certain degree be more influenced by their foreign mother organisation and regulated through internal statutes, conventions and customs.

Each local church may be looked upon as a state agency in so far as local churches have to perform different administrative functions, and civil legal activities, for the Central Administration. The parishes normally own some property, for instance real estate, which gives a certain income. The majority of local churches may thus be looked upon as legal persons or bodies with legal personality. The parish councils as the board of directors for the local parishes are independent legal bodies with legal capacity in many areas, not only locally as an administrative authority, but also in relation to the election of priests, services, rituals etc.

The different religious communities other than the Folk Church are independent autonomous, private institutions and are often organised as private associations with members paying some sort of subscription or dues. The establishment of such religious communities does not secure any special advantages or legal status from the State. But if they own real estate or a foundation (a charitable institution, a school, a hospital or the like) is established, of course the particular community must submit to Danish legislation about such matters, but they may also obtain some advantages or subventions.

IV. Legal Status of Religious Bodies

1. Legal Status

Religious bodies are in law to be divided into three groups: acknowledged communities, communities with authorization for weddings, and other religious communities without any formal recognition. The concept of acknowledged religious community was already used in Danish pre-constitutional legislation in relation to the German and the French Reformed Churches, the Roman Catholic Church and the Jewish Community. The concept of acknowledgment was mentioned in the oldest constitutions from 1849 and 1866, but from 1915 article 69 only mentions "religious communities other than the Folk Church". The acknowledgment was until 1969 given by a royal decree to the priest of a specific parish, who was authorized to marry and baptize and to keep registers of individual status. Such acknowledgments were given in accordance with this earlier practice to the Baptists, the Methodists, the Swedish Gustaf's Church, the Norwegian King Haakon Church, the Finnish Church, the Icelandic Church, the Danish Reformed Church, St. Albans' English Church and the Russian Orthodox Church.

The religious communities whose priests have authority to marry now number 90, which includes religious denominations of very different kinds, among which are 50 different Christian communities, 18 different Islamic communities and 4 Buddhist communities.

A condition for having an authorisation for the performance of weddings is that the community must be a religious denomination with a clear organisational structure and representatives. There must be a certain number of members, more than a few persons. It is not enough to be a religious movement or a philosophical or scientific association. The religious community must have a cult, a doctrine and a rite, which are legally acceptable and not contrary to morality or public order. The priests of such religious communities need not to have Danish citizenship, but they must know the Danish language well. They must declare that they will observe the Danish legislation and governmental decisions generally and that they will respect the secular aspects of ceremonial acts. Lately some imams have been criticized for failing to respect essential Danish cultural values and for making political propaganda. A consequence of the recognition limited to the solemnisation of weddings is that the authorised priests are not in the position to baptise with civil legal effect or to register personal information. Registration has to be by the local parish priest of the Folk Church, which has been heavily criticised in recent years. If a church or religious community is allowed to perform weddings, it will automatically have the right to tax exemptions for single gifts between 500 and 5.000 Danish Crowns by virtue of the Act on Assessment of Income Taxes to the State (791/2002). It is also possible for donors to accept unilateral obligations to pay bigger contributions for a period of at least 10 years to such associations, institutions or religious communities as are approved by the Minister of Taxation. The condition for such approval is that the religious community is domiciled in Denmark. The Taxation Authorities publish lists with the names of approved associations and religious communities.

If a church or denomination or an association of several religious associations is accepted as a religious community it will automatically obtain the tax exemption, while other organisations in which a religious purpose is one among a number of other purposes (such as charitable, social or cultural ones) will have to fulfil some special legal conditions as to number of members, a minimum number of donors, a secure financial basis etc. in order to get the exemption. Religious organisations inside the Folk Church with diaconal, social or cultural aims will probably not be covered by the Act on Assessment of Income Taxes.

Since 1868 it has been possible for members of the Folk Church to form a special parish and to choose a certain person as their priest and have this "Election Parish" (Valgmenighed) acknowledged as part of the Folk Church. The parish must have its own church building or an acceptable church hall. The members of the election parish pay all expenses themselves and do not receive contributions from the State. The parish must have a board or managing council with legal capacity. The Election Parish is a legal person with corporate rights and duties in relation to public and private institutions and persons. It stands under the supervision of the bishop in relation to the Ministry of Ecclesiastical Affairs. This type of election parishes has been used also for the establishment of special parishes for deaf persons with special trained "deaf chaplains".

It is also possible to establish "Free Parishes" (Frimenigheder) which are outside the Folk Church even if they confess the same Evangelical-Lutheran Faith. The Free Parishes want to be autonomous in matters of organisation and to have similar conditions to those of the Election Parishes. They have more privileges than other religious communities e.g. a right to use the churches of the Folk Church for their religious services and for their priests to wear the same gown as

priests in the Folk Church, if they have served a Free Parish for at least 7 years, and they have the right to make use of the special training in the "Priests High School" and the "Priests' Training College". They do not have the right to perform weddings and baptising with civil legal effect, but they can conduct ceremonies associated with weddings and baptisms.
The new religious movements, "New Age", and other more or less philosophical movements with alternative approaches to traditional western culture with interests in spiritual matters, mysticism, holistic ideas, theories about reincarnation etc. may be protected by article 67 about the freedom of worshipping God, although they will not be able to have an acknowledgment as a religious community, but they will clearly be protected by article 78 about freedom of associations. Article 67 also protects individuals such as Muslim imams, but of course only in places where public order will not be disturbed.

2. Activities of Religious Communities

In the modern society, public authorities at local or national level take responsibility for social and health-related problems, including education of children and young people. But the public sector is no longer the only provider of "Welfare". The crisis in the Welfare State has called on alternative resources and solutions to the different needs for charity and help. The concept of "welfare-mix" has been used to characterise the composition of different welfare suppliers from different sectors: the public sector (State, municipality) the market sector (profit-making, private organisations) and the civil society sector (voluntary, non-profit-making networks or associations). In Denmark there are probably around 100 free organisations with the status of private legal entity which are founded on Christian principles and are active either in Denmark or on overseas humanitarian work, and around 15 associations working in foreign missions. These free organisations are either connected to the Folk Church or attached to other religious communities, and they have established many different social welfare institutions, commercial enterprises and schools. They form an essential part of the Danish welfare system by running kindergartens, schools, post-primary schools, nursing homes etc. If they work together with public social authorities they will also get public subsidies.
Spiritual movements from the middle of the 19th century have formed an important part of the Christian life. The two very different bodies,

"The Christian Association for Inner Mission" and "The Grundtvigian Movement" named after the clergyman, hymn writer and author N.F.S.Grundtvig (1783-1872), are of equal importance to an understanding of this development. Inner Mission is a revival movement with a call to conversion and personal commitment to Jesus. The movement has mission houses throughout the country and has appointed 100 lay ministers. Inner Mission started Sunday Schools and from these schools developed YMCA-boy scouts and YWCA-girl scouts as well as FDF and FPF (The Boys' Brigade and the Girls' Brigade). The Grundtvigian movement was less organised, but very influential for the religious life of Denmark. The movement also built houses, but not for prayer alone, but first and foremost for the instruction of common people and for the physical and moral education of young people. Grundtvigianism created the "Danish Folk High School" which has been a tremendous success in popular education and an important supplement to the standard primary school.

All religious communities whether recognized or not have the right to arrange collections with social or humanitarian aims at their indoor services or meetings, when the initiative for the collection is taken by the religious community as such. All charitable humanitarian, private organisations have a right to arrange public collections. Among these organisations we find some with close connections to the Folk Church or other churches, for instance Caritas. In the Folk Church the parish councils may arrange collections and spend the money on different forms of voluntary work. A single parish council cannot give money to the running of voluntary Christian organisations without permission from the Ministry of Ecclesiastical Affairs, but two or more parish councils may work together and jointly find some money for such purposes under the Act on Participation by the Folk Church in Interchurch Cooperation (334/1989). This Act also offered the possibility of promoting closer links between the Folk Church and other religious communities: see Act on the Economy of the Folk Church (537/1997 § 12). But it was emphasised that the new Interchurch Board should in no way have a synodical character. The resources for this work come from different funds and subsidies from local parishes inside the relevant diocese.

"Folkekirkens nødhjælp" (Folk Church Relief) is a private Christian organisation which takes part in national and international ecumenical co-operation. "Kirkens Korshær" (The Cross-Army of the Church) has a closer connection with the Folk Church but cooperates with public authorities in a lot of institutions and services. In Copenhagen it works e.g. for prostitutes, drug addicts and in lodging-houses for homeless people.

Article 76 of the Constitution secures "a right for all children to receive a free education" (freedom of education). Parents or guardians who wants to make their own educational arrangements for their children are not obliged to send the children into the public primary school ("Folkeskolen"), if the instruction given otherwise is comparable with the general practice in the primary school. This "freedom of school" is a special right for the parents to give their children the necessary instruction either at home or in a private school. Parents may choose a private school for political, religious, cultural, pedagogical, national or personal reasons as provided in the Act on Free Schools and Private Primary Schools (619/2002).

No private schools have been established especially for children of parents belonging to the Folk Church. But several religious communities or denominations have opened such private schools, which receive public subsidies, if they fulfil prescribed conditions as to the quality of instruction, independence and good administration. They must not be controlled by special interests, and it is not allowed for such schools to co-operate with extraneous institutions or groups, which are not relevant to the curriculum, e.g. in order to practise political indoctrination as seen in some Muslim schools which have been closed by the authorities.

A High Court decision held that a municipal refusal to make a new building available to a Free School for children of parents belonging to the Scientology movement correct and not in conflict with ECHR article 9. The court did not take a decision on the still open question, whether Scientology is a real religious community or not (VLD 12/1 1999).

V. *Church and Culture*

1. *Religious Education*

The "teaching of Christianity" in the primary schools was in 1975 changed into teaching of "religious knowledge". But the Act on the Primary School (730/2000) has now chosen to speak of teaching of "knowledge of Christianity". The subject is a compulsory part of the

curriculum on all levels from the 1st to the 10th class, except the 7th and 8th level, where the children are given the opportunity to receive preparation for confirmation from the priest of the parish.
The central theme in this subject is the Christianity of the Evangelical-Lutheran Folk Church. In the higher classes the pupils are to be presented with other religions and different forms of philosophy of life. The teaching of Christianity comprises the history of Christianity in Europe and Denmark, the Reformation and the relation between State and Church in Denmark. It also aims to make the pupils familiar with fundamental values in Danish culture on the basis of the Bible. In the gymnasium or grammar schools, religion is a compulsory discipline, but only during the last of the 3 years of study; it comprises religion and not especially Christianity.
Children who do not want to be confirmed are not obliged to follow the normal education in Christian knowledge instead of going to the priest of the parish. A child can be exempted from the instruction in Christianity when its parents so request, but the child must itself join in the request if it has reached the age of 15 years. A teacher can ask for exemption from the duty of giving instruction in Christianity.
A special feature in the Danish system of education is the "Folk High School" for adults, younger or older people, and the so-called "Efterskoler"(post primary schools) for young people between 14 and 18, who have left primary school and do not want to go to a gymnasium. They will get instruction in a few topics, which they learn to study more seriously and independently, than is the case in the normal primary school.
Theological education is primarily given in the two theological faculties at the university of Copenhagen and the university of Aarhus. Normally all priests, deans and bishops must have graduated in theology. Persons who have been priests in the Church of Greenland and have passed the special course in Christian Teaching in Greenland, can, if they speak Danish, be priests in the Folk Church. The Minister of Ecclesiastical Affairs can grant exemptions to enable persons with different educational backgrounds to be priests. Such exemptions are typically granted to persons with another university education e.g. in history, knowledge of Christianity, or languages, if they have shown the specific qualities needed for the work of a priest. Also persons appointed as missionaries in the Foreign Mission may have other qualifications than a theological degree.
As an alternative to the ordinary theological education at the two universities, an institution for theological students on a clear confessional basis has been established in Aarhus. The aim is to provide a

complete education for priests on the basis of the Bible and the Evangelical-Lutheran confessional writings, in contrast to the two theological faculties which are non-confessional. The institution in Aarhus is called "Menighedsfakultetet" (the Parish Faculty). A corresponding institute in Copenhagen is called "Dansk Bibel-Institut" (the Danish Bible Institute). Neither currently offers a complete theological education, although it is the aim for the future.

The Folk Church has different institutions for education, post education or supplementary training on a university-level. For new theological graduates the "Priests' Training College" (Pastoralseminariet) as a compulsory school gives preparatory training in pastoral or liturgical theology. Post educational or supplementary training for priests in practical and general theology is given in the "Priests' High School" (Præstehøjskolen). Furthermore there are three "Church Music Schools" for organists, singers and carillon players. The two colleges for priests and the musical education are financed by the Folk Church through the so-called "Common Fund".

2. Media

The Radio and Television system in Denmark consists of 2 units: 1. "DR" (Danish Radio and Television) which is a public agency with a certain autonomy, 2. "TV 2/Danmark" which is a private foundation. It has 8 regional TV undertakings with public service activities. Particular organisations may receive grants to make programmes for radio or regional or local programmes for TV. Associations and private communities as well as municipalities may also get special grants to make programmes, under the Act on Radio and Television Activities (1052/2002).

DR, TV 2/Danmark and the 8 regional undertakings are all obliged to deliver public service activities through television, radio or the Internet. Public service includes "news, information, education, art and entertainment". The programmes must reflect a certain broadness and make provision which reflects the plurality or multiplicity of cultural interests in the Danish society. The special Christian interests of the Folk Church are not explicitly mentioned.

The Act has been followed by some departmental regulations about the content of advertising. Transmission of programmes which might instigate hatred based on race, gender, religion, nationality or sexual orientation is forbidden, see 1174/2002 which corresponds to the EU Directive concerning broadcasting.

There are no specific regulations about the right of religious communities to get programme time. But the general rules and the structure of the system allow for such activities. DR broadcasts on radio each weekday morning the morning prayer from Copenhagen Cathedral, and on each Sunday and special major religious festivals DR broadcasts on radio and TV morning or afternoon services from different churches, not only from the Folk Church but also from other Christian Communities. Each Saturday afternoon a programme with children's choir and the readings set for the following Sunday is broadcast by DR. During a year different churches and choirs are in this way seen on television. Such programmes in television and radio seem to be very popular. A suggestion by DR that they might be discontinued let to many protests to the board of DR.
Many individual programmes take up problems of religion and Christian life. Some of the Christian communities have established their own local TV stations. In Aarhus, a Programme Centre for videos, CDs and special TV programmes was established in 1998 as a commercial foundation under the name "Danmarks Kirkelige Mediecenter" (The church media centre of Denmark). Some newspapers specialise in religious and Christian questions although also containing general news. In Denmark a political party, the Christian Democrats, bases its political programme upon Christian principles.
The problem of the interruption of religious programmes by commercials does not arise in Denmark, because the Act on Radio and Television requires that commercials can only be transmitted in blocks between the programmes (1052/2002 § 73).
The different radio and television institutes are organized with separate, special boards. In DR 10 members are nominated by the Minister of Cultural Affairs, 6 by the Parliament and 1 by the staff of DR. The members must be knowledgeable about culture, media, management and business. If there are priests or other clergy who have such knowledge, they may be nominated. In TV 2/Danmark the Minister of Cultural Affairs nominates 9 members and the staff 1 member with the same qualifications as mentioned above. In the regional institutions, the boards are nominated by a council and by the staff. Members of Parliament or local or regional municipality politicians cannot be nominated.

VI. Labour Law within Religious Communities

1. Individual Labour Law

The Act on Employment in Positions in the Folk Church (310/1990) deals not only with the clergy but also with all other positions in relation to church services, church administration and churchyards. The clergy will normally be appointed in accordance with the rules in the Act on Civil Servants (678/1998) and are in that respect looked upon as belonging to the normal body of civil servants. The clergy are appointed and dismissed by the Minister of Ecclesiastical Affairs, but the appointment will take place after nomination by the parish council. The Act on Civil Servants has a special chapter about the civil servants of the Folk Church, because of the special relationship between the clergy and the parishes.

The normal rules of suspension and disciplinary actions against civil servants may be used against priests, but not in cases raising doctrinal questions. The rules of dismissal can be used in cases where the priest and the parish have for several years been in serious disagreement, which has adversely affected church life in the parish.

For the other religious communities the main principle must be that they have to follow the common labour rules both as to individual labour law and collective labour law. But the Act on Prohibition of Discrimination in the Labour Market (459/1996) allows employers to dismiss persons who do not have a certain religious conviction, if it is relevant for the job, e.g. as a teacher in a religious school. The Act on Protection Against Dismissal because of Membership of a Special Association (443/1990) does not prevent employers in bodies which promote a certain religious conviction, e.g. a religious community, from requiring that a priest looking for employment is a member of that particular religious community.

2. Collective Labour Law

The different groups of employees have their own trade unions under a few central organisations, which have the right to negotiate salaries and other terms and conditions of employment with the Minister of Finance on behalf of the State. The central organisations for priests and deans and other officials also have the right to negotiate with the

Minister of Finance. The central organisations for church officials are:

1) The National Association of Publicly Employed University Graduates. It can negotiate for priests, deans, bishops, gardeners with horticultural qualifications and the higher educated organists and cantors.
2) The Central Organisation for Servants in the State with more specific qualifications (not at university level): it can negotiate for parish clerks, some organists, supervisors and assistants in cemeteries.
3) The Union of State Employees. It can negotiate for non-skilled gardeners and gravediggers etc.

Each group of church employees has its own trade union, e.g. "the Danish Priests' Association" (Den danske Præsteforening) and "the Deans' Association" (Provsteforeningen), which has the right to negotiate on all matters concerning the members' relationship to the church authorities. Although the members of the parish councils are democratically elected, they do have an organisation for their special interests, which of course is not a trade union.

While the basic agreements are negotiated between the Minister of Finance and the central organisation, the Minister of Ecclesiastical Affairs can be authorised to negotiate on particular matters with the individual trade unions for church officials. The employees have the right to be represented by their trade unions in negotiations with the parish council about working conditions. The bargaining topics for the central organisations are those of wages and conditions of employment, for instance the length of a probationary period, contributions to housing costs, travelling expenses, removal expenses, sickness and unemployment benefit.

Civil servants of the State administration, including the clergy, have a more explicit loyalty to the State and have no right to strike. In return the State has no right to "lock out" its civil servants. But other employees in the Church who are not civil servants do have all normal collective rights in the labour market, including the right to strike.

VII. Matrimonial and Family Law

The Marriage Act (147/1999) provides that both parties must have Danish citizenship or a legal residence permit under the Act of Aliens (608/2002). The Act of Aliens has been amended in recent years to include several new and very strict conditions especially concerning family reunions. If a marriage seems to be a forced marriage or a marriage of convenience entered into in order to get a residence permit, the permit will not be given and the marriage will not be recognised. Under the Act on Aliens there is no longer a right to a residence permit in order to bring about a family reunion. The aliens' authorities must subject to ECHR articles 8 and 12 and the UN conventions test the existence of all the legal conditions. The result of the new rules is that the number of family reunions among immigrants is sharply reduced. But the rules have caused problems for Danish citizens studying or living abroad for some years, when they want to return to Denmark together with a foreign wife or husband. In order to get a residents permit for the spouse, they have to demonstrate a closer affiliation to Denmark than to the foreign country from which the spouse comes, and there is a minimum age-limit of 24 years. The number of forced marriages of young immigrant women has been reduced during recent years.

The wedding ceremony may be either religious or civil, at the choice of the parties. The religious wedding may take place in the Folk Church if one of the parties is a member. The same condition holds good in the acknowledged churches, that is: one of the parties must be a member of the religious community. In the case of the other religious communities, one of the parties must be a member and the community must have a priest who is authorised to perform weddings. Everyone has a right to civil weddings.

There are now 90 religious communities other than the acknowledged churches, whose priests have been authorised to solemnise weddings. The most recent such community which obtained this right in November 2003 is the so-called "Forn Sidr", a community which believes in the ancient Nordic gods Wodan and Thor. This provoked some protests from those objecting to the old heathenism from the Viking Age being accepted as a religious community with the right to tax exemptions.

Conciliation by a priest in case of separation or divorce is voluntary; the same is true of counselling from a civil servant or a psychologist.

VIII. Finances of the Church

The revenues of the Folk Church amount to about 4.5 milliard, 75 % of which is paid as church taxes by members. The State subvention amounts to 12 % and the remaining 13 % comes from funds and real property and special contributors.
The expenditure of the Folk Church is distributed as follows: 50 % for wages to priests, deans, bishops and other staff members, 25 % for daily working expenses, 10 % for pensions and 15 % to new investments.
60 % of the church taxes are used for wages to priests and deans. The State subvention goes to the Ministry of Ecclesiastical Affairs, wages for bishops, pensions for priests and deans and for the remaining 40 % of wages for priests and deans, the administration of parishes and dioceses, education, special grants for restoring historic churches, furnishings, graves and monuments deserving preservation.
All revenues go into the Common Fund, which is administered by the diocesan authorities.

IX. Religious Assistance in Public Institutions

The Ministry of Ecclesiastical Affairs can decide that theologically trained persons shall or may by appointed in the service of public institutions or groups who do not constitute a parish, e.g. for university students, for private religious and humanitarian organisations, for hospitals and for prisons. During the last 10 years priests have become more visible in many social context as trained helpers in disaster situations, among street children, for AIDS sufferers etc.
Under the Act on Personnel of the Defence Forces (249/2001), military personnel include clergy. Military chaplains are an integral part of the organisation of the different military forces (army, navy and air force). Not a few of the chaplains have in the recent years been in service with UN forces, and in other international peace-keeping activities with NATO and lately in Iraq both in war and humanitarian activities.

X. Criminal Law and Religion

Anyone who tries to hinder, obstruct or disturb divine services or other church ceremonies can be punished under the Penal Code § 137, and under § 140 persons who publicly mock or insult the confession of faith or worship of God of a legitimate religious community may be punished with imprisonment for up to 4 months or in case of mitigating circumstances to a fine. The condition of "legitimacy" does not concern the status as acknowledged or not, but the general constitutional condition that each association must be lawful. The Penal Code § 266b, penalises statements or information made publicly or with the intention of disseminating them widely, by which a group of persons are threatened, insulted or degraded because of their race, colour of skin, national or ethnical origin, faith or sexual orientation. If the activities or information have the character of propaganda this will be looked upon as aggravating circumstances. The extreme right-wing political Party, "Dansk Folkeparti", has on the basis of a court decision (U 1999. 1113) criticised § 266b. They argue that it limit their freedom of expression, if they cannot express their critical view of immigrants and especially of Muslims. They want § 266b to be repealed.

The Act on Festivals (279/1983) is in fact a supplement to the Penal Code § 137, which only covers wilful noise and disorder. The Act on Festivals § 1 forbids every action on Holy Days of the Folk Church, which might disturb the church service. The act does not protect the festivals or Holy Days of other churches or religious communities.

As to Danish Procedural Law taking the oath is no longer a possibility. It was abolished in 1965.

Prisoners serving a sentence in open or closed prisons have the opportunity to participate in religious services performed in the institution and a right to see a clergyman or minister or equivalent from his own religious community according to the Act on the Execution of a Sentence (432/2000 § 35). When in custody this right may be limited because of an ongoing investigation. If the prison authorities are responsible for the preparation of the prisoners' food, a special diet must be provided for Muslims, Jews and others whose religion requires it.

XI. Legal Status of Clergy

Priests enjoy the full civil rights and liberties of the Constitution and the European Convention of Human Rights. They also have freedom of expression. In the Act on Parish Councils (571/1996) § 37 it is emphasised that the priest in exercising his function and in giving spiritual counsel is independent of the parish council. This principle is called "freedom of confession".

The Act on Civil Service declares in § 17, that civil servants can only have another occupation in addition to their main employment, if it is possible to combine it with a conscientious performance of all duties in the service and with the necessary esteem and trust. The Act on Civil Servants has a "general duty" of "decorum" in article 10 requiring the civil servant to observe conscientiously the rules about his employment and both within the service and in his private life to show himself worthy of the esteem and trust which his position requires.

The priest has a right to professional secrecy not only concerning confessional secrets, but also concerning all information which he receives during his office, if secrecy is appropriate, e.g. information concerning personal registration. See also the Act on Administration chapter 8 and the Penal Code § 152.

If any civil servant, including a priest, is elected to be a member of Folketinget, the Constitution says explicitly in article 30(2), that he need not have permission from the Government to accept election. At present there are 4 priests in Folketinget. Normally it will be necessary to apply for complete or partial leave of absence under the rules of the Act on Civil Servants § 58 in order to serve. This also holds good for civil servants which are elected to local municipal councils. The performance of an honorary office may make it impossible to fulfil the normal duties to the full extent. But civil servants, including priests, are under no duty to notify their superiors if they take up some sort of private activity provided that it can be combined with their main job.

Priests and clergy have the right to take part in all forms of public life and to sit on public boards in the field of culture, if it is not in conflict with the duties and with decorum. Both in relation to the preparation of church legislation in the Ministry of Ecclesiastical Affairs and in many other administrative fields, the clergy will often be asked to take part as representatives, e.g. in the trade union for the priests. The only proviso is that no one can speak on behalf of the

Folk Church as such, because of the special Danish structure without a central synod or council.

The Act on Doctrinal Cases (336/1992) is to be used in cases brought before the so-called Priests' Court or Bishops' Court in cases where a cleric through his preaching of the Gospel has disregarded the confessional basis of the Folk Church, and in this way has disregarded his vow in which he had promised to "preach the words of God clean and pure" The doctrinal cases concern breach of discipline, and they are not ordinary penal cases. The ordinary court and the ordinary judge become the Priests Court when two theological experts are added. The decision may be challenged on appeal to the High Court, where three theological experts will join the court. The experts in the Priests Court need not be ordained priests. They will be chosen by lot from a list which is prepared by the Ministry of Ecclesiastical Affairs with the consent of the central organisation. If the case concerns a bishop it will start in the High Court and an appeal lies to the Supreme Court. The experts in the Bishops' Court will be the two most senior bishops by length of service. The priest or bishop against whom a doctrinal action is brought has the right to chose an advocate as assessor. Only two cases have until now been brought before these special courts.

XII. Bibliography

Inger Dübeck, in: *European Consortium for State-Church Research* (ed.), Church and Labour Law in the EC-Countries, Milano, 1993.

Inger Dübeck, in: *European Consortium for State-Church Research* (ed.), Marriage and Religion in Europe, Milano, 1993.

Inger Dübeck, in: *European Consortium for State-Church research* (ed.), Status of Churches in the European Countries, Milano 1995.

Inger Dübeck, in: *European Consortium for State-Church Research* (ed.), The Constitutional Status of Churches in the European Union Countries, Milano 1995.

Inger Dübeck, in: *Gerhard Robbers* (ed.), State and Church in the European Union. Baden-Baden, 1996.

Inger Dübeck, in: *European Consortium for State-Church Research* (ed.), New Liberties and Church and State relationships in Europe, Milano 1998.

Inger Dübeck, in: *European Consortium for State-Church Research* (ed.), Citizens and Believers in the Countries of the European Union, Milano 1999.

Inger Dübeck, Kirchenfinanzierung der nordischen Länder, in: Zeitschrift für Evangelisches Kirchenrecht, Band 47, Tübingen 2002.

Inger Dübeck, in: *European Consortium for State-Church Research* (ed.), Social Welfare, Religious Organisations and the State, Milano 2003.

Lisbet Christoffersen, Kirkeret mellem stat, marked og civilsamfund, Copenhagen 1998.

Preben Espersen, Kirkeret. Almindelig Del, Copenhagen 1993.

Preben Espersen, Kirkeret i Grundtræk, Copenhagen 2000.

Ingrid Lund-Andersen et al., Familieret, 5. edition, Copenhagen 2003.

Karsten Nissen et al., Huset mellem himmel og jord – en bog om folkekirken, Skive 1993.

Henrik Zahle (ed.), Danmarks Riges Grundlov med kommentarer, Copenhagen 1999.

Gerhard Robbers
State and Church in Germany

I. Social Facts

Within Germany there are two major Churches which are nearly equal in size and importance. The German population amounts to about 82.5 million in total; the Catholic Church has about 26.5 million members, while the Protestant Church has 26.2 million members. The Protestant Church consists of numerous separate territorially based *Landeskirchen*, each of these Churches being an independent unit. Together they form the Evangelical Church in Germany. There is also a number of smaller Protestant Churches that have chosen to stay outside this federation; they are known as the *Freikirchen* (Free Churches). The Protestant Churches are either Lutheran or Reformed Churches; some follow a unified confession, shaped in various ways from these two creeds. Islam in Germany has approximately 3.2 million members. The Jewish communities consist of somewhat over 100,000 members, Orthodox Christians amount to about 1.2 million. There are also many smaller religions in the country, some having a long-established tradition in Germany, others having been in Germany for only a short while. Their membership is estimated at about 1.6 million persons. There is also an estimated 22 million inhabitants of Germany who profess themselves to be without any confession.[1] This stems in part, although not entirely, from the reunification of Germany, as the political system of the former East Germany took a hostile stance towards the churches. Furthermore, the confessional viewpoints in Germany tend to change very rapidly as a result of immigration and other social shifts, so that estimates remain uncertain and tentative.

---

1 www.destatis.de.

II. Historical Background

The religious situation in Germany, even today, is strongly influenced by the Reformation of 1517. The relationship between the Lutheran Reformation and the territorial sovereignty and activities of the local princes led to the existence of the *Landeskirchen* of today, for the supreme bishops of such Churches were often the local sovereigns themselves. They worked out a close relationship between the Throne and the Altar that existed until 1919. Since the Middle Ages the Catholic Church had possessed a great deal of direct secular sovereignty and power. The archbishops of Trier, Cologne and Mainz were themselves Prince Electors of the Holy Roman Empire; their worldly power was not very different from that of other Electors.

These positions of sovereignty came to an end with the *Reichsdeputationshauptschluss* of 1803; a sort of recovery of damages was made by the majority of the lords of the "right of the Rhine", as a result of the Peace of Lunéville of 1801, for their "left of the Rhine" losses to France. In the process, the worldly sovereignty of the ecclesiastical princes was abrogated and the majority of their territory reallocated. The property of the Catholic Church was for the most part secularised, so that not much more remained than the property belonging to local parishes.

In the Religious Peace of Augsburg of 1555, the Lutheran and Catholic confessions were recognised as essentially equal. At the end of the Thirty Years War, 1618-1648, both religious parties emerged without victory. Even today, the territorial distribution of religious congregations is enduringly marked by these events.

Throughout the 19th century, the ties between the State and the Protestant Church were gradually loosened. The Weimar Constitution of 1919 resulted in the establishment of a separation of Church and State, nevertheless recognising and allowing for the existence of co-operation in matters such as religious instruction in the public school system, the Church tax and military chaplaincy. Taking responsibility for the murder of millions of European Jews by Nazi Germany in the 1940s has led Germany to give to the Jewish religious communities, though still small in numbers, a very visible role in society.

III. Legal Sources

Article 4 of the Basic Law guarantees the freedom of religion. Freedom of faith, of conscience, and freedom of creed, religion or ideology, are inviolable. The undisturbed practice of religion is guaranteed.
These individual rights guaranteeing the free existence of religion are complemented by and spelt out in Article 140 GG. These norms incorporate Articles 136-139 and 141 of the Weimar Constitution of 11 August 1919 into the Basic Law, so that they are fully fledged constitutional rights. Moreover, Article 7(2) and (3) of the Basic Law guarantees religious education in the public schools. Numerous other regulations, such as the existence of theological faculties at State universities, are contained within the Basic Law and other laws of the *Bundesländer* (Federal States). A large part of Church-State relations in Germany is assigned to the competence of the *Bundesländer*. The detailed arrangements of the constitutional foundation for a Church-State system are established in numerous regulations in the legal provisions ranking below the Basic Law.
The Federal Republic of Germany and its *Bundesländer* have established many concordats and Church-State treaties with the Churches in Germany.[2] In relation to the Catholic Church, the *Reichskonkordat* of 1933 is an essential basis which is recognised as a treaty under international law. Church-State treaties with the Evangelical Church and those made with Catholic dioceses are sui generis but are treated as being in a category similar to that of international treaties. Treaties or agreements also exist with a whole range of other smaller religious congregations. The subject matter of such Church-State treaties include the co-operation between the State and the bishops, the guarantees and arrangements for religious education in public schools, the theological faculties, the military chaplains and the position of the Church in the public sphere, such as the financing of religious parishes.

---

2 Cf. *Joseph Listl* (ed), Konkordate und Kirchenverträge in der Bundesrepublik Deutschland, 2 vols., 1987.

IV. Basic Categories of the System

Under the Church-State systems of Europe, Germany takes a middle of the road approach between that of having a State Church and having a strict separation between Church and State. The Basic Law lays down a system under which there is a separation of Church and State while at the same time a constitutionally secured form of co-operation exists between the two institutions. This is done in order to care co-operatively for the needs of the people. The legal basis of the German State-Church system is therefore structured around three basic principles: neutrality, tolerance, and parity.

Neutrality requires the State not to identify with a Church; there is to be no Established Church (Art. 137(1) WRV in conjunction with Art. 140 GG).[3] The State is not allowed to have any special inclination to a particular religious congregation or to judge such a congregation's particular merits or ideologies to be true. Ideological institutions are to be on equal footing with religious institutions; this deals with congregations which have a humanistic ideology or a position without reference to the question of a God or gods. This has however only minimal social consequences. On the other hand, religious institutions must not be placed in a more disadvantageous position than societal groups; this prohibits a decision in favour of State atheism. Neutrality therefore means, more than anything else, non-intervention: the State is not allowed to take decisive action in the affairs of religious communities. This is made particularly clear in Article 137(3) WRV: Every religious community regulates and administers its own affairs independently within the framework of the general law. This right of self-determination is valid, regardless of the legal status of the religious congregation.

The principle of tolerance obliges the State not only to be impartial as between all the different religious views, but also to maintain a sphere of positive tolerance that makes room for the religious needs of society.

Parity, as the last of the principles, means the obligation to treat all religious communities equally. This means that through a constitutional differentiation of legal status, a sort of graded parity exists that provides an adequate basis for dealing with the various social phenomena. This parity is a specific, group-orientated shaping of the idea of equal treatment that finds its historical roots in the equality of

---

3 Cf. also Art. 136 WRV in conjunction with Art. 140 GG, Art. 4, 33(3) GG.

confessions – the result of the religious wars of the 16th and 17th century.

These basic principles are also to be seen in the setting out of the freedom of religion according to Article 4 GG. It is here that one finds the requirement of positive tolerance. Freedom of faith is guaranteed in order to give every individual the right to believe what they will. Also included is the freedom of faith in a negative aspect, that is the right not to have a creed and/or not to belong to a particular religious faith. Religious freedom also guarantees the right to act according to one's beliefs. As a result, conscientious beliefs present a problem in criminal cases: a Jehovah's Witness was critically ill, but refused medical treatment on the basis of her faith. Her husband, of the same faith, respected her wishes; the woman died as a result. The *Bundesverfassungsgericht* (Federal Constitutional Court) quashed his conviction for neglect of a duty to help, because the man could not be held responsible; truly acting in accordance with one's faith and conscience can result in an absence of criminal liability for those who break the law.[4]

Freedom of faith in the sense of positive tolerance also allows for the possibility of the State offering in public schools the opportunity for inter-denominational school prayer, so long as participation is a part of the existing social attitude and as such is completely voluntary. The State must make sure that it provides for an atmosphere of tolerance. The State in certain circumstances, in which it has control over a person's surroundings, such as when one is obliged to attend school, is required to provide for the religious needs of those persons put into such a position.[5] This applies equally to the National Defence Force and penal institutions.

Religious institutions may also rely on the freedom of faith, which exists as a collective right.

V. *The Legal Status of Religious Communities*

The religious communities with large memberships in Germany, and also a considerable number of the smaller religious communities, have the status of public law corporations. Under various diverse

---

4   Cf. BVerfGE 32, p. 98.
5   Cf. BVerfGE 52, p. 223.

individual arrangements, Church parishes, dioceses, *Landeskirchen* and Church federations are considered public law corporations. Unlike other public law corporations, the religious communities with this status are not integrated into the State structure. They retain their complete independence, even as public corporations. Under this legal norm, no particular identification between the Church and State is intended: quite the contrary, as the State's view accepts that circumstance as a justification for the religious communities being part of public life. Only a few particular rights are associated with this status. Every religious community, upon application to the responsible federal state, will receive the status of a public law corporation, when they can prove through their bye-laws and the number of their members that they are indeed a permanent community (Art. 137(2)(2) WRV; Art. 140 GG). In the struggle of Jehovah's Witnesses for recognition as a public law corporation the Federal Constitutional Court has stated that a general loyalty to the law is also required to obtain this status. In 2004 their case was still pending in the administrative courts.

Other religious communities receive their legal capacity as a result of civil law. Their status will be at least that of a private registered association. As a result of the guarantees of freedom of faith, the peculiarities of a religion must be taken into account; where necessary, the civil law conditions must be adjusted to meet the religious requirements.[6] Consequently the Federal Constitutional Court has seen it to be a constitutional requirement that, contrary to the general requirements of civil law, a local spiritual advisory board of the Bahá'i that applies for legal status should be entered in the register of associations, even though it is considered not to be independent of other organs of the Bahá'i religious movement.

VI. *The Meaning of Religious Community and the Right of Self-Determination*

The right to self-determination (Art. 137(3) WRV, in conjunction with Art. 140 GG), may be considered to be the central reference point for the legal and social existence of religious communities in the Federal Republic of Germany. Every religious community inde-

---

6 Cf. BVerfGE 83, p. 341.

pendently regulates and administers its own affairs within the boundaries of the general law. Every religious community may, then, regardless of its legal status, manage its own affairs independently. This right of self-determination covers such things as religious dogma and teaching, making official appointments, religious services, the organisation of charitable activities, matters concerning the important parts of the relationship between employer and employees, and data protection. The list of possible examples should not mislead one into supposing that the right of self-determination is not all-encompassing, nor should it be taken to suggest that the operating spheres of the Churches are to be restricted into certain defined areas. The meaning and formulation of the limits of the right of self-determination is not uncontroversial. It exists only within the boundaries of the general law. For some time, the Federal Constitutional Court used the formula that a law would not be contrary to the right of self-determination of religious communities when the law did not particularly affect the religious community but instead affected everyone. Subject to that, a law breaches a Church's right of self-determination when the Church itself is not affected to the same extent as everyone else, but rather, within its special qualities as a Church, its self-identity and in particular its spiritual-religious duty is subject to particular disadvantages. More adequate is another formula created by the Federal Constitutional Court whereby the right to self-determination cannot prevail against an general law that represents a provision of particular importance to the common weal.[7]

It is important for the understanding of this matter to note that the Federal Constitutional Court attributes major importance to the Church's self-identity: what is meant by the Church's own affairs is determined particularly by how the Church itself views its own affairs, although the competence to take a final decision on the basis of the Basic Law is still reserved for the State Courts. The central relevance of the right of self-determination of a Church must furthermore be taken into account when defining the boundaries of this right.

A Church's right of self-determination is not restricted to a narrowly-drawn field of specifically "ecclesiastical" activities. The idea of freedom of religious practice extends to preserve the right of self-determination in other areas that are also based on religious objectives, such as the running of hospitals, kindergartens, retirement homes, private schools, and universities.

---

7 Cf. BVerfGE 42, 312/334; 66,1/20.

In very substantial ways, the large churches in Germany provide social services, particularly in the form of the Caritas of the Catholic Church and the Diaconical Works of the Evangelical Church. Without these services, the guarantees of a social State in Articles 20(1) and 28(1) GG would be mere empty platitudes. All these activities are part of what religious communities and the Church really means. The service rendered by the Churches is also understood by State law to be a single whole. The right of self-determination is therefore not merely attributed to a Church itself as a distinct entity, but instead it is something common to all institutions which are connected in some way or another with the Church regardless of the legal form taken by those links. This is true so long as, according to their self-identity, their goals or duties are suitably carried out and are held to be true mandates of the Church.[8]

Taking also into account the status of a public corporation, this approach has led the Federal Constitutional Court to regard religious hospitals as not falling under the State's insolvency laws, even when according to the hospitals' statutes they are only loosely associated with the particular organised Church. It would not be compatible with the idea of the right of self-determination that a judicially ordered administrative receiver should act within the particular structure or organisation of a religious establishment.[9]

The space which the framework of the right of self-determination offers to the religious communities has been used by the large Churches in Germany to work out their own detailed and voluminous internal legal systems with their own peculiarities and particular Church emphases, which operate in parallel with State law. Within the framework of the right of self-determination, there is also a jurisdictional system belonging to the Church. So far as the right of self-determination applies, the jurisdiction of the Church is exclusively the Church's own affair and Church matters settled internally are not reviewed by the public courts. In detail, however, there is still much that is a matter of debate. New developments indicate that the State courts are becoming more ready to interfere in church matters, but they give ample space to the right of self-determination in assessing each individual case.

---

8 Cf. BVerfGE 70, 138/162 with further references.
9 Cf. BVerfGE 66, p. 1.

VII. Churches and Culture

The large Churches in the Federal Republic of Germany operate a significant number of private schools. The majority of them are recognised as replacing public schools. This means that they offer a standard of education equal to that offered in State schools. As a result, they are made subject to various important regulations that apply to the public schools. The entire school system of Germany exists on the basis of Article 7(1) GG and is thus under the supervision of the State; compared with the number of State schools, Church or other private schools or educational establishments form a small minority. Concerning the financing of private schools, the Churches, like other organisations running private schools, receive public funding. The large Churches operate a considerable number of kindergartens for children between about 4 and 7 years of age.
According to Article 7(3) GG, religious instruction in public schools, with the exception of non-confessional schools, is to be a standard subject. Notwithstanding the State's right of visitation, religious education is to be conducted in accordance with the guidelines of the religious communities. No teacher is obliged, against his or her will, to teach religious education. Parents or guardians have the right to control the participation of their children in religious education; in principle when the child reaches the age of 12 years, the parental decision is not allowed to conflict with the child's. Upon reaching 14 years of age, the child may decide for him- or herself. Religious education, according to the requirements of Article 7(3) GG, is to be a standard subject in public schools, and it is therefore not permissible to put it into the position of simply a minor or an optional subject. The content of religious education is to be decided by the confessional teachings of the relevant religion. When a minimal number of students of the same confession is reached, normally between six to eight pupils, a public school is obliged to offer corresponding religious education. Children, parents and religious communities have a constitutional right to such educational services.
A question not yet adequately settled relates to the religious instruction for Muslim school children; despite a basic standing entitlement to such religious instruction, claims for the service often founder because of the lack of representation on the part of the Islamic communities. Instruction in Muslim religion and culture is very often provided for in classes of Turkish and Farsi language and culture offered to the immigrant children. There are more than 600,000 Muslim pu-

pils in German schools. Pupils are allowed to wear religious symbols such as the Muslim headscarf in public schools. The same applies in most of the federal *Länder* for teachers. Some *Länder*, however, have started to forbid teachers in public schools from exhibiting religious symbols in class to varying extents. This highly controversial issue relates predominantly though not exclusively to the Muslim women's headscarf.

At numerous public universities there are theological faculties of a specific confession. In a variety of differently fashioned State-Church agreements, the Churches have a more or less determinative influence upon the appointment of professors and on the curriculum and examinations. In this area the Catholic Church enjoys a greater area of control than does the Evangelical Church. The professors of the theological faculties at State universities are State officials; nevertheless at Catholic faculties they need the *missio canonica* from the Catholic Church. If it is withdrawn, the particular professor is not allowed to remain a member of the theological faculty. He or she will however still retain the rights and duties as a State official and must be given another position within the university. For vacant theological professorships, the State is obliged to find the necessary replacement.

Moreover, the large Churches also have their own theological faculties. The Catholic Church has its own university in Eichstätt, which also has a significant number of non-theological faculties. There is also a large number of Church-run colleges, offering an education that is more vocationally orientated than that of a university.

It is part of the special position of the Churches that they have a special public mandate. This public mandate is secured by State-Church treaties and has its foundations in the religious freedoms of the Churches. This accordingly allows them to have a say and a right to information in the matters and affairs of public life. On the basis of their public mandate, religious institutions have designated time-slots on television and radio. They are also, as a result, given a representative position on the supervisory boards of public institutions where a particular societal representation is necessary. The Churches' position is relevant to the broadcasting commissions of public broadcasting corporations such as ZDF, ARD and the *Land*-based broadcasting corporations, the supervisory commissions for the private television and radio stations, and also appraisal and classification boards in order to identify and restrain scripts and films that are deemed harmful to young viewers and listeners. Mirroring their historic and cultural impact, the Jewish communities usually also have representation in these bodies. It is a matter of future development as to whether and how the Muslim population can also be represented here.

VIII. Labour Law within the Churches

The large Churches of the Federal Republic of Germany employ together more than one million persons: this is evidence of the importance of their position as employers.

As public corporations, the Churches are considered to be entitled to confer public office. This means that they are able to have employees who are considered to be civil servants; reciprocally Church administrations are structured along the same lines as their State counterparts. The Churches frame their own civil service law along the same lines as the public civil service law, even in respect of salaries and benefits. For priests and ministers, a separate service law is in force that also mirrors public civil service law as far as possible, considering the special context.

However, for the large majority of the employees in the service of a church, normal labour law applies. It is nevertheless modified in many circumstances, on the basis of the Church's right of self-determination and its particular religious context. Freedom of religion demands that the special conditions which result from the duties of the Churches must be taken into consideration when examining their labour status.

A particular expression of this is in that Church employees owe a particular obligation of loyalty to their Church employer. It is the Church itself which, within the constitutional framework of the notion of *ordre public*, good faith, and prohibition of prejudice, determines the contents of these obligations. The right of self-determination of the religious communities allows the Churches, within the limits of the general law, to regulate Church working conditions according to their own terms and to make obligatory specific duties of the Church employees. Which basic duties of the Church are important as part of the terms of employment is judged according to the organised Church's own acknowledged standards. In cases of dispute, the labour courts have to respect the standards of the Church in assessing contractual obligation of loyalty, insofar as the Basic Law recognises the right of the Church to determine the matter internally.

It is thus normally left to the organised Church to decide what is required for the credibility of the Church and its teaching, what the specific Church duties are, what are essential principles of the faith and morality, and what is to be considered contrary to these norms. In the case of a violation of such an obligation of loyalty by the employee, the public labour courts are the final judge of whether termination of employment of a Church employee is justified or not.[10] As a result of their religious mandate, Churches have the right to give notice to an employee when in their public way of life or in their publicly expressed opinions they act contrary to Church teachings. The Federal Constitutional Court ruled that it was constitutional to give notice of termination to a physician employed at a Catholic hospital who had publicly taken a stance against the Church on television and in a magazine concerning the right of women to have an abortion. This decision was reaffirmed by the European Commission of Human Rights.[11]

In the sphere of collective labour rights, the Churches are also in a special position as a result of the notion of freedom of religion and consequently the right of self-determination. Their structures are not subject to the public co-determination laws.[12] The State is in principle not allowed to intervene in the internal organisational structures and set-up of the Churches.[13] The Churches have developed the so-called third way in this area. They understand their vocation, especially in the area of charity, as part of one undivided, religiously-based commitment. This in principle makes it impossible for them to accept a legal structure of labour relations which is based on the idea of a fundamental opposition between employer and employee. The Catholic Church along with most of the Protestant Churches therefore rejects the conclusion of agreements through collective bargaining with trades unions.[14] Within the Church structure there exists no right to strike, just as there is no possibility by way of internal Church decision of locking out employees. The Churches have created their own system of employees' representation and co-determination. It confers, to a considerable extent, more extensive rights on their employees than does the public co-determination system.

---

10 Cf. BVerfGE 70, p. 138.
11 Cf. BVerfGE 70, p. 138; EKMR, 12242/86, decision of 6 September 1989.
12 § 118 BetrVerfG; § 1 IV MitbestG.
13 Cf. BVerfGE 53, p. 366/400.
14 Some Protestant Landeskirchen (Nordelbien, Berlin-Brandenburg) have concluded collective bargaining agreements for their employees instead.

IX. Financing of Churches

As a result of repeated appropriation of church property in the past, the Churches in Germany now have only a small amount of property. As compensation for this secularisation following the *Reichsdeputationshauptschluss* of 1803, a series of government decisions guaranteed funds for the Churches. They are guaranteed by Article 138(1) WRV in conjunction with Article 140 GG. This provision also envisages the ending of those payments which are necessarily linked to the payment of compensation; this so far has not been pursued on grounds of impracticality. In addition, other subsidies granted by the State are often related to long-standing claims of the Churches; an important example is the fact that the local authorities must discharge their public duty to contribute to the maintenance of church buildings. Likewise, on the basis of contractual terms, there are some obligatory contributions to be made by the State to the Church, such as subsidies to the salaries of Church officials.
Approximately 80% of the entire Church budget, however, is covered by the Church tax; guaranteed by Article 137(6) WRV in conjunction with Article 140 GG. On the basis of the civil tax lists, in accordance with the law of the *Länder*, the religious communities that are public corporations are allowed to levy taxes. The large Churches have made ample use of this opportunity, but smaller religious communities with the status of public corporation, such as the Jewish communities, have also done so. Only members of the particular Church authorised to levy the Church tax are obliged to pay. The Church tax was instituted at the beginning of the 19th century in order to relieve the national budget of its obligations to the Churches, which were in turn based on the secularisation of Church property.
Those desiring to be free of the tax may achieve that result by leaving the Church. Withdrawal from the Church is effected by de-registering with the proper State officials and simply means that one has, according to the State classification, officially ended one's membership of the particular Church in question. However, most Protestant Churches see the withdrawal as a withdrawal from their particular Church as well. The Catholic Church, as a general rule, views the withdrawal as a serious violation of the person's obligations to the Church, without bringing into question the theological dimension of Church membership.
The rate of the Church tax is between eight and nine per cent of the individual's wage and income tax liability. Other tax standards may

also be used. Although this concept is not a requirement, in most cases the Church tax is collected by the State tax authorities for the larger Churches, as a result of an arrangement with the State. For this service, the Churches pay between three and five per cent of the tax yield to the State by way of compensation. If a Church member refuses to pay the required tax, legal means can be used to collect the tax; the Churches however are not required to pursue legal action in the case of non-payment. In so far as the Church tax is tied to the income tax of employees, the employer will directly provide the financial authorities with the Church tax along with income tax.

Because of the links with State taxes, tax exemptions also affect the Churches' own Church tax. It is estimated that about one-third of all Church members pay no Church tax because they are not liable to income tax. In some cases the Churches attempt to make this good by demanding an alternative contribution to the Church, which is independent of income tax.

A further important source of income for some Church institutions is being part of general public funding systems. Church-run hospitals, which in some parts of Germany make up the majority of the available hospital beds, are thus part of the publicly-run financing systems for hospitals, supported mainly by money paid in medical insurance for the number of beds filled. Further, many Churches receive allocations from the State for activities in the same way as other publicly funded activities: it is part of the idea of State neutrality that Church activities are not to be put in a worse position than that of, say, State funded local athletic clubs.

Churches also receive a certain number of tax exemptions. The Church tax and charitable donations to the Church may be deducted from income tax; this applies equally to donations to non-profit organisations. Churches are also not required to pay certain taxes and duties.

X. *Religious Assistance in Public Institutions*

In so far as the need for religious services and religious assistance in the armed forces, hospitals, penal institutions or other public institutions is concerned, the various religious institutions are permitted to undertake such activities. They have a right to give religious assistance in hospitals and for prisoners. Religious activities within the police and the military forces are governed by contracts. Military chaplains are sent from the Churches for a specific time. For the duration of their service they are given the status of State officials; a contractual status is also possible. Their overall superior in matters of their State position is the Head of the Federal Defence Ministry. German military chaplains have the status of normal civilian State staff without a uniform or military rank. As part of the State administration, there is an Evangelical Church office for the Defence Forces for Protestant military chaplains, and for the Catholics a Catholic military bishop's office. Their sphere of duties is considered to be part of both Church and State administration. In Church matters they are subordinate to their respective military bishop, acting for his Church, and in matters of public administration to the Federal Defence Minister.

XI. The Legal Position of Priests and Members of Religious Orders

There is in general no special status in State law for priests, ministers, and members of religious orders within the German legal system. There is only a small number of particular considerations. The Federal Constitutional Court has declared it to be constitutional that a religious institution may deny their own Church office holders the right to stand for public office while they exercise a religious office.[15] According to State law, the right to vote and to be elected is in no way restricted and there are no legal impediments whatsoever. Such regulation would not be in harmony with Article 3(3) GG, whereby no-one on the basis of their faith is to be disadvantaged or privileged. Furthermore, Article 33(3) GG states that the enjoyment of civil rights and the admission to public office and the rights acquired in the civil service are independent of one's confession. No-one as result of their confession or ideology is to be disadvantaged. Similar stipulations are to be found in Article 138 WRV in conjunction with Article 140 GG. This prohibition against discrimination is however independent of the occupation of a religious office. Ordained Protestant ministers and Roman Catholics ordained to the diaconate are exempt from service in the Defence Forces, as are full-time active

---

15 BVerfGE 42, p. 312.

ministers of other denominations. Ordinands are able to defer their Defence Force service (paras. 11, 12 WPflG). Ministers do not have to give evidence, especially in court, concerning events which were made known to them in their function as ministers (e.g. para. 53.1.1 StPO).

XII. Matrimonial and Family Law

Contrary to the position in some other European countries, the Churches in Germany have no competence in the areas of marriage and family law. Marriage according to the German legal system is wholly a civil affair: it takes place in the register office. A different form, especially a religious marriage with legal effect, may be contracted only between foreigners before a body recognised by their home country as having the right to conduct a marriage. For German nationals, a religious wedding in Germany has no civil legal effect. On the other hand, though, everyone is free to have a religious wedding service. A constitutionally-questionable rule states that a religious wedding is not to precede the civil marriage. However, sanctions for the violation of this rule do not exist.

XIII. Religion and Criminal Law

Religion enjoys considerable protection in German criminal and procedural law. According to paragraph 130(2) of the Criminal Code a person inciting hatred against a religious group in specifically defined ways is punishable by up to three years imprisonment or a fine. Equally punishable is a person who attacks the contents of religious or philosophical beliefs in a way that threatens to disturb the public peace. The same applies to a person who interrupts the worship of a religious community existing in Germany or commits vituperating mischief in a place dedicated to worship by such a community. The ceremonies of philosophical, non-religious communities are equally protected. Interrupting funeral ceremonies as well as disturbing the peace of the dead is equally punishable (paras. 166-168 Criminal Code).

A person who without being authorised uses titles, ranks, uniforms or ensigns of a public law religious community is liable to punishment of up to one year's imprisonment or a fine. The destruction or suppression of official documents of a public law religious community is punishable by up to two years imprisonment or a fine; in severe cases this rises to up to five years of imprisonment (paras. 132 and 133 Criminal Code).

The confessional secret is broadly protected. Clergy are not obliged to report under any circumstances what they have learned in performing spiritual care (e.g. para. 139(2) Criminal Code, para. 53 Criminal Procedure Code, para. 383 Civil Procedure Code, etc.). Under these circumstances they are also not obliged to inform of planned crimes (para. 139(2) Criminal Code).

XIV. Particular Questions of Civil Ecclesiastical Law

In the last 50 years, German State-Church law, thanks also to the (mostly prudent) case law of the Federal Constitutional Court, has proved to have a clearly structured firm basis, and to be able to respond to social needs in particularly suitable ways. Its further development will include the recognition of new religions and non-religious groups, in particular Islam on one hand, and widespread religious scepticism on the other: important tasks that lie in the future.

XV. Bibliography

Axel Frhr. von Campenhausen, Staatskirchenrecht, 3rd ed., 1983.

Alexander Hollerbach, "Grundlagen des Staatskirchenrechts", in Josef Isensee/Paul Kirchhof (ed.), Handbuch des Staatsrechts der Bundesrepublik Deutschland, vol. VI, 1989, p. 471.

Alexander Hollerbach, "Der verfassungsrechtliche Schutz kirchlicher Organisation", ibid., p. 557.

Alexander Hollerbach, "Freiheit kirchlichen Wirkens", ibid., p. 595.

Axel Frhr. von Campenhausen, "Religionsfreiheit", ibid., p. 369.
Bernd Jeand'Heur/Stefan Korioth, Grundzüge des Staatskirchenrechts, Stuttgart 2000.
Jörg Winter, Staatskirchenrecht der Bundesrepublik Deutschland. Eine Einführung mit kirchenrechtlichen Exkursen, Neuwied 2001.
Joseph Listl, "Das Verhältnis von Kirche und Staat in der Bundesrepublik Deutschland", in Joseph Listl/Hubert Müller/Heribert Schmitz (ed.), Handbuch des katholischen Kirchenrechts, 1983, p. 1050.
Joseph Listl (ed.), Konkordate und Kirchenverträge in der Bundesrepublik Deutschland, 2 vols., 1987.
Joseph Listl/Dietrich Pirson, Handbuch des Staatskirchenrechts der Bundesrepublik Deutschland, 2 vols., 2. ed. 1994.
Gerhard Robbers, "Das Verhältnis von Staat und Kirche in der Bundesrepublik Deutschland", in Gottfried Zieger (ed.), Die Rechtstellung der Kirchen im geteilten Deutschland, 1989, p. 7.

Periodicals:
Archiv des katholischen Kirchenrechts
Zeitschrift für evangelisches Kirchenrecht
Kirche und Recht

Merilin Kiviorg
State and Church in Estonia

I. Social Facts

After regaining independence at the beginning of the 1990s, Estonia experienced what can be called a "return of religion", in common with other Eastern European post-communist societies. This process was partly an expression of national identity and partly a reaction to the lifting of the suppression of individual freedoms that had been practised by the Soviet regime. But the new religious enthusiasm petered out rapidly, and the sudden, major growth in the membership of religious organisations ceased.

Although Estonia is a country with a predominantly Christian background and history, it cannot be called homogenous in terms of religion. Today's religious picture in Estonia is a mosaic of different faiths and denominations. Secularisation has also played a significant role, especially in the last 100 years, and has shaped the attitudes towards religion of contemporary society. Today, only approximately 23 % of the Estonian population (estimated to be 1,356,045 people in January 2003[1]) is officially connected with the various Christian Churches. The Estonian Evangelical Lutheran Church has been the dominant church in Estonia since the middle of the 16th century. Today, only about 11 % of the population officially belongs to this Church.[2] The next in size, also with a long historical tradi-

---

1   Statistical Office of Estonia. Data available at http://www.stat.ee.
2   In contrast, in the 1920s and 1930s, before the Soviet occupation, Estonia was more or less religiously homogenous. Most of the population (ca 76 %) belonged to the Estonian Evangelical Lutheran Church. According to the national census of 1934, there were 874,026 Evangelical Lutherans in Estonia of a total population of 1,126,413. See http://www.estonica.org/culture/religion, 17.01.2004. It has often been argued that the low membership of the Church today is due to the Soviet occupation and atheistic education. This is only partially true. Some scholars are of the opinion that statistics of church membership from before World War II and the Soviet occupation give a false impression that the Lutheran Church could be regarded as the national church. Moreover, a bitter conflict between the dominant German clergy and national clergy during the 1920s and 1930s gave some indication that the Church had some way to go in successfully winning the hearts and minds of the nation. 'The Lutheran Church had not enough time to establish itself as an essential part of the Estonian people's national identity. If it had, atheistic education probably would

tion, is the Orthodox community (about 10 % of the population).[3] The percentages presented reflect both active and passive membership of the Churches. There are smaller communities of Roman Catholics, Baptists, Jews, Methodists, Muslims, Buddhists, and others.

II. Historical Background

It is likely that Christianity was already established in Estonia by 1054. Estonia was christianised by the middle of the 13th century. Bishop Albert and Brethren of the Order of the Sword combined forces so that the knights of the Order could conquer the land and the priests could baptise the people. As a result of the conquest, the Pope, as head of the universal church, became the highest suzerain of Estonia. The Pope personally took the Estonian neophytes under his protection, establishing a Church State on Estonian territory. In the 17th century, when Estonia came under the sovereignty of Sweden, a systematic ordering of life under the Lutheran Church began, and the Catholic Church was practically expelled from Estonia. The Reformation turned the Church-State relationship upside down to that of a State Church or, more precisely, a Land Church.[4] The subjection of the country to Russian rule from the beginning of the 18th century did not change anything in principle. Some liberties were guaranteed in the 19th century: for example, the Grace of Czar Alexander I in 1817 permitted the activities of the Herrnhut Movement. In 1840s it was possible to convert from the Land Church to the Czar's Church, the Russian Orthodox Church (with no way back!), and in the 1880s the first Free Church (Baptist) congregations were established. The free-

---

never have taken root to the depth it did.' *M. Ketola*, 'Some aspects of the Nationality Question in the Lutheran Church of Estonia, 1918-39', in *Religion, State and Society* (Oxford: Keston Institute, 1999), vol. 27, no. 2, p. 239-243.

3 There are two Orthodox churches in Estonia: the Estonian Orthodox Church, subordinated to the Moscow Patriarchate, and the Estonian Apostolic Orthodox Church, subordinated to the Ecumenical Patriarchate of Constantinople. These two Orthodox Churches are also partly divided on the basis of nationality. The Estonian Apostolic Orthodox Church has mainly Estonian speaking members and the Estonian Orthodox Church has mainly Russian speaking members.

4 For a more detailed history of religions in Estonia, see website http://www.estonica.org, 16.01.2004.

dom of religion was formally guaranteed to all the subjects of the Czar by the Tolerance Act of 17 April 1905.

The history of the law on religions in the Republic of Estonia may be divided into four main periods. The first started with the formation of the independent State in 1918[5] and with the adoption of the 1920 Constitution, which set forth the principle of a strict separation of State and Church.[6] This was followed by the 1925 Religious Societies and their Associations Act, which reaffirmed the principle of equal treatment of all religious organisations, and the separation of state and church.[7]

The second period (the 1930s) saw significant political changes in Estonian society, which were characterised by the centralisation of State administration, the concentration of power, a decline of democracy, and the expansion of State control. In 1934 the Churches and Religious Societies Act was enacted, not by Parliament but by decree of the State Elder (President).[8] This Act established different legal treatment for churches and for other religious societies. The status of some churches, especially large ones, was to a certain extent similar to the status of a State Church. According to section 84(1)(b) of the 1938 Constitution, the leaders of the two largest and most important churches gained *ex officio* membership of the *Riiginõukogu* (Upper House of Parliament).[9] The government of all churches was subjected to control by the State.

The third period began with the Soviet occupation of Estonia. The law on religions in the Soviet Union was based on the 1918 Leninist decree on the separation of church from state, and school from church. The bizarre fact is that the separation of state and church (religious organisations) was actually a non-separation, because the state controlled all the aspects of religious organisations, including their leaders and sometimes even their members. Estonia became part of the USSR in 1940 and had little legislative independence during the occupation. USSR law dictated the laws on freedom of religion for the entire occupation period.

The fourth period began with the regaining of independence at the beginning of the 1990s and with the adoption of the 1992 Constitution.[10] Estonia started to rebuild its legal order on the principle of res-

---

5 Prior to the 1917 revolution in Russia, Estonia was part of the Russian Empire.
6 RT 1920, 113/114, 243.
7 RT 1925, 183/184, 96.
8 RT 1934, 107, 840.
9 RT 1937, 71, 590.
10 Eesti Vabariigi põhiseadus [The Constitution of Estonian Republic] (Riigi Teataja toimetuse väljaanne. Tallinn, 1994).

titution, while at the same time acknowledging the changes over time in European legal order and thinking. The Estonian Constitution provides express protection to the freedom of religion. Article 40 provides that:

> "Everyone has freedom of conscience, religion and thought. Everyone may freely belong to churches and religious associations. There is no state church. Everyone has the freedom to practise his or her religion, both alone and in a community with others, in public or in private, unless this is detrimental to public order, health or morals."

The religious freedom clauses in the 1992 Constitution were followed by the 1993 Churches and Congregations Act (hereinafter the 1993 CCA).[11] On 1 July 2002, the 1993 law was replaced by a new Churches and Congregations Act (hereinafter the 2002 CCA).[12] The 2002 CCA differed from the earlier law principally in the way in which religious organisations were registered by the government. Previously, under the 1993 CCA, religious associations were registered by the Ministry of Internal Affairs. According to the new law, religious associations are registered by the registration departments of county and city courts.

Estonia has been a newly independent state for approximately 12 years. In its law-making and the implementation of law, one can see the effects of both the first independence period (1918-1940) and the later Soviet occupation which lasted over fifty years. Estonia is still a country in transition.

III. Basic Structure

1. Legal Sources

The legal sources of the law on religion in Estonia are: (1) provisions set forth in national law[13] (the Constitution of Republic of Estonia,

---

11 RT I 1993, 30, 510; RT I 1994, 28, 425.
12 RT I 2002, 24, 135; RT I 2002, 61, 375.
13 Translation of the texts of selected Estonian legal acts can be found at www.legaltext.ee. It should be noted that these translations are unofficial translations (there are no official translations of legal acts in Estonia) and these translations do not always take account of the latest amendments to the law.

the Non-profit Organisations Act,[14] the Churches and Congregations Act and the other Acts directly or indirectly regulating the individual and collective freedom of religion), (2) provisions set forth in international law, and (3) the interpretation of fundamental freedoms and rights by courts (including decisions of the European Court of Human Rights and the European Court of Justice). Estonia joined the European Union on 1 May 2004.[15] The law of the European Union takes precedence over Estonian Law, as long as it does not contradict the Estonian constitution's basic principles.[16]

The right to freedom of religion in Estonia is protected by the Constitution of 1992 and by the international instruments that have been incorporated into Estonian law. Starting with protection by international instruments, Article 3 of the Estonian Constitution stipulates that universally recognised principles and standards of international law shall be an inseparable part of the Estonian legal system. By Article 3 of the Estonian Constitution the universally recognised principles and standards of international law have been incorporated into the Estonian legal system and do not need further transformation. They are superior in force to national legislation and binding for legislative, administrative, and judicial powers. It should be noted that Article 3 incorporates into the Estonian legal system both international customary norms and general principles of law.

The international treaties (ratified by Parliament[17]) are incorporated into the Estonian legal system by Article 123(2) of the Constitution. Article 123 states that if Estonian Acts or other legal instruments contradict foreign treaties ratified by the Riigikogu (Parliament), the provisions of the foreign treaty shall be applied. Estonia is also a party to most European and universal human rights documents.[18] The Constitution is silent on the legal position in the hierarchy of norms of international treaties concluded by the Estonian government but not ratified by the parliament. In practice, many such international treaties exist, and the majority view among legal scholars is that these treaties have the same position in the hierarchy of norms as

---

14 RT I 1996, 42, 811; RT I 1998, 96, 1515 (revised text); RT I 2002, 53, 336.
15 Treaty of Accession, RT II, 2004, 3, 8.
16 Amendments to the Constitution of Estonian Republic, RT I 2003, 64, 429.
17 According to section 121(1) Parliament ratifies treaties: (1) which amend state borders; (2) the implementation of which requires the adoption, amendment or voidance of Estonian laws; (3) by which the Estonian Republic joins international organisations and leagues; (4) by which Estonia assumes military or financial obligations; (5) where ratification is prescribed.
18 *Inter alia*, the European Convention for the Protection of Human Rights and Fundamental Freedoms (1950), and the International Covenant on Civil and Political Rights (1966).

those international treaties that have been ratified by Parliament. This interpretation also conforms to the international obligations of Estonia under the 1969 Vienna Convention on the Law of Treaties.[19]

Article 40 of the Estonian Constitution quoted above expressly protects the freedom of religion. Even during a state of emergency or a state of war, the rights and liberties in Article 40 of the Constitution may not be restricted (Article 130). Article 41 on the freedom of belief and Article 42 on the privacy of one's religion and belief add strength to the commitment to freedom of religion. In addition, other constitutional provisions complement the basic freedom of religion. For example, Article 45 concerning the right to freedom of expression, Article 47 concerning the right to assembly and Article 48 concerning the right to association: each provides specific protection for different aspects of religious freedom.

In addition to constitutional law and international human rights law, Estonia regulates the freedom of religion and belief and church-state relations by a number of statutes and regulations. The principal statutes for church-state relations are the Non-Profit Organisations Act, and the 2002 Churches and Congregations Act. There are many other Acts directly or indirectly regulating freedom of religion for both individuals and groups: for example, the Acts concerned with tax exemptions, education and criminal liability.

In Estonia, church-state relations are governed not only by general laws but also by formal agreements that are negotiated directly between the Government and religious institutions. Some of these agreements are considered to be international treaties (such as the agreement between the State and the Holy See for the Roman Catholic Church). The agreements between the State and religious organisations may also have the nature of administrative agreements or co-operation agreements under civil law. The purpose of these agreements may vary from co-ordination and co-operation on issues of public interest to contracting for the specific religious needs of a religious community. The agreements are perhaps becoming an increasingly important source for regulating the relationship between religious communities and the State. As a relatively new way of approaching this relationship in Estonia, it is not without difficulties and controversies – mainly concerning the equal treatment of religious communities.

---

19 Eesti Vabariigi Põhiseadus. Kommenteeritud väljaanne [Commentaries on the Estonian Constitution], Tallinn: Juura, 2002; *K. Merusk/R. Narits,* Eesti Konstitutsiooniõigusest [About Estonian Constitutional Law], Tallinn, 1998, p. 26-32.

2. Categories of System Approach

The mere fact that a State does not have a formally established church does not necessarily mean that it maintains a rigorous policy of non-identification with religion. After Estonia became an independent state at the beginning of 1990s, the historically dominant Evangelical Lutheran Church started to re-establish its position in society and in relation to the State, actively lobbying Government and Parliament for more a privileged position. In constitutional terms Estonia does not have a State Church; indeed the present Constitution states inter alia that *"there is no state church"* (Article 40). But the separation of State and Church (especially the Evangelical Lutheran Church) has not been interpreted in administrative practice strictly and inflexibly; as a consequence of this some have argued that Estonia has a State Church *de facto*. Although this is clearly an exaggeration, the Estonian Evangelical Lutheran Church has, in fact, enjoyed a certain amount of preferential treatment from the State. This raises the question as to whether all forms of this co-operation can be accepted in the light of the constitutional principles of the separation of State and Church and the equal treatment of religious communities. There are also several other forms of preferential treatment of Christian Churches. The Estonian Council of Churches, which consists of 10 Christian Churches[20] has been very active in determining relations between Church(es) and State. The State has treated the Council as a partner in decision-making on religious freedom questions in Estonia. The privileged position of the Council is visible, and perhaps most sensitive, in matters of financial support and education. On 17 October 2002 the Government and the Estonian Council of Churches signed the Protocol of Common Concerns. Although it has been argued that other religious organisations have in principle the right to seek the same type of co-operation, no other religious organisation has yet been able to establish it. There has also been criticism of the current law (the 2002 CCA) imposing Christian terminology on non-Christian faiths, especially regarding their names, and for favouring Christian religions generally. The non-Christian organisations filed a petition to the Legal Chancellor in order to test compatibility of current law with the constitution.[21] Amendments to this law are already under preparation in the Ministry of Internal Affairs. According to the draft amendments to the

---

20 The Council decides according to its own statutes which churches to admit to membership.
21 Petition to check the constitutionality of § 2, § 7 and § 11 of the Churches and Congregation, Registered No. 1-14/158, 22. 05. 2002, Office of Legal Chancellor.

2002 CCA, religious associations will be entitled to use their historical names instead of the Christian terminology imposed by the 2002 CCA.

In the context of Estonia it is rather difficult to determine if there is a strong enough social need or tradition (including a legal tradition) in existence to justify differing legal treatment of religious organisations. Moreover, the principle of equality is anchored in the first sentence of the first paragraph of Article 12 of the Estonian Constitution, which states that all persons shall be equal before the law. The second paragraph of article 12 of the Constitution sets forth the principle of non-discrimination, prohibiting discrimination *inter alia* on the basis of religion or belief. As the Constitution protects both the individual and the collective freedom of religion, these principles have also to be applied to religious communities. The principle of non-discrimination is a special equality right and is deemed to protect minorities. According to Article 11 of the Constitution, "rights and liberties may be restricted only in accordance with the Constitution. Such restrictions must be necessary in a democratic society, and their imposition may not distort the nature of the rights and liberties." Thus, every case of restriction of rights and liberties including the general equality right (the principle of equality) and special equality right (the principle of non-discrimination) has to be justified and to pass the test of proportionality.

IV. Legal Status of Religious Bodies

1. Legal Status of Religious Communities

In Estonia a religious association is a legal person in private law (2002 CCA, Article 5(1)). The 2002 CCA expressly states that the Non-Profit Organisations Act[22] and 2002 CCA are related as general and special legislation (2002 CCA, Article 5(1)). Estonian law addresses five different types of religious organisation: churches, congregations, associations of congregations, monasteries, and religious societies. The 2002 CCA gives legal definitions for all five catego-

---

22 RT I 1996, 42, 811; RT I 1998, 96, 1515 (revised text); RT I 2002, 53, 336.

ries of religious organisation.[23] The 2002 CCA regulates the activities of only the first four. The activities of religious societies are regulated not by the CCA but by the Non-Profit Organisations Act.

The legal capacity of a religious association commences with its entry in the register of religious associations. The law does not prohibit the activity of religious associations which are not registered. Rather, the main disadvantage for these unregistered entities is that they cannot present themselves as legal persons, and therefore cannot exercise the rights or seek the protections accorded to a religious legal entity.

Estonia has so far been very liberal towards the so-called non-traditional religious movements. Nevertheless, just before the adoption of the 2002 CCA by the Estonian Parliament, the Estonian Council of Churches sent a letter to the Parliamentary Commission asking it to take steps in the new law to limit the activities of "non-constructive religious communities." These proposals were not enacted into law. The Council's intention was probably an attempt in good faith to avoid harmful experiences to individuals, and it raised questions about proselytism. Yet, raising this issue created alarm when seen in the larger Eastern European or even pan-European context.

---

23 (1) A church is an association of at least three voluntarily joined congregations which has an Episcopal structure and is doctrinally related to three ecumenical creeds or is divided into at least three congregations and which operates on the basis of its statutes, is managed by an elected or appointed management board and is entered in the register.
(2) A congregation is a voluntary association of natural persons who profess the same faith, which operates on the basis of its statutes, is managed by an elected or appointed management board and is entered in the register.
(3) An association of congregations is an association of at least three voluntarily joined congregations professing the same faith and which operates on the basis of its statutes, is managed by an elected or appointed management board and is entered in the register.
(4) A monastery is a voluntary communal association of natural persons who profess the same faith, which operates on the basis of the statutes of the corresponding church or independent statutes, is managed by an elected or appointed superior of the monastery and is entered in the register.
(5) A religious society is a voluntary association of natural or legal persons the main activities of which include confessional or ecumenical activities relating to morals, ethics, education, culture and confessional or ecumenical diaconal and social rehabilitation activities outside the traditional forms of religious rite of a church or congregation and which need not be connected with a specific church, association of congregations, or individual congregation.

2. The Meaning of Religious Community and the Right of Self-Determination/Autonomy

The general right to self-determination of persons (both individuals and groups) stems from Article 19 of the Estonian Constitution. Article 19(1) states that: "all persons shall have the right to free self-realisation." The right to religious (church) autonomy is also considered to be an essential part of collective freedom of religion protected by Article 40 of the Constitution and also by Articles 48, 19(1) and Article 9(2).[24] The autonomy of religious associations also means the right to self-administration in accordance with their internal laws and prescriptions.

The 2002 CCA gives considerable latitude for religious associations to organise themselves in accordance with their own teachings and structures. The statutes of a religious association may differ from the provisions of the Non-Profit Organisations Act concerning membership and management if such differences arise from the historical teaching and structure of the religious association (Article 5(2)). Other associations and religious societies registered under the Non-Profit Organisations Act do not have the same amount of freedom. The Non-Profit Organisations Act prescribes a structure and a way of (democratic) governance for the organisation. Thus, religious associations and religious societies have different degrees of autonomy as to their internal affairs. Religious societies are treated as regular non-profit-making organisations and enjoy considerably less autonomy in their internal affairs than do religious associations. However, the distinction between a religious association and a religious society is problematic.

V. Church and Culture

Religious education is a sensitive and long debated topic in Estonia. As to the current law, Article 37 of the Constitution creates the basis for the entire school system and states, inter alia, that the provision of education shall be supervised by the State. The Estonian school system consists mainly of state schools. Thus, the principal place for

---

[24] Presidential veto to the 2002 Churches and Congregations Act in RTL, 03.07.2001, 82, 1120.

religious education is in state schools. The law provides and prescribes possibilities for organising religious education.

According to Article 4(4) of the Education Act,[25] the study and teaching of religion in general education schools is voluntary and non-confessional. In accordance with the Act on Basic Schools and Gymnasiums[26] the nature of the religious education is non-confessional and a voluntary subject for students (Article 3(8)). In 1999 the Estonian Parliament passed amendments to the Law.[27] Religious education is now compulsory in a school if at least fifteen pupils wish it to be taught. Before the adoption of that provision it was likely that schools just did not provide religious education even if there were pupils who wished to be taught.

The principles and topics of religious studies are set out in a curriculum approved by the Ministry of Education. Religious study in schools is a subject in which the views and contributions of various religions to the development of humanity are analysed. In the primary classes, parents make the decision as to whether their children should participate in religious studies lessons. At the gymnasium level (secondary school), pupils decide this independently. Teachers of religious studies have to have both theological and pedagogical training. Confessional instruction is provided for children by Sunday schools and church schools run by congregations.

There have been debates on whether to make religious education compulsory. This would give a non-confessional overview of Christianity and other world religions, to help pupils understand the impact of different religions on world culture. The aim of this change would be, perhaps most importantly, to prepare them for life in a pluralistic and multicultural world.

There are various factors hindering the reorganisation of religious education. One major concern is the protection of the religious freedom of pupils and their parents. One of the reasons for opposing reorganisation goes back to negative experiences in the first days of religious education in state schools. When schools became open to religious education, many eager people without teaching experience and professional skills rushed in to teach.[28] Sometimes religious education in schools turned into confessional instruction. The lack of

---

25 RT I 1992, 12,192; RT I, 2003, 78, 526.
26 RT I 1993, 63, 892; RT I, 1999, 42, 497.
27 RT I 1999, 24, 358.
28 See also P. *Valk*, 'Development of the Status of Religious education in Estonian School. European and Local Perspectives', Conference on Law, Religion and Democratic Society, Estonia, University of Tartu, 1999.

teachers with sufficient professional and pedagogical skills to communicate this subject in schools is acute even today.

At university level, there has been a Faculty of Theology at the University of Tartu since 1632, but in 1940 the Soviet authorities abolished the theological department. In 1941, German occupation forces refused to allow the faculty to be reopened; however, they granted permission for the founding of a Theological Examination Commission at the Consistory, thus providing an opportunity for students to complete their theology degrees. After the Second World War, theological education continued, and the Examination Commission was converted into the Theological Institute of the Estonian Evangelical Lutheran Church, which operates to this day. In 1991, the Faculty of Theology was reopened at the University of Tartu. It offers higher theological education, but does not automatically authorise graduates to serve as church ministers. This situation has been solved in co-operation with the Theological Institute of the Evangelical Lutheran Church. The Faculty of Theology, as part of a public university, is fully funded from the State budget.

As to the churches and the media, freedom of expression is protected primarily by Articles 44, 45, and 46 of the Estonian Constitution. The religious organisations' right to receive and impart information is regulated by law. The Broadcasting Act establishes general provisions for public and private broadcasting organisations.[29] In accordance with the law and their broadcasting permits, the broadcasting organisations have a right freely to decide upon the content of their programmes. The public broadcasting organisations are Estonian Television and Estonian Radio. Both of these organisations have contracts with the Estonian Council of Churches to provide programmes on religious issues. The Estonian Council of Churches decides upon the air-time that is given to members of the Council and the content of programmes, while the financing of programmes comes mainly from religious organisations. The Estonian Council of Churches has also used allocations from the State budget for support. There are also many private radio stations providing mainly confessional programmes.

Currently, anyone may freely publish newspapers, periodicals or books. The Penal Code prohibits the printing of certain materials, such as war propaganda and the incitement of racial or religious hatred. Many religious organisations have their own newspapers. In 1991 a non-profit-making organisation was established – the Esto-

---

29 RT I 1994, 42, 680; RT I 2003, 83, 560.

nian Press Council – which since 1997 has been a joint organisation of the Newspaper Association, the Association of Broadcasters, the Journalists' Union, the Union of Media Educators, the Consumers' Union, the Network of Non-Profit-Making Organisations and Foundations, and the Estonian Council of Churches. Every member organisation nominates one to three members to the Press Council. The aims of the Press Council are: to protect press freedom; to examine complaints about print media (and broadcasting) from the aspect of media ethics; to support the development of journalists' professional skills (including ethics); and adherence to the good tradition of journalism.

VI. Labour Law within the Religious Communities

According to Article 7 of the Labour Contract Act, labour law does not apply to persons who conduct religious activities in religious organisations, unless prescribed by the bye-laws of the religious organisation.[30] The latter would be the case when the bye-laws prescribe entering into an employment contract with these persons. The literal interpretation of this provision is not free from problems. It could be argued that the Article embraces only priests, ministers, and spiritual leaders of religious organisations, but the real scope of the Article is not entirely clear. It also has to be pointed out that religious organisations are free to choose whether or not to enter into an employment contract with the aforementioned persons. Different religious organisations have different approaches.[31] The purpose of the law is to give more autonomy to religious organisations in employment decisions.

---

30 RT I 1992, 15, 241; RT I 2000, 25, 144.
31 For example, in the Estonian Evangelical Lutheran Church priests do not have labour contracts. Their stipends are generally determined by the Board of Congregation. Thus the protocols of the board meetings are the main ground for paying social tax and income tax.

VII. Matrimonial and Family Law

During the first period of independence in Estonia (1918-1940) clergy had the right to register marriages under the 1926 Personal Status Act.[32] This right to register marriages with civil validity was annulled in 1940 and only restored in December 2001. After Estonia regained independence, the issue of granting authorisation was discussed several times. But at the beginning of the 1990s neither society nor the church was ready for change. The topic was brought up again in 2000, when several proposals to change the law were put forward. Finally, in May 2001, the Estonian Parliament passed amendments to the Family Law. The amendments came into force in December 2001. In accordance with the Law a clergyman who has received authorisation from the Ministry of Internal Affairs is entitled to perform civil marriages. Thus, the State has not recognised the concept of religious marriage per se but, rather, has established the possibility of delegating the obligations of the register office to a clergyman of a church, congregation, or association of congregations. According to the Family Law an authorised minister can refuse to perform the marriage if those being married oppose the conditions set for marriages by the confessions of the church, congregation or association of congregations.[33]

The Ministry of Internal Affairs may authorise clergy to perform civil marriages only if they have successfully undergone training organised by the Ministry in conjunction with the register offices. The Ministry of Internal Affairs may refuse to authorise clergymen only on very limited grounds. Thus, the discretion of the Ministry has been reduced to a minimum. Only churches, congregations, or associations of congregations registered under the CCA may apply for authorisation to perform civil marriages. The Ministry of Internal Affairs may declare such authorisation void if, *inter alia*, a minister does not perform civil marriages in accordance with the law. The Ministry of Internal Affairs may also declare the authorisation to perform civil marriages void on the recommendation of a church, congregation, or association of congregations.

---

32 RT I 1925, 191/192, 110.
33 In contrast, according to the 1926 law clergy were obliged to register anyone, not just members of their Church. Yet, this was seen as necessary even by clergy themselves as it provided correct and up-to-date statistics about changes in personal status that the previous system was not able to do.

VIII. Finances of Churches

Since there is no State Church in Estonia (Constitution, Article 40), there are no direct church taxes in Estonia. There are several indirect ways in which the State supports religious organisations. A few examples follow:

By taking into account the fact that sacred church buildings usually have historical, cultural, and artistic value, the State is obliged, according to law, to find additional finances to support the Churches and other religious organisations in the preservation of these buildings. Provision of such funds, of course, very much depends on the availability of financial resources.

Moreover, on the basis of the Income Tax Act[34] and by Government of the Republic Regulation No. 89 of 21 March 2000, the Estonian Government has established an order which regulates the list of non-taxable organisations.[35] In accordance with Article 11(2) of the Income Tax Act, religious associations are automatically exempt from income tax. Other non-profit-making organisations (including humanist associations and religious societies) have to apply to be included on the list of non-taxable non-profit-making organisations. This means that this status can also be refused on certain grounds. In practice, it has not been very difficult to get on the list.

Religious associations have also certain privileges concerning Value Added Tax (VAT), usually applied as discounts against the ordinary tax rate. For example, until 1 July 2005, religious organisations can buy electricity attracting a rate of 5 % VAT (instead of the normal 18 %).[36] The same does not apply to other non-profit-making organisations.

Religious associations are exempt from land (property) tax. Land tax is not imposed on land under the places of worship of churches and congregations (Land Tax Act, Article 4(5)). This exemption does not apply to the properties of secular non-profit-making organisations.

The above-mentioned examples also illustrate differences in the treatment of religious associations and other non-profit-making organisations, including religious societies. Moreover, since the beginning of 1990s the State has been giving regular support to the Estonian Council of Churches. The Estonian Council of Churches con-

---

34 RT I 1993, 79, 1184.
35 RT I 1996, 48, 946.
36 RT I 2001, 64, 368 (in force 1. Jan. 2002).

sists of 10 Christian Churches, including the two biggest Churches of Estonia – the Evangelical Lutheran Church and Estonian Apostolic Orthodox Church. The Council decides according to its own statutes which Churches it admits. The progress in allocating more funds to the council can be seen when you compare State budgets over the years. For example, 4,900,000 million EEK (about €314,103) was allocated from the 2004 State budget,[37] compared with 1,945,000 EEK in 2000.[38] It is debatable whether this can be viewed as a breach of the religious freedom of taxpayers who do not belong to the member Churches of the Council. The State does not prescribe how the money has to be used by the Council.

In addition, allocations have been made to support the publication of the newspaper of the Estonian Evangelical Lutheran Church. The constitutionality of these allocations and preferential treatment of the Estonian Council of Churches and the Lutheran Church have been questioned by non-Christian religious communities.

Significant compensation has been paid to the Estonian Apostolic Orthodox Church – 35,500,000 million EEK.[39] This is connected to the fulfilment of the agreement between the Estonian state, Estonian Apostolic Orthodox Church and Russian Orthodox Church, to settle a legal dispute between these two Orthodox Churches over property.[40]

IX. Religious Assistance in Public Institutions

The realisation of religious freedom in public institutions is regulated by Article 9(1) of the 2002 CCA. This article stipulates that: 'Persons staying in medical institutions, educational institutions, social welfare institutions and custodial institutions, and members of the Defence Forces have the right to perform religious rites according to their faith unless this violates public order, health, morals, the rules established in these institutions, or the rights of others staying or serving in these institutions'. The general conditions for religious

---

37 RT I 2004, 1, 1.
38 RT I 2000, 1, 1.
39 RT I, 2003, 3, 18; RT I, 2004, 1, 1.
40 The two agreements (protocols) were signed by Estonian Republic and Estonian Apostolic Orthodox Church and Estonian Republic and Estonian Orthodox Church of the Moscow Patriarchate on 4 October 2002.

assistance in public institutions are regulated by the Article 9(2) of the 2002 CCA. Article 9(2) of the CCA provides that a religious association shall conduct religious services and religious rites in a medical institution, educational institution or social welfare institution only with the permission of the owner or the head of the institution, in a custodial institution with the permission of the director of the prison, in the Defence Forces with the permission of the commanding officer of the military unit and in the National Defence League with the permission of the chief of the unit.

Army and prison chaplains are civil servants and are paid in full by the State budget. Only those from the member Churches of the Estonian Council of Churches are entitled to serve as chaplains. Members of other religious organisations (including non-Christian ones) have access to these institutions at the request of the people staying there. The institution of the chaplaincy is meant to be inter-denominational and ecumenical. According to unofficial sources, however, religious freedom is not always respected in the army when it comes to the celebration of public holidays. For example, conscripts are often required *in corpore* to attend services in the Estonian Evangelical Lutheran Church, regardless of their religious beliefs.

X. *Criminal Law and Religion*

The new Penal Code,[41] adopted on 6 June 2001, has several provisions protecting the individual and collective freedom of religion. It also contains necessary restrictions on the manifestation of the freedom of religion. Article 154 of the Penal Code lays down the penalty for interfering with the religious affiliation or religious practices of a person, unless the religious affiliation or practices are detrimental to the morals, rights or health of other people or violate public order. Compelling a person to join or be a member of a religious association is punishable by a fine or by imprisonment for up to one year (Penal Code, Article 155). Article 152 of the Penal Code also provides the penalty for the violation of the principle of equality. "Unlawful restriction of the rights of a person or granting of unlawful preferences to a person on the basis of his or her...religion...is punishable by a fine or up to one year's imprisonment." Activities which

---

41 RT1 I 2001, 61, 364 (in force 1 Sept. 2002).

publicly incite hatred or violence on the basis of religion are punishable by a fine or up to 3 years' imprisonment (Penal Code, Article 151).

The new Criminal Code also introduced into Estonian law the concept of criminal liability for legal entities. For certain crimes a religious organisation can be subjected to compulsory dissolution. The basis for this may be found in Article 48(3) of the Constitution: 'associations whose aims or activities violate criminal law are prohibited'.

The new Code of Criminal Procedure,[42] which came into force on 1 July 2004, sets forth the right of the clergy to keep confessional secrecy. This Code obviously tries to find a compromise between the right of a defendant to a fair trial and the clergy's freedom of religion. According to the Code, ministers of the religious organisations registered in Estonia have the right to refuse to give testimony as witnesses concerning circumstances which have become known to them in the course of their professional activities (Code of Criminal Procedure, Article 72). The same right, according to the law, applies to the professional support staff of the ministers. This right of ministers and their support staff is qualified by the requirement to give testimony if their testimony is requested by the suspect or the accused. Moreover, when a court is convinced that the refusal to give testimony is not related to ministerial or professional activities of support staff, the court may require a person to give testimony. The latter provisions may conflict not only with ecclesiastical law but also with Article 22 of the 2002 CCA.[43] This article categorically declares that a minister of religion shall not disclose either information which has become known to him or her in the course of a private confession or pastoral conversation, or the identity of the person who makes a private confession or has a pastoral conversation with a minister of religion. One further aspect should be noted here, that the court deciding upon the question of testimony will have to interpret notions such as 'minister', 'support staff' and 'related to professional activities'. Thus, it will be for future court practice to determine how much autonomy religious organisations themselves have in the determination of these notions.

---

[42] RT I 2003, 27, 166.
[43] Attention should be drawn to the fact that Article 22 is not formulated as a right, but as an obligation of clergy.

XI. The Legal Status of Clergy

In Estonia, clergy do not generally enjoy any special status in law; there are, however, a few exceptions to this. As mentioned above, labour law establishes exceptions to the general rules with regard to clergy. This cannot be considered as priestly privilege. The exceptions have been established to respect the autonomy of Churches and other religious organisations. The salaries of priests and other people working for the Church or religious organisation are paid by the religious organisations themselves.[44] As mentioned before, the confessional secrecy is protected by law. Some special provisions have been made to protect professional attire of minister of religion. Only a person to whom a religious association has granted the corresponding permission has the right to wear the professional attire of a minister of religion as prescribed in the statutes of the religious association concerned. The specified restriction does not apply if the professional attire of the minister of religion is ordinary clothing (2002 CCA, Article 21).

There are no restrictions in law on the holders of a spiritual office being elected either to Parliament or to the representative bodies of local government. Many members of the clergy are politically very active.

XII. Particular Questions of Civil Ecclesiastical Law and Developments

So far there have been only a few cases in the Estonian Supreme Court where the provisions of international instruments concerning freedom of religion were invoked. In general, there have been only a few freedom of religion or belief cases in courts anywhere in the country. Although individual and collective freedom of religion is protected in Estonia, many aspects of the relationship between State and Church (religious organisations) are in a process of development. There are signs of hesitation and a lack of knowledge on both sides – State and religious organisations – that obstruct the formation of the concept of a real State-Church relationship.

---

44 See also 'Labour Law Within the Religious Communities' above.

XIII. Bibliography

M. Ketola, 'Some aspects of the Nationality Question in the Lutheran Church of Estonia, 1918-39', Religion, State and Society (Oxford: Keston Institute, 1999), vol. 27, no. 2.

M. Kiviorg, 'Church Autonomy in Estonia' in *Robbers, G. (ed.)*. Church Autonomy. A Comparative Survey, Peter Lang: Frankfurt am Main, 2001, p. 285-301.

M. Kiviorg, Law, Religion and Politics, Rechtstheorie. Zeitschrift für Logik, Methodenlehre, Kybernetik und Soziologie des Rechts, Berlin: Duncker-Humblot, 2001.

M. Kiviorg, Legal Status of Religious Communities in the Realms of Public and Private Law, Juridica International. Law Review University of Tartu, 2001, VI, p. 169-177.

P. Valk, Development of the Status of Religious Education in Estonian Schools. European and Local Perspectives, Conference on Law, Religion and Democratic Society, Estonia, University of Tartu, 1999.

P. Roosma, Protection of Fundamental Rights and Freedoms in Estonian Constitutional Jurisprudence, Juridica International, Vol. IV, 1999, p. 35-44.

R. Ringvee, Religious Freedom and Legislation in Post-Soviet Estonia, 2001 BYU L. Rev. 631-642.

Charalambos Papastathis
State and Church in Greece

I. Social Facts

The majority of the Greek people – 95 % of the total population of the Greek citizens in the country – are considered to have been baptised into the Eastern Orthodox Church. There are smaller numbers, in order of size, of Muslims (living mainly in Western Thrace), Roman Catholics, Protestants, Jehovah's Witnesses, Armenians, and Jews. It follows that when we refer to relations between the Greek State and the Church, we mean the Orthodox Church. In recent years considerable numbers of legal and illegal immigrants have come to live in Greece: most of them are Albanians of Muslim origin.

II. Historical Background

The theoretical basis for relations between State and Church is an advanced form of caesaropapism, a system referred to in Greek literature as that of "State-law rule". According to the Constitution, the State has the right to legislate in respect of all administrative matters concerning the Church, even as to its internal structure. The frequent criticisms advanced on this point are usually refuted by alluding – incorrectly – to long-established tradition. It is true, of course, that in the Christian Byzantine Empire, a form of caesaropapism was in force. However, after the fall of Constantinople (1453), the institutional framework changed. Mehmet II the Conqueror conceded political power to the Church: the Ecumenical Patriarch of Constantinople was held responsible to the Ottoman state for all Orthodox Christian activities concerning State rule. During the War of Independence of 1821, a new relationship developed: the Constitutions of the emerging Greece not only established the Eastern Orthodox faith as the prevailing religion or "religion of the State", but also guaranteed freedom of worship to the followers of other religions. The Constitutions contained no provisions giving the State the right to legislate on Church matters. In 1831, the Great Powers imposed on Greece an absolute monarchy with Prince Otto of Bavaria as King. As he was under age, a three-member regency, consisting of German officers, was proclaimed. The Regency published the decree of 3 (15)/14(27) April 1833, which established the "State-law rule". A short time after, on 23 July (4 August) 1833, with the decree on "The Independence of the Greek Church", the State was made the exclusive legislative body and the Church was declared subject to the monarch, who was proclaimed its Head. Article 105 of the 1844 Constitution contained a provision concerning Church administrative matters, stipulating that they could be regulated by law of the State.

This new state of affairs was introduced in 1833 by Georg Ludwig von Maurer, a member of the Regency and a well-known jurist. Modern Greece owes to Maurer a particularly significant work of codification. However, Maurer was not successful in his provisions concerning Church affairs – framing relations, together with the imposition of the state of autocephaly.

There were several reasons for the imposition of the State's rule on the Orthodox Church: the very nature of monarchy, and Maurer's fear of the Church becoming a focus for opponents of the regime – the latter a not inconsiderable threat, given the political stance of the Church throughout the Turkish occupation. We may also note his efforts to raise the cultural and living standards of the clergy, which had been far from satisfactory.

III. Legal Sources

1. Constitution

The provision of the 1844 Constitution concerning "State-law rule" over Church matters was not repeated in the Constitutions of 1864, 1911, 1927, and 1952. This, however, does not mean that it ceased to be operative. A similar provision existed in the corresponding statutory Charter of the Church, which had the force of State law. The stipulation appears again in the 1968 Constitution, promoted by the military junta. Article 1(5) provided that no Bill concerning church administration was to be discussed without consultation with the Holy Synod, unless a period of twenty days had elapsed without agreement. A similar stipulation exists in the 1975 Constitution which is currently in force, (Art. 72(1)): Bills relating to Article 3 (position of the Church) and Article 13 (religious freedom) may be discussed by Parliament in plenary session only and not during the summer session.

2. Basic Categories of the System

Article 3(1) of the Constitution contains the following fundamental statements concerning the position of the Church of Greece and its relations with the State: the dogma of the Orthodox Church is the prevailing religion; the Church of Greece is inseparably united in doctrine with the Ecumenical Patriarchate of Constantinople and with all other Orthodox Churches; the Church is self-governing; and it is autocephalous.
The provisions of Article 3 are not all new: they existed in various forms in all previous Constitutions.

a) The prevailing religion

The present Constitution, however, differs from that of 1952 at several points concerning particular aspects of the prevailing religion. These include the provisions according to which the heir to the throne should be an Orthodox, and that on assuming his duties, the King swears to protect the State religion and even has to take his oath before the Holy Synod. As for the rest, the opening phrase of the Constitution (invoking the Holy Trinity) remains the same; this also holds for the oaths given by the President of the Republic (Art. 33(2)) and by Members of Parliament (Art. 59(1)). The legal significance of the term "prevailing" has not changed. As in the past it means that (1) the Orthodox Christian faith is the official religion of the Greek State; (2) the Church, which embodies this faith, has its own legal status: it is a legal person under public law in its juridical relations, as are its various services (Art.1(4) L. 590/1977 concerning the statutory Charter of the Church of Greece); and (3) it is treated by the State with special concern and in a favourable manner, which is not extended to other faiths and religions. This is not inconsistent with the constitutional principle of equality, as explained below.

This special treatment (1) concerns the Church itself and not its members individually; this is in accordance with the principle of equality because otherwise, in treating non-Orthodox differently, there would be discrimination between citizens on the basis of their religious convictions; (2) concerns initially the Orthodox Church of Greece and all other Sees of the Ecumenical Patriarchate having their seat in Greece, but is also extended to all other Eastern Orthodox Churches of the East, as well as to those of the Diaspora (e.g. Art. 18(8)); (3) is favourable in general and does not involve opposing a specific faith or religion and its cult; and (4) should not be considered as unconstitutional. We mention here as an example, the case of the city of Patra (County Court decision 261/1983) that the provision of Article 11 of L.D. 3485/1955 compelling all consumers of electricity in that city to pay with their bill every month a special contribution for the construction of the Cathedral of St. Andrew was unconstitutional.

With regard to the real content of the term "prevailing" we should note that, with the exception of the establishment of the Orthodox faith as the official religion (or religion of the State), other privileges are not limited to that Church only. In fact, it has been maintained in theory – at least in part – that the Roman Catholic and Protestant Churches in Greece are also legal persons in public law and therefore exercise public administration. This is true for the situation prevailing before the enforcement of L.1230/1982 concerning civil marriage, when a licence for such a marriage could be obtained by a non-Orthodox bishop for a member of his Church (according to Art. 1368 of the Civil Code, then in force). As regards the favourable treatment of the dominant religion by the civil legislator, it is important to bear in mind that this is also extended to other religions. Mention may be made of L. 1763/1988 on army conscription (Art. 6(1)(c)) which exempts all monks or novices, regardless of whether they are Orthodox or belong to another faith. And again, L.D. 3843/1958 on income tax and L.D. 1249/1982 on property-tax, which exempt not only Orthodox but also non-Orthodox churches and monasteries. It was also decided that the provision of Article 21 of L.D. 22 April/6 May 1926, which states that real property of all monasteries cannot be taken over by third parties, was applicable to Roman Catholic monasteries too.

b) *The spiritual unity of the Orthodox Church*

Depending on the mode of its administration, an Orthodox Church may be autocephalous or autonomous. A church is autocephalous when it is spiritually self-sufficient and independent in administration. It is autonomous when it is only independent in administration. At present, the following are autocephalous: the Ecumenical Patriarchate of Constantinople, and the Patriarchates of Alexandria, Antioch, Jerusalem, Russia, Serbia, Romania, Bulgaria, and Georgia, together with the Archbishoprics of Cyprus, Greece, Poland, Albania, and the Czech Republic-Slovakia. The Orthodox Churches of Finland and Estonia are autonomous. Autocephalous churches are independent as regards their administration, but within a dogmatic and canonical framework; deviation from it can lead to heresy or schism. This framework constitutes the spiritual unity of Orthodoxy, which is treated under the headings of dogmatic and canonical unity. Dogmatic unity consists in following the teachings of Holy Scripture, respecting tradition, and strict observance of the dogma as defined by the Ecumenical Councils and the local Synods. Canonical unity consists in the observance of at least the most important institutions of Church administration, which were also defined and acknowledged by the same Councils and Synods, as well as through the relations between Orthodox Churches.

The constitutional legislator of 1844 had already defined the Church of Greece as inseparably united in doctrine with the Great Church of Christ in Constantinople and with every other Orthodox Church. How is this unity achieved? At this point in the Constitution, we have after "inseparably united in doctrine" the phrase "observing unwaveringly, as they do, the holy apostolic and synodal canons and sacred traditions". The above formulation, which has remained unchanged since 1844, was addressing spiritual unity. However, when the "State-law rule" was established, it led legal theory and jurisprudence to the view that at this point the Constitution safeguards the Holy Canons. This different approach led to diametrically opposite interpretations, controversies over the constitutional validity of one or the other law, and countless appeals to the Council of State (the supreme administrative court) against decisions of public and ecclesiastical administration. The conflict over the constitutional validity of the Holy Canons is perpetually active in Greece.

bb) *The so-called constitutional validation of the Holy Canons*

All the Holy Canons, as defined by the seven Ecumenical Councils (325 to 787 A.D.), the local Synods and the Fathers of the Church, whether they concern dogmatic or administrative issues, are validated by the Constitution. So any legislation enacted by the Greek State, regardless of its object, is unconstitutional if it is in opposition to the Holy Canons. This theory is supported by the Church, theological doctrine, and some jurists.
However, according to another view, only the Holy Canons concerning the dogma of the Church and not those concerning its administration are constitutionally validated. Accordingly, the legislature may deal freely with all issues concerning Church administration in general. This is the theory supported by jurisprudence, most jurists, and public administration.
Both views agree in contrasting the phrase "inseparably united in doctrine" with that of "observing unwaveringly as they do...". According to both views, the Constitution introduces two quite different rules: (a) dogmatic unity; and (b) constitutional validation (or non-validation) of the Holy Canons and Tradition.
Both theories are liable to lead to difficulties. Were the former to be followed, it would impose a theocratic State, and would require equality of citizens to be considered as unconstitutional, since the Holy Canons will always support Christians (see Canon II of the Synod of Troullo, concerning relations between Christians and Jews). On the other hand, the second theory turns the Church into a civil service. In addition to matters of dogma, there exist the Holy Canons confirming the Orthodox character of the Church, including its synodical regime. However, according to this second theory, the legislator may deal freely with this regime because the Holy Canons referred to it are administrative.
It all comes down to one provision of the Constitution: the engagement of both State and Church to ensure the spiritual unity of the latter. This conclusion is reached by considering both the text of the provision and the historical circumstance of its initial application (1844 Constitution). At that time, there was a break in relations between the Church of Greece and the Ecumenical Patriarchate and other Orthodox Churches, because the Church of Greece was proclaimed autocephalous by a sudden decision in 1833. The provision of the 1844 Constitution was formulated in Parliament in order to proclaim the Orthodox character of the Church of the new kingdom.

The Council of State reached a similar conclusion in 1967. It not only admitted the constitutional validation of the Holy Canons concerning dogmatic matters, but also stated that the common legislator could not proceed to change fundamental administrative institutions which had long been established in the Orthodox Church. The Council of State reached this conclusion by citing principally the 1875 Constitution, Article 13(1) and (2) – on religious liberty.

c) *The self-government of the Church*

The present Constitution, like its predecessor, guarantees the self-government of the Church. The Church is administered by the Holy Synod which is made up of the bishops. However, there is a new point in the Constitution of 1975 specifying that the Orthodox Church of Greece is governed by the Holy Synod (of the Hierarchy) formed by all serving bishops (Metropolitans) and by the Permanent Holy Synod formed also by them.

These active bishops are the prelates who actually administer Church sees; those bishops who are not in active service (retired bishops) are excluded, as are titular metropolitans. In the past, during periods of strife between State and Church or in irregular political situations, the government could call together a Synod formed by bishops chosen from among metropolitans sympathetic to the regime, and in this way could settle matters according to its wishes. This danger is now averted.

The same provision states that the Patriarchal Tome (1850) must be implemented as must the Patriarchal Synodal Acts (1928), examined below. All the debates in Parliament or in the Council of State concerning the Constitution point to the fact that these two patriarchal documents are valid only as regards the formation of the Permanent Holy Synod. The self-government of the Church, its content and implementation are guaranteed by the Constitution, according to the provisions of Article 72(1), namely "state-law rule". At the same time, all acts effected by persons entrusted by the State with the administration of the Greek Orthodox Church may be submitted to or cancelled by the Council of State. This holds for acts concerning the implementation of legal provisions on administration only, not on religious or dogmatic matters. The actual jurisprudence of the Council of State is very rich and at the same time its field of application is growing ever wider.

d) Church autocephaly in Greece and its field of application

Article 3(1) of the Constitution decrees that "the Orthodox Church of Greece is autocephalous". This is stated not only as a fact, but also as a guarantee of the continuation of this state of affairs. Abolition of autocephaly would require a revision of this provision; it should be noted that Article 110(1) of the Constitution considers this provision as not exempt from revision.

The "Orthodox Church of Greece" referred to in Article 3(1) does not unite all the Orthodox members in the Greek State: its jurisdiction does not extend to the whole country. The Greek State is divided into five distinct ecclesiastical provinces, each with a different Church, though some are under the same synodical hierarchy but on a different administrative or spiritual basis.

The provinces, which today constitute the autocephalous Church of Greece formerly belonged to the jurisdiction of the Patriarchate of Constantinople. During the 1821 War of Independence, relations with the Patriarchate were interrupted because of the war. When the new Greek State was founded, certain circles favoured and finally imposed the state of autocephaly for the Church of the liberated provinces for reasons of ecclesiastical and, chiefly, State policy. After King Otto, formerly a Prince of Bavaria (1833), came to the throne, the Bavarian Regency proclaimed the autocephaly of the Church without fulfilling certain conditions required by canonical tradition. In this way, the decree of 23 July/4 August 1833 (on the independent Greek Church) declared the Church of the realm to be autocephalous, in what amounted to a coup d'etat. This was met with opposition in Greece as well as in Constantinople and other Orthodox Churches, and resulted in a break in the spiritual unity of the Church. Finally, on 29 June 1850 the Patriarchate published a Synodal Tome, according to which the Church of Greece was proclaimed autocephalous ex nunc. When the Ionian Islands (1864) and later Thessaly, the province of Arta and some villages of Epirus and Macedonia (1880) were united with Greece, the Ecumenical Patriarchate conceded all these new provinces to the autocephalous Church of Greece by Acts dated 9 July 1866 and May 1882.

The Patriarchal and Synodal Act of 1882 determined the final jurisdiction of the autocephalous Church. Since then, when new lands have been liberated and united with Greece, they have not been under the jurisdiction of the autocephalous Church of Greece. Thus, when the autonomous authority of Crete was founded (1898), it came to an agreement with the Ecumenical Patriarchate (14 October 1900) which regulated its canonical dependence and organisation. The Church of Crete remains spiritually dependent upon the Patriarchate of Constantinople and is administratively semi-autonomous to the present day.

After the Balkan wars of 1912-13 and the First World War, Macedonia, Epirus, Western Thrace and the Aegean Islands were also liberated and united with Greece; these provinces too, were dependent upon the Ecumenical Patriarchate. The regime prevailing in these provinces, the so-called "New Lands", has been the subject of much discussion. These resulted in a rather unusual solution (L. 3615/1928 and the Patriarchal and Synodal Act of 1928): the "New Lands" would be spiritually dependent upon the Ecumenical Patriarchate but at the same time they would be administered by the autocephalous Church of Greece. This meant, firstly, that the autocephalous Church of Greece assumed responsibility for the day to day government of the New Lands, extending into them the administration as exerted in her own provinces; and secondly, that this regime would be temporary. Both texts contain a number of conditions which the Church of Greece is obliged to apply. However, the Church of Greece has not in practice respected the Patriarchal Act of 1928. In 2003 a conflict between the two Churches began, which ended in June 2004 with the assurance of the Holy Synod in Athens that it will apply all the conditions of the Act, while the Hellenic Republic guarantees the application of the same Act.

Following the union with Greece of the Dodecanese Islands (7 March 1947), the ecclesiastical regime was not changed; thus the four metropolitan sees and the exarchy of Patmos remain within the spiritual and administrative jurisdiction of the Ecumenical Patriarchate.

Finally, the peninsula of the Holy Mountain-Athos, which was liberated in 1912, retains its ancient, privileged, regime of self-government, while remaining under the spiritual jurisdiction of the Ecumenical Patriarchate.

This division of the Greek lands into five ecclesiastical provinces is in no way detrimental to the position of the Orthodox Church as the prevailing Church. Article 3(1) of the Constitution refers to the autocephalous Church and in Article 3(2) stipulates that the ecclesiastical regime existing in certain provinces is not in opposition to the previous paragraph.

Orthodox members resident in the province of another autocephalous Church are subject to that Church. The Greek Orthodox Diaspora

(Western, Central and Northern Europe, America, Australia and the Far East) is dependent upon the Ecumenical Patriarchate.

IV. Religious Freedom

Religious freedom in Greece is guaranteed by Article 13 of the Constitution. Religious freedom consists of freedom of conscience (Art. 13(1)) and freedom of worship (Art. 13(2)).
Freedom of religious conscience covers all religious, non-religious or atheistic beliefs, as well as dogmatic and administrative differences within any religion (heresy or schism) and all persons, Greek or alien, according to the principle of equality (Constitution, Articles 4 and 13(1)).
There have been some deviations from this principle of equality, especially regarding the appointment of teachers in primary education. At elementary schools religious education conforms to the creed of the prevailing religion, and it is taught by regular teachers. There was a decision of the Council of State (1417/1949) that only an Orthodox may be appointed as a primary school teacher; teaching by a non-Orthodox according to the dogma of the Eastern Church was not held to be possible. In practice, it also applied to nursery school teachers. This state of things, with an exception in the case of schools of religious minorities, was in force until 1988, when it was abolished (L. 1771/1988). Accordingly, a non-Orthodox may now be appointed as teacher (in a school with at least two posts), and religion will be taught by his or her Orthodox colleague.
Similarly, the President of the Republic can take only a Christian oath. Article 33 of the Constitution does not contain a stipulation similar to that of article 59, concerning the oath of non-Christian members of Parliament. This is an indirect way of promoting the election of a Christian President only and does not conform to the principle of equality.
In contrast to the position concerning the freedom of religious conscience, freedom of worship is subject to certain restrictions. According to Article 13(2) of the Constitution, a religion must be a "known religion", that is a religion without a secret dogma or a hidden cult. Furthermore, this religion should not offend public order and moral principles. This includes the whole set of civil, moral, social, and economic principles and beliefs prevailing in Greek society at any

given period. The above conditions are enforced by the public administration and, ultimately, by the courts. At the same time, another point is stressed by both theory and judicial practice: members of a certain religious denomination are not allowed to proselytise.

Proselytism is treated in Greece as an offence under the criminal law; this was established by F.L.1363/1938, and replaced by a provision of F.L. 1672/1939; both laws were promulgated during the dictatorship of Metaxas. Proselytism is a criminal offence when it is carried out systematically and pressingly, directly or indirectly, by use of unlawful or immoral means amounting to a violation of the religious conscience of a person of a different religion in order to change his or her religious beliefs. Proselytism is punished severely: imprisonment, fines, police surveillance and even expulsion in the case of a foreigner. In the 1952 Constitution, proselytism was considered an offence when directed at an Orthodox. The present Constitution (Art. 13(2)) protects all religions from similar injury.

The establishment of a place of worship for the various religions (church, house of prayer, synagogue, or mosque) is licensed by the Ministry of Education and Cults. Among other prerequisites is the permission of the local Metropolitan of the prevailing Orthodox Church (F.L. 1369/1938, Art. 41(1)). It was decided by the Council of State that this applies to the establishment of houses of prayer, although the relevant law is not specific on the point. The Council of State has also ruled that the Metropolitan's permission is only a recommendation, which does not bind the Ministry; but if the Ministry did permit an establishment against the Metropolitan's recommendation, it would have to justify its decision. In practice, the Metropolitans are almost always against such developments and the Ministry does not as a rule oppose them. Therefore, the interested party has to appeal to the Council of State, and the appeal is usually upheld. The same holds good for the Orthodox following the Julian calendar (since 1924): they have their own hierarchy, clergy and parishes. New religious movements are protected by Article 13 of the Constitution only insofar as they are considered as a religion. Scientology has not been recognised as a religion by the Council of State.

Non-Orthodox congregations are usually recognised as associations according to civil law, since no law admits their legal personality under public law. A special committee was formed in 1988 by the Ministry of Education and Cults in order to study questions of religious freedom in general; since the resignation of the Minister Anthony Tritsis (May 1988) the committee has not been summoned by his successors.

V. State Supervision of Religion

1. The Administration

The general State supervision of all religions is entrusted to the General Secretariat of Cults of the Ministry of National Education and Cults. Each duty includes: supervision of the implementation of government policy in the area of cults; and the duties of the following departments of the above Ministry: the Department of Ecclesiastical Administration: duties are limited exclusively to the matters of the prevailing religion and only within the Hellenic territory; the Department of Ecclesiastical Education and Religious Instruction; and the Department of Persons of a Different Cult and a Different Religion. The title of this department is somewhat paradoxical for a modern State. The department deals with proselytism, the procedures for the foundation and the operation of the places of worship of non-orthodox Christians, of divinity schools, seminaries, foundations and other legal entities, as well as the supervision of all the above. The department is also in charge of the appointment, discharge, and the matter of the official status of the general chief Rabbi of Greece, the chief Rabbis of the Israeli communities, and the three Muslim Muftis of the Muslim minority of Western Thrace.

The Ministry of Foreign Affairs also has responsibilities towards religion. Each Department of Ecclesiastical Affairs is responsible for the supervision, study, and recommendations as to the solution of all matters and affairs pertaining to the Orthodox, the other Christian churches and other religions outside Greece, the Orthodox Divinity Schools and Ecclesiastical Centres outside Greece, the Orthodox Greek clergy living abroad, and the civil administration of Mount Athos.

2. The Council of State

The Orthodox Church in Greece is a spiritual and religious foundation, but at the same time it exercises a conferred administrative power, implementing as a public legal entity the provisions of State legislation. The Council of State (which is the Supreme Administrative Court) has subjected to its review all Acts that pertain to administrative matters. The Council uses three relevant criteria: firstly, the

Act should originate from those ecclesiastical agencies to which the state has entrusted the administration of the Church (i.e. Holy Synod, Bishoprics, parish councils); secondly, the contested Act should be issued in compliance with state legislations; and finally, the contested Act should be both an exercise of administration – that is, it should regulate an administrative matter, not doctrine, worship or matters of a spiritual nature – and be not yet in force.

VI. Organisation of the Church

The Church of Greece is organised according to the synodical system; this is a fundamental administrative institution for every Orthodox Church, and it is found at central and local levels. The supreme authority is the Holy Synod of Hierarchy with the Archbishop of Athens as its President, and all the serving bishops (Metropolitans) as its members. Currently, there are eighty metropolitan sees in the entire Archbishopric: 43 in the autocephalous Church and 36 in the New Lands. The Church of Crete has an archbishopric and seven metropolitan sees, the Dodecanese Islands have four, and the Holy Mountain is under the episcopal jurisdiction of the Ecumenical Patriarch himself.

The Holy Synod has administrative, legislative and juridical competence. In its legislative competence, it may publish regulations and canonical orders according to authority given in several areas by the constitutional Charter of the Church (L. 590/1977). The Synod is summoned *ipso jure* annually on 1 October, and at other times exceptionally according to need. A permanent administrative service is assured by the Permanent Holy Synod; this is formed by twelve metropolitans (six from the autocephalous Church and six from the Churches of the New Lands), with the Archbishop of Athens as President. It has a yearly tenure and prescribed powers.

At the same time, there exist several synodical committees, which also assist the Synod. It also has attached to it certain organisations as legal persons: the Apostoliki Diakonia and the Inter-Orthodox Centre.

The Church of Greece is organised locally as follows:
(1) The Archbishopric of Athens and the metropolitan sees; their boundaries, name and see are defined according to resolutions of the Holy Synod of the Hierarchy. The metropolitan sees are legal per-

sons of public law. The bishop is the principal administrator in every province, and his title is that of metropolitan; questions concerning churches and parishes are in general decided by the metropolitan council consisting of a judge, an official from the Ministry of Finance, two priests, and a parish councillor. The election of the Archbishop of Athens and of the metropolitans is carried out by the Holy Synod of the Hierarchy. All active metropolitans are eligible for the archbishopric, together with those priests who are included in the list of candidates. Priests who are candidates for election as metropolitan must be included in the list of those eligible as archbishops. This list is established by the Holy Synod. New names are added every year, according to criteria stated in the constitutional Charter of the Church. The Ecumenical Patriarchate of Constantinople also has the right to add new names to the list, but only for the sees of the New Lands. Also eligible are prelates who are not active metropolitans. Official records on the election of archbishops and metropolitans are submitted to the Minister of Education and Cults, and he orders the publication of a presidential decree; following that, the elected prelate submits his confirmation to the President of the Republic and assumes his duties.

(2) A parish is a legal person of public law. It is founded by a presidential decree and administered by the parish priest and a five-member council of lay persons. The parish priest must be married; non-married priests may be ordained temporarily. Vacancies are filled by decree.

(3) Monasteries are also legal persons of public law, and also founded by presidential decree. Monasteries in the Church of Greece are divided into those which are under the supervision of the local metropolitan and those which are supervised by the Holy Synod. There are also monasteries in Greece which are supervised by the Ecumenical Patriarchate or are dependent upon the Monasteries of Mount Athos, the Holy Sepulchre, or the Mount Sinai Monastery.

VII. Church and Culture

In primary and secondary schools, courses in religious education are taught according to the dogma and the tradition of the Eastern Orthodox Church. Teaching is carried out by teachers in primary schools, and graduates of theology in secondary schools. Both are considered as civil servants and receive a salary from the State, while their appointment and syllabus are controlled by the Church. According to the principle of religious freedom, non-Orthodox pupils are not obliged to follow the courses. Parents raise their children according to their own religious beliefs.

Each religious denomination may have its own schools in Greece. The State is also in charge of schools for the Muslim minority in Western Thrace as well as a training college for future teachers in these schools.

Training for Orthodox ordinands is given in twenty-one schools (secondary schools, higher schools and schools for accelerated training). These establishments also provide board and lodging for the students. All expenses are met by the State, and the teachers are considered civil servants.

Both the Universities of Athens and Thessaloniki have theological faculties, which non-Orthodox students may also attend.

VIII. Criminal Law

The penal jurisdiction of the Church, its offences, sentences, and procedures is governed by State Law 5383/1932. Under the regime of "state-law rule", the jurisdiction of the ecclesiastical courts has been limited to clergy and monks. These courts do not judge lay people. If a lay person has committed a serious violation of faith or ecclesiastical order – such as heresy or schism – the Holy Synod of Hierarchy can impose aphorism (anathema) or excommunication. The ecclesiastical courts are: for priests, deacons and monks the episcopal court; the first instance synodal court and the second instance synodal court; for bishops the first and second instance courts; and, solely for the members of the Permanent Holy Synod, a special court. All bishops found guilty by the second instance court have the right of appeal to the Ecumenical Patriarchate. The penalties of the ecclesiastical courts are: demotion, suspension, dethronement (only for bishops), fine, internment, and unfrocking (see also Section X, below).

IX. Financing of Churches

In Greece there is no Church tax. Every religion has its own revenues from movable and immovable property, and the offerings of members. The State has, however, almost entirely assumed the financing of the prevailing religion; this is done under a variety of forms:
Direct or indirect subventions, such as the yearly subvention to the "Apostoliki Diakonia" (L. 976/1946, Art. 24(1)(8)) and another granted to the Cathedral of Athens (L. 2844/1954), together with various grants to churches and monasteries for different reasons. At the same time, the State is charged with all the expenses of Orthodox clerical education.
The State pays the salaries of prelates, priests who serve a parish, deacons (priests and deacons number up to 10,000), preachers, and also laity employed by the Orthodox Church. The same persons also receive pensions from the State when retired. The law which imposed a State levy of 35 % of all parish revenues was abolished in 2004. The monks are also insured (for health and pension) by the "Farmers' Security Organisation". Priests serving in cemeteries and hospitals receive their salary from the local municipality or hospital administration. Priests serving in the Army and the Police Force are raised to the rank of officers and receive the salary or pension of their rank. They may also hold posts in the public or private sector – usually as teachers – with the appropriate income.
Tax exemption: both the Orthodox Church and Churches of other religious denominations enjoy various tax-exemptions such as those from real-estate tax, real-estate income tax, tax from real-estate transfers, donations, and inheritance tax. More favourable tax-exemptions apply to Mount Athos.
Other financial privileges comprise the inalienability of real property belonging to the Orthodox Patriarchates of the Middle East as well as to the monasteries of the Ecumenical Patriarchate, and the fact that real property belonging to monasteries cannot be taken over by third parties. The Court of Appeal in Thessaloniki has accepted that this also holds for Roman-Catholic monasteries (1161/1983).
The State does not pay the salaries of precentors and sacristans; these persons, however, are not employees according to general labour laws because, according to the Holy Canons, they are considered as inferior clergy.
Although only a few of these persons have this status, the old financial regime still holds in their case: that is, when they are appointed

by the metropolitan they receive from the church a salary which has been agreed by the parties. Other Church employees are remunerated as civil servants of similar categories.

X. Ordination and Legal Position of Priests and Monks

The qualifications required of candidates for ordination are the following:
(a) He must be a member of the Orthodox Church, (b) with a correct and sound faith, (c) he must be a male, (d) of the right age (minimum age 25 years for a deacon, 30 for a priest, 34 for a bishop), (e) have the necessary education, (f) be physically and spiritually healthy, (g) if he is married, his marriage must conform to the Holy Canons, (h) he should not have extramarital relations, and (i) he must be of irreproachable conduct.
If he is found guilty by an ecclesiastical court, a priest may lose his attributes and may be defrocked. A defrocked priest resumes the status he held before ordination, as a lay person or monk. The Eastern Church accepts that the conferring of orders is reversible: the acts of the defrocked priest are invalid.
Priests must accept the following restrictions: they cannot be appointed guardians of minors or of legally condemned persons. The Holy Canons prohibit trading by priests; if a priest is found to be practising trade systematically, he is considered a trader and accordingly punished. There exist in the Penal Code certain offences, which can be perpetrated only by a priest. These include: the abuse of clerical rank (Art. 196), the abuse of a spiritual child with indecent assault (Art. 342(1)), violation of confidentiality (Art. 371(1)). Another offence is the celebration of betrothal before a marriage or marriage without the bishop's permission, according to the constitutional Charter of the Church (Art. 49(2) and (3)). This offence may be punishable by up to a year's imprisonment by a State court and is also punishable by the ecclesiastical courts.
According to penal and civil jurisprudence, when an oath is necessary, priests must only give an affirmation; they are not asked to divulge any information gained through confession. A prelate's testimony is taken at his residence and then read out in court. Bishops enjoy a special penal jurisdiction according to the Code of Criminal Procedure. Petty offences committed by a prelate are judged at the

"crown court", not at the police court; while an offence is judged at the court of appeal, not at the "crown court". Although this was standard practice in the past, lay people do not now take part in the administration of ecclesiastical establishments and the election of prelates and parish priests.

Monastic status is acquired by tonsure which is a ceremony and not a mystery. Tonsure takes place at the monastery where the new monk will live. During the ceremony the monk takes vows of obedience, poverty and chastity. Before tonsure, a future monk has to remain a novice, usually for a period of three years. A novice cannot be less than 16 years old.

As with priesthood, tonsure is an obstacle to marriage; tonsure will not automatically annul a former marriage. It constitutes, however, a reason for a demand of divorce by the other partner. Succession to the property of a monk is subject to particularly complicated legal arrangements in Greece. It will suffice to mention here that a monk's estate is inherited twice: after tonsure and after his death. After tonsure, his estate goes to the monastery and to his wife and children if he was married. After death, his estate is equally divided between the monastery and the Church.

XI. Matrimonial and Family Law

Marriage is not considered incompatible with priesthood in the Eastern Church. It must have taken place, though, before ordination. Bishops are elected only from among non-married or widowed priests.

Civil marriage was introduced in Greece in 1982. Until that year, religious marriage was the only valid form; a civil marriage could only take place abroad and was not recognised in Greece. L.1250/1982 introduced the equal validity of religious and civil marriage, and at the same time abolished many marriage-impediments in the Civil Code. However, the Church of Greece decided to keep many of these impediments. Thus, an Orthodox may not be married to a person of a different religion; nor when a third marriage has already taken place; nor when there is a close blood-relationship or spiritual affinity after baptism; nor when both parties have been convicted by a criminal court of adultery between them (although adultery is no longer considered a criminal offence). Marriage is not permitted to priests and monks and to a woman before ten months have elapsed after the dissolution of a previous marriage.

Marriage in church requires a licence from the Metropolitan. In practice, this amounts to the same licence required by municipalities or communities for a civil marriage. The officiating Orthodox priest should be "in a regular position", that is entrusted with performing the mysteries of the Church. Otherwise, the marriage is not valid. Mixed marriages are celebrated according to both dogmas (Civil Code 1371).

Divorce is granted only by a civil court. The Church may intervene in the proceedings twice: before a divorce suit in an attempt at reconciliation (Code of Civil Procedure, Art. 593 and f.) (this was abolished after the introduction of civil marriage); and after the court's decision, the Church dissolves the marriage spiritually. This is still in force today for persons who after a first religious marriage wish to proceed to another.

XII. Mount Athos

Organised coenobitic monastic life on the Athos Peninsula is considered to date from the year 963, when the Monastery of Great Lavra was built. The Byzantine Emperors were in the habit of granting to Mount Athos privileges of self-administration (relating to the exercise of legislative, judicial, and administrative power), as well as privileges of a religious, personal, and financial nature. Mount Athos became the pan-Orthodox monastic centre, with monks from all the Orthodox nations. Nowadays, almost 2,500 lead the monastic life there.

According to the Constitution of the Hellenic Republic (Art. 105) the Athos Peninsula is a self-governing part of the Greek State, whose sovereignty remains intact. Spiritually, Mount Athos is under the direct jurisdiction of the Ecumenical Patriarchate of Constantinople. All persons leading a monastic life there acquire Greek citizenship *ipso jure* upon admission to a monastery as monks or novices. Mount Athos is governed, according to its privileged regime, by its twenty monasteries, and the entire peninsula is divided among them. The whole territory of the peninsula is exempted from expropriation. The administration is exercised by representatives of the twenty monasteries constituting the Holy Community, and its executive body the

Holy Epistassia (Superintendence), which comprises four monks drawn annually from four different monasteries in rotation. The constitution does not permit any change in the administrative system or in the number of the monasteries or in their hierarchical order or in their relationship to their subordinate dependencies (sketes, cells, hermitages). Non-Orthodox Christian persons or Orthodox schismatics are prohibited from living there. The determination in detail of the regimes of Mount Athos entities and their manner of operation is regulated by the Charter of Mount Athos. This Charter was drawn up and voted for by the twenty monasteries, and ratified by the Ecumenical Patriarchate and the Hellenic Parliament. The Charter in force came into operation in 1927.

Proper observance of the Athonite regimes by its entities is in the spiritual field under the supreme supervision of the Ecumenical Patriarchate, and in the administrative field under the supervision of the Hellenic Republic, which is also exclusively responsible for safeguarding public order and security. These powers of the State are exercised through a civil governor, whose rights and duties are determined by law, and who is appointed by the Ministry of Foreign Affairs. The law determines also the judicial power exercised by the monastic authorities and the holy community as well as customs and taxation privileges, (Legislative Decree of 10/16-9-1926).

In addition to the Constitution, the Charter and the L.D., two other basic legal sources are in force: Article 13 of the 16th protocol of the Treaty of Lausanne (1923), which safeguards the rights and liberties of the monastic communities that are non-Hellenic in origin; and the joint declaration no. 4 of the Final Act (1979) of the Agreement concerning the accession of Greece to the European Community, which states that the Community must preserve the status of Mount Athos, in particular in relation to customs franchise privileges, tax exemptions, and the right of establishment.

XIII. *The Special Legal Status of the Various Cults and Religions*

1. Non-Orthodox Christians, as well as the Orthodox who follow the Julian calendar, are almost always assembled into associations of the type provided for in the Civil Code, since there are no special laws that would recognize their moral personality of public law.

The 3rd London Protocol (1830) on the foundation of the Greek State, dealt in the first place with the position of the Roman Catholic Church in Greece. Under the provisions of this Protocol: a) France – which had assumed the protection of the Roman Catholics during the period of the Ottoman rule –, abandoned this role in the liberated territories, entrusting this task to the sovereign of the newly formed State, and b) it was determined that the Roman Catholic religion would enjoy the free and public exercise of its cult; that its property would be guaranteed; that its bishops would be maintained in the integrity of functions, rights and privileges which they enjoyed under the patronage of the kings of France; that the property which had belonged to the old French missions, or French settlements, would be recognized and respected.

Protocol n° 33 (1830) which followed, stipulated that the privileges which the Catholics had benefited from could not impose, on the Greek government, obligations which would eventually entail prejudice towards the dominant religion. When the Ionian Islands were reannexed to Greece (1864), the 3rd Protocol was also put in effect. After the ratification (1923) of the Treaty of Sèvres dealing with the protection of the minorities in Greece, the prevalent opinion in Greek theory and jurisprudence maintains that the London Protocol ceased to be in effect. This interpretation creates various problems within the Catholic Church, concerning the creation of new dioceses, the official recognition of prelates, the nature and function of its administrative organs, or even the very application of its Canon Law.

There is no legislative text regarding Protestant cults. Several years ago, the question of the legal personality of the Evangelist Church was raised. The justice of the peace of Katerini (1961) had accepted that this Church constituted a moral person of private law. The tribunal of the first instance of the same city and the Appellate Court of Thessaloniki had ruled, to the contrary, that the Evangelist Church is deprived of any legal personality. The Areios Pagos has however attributed to this Church the moral personality of private law. The same was maintained for the Armenian parishes in Greece. As concerns Jehovah's Witnesses, the Council of State has decreed that it is a "known" religion according to art. 13 of the C., whereas the Areios Pagos and the other civil tribunals always maintain their negative position on this subject. Also, the Scientologists have not been recognized as a known religion.

2. *Muslims*. The Muslim minority installed in Western Thrace is governed by the provisions of the Treaty of Lausanne (1923) and by various more recent laws. At the head of the minority, divided into

three districts (Xanthi, Komotini, Didymoteicho), there are three *muftis*, appointed by the Minister of National Education and Cults. The jurisdiction of the *mufti* is exercised over all the ministers of the Muslim religion of his district and he judges suits relevant to the family law and inheritance law of his fellow Muslims. Next to each *mufti* there sits a committee which manages the property (*evkaf*) which belongs to the religious collectivities and to the pious establishments of its district. The Greek State looks after the maintenance of schools for the Muslim minority, as well as after the *mendressés* (seminaries) and the school teachers in Thessaloniki.

3. *Israelites*. In Greece, the legal status of the Israelite religion is secured by several laws (L. 2456/1920, M.L. 367/1945, L. 1657/1951, R.D. of 25.6.1951, D.L. 01/1069). In cities where more than five Israelite families reside, an Israelite Community may be founded, by Presidential Decree. These communities are moral persons of public law, administrated by the Assembly and the Council of the Community, organs elected by their members. All the Israelite Communities of Greece are represented by the "Central Israelite Council of Coordination and Consultation", elected for three years by a general assembly, comprised of their special representatives.

Each religious community is headed by a rabbi, appointed by Presidential Decree on the proposal of the respective community. There is likewise a council of rabbis, which also acts as religious tribunal (*Beth-Din*). The Civil Code (1946) has however abrogated its civil jurisdiction. The Beth-Din continues, nevertheless, to exercise its competence over the Israelites that don't have Greek citizenship, as well as for pronouncing the spiritual dissolution of marriages for which the civil court granted the divorce.

XIV. Bibliography

Alivizatos H., Die Oikonomie nach dem Kanonischen Recht der Ortodoxen Kirche, Frankfurt a M., 1998.

Deliyannis J., Le mariage religieux et son efficacité civile en Droit hellénique, in: Marriage and Religion in Europe, Milano (European Consortium for Church-State Research) 1993, p. 121-151.

Ioannou N.-N., Discipline générale antique (IIe-IXe ss.), Rome (P. Comm., Redazione di Codice di Diritto Canonico Orientale – Fonti, IX) 1962-1964.

Konidaris J., Legal Status of Minority Churches and Religious Communities in Greece, in: The Legal Status of Religious Minorities in the European Union, Thessaloniki-Milano (European Consortium for Church-State Research), 1994, p. 171-181.

Konidaris J., Die Orthodoxen Kirchen in Griechenland nach der neuen Grundgesetzgebung, in: Zeitschrift für Evangelisches Kirchenrecht 23 (1978) p. 189-201.

Koukiadis I./Papastathis. Ch., Droit du travail et religion en Grèce, in: Churches and Labour Law in the EC Countries, Milano-Madrid (European Consortium for Church-State Research) 1993, p. 115-125.

Kyriazopoulos K., Church and State in Modern Europe, in: *Catharine Cookson* (ed.) Encyclopaedia of Religious Freedom, Routledge, New York/London, p. 56-60.

L'Année Canonique, vol. 45 (2003) with several reports.

Manitakis A./Photiadou A., New Liberties and Church-State Relationships in Greece, in: New Liberties and Church and State in Europe, Milan, (European Consortium for Church-State Research) 1998, p. 141-158.

Mavrakis A., The Law of Marriage and Divorce in the Church of England and the Church of Greece in Recent Times, 1850-1980, Athens 1992.

Maximos Metropolitan of Sardes, The Ecumenical Patriarchate in the Orthodox Church, Thessaloniki (Patriarchal Institute for Patristic Studies) 1976.

Naskou-Perraki P., The Legal Framework of Religious Freedom in Greece, Athens-Komotini, (A. Sakkoulas), 2000.

Nicodemus and Agapius, The Rudder of the Orthodox Catholic Church. The Compilation of the Holy Canons, Chicago, 1957 (Reprinted, New York 1983).

Papageorgiou Const., Freedom of Religion: A Case of Discrepancy between the Greek and the European Legal Order before the European Court of Human Rights, in: Erasmus Intensive Seminar on Legal Theory: Jurisdiction in Europe. Towards a Common Legal Method, Münster, 1997, p. 215-22.

Papastathis Ch., State Financial Support for the Church in Greece, in: Church and State in Europe: State Financial Support – Religion and the School, Milano (European Consortium for Church-State Research) 1992, p. 1-18.

Papastathis Ch., The Hellenic Republic and the Prevailing Religion, in: Brigham Young University Law Review (1996), p. 815-852.

Papastathis Ch., The Status of Mount Athos in Hellenic Public Law, in: Mount Athos and the European Community, Thessaloniki (Institute for Balkan Studies) 1993, p. 55-75.

Papastathis Ch., The Legal Status of the Monks of Non-Greek Origin in Mount Athos, in: Huit Siècles du Monastère de Chilandar, Belgrade, 2000, p. 179-185.

Papathomas Gr., Le Patriarcat Oecuménique de Constantinople (y compris la Politeia Monastique du Mont Athos) dans l' Europe Unie, Katerini, 1998.

Perrakis S., L' objection de conscience dans l' ordre juridique hellénique, in: Conscientious Objection in the EC Countries, Milano (European Consortium for Church-State Research) 1992, p. 195-210.

Phidas Vl., Droit Canon. Une perspective orthodoxe, Chambésy/Genève, 1998.

Pitsakis C., La synallelia principe fondamental des rapports entre l' Eglise et l'Etat, in: Kanon 10 (1991), p. 17-35.

Poulitsas N., Die Orthodoxe Kirche in griechischer Sicht, in: Die Beziehungen zwischen Staat und Kirche in Griechenland, B. II, Stuttgart (1960), p. 38-48.

Schaff P./Wace H., A Select Library of Nicene and Post-Nicene Fathers of the Christian Church, 2nd Ser. Vol. XIV: The Seven Ecumenical Councils of the Undivided Church. Reprint: Edinburgh-Grand Rapids, Mich. 1991.

Spyropoulos N., Die Beziehungen zwischen Staat und Kirche in Griechenland, Athens, 1981.

Troianos S., Die Beziehungen zwischen Staat und Kirche in Griechenland, in: Orthodoxes Forum 6 (1992), p. 221-231.

Troianos S., Die Synode der Hierarchie als höchstes Verwaltungsorgan der einzelnen Autokephalen Orthodoxen Kirchen, in: Kanon 2 (1974) p. 192-216.

Tsourkas. D., Les Juridictions Musulmanes en Grèce, in: Hellenic Review of International Law 2 (1981-1982), p. 581-598.

Zhisman J., Das Eherecht der Orientalischen Kirche, Vienna (W. Braumüller), 1864.

Iván C. Ibán
State and Church in Spain

I. Social Facts

No mechanisms exist under Spanish Law that enable us to ascertain accurately the number of members of different religious groups. No register exists containing such information nor is there any other instrument that enables us to acquire it indirectly (e.g. religious taxation). Moreover, the Spanish Constitution would prohibit any such mechanism since it clearly states that, "Nobody may be compelled to make statements regarding his religion, beliefs or ideology" (Art. 16 [2]). Therefore, in order to provide any data to this effect, one has to resort to studies that have been made, starting with surveys. The most recent, fairly reliable, survey provides the following figures in relation to stated religious beliefs:

Catholics	80,3 %
Other religious believers	1,9 %
Non-believers	10,6 %
Atheists	5,2 %
No answer given	2,1 %
SOURCE: Centro de Investigaciones Sociológicas. Survey N° 2,474 of December 2002	

This data makes it clear that the only religion with a strong social presence is Roman Catholicism. However, I suggest that the strong presence of Catholicism should be played down for two reasons. The first of these is that the number of self-proclaimed Catholics is in annual decline. And second, this does not necessarily mean that standards of conduct correspond to the official doctrine of the Catholic Church. In order to highlight the truth of the second statement, we should take into account that in the afore-mentioned survey, nearly half of the Catholics stated that they almost never attended mass, whilst less than one-fifth admitted attending almost every Sunday, while attendance at mass is an obligation imposed by the Catholic Church on all those who profess to follow its teachings.

I feel that we can summarise the above by asserting that the only strong religious presence in Spain is Catholicism, but this should be seen in the context of an increasingly secular society which considers that standards of conduct should not be determined by any official religion. Nor can any significant increase be appreciated in followers of other religions, which continue to be in a clear statistical minority. This trend towards a wholly secular society is clearly perceived by its own members, since 65 per cent of those surveyed considered that religion will be less influential in ten years time; while three-quarters thought that it was more influential only a decade ago.

II. Historical Background

The strong presence of Catholicism in a secular society, as is the case of Spain, has an historical explanation. Whilst it is not appropriate to go into detail here about the origin of Spain as a political entity, it should be mentioned that in such distant times as that of the Third Council of Toledo (589), Catholicism was proclaimed as the official religion of Spain. It is quite clear that the three religions of the Book (Christianity, Judaism and Islam) had cohabited the Iberian Peninsula for centuries, but it is no less clear that the most significant step towards the full unity of Spain (1492) coincided with the military defeat of Islam and the expulsion of the Jews. National identity is thus based, to a large degree, on religious unity.

The Reformation was a key element in identifying the Nation (and subsequently the State) with one specific church, thus giving rise to the phenomenon of national churches. The Reformation barely touched Spain, but the Spanish Catholic monarch, like those in other Catholic monarchies, knew how to take advantage of it. On the one hand, without breaking from Rome, the monarch gained control over the Catholic Church in his territories in the same way as the Protestant monarch did in a more intense way in his realms: this became known as Regalism. On the other hand, defending Catholicism from the reformers enabled it to establish mechanisms of social control that clearly went beyond the purely religious and into the political realm. The Inquisition is the clearest example of this. Thus, most notably in the 18th century, but also much earlier, and continuing into more recent times, the Spanish monarchy both manipulated the Catholic religion as an instrument of social control, with the tacit approval of Rome, and exercised strong control over the Catholic Church in its territorial area of sovereignty, without the approval of Rome. There is only one exception to the papal opposition to Regalism and its techniques of control, and that exception occurred in relation to the Spanish Crown: American Regalism. This is understood as being the Regalism which developed in the American territories, where Rome was forced to consent to it since it was the only way of imposing Catholicism in those lands.

The 19th century, from a legal-political point of view, was characterised by an avalanche of constitutions, proclaimed at the same time as various political changes, ranging from liberalism to conservatism. Nineteenth century liberalism used anti-clericalism as a recruiting tool. However, that did not in any way mean that liberalism was decisively influential in breaking the identification of Spain with Catholicism. Remember, for example, that the Constitution of Cadiz (1812), which is seen as the paradigm of Hispanic liberalism, proclaimed Catholicism as the official religion and prohibited the practice of any other. Such a principle should come as no surprise if we take into account the fact that one-third of the assembly was made up of either Catholic clerics or members of religious orders.

The first clear break between the identification of the legal-political structures and the Catholic Faith occurred as recently as 1931. In that year the Constitution of the Second Republic was proclaimed, in which it was established that "the Spanish State has no official religion" (Art. 3), religious teaching was banned, and financing of the Catholic Church was abolished, among other changes. The Second Republic was probably not mistaken in the content of these reforms, but rather in their timing. It was going not too far but too fast. This secularising policy, with anti-clerical traits, was one of the factors in the chain of events that led to the frustrated *coup d'état*, which was the origin of a bloody civil war (1936-1939).

The military faction which played a principal role in the outbreak of the civil war used the defence of Catholic unity in Spain to justify its attempted *coup d'état* and to wage a prolonged civil war. The Spanish Catholic hierarchy (Rome showed initial caution) was almost unanimous in its support for the said faction, and did not hesitate to classify the war as a religious Crusade.

Given the history, it comes as no surprise that the political régime that arose from the civil war adopted the most traditional stance in identifying the Nation with the Church. Catholicism was declared the official State religion, non-university education was practically monopolised by the Catholic Church, there was a notable presence of members of the Catholic hierarchy in political bodies, a Concordat was signed in 1953 in which all kinds of privileges claimed by the Church were recognised, and so on. A very strict and very anachronistic model was thus created, which could not survive the end of the autocratic regime of General Franco. Although the political system certainly evolved during its forty-year life span, any fundamental change had to wait until the death of Franco in 1975.

The swift and effective transition process following the death of Franco wholly altered the legal framework from an autocratic system to a democratic one. This, as was inevitable, also took place in the field of Church and State relations. By 1976, an agreement had been signed with the Holy See laying down the foundations for the replacement of the 1953 Concordat. In 1978, a new Constitution was drawn up, declaring the non-denominational nature of the State and full religious freedom. A series of agreements with the Holy See that replaced the Concordat (1979) and an Act of Religious Freedom (1980), along with another series of reforms (e.g. the introduction of divorce), resulted in the Spanish system being the antithesis of what had been in force but a few years previously. It was not until the Socialist Government came to power that educational reforms and the signing of agreements with minority religions in 1992 completed a series of reforms that produced the system of Ecclesiastical Law currently in force, which is analysed below.

III. Basic Structure

1. Legal Sources

The Constitution occupies the supreme hierarchical position of our sources of law. Article 16 establishes the foundations of the system of Ecclesiastical Law in the following terms:

> "1. Freedom of ideology, religion and worship of individuals and communities is guaranteed, with no other restriction on their expression than may be necessary to maintain public order as protected by law.
> 2. Nobody may be compelled to make statements regarding his religion, beliefs or ideology.
> 3. There shall be no State religion. The public authorities shall take the religious beliefs of Spanish society into account and shall in consequence

maintain appropriate co-operation with the Catholic Church and the other religious Communities".

Other rules are also relevant in Church and State matters. Article 14(2) states:

"Spaniards are equal before the law and may not in any way be discriminated against on account of [...] religion [...]".

And Article 27(3):

"The public authorities guarantee the right of parents to ensure that their children receive religious and moral instruction that is in accordance with their own convictions".

International Law also enjoys a leading position among the sources of Spanish domestic law. It is not simply the fact that the main declarations of rights have been signed by Spain, but rather that the Constitution makes clear reference to the matter in the following terms: "The rules relating to the fundamental rights and liberties recognised by the Constitution shall be interpreted in conformity with the Universal Declaration of Human Rights and the international treaties and agreements thereon ratified by Spain" (Art. 10(2)).

Spain has traditionally had concordats with the Holy See. Even despite the notable changes in the political and constitutional sphere, and without detracting from the fact that the current content is quite different from what existed before, the system still exists. Relations with the Holy See are expressed in five agreements. There are four from 1979 whose objects, respectively, are the following: legal matters (fundamentally matters relating to legal personality and marriage), education and cultural affairs, the Armed Forces, and economic matters. The agreement of 1962 regulates the non-ecclesiastical studies taken in Church Universities. These agreements have the status of Treaties under International Law, as is evidenced not only by the parliamentary procedure adopted but also by repeated legal judgments, both of the Spanish Supreme Court and the Spanish Constitutional Court.

As mentioned above, the Act of Religious Freedom was passed in 1980. In addition to declaring individual and collective religious freedom, and attempting to define the content and scope of such law, its essential function is to determine the position of those religious communities other than the Catholic Faith within our legal system. It clearly does not apply to the Catholic Church, as the position of the Catholic Church is already established by means of the concordats. The Act of Religious Freedom outlines a possibility that is a complete novelty in Spanish Ecclesiastical Law:

> "The State, taking account of the religious beliefs existing in Spanish society, shall establish, as appropriate, Co-operation Agreements or Conventions with the Churches, Faiths or religious Communities enrolled in the Registry where warranted by their notorious influence in Spanish society, due to their domain or number of followers. Such Agreements shall, in any case, be subject to approval by an Act of Parliament" (Art. 7(1)).

Based upon this legal principle, three agreements came into force in 1992, signed with the Protestant Churches, the Jewish Community and the Islamic Community respectively. Their exact legal nature is highly arguable: whether or not Parliament could amend these agreements unilaterally is, for the time being at least, a theoretical question. The clear point of reference for the content of these agreements is the concordats with the Holy See, although it is evident that the rights obtained by the Catholic Church are more numerous, and above all, the content is more effective. For example, the possibility of religious teaching is laid down both by the Catholic Church and by other denominations; however, in the former case the offer is obligatory and the costs are borne by the State, while this is not so in respect of the latter case. In the same way, the costs of Catholic hospital assistance are borne by the State, but not if this is provided by those minority religious communities that have signed an agreement. Apart from its legal scope, its symbolic role should not be forgotten: minority religious communities are placed, albeit at a strictly instrumental level, on a par with the Catholic Church. Whether or not this is so in reality does not detract from its symbolism.

Naturally there are numerous specific provisions for minority religious communities in more wide-ranging laws, for example, in tax, employment or urban matters, but these are beyond the scope of the present discussion.

Without going into detail as to whether they should properly be considered sources of law, we should not forget the legal judgments of the Spanish Supreme Court and the Spanish Constitutional Court in the make-up of Spanish Law and, consequently, Spanish Ecclesiastical Law. Remember, merely by way of example, that the sole legal basis for recognising the right to conscientious objection to abortion on religious or ethical grounds is found in a decision by the Constitutional Court. Lastly, whilst it is evident that these are not sources of law, there are numerous acts and provisions of the Spanish Administration that are significant in our field: recording a religious community in the corresponding register, establishing a practical method of providing religious assistance in hospitals, to mention a few examples.

This brief summary of the sources of law would not be complete without mentioning two issues. The first is the so-called 'Autonomous Region Law'. The politico-administrative organisation established under the 1978 Constitution has developed into a novel system in which the various regions (Comunidades Autónomas) have full legislative authority within their areas of competence. They are not directly empowered in areas of religious freedom, religious denominations, and so on; indirectly, however, they are becoming increasingly more important in the establishment of the actual model of Ecclesiastical Law. It should be remembered that the Autonomous Regions are competent in matters such as public health (religious assistance in hospitals), education, and town planning, which clearly impinge upon matters relating to minority religious communities.

The other issue is the relevance of denominational legal systems. Apart from their consideration as Statute Law, remnants of the direct effects of Confessional Law survive under Spanish Law. As we shall see, this affects Canon Law in matrimonial matters. However, such survivals have a merely residual effect.

2. *Characteristics of the Model*

I do not believe that traditional classifications are relevant to the current models of Church and State relations. Besides, it is clear that the Spanish system cannot be classified as an example of a State Church, nor even as a denominational model. Nor does it correspond to a separatist model in the strict sense.

The Constitution obliges us to take into account the religious phenomenon, but goes little further in defining what that should actually comprise. It should also be remembered that the current legal system is a reflection of history and that, therefore, certain remnants of Catholic denominationalism still survive, albeit on the wane. Even though the mention of the Catholic Church in the Constitution has no particular legal consequences, the fact that it is taken into account is a sign both of its historical and of its sociological importance.

In practice the system revolves around two ideas. On the one hand, religious denominations should receive some recognition by the State and certain specific treatment as a result of that. On the other hand, the idea of religious freedom is fundamental to the system, not only through the recognition of the fundamental right to religious freedom with the maximum protection available in law, but also limiting the level of recognition given to minority religious communities: minority religious communities may receive State aid, provided that this is not detrimental to religious freedom and equality.

At a level of legal instruments, the legal system has opted for a precise mechanism – that of the agreement – for fixing the position of minority religious communities. In this respect, as will be outlined below, we can show that a pyramidal system has been adopted; the Catholic Church receives maximum rights via Concordats; at a second level are found those minority religious communities that have signed agreements; the third level is comprised of those minority religious communities that are recorded in their corresponding register; and finally are those without any specific legal status.

The origin of this pyramidal structure of the treatment received by minority religious communities lies in the system of sources of law, which also adopts this structure. In a simplified way, and with regard to the specific rules of Ecclesiastical Law, we could say that the Constitution is the apex. A series of international agreements signed with the Holy See which together form a Concordat, regulates the legal position of the Catholic Church. The position of the three groups of the minority religious Communities is regulated by agreements that have the regulatory status of laws, but, in some way reinforced by their conventional nature. The Act of Religious Freedom establishes the framework of religious behaviour not included in any of the four religious communities that have signed an agreement with the State.

IV. Legal Status of Religious Bodies

The Act of Religious Freedom 7/1980, of 5 July 1980, establishes that "Churches, Faiths and Religious Communities and their Federations shall acquire legal personality once registered in the corresponding public Registry created for this purpose and kept in the Ministry of Justice" (Art. 5(1)). Therefore, in the first place it is the role of the Public Administration to recognise the legal personality of minority religious communities. It is clearly the role of the Courts of Justice to review any potential refusal by the Administration to register them. The law itself establishes the requirements for registration, "Registration shall be granted by virtue of an application together with an authentic document containing notice of the foundation or establishment of the organisation in Spain, declaration of its religious purpose, denomination and other particulars of identity, rules of procedure and representative bodies, including such body's power and requisites for valid designation thereof" (Art. 5(2)).

In practice, after an initial period in which the criteria for registration were very broad, a second phase took place in which the Public Administration and the Courts of Justice were more restrictive, demanding that the existence of religious beliefs be demonstrated, along with a certain number of followers, an organisational structure, and so on. A recent judgment by the Spanish Constitutional Court (Judgment 46/2001, of 15 February 2001), will perhaps result in a return to a system whereby registration is more straightforward. The number of religious bodies registered must now be in excess of one thousand, which does not necessarily indicate that all of these are minority religious communities in the strict sense*.

Apart from obtaining legal personality, the following rights established in the law itself proceed from registration: "Registered Churches, Faiths and religious Communities shall be fully independent and may lay down their own organisational rules, internal and staff by-laws" (Art. 6(1)).

However, and as mentioned above, the procedure for acceding to a wider range of privileges is to sign an agreement with the State. To achieve this, three groups of minority religious communities have created their own federations that enabled them to reach an agreement, approved by means of successive laws at the same time: Spanish Federation of Protestant Churches [Law 24/1992], Spanish Federation of Jewish Communities [Law 25/1992] and the Islamic Commission [Law 26/1992]. The content of these agreements is practically identical, which, added to the fact that the date on which they were passed is the same, means that we can assume that, to a

---

* According to data provided by the General Directorate for Religious Affairs (Dirección General de Asuntos Religiosos) in respect of 1998, the following number of bodies is registered: Protestant Churches and bodies: 744; Orthodox Churches: 5; Christian Science: 3; Jehovah's Witnesses: 1; Mormons: 1; Other Christian Denominations: 10; Judaism: 15; Islam: 99; The Bahá'í Faith: 2; Hinduism: 3; Buddhism: 13; Others: 3. *Guía de Entidades Religiosas de España*, Secretaria General Técnica. Ministerio de Justicia, Madrid, 1998, p. 23.

great extent, they are not just specific agreements but in reality texts presented by the State to be generally accepted. That notwithstanding, it appears that for the time being the Public Administration is not in favour of generalising the system; however, minority religious communities may obtain those privileges conferred through the agreements provided that they join one of the existing federations. This system of obtaining those privileges conferred through agreements is based on the incorporation of a new minority religious community in one of the signatory federations that has signed thereto and was proposed by the Public Administration in order to avoid a plethora of agreements, yet it has produced paradoxical results. To take an extreme example, the method adopted by the Orthodox Communities to reach an agreement was to join the Protestant Federation. Certain minority religious communities have attempted to join one of the existing federations yet their hopes have been dashed since, as is natural, it is the role of the federations to approve the admission of new members. Finally, by adopting the method of joining one of the federations that has signed an agreement with the State, any possibility of State intervention is avoided; in other words, the fact that a certain minority religious community obtains those privileges outlined in the agreements does not in any way depend upon the State, but rather on the will of those minority religious communities that are already members of the federation concerned.

At all events, and as indicated above, the system of agreements was contrived by Spanish Law as the method of conferring privileges on the minority religious communities, in such a way that those that are simply registered receive only marginally more favourable treatment, with all special privileges reserved for those under the agreements.

The Catholic Church is a case apart. As such, it is not recorded in the Registry of the Spanish Ministry of Justice. Essentially, its position is regulated through international treaties. At all events, and apart from the consideration of the Holy See being subject to International Law, the Catholic Church moves as idiosyncratically as it wishes within the scope of Private Law. There is no place in Spanish Law relating to minority religious communities for bodies such as Public Law entities. The broad organisational framework of the Catholic Church means that the systems of acquiring legal personality vary depending on the different types of body dealt with. The Episcopal Conference has legal personality due to a provision of law; the dioceses and other territorial divisions (parishes, etc.) acquire that through simple notification to the State; religious orders and congregations should be registered, and associations and foundations are in principle subject to Common Law.

In respect of the remaining collective religious groups, Spanish Law does not stipulate any specific treatment. Common Law is applied to those non-registered minority religious communities. In the same way, the so-called "new religious movements" do not receive any specific treatment, and are thus subject to Common Law in such matters as association, worship, and freedom of expression.

Nor does an individual religious state have any importance under Spanish Law. There are neither prohibitions nor privileges for professing a certain faith or for occupying any position in the hierarchy of a minority religious community (with the occasional anachronistic exception relating to the Catholic hierarchy).

V. Church and Culture

In principle it should be said that the minority religious communities do not enjoy any special treatment in the world of education and culture. But this needs to be qualified in several respects.

In relation to the creation of non-university educational centres, the minority religious communities are on an equal footing with any other body, or any other individual. In Spain, there are both free state schools and the freedom to set up private centres. These private centres may be self-financing, or may receive state funding. Those private centres that receive state funding, which may even cover all expenses, are subject to a series of requirements which in short are as follows: they should be free of charge, entry requirements for pupils should be very similar to those of state centres, and with parents, teachers, pupils and representatives of the rest of the personnel actively participating in managing the centre's affairs. Whilst state schools should be ideologically neutral, private centres may be ideologically orientated. This possibility of a certain ideological orientation means, among other things, that the staff's freedom to teach is more restricted, to the extent that they cannot contradict the ideology of the centre when teaching. In other words, it is possible in Spain to have privately funded educational centres with public funding and a certain religious ideology, but in exchange for this public funding they are subject, with justification, to more restrictive conditions than those private educational centres without public funding.

A quite different question is that of religious teaching. In all educational centres financed through public funding, teaching of the Catholic religion is offered on an optional basis. The teaching staff is selected by the Episcopal Conference, but paid for by the State. One of the traditional problems is the decision as to what alternatives should be offered to those pupils who do not take this subject, and whether the marks should be taken into account to pass the academic year. The solution given has depended on the political viewpoint of the government in office.

In relation to other minority religious communities, the agreements with the three Federations (Art. 10) envisage the possibility that such curricula may be offered both in state centres and in those private centres with public funding, provided that, in the latter case, they are not in contradiction to that private centre's ideological leanings. However, the State will only bear the teaching costs should a minimum of ten pupils opt for these subjects, which means that in the Spanish sociological reality, with the exception of the special cases of Ceuta and Melilla (geographically located in North Africa but under Spanish sovereignty), the costs of these subjects are to all intents and purposes borne by the respective minority religious communities.

At university level, in principle, minority religious communities are subject to Common Law. They may establish universities in the same way as any other body or individual. The only exception, once again, is the Catholic Church. Four Church Universities (governed by the Episcopal Conference in the case of Salamanca, Opus Dei in the case of Navarre and the Jesuits in the cases of Deusto and Comillas) have their status regulated by a specific Agreement of 5 April 1962. However there are currently new Church Universities that cannot subscribe to this Agreement, but must resort to general legislation in matters relating to the foundation of universities.

There are no existing Theology Faculties in the Spanish State Universities, nor does it seem probable that any will be set up in the next few years. This represents a break with tradition. However, theological studies and any other ecclesiastical studies undertaken in a Catholic Church University are recognised for civil law purposes.

In respect of the media, the religious communities are on the same footing as other social groups. They may set up radio, press or television stations. They do not form a part, as such, of any public media watchdog body. In practice, both in the field of state-owned television and radio, they have been assigned air time by the Board of Directors of those bodies. In conclusion, the Directive 89/552 of the

European Community in relation to advertising has been included in our legal system by means of Law 25/1994 of 12 July 1994.

VI. Employment Law within the Religious Communities

In principle minority religious communities are subject to the application of employment regulations, albeit with those special characteristics pertaining to a religious body.
The position of work carried out by certain religious individuals under the authority of their own religious order, or under its instructions, has generated a certain amount of case law, not always uniform, but this is not the place to go into details.

VII. Matrimonial and Family Law

In parallel with civil matrimony there are also certain religious forms of matrimony that have civil law consequences under Spanish Law. The Spanish Civil Code establishes that "marriage contracted according to the rules of Canon Law... may also have effects at civil law" (Art. 60). The validity of matrimony contracted in accordance with that outlined in the rules of the Protestant Church, the Jewish Community and the Islamic Community (Article 7 of the respective agreements) is also established. That does not in any way mean that such matrimony detracts from the civil regulations relating to matrimony. In other words, and avoiding technical minutiae, we can say that only one class of matrimony exists in Spain, civil matrimony, but in a variety of forms: civil, Catholic, Protestant, Jewish and Islamic.
The interpretation of the following regulation is more complex, "Those parties contracting matrimony, in accordance with the provisions of Canon Law, may resort to the Ecclesiastical Courts, requesting a statement of nullity or requesting a papal decision in relation to a brief but unconsummated marriage. At the petition of either party, the said ecclesiastical decisions shall have full legal effect under civil law if they are declared to be in accordance with State Law" (Art.

6(2) of the Agreement on Legal Matters). It can be seen that the difficulty lies in determining exactly what is in accordance with State Law. However, the problem is more theoretical than actual, since the parties to the conflict may reach the desired result by recourse to civil divorce by mutual agreement, which is practically automatic under Spanish Law.

VIII. Finances of the Church

The Catholic Church is the only church to receive direct state funding. The procedure established is that the Personal Income Tax-payer may state that 0.5 % percent of the amount payable shall go directly to the Church. We should make it clear that this does not amount to an independent taxation, since the amount to be paid does not alter because the taxpayer decides to allocate this percentage to the Church, for other social ends, or directly to the State. The other religious communities do not have the right to adopt this mechanism. It is quite clear that this mechanism, designed to fund the Catholic Church by budgetary means, and dependent on the wishes of the taxpayers, has been adversely affected by the survival of a situation that is seen as temporary. The Agreement with the Holy See on economic affairs established that from the introduction of this system of financing, and during the following three years, the State would make up the difference between the amount received through this method, and the amount that up to then had been received from direct budgetary allocation. After these three years, it would thus depend on the wishes of the taxpayers as to how much money would be received. However, year after year, the difference continues to be made up in the same way as was established for the supposedly temporary period of three years.

A method of financing alternative to that of budgetary allocation is that of granting certain tax advantages. With all the complexity typical of Tax Law, the Spanish legal system envisages certain advantages to this effect. It is not necessary to go into detail here. It is perhaps enough to say that the religious communities who have subscribed to an agreement (Catholic Church, Protestant Church, the Jewish Community and the Islamic Community) are treated in the same way as non-profit making organisations in relation to Corporate Income Tax; in other words, they are exempt from such taxation, provided that their economic income is allocated to ends related to their Community. In addition, certain activities with a definite religious end are exempt from taxation: certain publications, the acquisition of religious objects, and so on.

IX. Religious Assistance in Public Institutions

Religious assistance is provided in three types of public institution: the Armed Forces, penitentiaries and hospitals. In the recent past this was structured in such a way that there were certain specific bodies of civil servants who were Catholic chaplains for each of these institutions. There was no other form of assistance. However, the system has evolved in such a way that the administrative relationship has disappeared and a contractual relationship has been substituted; the intention is to extend this to other religious communities. However, for the sake of respecting those acquired rights, certain remnants of the old system have been preserved. I shall only outline the current regulations without referring to those remnants that will disappear at some point in the future.
Catholic religious assistance in the Armed Forces is provided through the military Bishopric of the Armed Forces (a personal and not territorial diocese), headed by a bishop who is appointed by mutual agreement between Church and the State. He is assigned a group of clergy who are contractually bound either on a temporary or a permanent basis. They are paid from public funds and are under a legal obligation to render their services. Other clergy or members of religious orders may collaborate with them, without being contractually bound. Non-Catholic religious assistance is established both by the Royal Decrees of the Armed Forces and in the agreements of 1992. The corresponding denominational ministers are entitled to gain access to the military establishments to provide assistance but are neither obliged to do so nor are they financed through public funding. A similar regime applies to the National Police Force.
Catholic assistance is provided in the prison service by chaplains appointed by the Bishop of the area in which the prison is situated and are authorised and remunerated by the State. In the case of non-Catholics there is only a right of access.
This system is virtually identical to that in public hospitals.

X. Criminal Law and Religion

A section of Chapter XXI of the Criminal Code (Crimes against the Constitution) is entitled "Crimes against the freedom of conscience, religious sentiments and respect for the deceased", and includes five articles (Arts. 522-526). The following are classified as crimes: impeding religious acts, forcing the practice of religious acts, disturbing religious acts of "registered religious communities", offending religious sentiments in places of worship, the public ridicule of religious sentiments, and the violation of tombs.
Moreover, the fact that discriminatory treatment might stem from religious motives is considered by the criminal legislator to be aggravation.

XI. The Legal Status of Clergy

The first difficulty to arise is determining when, under Spanish Law, we are dealing with a religious minister. In the case of the Catholic Church there is no problem. Nor is there a problem in respect of other religious communities that have subscribed to an agreement since it is outlined therein what constitutes religious authority (Art. 3).
It was historically correct to speak about clerical status in terms of a series of specific rights and obligations; however, the situation has changed. The fact that, for example, there are provisions in matters of Social Security for religious ministers of certain denominations or for religious members of certain orders, cannot be considered as favourable treatment enabling us to speak about specific status. It is simply a case of trying to provide the most appropriate framework for certain individuals who perform certain specific functions within this universal system of protection.
There are undoubtedly still some remnants of the old system without significant practical importance, such as, for example, the fact that the Bishop should be notified whenever one of his Catholic clergy or member of a religious order is criminally charged (Art. II of the agreements with the Holy See of 28 July 1976), or where the Act of Military Procedure excuses "senior dignitaries of officially recog-

nised religious communities" from the obligation of attending court to give a statement when this can be given in writing (Art. 135(2)). With regard to confessional secrecy, which I believe falls within the framework of professional secrecy, the Act of Criminal Prosecution excuses religious ministers from the obligation of reporting or bearing witness "in relation to information that they were privy to in the exercise of their functions in their ministry" (Art. 263), and which applies to any religious minister.

XII. Bibliography

Legislation

A.-C. Álvarez Cortina/M.J. Villa Robledo, *Repertorio Legislativo y Jurisprudencial de Derecho Eclesiástico Español*, Universidad de Oviedo–EUNSA, Pamplona, 1998.

A. De la Hera/R..M. Martínez De Codes, *Spanish Legislation on Religious Affairs*, Centro de Publicaciones. Ministerio de Justicia. Madrid, 1998.

M.E. Olmos/J. Landete Casas, *Legislación Eclesiástica*, Thomson-Civitas, Madrid, 2004.

I.C. Ibán/M. González, *Textos de Derecho Eclesiástico (Siglos XIX y XX)*, Centro de Estudios Políticos y Constitucionales–Boletín Oficial del Estado, Madrid, 2001.

Journals

"Anuario de Derecho Eclesiástico del Estado", 1985 and following years.
"Laicidad y Libertades. Escritos Jurídicos", 2001 and following years.

Textbooks

I.C. Ibán/L. Prieto Sanchís / A. Motilla, *Manual de Derecho Eclesiástico*, Editorial Trotta, Madrid, 2004.

J. Ferrer Ortiz (ed.), *Derecho Eclesiástico del Estado Español*, EUNSA, Pamplona, 2004.

J.M. González del Valle/M. Rodríguez Blanco, *Derecho Eclesiástico Español*, Civitas, Madrid, 2002.

Brigitte Basdevant-Gaudemet
State and Church in France

I. *Social Facts*

France is a country in the Catholic tradition, even if religious observance is less wide-spread today.[1] There are "six great religions" and their adherents include about 750,000 Protestants, 650,000 Jews, 200,000 Orthodox and 6,000,000 Moslems, Islam being the second religion of the country.
The Protestant Churches are not part of a single unified organisation, but they share a particular "associative" structure. Within each parish, a parish association elects a parochial council. The parishes are grouped into "consistories" [circuits] comprising all the pastors active in the area with twice as many lay representatives. At higher levels, the organisational pattern is not uniform. To mention only the two largest churches: in the Reformed Churches, which contain the largest number of French Protestants, there are regional synods and a national synod. The Churches of the Augsburg Confession in Alsace and Moselle have superintendent ministers and the Higher Consistory. In the wake of the Law of 1905 there was created the *Fédération Protestante de France*, formed under the Law of 1901, which remained for a long time a sort of confederation of Churches each jealous of its independence from the others. The *Fédération Protestante de France* could take decisions only by a unanimous vote of its members, a token of deep mistrust. New Statutes adopted in 1962 gave a new look to the organisation which could now take decisions (except in the field of doctrine) by a simple majority. The *Fédération* has among its objects that of "representing French Protestantism in relations with the public authorities and foreign and international institutions", even though it does not include all Protestant communities. A number of agencies, which can only operate in collaboration with secular bodies, are part of its structure (information, youth, external relations, radio and television, prison chaplaincy work...).

---

1   Almost 80 % of French people declare themselves to be Catholic, although less than 15 % regularly attend Sunday Mass.

Judaism has a similar structure, with a consistorial form of government. The central consistory has its seat in Paris; formed from all the Jewish religious bodies, it is the representative organ of French Jewry in dealings with the State authorities, and it elects the Chief Rabbi of France. The Representative Council of French Jewish Institutions also plays an important role.

Islam unites people from a variety of backgrounds and nationalities, but 80 % of Moslems living in France are workers with poor qualifications. They belong to different religious groupings, with resulting difficulties in co-ordinated action. The *Bureau des Cultes* in the Ministry of the Interior is responsible for relations with them. In April 2002 a French Council of the Muslim Cult (CFCM) and regional councils were elected by the mosques. The Moslems have a very large number of places of worship, but they are often in a precarious situation with meagre resources. France has only eight mosques in the architectural sense of the term.

The Orthodox dioceses, organised on an ethnic or national basis, are coordinated by the Interepiscopal Committee presided over by the Metropolitan who acts on behalf of the Patriarch of Constantinople.

Finally, the Union of Buddhists includes 80 % of the pagodas, centres and institutes which claim to follow the Buddhist tradition.

II. Historical Background

In France, the legal status of the churches is very heavily dependant on history.

a - The Declaration of the Rights of Man and of the Citizen of 26 August 1789 declared the freedom of belief (Art. 10) and the Constitution of 1791 (Title I) guaranteed the freedom of religious observance. The decree of 2 November 1789 effected the nationalisation of the property of the clergy; in return, the State undertook to meet the running expenses of the Church and those of the maintenance of its ministers. The Civil Constitution of the Clergy (12 July 1790), a unilateral act by the state, regulated the status of ministers of religion and the organisation of the practice of the Catholic faith which found itself subordinated to the state and treated as a public service. Pius VI condemned it (10 March 1791, in the brief *Quod Aliquantum*). Progressively, the régime of the Convention, especially under the terror (May 1793 to July 1794) adopted a policy of systematic de-Christianisation. The decree of 21 February 1795 established a régime of separation of Church and State; although affirming freedom of religious observance, the Republic provided no salaries, no premises, and recognised no ministers of religion. The Church suffered intense persecution.

b - Bonaparte restored religious peace by negotiating a Concordat, signed on 15 July 1801 (26 Messidor year IX) with Pius VII. In its short text of 17 articles, Bonaparte left some ambiguities.[2] The Concordat was completed by the Organic Articles (77 articles), a unilateral act of the French Government and never accepted by Rome, but promulgated at the same time as the Concordat (Law of 18 Germinal year X), and applied by successive Governments throughout the 19th century. These Organic Articles set out the relationship between Church and State. They allowed the civil authorities to exercise a tight control over ministers of religion and the progress of religious life. To this Law, Bonaparte added 44 organic articles relating to the Protestant Churches, subjecting the organisation of the Reformed Church and the Church of the Augsburg Confession to measures of control comparable to those applying to the Catholic Church. Judaism was organised in three decrees of 1808.

Other texts completed this corpus, spelling out the legal position of ministers of religion and their stipends, as well as the legal rules applying to the property assigned to the use of the churches. Some of the public religious bodies managed this patrimony; in particular those the structures and powers of which were regulated by the decree of 30 December 1809. Throughout the whole of the 19th century, the four "recognised Churches" enjoyed certain, and especially financial, advantages, but were subject to the constant supervision of the public authorities.

This body of legislation was applied in extremely diverse political contexts. Governments favourable or hostile to the Catholic Church, or even to all religion, followed one another in rapid succession. In the 19th century, in France as elsewhere, religious interests were part of what was at stake in fundamental policy debates for all Governments. The Revolution had laid the basis for later conflicts and from the July Monarchy (1830) onwards important currents of opinion,

---

[2] Article 1 guaranteed the public practice of religion "in accordance with such regulations as the Government deems necessary for the public peace". Religious boundaries were redefined by agreement between the religious and the State authorities. The stipends of bishops and parish priests were a charge on State funds. Those churches which were not given up, and which were needed for worship, were left available to the bishops (the *Conseil d'État* later decided which were the property of the State and which of the communes).

within the Catholic Church as well as within the political world, contributed to the formation of two rival groups. One comprised the partisans of the traditional order, concerned with the revival of the *Ancien Régime*, and seen as unconditional supporters of clerical power. The other, the partisans of the new order, were attached to the values of 1789 and implacable opponents of the Catholic Church and its clergy. A more complex pattern can be detected behind this simple picture of two rival parties, but the two opposed tendencies made the legal status of the Churches a political issue of the first order of importance. Once the republicans had again taken power after 1879-1880, anticlericalism was at the top of their political programme. To them, the very existence of the republican régime was incompatible with the preservation of a Church with any vitality. With this in mind, they enacted the anti-clerical Laws of the 1880s which were unacceptable to the Church. Most of these Laws are still in force today. After the breaking of diplomatic relations with the Holy See in 1904, the Law of 9 December 1905 installed in France the régime of Separation of Church and State.

c - The fundamental principles of the new status of the churches are set out in the first two articles. The Republic guarantees the freedom of public worship but ends the status of the "recognised Churches". No religion is to receive any legal establishment. The churches ceased to be public institutions, and had to become part of the private sector. After a certain delay, the Pope, in the encyclical *Vehementer Nos* (11 February 1906), condemned the Separation of Church and State and asked the episcopate to oppose the application of the Law of 1905. Some later Laws attempted to fill the legal void left by the refusal of the Catholic Church to co-operate.

In 1870, three *départements* of the east of France came under German rule (Haut-Rhin, Bas-Rhin, Moselle). The German Emperor and the Holy See agreed to preserve in the dioceses of Strasbourg and Metz the French religious law in force at the time of their annexation. Imperial decrees modified or supplemented some provisions. After the return of the three *départements* to France in 1918, political leaders and the local population wished to preserve the *status quo*. The local law of Alsace Moselle preserves the system of Recognised Churches, supported financially by the State. The Law of 1905 does not apply to them.

III. Legal Sources and the Constitutional Régime

The fundamental principles are enshrined in the Law of 1905. In fact the Constitution of 1958 does not fix the constitutional régime of the Churches, and contains only two provisions dealing with the status of the Churches.[3] These constitutional sources are meagre but fundamental in that they establish the régime of the neutrality of the state. The Law of 1905 puts forward the fundamental principles in its two first articles: Freedom of the exercise of religion, but no "recognition" and no subsidies.[4]

Under the régime of positive neutrality as it is conceived by the current doctrines of the "French *laïcité*" the principle of freedom of belief imposes positive obligations on the State compatible with a régime of separation. The state must ensure that everyone has the possibility of attending the ceremonies of his Church and of being instructed in the beliefs proper to his chosen religion. Gradually, there is coming to prevail in France a new understanding of the role of the state requiring frequent intervention in order to bring into being everywhere the necessary practical conditions for public worship in respect of each religion.

Equality between the various religions implies that there is no state religion, no "official" or dominant religion, no recognised Churches ... No religion has a particular public status. The legislator of 1905 wanted to make religion a private matter and as such subject to private law. However, the state does not always treat the religions as purely private, but instead sometimes accords them a different status. But to which groups or activities does this special régime apply? What is a religion? The question is delicate; the legislator, the courts, the doctrinal writers have not provided a solution. A priori they are not entitled to pronounce on the point, given the neutrality of the State which recognises no religion. In practice it is the judge (the

---

3   The Preamble refers expressly to the Declaration of the Rights of Man and of the Citizen of 1789 and to the Preamble of the Constitution of 1946 guaranteeing the freedom of belief. Article 2 provides that France is "... a lay Republic (which) ... assures the equality before the law of all its citizens without distinction of origin, race or religion. It respects all beliefs."
4   Art. 1: "The Republic assures the freedom of conscience. She guaranties the free exercise of religion subject only to the restrictions mentioned hereafter in the interest of the public order". Art. 2: "The Republic does not recognise, fund or subsidize any religion. ... Nevertheless there can be included in these budgets (of the state or the public entities) the expenses in relation to chaplaincy services designed to assure the free exercise of religion in public establishments such as secondary schools, colleges, schools, nursing homes, asylums and prisons ..."

Conseil d'État or the *Cour de Cassation*) which decides, case by case and avoiding giving a general definition which could be prayed in aid in other cases. So the courts decide in respect of each group or association whether it should be recognised as having the character of a church and whether the legal rules, advantageous or disadvantageous, in force in respect of religious groups should be applied. The silence of Constitutions, the régime of Séparation, the neutrality of the State, and the prudence of the legislator ensure that French ecclesiastical law is derived largely from judicial decisions. Granted, there are laws, decrees and other provisions. But France needs sources of law which are more flexible and more precise in their application. They are of two forms: ministerial circulars issuing from the *Bureau des Cultes* of the Ministry of the Interior, and the abundant case-law of the *Conseil d'État*, of the *Cour de Cassation*, and also, more recently and to a lesser degree, that of the *Conseil constitutionel*.
Le regime français de "laïcité neutralité" a pris de nouvelles orientations lors du vote de la loi du 15 mars 2004 qui interdit, "dans les colleges et lycées publics le port de signes et tenues par lesquels les élèves manifestent ostensiblement une appartenance religieuse".

IV. Legal Status of Religious Groups – Situation of the New Religious Movements

Despite the principle of non-recognition of churches, religious groups are subject in French law to some special rules. It is not a matter of a status conferred upon a Church as a general matter, but rather of legal rules applicable to a series of institutions, organisms or groupings essential to the life of a Church. We mention the principal cases, noting that there exist other bodies (foundations, church companies, etc) and legal principles not dealt with here.

1. Religious Associations [associations cultuelles]

Article 4 of the Law of 1905 provided for the formation of *associations cultuelles*, capable of receiving the property of the former public church establishments suppressed in 1905. The relevant associations are subject to the Law of 1 July 1901, which governs all associations,[5] and must comply with some additional rules set out in the Law of 1905: article 19 requires them to be "exclusively for the purpose of the church"; they are not to be "in any form which would enable them to receive subventions from the State, the *départements* or the *communes*". The Law also specifies the required composition of associations, their size related to that of the local population. The permitted sources of funds are set out; they must always be provided by the faithful, except for sums made available for the repair of listed monuments which payments are not treated as prohibited subventions.[6] These *associations cultuelles* have benefited progressively from advantages under tax law, which means that the "label" is now sought after. Since 1905, Protestants and Jews have made use of the law and established *associations cultuelles*, which remain active today, in accordance with all the provisions of the Law of 1905.

2. Diocesan Associations [associations diocésaines]

In speaking of the *associations cultuelles*, we have made no mention of the Catholic Church. This silence is significant. The Catholic Church refuses to put the Law of 1905 to use because of the opposition of the Holy See and of a part of the episcopate concerned precisely with the issue of *associations cultuelles*. The Catholic hierarchy fears the emergence of a multitude of different associations, all claiming to be of the Catholic Church but which the hierarchy could not control and in which the laity would have the power of decision-making. When the Law was under consideration, a number of personalities in the Church in France had expressed their anxiety, and their opinion found echoes in the parliamentary debates. Eventually, article 4 of the Law provided that *associations cultuelles* must comply with "the general organisational rules of the religion which

---

[5] The Law of 1 July 1901, which remains in force, enshrines the principle of freedom of association of all who share their knowledge or activity for a purpose other than making a profit. The association can be lawful without this entailing any recognition of its objects. It is formed by depositing its statutes at the *préfecture* (or *sous préfecture*) and acquires legal capacity; it can be recognised by decree as being "of public utility" [*d'utilité publique*]. An association so recognised may receive grants, to the extent and on the terms authorised in each case by the decree. But this same Law contains disadvantageous and very constraining rules applying to religious orders: article 13, Title III provides "No religious order may be formed without authorisation in a Law which will specify the conditions set on its activity".

[6] This provision was amended by the Law of April 1908, in a manner advantageous to the churches, by authorising the local authorities to bear the cost of repairing church buildings belonging to them.

the association is to advance". By this formula, although it is not mentioned by name, the Catholic hierarchy could hope to maintain its authority. Despite this guarantee, the Catholic Church has established no *associations cultuelles*. To fill the legal void, the Law of 2 January 1907 provided that the public exercise of religion could be advanced by associations conforming simply to the Law of 1901, or by meetings, called on an individual initiative, under the Law of 1881 on the freedom of public assembly.

Following the First World War, relations between Church and State were seen to have improved. Diplomatic relations were re-established with the Holy See; equally, after long negotiations with the Holy See, it was agreed that the Catholic Church could establish *associations diocésaines* under a special set of model provisions. The *Conseil d'État* recognised this special status as being in conformity with French law, notably with the Laws of 1901 and 1905 (opinion of the *Conseil d'État*, 13 December 1923) and Pius XI authorised the establishment of the associations (encyclical *Magnam Gravissimamque*, 18 January 1924). Since 1924 the French bishops have put into place *associations diocésaines* which are *associations cultuelles*, complying with the Laws of 1901 and 1905, even if meeting the expenses of the Church is no longer mentioned as the "exclusive" object of the association. The rules of Canon Law are also followed, the associations acting "under the authority of the bishop, in communion with the Holy See and in conformity with the constitution of the Catholic Church" (article 2 of the model statutes).

This development had repercussions on the legal status of the Catholic religion, as the new bodies had as their purposes the organisation of the exercise of the religion and the management of the property used for that purpose. So, in the matter of the ownership of church buildings, following the Law of 1905 the buildings of the Protestant churches and of the Jews were vested in the relevant *associations cultuelles*. The Laws of 2 January 1907 and of 3 April 1908, on the other hand, transferred the ownership of existing Catholic church buildings, and responsibility for their repair, to the State (cathedrals and bishops' houses to the state; parish churches and presbyteries to the *communes*). By contrast, after 1924 it fell to the *associations diocésaines* to decide upon and to finance the construction of new places of worship, and as owner to ensure their good repair.

These vicissitudes of history explain the co-existence of *associations cultuelles* under the Law of 1905, associations for the purposes of a church under the terms of the Law of 1907 and which conform to the requirements of the Law of 1901, and also *associations diocésaines*, complying with the Laws of 1901 and 1905 but also meeting additional criteria. In addition, the freedom of association provided under the Law of 1901 has allowed the development of a multitude of associations, notably for charitable and educational purposes, which work in liaison with the religious authorities but which do not have exclusively religious purposes and are therefore not "*cultuelles*". In this last category feature numerous cultural associations with educational purposes, directed out of a sense of religious conviction. The Moslems currently use this legal form of the Law of 1901: the presence of a Koranic school justifies the qualification as "cultural" notwithstanding the fact that alongside the school there is the mosque, managed by the same cultural association. The distinction between an association which is *cultuelle* and one which is cultural reflects an essentially legal distinction: the former is governed by the Law of 1905, the latter by the Law of 1901. The financial and fiscal régimes differ.

3. The Religious Orders[7]

French legislative texts do not define the term *congrégation* [religious order], for the essential purpose of the legislator of 1901 was to banish the orders from the national territory. There was little point in tying oneself to a definition of an institution which one wished wholly to wipe out. It falls to the judges to say what groupings can be categorised as religious orders. There will be taken into account some matters of fact: the existence of religious vows, pious works undertaken by the order, the submission of members to statutes approved by the religious authorities ...
The current position of the religious orders is again best understood by its history. The legislation of the 19th century took various forms and generally speaking a Law or decree was required to authorise a religious order. Nonetheless, most orders existed without such authorisation in good and due form. Under the Third Republic the orders had to disappear. In that sense, Title III of the Law of 1901 declared prohibited every order which had not received legal recognition (article 13). And the Parliament systematically rejected every request for recognition which an order presented. However, from

---

[7] Les congrégations et l'Etat [The religious orders and the State], ed. *J.P. Durand*, Paris, La documentation française, 1992, 139 p.; *J.P. Durand*, Les congrégations religieuses : droit canonique et droit français, [Religious Orders: Canon Law and French Law] thesis, Faculty of Law, University of Paris XI and ICP, Paris, Cerf, 1999, 3.

1914 the unauthorised orders returned to France; they were illicit but they were not persecuted. The Law of 8 April 1942 improved their position by abolishing the offence of being an "illicit order". They could exist as groups de facto, without legal existence or personality. On the other hand, the procedure for according legal recognition was simplified: "authorisation" became simply "legal recognition" accorded by a decree of the *Conseil d'État* and conferring legal capacity. It was only after 1970 that this process affected new orders and it has accelerated since 1987.

In 1987, the procedure of legal recognition was opened to non-Catholic orders.[8] A recognised order possesses full civil capacity: under French law its position is close to that of an association recognised as being of *utilité publique* (this does not imply that an order is an association). An order is subject to a form of trusteeship supervision on the part of the State, which recent measures have notably lightened.

4. The New Religious Movements and "Sects"

French law faces some difficulties in taking account of new religious movements given its refusal to define a religion. However, the courts, the *Conseil d'État* in the first place, have not recognised as "religious" every group which tries to present itself as such. If the public authorities accept that a religious movement organises itself under the form of an *association cultuelle* they admit by that very fact that it belongs to a religion, even if they prohibit themselves from using the term. The category of *association cultuelle* is allocated sparingly, especially where new religious movements are concerned. The courts hesitate to say whether a group is "religious", and thus to acknowledge that an association is *cultuelle*. Some "sects" have attempted to form themselves as *associations cultuelles* under the Law of 1905; the *Conseil d'État* has always disallowed this, on the ground that article 19 of the Law of 1905 specifies that *associations cultuelles* must have exclusively religious purposes. In each case, it has been held that the purposes of the association seemed incompatible with the maintenance of *ordre public*, or that the association had other forms of activity (cultural, commercial, medical...). How to distinguish between "religion" and "sect"? For a long time the French legislator in the name of freedom of conscience and relig-

---

8   Buddhists, Orthodox, Protestants.

ion declined to legislate about the sects. The fight against these movements was essentially the work of the judges who refused to give them financial advantages attributed to the *associations cultuelles* and who kept in check their illegal activities. The Law of 12 June 2001 introduced various means by which "sectarian dealings" could be checked. A judge can dissolve a legal person whose activities present certain dangers. The regime of criminal responsibility of legal persons has been enlarged. The Law creates the offence of "fraudulent abuse of the state of ignorance or of a situation of weakness". The recognised associations of public utility fighting against the sects can become party to a litigation process.
The great religions have expressed their concern that the public authorities while applying this new Law should not limit the freedom of religion.

5. *Church Organisations providing Social Services*[9]

The churches provide assistance of general interest and take part in public services by institutions of a "special character". They run organisations of a confessional character in collaboration with the public authorities, especially in the field of education (cf. infra: 6) and of *assistance*.
In France, *assistance* and health care are primarily State services, more so than in other European countries (Germany, the Netherlands, for example).[10] However, providing care is an essential part of the Church's work. French law allows the churches to control their own caring institutions, whether offering humanitarian assistance or health care. It is essentially the Catholic Church which is concerned, given its place in this country.
Works of charity from a religious motivation do not have, by virtue of their confessional character, a special and uniform legal structure from the point of view of State law. They operate like any other private initiative. Private hospitals of a religious character can be foundations, declared to be of *utilité publique* by decree of the *Conseil d'État*, or companies, or follow the pattern of associations in one of

---

9 B. *Basdevant-Gaudemet et F. Messmer*, " Les établissments de santé et les institutions d'assistance confessionnels en France ", Revue de Droit canonique, tome 52/1, 2002, p. 187-213; reproduits dans Les Établissements d'assistance, l'État, les Eglises et la société, European Consortium for Church-State Research, Guiffré, Milano, 2003, p. 73-99.
10 Cf. paper presented by *B. Basdevant-Gaudemet*, "les activités d'assistance", 8th Congress of Canon Law, Lublin, September 1993.

two forms: that of associations under the Law of 1901 with legal personality, and that of associations recognised as of *utilité publique*, with an enlarged legal capacity, able to receive gifts and legacies but subject to a higher degree of administrative control. The recognition of *utilité publique* is independent of the confessional character, it is given in regard of the social aims pursued and acquired for the work in question.

The confessional character of some of this type of work is not opposed, and is taken into account by the public authorities even if it is not enshrined in any specific legal status. Such is the case with humanitarian aid,[11] and hospital work.[12] The legal position of these establishments can vary. The order, company, or association running the establishment may or may not own the buildings, the land on which they stand, the equipment... They may depend upon private funds, the property of the order, foundations, donations and collections.... To these resources will generally be added subventions from public funds, from the State or local authorities, as these are not regarded as subventions to churches, prohibited by the Law of 1905, but as support for work in the general interest.

The ecclesiastical authorities can authorise or prohibit certain medical treatments in the establishments which have a "distinctive character".[13] They have control over the personnel working in the confessional hospitals. Religious continue to be dependant upon their order, not the hospital. The contract of employment, if any, is between the establishment and the order; the religious are not individual parties to the agreement. The personnel in hospitals with a religious foundation tend increasingly to have a majority of lay persons. Their legal position (conditions of recruitment, of work, of authorisation...) is governed by secular law and existing collective bargains. Employment qualifications depend on State diplomas. The church authorities, however, may have their own requirements which they impose on their employees, and the civil judge will respect them.[14] They bear on

---

11 *Secours Catholique*, the CCFD, etc. are fully recognised by the public authorities as Church entities, possessing their "distinctive character" and their particular purposes, but able to work with the public authorities, French or international, in their varied activities.

12 *A. Bamberg*, Hôpital et Eglises [Hospital and Churches], cerdic, Strasbourg, 1987, 408 p.

13 *A. Bamberg*, Hôpital et Eglises [Hospital and Churches], Strasbourg, 1987, 408 p. The diversity of legal conditions does not prevent the State from recognising and respecting their "distinctive character", or from recognising that specific activities are, or are not, practised within the particular institution. In particular, voluntary terminations of pregnancy may be prohibited. The Church takes care that the "distinctive character" is written into the statutes, which the judge will respect in any civil litigation.

14 Cf. section VI., below, Labour Law and the Churches.

some matters which are of fundamental importance, but highly specific and relatively few in number. To whatever is not dealt with by the religious authority in this way, the ordinary employment law will apply.

V. Relations with the Political System

Under the French régime of séparation and *laïcité* the religious denominations in principle do not have any direct and officially approved relations with the political systems. However, the representatives of the major denominations are regularly consulted in the great debates of society, especially on questions of ethics. On the other hand there are several legal systems concerning the religions which all rely on the *laïcité*. Nevertheless the Law of 1905 only applies to the metropolitan territory and not to the whole of that territory.

In three departments of the east of France (Haut-Rhin, Bas-Rhin and Moselle), there is a regime of "recognised cults", inherited from the Napoleonic system, modified by the German legislation between 1871 and 1918 and which has been amended in some respects since the return of Alsace-Moselle to France in 1918.[15] The clergy of the cults are paid by the State; religious instruction is taught in the state schools; the archbishop of Strasbourg and the bishop of Metz are appointed by the Head of the State....

Some overseas departments and territories also have a specific régime. The Law of 1905 does not apply in three departments (Réunion, Martinique, Guadeloupe), in which the concordat régime had been introduced at the beginning of the 19th century. French Guyana is governed by a royal ordonnance of August 27, 1828, according to which the Catholic religion is financed by public funds. The "décrets Mandel" of 1939 permit other religions to enjoying certain rights, and above all, to obtain important financial assistance from local communities. These rules apply in most of the overseas departments and territories, however with numerous specific provisions.[16]

---

15 *J.-L. Vallens* (ed.), Le guide du droit local; le droit applicable en Alsace et en Moselle de A à Z, Paris, Économica, 1997.

16 *F. Messner, P.-H. Prélot, J.-M. Woehrling*, Traité de droit français des religions, Paris, Litec, 2003, p. 835-838.

VI. The Field of Culture: Private Schools – Religious Education – Faculties of Theology in Public Universities – the Media

1. Private Schools[17]

Freedom of education is a constitutional principle guaranteed since the Constitution of 1848 (Art. 9). Whilst the recent constitutional texts (the Constitutions of 1946 and of 1958) make no express mention of this freedom, the *Conseil constitutionnel* has in two judgments affirmed that the freedom of education is "one of the fundamental principles recognised by the laws of the Republic".[18]

Freedom of education is governed by a number of Laws of the 19th century, each drafted during a particular phase in the developing political relationship between Church and State. This particular history explains the diversity in the organisational and financial régimes for private schools, according to the various levels of education, and the diversity of the place held by the Church at different levels within the public educational system.[19]

The legislative texts establishing the freedom of education remain in principle in force. They allow the creation of a "free" educational sector, existing alongside the great public service established by Napoleon in 1806 as having an absolute monopoly throughout the educational system.[20] Today, private education accounts for some 18 % of all pupils. 90 % of private establishments are Catholic, the remaining 10 % being shared between Protestant and Jewish schools and a small number of non-confessional schools. This private education is

---

17 Cf. *N. Fontaine*, La liberté d'enseignement, guide juridique de l'enseignement associé à l'Etat par le contrat, [Freedom of education: the law relating to education under contract with the State] 3rd ed. Paris, UNAPEC, 1980, 665 p.
18 (C.C. 23 November 1977, A.J.D.A. 1978, p. 565, note Rivero; C.C. 18 January 1985, R.F.D.A. 1985, 5, p. 633, art. Delvolvé). The same court has held that the fundamental principles recognised by the laws of the Republic enjoy a constitutional status (C.C. 16 July 1971).
19 Major laws guaranteeing the freedom of education: - Primary education, *loi* Guizot, 28 June 1833 (the Laws of 28 March 1882 and of 30 October 1886 deal with the *laïcité* of the public primary school); secondary education, *loi* Falloux, 15 March 1850; higher education, *loi* Dupanloup, 12 July 1875; technical education, *loi* Estier, 23 July 1919.
20 The Law of 10 May 1806, creating the Imperial University, reserved to the State this educational monopoly. The Church played a part in the operation of this public educational service, but under the control of the State authorities. There was no place for a free sector, created by private initiatives.

seen as part of the whole national provision of educational services.[21] By the *loi* Debré (31 December 1959), private education, confessional or not, was fully recognised; its "distinctive character" is guaranteed. The private establishments can enter into a contractual relationship with the State, as has happened in the great majority of cases.[22]

Religious education is provided in private confessional schools. However the schools with a State contract undertake to take pupils without distinction of race or religion; there religious education is not obligatory.

2. Religious Education in Public Schools - the "aumôneries" [chaplaincies][23]

For historical reasons, except in the three *départements* of the East of France, public education is secular, but this *laïcité* takes different forms according to the level of education concerned. The present picture is as follows:

- For the primary schools, the Law of 28 March 1882, an essential part of the platform of the republicans of that time, provides that the school must leave clear one day a week to enable parents, if they so wish, to arrange for religious education outside the school; it may not take place within the school. In school, "moral and civic" rather than "moral and religious" education is offered. In practice, primary school children do not have classes on Wednesdays.[24]
- So far as secondary schools are concerned, when Napoleon established *lycées* for boys, he created posts of *aumôniers* [chaplains]

---

21 Even under the 4th Republic, by the *lois* Marie and Baranger, the State had accorded a certain recognition, and some material advantages, to the private establishments.
22 These contracts are of two types: *contrats simple*, allowing the payment of staff by the State; and *contrats d'association*, the more common, under which the staff are paid by the State and local authorities provide certain subventions, similar to those given to public schools, to assist the operation of the schools. The system is a complex one; the State subventions cover a greater or lesser part of the expenses of the school depending on the level of education concerned. This complexity is the result of history; some reforms have recently been under consideration, but have not been adopted.
23 J.M. Swerry, Les aumôneries catholiques dans l'enseignement public, [The Catholic chaplaincies in public education], thesis, Faculty of Law, University of Paris XI, 1990, ed. cerf, 439 p., 1995.
24 There is a debate on this issue; in certain regions the Saturday-classes have been changed to Wednesday so as to clear the weekends for family activities, which the episcopate is criticising.

as an integral part of the establishment. In 1880, the *loi* Camille Sée established *lycées* for girls and provided for church teachers, not part of the establishment and with a less favourable position than their counterparts had enjoyed since the start of the century in the boy's schools.
- The Third Republic abolished the church teachers. Since 1905, chaplaincies can exist; the State is under no obligation to meet the cost, and does not do so. Various legal texts (a decree of 22 April 1960, an order of 8 August 1960 and a ministerial circular of 22 April 1988) govern the matter. The posts are created by the head of the school on the request of parents, and function sometimes within and sometimes outside the school. The cost is met partly by contributions from the parents and partly by the diocese. The actual appointment is made by the head of the school on the nomination of the relevant religious authority.
- The local law in Alsace-Lorraine: Religious education in the three *départements* of the east of France remains, in general principle, as it was under the law in force before 1871. In the public schools, both primary and secondary, religious education is part of the general curriculum, the teachers being in principle paid by the State (though in fact donations are often sought in primary schools). The families are quite free in deciding whether their children should attend these classes. The grades do not count for the evaluation of pupils.

3. Faculties of Theology in State Universities[25]

In State Universities, education is secular; at the end of the 19th century, this led to the virtual disappearance of teaching on religious matters. Church History retains a place in Arts Faculties, though Law Faculties give very little space to the law as it affects the churches; Canon Law is only touched on in the context of Legal History. Ecclesiastical Law is not the subject of any special course, and is touched upon in a fragmentary fashion by some teachers of public law in the context of constitutional or administrative law or on public

---

25 *P.H. Prelot*, Naissance de l'enseignement supérieur libre, la loi du 12 juillet 1975, [The birth of free higher education; the law of 12 July 1875], Paris, P.U.F., 1987, p. 139; [same author] Les établissements privés d'enseignement supérieurs, [Private higher education establishments], thesis, Faculty of Law, University of Paris II, L.G.D.J., 1989.

liberties, and by teachers of private law in relation to marriage, the family, and notions of *ordre public*.[26]

A "free" higher education sector exists, under the terms of the Law of 12 July 1875. In 1880, at the height of anticlericalism, the republicans forbade these establishments from using the title "university". They awarded their own diplomas, not those of the State. However, since 1970, there have been many agreements between the state Universities and the other higher education institutions under which students in the "free" sector can be examined by mixed boards of examiners (made up of teachers from both types of establishment) and obtain, at one and the same time, both the State diploma and that of the private institution.[27]

4. The Church and the Media[28]

The Churches have their own press departments and can also make their views known via the secular media, public or private.
- There are newspapers, radio stations such as Radio Notre-Dame, and particular programmes which are the Church's. For Catholics, the work is co-ordinated by a body created by the secretariat of the episcopate, "*Chrétiens-médias national*". The Catholic press has a large circulation, including dailies (*La Croix*), weeklies (*La Vie, Témoignage Chrétien...*) and specialist publishing houses (Bayard Presse...). In addition, the *Fédération française des radios chrétiennes* includes in its governing council the *Fédération protestante*, the Catholic Church, the Armenian Apostolic Church, and the Orthodox Church; it has some 30 stations.
- The secular media also devotes space to religious questions and will give churchmen a hearing. This task is partly discharged by the State radio and television service. After the Second World

---

26 P. Coulombel, "Le droit privé français devant le fait religieux depuis la séparation de l'Eglise et de l'Etat", [French private law as to religion since the separation of Church and State] Rev. trim. dt civ., 1956, p. 1-54.

27 Currently there are operating Catholic institutes (those of Paris, Lille, Angers, Toulouse, and Lyon) which cover the major branches of learning to a high level. They are widely funded from private sources, including the fees of the students; but they also receive subventions from the State and local authorities, although such are not required by law. The University of Strasbourg is in a very special situation. In 1902 a convention between the Holy See and Germany created a faculty of theology. This was continued in being after 1919, and awards State diplomas which are also pontifical diplomas.

28 Cf. the paper by L. De Fleurquin, "L'Eglise et les médias", [The Church and the media] 8th International Congress on Canon Law, Lublin, September 1993.

War, there was established on television "le jour du Seigneur" [the day of the Lord]. On a State network, there are now each Sunday programmes devoted to each of the principal religions of France.[29] This practice is an obligation of the public service, under article 56 of the Law of September 30, 1886.

VII. Labour Law and the Churches[30]

The Preamble to the 1946 Constitution, to which the Constitution of 1958 refers, provides "No-one may be discriminated against in his work or employment on account of his origins, his opinions or his beliefs". Can it be that religious convictions, perhaps even ministry in a church, have no effect on Labour law? The reality is more subtle, and the position varies depending on whether the individual is ordained or lay.

1. French Labour Law and Ministers of Religion

- In principle, ecclesiastical status has no civil consequences in French law. It is immaterial in considering the existence and validity of a contract of employment. In seeking employment by a lay employer, a candidate is under no obligation to declare his ecclesiastical status; case-law has held improper a dismissal on the ground of failure to disclose this fact.[31] This is the position of

---

29 In 1933, when the radio services were nationalised, all religious broadcasting ceased under the principle of *laïcité*. Some religious programmes were soon brought back, but it was only after 1944 that religious broadcasting became well established.

30 N. *Guinezames*, "L'Église et le droit du travail", Les Églises et le droit du travail dans les pays de la Communauté européenne, Milan-Madrid, Giuffrè, 1993, p. 83-103.; J. SAVATIER, "L'animateur pastoral selon le droit du travail", l'année canonique, t.35, 1992 p. 29-43; G. DOLE, Les professions ecclésiastiques, fiction juridique et réalité sociale, Paris, LGDJ, 1987, 590 p.; Idem, La liberté d'opinion et de conscience en droit comparé du travail; Union européenne t.I : Droit européen et droit français, Paris, LGDJ, 1987, 256 p.

31 We should mention, however, the celebrated case of abbé Bouteyre, C.E. 10 May 1912; the *Conseil d'État* held that it was correct that an ecclesiastic should be barred from the competition for qualification as teacher in public secondary schools. In explaining the decision, two points may be noted: the matter was one of public education and not of the ordinary law of employment; and the decision was reached at the height of anticlericalism under the

worker-priests in respect of the labour law.
- Different considerations apply to ministers of religion in their essentially pastoral function, the parish priest or pastor for example. Is the minister an employee of his superior in the hierarchy, of an *association cultuelle*, or an *association diocésaine*, of the authority (the individual or the body with legal personality) which appoints him to his charge, or which pays his stipend? Since a decision of the *Cour de Cassation* in 1912, case-law has been consistent. There is no contract of employment between a clergyman and his superior; the first is not the "employee" of the second. Their relationship is of a different type, and secular law, holding itself neutral, refuses to categorise the bonds resulting from the internal organisation of the Churches. So the civil courts regard themselves as incompetent to review the decisions of a bishop in suspending a priest or religious from his ecclesiastical functions, a step which could ultimately lead to his removal.
- A minister of religion does however possess some of the rights of an employed person, including those relating to national insurance. The Protestant clergy and Jewish rabbis benefited from the social security system on its introduction in 1945. For Catholic priests and religious, special social security bodies dealing with first health and later retirement were established from 1959. Their management was more and more closely aligned to that of the general system of social security. Eventually, by the Law of 2 January 1978, the Catholic clergy came within the Social Security provision, but with a limited régime.[32]

2. *French Labour Law and Lay Persons working in a Religious Context*

The position of lay people working for the Church is varied.[33] They can be carrying out secular tasks or joining in the religious mission of the Church, assisting the ministers of religion in their pastoral functions, as do the "pastoral workers".

Third Republic. One wonders whether the *Conseil d'État* would hold to its view were the matter to arise today.

32 *J.P. Durand*, in Valdrini, Durand, Echappé, Vernay: Le droit canonique, précis Dalloz, Paris, 1989, p. 622.

33 The situation of honorary assistants, for whom most of the labour law rules do not apply, is not treated here.

- The ordinary labour law applies to all these lay people, but with some important emphases. The laity working in a Church body generally have a contract of employment. The employer can be an *association cultuelle* or an *association diocésaine*. The parish does not, in French law, have legal personality and cannot be an employer. The employer can also be an association under the Law of 1901 linked to a Church. The general rules of labour law apply to the relations of employer and employee.
- But may the Church impose additional terms when the laity have a pastoral function? The diocesan bishop gives each pastoral worker a personal "*lettre de mission*" setting out the work which the worker is authorised to carry out, which is always revocable. It is only through the possession of the *lettre de mission* that the pastoral worker can become an employee of an *association diocésaine*. Does the withdrawal of the *lettre* by the bishop involve, ipso facto, the ending of the contract of employment or is an express dismissal by the employer needed? What is in issue is the amount of compensation payable by the association which is the actual employer. Discussions are under way to draft a model contract of employment for pastoral workers which would take into account the episcopal licence.

The courts have pronounced on the legality of the dismissal of remarried divorced persons working perhaps in Catholic clinics or in Catholic private schools. These employees do not have to hold a *lettre de mission*, but they do work in what is called an "*entreprise de tendance*", one in which religious convictions are taken into account. After several twists and turns in the case-law, the *Cour de Cassation* has held proper the dismissal of a teacher in a Catholic school who had divorced and remarried.[34] Commentators are not unanimous in supporting this rigorous conclusion, which does not apply to those working in a Catholic clinic, where there is not the same educational objective.

---

[34] C. Cass. Ass. Plén. 19 May1978, D. 1978, p. 541, concl. Schmelck, n.Ph. Ardant. The decision is already old. The Church avoids to bring this kind of case into court since the position of the courts in this matter seems to be subject to modifications; "Les motifs de licenciement dans les entreprises de tendance", synthèse du colloque du centre Droit et Sociétés religieuses, par *E. Hirsoux*, l'année canonique, 39, 1997, p. 151-174

VIII. Financing of Churches

1. Historical Summary

Under the *Ancien Régime*, the Church possessed large estates which enabled it to pay its way. By the decree of 2 November 1789, the Constituent Assembly decided to nationalise the property of the clergy, and its sale to meet the deficit in the State's treasury. In return, the State promised adequate stipends for ministers of religion.

During the period of the Concordat, the State and the local authorities, especially the *communes*, continued to finance, more or less generously according to the period, the four recognised churches, in terms of the stipends of ministers, the construction of buildings, assistance with repairs, and above all with operational expenses. In general terms, this régime remains in force in the three *départements* of the East of France.[35]

Article 2 of the Law of 1905 ended the church budget, the payment of ministers' salaries and all other subventions from public funds. This remains the law. However, the systematic harassment of the churches is a thing of the past. As a result, the churches have two sources of finance: private giving on one hand, and on the other indirect help from the State in forms which do not amount to subventions. Moreover, associations which are not *associations cultuelles*, but which are nonetheless in the Church orbit, can receive public subventions.

2. Finance from Private Funds after 1905

This is the normal, fundamental, source of income. Now that the State no longer pays the clergy, almost all the Churches' resources must be found from private sources. Each church is free to decide how it will seek to collect funds, and how it will apply them. In fact the methods vary; we give some examples:
- In the Reformed Church of France, the funds come from the giving of the faithful.[36] Each local church manages its own resources,

---

[35] Fr. *Messner*, Le financement des Eglises, [The Financing of Churches] Strasbourg, cerdic, 1984, 259 p.
[36] These can take two forms (1) regular giving, no fixed sum being prescribed, to the parish association to which each individual belongs; (2) offerings given at the Sunday services.

but a principle of solidarity operates to mitigate the differences between parishes and between rich and poor regions. The pastors' stipends vary according to their age and family circumstances, but not according to locality.
- In the Catholic Church, the gifts of the faithful are equally essential.[37] The use of resources and their allocation is determined at diocesan level.

Gifts can also take the form of foundations, the irrevocable settlement of property for a purpose which is in the public interest and which can be created and/or managed by a Church entity.

3. Indirect Assistance by the State since 1905[38]

This can be put into four categories:
Certain ministers of religion are paid by the State, without any violation of the Law of 1905. These are those working in prisons or hospitals,[39] or the church teachers in private schools when the school has entered into a contractual relationship with the State under the Law of 1959.

The State can guarantee sums borrowed by *associations cultuelles* or *associations diocésaines* for the construction of new places of worship.[40] In the same spirit is the appearance since 1930 of a form of mortgage funding by the *commune* to an *association cultuelle*, generally for a term of 99 years with a peppercorn rent of 1 franc a year. First used for the construction of churches in the Paris area, the practice has spread, without administrative objection.

Finally, the State is owner of Catholic places of worship built before 1905. It undertakes the major works of repair.

Finally, the tax régime applying to *associations cultuelles* and *diocésaines* is extremely favourable. Article 238 bis of the General Tax Code allows enterprises and individual taxpayers to deduct, up to a certain limit, donations to the work of organisations serving the

---

37 The collection of the Church is a voluntary contribution of the faithful; given in practice by less than half of those Catholics who attend church regularly, this can seem a precarious flow of income, even if it seems to allow the payment of the diocesan clergy. Fund-raising outside Mass augments it.
38 J. Gueydan, X. Delsol, P. Desjonqueres, Cultes et religions, impôts et charges sociales, [Churches and religious groups: taxation and social charges], Paris, LGDJ, 1991, 270 p.
39 cf. infra, section VIII.
40 The *loi de finance rectificative* of 29 July 1961 (Art. 11) allows *départements* and *communes* to give these guarantees; the State, through the Ministry of Finance, can do the same.

public interest. The *Conseil d'État*, in an opinion of 15 May 1962, held that this applied to *associations cultuelles* in respect of funds devoted to the construction and maintenance of church buildings, or to certain works of a philanthropic, educational, social or family nature. In contrast, however, in 1962 the power of deduction was held inapplicable to donations for the purpose of paying the stipends of ministers of religion.

The possibilities of tax deductions in favour of *associations cultuelles* have been much increased by the *loi* du Mécénat.[41] One can understand the interest which different groups have in obtaining the label of *association cultuelle*; the judges, as we have said, are watchful against abuses.

4. Financing Associations under the Law of 1901

Failing being an *association cultuelle*, a group working in the Church field is generally constituted as an association under the Law of 1901, authorised to solicit subventions from the State, local authorities, and other public bodies. These associations can only receive donations from individuals, who benefit from no tax exemption.[42] Donations in favour of associations recognised as of *utilité pratique* enjoy tax exemptions.

IX. Religious Assistance in Public Institutions

The doctrine of positive *laïcité* implies that the State ensures that every individual has the means of exercising his or her religion. If the individual lives in an establishment managed by the State, and which he cannot leave to follow religious observances outside, he ought to be enabled to practise his religion within the establishment.

---

41 *J.P. Durand*, "Chronique de droit civil ecclésiastique", *l'année canonique*, 1988, p. 443-462; increase of the amount of tax deductions allowed and possible deductions of the "church contribution".

42 This is the position of many *associations cultuelles* of Moslems, associations whose object is not exclusively worship but also the construction of Koranic schools, libraries, etc., which generally accompany mosques. It is also the legal form chosen by many educational bodies in the Church orbit.

Therefore the State accepts a responsibility for this spiritual assistance in places with a population unable to leave. Article 2 of the Law of 1905 envisages "*lycées*, colleges, hospitals, prisons". In practice, the régimes applying to these very different establishments differ, for one can more readily leave a *lycée* or a college[43] (even as a boarder) than a hospital or a prison. Military chaplaincies meet similar needs.

1. Hospitals and Prisons

The Law of 1905 allows the organisation of chaplaincies, and their being at the charge of public funds without creating any obligation to this end. The case-law of the *Conseil d'État* together with a number of ministerial circulars fashioned a relevant legal régime.

In hospitals, it falls to the head of the establishment to take the necessary measures to enable the residents to practise their religion within the establishment. Local arrangements must be made. Greater precision is given by a ministerial circular of 26 July 1976. Hospital administrations could call on the ministers of religion of the various churches to help those patients who sought it. These chaplains would enter into an agreement with the hospital administration having obtained the approval of the religious authority concerned. They are salaried, must respect the rules of the hospital, and are within the general régime of Social Security. Their contract of employment can be varied by agreement, or withdrawn unilaterally by the administration on three months' notice (except for grave misconduct) after consultation with the religious authority.

In prisons, spiritual assistance to the inmates is currently regulated by a decree of 12 September 1972. The Minister of Justice appoints the chaplains of different churches, after consultation with the competent religious authority. The persons appointed have no contracts, but are subject to special rules as non-established public officials. They receive a stipend and are within the general régime of Social Security.

---

43 cf. supra, section V.

2. Army Chaplaincy[44]

The military chaplaincy was organised by the Law of 8 July 1880. The *Conseil d'État* considered that the silence of the Law of 1905 on this subject did not imply any prohibition on this service being a charge on public funds. In practice in the department of the *État-major des armées* are three military chaplains, representing respectively the Catholic, Protestant and Jewish faiths. Each is responsible for the chaplaincy work of his own church and ensures co-operation between the administration and the religious authorities.[45] Two difficulties hinder the smooth running of the chaplaincies: insufficient numbers of chaplains of the various churches, in hospitals as well as prisons; in particular there is a grave shortage of Moslem chaplains.

X. Status of Priests and of Religious[46]

Priests, religious, and ministers of religion are subject to the general law applying to every individual on French territory. There is, in principle, no special status of minister of religion. However, by virtue of his function, he is subject to numerous special rules having no relevance to the life of other individuals.[47] One cannot speak, though, of a particular status.

---

44 G. *Dole*, Les professions ecclésiastiques, op. cit. p. 312.
45 The personnel of these chaplaincies fall into three categories: (1) the military chaplains properly so called, appointed by the Minister and whose career is assimilated to that of an officer; (2) chaplains engaged in a civilian capacity, who have a contract of employment; their position is similar to that of civilian employees of the Ministry of the Armies; (3) voluntary chaplains, unpaid, but benefiting from State insurance in case of an accident at work.
46 J. *Kerleveo*, l'Eglise catholique en régime français de séparation, [The Catholic Church under the French régime of separation] T.III, Le prêtre catholique en droit français, [Catholic Priests in French Law] ed. Desclé, Paris, 1962; P. *Barbier*, "Le ministre du culte peut-il voir sa responsabilité civile engagée à l'occasion des actes qu'il accomplit dans l'exercice de son ministère", [Civil liability of ministers of religion for acts involved in the exercise of their calling], l'année canonique, 1987, p. 235-256.
47 Some examples of these rights and obligations special to ministers of religion: 1.) Some professions, few in number, are incompatible with the position of minister of religion. The Laws of 1882, 1886 and 1904 progressively prohibited ministers from teaching in primary schools, a prohibition which perhaps extends to secondary education (cf. above, section V). 2.) Article 909 of the Civil Code prohibits a minister of religion from receiving gifts or legacies from a sick person who has been in his spiritual care during the person's final ill-

XI. Matrimonial and Family Law[48]

For many centuries, in France as in most European countries, the Church regulated the law as to marriage and the family. Progressively under the *Ancien Régime*, there was a move towards the secularisation of those institutions. The French Revolution achieved the secularisation. Today, in this field, French Law and Canon Law are autonomous, but not able to ignore one another. We will note the extent to which French civil law takes into account facts relating to religion.

1. Formation of Marriage

The existence of the two legal orders presents few difficulties. The Napoleonic codification required that two persons wishing a religious marriage must have first contracted a civil marriage before the officer of civil status. A purely religious ceremony can never constitute a marriage valid under French law, and the minister of religion who conducts it will be criminally liable.[49] However, a marriage celebrated only in religious form abroad, and complying with the foreign law of the place of celebration, will be recognised in France.

---

ness. 3.) The exercise of some pastoral functions must be undertaken with respect to the provisions of secular law, on pain of liability: the prohibition on a minister of religion celebrating a religious marriage before the civil ceremony; prohibition on carrying out the burial ceremonies without administrative authorisation given by the officer of civil status, who in turn cannot act without sight of the death certificate signed by the doctor; prohibition on the administration of a sacrament (e.g. baptism) without the consent of the interested parties (or of those with parental authority in the case of an infant); this is to protect the freedom of conscience of the citizen (Cf Liège, 5 May 1909, D.P. II.2.364; a grand-mother had had a child baptised without the consent of the widowed father, and was ordered to pay token damages). 4.) Certain penalties are aggravated when the wrong is committed by a minister of religion. 5.) The obligation of professional secrecy (not limited to the confessional) allows a minister of religion to refuse to give evidence of facts of which he became aware in the exercise of his office. Etc.

48 G. *Cornu*, Droit civil, la famille, Domat, 2003; *J. Carbonnier*, Droit civil, la famille, Paris, Montchrétien, 1999, 20°éd.; *Malaurie etAynes*, Droit civil, la famille, Paris, Cujas, 1998, 6° éd.; *H. Gaudemet-Tallon*, v° "Famille", Répertoire Dalloz, 1997; "Divorce et nullité de mariage, colloque de droit canonique et de droit civil", actes du colloque de Poitiers, avril 1989, l'année canonique, t. 32, 1989, p. 13-195; *Y. Geraldy*, La religion en droit privé, thèse droit Limoges, 1978; numerous articles in the Revue de Droit Canonique, Strasbourg.

49 Art. 199 and 200 C. pen. Cf. *T. Revet*, "De l'ordre des célébrations civiles et religieuses du mariage", [Of the order of celebration of civil and religious marriage], la Semaine Juridique, G. no. 49, 1987, 3309, p. 1-8.

Can matters of religious fact be taken into account after the conclusion of a civil marriage? If so, it is only indirectly. For example, the validity of the marriage of a priest cannot be challenged in French law,[50] were the courts to declare such a marriage void, it would not be because of the Church's prohibition but on account of a mistake as to an essential quality of the person, the priest having concealed his ecclesiastical status. Further, the remarriage of a divorced person can be annulled, not because the Catholic Church forbids the second union but because one party has concealed his or her status as a divorced person which can be treated as a mistake as to an essential quality of the person so long as the other party proves that the fact, if known, would have been a barrier to the marriage.[51] Taking another example: when the spouses are not French, the judge applies their national law to determine the essential validity of the marriage; religious matters may be taken into account, as elements in that national law but not simply as confessional rules. However, such matters (for example a prohibition on marrying a person of another religion) may sometimes be ignored on the basis of *ordre public*.[52]

2. The Dissolution of Marriages

French law makes full provision for divorce, under legislation which has developed over the years.[53] Currently it is governed by the Law of 11 July 1975 which ignores confessional rules. The two legal orders each have their proper domain. Civil divorce is recognised by the organs of the State and has only civil effects; canonical nullity has no effect on the possible civil nullity of the marriage. Religious factors can, however, be relevant in the secular courts:
- refusal by a spouse to carry out the religious marriage to which he has agreed before the civil ceremony is a grave wrong, a ground for divorce. The courts note the breach of the promise as well as

---

50 This, the current position of the courts, had already been adopted in the 19th century; the Law of 1905 had no effect on the matter (C.Cass. civ. 25 January 1888).
51 T.G.I. Le Mans, 7 December. 1981, J.C.P. 1986, 20573.
52 *H. Gaudemet-Tallon*, La désunion du couple en droit international privé, receuil des cours, académie de droit international de La Haye, 1991, I, 279 p.; on religious questions, see p. 179-273.
53 The Law of 20 September 1792 introduced divorce for the first time, seeing it as an essential corollary of individual liberty; later reforms reduced the available grounds. Divorce remained open under the Civil Code of 1804, being easier for the man to obtain than the woman. It was abolished at the Restoration in 1816. Finally, the *loi* Naquet, 27 July 1884, re-established divorce in France.

the affront to the religious convictions of the injured party.
- When after many years of life together the wife withdraws to take religious vows, there is a grave wrong to the husband who may obtain a divorce on the basis of the wrong done by the wife.[54]
- The court generally ignores the position of the Catholic Church in its refusal to allow any divorce; however, it has taken into consideration the fact that a divorce would be against the wishes of a spouse, a Catholic particularly committed to the Church, and that the divorce would lead to "exceptional hardship" given the teaching of the faith on the indissolubility of marriage. The judge will apply the "hardship clause" of article 240 of the Civil Code.[55]
- The civil judge finds it easier to deal with religions which allow divorce and remarriage, such as Judaism. In the Jewish faith, the repudiation of the wife by the husband, who delivers a *gett* in the presence of a rabbi, allows the wife to remarry in religious form. The civil judge, when pronouncing a civil divorce, can take into account a refusal by the husband to deliver a *gett*. He can order the husband to pay damages to compensate the wife. But he has no power to order a positive religious action by the husband.[56]

3. *Internal Organisation of the Family*

In the internal organisation of the family, the judge also takes some notice of religious elements. He pays respect to the principle of freedom of conscience, in allowing a spouse to change religion or religious observance during the marriage, excluding such a fanaticism as would amount to neglect of the fundamental obligations of marriage. So, while adherence to a sect is not itself a matter of which the judge will disapprove, it can lead to a situation which involves a spouse in "grave errors".
The religious education of children can lead to disagreements between the spouses.[57] The parents should together chose what provi-

---

54 C. A. Amiens, 3 March 1975, D.S. 1975, p. 706.
55 Civ., 2, 23 October 1991, D. 1993, p. 193, 1° esp. n. Villaceque. However, a recent view is that even a deeply Catholic spouse should, in the circumstances of modern society, accept divorce.
56 *P. Barbier*, "Le problème du Gueth", G.P. 1987, doct. p. 485 et C. Cass. 15 juin 1988, Bull. Civ. II, no. 146; C. Cass. 21 November 1990, D. 1991, 434, n. E. Agostini; *H. Gaudemet-Tallon*, op. cit. p. 248-253.
57 *Cl. Castellan*, L'éducation de l'enfant, puissance paternelle en droit canonique et autorité parentale en droit français, Thèse, droit, Paris XI et ICP, 2001. For a long time, in the case

sion they will make (Art. 371-2 of the Civil Code). Once made, a choice will be respected by the court. In the case of divorce, or of disagreement between the parents on this matter, the judge will uphold the practice previously agreed upon.[58] Moreover, France is bound by article 14 of the Convention of New York of 29 November 1989 on the Rights of the Child, and must take into account the child's capacity for discernment.[59]

Family law, then, often takes account of religious facts, but it is rare for the legislator to refer to them. It is a matter for case-law, working sensitively on the varying facts of each case. The judge will not apply canonical rules as such, but will note their possible effects on the "civil" relationship between the parties.

XII. Bibliography

The essential work is:
Messmer Fr./Prélot P.-H./Woehrling J.-M. (eds.), Traité de droit français des religions, Paris, LITEC, 2003, 1317 p.

Other sources are:
Basdevant-Gaudemet B., Le jeu concordataire dans la France du XIX° siècle, Paris, P.U.F., 1988, 289 p.
Basdevant-Gaudemet B./Messner Fr. (eds.), Les origines historiques du statut des confessions religieuses dans les pays de l'Union européenne, Paris, PUF, coll. Histoire, 1999.
Basdevant-Gaudemet B., "Droit et religions en France", Revue internationale de droit comparé, 1998, p. 23-55, reproduits dans :La religion en droit comparé à l'aube du XXI° siècle, (ed. *Caparros*), Bruylant, Bruxelles, 2000, p. 123-164.
Bauberot J., Histoire de la laïcité française, Paris, PUF, que sais-je ?, 2000, 128 p.
Bauberot J., Vers un nouveau pacte laïque, 1990.
Berlingo S. (ed.), Code européen, Droit et Religions, T.I, Union européenne ; les pays de la Méditerranée, Milan, Giuffré, 2000 (p. 153-273 sur la France).

---

of mixed marriages, the Church required the non-Catholic spouse to promise to allow the Catholic spouse to bring up the children in that faith. Such an agreement was valid in the eyes of the Church, but not in the civil courts. However, the civil judge could not ignore it, and could hold that there had been a breach of a prior agreement without entering into questions as to the content of that agreement.
58 Paris, 6 April 1967, J.C.P. 1967, II, 15100
59 Cass. Civ. 1° 11 June 1991, D. 1991, 521 n. *Malaurie*.

Boyer A., Le droit des religions en France, Paris, P.U.F., 1993, 260 p.

Durand J.P., in Durand, Echappé, Vernay, Valdrini, Le droit canonique, Paris, Dalloz, 1989, 747 p.

Jeuffroy B./Tricard F. (eds.), Liberté religieuse et régimes des cultes en droit français, Textes, Pratique administrative, jurisprudence, Paris, cerf, 1996, 1242 p.

Kerleveo J., L'Église catholique en régime français de séparation, 3 vol. Paris, Desclé, 1962.

Mayeur J.M., La Séparation des Églises et de l'État, Paris, ed. Ouvrières, 1991, 188 p.

Messner F. (ed.), Les "sectes" et le droit en France, Paris, PUF, 1999.

Poulat E., La solution laïque et ses problèmes, Berg international, 1997, 229 p.

Prélot P.-H., "Chronique de droit français des religions", dans chaque numéro de la Revue européenne des relations religions États, Leuven, Peeters.

Robert J./Duffar J., Droits de l'homme et libertés fondamentales, Paris, Montchrestien, 7° éd., 1999, 855 p.

James Casey
State and Church in Ireland

I. Social Facts

Two preliminary points should be made by way of background. The first is statistical and social. Though its population embraces people of all faiths, and none, Ireland is a predominantly Roman Catholic country. Over 88 % of the population was baptised into that faith,[1] and a high proportion of these people continue to observe the tenets and practices of that church. The remainder of the population is divided between various Protestant churches, and there are also small Jewish, Muslim and Orthodox communities.[2]

The second point is a legal one. Like the United Kingdom, Ireland belongs to the common law tradition; but it also has a written constitution enshrining judicial review of legislation, and in that respect resembles certain continental states such as Germany, Italy, Portugal and Spain. Unlike them, however, it has no specialised constitutional court. The task of judicial review is instead entrusted to the High Court and, on appeal therefrom, the Supreme Court. This, coupled with the fact that constitutional adjudication has become a familiar institution in practice, has generated a symbiotic relationship between the Constitution's precepts and the common law as administered in Ireland.

II. Historical Background

Until 1871 the (Anglican) Church of Ireland was the church established by law; under the tithe system, as modified, it was legally enti-

---
1 The figures from the 2002 census give the Roman Catholic population as 3,462,606: *Census 2002: Principal Demographic Results* (Central Statistics Office, Dublin 2003), p. 82.
2 Church of Ireland 115,611: Presbyterians 20,582: Methodists 10,033: Jews 1790: Muslims 19,147: Orthodox 10,437.

tled to financial support even from those who did not belong to it,[3] and its courts alone had jurisdiction over matrimonial causes.[4] Before 1829 Roman Catholics were subject to a number of legal disabilities, including ineligibility for public office, and their church received no support from public funds.[5] The main legal disabilities were removed by the Roman Catholic Relief Act 1829, and the Church of Ireland was disestablished by the Irish Church Act 1869. Matrimonial jurisdiction was transferred to the ordinary courts by the Matrimonial Causes and Marriage Law (Ireland) Amendment Act 1870.

By the terms of the Roman Catholic Relief Act 1829 certain disabilities continued to attach to members of Roman Catholic religious orders, such as the Society of Jesus; they could not, for example, lawfully be ordained in Ireland and donations or bequests in favour of such orders were invalid. But these were all swept away by section 5 (2) of the Government of Ireland Act 1920.[6]

The Anglo-Irish Treaty of 6 December 1921 provided for the establishment of an independent Irish Free State. Article 16 of that Treaty gave guarantees of religious liberty,[7] and these were implemented by Article 8 of the 1922 Irish Free State Constitution. It provided:

> "Freedom of conscience and the free profession and practice of religion are, subject to public order and morality, guaranteed to every citizen, and no law may be made either directly or indirectly to endow any religion, or prohibit or restrict the free exercise thereof or give any preference, or impose any disability on account of religious belief or religious status, or affect prejudicially the right of any child to attend a school receiving public

---

3 See further *Kevin B. Nowlan*, "Disestablishment: 1800-1869" in *Michael Hurley S.J.* (ed.), Irish Anglicanism 1869-1969 (Dublin 1970), p. 1-22.
4 See *R.B. McDowell*, "The Irish Courts of Law 1801-1914", 10 Irish Historical Studies (1957) p. 363-391.
5 Though St. Patrick's College, Maynooth – the principal Irish seminary – was founded in 1795 with aid from public funds and received an annual grant until the coming into force of the Irish Church Act 1869. See further *Nowlan*, op.cit., No. 3 supra.
6 Which provided as follows: "Any existing enactment by which any penalty, disadvantage, or disability is imposed on account of religious belief or on a member of a religious order as such shall, as from the appointed day, cease to have effect in Ireland". See Re *Byrne* [1935] I.R. 782.
7 Which provided as follows: "Neither the Parliament of the Irish Free State nor the Parliament of Northern Ireland shall make any law so as either directly or indirectly to endow any religion or prohibit or restrict the free exercise thereof or give any preference or impose any disability on account of religious belief or religious status or affect prejudicially the right of any child to attend a school receiving public money without attending the religious instruction at the school or make any discrimination as respects state aid between schools under the management of different religious denominations or divert from any religious denomination or any educational institution any of its property except for public utility purposes and on payment of compensation."

money without attending the religious instruction at the school, or make any discrimination as respects State aid between schools under the management of different religious denominations, or divert from any religious denomination or any educational institution any of its property except for the purpose of roads, railways, lighting, water or drainage works or other works of public utility, and on payment of compensation."

The 1922 Constitution was the subject of frequent, and occasionally radical, amendment – though Article 8 was not affected. By 1936 the prime minister, Mr. de Valera, had concluded that a new constitution was necessary and the task of preparing one began. In many respects the new constitution simply reproduces the text of its predecessor,[8] but the provisions on religion were markedly different. Whereas the preamble to the 1922 Constitutional merely acknowledged that "...all lawful authority comes from God to the people...", that of the 1937 Constitution opens as follows:

"In the Name of the Most Holy Trinity, from Whom is all authority and to Whom, as our final end, all actions both of men and States must be referred,
We, the people of Éire
Humbly acknowledging all our obligations to our Divine Lord, Jesus Christ, Who sustained our fathers through centuries of trial...."

And Article 44.1 No. 2, as originally enacted, provided that:

"2. The State recognises the special position of the Holy Catholic Apostolic and Roman Church as the guardian of the Faith professed by the great majority of the citizens.
3. The State also recognises the Church of Ireland, the Presbyterian Church in Ireland, the Methodist Church in Ireland, the Religious Society of Friends in Ireland, as well as the Jewish Congregations and the other religious denominations existing in Ireland at the date of the coming into operation of this Constitution."[9]

For a long time the words "special position" were the subject of controversy. One view was that they conferred a juridical privilege on the Roman Catholic church, another that they merely reflected social

---

8 See further *James Casey*, Constitutional Law in Ireland (3rd ed., Dublin 2000) p. 21-23.
9 On the difficulties of drafting this provision – a version of which was shown to Pope Pius XI – see *Dermot Keogh*, "The Irish Constitutional Revolution: An Analysis of the Making of the Constitution" in *Frank Litton* (ed.), The Constitution of Ireland 1937-1987 (Dublin 1987), p. 4-84.

reality and had no legal significance.[10] In *Quinn's Supermarket Ltd. v. Att. Gen.*[11] the Supreme Court declared in favour of the second view. Walsh J, speaking for the court, said:[12]

> "This declaration is an express recognition of the separate coexistence of the religious dominations, named and unnamed. It does not prefer one to the other and it does not confer any privilege or import any disability or diminution of status upon any religious denomination, and it does not permit the State to do so."

In a referendum not long afterwards the electorate approved the Fifth Amendment of the Constitution Act 1972, which deleted Article 44.I. No. 2 and No. 3.

III. Legal Sources

The principal source of law on Church-State relations is Article 44 of the Constitution (as now amended). Its provisions are as follows:

(1) The State acknowledges that the homage of public worship is due to Almighty God. It shall hold His Name in reverence, and shall respect and honour religion.

(2) 1. Freedom of conscience and the free profession and practice of religion are, subject to public order and morality, guaranteed to every citizen.

2. The State guarantees not to endow any religion.

3. The State shall not impose any disabilities or make any discrimination on the ground of religious profession, belief or status.

4. Legislation providing State aid for schools shall not discriminate between schools under the management of different religious denominations, nor be such as to affect prejudicially the right of any child to attend a school receiving public money without attending religious instruction at that school.

5. Every religious denomination shall have the right to manage its own affairs, own, acquire and administer property, movable and immovable, and maintain institutions for religious or charitable purposes.

---

10 See *J.M. Kelly*, Fundamental Rights in the Irish Law and Constitution (Dublin 1967),p. 248.
11 [1972] I.R.I.
12 At 24.

6. The property of any religious denomination or any educational institution shall not be diverted save for necessary works of public utility and on payment of compensation.

Any legislation or administrative arrangements incompatible with these principles would be unconstitutional. It should be noted that there is no constitutional or legal prohibition upon proselytisation. It will be clear, however, that Article 44 hardly presupposes a *laic* state; indeed, as mentioned above, the preamble of the Constitution, like that of Greece, opens with a reference to the Most Holy Trinity.

The Supreme Court has held that the primary purpose of Article 44 is to guarantee the full and free practice of religion.[13] Therefore distinctions created by law on the basis of religious profession, belief or status which are drawn for that purpose are compatible with the Constitution. So where the free practice and profession of a religion necessitates an exemption from the provisions of a generally applicable statute, such exemption may validly be given.[14]

Relations between the State and the Roman Catholic Church are not regulated by concordat[15] and the State has no formal role in respect of higher ecclesiastical appointments.[16] Nor does Irish law make any provision for agreements between the State and the churches, such as are contemplated in Article 16.3 of the Spanish Constitution of 1978.

IV. Separation of Church and State

Since the Church of Ireland was disestablished in 1871, Irish law – save in regard to education – has accepted the principle of separating church and state. The Constitution, as has been shown, forbids the endowment of religion. As interpreted by the Supreme Court this is

---

13 *Quinn's Supermarket Ltd v. Att. Gen.*, supra: *Mulloy v. Minister for Education* [1975] I.R. 88.
14 *Quinn's Supermarket Ltd. V. Att. Gen.* supra.
15 See *J.H. Whyte*, Church and State in Modern Ireland, 1923-1979 (2nd ed., Dublin 1980), p. 15: "No concordat between the Irish State and the Catholic Church has ever been negotiated, nor, so far as is known, has one ever been suggested."
16 With regard to the appointment of bishops *Professor Whyte* (op.cit) wrote: "The civil government has no part in the formal nominating procedure and, despite rumours to the contrary in one or two rare instances, I have been unable to find any case where it has made even informal representations to the ecclesiastical authorities." But *Dr. Keogh* suggests that in 1940 the Taoiseach (prime minister), *Eamon de Valera* played a role in securing the appointment of *John Charles McQuaid* as Archbishop of Dublin: op.cit, No. 9 supra, at p. 61.

more comprehensive than might at first appear. In *Campaign to Separate Church and State* v. *Minister for Education*[17] it was held also to prohibit

> (a) concurrent endowment – i.e. conferring of financial or economic benefits on *all* religions, and
> (b) the establishment of religion.

Article 44.2. No. 5 guarantees every religious denomination the right to manage its own affairs. The phase "religious denomination" is nowhere defined in the Constitution, and the courts have had no opportunity to elucidate it. It would obviously cover the traditional Christian churches, Judaism, Islam, Hinduism, etc. Whether it would extend to bodies such as the "Church of Scientology" is unclear.

A denomination's right to manage its own affairs would seem to include drawing up rules for its own governance. *Prima facie*, therefore, the contents of a church's code of canon law are its own business; and certainly changes in those contents require neither ratification by State law nor administrative sanction. If, however, it was established that alterations in a church's rules of governance had been effected in violation of that church's self-devised constitution, the courts, if called upon, could rule them *ultra vires*.[18]

In *O'Callaghan* v. *O'Sullivan*[19] the Supreme Court held that the canon law of the Roman Catholic Church ranks as foreign law, with the consequence that its precepts must be proved by the evidence of expert witnesses. The same would apply to the canon law, or similar provisions, of any church, for Kennedy C.J. (O'Connor and Fitzgibbon JJ. concurring) said:[20]

> "In my opinion all law is foreign to these Courts other than the laws which these Courts have been set up under the Constitution of Saorstát Éireann to administer and enforce, that is to say, other than the laws given force and validity by Article 73 of the Constitution and the enactments of the Oireachtas made after the coming into operation of the Constitution. No other laws are known to us judicially; nor can we take judi-

---

17 [1998] 3 I.R. 321.
18 [1925] 1 I.R. 90.
19 At 09.
20 In *Colquhoun v. Fitzgibbon* [1937] I.R. 555 the plaintiff challenged the authority of the Court of the General Synod of the Church of Ireland to entertain certain proceedings against him. The High Court (Meredith J.) ruled against him, plainly having no doubt as to its jurisdiction in the matter. And in *McGrath and Ó Ruairc v. Trustees of Maynooth College* [1979] I.L.R.M. 166 the Supreme Court accepted that there was jurisdiction to review decisions of an ecclesiastical body.

cial notice of any other laws, unless they are proved to us as facts. All other laws are extrinsic to these Courts of Justice of the Saorstát and in that sense "foreign" to the Courts. So it is that Scots law is "foreign" in that part of Great Britain which is England."

V. Legal Status of Religious Bodies

Under modern Irish law all churches and religious groupings stand upon the same footing[21]. Since none is established by law, they all have the status of voluntary associations. As *Sullivan P.* put it in *State (Colquhoun)* v. *D'Arcy*:[22]

> "The status of a church not established by law is, in the words of *Barry J.* in *O'Keeffe* v. *Cullen* "The status of a voluntary association the members of which subscribe or assent to certain rules and regulations, and bind themselves to each other to confirm to certain laws and principles, the obligation to such conformity and observance resting wholly in the mutual contract of the members, enforceable only as matter of contract by the ordinary tribunals of the land when brought within their cognisance and not enforceable under any independent coercive jurisdiction."

Churches and religious groups do not automatically have legal personality; in general their legal status is that of unincorporated associations. The Companies Acts provide machinery under which they could acquire corporate status,[23] but this does not appear to have been availed of. There is no procedure – short of legislation for the purpose – for making churches and religious groupings corporate bodies under public law.

As a result of this lack of legal personality – which does not seem to pose any practical problems – church property is normally vested in trustees, in some cases for a parish, in others for a diocese (or their equivalents). In the Church of Ireland, however, a centralised arrangement exists. As part of the process of disestablishment that church voluntarily created the Representative Church Body (R.C.B.) to hold its property. This body was incorporated by Royal Charter of

---

21 As to this, see the late *Professor Whyte's* magisterial work: Church and State in Modern Ireland 1923-1979 (2nd ed., Dublin 1980); also *G.W. Hogan,* "Law and Religion: Church-State Relations in Ireland from Independence to the Present Day" (1987), xxxv American Journal of Comparative Law 47.
22 [1936] I.R. 641 at 650.
23 See *Patrick Ussher,* Company Law in Ireland (London 1986), p. 7-8.

15 October 1870,[24] which declared it to be subject to the order and control of the General Synod. It may sue and be sued in respect of church property vested in it – *R.C.B.* v. *Hall:*[25] *Kirwan* v. *R.C.B.*[26]

In general, the acquisition or disposal of property by a church or religious grouping will be governed purely by its own internal rules and procedures. The civil law would intrude only if the relevant property was subject to a trust and its disposal was alleged to be in breach thereof.[27] Public law, in the form of the planning legislation, features a procedure under which the planning authorities may list buildings for preservation on grounds *inter alia* of historic or architectural interest. Such listed buildings may be altered or demolished only with permission – a matter clearly relevant to the problem of redundant churches. In addition, a monument associated with the religious history of the place where it is situated constitutes "a historic monument" under the National Monuments Acts 1930-1987. It may therefore be entered on the register of such monuments, in which case any alteration of or interference with it requires the consent of the Commissioners of Public Works.[28]

Churches and religious groups are given a limited exemption from the provisions of the planning legislation. Ministerial regulations made under statutory authority[29] classify as "exempted development" a change in the use of an existing structure to:

> "Use as a structure for public worship or religious instruction; use of such structure for the social or recreational activities of the religious body using the structure; as a monastery or convent."[30]

But this change of use must not require the carrying out of any works on the structure. It follows that the construction *de novo* of a church, school, hospital or the like would be subject to the ordinary law and thus require planning permission.

In the interests of protecting the architectural heritage, Part IV of the Planning and Development Act 2000 imposes controls over changes

---

24 Authority to grant this charter was provided by section 22 of the Irish Church Act 1869.
25 [1928] I.R. 334.
26 [1959] I.R.215.
27 Or where supervening events have made performance of the trust impossible, and the High Court is asked to permit the application of the trust property cy-prés – e.g. *Representative Church Body* v. *Att. Gen.* [1988[I.R.19.
28 Contravention of this requirement is an offence punishable, on summary conviction, by a fine of up to £1,000 and/or six months imprisonment; on conviction on indictment, by a fine of up to £50,000 and/or up to twelve months imprisonment.
29 Planning and Development Act 2000, section 4 (2).
30 Planning and Development Regulations 2001 (S.I. No. 600 of 2001), Art. 10.

in the interior, *inter alia*, of churches: section 52 (2). This innovation has provoked protests from some clerics.

The property of churches and religious groups is given special – though not absolute – protection by Article 44.2. No. 6 of the Constitution. It provides as follows:

> "The property of any religious denomination or any educational institution shall not be diverted save for necessary works of public utility and on payment of compensation."

The scope of this guarantee still awaits judicial elucidation.[31]

VI. Church Autonomy

Article 44.2. No. 5 of the Constitution, it will be recalled, provides as follows:

> "Every religious denomination shall have the right to manage its own affairs, own, acquire and administer property, movable and immovable, and maintain institutions for religious or charitable purposes."

The meaning of this provision was considered by the Supreme Court in *McGrath and Ó Ruairc v Trustees of Maynooth College*.[32] The plaintiffs – both former priests – had been dismissed from their teaching posts at the college, which was (then) in law a seminary but functioned also as a Pontifical University and as a recognised college of the National University of Ireland. (In the latter role – alone – it received State funding.) The ground of the dismissals was that the plaintiffs had violated certain of the college statutes. They claimed that those statutes discriminated between clerical and lay teachers and thus infringed Article 44.2. No. 3 of the Constitution. The Supreme Court rejected this argument. Henchy J. (Griffin, Kenny and Parke JJ. concurring) said (at p. 187-188):

> "The *raison d'etre* of the college, whatever academic or educational accretions it may have gathered over the years, has been that it has at all

---

31 See further *Ronan Keane*, The Law of Local Government in the Republic of Ireland (Dublin 1982), p. 225-226: *Casey*, op.cit., No. 8 supra, p. 572-574.
32 [1979] I.L.R.M. 166.

times been a national seminary where students are educated and trained for the Roman Catholic priesthood. This inevitably means that at least some of the academic staff must not only be priests but priests with particular qualifications and with a required level of religious orthodoxy and behaviour. It is part of the purpose of the statutes (which, incidentally, were drawn up by the trustees, who were all bishops of the Roman Catholic Church, and were not imposed by the State) that due standards are to be observed by those of the academic staff who are priests. Even if it be said that the statutes are, by recognition or support, an emanation of the State, the distinctions drawn in them between priest and layman, in terms of disabilities or discriminations, are not part of what is prohibited by Article 44.2. no. 3. They represent no prejudicial State instruction where priest is advanced unjustifiably over layman, or vice versa, as was the case in *Molloy* v. *Minister for Education* [1975] IR 88. On the contrary, they amount to an implementation of the guarantee that is to be found in subs. 5 of the same section that 'every religious denomination shall have the right to manage its own affairs, own, acquire and administer property, movable and immovable, and maintain institutions for religious or charitable purposes'. These statutes are what the designated authorities of the Roman Catholic Church in Ireland have deemed necessary for this seminary. Their existence or their terms cannot be blamed on the State as an unconstitutional imposition..."

It would thus appear that Article 44.2.5 gives religious denominations *carte blanche* in framing their constitutions and the other rules to be observed by their adherents. This would preclude any administrative supervision by the State of such matters, whether they involve doctrine or discipline, and none such exists. Since the State provides no funding for churches or religious groups, it has no concern with questions of ecclesiastical administration, such as the number of dioceses or the number of clergy assigned to a parish.

Any church or religious grouping is at liberty to organise economic enterprises, such as a publishing house, on the same terms as any group of private individuals. (This would normally be done by setting up a company for the purpose.) And there is no legal barrier to a church or religious group seeking permission to run a sound broadcasting service.[33] They are equally free to establish social welfare institutions, such as hospitals,[34] orphanages or charitable organisa-

---

[33] The Radio and Television Act 1988, which governs this matter, does not impose any such barrier. In regard to television, however, it provides for only one national service additional to those provided by Radio Telefis Éireann (a public corporation), and it is unlikely that any church, or combination of churches, could afford to fund this.

[34] But it would not be practicable to establish a denominational hospital unless State funds were forthcoming. However, the State is not legally obliged to provide such funds (*Governors of Barrington's Hospital v. Minister for Health* [1988] I.R.56) and it would hardly do so if there was already adequate hospital provision in the relevant area.

tions[35] (In practice hospitals and orphanages are run not by churches as collective bodies, but by entities within them, such as religious orders).

VII. Churches and Culture

1. Schools

Primary and secondary education in Ireland is organised predominantly on denominational lines – but extensively supported by State funding. Article 42.4 of the Constitution provides:

> "The State shall provide for free primary education and shall endeavour to supplement and give reasonable aid to private and corporate educational initiative, and, when the public good requires it, provide other educational facilities or institutions with due regard, however, for the rights of parents, especially in the matter of religious and moral formation."

Primary education is mainly provided in "national schools" – which despite their name, are not owned, run or fully financed by the State. With a few exceptions they are denominational in character. The State, through the Department of Education, will provide financial assistance to any group of parents (whether organised on a denominational basis or otherwise) who wish to establish such a school, provided that they can show that potential enrolments justify the establishment of the school.[36] It will be obvious, therefore, that the availability of schools affiliated to minority churches depends upon demographic factors. If these result in the local unavailability to certain parents of a school reflecting their religious convictions, the free school transport system may enable their children to attend one in an adjoining area; but this option would not assist those who belong to very small religious groups. The High Court has held that if otherwise adequate educational provision exists in a given area, a school voluntarily established by a group of parents will not automatically

---

35 Many such exist, most notably perhaps the (Roman Catholic) Society of St. Vincent de Paul.
36 See *John Coolahan*, Irish Education: History and Structure (Dublin 1981), Chapter 10.

become entitled to State funding: *O'Sheil & Ors v. Minister for Education*.[37]
In this connection it is appropriate to note Article 44.2. No. 4 of the Constitution, which provides:

> "Legislation providing State aid for schools shall not discriminate between schools under the management of different religious denominations, nor be such as to affect prejudicially the right of any child to attend a school receiving public money without attending religious instruction at that school."

For many years it was a requirement that periods of formal religious instruction should be indicated on national school timetables, and be fixed so as to facilitate the withdrawal of pupils whose parents disapproved of that instruction.[38] But a new curriculum introduced in 1970 stated that religious instruction should be integrated with that in secular subjects, and it appears that this has been acted upon. Plainly, these new arrangements make it more difficult for pupils to avoid religious instruction of which their parents or guardians disapprove. This matter was discussed by the Constitution Review Group in its *Report* of May 1996.[39] It concluded as follows:[40]

> "...the present reality of the denominational character of the school system does not accord with Article 44.2.4... either Article 44.2.4 should be changed [a possibility the Group rejected] or the school system must change to accommodate Article 44.2.4."

Save for the issue just mentioned, the constitutionality of the primary education arrangements described is unassailable. Pointing out that the State's constitutional obligation is not to provide, but to provide for, free primary education, the Supreme Court upheld them in *Crowley v. Ireland*.[41]
Religious instruction in national schools is normally given by those who teach in them. Unlike secular instruction it is not supervised by the Department of Education inspectors. Such supervision is the responsibility of the relevant church authorities.

---

37 [1999] 2 I.R. 321.
38 Rules for National Schools (Stationery Office, Dublin, 1965), Rule 69.
39 *Report of the Constitution Review Group* (Stationery Office, Dublin, 1996), p. 374-375, 385-387.
40 Ibid., p. 375.
41 [1980] I.R. 102.

2. Secondary Schools

Second – level education is provided in a variety of institutions, the majority of which have a religious ethos. The oldest group are the secondary schools, in their origin private voluntary institutions linked to the churches. Most belong to Roman Catholic religious orders, though some are affiliated to the Protestant churches and there is a Jewish secondary school in Dublin. All these schools benefit from State funding, ranging from administration and maintenance costs to the salaries of teachers and 80 % of the cost of new buildings.[42] The basic funding mechanism (apart from salaries and building costs) is direct capitation grants in case of Roman Catholic schools; in that of the Protestant schools the State pays a block grant to the inter-church Secondary Education Committee, which distributes it. Since there are many areas of the country where no Protestant secondary schools are available, so that students wishing to attend one may have no alternative but to become boarders, the Secondary Education Committee may use its funds to provide boarding grants.

Of their very nature such schools provide religious instruction, supervision of which is the responsibility of the authorities of the relevant church. They are required to make arrangements under which pupils whose parents disapprove of such instruction may withdraw from it.[43] The same holds for the institutions of more recent vintage, the comprehensive schools and community schools. These are the product of demographic and other social trends – including a decrease in the numbers of religious, leading to the closure of schools – which meant that there were areas of the country where post-primary education was in jeopardy. The comprehensive schools are fully-funded – as to building and running costs and salaries – by the State, but they are nonetheless essentially denominational in character. The same is true for the community schools, in which the State funds the running costs and salaries, and subject to a local contribution, the greater part of the building costs[44].

The State is not constitutionally obliged to fund second-level education, but it is permissible for it to do so. Nor do existing arrangements violate Article 44.2. No. 2's non-endowment of religion principle, for Article 44.2. No. 4, as we have seen, specifically contemplates State aid to denominational schools. Thus the arrangements

---

42 *J. Coolahan*, op.cit., No. 36 supra, chapter 12.
43 Ibid., p. 159.
44 Ibid., p. 218-220; see also *Louis O'Flaherty*, Management and Control in Irish Education: The Post-Primary Experience (Dublin 1992), Chapter 3.

described above were upheld by the Supreme Court in *Campaign to Separate Church and State* v. *Minister for Education*.[45]

3. Culture

The Irish universities are open to those of any faith or none. Nor could religious *status* – such as being a minister, priest or nun – be invoked to refuse a person entry to a course. And scholarships or other public subventions must be available to church personnel on the same conditions as to any other students; the non-discrimination guarantee of Article 44.2. No. 3 of the Constitution would rule out any other arrangement.

Theology is taught at university level only at the National University of Ireland, Maynooth[46] and the University of Dublin. Students of any denomination – or none – would be eligible to take these courses.

Several statutory bodies impinge upon the field of culture; these include the Radio Telefis Eireann Authority,[47] the Broadcasting Commission of Ireland,[48] the Censorship of Publications Board[49] and the Arts Council.[50] No church or religious group is guaranteed representation on any such body, thought it would be usual to appoint at least one member of a minority church.

---

45 [1998] 3 I.R. 321.
46 This institution, founded under statute as a seminary – St Patrick's College – in 1795, became a constituent college of the National University of Ireland under the Universities Act 1997. On the same campus are the seminary and the Pontifical university. The arrangements for the government of the NUI college – alone – are laid down in the 1997 Act.
47 Established under the Broadcasting Authority Act 1960, as amended, to administer the publicly funded radio and television service. It consists of not less than seven and not more than nine members, who are appointed by the Government for a five year term.
48 Originally called the Independent Radio and Television Commission – and charged with licensing commercial broadcasters – it was re-named the Broadcasting Commission of Ireland under the Broadcasting Act 2001, which also expands its role. It consists of 7-9 members, appointed by the Government for a five year term.
49 Established under the Censorship of Publications Act 1946. There are five members, who are appointed by the Minister for Justice. There is also an Appeal Board, whose members are likewise appointed by the Minister.
50 Constituted under the Arts Act 2003, it consists of a chairperson and twelve members, appointed by the Minister for Arts, Sport and Tourism.

4. Religion in the Mass Media

Irish newspapers and magazines have a virtually unfettered discretion with regard to coverage of religious matters, and churches and religious groups are free to publish their own material. The only limitations are those of the general law, specifically that on contempt of court and defamation.[51]

The treatment of the electronic media is slightly different. Originally, broadcasting organisations, whether publicly or privately funded, were forbidden to transmit advertisements directed to any religious end.[52] The constitutionality of this prohibition was upheld by the Supreme Court in *Murphy* v. *Independent Radio and Television Commission*.[53] And the European Court of Human Rights found it compatible with the Convention in *Murphy* v. *Ireland* (10 July 2003). The original ban has now been relaxed somewhat under section 65 of the Broadcasting Act 2001, so as – for example – to permit the broadcasting of a notice that a particular religious ceremony or event will take place. The Minister for Communications has announced a review of the matter.[54]

On the other hand, broadcasting organisations are free to broadcast religious services and programmes of religious significance, and they do so.

VIII. Labour Law within the Churches

Though clear modern authority on the point is lacking, it seems probable that persons in Holy Orders or under religious vows do not have a contractual relationship with their ecclesiastical superiors.[55] If this is correct they would not fall within legislation regulating the employment relationship, for as a rule that legislation confers rights only on "employees" – defined as persons who work under a contract of employment.[56]

---

51 As to which see Casey, op. cit., No. 8 supra, Chapter 15.
52 Broadcasting Authority Act 1960, section 20 (4): Radio and Television Act 1968, section 10 (3).
53 [1999] 1 I.R. 12.
54 *The Irish Times*, 3 March 2003.
55 *Wright v. Day* [1895] 2 I.R. 337. See also *O'Dea v. O'Briain* [1992] I.L.R.M. 364.
56 E.g. the Employment Equality Act 1977 and the Unfair Dismissals Act 1977.

In contrast, lay persons employed by a church or religious group *will* have a contractual relationship with their employer, and will consequently benefit under the legislation referred to. Thus a lay teacher employed by a religious order is entitled to the protection of the Unfair Dismissals Act 1977. But in the *Employment Equality Bill* case[57] the Supreme Court ruled that legislation permitting e.g. denominationally sponsored schools or hospitals to discriminate on religious grounds in hiring and firing was compatible with the Constitution. Such a body may therefore, in the interests of the religious ethos of the institution, require from its employees standards of behaviour that no lay employer could demand.

Collective bargaining between trade unions and the churches *as such* does not exist, despite the significant involvement of the latter in education and in hospitals. The salary levels, etc. of teachers in denominational schools in receipt of public funds are regulated by collective agreements negotiated between the Department of Education and the teachers' unions. Those employed in hospitals (of whatever kind) are covered by collective agreements between the Department of Health and the various unions. But the terms and conditions of employment of teachers employed in denominational schools which receive no State funding would be fixed by agreement between their employers (usually religious orders) and the relevant union.

Churches and religious groups are obliged to find their own funds for such things as the provision and maintenance of places of worship and the financial support of pastors. The State does not provide any subventions, or contributions towards such costs, and it could not do so. The constitutional guarantee against endowment of religion, as interpreted by the Supreme Court,[58] would preclude this.

Salaries paid to ministers, nuns, priests, etc. – from whatever source – are liable to income tax: *Donlan v. K*.[59] But income received by a church, religious order or religious group from the product of a gift or a bequest which qualifies as "charitable" is exempt from taxation. The gift or bequest so qualifying will not attract inheritance taxes.[60]

Under section 63 of the Poor Relief (Ireland) Act 1838 exemption from rates (local taxes) is given to

---

57 [1997] 2 I.R. 321.
58 *Campaign to Separate Church and State* v. *Minister for Education* [1998] 3 I.R. 321
59 [1944] I.R. 470.
60 The law of charities (or charitable trusts) is a very complex topic. See *James C. Brady*, Religion and the Law of Charities in Ireland (Belfast 1976).

"...any church, chapel or other building exclusively dedicated to religious worship..."

This is clearly comprehensive enough to cover anything from an Anglican or Roman Catholic cathedral to a synagogue, by way of a mosque. A similar exemption is given to hospitals,[61] but secondary schools are subject to a different, and very complex, regime.[62]

IX. Religious Assistance in Public Institutions

Given the structure of the Irish educational system, the question of providing religious assistance – e.g. chaplains – could scarcely arise. But the deeds of trust under which community schools are governed requires the board of management to appoint a chaplain. This person is to be employed outside the normal teacher quota, to receive a salary equivalent to that of a teacher, to be a member of the full-time staff and to be "...nominated by the competent religious authority"[63]. The constitutional validity of these arrangements has been upheld by the Supreme Court.[64]
Chaplains are appointed to the Defence Forces and to prisons, and the perssons so appointed are paid a whole or part-time salary out of public funds. This arrangement, in those cases, would seem to be proof against a constitutional challenge based on the non-endowment principle of Article 44.2.2. For it may be argued that no other arrangement can guarantee to service personnel, or prisoners, the full and free practice of religion which it is the main purpose of Article 44 to secure.

---

61 For an extended discussion of section 63 see *Keane*, op. cit., No. 31 supra p. 289.
62 Under the Local Government (Financial Provisions) Act 1978.
63 Defined to mean "...in relation to the Roman Catholic Church or the Church of Ireland, the Ordinary and in any other case the person or persons who according to the rules or the constitution of the Church or Faith concerned is or are for the time being the religious superior of the members of that church or Faith living in the area in which the school is situated."
64 *Campaign to Separate Church and State* v. *Minister for Education* [1998] 3 I.R. 321.

X. Criminal Law and Religion

Article 40.6.1 of the Constitution, which guarantees freedom of expression, concludes as follows:

> The publication or utterance of blasphemous...matter is an offence which shall be punishable in accordance with the law.

But the Supreme Court's decision in *Corway* v. *Independent Newspapers (Ireland) Ltd.*[65] makes it virtually impossible to prosecute blasphemy cases. The plaintiff claimed that the defendant company had published a blasphemous libel, contrary to section 13 (1) of the Defamation Act 1961, and under section 8 of the Act he sought the High Court's leave to commence a prosecution against it. The High Court refused leave and the Supreme Court confirmed this ruling on appeal. Barrington J., for the Supreme Court, noted that there was no constitutional or legislative definition of blasphemy. The common law definition – which presupposed an established church – could hardly apply in modern Ireland. Thus it was impossible to say what the offence of blasphemy consisted of, and the court could not authorise the institution of proceedings against the defendant.[66]

The Prohibition of Incitement to Hatred Act 1989 makes it an offence to publish, distribute or display material which is "threatening, abusive or insulting" *and* intended, or likely, to stir up hatred. This would cover material intended or likely to stir up hatred against a group of persons on account of their religion.

XI. Legal Status of Clergy

Any legislation or administrative arrangement which discriminates against ministers, priests, etc., would not survive constitutional scrutiny. So much is clear from the Supreme Court's decision in *Mulloy* v. *Minister for Education.*[67] In that case the plaintiff challenged the validity of regulations made by the Minister in relation to time spent

---

65 [1999] 4 I.R. 484.
66 See further *James Casey*, "Church and State in Ireland in 1999", *European Journal for Church and State Research*, vol. 7 (2000), p. 93-95.
67 [1975] I.R. 88.

teaching in certain developing countries. Under these, lay teachers – alone – could count such service for salary increment and pension purposes when they returned to Ireland. Father *Mulloy*, who was otherwise amply qualified under the scheme, argued that the exclusion of religious personnel violated Article 44.2 No. 3 of the Constitution. The Supreme Court ruled in his favour, holding that the scheme created a distinction on the ground of religious status by enabling a person who was not a religious to obtain a greater financial reward for the same work than one who was.

Ministers, priests, nuns and other religious personnel are entitled to seek election to, and if elected to take their seats in, either House of the Oireachtas – though no such person has ever been elected. Disqualification for election to, or from membership of, Dáil Éireann[68] is the subject-matter of section 41 of the Electoral Act 1992, which makes no reference whatever to religious status.

In *Mulloy* v. *Minister for Education, supra,* the Supreme Court said that a distinction between religious personnel and others would be valid where it was necessary to guarantee the full and free practice of religion. This would presumably validate the provisions of the Juries Act 1976 giving a right to be excused from jury service, upon application, to:

> "A person in Holy Orders.
> A regular minister of any religious denomination or community.
> Vowed members of any religious order living in a monastery, convent or other religious community."

And it would also appear to confirm those judicial decisions which recognise a special sacerdotal privilege in the law of evidence.[69]

Since compulsory military service has never existed in Ireland, the question of exempting religious personnel therefrom has never arisen.

---

[68] And, by extension to Seanad Éireann, since Article 18.2 of the Constitution provides: "A person to be eligible for membership of Seanad Éireann must be eligible to become a member of the Dáil Éireann."

[69] Such as freedom from compulsion to testify about confidential communications – *Cook* v. *Carroll* [1945] I.R. 515: *E.R.* v. *J.R.* [1981] I.L.R.M. 125, both decisions of the High Court.

XII. Matrimonial and Family Law

While civil marriage has been available in Ireland since 1844[70] it is not compulsory. Most marriages are solemnised according to religious rites, and a complex set of legal arrangements gives such marriages civil law efficacy provided that the relevant conditions are fulfilled. These conditions may not necessarily be those of the relevant church's internal law; thus the civil law validity of a Roman Catholic marriage does not depend upon compliance with the rules of canon law regarding the presence of witnesses.[71] Though all marriages – whether by civil ceremony or religious rites – must be registered, failure to register does not affect the validity of the marriage.[72]

It appears that only the Roman Catholic Church in Ireland has a system of tribunals with jurisdiction in matrimonial matters. No decree of any such tribunal could have civil legal effect; the judicial power of the State is bestowed only upon the courts established under the Constitution.[73] There is no provision for recognition of such decrees, e.g. by registration, and it must be doubted whether any such provision would be compatible with the Constitution, in particular with Article 44.2. No. 3.

There is no reported case in which religious factors have grounded a civil decree of nullity or of judicial separation or divorce. It would not appear that failure to fulfil a confessional obligation to go through a religious ceremony of marriage could invalidate a marriage valid at common law or under statute. It is possible, however, that failure to bring up the children of a marriage in an agreed faith might found an application for a judicial separation. Under section 2 of the Judicial Separation and Family Law Reform Act 1989, one ground for granting such a decree is that

> "...the respondent has behaved in such a way that the applicant cannot reasonably be expected to live with the respondent."

Under Irish law a child's religious upbringing is a matter for joint determination by the parents. An agreement on this issue, whether

---

70 Marriages (Ireland) Act 1844.
71 See further *James Casey*, "Religious Marriage and its Civil Effectiveness in Ireland" in European Consortium for Church – State Research, Marriage and Religion in Europe (Milan 1993), p. 112-115.
72 Ibid., 116.
73 See further *J. Casey*, op. cit., No. 8 supra, p. 194.

express or implied, binds both parties and may not be unilaterally revoked by either.[74]

XIII. Sites of Religious Significance

A recent High Court decision – *Tara Prospecting Ltd.* v. *Minister for Energy*[75] – holds that religious factors may properly influence certain administrative decisions in the environmental field. In that case the plaintiff company had for some years been engaged in mineral exploration in Co. Mayo, including part of the mountain known as Croagh Patrick. This was done on foot of a series of prospecting licences issued under statutory authority by the defendant. By 1990, the company – which had spent some £1.8 million on the exploration work – was concentrating on gold prospecting, and this had become a matter of public knowledge and public concern. For the mountain has been associated with St. Patrick – Ireland's national saint – since the early middle ages, and it has long been a place of pilgrimage for individuals and groups. In May 1990 the defendant Minister refused to renew the company's prospecting licence insofar as it related to Croagh Patrick. The company argued that this decision was invalid, since it was confessedly based on religious, cultural and heritage grounds. Under the relevant legislation, it contended, the Minister was not entitled to have regard to such matters.

Costello J. dismissed the plaintiff company's claim. He pointed out that under the relevant Act the Minister was entitled to have regard to "... the public interest." This concept was wide enough to enable him to consider whether a proposed operation would be offensive to many people on religious grounds. The judgment continues:[76]

> "He should have regard to the Constitution when exercising his ministerial discretion. Its preamble contains a clear affirmation that the Irish are a religious people and Article 1 provides that the Irish nation will develop its political, economic and cultural life in accordance with its own genius and traditions. If, therefore, a Minister in the exercise of a statutory power is required to have regard to the public interest it seems to me he is entitled to bear in mind what the Constitution says about the Irish nation

---

74 Re *Tilson* [1951] I.R. I: Re *May* [1959] I.R. 74.
75 1993] I.L.R.M. 771.
76 At 781.

and the Irish people. It would follow that it would not be *ultra vires* for him to prohibit activities which he concluded were offensive on religious grounds to many members of the Irish public. I must hold therefore that the Minister's decision was not an *ultra vires* one."

XIV. Bibliography

James Casey, Constitutional Law in Ireland, 3rd ed., Dublin 2000, Chapter 19.

Desmond Clarke, Church and State: Essays in Political Philosophy, Cork 1985.

Michael Forde, Constitutional Law of Ireland, Cork/Dublin 1987, Chapter XIX.

G.W. Hogan, "Law and Religion: Church-State Relations in Ireland from Independence to the Present Day", 1987, XXXV America Journal of Comparative Law 47-96.

J.M. Kelly, the Irish Constitution, 3rd ed. By *G. Hogan and G. Whyte*, Dublin 1994, p. 1092-1116.

G. Whyte, "Education and the Constitution", in: *Dermot A. Lane* (ed.), Religion, Education and the Constitution Dublin 1992, p. 84-117.

J.H. Whyte, Church and State in Modern Ireland 1923-1979, Dublin 1980.

Silvio Ferrari
State and Church in Italy

I. Social Facts

Italy is a predominantly Catholic country, though it is not easy to give even an approximate estimate of the number of Italians practising this faith. Apart from the problem of the reliability of the relevant statistical data, the available figures differ substantially. More than 90 % of the pupils at State schools take part in Catholic religious education classes, whereas less than 40 % of taxpayers give that part of income tax (imposta sulle persone fisiche, IRPEF) intended for the denominations or State social welfare institutions to the Church. Seventy percent of all religious marriages take place according to Catholic rites, but in spite of the high percentage of citizens who have received Catholic baptism, less than 30 % regularly take part in Sunday mass.
In addition, the Papacy resides in Italy, which gives the Catholic Church great influence over political and social events in the country regardless of the statistical figures on the religious beliefs of Italians. Amongst the other denominations, Muslims now form a larger group than Jehovah's Witnesses, because of the massive stream of immigrants from North African countries. The presence of Jews and Valdensians, though they have a long tradition, is numerically less significant; the spread of the "new religious movements" (an inappropriate expression which has however become common) is similar to that in other Western European countries.

II. Historical Background

The unification of Italy (1860-70) caused a serious crisis in the relationship between the Catholic Church and the new State. The liberal governments of Cavour and his successors began a process of secularisation of institutions and public life, for example the introduction of obligatory civil marriage in 1865; restriction of Catholic religious education in State schools, 1877; reform of the penal laws for the protection of religion, 1889; State control of the welfare and charitable institutions, 1890. These changes were opposed by the Church hierarchy, which was further concerned by measures aiming to diminish the economic power of the Church, especially by way of abolishing certain Church entities and confiscating their property, between 1866 and 1867. The fact that the unification of Italy was attained by destroying the secular power of the Popes, through the capture of Rome in September 1870, gave particular strength to the hostility felt by many Catholics towards the Kingdom of Italy, which was accused of trying to rob the Pope and the Church of their remaining liberty. The predominantly moderate policy of the Italian Government, particularly after the promulgation of the Law of Guarantees (*legge delle Guarentigie*) in 1871, gradually reduced the tensions in Church-State relations, which were further improved by the more flexible attitudes of Pope Leo XIII (1878-1903) and of Giovanni Giolitti, who led Italian politics in the first fifteen years of the twentieth century. However, the outbreak of World War I prevented this rapprochement having any concrete effects. Following the war, the Fascist party, which was in power from 1922 until the end of the Second World War, initiated a policy of conciliation towards the Catholic Church, culminating in the signing of the Lateran Treaties in 1929. These resolved the 'Roman question' (the conflict between the Pope and the Italian State about sovereignty on Rome) by creating the Vatican State. The Treaties also restored some of the Church's privileges – in matrimonial and economic matters and in the field of religious education in State schools – which it had lost during the liberal period.

The promulgation of the Republican Constitution in 1948 formed the basis for the revision of those provisions of the Lateran Concordat which were least compatible with the principles of freedom and equality in religious matters enshrined in the Constitution. However, for a number of national and international reasons, the reform of Italian ecclesiastical law could not be initiated until the 1980s, after a significant process of secularisation (the most important results of which – in the field of legislation – were the introduction of divorce in 1970 and the legalisation of abortion in 1978) had profoundly changed Italian society.

III. Legal Sources

The fundamental provisions of Italian ecclesiastical law are contained in the Constitution and aim, on the one hand, at safeguarding the liberty and equality of the individual in religious matters and, on the other, at guaranteeing a system of co-operation between the State and the religious denominations.
Article 19 of the Constitution declares that "every man has the right to freely profess his faith in every possible form, alone or in association with others, to promote it and exercise its worship in public or in private, provided that the rites involved do not offend common decency." Article 3(1) for its part affirms that "all citizens have the same social dignity and are equal before the law, regardless of their sex, race, language, religion, political opinions or of their personal or social circumstances".
As has already been mentioned, the Italian system of ecclesiastical law is bipartite. On the one hand it is aimed at guaranteeing everybody (including non-citizens) religious freedom and equality: the predominant interpretation of the term "religion" supports the extension of the guarantees of Articles 3 and 19 to the profession of atheist or agnostic beliefs. From the point of view of individual rights to religious freedom and equality, the Italian legal order appears to be in step with the main provisions of international law in this area and with the principles contained in most Constitutions of the other Western countries.
The introduction of special rules allowing conscientious objection to military service (1972) and – limited to medical employees – to participation in abortions (1978) has contributed towards solving some important problems of religious freedom. Others, however, remain unsolved. Here the main problems are those caused by religious groups which have appeared in Italy only relatively recently. Particular cases that can be called to mind here are those of the refusal of medical treatment (the prevailing jurisprudence acknowledges the possibility of refusing any medical treatment which is not obligatory by the law, insofar as such a refusal – for instance of a blood transfusion – does not endanger the life of another person) as well as those of the refusal to work on religious holidays (this right is granted only to the adherents of denominations which have come to an agreement with the Italian State; others, including Muslims, do not enjoy the right).

In addition to these provisions concerning individual rights, there are several provisions concerning the legal position of the denominations. Article 8(1) affirms that "all denominations are equally free before the law." This article further contains provisions concerning the minority denominations: "The non-Catholic denominations have the right to organise themselves according to their own statutes insofar as they are not in conflict with Italian law. Their relations with the State are ruled by laws on the basis of agreements with the relevant representatives". A special ruling however applies to the Catholic Church according to Article 7: "The State and the Catholic Church are, each according to its own order, independent and sovereign. Their relations are ruled by the Lateran Treaties. Amendments to these treaties which are agreed by both sides do not have to follow the procedure prescribed for constitutional amendments." Finally, Article 20, which is also directed at all the denominations, establishes that "the ecclesiastical character or the purpose of religion or worship of an association or institution may not justify particular legislative restrictions or tax burdens on its foundation, legal capacity or any form of activity."

Under Article 7, the Agreement of Villa Madama (*Accordo di Villa Madama*) was concluded between the State and the Catholic Church in 1984, replacing the Lateran Concordat of 1929. The Agreement was followed by a series of special agreements, the most important of which are concerned with the regulation of Church entities and property (1984), Catholic religious education in State schools (1985), Church holidays (1985), protection of cultural and religious heritage (1996), and pastoral care in the police force (1999). Under Article 8(3), agreements (*intese*) were reached between the Italian State and the *Tavola Valdese* (Valdensians) (1984), the Christian Churches of the Seventh-Day Adventists (1986), the *Assemblee di Dio* ("Assemblies of God", a Pentecostal Church) (1986), the Union of Jewish Communities (1987), the Christian Evangelical-Baptist Union (1993) and the Lutheran Church (1993). Two further agreements, with the Christian Congregation of Jehovah's Witnesses and the Buddhist Union, were signed in 2000 but have not yet been approved by Parliament.

The remaining denominations are still governed by the Law No. 1159 of 24 June 1929. This law, because of the historical background to its enactment, contains several provisions which appear to be incompatible with the principles of the Constitution; however, a proposal for its reform which was approved by the Council of Ministers in 1990 has not so far been submitted to Parliament for approval.

The discussion becomes more complex when one passes from the rights of individuals to the legal classification of churches. In this field the system of concordats and agreements introduces elements of differentiation among the denominations. They are not excluded by Article 8(1) which refers to 'equal freedom', not equality, but in some cases they may have an effect on the legal position of individuals; examples may be found in the later sections of this chapter on the financing of the denominations and religious education in State schools. For this reason, the correct relationship between liberty (i.e. the possibility of a special regulation for each denomination) and equality (i.e. the necessity of a common set of rights and duties for all) is a central problem of Italian ecclesiastical law in its present stage of development.

Italian ecclesiastical law is a three-tier system. The most prominent position is held by the Catholic Church, which, because of the number of its adherents and its special significance in Italian history, enjoys a preferential position secured by the Agreement of Villa Madama and numerous other regulations. An intermediate position is held by those denominations which have come to an agreement with the State. The groups concerned here are those which have existed in Italy for a long time (i.e. the Valdensians, Jews and Protestants) or more recent groups which however have no characteristics incompatible with Italian law. By these separate agreements they are guaranteed a position equivalent, if not equal, to that of the Catholic Church. In the lowest tier are denominations – some of them with a significant number of adherents, such as Muslims – which have only relatively recently settled in Italy and which are, above all, characterised by doctrines and practices which are, according to the predominant interpretation, in more or less open conflict with public order; this includes some of the highly controversial "new religious movements", such as the Scientology Church. These groups are regulated by the Law No. 1159 of 1929 and/or the general laws on associations, and are excluded from some important privileges (for instance with respect to financing, religious education and pastoral care) which have – at least up to the present day – been granted only on the basis of a concordat or agreement.

Roughly speaking, this three-tier system is based on Italian history and culture: however this does not mean it should not be examined from other angles.

The first point concerns the extent of the system of treaties and agreements which was expanded to include matters which could have been dealt with by State law and produced more satisfactory results with respect to the principle of equality. For instance, in the field of the financing of denominations, the present system excludes Muslims and Jehovah's Witnesses (which form, numerically, the second and third largest religious communities in Italy), who without an agreement can neither participate in the distribution of the 0.8 % IRPEF nor deduct sums donated to their religious community from their taxable income. A State law opening these channels of funding to all denominations recognised as such by Italian law would show more respect for the "equal freedom" guaranteed by Article 8 of the Constitution.

A similar criticism applies to other areas of Italian ecclesiastical law. There is no law common to all religious communities concerning problems that could be solved uniformly (besides financing, this applies to pastoral care in public institutions, access to schools etc.). Were that to be in place, it would leave only the regulation of issues – possibly in differing fashion – of special interest to separate denominations to the treaties and agreements. These issues include, for example, the refusal of blood transfusions for Jehovah's Witnesses, the ritual slaughter of animals for the Jews, and Sabbath rest for Jews and Adventists.

Another aspect of Italian ecclesiastical law which attracts criticism concerns the excessive amount of discretion which the public powers possess in deciding whether to accept or reject the proposal of a denomination to enter into negotiations for an agreement. Certainly a margin of flexibility in dealing with applications, and especially as to their contents, seems sensible; however, decision-making by public bodies which is not based on objective criteria (number of adherents, duration of their presence in Italy or other countries, type of organisation, etc.) facilitates abuse.

IV. The Legal Status of the Religious Communities

Initially it must be emphasised that any group with religious aims may be founded without the necessity of any authorisation or prior registration and may operate within the Italian legal system. The only limits are set by considerations of public order and common decency. For these purposes the denominations (or, more precisely, their legal entities) may choose between the various types of legal capacity prescribed by Italian law.

First of all, they may constitute themselves as non-recognised associations (*associazione non riconosciuta*) under Articles 36-38 of the Civil Code. This is the most simple model which is also made use of by political parties and trades unions. In this way, the denomination attains legal capacity (including independence in property matters and the ability to receive donations, take legal action, etc.) with complete freedom, and their constitutive act or statute does not have to be submitted to any form of State control. More precise and binding rules apply to recognised associations (*associazioni riconosciute*) under Articles 14-35 of the Civil Code and Dpr. 10 February 2000, No. 361. They obtain legal personality through registration with the Prefecture, provided they fulfil a socially useful purpose and have sufficient economic means.

Civil law legal capacity may also be obtained under Article 16 of the *Disposizioni sulle legge in generale* (the provisions on the law in general), which grants to foreign legal entities the rights of Italian legal entities on terms of reciprocity, and furthermore according to Article 2 of the Treaty of Friendship, Commerce and Shipping with the United States, concluded in 1948. About thirty denominations (or denominational legal entities) have in this way applied for and obtained legal capacity, attracted by the possibility of tax advantages for denominational bodies. Following some variations in interpretation which resulted in the loss of these privileges, they have now been granted a legal status similar to that of recognised associations.

Up to now this chapter has considered only the possibility of obtaining legal capacity in the forms provided by general law for all groups independently of their religious or other aims. For the religious groups however there is a further possibility of which the most important minority denominations (amongst them Muslims, Mormons, and Jehovah's Witnesses have made use: that is, to obtain legal capacity for their organisations on the basis of a law conceived especially for groups with religious aims, Law No. 1159 of 1929, which governs the exercise of the religions registered in Italy. This Law, by establishing the equal treatment of religious aims with those of welfare and education, grants important tax privileges thus extending the advantages instituted for the associations of the latter type to the former. On the other hand, this law subjects groups with religious aims to the control of the government and gives the State authorities the right to replace the administrative bodies of the associations by a State commissioner and to annul their decisions. But in spite of all the advantages and disadvantages linked with this provision, the acknowledgement of legal capacity under Law No. 1159 of 1929 has

great significance, because it confirms the religious nature of the recognised group. It forms the basic precondition (in fact, if not in law) for an application for an agreement with the Italian State according to Article 8(3).
The six denominations which have come to an agreement with the Italian State are no longer subject to Law No. 1159 of 1929, which has been replaced in their cases by the far more favourable provisions contained in their separate agreements. However, the legal capacity obtained on the basis of this law is maintained by the six denominations. The Jewish communities and their Union, on the other hand, were never subject to the law named above. They obtained legal personality by Law No. 1731 of 1930, created especially for them, which regulated their activity in detail. The law was abrogated when the agreements were concluded, but the communities and their Union have maintained the legal capacity granted them on the basis of this law. Parallel provisions apply to the *Tavola Valdese* and the consistories of the churches in the Vaudois Valleys, which have – even after the completion of the agreements – kept the legal capacity which they had obtained not on the basis of legal provisions, but because of "*antico possesso di stato*" (long-standing possession of status), which means they had legal capacity even before the foundation of the State of Italy.
A special comment must be made about the Catholic Church which has public law legal capacity, even if it is in no way comparable to the bodies which form part of the State organisation. If anything, it may be compared with foreign States which are public law subjects in Italian law.
As has been said, only the bodies of *denominations* can obtain legal capacity according to Law No. 1159 of 1929, and only *denominations* can (according to Article 8 of the Constitution) conclude agreements with the State. So there is the problem of defining the term "denomination", a problem which has become significant in Italy recently with the spread of the "new religious movements". As there is a complete absence of statutory definition, some commentators are of the opinion that the State is neither able nor competent to determine what a denomination is. From this the conclusion is drawn that the question must be left to the self-assessment of the adherents of those groups which are aiming to be recognised as denominations. If the adherents are of the opinion that they form a denomination, then the State authorities are bound to accept this assessment. Some more recent decisions of the Constitutional Court (and in particular Decision No. 467 of November 1992) appear however to be moving

in another direction in insisting that the term "denomination" must have an objective and not a subjective basis. From this point of view another group of writers has tried to identify characteristics which must be recognisable in every group which aims to be classed as a denomination. Such characteristics are: the belief in a transcendental reality (not necessarily God) which is capable of giving answers to fundamental questions as to the existence of humans and things; is able to furnish a moral code, and to create an existential interdependence of the faithful manifesting itself (amongst other things) in the form of worship; and the existence of a structure, however minimal. Besides the three religions of Abrahamitic derivation, many religions of oriental origin fit this paradigm, while para-psychological, spiritualist and occult groups would be excluded. Some of the "new religious movements", such as the Scientology Church, are borderline cases, as is testified by the contradictory decisions of the courts on this matter.

V. The Right of Self-Determination

In the same way as Article 7(1) of the Constitution which recognises the sovereignty and independence of the Catholic Church in its own order, Article 8(2) which grants all other denominations the right to organise themselves according to their own statutes, insofar as they are not in conflict with Italian law, gives the denominations a guarantee of a high degree of internal autonomy. They are free to organise themselves in the manner they regard as being opportune, and they are protected from any assertion of jurisdiction by the State.
But, even more strongly than in the provisions just quoted, the autonomy of religious denominations is guaranteed by the final sections of Articles 7 and 8 respectively. These provide that the State may deal with the legal organisation of a denomination only by way of an agreement, i.e. under the condition of reaching an understanding with that denomination. The two sections also provide that, once this arrangement has been arrived at, whether it is described as an agreement or a concordat, any amendment may be made only on the basis of an arrangement between State and denomination. Amendments may not be made on the unilateral initiative of the State, except, of course, that it is possible to amend Articles 7 and 8 by the procedure for constitutional amendments. In this way the Catholic

Church and the six denominations which have reached an agreement with the State have the security that the legal status that they have at present will not be altered *in peius* against their will. This is a further factor which differentiates between these denominations and the others which do not benefit from a similar guarantee.

Finally it must be noted that in contrast to other countries the institutions (hospitals, schools, etc.) dependent on the Catholic Church and other denominations have no special autonomy; some exceptions to this rule are discussed below in section VI.

VI. Churches and Culture

In Italy there are no theological faculties in the State universities. There are no particular problems regarding the right of denominations to establish schools and other educational institutions of every level and type: this is in fact granted to all private law persons by Article 33 of the Constitution; the provisions of the Agreement of Villa Madama and some of the agreements with other denominations merely repeat and apply this rule. For a long time private schools (including those run by a religious denomination) received no financial support from the State, but in 2000 a new law established that families who send their children to private schools recognised by the State are entitled to a partial refund of their fees.

In the field of education, discussion has concentrated mainly on the topic of religious education in State schools. On this subject there is a clear difference between the provisions applying to the Catholic Church on one hand and the other denominations on the other. The Agreement of Villa Madama stipulates that two hours of religious education will be taught in play school and primary school, and one hour at senior school per week; no religious education is provided for at university. The State bears the total financial burden of Catholic religious education.

Every year at enrolment the pupils – or, up to the end of intermediate school, which is usually completed at the age of 13, their parents – must declare whether or not they intend to take part in Catholic religious education classes. If they decline, the pupils may concentrate on other subjects during this period or may leave the school grounds; this right was granted the pupils alter lengthy conflict by decision No. 13 of the Constitutional Court in 1991.

The teachers of religious education are chosen by the diocesan bishop from a list of people with certain certificates of training which are proof of their qualification in theology and Church disciplines, and have succeeded in a national competition. Additionally they must be recognised by the Church authority in the person of the diocesan bishop, who provides written confirmation they are suitable to teach religious education. If this recognition is withdrawn, the teacher must cease to teach Catholic religion and he or she will be assigned to the teaching of a different subject (if qualified to do so) or will be given a different job in the public sector.

The curricula for Catholic religious education are arranged by agreement between the Minister for Public Education and the Chairman of the Italian Conference of Bishops for each type of school. The school books must be furnished with the *nihil obstat* of the Conference of Bishops and the bishop of the diocese in which the school where the books will be used is located.

The six denominations which have reached an agreement with the Italian State may send teachers of their own to the State schools if pupils, their parents, or the school bodies apply for classes in a certain religion (e.g. Judaism) or the study of "the phenomenon of religion and its implications" in general (as Article 10 of the agreement with the Tavola Valdese is worded). The arrangement of these classes is agreed by the competent school authority and the representatives of the denomination, while the financial burden is borne by the denomination. Denominations without an agreement do not have the right to send representatives of their own to State schools.

The agreements between some of the minority denominations and the Italian State also contain provisions of general importance excluding forms of "diffuse" religious education which takes place under cover of other subjects, and prohibiting pupils being forced to participate in religious acts or acts of worship. This has led to problems as to the compatibility of some practices traditionally widespread in State schools with these provisions, for instance the blessing of the school-rooms (which is done once a year by a member of the Catholic clergy), the participation of the pupils in religious ceremonies during school hours (usually mass celebrated according to the Catholic rites) and meetings of the pupils with the diocesan bishop on the occasion of a pastoral visit. A decree of the Ministry of Public Education (1992) granted the collegial bodies of the schools the right to decide on such activities, provided that the participation of pupils is voluntary, but the courts have subsequently reaffirmed that these activities are illegal.

The regulation of religious education contained in the Agreement of Villa Madama and the agreements has been the cause of numerous conflicts. However, since the intervention of the Constitutional Court, the system seems to have gained an equilibrium of its own. Some doubts remain as to some features of the new legal provisions: the obligation of the pupils to declare whether or not they wish to take part in Catholic religious education (with reference to the protection of confidentiality as to the denomination chosen); the fact that the State is charged with the financial burden of Catholic religious education but not that of the other denominations (in some cases it is the denominations themselves which reject the possibility of State financial support) and the limitation of religious education classes provided in response to the requests of pupils to the denominations which have concluded an agreement. These problems of religious education – some of which have already been discussed above – are, however, general problems which really depend on the fundamental decisions that are the basis of the whole reform of Italian ecclesiastical law, reappearing in all parts of the system, albeit in other forms. Finally it must be noted that special provisions in the Agreement of Villa Madama (Article 10, which reappears in the agreements with some of the other confessions), state that the seminaries and educational institutions in Church disciplines are free from any kind of State interference and are solely under the authority of the Church. This same article stipulates that the appointment of professors at the Catholic University of the Sacred Heart (*Università Cattolica del Sacro Cuore*) is subject to the consent of the Church authorities so far as the religious aspects are concerned.

VII. Labour Law within the Churches

According to the general rules of labour law the religious beliefs of the individual may not give rise to any kind of discrimination, that is that they are irrelevant to employment, the giving of notice, professional advancement, and so on. A partial exception to this rule is employment in organisations with a clearly religious character (e.g. a hospital or school run by a religious order). They are so-called organisations of a special tendency, as are political parties, trade unions, etc., and thus are subject to special rules. These aim to ensure that the religious purposes of the organisation are respected by all its employees. In particular, religious organisations can refuse to employ a person on religious grounds and give notice to an employee who professes an ideology or demonstrates behaviour that is in conflict with the religious orientation of the organisation; for example, a teacher at a Catholic school who voices doubts on fundamental principles of Catholic doctrine or contracts a civil law marriage. This trend has been recently confirmed by the decree of 9 July 2003, No. 216, enforcing the EU directive 2000/78/CE in Italy.

Special problems have surfaced in the case of members of religious orders working both within their own order and outside the order, on the basis of a contract concluded between the religious order and another legal person, for example a hospital in which members of the order do nursing tasks without receiving remuneration. In this case it has frequently been denied that the activity of the members is professional activity, and argued that these are works of evangelisation accomplished for the sake of religion (*"religionis causa"*). In consequence, the member of the order does not have normal employment rights (payment of outstanding salaries, severance pay, social security contributions), even should he or she leave the order.

VIII. Financing of Churches

The Agreement of Villa Madama of 1984, which also makes use of the new possibilities created by the *Codex Iuris Canonici,* has fundamentally changed the system of State funding of the Catholic Church. For centuries the livelihood of the clergy was secured by the *beneficium* (benefice), an amount of property connected to the office exercised by each clergyman. This system secured a certain degree of economic independence, as each clergyman could directly administer the returns on his own *beneficium*; however it caused great disparities between the holders of rich and poor *beneficia.* If the returns of a benefice were excessively low, the State supplemented it by paying a sum of money called the *"supplemento di congrua"* ("supplement of adequacy", because it was meant to secure an "adequate" living by supplementing the returns of the benefice). As this money was part of the general State budget consisting of the taxes paid by all citizens, this arrangement meant that all citizens automatically contributed towards the payment of Catholic clergy, even if they were of no declared religious persuasion or belonged to another religion.

The agreement on Church entities and property reached between the Italian State and the Catholic Church in 1984 was given effect by Law No. 222 of 20 May 1985. Benefices were abolished and their property transferred to newly established bodies, the diocesan institutes for the support of the clergy. These are to provide for the financial support of the clergymen in office in each diocese. Directly afterwards a central institute for the support of the clergy was founded which is to supplement the financial resources of those diocesan institutes that cannot deal with their tasks on their own. Through this reform, the Catholic clergy has been transformed into a stipendiary clergy, according to a model already in operation in the Church of England. This is supposed to secure a substantial equalisation of payment between all clergymen, even at the risk of restricting their economic freedom. The abolition of benefices has also caused the end of the *supplementi di congrua* paid by the State. In its place two systems of financing have been established, benefiting not only the Catholic Church, but also the other denominations which have signed an agreement. The first type concerns a quota of 0.8 % of the revenue from IRPEF (*imposta sul reddito delle persone fisiche* – income tax) which is paid annually by all Italians liable to taxation who earn more than a certain minimum income. In his or her income tax declaration the person liable to taxation can, by ticking the respective box, determine who is to benefit:

a) the Italian State for extraordinary measures against famine in the world, natural disasters, aid to refugees, the conservation of cultural monuments;
b) the Catholic Church, for the worship needs of the population, the support of the clergy, welfare measures benefiting the national community or third world countries;
c) one of the denominations which have signed an agreement with the Italian State; this declaration is subject to the special conditions explained below.

The quota of 0.8 % is distributed on the basis of the declarations of the persons liable to taxation. The percentage which equals the proportion of persons who have not declared their preference is distributed among the different recipients in proportion to the choice made by the rest of the population liable to income tax.

The data available up to now (for 1997) show the following distribution: 40 % of taxed persons have made a choice, and 81 % of these (which roughly equals 32 % of all persons liable to income tax) have opted in favour of the Catholic Church, whereas 15 % preferred the Italian State and the remaining 4 % are divided among the Seventh-Day Adventists, the Assemblies of God (Pentecostals), the Valdensians, the Lutherans and the Union of Jewish Communities. Of the sums thus attributed to the Italian Conference of Bishops, 35 % were used for the maintenance of the clergy, about 20 % for welfare measures and the remainder (about 45 %) for purposes of worship for the benefit of the population.

The second type of financing, also created by agreement for members of the Catholic Church as well as of other denominations, is the possibility of off-setting donations from taxable income up to Euro 1,032.91 to the Central Institute for the Support of the Clergy or similar institutions of other denominations.

As has been mentioned, the two channels of funding just described are also open to the six denominations which have signed an agreement with the Italian State. However, there are certain peculiarities which must be mentioned. The Christian Evangelical-Baptist Union has declined to take part in the distribution of the 0.8 % of IRPEF; the Valdensians and the Pentecostals have decided to relinquish their right to the proportion of the 0.8 % IRPEF equivalent to the "choice not expressed" persons and, together with the Adventists, they chose to use these revenues for social and humanitarian purposes only, because they are of the opinion that the financing of the Church and the maintenance of the clergy should rely exclusively on donations by their members.

Scattered amongst various other legal provisions are additional forms of direct or indirect funding of the denominations. For instance, the regional laws which allocate lots and parcels of land for the erection of Church buildings, and Law No. 390 of 1986, which facilitates the loan or hire of State real property to Church bodies with only minimal rental payments. In both cases it is uncertain whether these provisions apply to only the Catholic Church and the denominations with an agreement or to all denominations.

There is no doubt that the present system of financing, which follows the Spanish model, is a step forward compared with the situation in Italy before 1984. It is in certain respects preferable to the systems in other European countries, which are characterised by inflexible mechanisms that may sometimes come into conflict with fundamental rights of religious freedom. However, in addition to the distribution of the quota of IRPEF pertaining to persons who have not declared their preference, there are certain fundamental characteristics of the present provisions which may present problems. In particular, the precondition for access to the two main channels of finance (0.8 % IRPEF and donation deductible from taxable income) is the setting up of a concordat or an agreement with the Italian State. This means that many denominations are excluded from all forms of state funding, either because they cannot or do not want to come to such an agreement, or because their application has been rejected by the State which, according to the most recent view of the matter, enjoys a large disactionary power freedom in the making of this decision.

In the area of taxation the denominations enjoy numerous privileges. As, however, the legal provision is particularly fragmentary, only the basic principles of the system may be mentioned here. The legal basis is, as already noted, the equal treatment of the religious aims and those of worship of the Church entities with those of welfare and education. This equal treatment is provided for the Catholic Church bodies in Article 7(3) of the Agreement of Villa Madama and for the other denominations by Article 12 of the Royal Decree of 28 February 1930, which was passed for the implementation of Law No. 1159 of 1929. The same provision is contained, in more or less unaltered form, in the text of the agreements between the State and some denominations. Because of this equal treatment the Church entities enjoy numerous advantages, for instance a rebate of 50 % on corporation tax (*imposta sul reddito delle persone giuridiche*, IRPEG), and exemption from inheritance and donation tax. Further exemptions concern value added tax (*imposta sul valore aggiunto*, IVA), local land transfer tax (*imposta comunale sull'incremento di valore dei beni immobili*) and other indirect taxation.

Finally it must be noted that such real property of the Holy See as is located on Italian territory (Articles 13 and 14 of the Lateran Treaty) as well as the other real property named in Articles 13 and 14 of that Treaty is exempt from any kind of tax or duty toward the State or other public entities.

IX. *Religious Assistance in Public Institutions*

Article 11 of the Agreement of Villa Madama states that the pastoral care of soldiers, prisoners and patients in hospitals and nursing homes is the responsibility of Catholic clergy appointed by the competent State authorities on the nomination of the Church authorities. The details of their legal status and the rules governing the provision

of pastoral care are to be dealt with in special agreements, of which only that concerning the police has been completed thus far.
In the case of the army, pastoral care is the responsibility of army chaplains who are appointed by decree of the President of the Republic on the nomination of the Bishop for the Army. The army chaplains are permanent employees of the State, which is responsible for their payment, and are integrated into military hierarchy in the officer ranks.
In the prisons there are also chaplains, but they are not counted as regular State employees even if they are paid by the State. They serve on the basis of an open term assignment granted by the Minister of Justice after receiving the *nihil obstat* of the diocesan bishop. The assignment becomes invalid if the *nihil obstat* is withdrawn or on the ground of evident incompatibility between the chaplain and the prison community in which he serves. In the hospitals, pastoral care is the duty of clergy who are included in the budget employment plan of the local medical services (*azienda sanitaria locale*) or who work on the basis of contracts with the health administration, which takes responsibility for the payment of the clergy involved and for securing the necessary preconditions for pastoral care. Such clergymen are appointed by the diocesan bishop.
The agreements concluded with the minority denominations provide that their ministers have right of access to prisons without the need for any special permit, and to hospitals without limitations as to time, so as to be able to exercise pastoral activities mainly but not exclusively at the request of the prisoners or patients. Soldiers belonging to these denominations have the right to take part in religious activities which their clergy organise at the soldiers' place of posting or its vicinity. If these activities take place at an excessively distant location, the soldiers may take part in specially organised prayer meetings in rooms placed at their disposal by the military authorities. The financial burden of pastoral care must be borne by the denominations.
Ministers of the denominations without an agreement have access to prisons and hospitals to give assistance to prisoners or patients who seek it: this right is based on Articles 5 and 6 of the Royal Decree of February 1930 for the denominations recognised according to Law No. 1159 of 1929 and on the basis of the general legal provisions for the other denominations. They also have access to barracks so as to give pastoral care to sick soldiers if they so wish.
No form of pastoral care is provided for in schools (however, religious education classes take place, see section V, above).

X. The Legal Status of the Clergy and Members of Religious Orders

In Italian law there is no definition of the term clergyman or minister, so this has to be derived from an examination of the legal structure of the various confessions. The term is sufficiently clear in Canon Law, according to which clergy are persons who have received the sacrament of ordination in at least one of its three degrees: as deacon, priest, or bishop. The term becomes more complicated in some minority denominations and especially in the so-called "new religious movements", in the case of which it is not always clear to whom this term applies.

The clergy enjoy a special legal status in Italian law. In part this status signifies preferential treatment: under some conditions clergymen may validly take under a will; crimes committed against them are treated as having aggravating circumstances, and so on. More often however it involves examples of legal incapacity, such as non-eligibility for certain public offices (for instance that of mayor, but not the office of Member of Parliament), incompatibility with the exercise of certain professions (notary, lawyer, tax collector) and ineligibility for some legal functions such as jury service. Some of these rules, which date from a former time when clergymen could easily influence public opinion, appear to be obsolete now that the process of secularisation has transformed society.

Apart from the provisions of general law which have just been mentioned, the Agreement of Villa Madama and the agreements with other denominations also contain rules seeking to regulate the status of the clergy.

These rules apply first of all to exemption from military service, but this issue has now lost the significance it had in the past because compulsory military service was abolished in Italy in 2004. The other matter regulated by agreement (and partly also by the provisions of general law) is that of the obligation of secrecy. Article 4 of the Agreement of Villa Madama provides that the clergy are not bound to impart information about persons or matters to judges or other authorities when they have obtained the information in the exercise of their office. The same provision is made in the agreements with the Union of Jewish Communities and the Protestant Lutheran Church, but not in the other agreements. However this causes no significant discrimination, because the provisions of the Codes of Civil and Criminal Procedure allow all ministers to maintain official secrecy in court.

XI. Matrimonial and Family Law

Under the Civil Code of 1865 obligatory civil marriage was introduced in Italy as the only form of marriage recognised by the State. This reform was vehemently attacked by the Church which never accepted the fact that religious marriage had lost its significance in State law. For this reason the regulation of matrimony was of especial importance in the negotiations leading up to the conclusion of the Lateran Concordat. Article 34 restored the civil law validity of marriages *in facie Ecclesiae:* it provided that Church marriages could be registered in the registers of births, marriages and deaths kept in every Italian municipality and so obtain full validity in State law. Additionally it was ruled that the Church courts – not the State courts – were to be competent to deal with annulments and dissolution of the registered Church marriages (the so-called "concordat-marriages", *matrimoni concordatari*) and that the decisions of these courts, which were arrived at on the basis of Canon Law, obtained civil law validity by a (very summary) decision in the recognition procedure (*giudizio di delibazione*) in the Italian courts of appeal. It was of course still possible for the Italian citizens to opt for a civil law marriage which was completely regulated by State law and subject to the jurisdiction of the State courts. For the adherents of non-Catholic denominations, Law No. 1159 of 1929 made it possible to be married by a clergyman of their own denomination, while (in contrast with the "concordat-marriages") the regulation of these marriages and jurisdiction to declare their nullity were matters for the State legislation and courts.

Article 34 of the Concordat and Law No. 847 of 1929 which was passed for its implementation have – also as a consequence of faults in legal technique – caused numerous problems which the Agreement of Villa Madama has tried to remedy without compromising the fundamental principles of the system laid down in 1929.

Article 8 of the Agreement recognises the civil law effects of marriages conducted according to Canon Law provided that the certificate issued by the clergyman solemnising the marriage is transferred to the state register of births, marriages and deaths. The civil law effects begin at the moment of the marriage, even if the transfer is not made until some time later. It is not possible to register and so give civil law consequences to Church marriages of persons who have not reached the age of consent for civil law marriage (18 or, with a court authorisation, 16 years of age), or where there is an impediment to the marriage of the parties which is regarded as insurmountable in civil law: No. 4 of the Additional Protocol to the Agreement of Villa Madama treats as impediments insanity, previous marriage, crime and direct blood relationships. In order to establish possible impediments the parties must publish their banns at the town hall, according to the rules applying equally to civil marriage. In this way an attempt is made to prevent religious marriages from obtaining civil law validity by way of a registration which could not have been made under the provisions of the Civil Code, so as to protect the equality of citizens in matters of marriage regardless of the denomination to which they belong. The same article also provides that the court of appeal may on application of the parties declare valid in Italian law the annulment of a marriage declared by the Church courts and having force in Canon Law. To do this, however, the court of appeal must establish that (a) the Church court had jurisdiction to acknowledge the grounds of annulment; (b) during the canonical procedure the right of the parties to maintain and defend litigation was respected in a way not deviating from the fundamental principles of Italian law;[1] and (c) the further preconditions for the recognition of foreign judgments in Italy were met.

Of these conditions, enumerated in Article 797 of the Code of Civil Procedure, special significance attaches to that which says that the annulment of the marriage by the Church court may contain no provisions that are in conflict with Italian law. On the basis of this provision it is argued that Church decisions annulling a marriage for typically denominational reasons (for instance *disparitas cultus,* ordination and the vow of chastity) may not be declared valid in Italian law, because this would conflict with the principle of religious freedom. The Constitutional Court has also emphasised the existence of a similar conflict in Church decisions which annulled a marriage on the grounds of a deception by one of the parties only: in this case it is

---

[1] Recently Italy has been condemned by the European Court of Human Rights (Pellegrini v. Italy, No. 30882/96, July 20, 2001). The Court condemned the enforcement by the Court of Appeal of Florence of a Church court decision that had annulled a "concordat-marriage": according to the European Court, the Church judgment had not respected the principles of fair judgment granted by Article 6 of the European Convention for the Protection of Human Rights and Fundamental Freedoms.

possible to declare these decisions valid in Italian law only with the consent, or at least without the dissent, of the party who was in good faith or after proof that the deception was known, or at least recognisable, to the latter at the time of marriage.

On the subject of the jurisdiction of the Church courts Article 8 of the Agreement of Villa Madama is worded ambiguously – perhaps purposely so because of the difficulty of overcoming differences of opinion which appeared between the parties during the negotiations. Specifically, the Article does not repeat the clear wording of Article 34 of the Lateran Treaties which states that cases concerning the annulment of marriage and the dissolution of marriages which have been concluded but not consummated are reserved to the competence of the Church courts and dicasteries; Article 8 simply declares that the Church decisions of annulment are valid under the conditions enumerated, without referring to any reservation as to jurisdiction.

Because of the lack of any reference to a reservation as to jurisdiction in favour of the Church courts, some commentators have argued that this reservation no longer exists and that State courts are competent alongside Church courts to declare the nullity of concordat marriages. This opinion was adopted by the Court of Cassation in a decision of February 1993 and it is followed by the majority of the Italian courts.

Questions related to religious marriages have been of great relevance in the past, but one must however be aware of the fact that the problem – which remains of great theoretical interest – has now only small practical importance because, since the introduction of divorce in Italy in 1970, the number of applications to give validity to decisions of annulment of the Church courts has dropped to a few hundred a year.

As has been mentioned, citizens who do not wish to marry *in facie Ecclesiae* may contract a civil marriage or, if they are members of a denomination other than the Catholic Church, be married by a minister of their own denomination according to the provisions of Law No. 1159 of 1929. This Law is no longer applied to those denominations which have come to an agreement with the Italian State. But the provisions on matrimonial law contained in the agreements – even if they introduce significant innovations such as the abolition of the preliminary State authorisation for the minister conducting the marriage – do not change the structure of the institution of marriage, which remains wholly under civil law even if it is conducted within a religious context.

XII. Criminal Law

The Code of Criminal Law contains provisions that punish blasphemy against the Deity (of whatever religion), offences against ministers of religion and religious articles, disturbances to religious ceremonies (Articles 724 and 403-406). Incitement to violence or discrimination for religious motives is punished by Law 654 of 1975 (as modified by Law 205 of 1993), that enforces in Italy the U.N. international convention on the elimination of all forms of racial discrimination of 1965.

XIII. Bibliography

Legislation:
S. *Berlingò/G. Casuscelli* (ed.), Codice del diritto ecclesiastico, Giuffrè, Milano, 2003.

Textbooks:
F. *Finocchiaro*, Diritto ecclesiastico, Zanichelli, Bologna 2003.
C. *Cardia*, Ordinamenti religiosi e ordinamenti dello Stato, Bologna, Il Mulino, 2003.

Periodicals:
Il diritto ecclesiastico, Giuffrè, Milano.
Quaderni di diritto e politica ecclesiastica, Il Mulino, Bologna.

Achilles Emilianides
State and Church in Cyprus

I. Social Facts

The Republic of Cyprus was established as an independent sovereign republic on 16 August 1960, when its Constitution came into force and British sovereignty over Cyprus, as a crown colony, ceased. The establishment of the Republic was the outcome of the Zurich and London Agreements on which the Constitution was based.
In the 1973 census, the population of Cyprus totalled 631,778 inhabitants. Of these, 498,511 (78.9 %) belonged to the Greek Community, including Armenians, Maronites and Roman Catholics; 116,000 (18.4 %) were members of the Turkish community, and 17,267 (2.7 %) were from other ethnic groups and were mainly British.
On 20 July 1974 the armed forces of the Republic of Turkey, one of the guarantor powers of the independence, sovereignty and territorial integrity of Cyprus, invaded the country and occupied the northern part of the island. As a result of the occupation, the Greeks and other Christians from that region became refugees and fled to the southern part of the island. In addition, Turks living in the southern part of the island were encouraged to relocate to the north.
The Turkish occupation of northern Cyprus continues to the present day, and the Republic of Cyprus is thus prevented from exercising its powers over the whole island. Though there are no official statistics, it is estimated that 83 % of the present population of the Republic of Cyprus is Greek Orthodox, with 13 % Muslim (nearly all of whom live in the area not controlled by the Republic), 0.6 % Maronite, 0.6 % Armenian, and 0.3 % Roman Catholic, while 2.5 % belong to other churches.

II. Historical Background

With the exception of sporadic Arab invasions, Cyprus remained for more than eight and a half centuries – between 325 and 1191 – part of the Byzantine Empire. Thus, Christianity was the state religion of the island. During the period of Frankish rule (1191-1489), the Roman Catholic or Latin Church was established as the official church of the new kingdom at the expense of the autocephalous Greek Orthodox Church of Cyprus. Following the Venetian period, which lasted for 82 years (1489-1571), there were more than three centuries of Ottoman rule (1571-1878). During that time and the period of British occupation that followed it (1878-1960), the Orthodox Church had a dual role. It was both the ministering religious organisation of Orthodox Christians of the island, and the nation-leading political coalition of the Greeks under foreign sovereignty.

Great Britain acquired the rights of possession and administration of Cyprus by signing the 1878 Treaty of Alliance with the Ottoman Empire; the Sultan maintained limited ownership over the island and Cypriots remained Ottoman subjects. Great Britain agreed to preserve the status quo, including competencies granted by the Imperial prescript, Hatt-i-Humayun (1856), towards the Churches and religious authorities.[1] These competencies included spiritual advantages and exemptions. This state of affairs remained in effect, even after the annexation of Cyprus by Great Britain in 1914, the recognition of this annexation by Turkey in 1923, and the proclamation of the island as a Crown Colony in 1925.[2]

The 1914 Charter of the Orthodox Church was drafted and put into effect by the Church itself, with no intervention from the British authorities. It was in operation for 66 years, until the enactment of the 1980 Charter which is still in force. The Church of Cyprus was established as a legal entity, not further determining its nature (Article 94). It is safe to assume, however, that the Church considered itself to be a legal entity under private law. The Charter was never vested with state authority, nor was the Church subject to control on the part of the State, something that would have happened had the Church been considered a legal entity under public law. Acts of the Church that were of a legislative and administrative nature, the decisions issued by ecclesiastical courts on any subject, and marriages con-

---

1 See *A. Emilianides*, "Private International Law", 90, C. Tornaritis, "The Relations", 11.
2 *C. Papastathis, On the Administrative Organization*, 29.

tracted only through a church ceremony, were recognised by the state administration and justice, as a result of the aforementioned state of affairs that was preserved by Great Britain after the annexation of Cyprus.

The status of the Orthodox Church and the other Churches and religions was confirmed by a Law of 1935 regarding the Administration of Justice, which explicitly excluded from the jurisdiction of state courts "any marital disputes of members of the Greek Orthodox Church, whenever the marriage was celebrated in accordance with ceremony... [and] any other case, which according to the principles of the Ottoman Law that was formerly in force in Cyprus, was subject to the jurisdiction of an ecclesiastical court of the religious community of the litigants".

Election of Bishops and administration of ecclesiastical property were considered to be internal affairs of the Orthodox Church. Laws 33/1937 and 34/1937, which stated that the elected Archbishop should be approved by the colonial government, were an attempt to limit Church's privileges, but these were eventually superseded by Law 20/1946 after strenuous protests by the Church. The right of the Church to elect its Archbishop and generally administer its internal affairs without any state intervention was confirmed by a decision (343/1948) of the District Court of Nicosia.

III. Basic Structure

1. Legal Sources

The basic legal source for religions in general is the Constitution of Cyprus. Due to its bi-communal structure, which reflects the religion of its citizens, there are several Articles referring to religion. The main Articles of the Constitution that refer to religion are the following: Article 18 which safeguards the right of religious freedom; Article 23(9 and 10) which prohibit any limitation of the property rights held by Christian and Muslim corporations and institutions, without the consent of the appropriate ecclesiastical authority or of the Turkish communal chamber respectively; Article 87(1a), which bestows on both Communal Chambers legislative power with regard to all religious matters of the two Communities respectively; Article 110

which safeguards the administration of internal affairs and property of all creeds and Article 111(1) which concerns family law disputes.
Article 18 of the Constitution safeguards the right of religious freedom, including the freedom of religious conscience and freedom of worship. This Article corresponds in many ways to Article 9 of the European Convention on Human Rights (Treaty of Rome, which was ratified in Cyprus by Law 39/1962), but it is more detailed and its provisions cover aspects not recorded in Article 9.
By virtue of Article 18(1) "every person has the right to freedom of thought, conscience and religion". Freedom of thought is thus safeguarded for any person, either a believer or an atheist, a citizen or a non-citizen of the Republic of Cyprus. Article 18(2) stipulates that "all religions whose doctrines or rites are not secret are free".
According to Article 18(3) "all religions are equal before the law. Without prejudice to the competence of the Communal Chambers under this Constitution, no legislative, executive or administrative act of the Republic shall discriminate against any religious institution or religion". It should be noted that Communal Chambers no longer exist. The Greek Communal Chamber was self-dissolved. Its legislative competences were transferred to the House of Representatives, while its administrative competences were transferred to certain Ministries. The Turkish Communal Chamber is de facto non-existent because of the relocation of the Turks to the occupied part of the island.
Article 18(4) guarantees the religious freedom of the individual, stipulating that "every person is free and has the right to profess his faith and to manifest his religion or belief, in worship, teaching, practice or observance, either individually or collectively, in private or in public, and to change his religion or belief". Illicit proselytism in favour of or against any religion is prohibited for any individual, as Article 18(5) prohibits "the use of physical or moral compulsion for the purpose of making a person change or preventing him from changing his religion". However, this constitutional prohibition has not yet been supplemented by law.
The freedom to manifest one's religion may be restricted by virtue of Article 18(6), but only if such limitations are prescribed by law and are necessary in the interests of:
a) the security of the Republic,
b) constitutional order,
c) public safety,
d) public order,
e) public health,

f) public morals,
g) the protection of the rights and liberties guaranteed to every person by the Constitution.

In addition to the conditions mentioned above, any limitation of the freedom, in a democratic society, to manifest one's religion must be considered necessary under the mandate of Article 9(2) of the European Convention on Human Rights.

Article 18(7) of the Constitution states that, "until a person attains the age of sixteen, the decision as to the religion to be professed by him shall be taken by the person having the lawful guardianship of such person". Finally, by virtue of Article 18(8) "no person shall be compelled to pay any tax or duty the proceeds of which are specially allocated in whole or in part for the purposes of a religion other than his own".

Indirectly related to religious freedom are the constitutional provisions of Articles 10(3b) and 28(2). Article 10(3b) states that the term "forced or compulsory labour", which no person shall be required to perform, shall not include "any service of military character if imposed or, in case of conscientious objectors, subject to their recognition by a law, service exacted instead of compulsory military service". This constitutional statute implements Article 4(3b) of the European Convention on Human Rights, and empowers the legislative branch to exempt from compulsory military service those who object to it for reasons of conscience, and order them to provide services of another nature. The Supreme Court of Cyprus decided that limitations of one's religious freedom, occurring as a result of such service, were justified, due to the special conditions prevailing in Cyprus.[3]

Article 28(2) of the Constitution, implementing Article 14 of the European Convention on Human Rights, states that "every person shall enjoy all the rights and liberties provided for in this Constitution without any direct or indirect discrimination against any person on the ground of his community, race, religion, language, sex, political or other convictions, national or social descent, birth, colour, wealth, social class, or on any ground whatsoever, unless there is express provision to the contrary in this Constitution". It should be noted though, that the Constitution contains a number of provisions not currently in effect, which could lead to significant religious dis-

---

[3] And therefore the religious beliefs of Jehovah's Witnesses were not considered as legitimate reasons for them to refuse to be drafted in the National Guard. See Michael Andreou Pitsillides and Another v The Republic (1983) 2 C.L.R 374.

crimination, as a result of the bi-communal character of the Constitution.

It should also be noted that, under the mandate of Article 109 of the Constitution, each "religious group" has the right to be represented, by an elected member or members of such a group, in the Communal Chamber of the Community to which the group has opted to join as provided by a relevant communal law. Ever since the Greek Communal Chamber was self-dissolved, members of the three "religious groups", in addition to the rights of electing and being elected in parliamentary elections, also elect, as members of their religious group, one member of each group to represent their group in Parliament. That member oversees all matters concerning the group, but does not have the right to vote (Law 38/1976).

Articles 18 and 110 recognise the religious laws that govern the internal affairs of religions and creeds. Article 110(1) which establishes the right of the Orthodox Church to regulate and administer its own internal affairs and property, stipulates that this right shall be exercised "in accordance with the Holy Canons and its Charter in force for the time being". The Holy Canons whose force is safeguarded by the Constitution are not only those that relate to Church doctrine, but also those that refer to the administration of the Church's internal affairs and property. This includes both the strict observance of the doctrines (doctrinal unity) and the effect of those fundamental administrative institutions of canon law that give a Church its Orthodox character (canonical unity).

In addition to the Holy Canons, the Constitution also makes reference to the Charter of the Church of Cyprus. The question that arises here is whether the Church of Cyprus possesses its own legislative power and has, therefore, the right to draft and enact a new Charter.

According to canon law, the Church is entitled to legislate freely, subject to the condition that its new statutes do not contravene the Holy Scriptures, the Holy Tradition and those Holy Canons that are accepted by all Orthodox Churches. The same holds from the point of view of the Constitution. Article 110(1) stipulates that the Church "has the exclusive right of regulating and administering its internal affairs and property" and that "the Greek Communal Chamber shall not act inconsistently with such right". In addition, Article 111(1) recognises that the Church of Cyprus – as well as the other Churches – has legislative power, stipulating that certain matrimonial institutions "of members of the Greek Orthodox Church or of a religious group ... shall be governed by the law of the Greek Orthodox Church or of the Church of such religious group". As a result the Orthodox

Church of Cyprus does have the right to draft and enact a new Charter. Increased formal force is recognized by the Constitution for each Charter in force, so long as it was drafted and enacted by the Church according to the Holy Canons. If a new Charter contains provisions for issues that were not included in the 1914 Charter which was in force when the Constitution was enacted, these issues are not guaranteed by the Constitution.[4]

The new Charter of the Church of Cyprus came into operation on 1 January 1980. It consists of 355 Articles, divided into nine chapters. Its main characteristics are:
1) The reinforcement of the synodical system of Church administration,
2) The substantial participation of lay persons in ecclesiastical administration and in the election of metropolitans and of the archbishop,
3) The equality of men and women with regard to the administration of the ecclesiastical body and electoral assemblies – though not totally in matters of family law,
4) The financial remuneration of clergy and other persons attending to the Church and
5) The detailed audit of financial management.[5]

2. Categories of System Approach

The Constitution did not create a new internal legal regime for the various religions in Cyprus.[6] It maintains in effect the provisions of Ottoman law, especially Hatt-i-Humayun, with regard to the implementation of the religious law of each religious community and religious group, regarding:
1) their religious affairs
2) institutions of family law and adjudication of the relevant disputes by the appropriate religious tribunals. This jurisdiction is however, subject to the provisions of the Constitution. Any provisions of religious law that are inconsistent with the Constitution are not implemented.

According to Article 110(1) of the Constitution, the autocephalous Greek Orthodox Church of Cyprus shall continue to have an exclu-

---

4   C. *Papastathis*, *On the Administrative Organization*, 58ff.
5   C. *Papastathis*, "The New Statutory Charter".
6   C. *Tornaritis*, "The Relations", 13.

sive right to regulate and administer its own internal affairs and property in accordance with the Holy Canons and its Charter in force for the time being. The Greek Communal Chamber (now the House of Representatives) must not act inconsistently with such right of the Orthodox Church. Furthermore, Article 111(1) states that any matter relating to betrothal, marriage, divorce, nullity of marriage, judicial separation or restitution of conjugal rights, or to family relations (other than legitimation by order of the court or adoption) of members of the Greek Orthodox Church is to be governed by the law of the Greek Orthodox Church and shall be cognisable by a tribunal of such Church. The Greek Communal Chamber does not have the authority to act inconsistently with the provisions of the law, whereas the execution of the decisions issued by ecclesiastical courts must be carried out by the public authorities of the Republic (Art. 90(5) in conjunction with Art. 111(2)).[7] It should be noted that Article 111 "was intended to preserve and not to extend, the competence of the ecclesiastical tribunals of the Greek Orthodox Church as exercised at the time of the coming into operation of the Constitution".[8]

All these rights of the Orthodox Church are also granted to the other "religious groups" of the Republic, for which the provisions of Article 2(3) of the Constitution apply (Art. 110(3), 111(1)). A "religious group" in the constitutional sense is a group of persons, ordinarily resident in Cyprus, professing the same religion and either belonging to the same rite or subject to the same jurisdiction. The number of persons who were members of these groups on the date of the coming into operation of the Constitution exceeded one thousand, at least five hundred of whom became citizens of the Republic on that date (Art. 2(3)). The "religious groups" are the Armenians, Maronites and Roman Catholics (Appendix E of the Treaty of Establishment between the United Kingdom, Greece, Turkey and the Republic of Cyprus). They opted to belong to the Greek Community and now reside in the territory controlled by the Republic of Cyprus. Other religions and rites (such as Jehovah's Witnesses or the Orthodox Christians who follow the Old Calendar) enjoy religious freedom, but are not considered as "religious groups" in a constitutional sense.

Article 110(2) recognises the institution of Vakf and the principles and laws of vakfs in a manner favourable to the Muslim religion.[9] It stipulates that "All matters relating to or in any way affecting the

---

7 Article 111 was eventually amended. See part VIII.
8 Myrianthi Charalambous Christodoulou Tyllirou v Charalambos Christodoulou Tylliros 3 R.S.C.C 21.
9 See *K. Dizdar*, "The Origin and Administration of the Cyprus Evkaf".

institution or foundation of Vakf or the vakfs or any vakf properties, including properties belonging to Mosques and any other Moslem religious institution, shall be governed solely by and under the Laws and Principles of Vakfs (ahkamul evkaf) and the laws and regulations enacted or made by the Turkish Communal Chamber, and no legislative, executive or other act whatsoever shall contravene or override or interfere with such Laws or Principles of Vakfs and with such laws and regulations of the Turkish Communal Chamber". The Constitution does not contain a provision similar to Article 111(1), stipulating the competence of Muslim religious institutions concerning the family relations, because of the radical amendments to the Turkish Cypriot institutions following the acceptance of the Kemalic reforms.[10]

Article 23(9) states that no deprivation, restriction or limitation on the right to acquire, own, possess, enjoy, or dispose of any movable or immovable property belonging to any See, monastery, church or any other ecclesiastical corporation or any right over it or interest therein shall be made, except with the written consent of the appropriate ecclesiastical authority being in control of such property.

The same right is accorded to all Muslim religious institutions. According to Article 23(10) no such deprivation, restriction or limitation may be imposed on the immovable or movable property of any vakf, except with the approval of the Turkish Communal Chamber and subject to the Laws and Principles of Vakfs. Such property includes the objects and subjects of the vakfs and the properties belonging to the Mosques or to any other Moslem religious institutions, or any right thereon or interest therein.

From these constitutional provisions, it may be seen that no single religion or creed is established as the official religion of Cyprus. As a result:

a) there is no prevailing religion or state religion, and

b) the State is non-confessional.

Thus, when assuming their duties, State officials are not sworn in but rather affirm their faith to, and respect for, the Constitution and the laws made under it, and to the preservation of the independence and the territorial integrity of the Republic of Cyprus, pursuant to Articles 42(1), 59(4), 69 and 100 of the Constitution.

The constitutional provisions superseded the system of moderate separation of State and religion that prevailed under English rule,

---

10 *A. Emilianides*, "Private International Law", 91.

introducing instead a system of co-ordination between the Republic of Cyprus and all other religions and Christian creeds. Therefore,
1) all the religions and creeds in Cyprus deal purely with their own affairs, without in any way interfering in the affairs of the State;
2) the State recognises broad discretionary powers in their favour and has no right to intervene in their internal affairs; and
3) whenever matters of common interest arise, (such as religious education and family matters), the State and religious corporations debate on equal terms.[11]

This system is in effect, even though the Orthodox Christian and the Islamic religion fulfil one of the criteria of the bi-communal character of the Republic of Cyprus. Under the mandate of Article 2(1) of the Constitution, the Greek Community comprises citizens of the Republic who are members of the Greek Orthodox Church, whereas citizens who are Muslims belong to the Turkish Community (Art. 2(2)). As stated above, when members of "religious groups" had to choose to belong either to the Greek or to the Turkish Community within three months of the date of the coming into operation of the Constitution (Art. 2(3)), they opted for membership of the Greek Community.

This peculiar legal status of the two religions does not however signify the recognition of special status in favour of either the Orthodox Church or the Muslim religion at the expense of other religions.

IV. Legal Status of Religious Bodies

The former Charter established the Church of Cyprus as a legal entity (Art. 94). The current Charter contains a similar provision, though only for particular ecclesiastical corporations: metropolises (Art. 153), parish churches (Art. 80(3) and 160), monasteries (Art. 184), collective bodies of administration of Church property (Art. 210) and a number of Church-run charitable foundations (Art. 190), but not for the Church per se. It is indisputable however, that the Church remains a legal entity, since:
1) the pre-existing Charter is still in force twenty years after the coming into operation of the Constitution; and

---

11 C. Papastathis, On the Administrative Organization, 34.

2) the institutional status of all religions and creeds as well as that of the Charter of the Orthodox Church are determined by Article 110(1) of the Constitution. Furthermore, the Church should be properly viewed as a legal entity under public law, because the Constitution confers upon it powers that appertain to the State.[12]
According to the Supreme Court of Cyprus, however, the Church is not considered to be an "organ" of or "authority" in the Republic, under the sense of Article 139 of the Constitution.[13] According to Article 139, "organs" or "authorities" means specific juridical creations, bearing the features of individual and concrete organic institutions of Government and functioning for, and on behalf of, a primary legal entity such as the Republic of Cyprus.[14] It should be therefore noted that all known religions are currently recognised as legal entities under private law. Religions are not required to register with government authorities, unless they desire to engage in financial transactions.

V. Church and Culture

Religious lessons given in primary and secondary schools follow the teachings of the Eastern Orthodox Church. Attendance is compulsory for Orthodox pupils. In secondary education, the courses are given by graduates of university schools of divinity, while in primary education they are given by the class teacher. There are also educational institutions, both primary and secondary, for Armenian pupils. The Orthodox Church and other Christian churches also operate Sunday schools.

In the University of Cyprus there is no School of Divinity. Those who wish to study theology resort primarily to Greece, and also to other countries, where Orthodox Theological Academies enjoy the status of a University College. Under the supervision of the Holy Synod, the hieratic school "Apostolos Vanavas" operates in Nicosia, as a dependency of the Monastery of Kykkos.

---

12 C. Papastathis, *On the Administrative Organization*, 37ff.
13 Autocephalous, Saint, Orthodox and Apostolic Church of Cyprus v The House of Representatives, (1990) 3 C.L.R 338.
14 Fuat Celaleddin and Others v The Council of Ministers and Others, 5 R.S.C.C 102.

It should be noted that the Orthodox Church of Cyprus takes part in all important social and economic activities of the Republic. The Orthodox Church also currently owns a private radio station, called "Logos", and a private television channel which it has decided to let to the Greek "Mega Channel".

VI. Church Administration

The administration of the Orthodox Church is divided into central and local institutions.
1. The central institutions are a) the Holy Synod and b) the Archbishop.
   a) As in every Orthodox Church, the congregation (clergy, monks, laity) constitutes the highest authority in the Cypriot Church (Charter, Art. 5). This authority is exercised by the Holy Synod, which is constituted by the serving archbishop and the serving metropolitans and any serving bishops who do not have administrative duties but assist the archbishop with his work (Art. 6). If a prelate has been sentenced to a canonical penalty (with the exception of a reprimand), he is not entitled to participate in the sessions of the Holy Synod for the duration of his sentence (Art. 23). The archbishop chairs the Holy Synod. If he is impeded from presiding or if the see is vacant, a ranking metropolitan assumes the chair (Art. 8) in the following order of precedence: Metropolitan of Paphos, Kition, Kyrenia, Limassol and Morphou.
   The Chairman of the Holy Synod normally convenes it three times a year. The Synod is also convened for special sessions, when the chairman deems it necessary or when at least two of its members make such a request (Art. 9). The Holy Synod is in quorum when half of its members are present, including the Chairman (Art. 11). If some of its members refuse to participate or if there are vacant sees, so that the quorum is not reached, then one or two prelates may be called upon from the Patriarchates of the East or from the Church of Greece (Art. 14). The decisions of the Synod are reached by an absolute majority of all members present, while an increased majority

of its members is required for the revision of provisions of the Charter (Art. 12).

The Holy Synod supervises the clergy and the overall ecclesiastical corporation, and exercises legislative, judicial and administrative power. It also has the "presumption of jurisdiction", which is the jurisdiction over any matter that does not fall within the jurisdiction of another body (Art. 18). Furthermore, it is the highest court for the canonical offences of clergy, monks and lay persons (Art. 19). When it is called upon to try a prelate who is charged with an offence which under canon law is punishable with defrocking, then the Synod assembles as a Superior Court. This court, thirteen in number including the chairman, is comprised of members of the Synod and prelates from other Churches (Art. 25).

b) The Archbishop is a central instrument of administration, as well as locally as a bishop in his archdiocese. He presides over the Holy Synod and represents the Church before the Republic, other states and churches. According to the privilege, granted to him by the Byzantine emperor Zeno in the fifth century, the archbishop of Cyprus signs in cinnabar (red ink), is clad in imperial purple, and holds an imperial sceptre (Art. 33).

2. The local institutions are a) the archdiocese and the metropolises, b) the parishes and c) the monasteries.

a) In addition to the archdiocese, whose prelate is the archbishop (with his seat in Nicosia), there are five metropolises, each administered by a metropolitan (Paphos, Kition, Kyrenia, Limassol and Morphou). The metropolitan holds the hieratic rank of a bishop and exercises judicial, legislative, and administrative authority within his area. He controls and supervises the administration and management of the parishes and monasteries of his province, and is generally charged with all competencies conferred by the Holy Canons and the Charter (Art. 45). The archbishop and metropolitans are elected for life, unless they resign or are discharged on account of an illness or a conviction for a canonical offence (Art. 55).

b) A parish is a particular area whose Orthodox inhabitants meet their religious needs in a specific church (Art. 81). The Orthodox inhabitants of a parish become parish members upon completing one year's residence there. In order to establish a new parish, there need to be 2,500 inhabitants in cities, and 1,500 in small towns and villages. Any special conditions of the region may, however, be taken into consideration if the number of the faithful is smaller. The head of the parish is the parish priest, who must be a married clergyman (Art. 82). The staff of the parishes also comprises cantors and sacristans (Art. 83).

c) Monasteries are centres of monastic life. From an administrative point of view they are divided into royal monasteries, parochial monasteries, and monasteries of the see. The "royal" monasteries enjoy complete autonomy in their internal administration and management, and are spiritually (but not administratively) subject to the archbishop (Art. 89). Parochial monasteries enjoy self-administration and are spiritually subject to the local metropolitan (Art. 90). Monasteries that have been abandoned are called monasteries of the see and belong to the local metropolis (Art. 90). The administration of the monasteries is carried out by the abbot, the abbatial council and the brotherhood of the monks.

VII. Labour Law within the Religious Communities

According to Articles 52 and 75-79 of the Charter of the Orthodox Church of Cyprus, each of the five metropolises can employ clergymen or laypersons to assist in the spiritual and administrative work of the Church. Employees are appointed for a probationary two-year period, after which the bishop decides whether they should become permanent. The bishop can impose penalties for offences concerning the service or terminate the employment of any member of staff who demonstrates negligence, inability to perform his duties, indiscipline, inconsistency, or improper behaviour.

The bishop and the See Fund issue decisions concerning the appropriate salary for employees. Any members of staff who are occupied full-time in the Church are entitled to insurance cover and medico-pharmaceutical care, according to the regulations in force of the Republic concerning public servants. A lay person who is made redundant can also claim any compensation to redundant employees granted by the laws of the Republic.

VIII. Matrimonial and Family Law

Article 111 of the Constitution refers to the courts of the Christian creeds. The Orthodox Church, the Maronite Church, the Latin Church and the Armenian Church all have ecclesiastical courts.
Marital disputes between Christian Orthodox who had celebrated a religious marriage used formerly to fall under the jurisdiction of the courts of the Orthodox Church. When both of the spouses-to-be were Orthodox and citizens of Cyprus, it was not possible for them to contract a civil marriage in Cyprus. If however, they had performed a civil marriage abroad, it was recognized by virtue of lex loci celebrationis. In 1977 the Supreme Court of Cyprus held that a civil marriage between Orthodox is null to begin with, wherever it has been celebrated,[15] because Article 111 of the Constitution stipulated that "any matter relating to betrothal, marriage, divorce, nullity of marriage, judicial separation or restitution of conjugal rights or to family relations ... of the Greek Orthodox Church or of a religious group ... shall be governed by the law of the Greek Orthodox Church or of the Church of such religious group, as the case may be, and shall be cognizable by a tribunal of such Church". Thus the only appropriate form of marriage for the Orthodox, Armenians, Maronites and Roman Catholics was the religious form.
The Charter of the Orthodox Church makes detailed references to the institutions of family law that come under the jurisdiction of ecclesiastical courts, namely betrothal, marriage, divorce, and adoption (Art. 217-235), as well as the organisation and operation of ecclesiastical courts (Art. 236-335).
The need to adjust all personal matters to contemporary legal principles, social perceptions, and the commitments of the Republic of Cyprus towards international conventions led to the First Amendment of the Constitution (Law 95/1989), which amended Article 111. According to the provisions of Law 95/1989:
1) All matters relating to divorce, judicial separation or restitution of conjugal rights or to family relations of the members of the Orthodox Church came under the jurisdiction of a family court. In divorce cases the court is composed of three members. It is presided over by a clergyman, with two lay persons acting as the other two judges. If the Church does not appoint a presiding judge, which has been the practice until today, a judge is ap-

---
15 Metaxa v Mita (1977) 1 C.L.R 1.

pointed by the Supreme Court of the Republic. The family courts came into force with Law 23/1990.
2) All matters relating to divorce, judicial separation or restitution of conjugal rights or to family relations of the members of the three religious groups came under the jurisdiction of the family courts of the religious groups; this eventually came into force with Law 87/1994.
3) The grounds for divorce are mentioned specifically in the Constitution. The ground of irretrievable breakdown rendering the marital relationship intolerable for the plaintiff has been added to the grounds of divorce mentioned in the Charter, which remain in force. The House of Representatives may establish by law other grounds for divorce; they eventually established the new ground of irretrievable breakdown with the promulgation of Law 46(I)/1999.
4) Members of the Greek Community may choose to contract a civil marriage. This became possible after the promulgation of Law 21/1990, which established a dual regime of civil and religious marriage.
5) Matters relating to betrothal, marriage, and nullity continue to be governed by the law of the Greek Orthodox Church or the Church of a religious group as the case may be.

Thus, the marriage and divorce law of the Republic of Cyprus is today at the same level of modernisation as in most other European countries.

On 1 June 1983 the Church of Cyprus took an extremely important initiative for the premarital regulation of the health of future spouses, something that is disapproved of by most Churches in other countries. In Cyprus several incidents of sickle-cell anaemia are reported each year. The Holy Synod decided that among the documents that the spouses-to-be are required to submit to the Church for the issuing of a licence for the solemnization of a religious wedding ceremony, there should be a certificate from a state-appointed doctor proving that they had been examined for sickle-cell anaemia. Even when the test shows that the disease is present, the marriage may still go ahead. The test aims exclusively at assisting the prospective spouses in making grave decisions concerning the future of their family.[16]

---

16 Apostolos Varnavas 44 (1983) 63-64.

IX. Church Finance

The Republic of Cyprus does not provide funding to religions, nor does it impose any special religious tax. Therefore, each religion administers its own property without state intervention. All religious institutions enjoy exemption from income tax (Art. 8(13), Law 118 (1)/2002), while all constructional materials, fittings and furniture for churches and mosques and all vestments and other articles which are imported for religious purposes by any Ecclesiastical and Religious Authorities, are eligible for relief from import duty and excise duty.

It should also be noted that, as a result of an agreement between the Republic of Cyprus and the Orthodox Church, the Church has granted immovable property to the Republic, which in return contributes to the payment of the stipends of parish clergy in rural areas. The government decided that this agreement should also include the clergy of the three constitutionally acknowledged religious groups of the Republic (Maronites, Armenians and Roman Catholics). State aid towards the Orthodox Church and the three religious groups reached in 2003 a total of 2,319,000 Cyprus Pounds (approximately 3,500,000 euros).

The Orthodox Church has set up central and local institutions for the administration of its property.

1. The central institutions are a) the Central Ecclesiastical Fund, b) the Audit Department and c) the Ecclesiastical Financial Board. All of these are situated in Nicosia.
   a) The Central Ecclesiastical Fund is supervised by the Holy Synod. Its resources are comprised of percentages of the total resources of the metropolises and the monasteries (Art. 123). It subsidizes the various ecclesiastical legal entities when their own finances do not suffice, and the various ecclesiastical activities, such as the operation of the hieratic school, the publication of the official review "Apostolos Varnavas" and Cypriot participation in inter-ecclesiastical and inter-religious events (Art. 124).
   b) The Audit Department is supervised by the Holy Synod and inspects the management of the property of the archdiocese, the metropolises and the "royal" monasteries (Art. 125). It is staffed by lay persons (Art. 127).
   c) The Ecclesiastical Financial Board is made up of ten lay members, who serve a four year term (Art. 130). It drafts rec-

ommendations as to the best possible use of Church property (Art. 129). The recommendations are not binding unless they are adopted by the Holy Synod (Art. 137).
2. The local institutions are a) the See Committee, b) the See Fund, c) the Fund for the Wages of the Clergy, d) the Parochial Committees, e) the Abbatial Councils and f) philanthropic and charitable ecclesiastical foundations in general.
   a) There is a See Committee based in each metropolis. Its chairman is the metropolitan and there are eight other members, four clergy and four lay (Art. 140). The See Committee is charged with the study, supervision and management of the finances of its diocese (Art. 152).
   b) The See Fund operates under the directions of the See Committee and it is responsible for the fiscal management of the finances of each metropolis (Art. 155).
   c) The Fund for the Wages of the Clergy pays a special allowance to clergymen in addition to the revenues that they have from their parish, so that their overall income is levelled and equalised (Art. 157).
   d) The Parochial Committee manages the finances of the parish. This Committee is chaired by the parish priest and comprises two to four other members from among the laity, elected every four years by the parishioners (Art. 158).
   e) The Abbatial Council is chaired by the Abbot and manages the property of the monastery (Art. 181).
   f) Each metropolis may establish philanthropic and other charitable foundations such as orphanages, old-people's homes and boarding schools (Art. 187). Each of them is administered by a council, appointed and chaired by the metropolitan (Art. 188). Foundations that have been instituted by virtue of a last will and testament and placed under the jurisdiction of the Church, operate under the conditions of the testator.

X. *Criminal Law and Religion*

In addition to constitutional provisions, certain religious acts are protected by penal law. Criminal offences that are characterized as religion-related in the Cypriot penal code are: the defamation of religions (Art. 138), the disturbance of religious assemblies (Art. 139), unlawful trespass into burial places (Art. 140), the affront to religious sentiments by word or act (Art. 141), and the circulation of publications that are defamatory and injurious to religions, constituting criminal libel (Art. 142). It should be noted that under Cyprus law, clergy do not enjoy exemption from criminal or civil procedure as a result of any kind of confessional secret.

XI. Legal Status of Clergy, Monks and Laity

Becoming an Orthodox Christian is effected by baptism and unction, which in the Eastern Church are administered simultaneously. Members of the Church of Cyprus are:
a) all Orthodox Christians who permanently reside in the island, regardless of citizenship, sex, or age; and
b) all persons of Cypriot origin who were baptised in Cyprus but live abroad (Art. 2).

This latter provision is an innovation,[17] as according to the views of the Greek Orthodox Churches (the Ecumenical Patriarchate, the Patriarchates of Alexandria and Jerusalem and the Archdioceses of Cyprus and Greece) the greater Diaspora is subject to the Ecumenical Patriarchate of Constantinople. The Church of Cyprus has not, however, established any parishes abroad and as a result, Cypriots who live abroad continue to be ministered to by the Ecumenical Patriarchate. The status of Orthodox Christian is forfeited with death, excommunication or voluntary secession from the Church.

As in every Orthodox Church, members of the Cypriot Church are divided into 1) clergy, 2) monks and 3) laity.
1) Clergy are composed of deacons, presbyters and bishops. They hold ceremonial, administrative, and teaching authority. The ordination of a deacon or a presbyter is performed by at least one bishop. The ordination of a bishop is performed by the archbishop or, by order of the latter, by the most senior metropolitan (Art. 63(5)). If the see of a metropolitan is vacant, the archbishop acts as vicar of the see (Art. 33).

---

17 C. Papastathis, *On the Administrative Organization*, 66.

The archbishop and metropolitans are elected by an Electoral Assembly, which is composed of clergy, monks and laity (Art. 62-63). A candidate is expected to be unmarried, to be over thirty years old, to be a graduate of a Theology school, to be distinguished for his integrity and piety, and to have completed ecclesiastical service of at least five years as a clergyman (Art. 71).

The status of clergyman is forfeited, when a clergyman is unfrocked. The penalty of unfrocking is imposed by the Holy Synod, convened as a tribunal (Art. 22) In case of prelates, the penalty of unfrocking is imposed by a superior synodical court (Art. 25). The capacity of clergyman may be regained when a pardon has been granted by the same court that had issued a conviction (Art. 24).

The law of the Republic of Cyprus contains no provisions as to the legal status of the clergy. The Charter limits itself to the impediment of contracting marriage (Art. 220(2d)) and to the establishment of a provision concerning the succession of prelates and unmarried clergy. The succession of married clergy is governed by the rules of succession contained in the statutes of civil law, while the succession of unmarried deacons and presbyters is governed by the stipulations of the Charter concerning the succession of prelates (Art. 74), only if they served as employee of a metropolis, and regardless of whether they were still in such service at the time of their death (Art. 79). Under canon law, clergy are prohibited from practising certain professions: profitable activities, which are inconsistent with their presbyteral function; the assumption of state offices; and more generally of secular concerns.

2) The status of monk is acquired by tonsure (Art. 100). The minimum age for tonsure is eighteen, after the candidate has completed a three-year term as a novice (Art. 102). Tonsure is performed by a bishop or a presbyter with the permission of the local bishop; otherwise it is null and void (Art. 103). Hiero-monks and hiero-deacons, who have undergone tonsure in order to become presbyters and deacons respectively, also belong to the order of monks (Art. 100-101). The law of the Republic of Cyprus contains no provision as to the legal status of monks. The Charter limits itself to the impediment of contracting marriage (Art. 220 (2d)) and the prohibition of exercising property rights on real estates (Art. 107). The provisions of canon law apply together with the internal regulations of monasteries.

3) Lay persons participate in all aspects of the work done by the Church. The participation of laity in the Church of Cyprus is probably the strongest in the entire Orthodox world, both in the extent of its competencies and its elevation to the status of an organ of Church administration[18]. Lay people participate in most of the central and peripheral organs of administration of the Church, as well as in the management of property and in the Electoral Assembly which votes for the archbishop and the metropolitans on the island. In these functions they are not appointed, but are elected by secret and universal ballot by the congregation of the Church, with no discrimination between men and women.

In particular, lay persons participate in
a) the election of the archbishop and the metropolitans (Art. 62-63),
b) the central institutions for the administration of church property (Art. 127, 131),
c) the local institutions of Church administration (Art. 75, 146, 161, 178),
d) the administration of philanthropic and other charitable ecclesiastical foundations (Art. 188),
e) the ecclesiastical courts of family law (Art. 242, 250).

If a lay person commits a canonical offence, a penance or a canonical penalty may be imposed by either the Bishop or the Holy Synod, depending on the gravity of the offence.

XII. Bibliography

Chrysostomos, Archbishop of Cyprus, Introductory Report on the New Charter of the Church of Cyprus (in Greek), *Apostolos Varnavas* 40 (1979), 376-406.

Dizdar K., "The Origin and Administration of the Cyprus Evkaf", *Proceedings of the First International Cyprological Congress*, vol. II/1, 1973, 63-78.

Emilianides A., "Private International Law in Cyprus", *Symposium on Cypriot Juridical Issues*, (in Greek), Thessaloniki, 1974.

Mantzouneas E., Ecclesiastical Law of the Apostolic Orthodox Church of Cyprus (in Greek), Evrihou/Cyprus, 1988.

---

18 *C. Papastathis, On the Administrative Organization*, 84.

Papastathis C., "The New Statutory Charter of the Church of Cyprus" (in Greek), *Hydor ek Petras*, St Nicholas, Crete, 1980, no. 5-6, 5-17.

Papastathis C., On the Administrative Organization of the Church of Cyprus, (in Greek), Thessaloniki 1981.

Papastathis C., "The Legal Status of Religions in the Republic of Cyprus", *The Status of Religious Confessions of the States Applying for Membership to the European Union*, Strasbourg 2000.

Papathomas G., L' Église Autocéphale de Chypre dans l' Europe Unie, Approche Nomocanonique, Katerini 1998.

Polyzoides C., A Commentary on the Charter of the Church of Cyprus, (in Greek), Thessaloniki, 1997.

Serghides G., Internal and External Conflict of Laws in Regard to Family Relations in Cyprus, Nicosia, 1988.

Tornaritis C., "The Relations Between Church and State Under the Law of Cyprus", (in Greek), *Review of Public and Private Law* (in Greek), Nicosia 1967, 9-16.

Tornaritis C., The Ecclesiastical Courts Especially in Cyprus, Nicosia, 1976.

Ringolds Balodis
State and Church in Latvia

I. Social Facts

Latvia is a country of 2.3 million people, living in an area of 64,589 sq. km near the Baltic Sea. The ethnic composition of the Latvian population in 2000 was as follows:

Latvians	57.6 %
Russians	29.6 %
Byelorussians	4.1 %
Ukrainians	2.7 %
Poles	2.5 %
Lithuanians	1.4 %
Jews	0.4 %
Germans	0.1 %
others	1.6 %

Now, at the beginning of the 21st century, Latvia is a multi-confessional country, where the three largest denominations are the Catholics, the Lutherans and the Orthodox Church. Altogether, there are about 170 different denominations and religious groups.

According to a survey made by a Latvian public opinion research centre in 2003, 49.3 % of the inhabitants of Latvia do not read the Bible, 4 % read the Bible almost every day, and about half read the Scriptures from time to time. According to the survey data, the declared religious affiliations of the population are:

Orthodox	25 %
Lutherans	25 %
Roman Catholics	21 %
Old Believer Orthodox	2.7 %
Adventists	0.4 %
Jews	0.1 %

In this survey 9 % considered themselves to be believers without identifying themselves with any particular denomination, while 12 % declared themselves to be non-believers. There are significant numbers of atheists. Orthodox Christians, many of them Russian-speaking, non-citizen, permanent residents, are concentrated in the major cities, while many Catholics live in the east.

Data at the disposal of the Board of Religious Affairs seem to be more reliable since these are data from the denominations themselves. The membership figures derived from this data are:

Roman Catholics	433,480
Evangelical Lutherans	400,300
Orthodox	350,000
Old Believers	60,000
Baptists	6,788
Evangelical Religion Christians & New Generation	6,589
Seventh Day Adventists	3,869
Trinity (Pentecostal)	3,721
Muslims	1,000
New Apostolic	973
Methodists	750
Latter Day Saints (Mormons)	605
'Dievturi' neo-pagans	603
Jews	550
Lutherans of the Augsburg Confession	392
Armenian Orthodox Apostolic Church	275
Krishna followers	*135
Jehovah's Witnesses	115
Reformats	95
Buddhists	75
Bahai'i	48
followers of *Vissarion*	23
Presbyterians	14

Others religions have in total 1,253 members. With regard to the Evangelical Lutherans, it must be noted that in 2000 the Church reported a figure of 400,300, while in 2001 and subsequent years, objecting to what they considered overstated numbers of Catholics and Orthodox believers (apparently through the use of different counting

---

* in 1995 – 2 400!

methods) it returned a figure of 37,000 in its report to the Board of Religious Affairs. Taking into account data about the number of believers provided by other churches, it seems that a figure of 400,300 Evangelical Lutherans believers in 2001 would be more accurate. So far as the Muslims are concerned, it should be said that the number is rather approximate.

Statistics on Religious Confession Congregations Registered in the Latvian Republic by 1 October, 2003

Confession	Number of congregations			
	1980	1990	2000	2003
Roman Catholics	178	187	247	252
Evangelical Lutherans	206	252	302	307
Augsburg Confession Lutherans	—	—	9	10
Orthodox	88	89	112	117
Old Believers	68	65	66	67
Baptists	62	61	87	90
Seventh Day Adventists	23	28	46	47
Methodists	—	—	10	12
Jews	4	4	8	13
Muslims	—	—	6	5
Vaishna (Krishna followers)	—	—	10	10
New Apostolic	—	—	11	11
Trinity (Pentecost)	2	7	77	57
Evangelical Religion Christians & New Generation	—	—	16	43
Buddhists	—	—	3	5
God Supporters	—	—	13	13
Jehovah's Witnesses	—	—	10	12
Latter Day Saints (Mormons)	—	—	3	3
Others religions/sects	—	3	22	24
Total	631	693	1058	1098

II. Historical Background

Before the German expansion in the 12th century, the territory of Latvia was inhabited by many kindred Baltic tribes (zemgali, kurschi, latgali). The most widespread religion among these tribes was a kind of paganism, '*Dievturība*'. As a result of Latvia neighbouring Orthodox Russia, there were some unsuccessful attempts to convert Latgali tribes to the Orthodox faith. According to historical records, Russian priests started to preach the Orthodox religion in Latvia in the 9th and 10th centuries. In 1180, the German Monk *Meinhardt* who had a special authorisation from the Knyaz of Polozk (as part of the Latvia fell in the Russian sphere of interest) started to preach in Latvia. When he failed to convert the pagan tribes to Christianity, he approached the Pope with a request to open a crusade in the Baltic. The aim of this war was to introduce Christianity in the Baltic. The request was granted, following which the German invasion of Latvia began. Despite some isolated uprisings, Latvia was under German control until the 18th century. Under the influence of German landowners the Lutheran doctrine spread, which later served as good soil for other branches of Protestantism. The year 1524 is considered as the year of the foundation of the Latvian Evangelical Lutheran Church.
After Sweden lost the Nordic War, Latvia was included in the Russian Empire in the 18th century. Russia tried to convert the newly acquired lands to the 'Tsar's faith'. Orthodox religion did not become popular among Latvians; however, a certain number of Latvians adhered to it. In the second half of the 17th century, Old Believers became active in Latvia. Despite Latvia being part of the Russian Empire, the Old Orthodox believers had found a haven in Latvia due to the distinctive and more liberal religious policy implemented in this region compared to others. Latvian Old Orthodox believers are the world's biggest group of the Old Believer Orthodox denomination and in the Grebenschikov church in Riga (the largest worship building of this belief in the world) is to be found the largest congregation of Old Believers (5,000 adherents).
Currently in Latvia there are about 5,000 Jewish people, whereas before the Second World War there were 100,000. The reason for decrease of the number of adherents to the Jewish faith is the holocaust practised by Nazis.

Seventh Day Adventists and Baptists have been active in Latvia since the end of 19th century, and Methodists, Jehovah's Witnesses, Muslims and Christian Scientists since the beginning of 20th century. The first Republic of Latvia was established on 18 November 1918 and existed till the Soviet occupation in 1940. The second Republic of Latvia was established in 1991. The proclamation of the independent democratic Republic of Latvia in 1918 largely became possible due to the promise of the founders of the state, who were representatives of the Catholic religion, to sign an agreement with the Holy See on the legal status of Roman Catholics in the country. Thus, the territorial unity of the Latvian State depended on religious tolerance towards the Catholics.

III. Legal Sources

1. Legal Principles

The state-church relationship in the Republic of Latvia is based on the following principles:

a. Separation

Separation of church and state has never implied segregation of religion from society or the complete exclusion of the Church from social life. This would not be possible in a democratic country, as religion and religious associations form one of the structural elements of society. In Latvia state and the church are separate, which implies that state institutions have a secular nature and religious organisations can fulfil the functions of the state only in special cases provided by law. State institutions supervise and control the conformity of activities of religious organisations to the applicable legislation. The Board of Religious Affairs is in charge of handling relations between the state and religious organisations and, if religious organisations so request, provides assistance in solving organisational, legal and other issues.

b. Religious freedom

According to the International Religious Freedom Report 2002 published by the Bureau of Democracy, Human Rights, and Labour, the Constitution of the Republic of Latvia provides for freedom of religion, and the government generally respects this right in practice. The Republic of Latvia guarantees the right to freedom of religion, including the right to adhere to a particular religion individually or in association with others or to have no religious affiliation, to freely change one's religion or conviction, as well as to freely express one's religious opinions in accordance with the existing laws. According to Article 4 of the Law on Religious Organisations, the explicit or implicit restriction of the rights of inhabitants or the grant of privileges to inhabitants, as well as offence to their feelings or incitement of hatred due to their attitude to religion are prohibited. Persons guilty of violating this provision are liable in accordance with the procedure prescribed by law. No reference may be made to a person's attitude to religion or his or her religious affiliation in identification documents issued by the state. However, it is provided in Article 4(4) of the Law on Religious Organisations that state and municipal institutions, public organisations, enterprises and commercial companies may not require from their personnel and other persons information concerning their attitude to religion or their religious affiliation.

c. "Traditionality"

There is no state religion. The Constitution of the Republic of Latvia (*Satversme*) does not mention any specific religion. The Latvian legislation (unlike that of Lithuania) contains no concept of "traditional" denominations. No such distinction is drawn in the Law on Religious Organisations and that Law does not list religions or religious denominations that are regarded as traditional. For all that, the confessions included in the Article 51 of the Civil Law, as having the right to solemnise the marriages of their members, are called "traditional". These are the Lutheran, Catholic, Orthodox, Old Believer, Methodist, Baptist, Seventh Day Adventist churches and the Jewish religious communities.

d. Respectful neutrality

Relations between the various religious communities are generally amicable. Ecumenism is still a new concept in the country, and traditional religions have adopted a distinctly reserved attitude towards the concept. Mutual relations of the state and religious organisations are managed by the Board of Religious Affairs, which on the request of religious organisations provides them with assistance they may need in addressing organisational, legal and other issues. The state recognises the right of parents and legal guardians to educate their children according to their religious convictions. According to Article 5(3) of the Law on Religious Organisations, the state recognises the right of parents and guardians to bring up their children in accordance with their religious creed.

e. *Delegation of particular powers*

The Government has delegated the right to register marriages only to some denominations, the clergy of which discharge the responsibilities of state officials, but are not paid fees or allowances by the state.
In the Constitution of the Republic of Latvia religion is mentioned only in the Article 99, which declares that "Everyone has the right to freedom of thought, conscience and religion. The Church shall be separate from the State." This provision was included in the Constitution in 1998, when a new section on human rights was added to the Constitution. The principle of the freedom of religion is spelt out in the Law on Religious Organisations of 7 September 1995.
The object of the Law is stated in Article 2 to be to grant the inhabitants of Latvia the right to freedom of religion, including the right to freely state one's attitude towards religion, to adhere to some religion, individually or in community with others, or not to adhere to any religion, to change freely one's religion in conformity with the existing legislation. The Law on Religious Organisations, in compliance with the Constitution, as well as international agreements concerning human rights in the sphere of religion, regulates social relations established through the exercise of the right to freedom of conscience and through engaging in the activities of religious organisations. The state protects the legal rights of religious organisations. The state, municipalities and their institutions, non-governmental and other organisations may not interfere with the religious activities of religious organisations.
In practice Latvia is a partial separation state, where the constitutionally declared separation of church and state does not work in practice. Latvia does not associate itself with any specific religion, and the question is not about religious tolerance, but about the interpretation of the Article about the separation of church and state in the

Constitution, because there is no clear opinion about where the borderline between the state and church should be strictly marked. The state and the Church are separate; however, if we speak about the main conditions that may ensure the Church's separation from the state, then practically none of these conditions exists in Latvia. This is understandable, taking into account that the Republic of Latvia is still young. It is not possible to achieve a perfect balance of theory and practice at once. It requires time to develop appropriate legislative norms in a particular social environment. State practice is often in conflict with the principles declared in the Article 99 of the Constitution (for example, only one religious association may be registered for each denomination).

2. *Agreements between State and Church*

In 1996, a working group was formed, which was charged with the development of an agreement on the legal status of the traditional churches in the Republic of Latvia, to be signed between the Government and those churches. The draft was rejected in 1997 as insufficiently developed, and many Latvian lawyers found this standard agreement unnecessary. Indeed, the draft contained little more than generalities. It was only on 9 October 2000, when the agreement with the Holy See on the status of the Roman Catholic Church was reviewed in the Council of Ministers, that the issue came back on the agenda. Cabinet members indicated that it was necessary to provide a balanced system, with equal rights for other religions on the model of the agreement with the Holy See. The Government prepared amendments to the Law on Religious Organisations providing that "the Council of Ministers shall be entitled to enter into an agreement with a religious community regarding matters related to that religious community and affecting the interests of its adherents and of the relevant denomination. Special laws may regulate the relations of the state and the religious community". The Latvian Parliament considered these amendments for two years (2000-2002) until, shortly before the Parliamentary elections, they responded to pressure from the churches and on 12 September 2002 ratified the agreement with the Holy See and added a new Article 7(5) to the Law on Religious Organisations providing that "Special laws can regulate the relations of the State and a Religious community."

There is no reference to agreements with other churches in this amendment, as the parliamentary Human Rights and Public Affairs

Committee decided that legally-binding agreements would only complicate relations between the state and the churches. However, in the autumn of 2003 both the Latvian Evangelical Lutheran Church and the Latvian Orthodox Church, acting on the basis of Article 7(5) of the Law on Religious Organisations, formulated draft laws and submitted them for examination to the Board of Religious Affairs. On analysis of both drafts it was found that a large part of the rules proposed in the draft laws was taken over from the agreement with the Holy See, and the content of the draft laws themselves was modelled closely on that agreement. The issue of the possible legal personality of the churches under public law has become acute and the Board of Religious Affairs has advanced the opinion that it would be better to sign agreements with churches and afterwards adopt special laws on the basis of those agreements. Despite massive criticism from the press, the Latvian Government concluded agreements with the seven traditional denominations on 8 June 2004. Agreements at this moment are under discussion in the Latvian Parliament.

3. Churches and Internal Organisation

According to the Law on Religious Organisations, religious organisations which indicate as their governing authority a religious organisation registered abroad may be registered as "autonomous religious organisations" in the Republic of Latvia, which actually means that Latvia takes into account the link between of congregation and its foreign centre. However, responsibility for compliance with the law rests on the registered congregation itself.
A large number of religious organisations incorporated in Latvia has indicated that their centres are located abroad. The Latvian Orthodox Church is canonically subject to the Moscow Patriarchate. The Roman Catholic Curia of the Riga Archdiocese is a religious organisation through which the authority of the Roman Catholic Church in the Riga Archdiocese is exercised in compliance with the teaching and discipline of the Roman Catholic Church and by which all the Latvian dioceses are controlled. The theological centre of the Buddhist congregation "Drinkung Kagyu Dharmachakra Centre" is situated in India. The centre of the Church of Jesus Christ of Latter-Day Saints (Mormons) is Salt Lake City (USA). The Seventh Day Adventist church is part of the Baltic Union, which in turn is within the Adventist Church Worldwide (General Conference). Similarly, the "Salvation Army", registered in Latvia as a congregation, is part of

the international body of the same name, being regionally subordinated to the Swedish corps. The Latvian Methodist Church is a component part of the United Nordic and Baltic Methodists, which appoints the furthermore appointing leader (superintendent) of the Latvian church. Of the twelve Muslim congregations in Latvia, seven have declared as their theological centre the Muslim Spiritual Board registered in Russia. These congregations in their standing rules have acknowledged that they are subject to their centre in religious, administrative and financial matters. Other Muslim congregations have claimed an "autonomous" status, but it is certain that four of them are subject to the theological centre in Saudi Arabia, and one to Tatarstan. The Sukyo Mahikari Latvian congregation is a constituent part of the organisation with similar name registered in Japan. The congregation indicates that it is subject to the oversight of a Luxemburg-based regional centre for Europe and Africa. The highest governing body of the Latvian Bahai' congregation is situated in Haifa (Israel). The Riga congregation of Saint Gregory the Illuminator (Armenian) Church is within the Eparchy for New-Nahichevan and Russia of the Armenian Apostolic Church. The "parent church" of the Christian Science congregation in Riga is "The First Church of Christ Scientist".

According to Article 14(4) of the Law on Religious Organisations religious organisations are allowed to invite foreign clergymen or missionaries to engage in religious activities in the Republic of Latvia, only if they have arranged permits of residence for them in accordance with the procedure prescribed by law. Visa regulations effective since 1999 require religious workers to present either an ordination certificate or evidence of religious education that corresponds to a Latvian bachelor's degree in theology. The visa application process still is cumbersome. While the government is generally cooperative in helping resolve difficult visa cases in favour of missionary workers, problems still persist. In June 2002, an American religious worker successfully appealed against the refusal of a visa; however, that decision was later overturned after a further appeal by the government. Foreign evangelists and missionaries, including those from the United States, are permitted to hold meetings and to proselytize, but the Law stipulates that only domestic religious organizations may invite them to conduct such activities. Foreign religious denominations have criticized this provision. In 2002 religious organisations invited 176 foreign clergy.

4. Public Activities of Religious Communities within the Local Community Area

The objective of the state is to ensure that its citizens' exercise of freedom does not conflict with the interests of society and the core principles of democracy, ensuring at the same time that every individual can freely express his or her opinion in accordance with his or her religious or atheist conviction. Public activities of religious organisations are regulated in a particular way in Latvia. First of all, a refusal to accept an application for registration does not prevent individuals from exercising their freedom of religion and freedom to associate. The freedom to gather in peaceful groups is provided for in the law "On Meetings, Demonstrations and Pickets". Article 3 states that pursuant the law everyone has the right organise peaceful meetings, demonstrations and pickets or participate in the same. However, this does not refer to events organised by religious organisations. In accordance with Article 14(3) of the Law on Religious Organisations, religious organisations may engage in religious activities in public places only if they have received permission from the relevant municipality. Rules of public order must not be violated when engaging in religious activities.

IV. Legal Status

1. Legal Status of Religious Bodies

The legal status of legal entities in Latvia is defined by the Civil Law, but the status and the registration of religious organisations are regulated by the Law on Religious Organisations of 7 September 1995. Other public organisations (except trade unions and businesses, which are subject to a different law) are regulated by the Law "On Public Organisations and their Associations". Although the Latvian government does not require the registration of religious groups, the Law accords religious organizations certain rights and privileges when they register, such as status as a separate legal entity for owning property or other financial transactions, as well as tax benefits for donors. Registration also eases the rules for public gatherings.

According to the Law on Religious Organisations, twenty-five persons of full age registered in Latvian Citizens Register and sharing one confessional affiliation, may establish a religious organisation. Ten or more congregations of the same denomination with permanent registration status may form a religious association. As provided by the Law on Religious Organisations, religious organisations (church congregations, religious communities and dioceses), seminaries, monasteries and diaconal institutions are to be registered. Only churches with religious association status may establish theological schools or monasteries.

A decision to register a church is made by the Board of Religious Affairs which was established at the end of 2000. The Board of Religious Affairs is a state authority supervised by the Ministry of Justice, which acts pursuant to regulations of the Council of Ministers. The Board of Religious Affairs is a legal entity. Within the limits of its competence, it ensures the implementation of state policy and the co-ordination of religious affairs, manages issues related to the state-church relationship and monitors the working of the applicable regulations dealing with religious practices within the state. It also submits proposals aimed at preventing human rights violations related to religion in accordance with the Latvian Constitution and international agreements. The Head of the Board of Religious Affairs is appointed and dismissed by the Council of Ministers. The Head of the Board of Religious Affairs is responsible for the work of the Board and the performance of its functions.

The statutes of a religious organisation can contain by-laws regulating the internal matters of the organisation. The Board of Religious Affairs has to process applications within one month.

Having been registered at the Board of Religious Affairs, religious organisations are given the status of legal persons. It is not provided by legislation of the Republic of Latvia that registration is obligatory to express freedom of belief. Therefore, every unregistered religious group has right to conduct services, religious rituals and ceremonies and to carry out charitable work, unless those break the law.

The activity of religious organisations is based on statutes (regulations) filed with the Board of Religious Affairs, canonical rules, and the Constitution and legislation of the Republic of Latvia. In accordance with Article 14 of the Law on Religious Organisations the activities of these organisations are based on their canons and statutes. In conformity with the Article 1 of the Law on Religious Organisations, religious activities include the manifestation of a religion, faith or cult, the performance of religious ceremonies or rituals and the providing religious instruction by preaching. After it has obtained the status of a legal entity, the religious organisation can: (1) organise public services; (2) create monasteries and educational establishments for its clergy (only registered religious communities have this right); (3) perform religious activities in hospitals, residential homes, penal institutions and the National Armed Forces; and (4) use religious symbols, the regulations providing that "only religious organisations or institutions established by such have the right to use the name and symbols of religious organisations in their official forms and seals."

The activity of religious organisations is restricted in accordance with the Article 116 of the Latvian Constitution. Activities of religious organisations promoting religious intolerance and hatred, breaking the law and inciting others to do so, violating or failing to observe the statutes of religious organisations, or threatening state security, public order and peace or the health or morals of other persons, can be ordered to cease by court injunction. Article 14 of the Law on Religious Organisations also provides that the state has the right to restrict the activities of religious organisation and their followers on those grounds. The government must ensure that citizens can freely practise their religion; however, religious freedom does not release anybody from the obligation to observe the law. If necessary, the state has the legal power to restrict manifestations of religion in order to protect the rights of other people, the democratic nature of the state, public security, public order, public welfare, and the morals and health of other people.

A religious organisation has the right to submit a renewed application after its registration has been refused, if it has eliminated the reasons mentioned in the decision refusing registration. An appeal can be brought against a decision by the chairman of the Board of Religious Affairs on the registration of a religious organisation or the refusal to register within 10 days of its receipt.

Re-registration of religious organisations required under Article 8(4) of the Law on Religious Organisations applies only to congregations of denominations starting their activity in the Republic of Latvia for the first time and not belonging to religious communities already registered in Latvia. The aim of re-registration is to ascertain the loyalty of a certain congregation towards the Latvian state and the compliance of its activity with the applicable legislation. It should be added that after the tenth re-registration, a religious organisation obtains the status of permanently registered. At the present 1,160 religious organisations and their establishments are registered at the

Board of Religious Affairs; 81 congregations of those have to be re-registered annually.

Article 7(3) of the Law on Religious Organisations provides that a particular denomination may create only one registered religious community. Before this provision came into effect, the Trinity Confession had two registered religious communities, namely the Latvian Trinity Community Centre and the International Divine Community Latvian Trinity Parish Association. Nevertheless, a number of unregistered denominations campaign for the Latvian Law on Religious Organisations to provide the opportunity for the registration of an unlimited number of religious communities within one denomination, allowing for example the registration of the Confessional Lutheran Church and the Free Orthodox Church.

These rules as to the registration of congregations appear to comply with the principles of human rights: under the Law on Religious Organisations twenty-five persons of full age registered in Latvian Citizens Register and sharing one confessional affiliation, may establish a religious organisation, provided that all registration documents (the statutes of the congregation, minutes of meeting, etc.) are executed and submitted to the appropriate state institutions in a proper way. On the other hand, so far as the conditions for registering a denomination are concerned, the state seems to have an excessive interest in the registration process, contradicting the freedom of religion. A religious community can be registered only if ten congregations of the denomination are united and no religious community has been registered in the appropriate denomination before. This state restriction is not justified. It is not based on any threat to public order, state security, health or morals.

2. *New Religious Movements*

The United States State Department in its 1997 report on religious freedom criticises Latvia for violation of religious freedom on account of Latvia's refusal to register Jehovah's Witnesses. This problem was resolved, and in the autumn of 1998 the Latvian Ministry of Justice registered the first two Jehovah's Witnesses congregations. At present there are 12 congregations of this movement registered in Latvia, and Latvian law enforcement agencies have no information on any abuses with respect to the freedom of this movement. Before the Christian Science congregation was registered in 2002, the Ministry of Justice has six times declined its application as, according to the Latvian Medical Association, the main activity of this organisation, i.e. treatment of people with non-medical means, contradicted Latvian law and the Code of Medical Ethics.

3. Churches and Religious Communities within the Political System

Pursuant to the 1992 Law of the Republic of Latvia "On Nongovernmental Organisations and Associations", a political organisation may be established by 200 natural persons, and therefore the churches in Latvia have not established their own party. Existing Latvian legislation does not prohibit religious organisations from participating in the election campaign. During the parliamentary elections of 2002 the major churches (Lutherans, Catholics and Orthodox) took an active part in the election campaign of the political organisation "First Party". Though the churches are not sponsors of the party, this party, called "the clerical party", has got into the Parliament and is part of the governing coalition. The party tries to support traditional and other religious organisations as best it can. In 2002-2003 one of the members to this party, a Baptist minister, held office as Minister of State for Children and Family Affairs.

V. Churches and Culture

1. Religious Education

Under Article 6 of the Law on Religious Organizations, the Christian religion may be taught in state and municipal schools to persons who have requested it in a written application. Applications by minors to be taught Christian religion must be approved by parents or guardians. If the minor is under 14 years of age, the minor's parents or guardians submit the application. The concept of Christian religious instruction does not include and cannot include the Jewish Faith or Islam. Christian religion in accordance with the curriculum approved by the Ministry of Education and Science may be taught by teachers of the Evangelical Lutheran, Roman Catholic, Orthodox, Old Believers or Baptist denominations, if not less than 10 students of the same

school have expressed their wish to study the religious teaching of the relevant denomination. The teachers must be selected by the denomination leaders and be approved by the Ministry of Education and Science. Since 1998 the Law has been supplemented by Article 6(5), which provides that religious teaching and ethics classes are financed from the state budget. In 1998 the Government provided funds for this education 100,000 Ls (i.e. US$210,000). Ethics is offered as an alternative to religious instruction.
Students at state-supported national minority schools may also receive education in the religion "characteristic of the national minority" on a voluntary basis. Other denominations may provide religious education in private schools only.
In accordance with Article 15 of the agreement between the Republic of Latvia and the Holy See, the teaching of the Catholic religion shall be conducted exclusively on the basis of a programme approved by the Bishops' Conference of Latvia, in agreement with the Ministry of Education and Science, and must be undertaken only by qualified teachers who possess a certificate of competence issued by the Bishops' Conference of Latvia; the revocation of the certificate carries with it the immediate loss of the right to teach the Catholic religion.
According to the Law, everyone individually or in groups, has the right to religious instruction in the educational establishments of religious organisations. In national minority schools supervised by the state or municipalities, if such is the wish of the students and their parents or guardians, the religion appropriate to the particular national minority may be taught in compliance with procedures prescribed by the Ministry of Education and Science. Thus for example, the Orthodox, whose religion is not mentioned in the Law on Religious Organisations, can ensure religious classes for their children.

3. Theological Faculties at State Universities

The University of Latvia's Theological Faculty is nondenominational. The Faculty of Theology at the University of Latvia was established in 1920, however in 1940 in consequence of occupation by the Soviet Union it was abolished. On the collapse of the Soviet regime at the end of the 80s, the Faculty was restored. Now the Faculty of Theology, pursuant to the Faculty Regulations approved in 1998 by the University Senate, is an ecumenical Christian academic and research department of the University of Latvia grooming theologians, academic researchers in religious studies, lecturers and professional teachers of religion and ethics, as well as specialists in ethical issues. The Faculty is subordinate to no church; it co-operates with all churches. Students and lecturers are from various denominations. This non-denominational stance has rather specific consequences: the separation of state and church here manifests itself as separation of Theology and the Church. The work of the Faculty reflects the direction of Theology more towards social issues, which really should be within the sphere of church activities under the classical model, rather than ministerial training.

4. Religion and the Mass Media

The Law does not regulate or prescribe a special registration procedure for the media of religious organisations. Religious organisations can establish magazines, newspapers and periodicals according to the general procedure. This liberal attitude has sometimes created problems. An example is the religious paper *Latvian Lutheran* published by the Augsburg Institute, a company registered in Latvia. The opinions of this newspaper differ from the official position of the Latvian Evangelical Lutheran Church. This led the Board of Religious Affairs in 1999, responding to church complaints, to seek an explanation from the company, enquiring why it engaged in religious activities which only religious organisation were permitted to do according to the Law.

5. Shrines being officially recognised by the Republic of Latvia

In Latvia 881 temples and cult buildings in all are owned by religious organisations, including: 300 by Lutherans, 216 by Catholics, 122 by Orthodox, 66 by Old Believer Orthodox, 66 by Baptists, 79 by Seventh Day Adventists, 24 by Pentecostalists, and 8 by the Salvation Army. A large proportion of the churches are listed as historic monuments of national importance. The most famous and best-known churches are Riga Dome owned by the Lutherans and the Aglona Basilica of the Roman Catholics.
The Aglona Basilica of the Roman Catholics is currently the only officially recognised shrine of the Republic of Latvia. The Basilica was built in 1800 by the Dominican monks. The Aglona Basilica was

visited and consecrated by Pope John Paul II in 1993, and attracts many pilgrims. Every year on 14 and 15 August there are celebrations to mark the Catholic feast of the Assumption of the Blessed Virgin Mary. Large numbers take part; for example, on 15 August 2003 about 100,000 pilgrims participated in the Aglona celebration.

The Shrine has a particular legal regulation. According to Article 1 of the Law of 1995 "On the International Shrine in Aglona", Aglona is an international shrine as well as being a part of the cultural and historical heritage of Latvia, a cultural monument and a place for religious pilgrimages. The Shrine of Aglona must be used exclusively for religious and spiritual observances under the auspices of the Latvian Catholic Church. On the basis of this Law, the government of Latvia promulgated in 1999 regulations "Concerning the Activities of Natural and Legal Persons in the Protected Area of Aglona Shrine". In the regulations it was provided that timber felling and any work affecting the river or lake, any construction or installation of premises and buildings, hotels or places of entertainment may be carried out only with the written permission of the congregation. In the Shrine area, no-one may, without the congregation's permission, sell or advertise alcoholic drinks and amusement products. Without the same permission, hunting and fishing in the area are also prohibited.

In accordance to the Article 11 of the Agreement with the Holy See, the Shrine of Aglona is part of the cultural and historical heritage of the Republic of Latvia, and as such is protected under Latvian law. Besides the building of the Basilica itself, the sacred square in front of the Basilica and the cemetery and the spring area, the protected area of the Shrine includes all other buildings, structures and lands belonging to the Catholic Church.

VI. Labour Law within the Religious Communities

The employment relationship is mentioned only twice in the Law on Religious Organisations. First, Article 19 of the Law provides that in case of termination of a religious organisation's activity, this organisation terminates its work relationship with all its employees in accordance with the Latvian Labour Law. Secondly, Article 14 provides that religious organisations can appoint or elect and dismiss their ministers in accordance with its own statutes, and employ and dismiss other employees in accordance with the applicable labour legislation. The current Latvian Labour Law does not address the particular problems of religious organisations, which means that religious organisations are subject to the same legal rules as any other public or commercial companies.

Article 7(2) of the Labour Law of 20 June 2001 contains a prohibition on any direct or indirect discrimination based on a person's race, skin colour, gender, age, religious, political or other conviction. The Article 29 of the Labour Law provides for "Prohibition of Differential Treatment" barring differential treatment from an employer towards an employee based on race, skin colour, age, disability, political or other convictions, national or social origin, property or marital status and religious conviction. In the same Article it is further provided that differential treatment based on the religion of an employee is permitted only in cases where adherence to particular religion is an objective and justified precondition for performance of the relevant work or for the relevant employment. Likewise the said Law prescribes (Article 33(2)(4)) that a job interview may not include questions which do not apply to performance of the intended work or are not related to the suitability of the employee for such work, or any directly or indirectly discriminatory questions. The category of discriminatory questions includes questions concerning "religious conviction or membership of a religious denomination". Article 34(1) of the Labour Law prescribes that if when establishing an employment relationships an employer has violated the prohibition of differential treatment, an applicant has the right to request appropriate compensation. In case of a dispute, the amount of compensation is to be determined by the court at its discretion.

VII. Finances of the Churches

There is no single law in Latvia dealing with taxation as it affects the churches. The financial and tax issues of the churches are dealt with in many Laws and regulations. Particular Laws which address a number of issues related to the financial activities of religious organisations include the following:

- under Article 15 of the Law on Religious Organisations, these organisations are entitled to engage in business activities. If their

revenues exceed 500 minimal monthly salaries within a calendar year, the religious organisation has to establish a company and perform its activities in accordance with the Law "On Entrepreneurship";
- the Law on Entrepreneurship provides that religious organisations are entitled to engage in business activities, establish companies, and acquire shares in companies;
- under Article 16 of the Law on Religious Organisations, religious organisations may own movable and real property, however, they are prohibited from mortgaging church buildings or ritual artefacts, and creditors may not foreclose on the same.

The next important issue is related to *tax relieves* for religious organisations:

- according to the Law on Real Estate Tax, real property owned by a religious organisation and used for performing religious activities is not taxable with effect from 1 January 2001;
- the Law on Value Added Tax envisages that religious, ceremonial and other not-for-profit services of religious organisations are exempt from Value Added Tax. Money contributions and donations to religious organisations are also Value Added Tax exempt;
- companies that make donations to religious organisations in accordance with permissions issued by the Ministry of Finance may claim tax relief of 85 % as provided under Article 20 of the Law on Corporate Income Tax. These tax relieves are not applied to companies that have a continuing tax liability for the previous fiscal year as at the first day of the second month of the new taxation period. In accordance with the Law, the total tax relief may not exceed 20 % of the total tax liability of the company;
- under the Law on Individual Income Tax a physical person who has made donations to a public or religious organisation (which has a licence issued by the Ministry of Finance) can deduct this amount from his or her taxable income before accounting for individual income tax. This amount should not exceed 20 % of the individual's taxable income. It should be pointed out that religious organisations do not pay corporate or individual income tax. If religious organisations receive foreign technical assistance, they are granted customs tax and Value Added Tax relieves.
- religious organisations have the right to receive humanitarian aid.

Cargoes of humanitarian aid are tax and duty exempt according to the procedure provided under the law. Religious organisations that are entitled to be beneficiaries of humanitarian aid are listed on an annual basis according to special regulations issued by the Council of Ministers.

VIII. Religious Assistance in Public Institutions

The work of religious organisations at public institutions is mainly carried out through the chaplaincy service. In 2002 there were in Latvia 17 Lutheran, 10 Baptist, 7 Pentecostal, 4 Seventh Day's Adventist chaplains and 1 Old Believer Orthodox chaplain. Chaplaincy is the only approved profession in Latvia where ministerial status and recognition from the church is required. According to Article 1(8) of the Law on Religious Organisations chaplains are the spiritual personnel who perform their duties at penal institutions, units of the National Armed Forces and elsewhere, where ordinary pastoral care is not available. In accordance with Article 14(5) of the Law on Religious Organisations, chaplains in Latvia function according to the Regulations of the Council of Ministers on the Chaplain Service. The Council of Ministers issued the Chaplain Service Regulations on 2 July 2002.
Chaplains' activity is financed and given material and technical support by the appropriate state or self-governmental institution within its regular budget, or by the relevant religious organisation.
The Regulations govern the work of the chaplaincy service in the Republic of Latvia and provide that:

- *"Chaplains of custody institutions"* give ecclesiastical service to the personnel of places of imprisonment, conviction or confinement, morally support and advise on religious and ethical questions, make arrangements for moral education. The structure of chaplaincy service at places of confinement is determined by the Board of the Places of Confinement in agreement with the Board of Religious Affairs. The chaplaincy services are regulated by the byelaws of the institutions supervised by the Prison Administration. All prisoners may see a clergyman tête-à-tête once in a month.

- *"National Armed Forces Chaplains"* provide ecclesiastical service for the personnel of the National Armed Forces. National Armed Forces Chaplains are given service ranks. Chaplains do not carry guns. These chaplains, being military persons, start professional military service in the National Armed Forces and carry it out under their free will according to procedure provided for in the applicable legislation. National Armed Forces Chaplains' activity is supervised by the Chief Chaplain of the National Armed Forces, who is administratively directly subordinated to the Commander of National Armed Forces. In accordance with the Paragraph 14 of the Chaplain Service Regulations, National Armed Forces chaplains are subordinated in administrative questions to their unit commander, in questions connected with chaplaincy activity to the Chief Chaplain of the National Armed Forces, and in questions connected with religion to the spiritual leader of the appropriate religious organisation.
- *"chaplains of airports, sea-ports and land transport terminals"* render ecclesiastical service to the personnel of airports, sea-ports and land transport stations, giving moral support and necessary advice on religious questions within their competence.
- *"chaplains of institutions of medical and social services"* render ecclesiastical service to the personnel and clients of institutions of medical and social services, giving them moral support and necessary advice connected with religious questions within their competence.

Only the following religious organizations can nominate persons as Chaplains: the Board of the Latvian Evangelical Lutheran Churches, the Riga Archidiocesan Roman Catholic Curia, the Latvian Orthodox Churches, the Latvian Old Believers Church Central Council, the Latvian Associated Methodist Churches, the Latvian Baptist Community Association, the Seventh Day Adventist Latvian Community Association, the Riga Jewish Religious Community and the International God Latvian Trinity Community Association.

In accordance with Article 23 to 29 of the Part III "Religious assistance to Catholics in the National Armed Forces of the Republic of Latvia" of the Agreement between the Republic of Latvia and the Holy See, "the Holy See shall establish within the Catholic Church in the Republic of Latvia a Military Ordinariate which, according to a special memorandum of understanding between the Ministry of Defence and the Bishops' Conference of Latvia, shall offer religious assistance to the Catholics within the National Armed Forces of the Republic of Latvia".

IX. *The Legal Status of Priests and Members of the Religious Orders*

In 2003 875 clergy were serving in the religious organisations registered in Latvia. They included:

149	Lutheran
121	Catholic
80	Baptist
77	Evangelical Religion Christians
75	Orthodox
76	Pentecostal
35	Seventh Day Adventist
35	Old Believer Orthodox
26	Jehovah's Witnesses

According to Article 1 of the Law on Religious Organisations officials of religious organisations are members of elected bodies (councils, boards and audit committees), including clergy. Clergy of religious organisations are archbishop, bishop, pastor, minister, priest, dean, rabbi etc.

Under the legislation currently in force in the Republic of Latvia, no privileges attach to the possession of spiritual or administrative office in a religious organisation. The only exception relates to military service. Under Article 21(1)(7) of the Compulsory Military Service Law, ordained clergy affiliated with any approved religious organisation in Latvia and persons studying for ordination in the seminaries of such religious organisations are not liable to compulsory active military service. Exemption from discharging military service due to religious reasons, and any attempt to use military rank to impose religious conviction is prohibited in Latvia. According to amendments of 28 June 2002 to that Law, persons liable to military service objecting to its performance by reason of their opinions, conscience or religious conviction, may perform an alternative form of service.

In accordance with Article 7 of the Agreement between the Republic of Latvia and the Holy See, the seal of the confessional is recognised as inviolable. Nobody may ever question a Catholic priest on matters connected with a confessional secret, even if that priest appears as a witness or party before a civil tribunal. However, this right of priests is not secured by the existing Criminal Procedure Law of the Republic of Latvia. While the Criminal Procedure Code of Latvia has been amended many times, it was adopted in the Soviet era. At present a new code has been prepared in which the seal of the confessional is fully recognised. In the new draft of Criminal Procedure Law of the Republic of Latvia, which has received its first reading in Parliament, Article 121 named "Professional secrets protected under criminal procedure" is included. Clause 1(1) of the Article provides that there shall be no restrictions imposed on the right of clergy to refuse to give evidence about what is heard during confession, and to refuse to disclose any personal notes regarding such matters. There have been no cases in the courts of Latvia and there has been no discussion of an issue which has proved controversial in other countries as to the boundary between a mere conversation between an accused and a priest on the one hand and the making of a confession in a sacramental sense on the other; or whether a particular church regards confession in a sacramental sense.

X. *Criminal Law and Religion*

1. *Criminal Law*

Article 227 of the Criminal Law of the Republic of Latvia prescribes a penalty for unlawful activities of religious organisations and their members. For organising or managing a group which teaches or performs religious rituals creating a threat to public security and order, or person's health, rights or interests protected by law, or for participation in such activities, the penalty can be custody for the period up to 5 years or a fine of up to 100 minimal monthly salaries.[1] Article 150 of the Criminal Law prescribes a penalty for committing direct or indirect restriction of the rights of persons or of their freedom of

---

1 From 1 January 2004, the minimal salary stipulated by the government is LVL 80 or EUR 124.

choice on the basis of the attitudes of such persons towards religion (excepting activities in the institutions of a religious denomination), as well as for committing violation of religious sensibilities of persons or incitement of hatred in connection with the attitudes of such persons towards religion or atheism. The maximum penalty in these cases is custody for 2 years or a fine of up to 40 minimal monthly salaries.

For intentional interference with religious rituals (if such are not in violation of law and are not associated with violation of personal rights), Article 151 of Criminal Law provides for a penalty of community service, or up to 100 minimal monthly salaries.

2. *Administrative Legislation*

In accordance with the Latvian Civil Law (Article 1415) blasphemy constitutes misconduct. "Unsanctioned and indecent activities if their aim is contrary to religion, law or good morals, or they are aimed at avoiding law, cannot be the subject matter of a legal transaction and any such transaction is void." Article 4 of the Law on Religious Organisations also prohibits direct or indirect infringement of religious sensibilities of people.

Under Article 2 of the Law "On Trademarks and Geographical Indications", religious symbols cannot be registered as trademarks. The religious symbols fall into the group called "non-registrable marks". It is noteworthy that the legislator has included the religious symbols in the group of non-registrable marks which also includes state emblems.

Article 13(3) of the Law on Religious Organisations prohibits non-registered religious organisations from adopting the names and symbols of registered religious organisations. It is evident that the interest of the state is to preclude hatred caused by religious blasphemy.

Article 7 of the Law "On the Press and Other Public Means of Information" imposes a prohibition on the publication and dissemination of information advocating religious intolerance in Latvia. Equally there is a ban on commercials which infringe religious sensibilities. Article 4 of the Advertising Law prohibits in advertising express discrimination against a person due to his or her race, skin colour, gender, age, religious, political or other convictions, national or social origin, financial status or other circumstances. Moreover it is prohibited in advertising "to exploit the effect created by fear or superstition", to a certain extent being applicable also to religious conviction. Sanctions in respect of violation of these principles are not of criminal, but of an administrative and civil nature, but are severe enough to deter a producer or a disseminator of advertising from the publication of material offensive to religion. Also Article 20 of the Radio and Television Law provides that commercials may not injure human dignity and religious feelings.

XI. Matrimonial and Family Law

The practice of the registration of marriages by churches in Latvia derives from particular legal, historical and cultural conditions. During the Russian Empire period (when Latvia was a Russian province) marriage registration was not centralised and the legal registration of births, baptisms, death and burials, and also marriages was entrusted to the Russian Orthodox Church. In the Baltic states this privilege was extended also to the Lutheran and Catholic bodies. In 1917 the Russian Provisional Government adopted a law providing for freedom of religion and the right to have no specific religious affiliation. The law provided that persons who did not belong to any denomination could carry out civil status transactions in their local governments. This meant the replacement of the old system by an alternative (either Church or Register Office). Although in Russia the Bolsheviks deprived the churches of their right to execute civil status transactions and introduced civil status register offices, in the newly independent Republic of Latvia the law of the Russian Provisional Government as to freedom of religion along with other Russian laws related to civil status registration remained in force until 1920. In the 1922 the Constituent Assembly following a Swiss model issued the Matrimonial Law stipulating the duty of the state to execute civil status acts of its citizens. However, it allowed for certain churches to have the right to register civil status acts. Clergy could be criminally liable for failing promptly report such acts to government institutions. The Civil Law of 1937 indicated 10 confessions that were allowed to register the marriages of their members on behalf of the state. The member had right to choose whether to register their marriage in the state marriage register office or with the Church of their confession.

After Latvia became independent a second time, it restored the Civil Law of 1937 (as the Family Law section of the Civil Law); the practice of registration of marriages by the churches was also restored. In accordance with the Civil Law of the Republic of Latvia 8 confessions have the right to solemnise marriages. The renewed Civil Law provides that persons can register their marriage in the Marriage Register Office or with a clergyman. According to Article 51 of the Civil Law, if the persons wishing to marry belong to the Lutheran, Catholic, Orthodox, Old Believer, Methodist, Baptist, Seventh Day Adventist, or Jewish religion and they want to marry in their respective churches with the clergyman authorised by that church, the clergyman can register their marriage after due notice according to the regulations of the relevant church. Article 58 of the Civil Law provides that the clergy should inform the Marriage Register Office about the concluded marriage within 14 days. The Law on Civil Status Acts of 1993 (Article 13.2) provides that the clergyman needs to be authorised by the respective church to perform the marriage registration on behalf of the state.

The marriage validity problem is also mentioned in the concordat. In accordance with Article 8 of the Agreement between the Republic of Latvia and the Holy See canonical marriage from the moment of its celebration produces the civil effects determined by the legislation of the Republic of Latvia, provided no civil impediments exist between the contracting parties and the requirements of the laws of the Republic of Latvia have been met. The way and the time within which a canonical marriage is to be registered with the competent civil authority are determined by the laws of the Republic of Latvia.

At the moment, approximately one third of all marriages are solemnised in churches. In 2002, permissions to marry have been issued to 339 clergy. These clergy solemnized in 2002 2,276 weddings. Of those, 1018 were concluded by Lutherans, 679 by Catholics, 522 by Orthodox, 36 by Baptists, 12 by Seventh Day Adventists, 7 by Methodists and 2 by members of the Jewish community.

XII. Particular Questions of Ecclesiastical Law and Developments

In 2000 the Parliament of Latvia passed the Law "On Individual Data Protection". According to the Law, personal data are any information that relates to an identified or non-identified physical person. Personal information on religious adherence is "sensitive information". The Board of Religious Affairs can be considered as the "data controller" under the Law, because as provided by law, religious organisations are registered as legal persons and they provide state organisations with personal data of the founders of the particular religious organisation, including their addresses, and naturally, information on their religious conviction. If this sensitive information is not properly protected, it may happen that the availability of it causes a hidden discrimination. For example, there is a possibility that an employer who is a Catholic, when he obtains information that the interviewed individual is a Krishna follower, finds another excuse to refuse employment to this person. It should be noted that this happens at a time when religious conviction is not indicated in the person's identification documents and the Latvian Labour Law strictly prohibits inquiring about the religious conviction of the candidate.

XIII. Bibliography

Sources

1. Results of the 2000 population and housing census in Latvia – collection of statistical data. – Central Statistical Bureau of Latvia. Riga, 2002.
2. Item to mass media from the Board of Religious Affairs of the Ministry of Justice of the Republic of Latvia of June 2003 "On the activity reports of Religious associations (churches), dioceses and religious organisations in 2002".
3. *Balodis R..*, Valsts un Baznīca (*State and Church*). – R: Nordik, 2000.
4. *Balodis R..*, Baznīcu tiesības (*The Church Law*). – R: RBA, 2002.
5. State and Church in the Baltic States: 2001. (ed. *Balodis R..)* – R.: Latvian Association for Freedom of Religion, 2001 (94 l p.).

Legislation

1. Latvijas Republikas Satversme (*The Constitution of the Republic of Latvia*) //Latvijas Vēstnesis, 01.07.1993, Nr. 43;
2. 2000.gada 8.novembra "Latvijas Republikas un Svētā Krēsla līgums" (*"Agreement between the Republic of Latvia and the Holy See" of 8th November 2000*)// Latvijas Vēstnesis, 25.09.2002, Nr. 137 3.1995. gada 7.septembra

Reliģisko organizāciju likums (*Law on Religious Organisations of 7th September 1995*) //Latvijas Vēstnesis, 26.09.1995, Nr. 146;
3. Latvijas Republikas Ministru kabineta 2000.gada 19.septembra noteikumi Nr.321 "Reliģisko lietu pārvaldes nolikums" (*Regulations of Council of Ministers of the Republic of Latvia of 19th September 2000 "Rule of the Board of Religious Affairs"*)//Latvijas Vēstnesis, 22.09.2000, Nr. 331/333;
4. Latvijas Republikas Ministru kabineta 2002gada 2.jūlija noteikumi Nr. 277 "Noteikumi par kapelānu dienestu" (*Regulations of Council of Ministers of the Republic of Latvia of 2th July 2002 "Regulations on the Chaplaincy Service"*)//Latvijas Vēstnesis, 05.07.2002, Nr. 101.

Jolanta Kuznecoviene
State and Church in Lithuania

I. Social Facts

According to statistical data Lithuania is an overwhelmingly Roman Catholic country. The majority of the Lithuanian population – 79 % – consider themselves Catholics. Although most of them are not regular worshippers (only 3 % attend church once a week or more frequently), Lithuanian Catholics are strongly committed to the ceremonies of the Catholic Church. Approximately 90 % of them indicated that they consider baptism, marriage, and burial according to Catholic rites to be very important. Nevertheless, as the census data indicate, 80 % hold that priests should not take part in politics or influence the way people vote.[1]

In 2001 the religious affiliation of the population of Lithuania was as follows:[2]

Confession	Membership	Membership as %
Roman Catholics	2,752,447	79
Russian Orthodox	141,821	4.07
Old Believers	27,073	0.78
Evangelical Lutherans	19,637	0.56
Evangelical Reformed	7,082	0.2
Jehovah's Witnesses	3,512	0.1
Muslims (Sunni)	2,860	0.08
Pentecostals (all)	1,307	0.04
Jews Word of Faith	1,272	0.04
Baltic Pagans	1,270	0.04
Baptists (all)	1,249	0.04
Adventists	547	0.02
New Apostolic Church	436	0.01

---

1 *Matulionis A.* (ed.) (2001), Europa ir mes, Vilnius, Gervelė, p. 129, 139.
2 Data from population census, 2001. Source: www.std.lt.

Confession	Membership	Membership as %
Buddhists	408	0.01
Eastern Rite Catholics		
Greek Catholics	364	0.01
Hare Krishna	265	0.01
Karaite	258	0.01
Methodists	211	0.01
Mormons	197	0.01
Non-believers	239	0.01
No particular religion	331,087	9.9
No response	186,447	5.35

II. Historical Background

The rise of the Lithuanian State is synonymous with the Lithuanian King Mindaugas who was baptised in 1251. At that time the See of Lithuania was formed. However, only in 1387 was Lithuania officially proclaimed a Christian State. Under the privilege of Grand Duke Jogaila, the Bishop of Vilnius was granted a generous amount of state land, and the churches and monasteries were exempted from their fiscal obligations to the state.[3]
The Catholic Church became powerful in the social, political, and cultural life of Lithuania. It was supported by the Grand Dukes and by the State. In order to reduce the influence of Protestantism and the advancement of the Uniates, the Lithuania Seimas (Parliament), adopted laws (the Constitutions of 1630, 1648, 1666, 1674) prohibiting the construction of new churches for other denominations. In 1733 the Seimas excluded the other denominations from participation in State affairs. In the Constitution of 1791 the Catholic faith was declared as pre-eminent.
A period of suppression for the Catholic Church began when Russia annexed Lithuania in 1795. According to documents published by Catherine II in the period between 1769 and 1772, most of the privileges which had previously been conferred on Catholic priests were withdrawn. Moreover, the Government was given the right to inter-

---

3 *Jucas M., Luksaite I., Merkys V.* (1988), Lietuvos istorija, Vilnius, Mokslas.

vene in the internal life of the Church. It also withdrew the rights of the Catholic Church to appoint bishops independently, to establish new parishes, to appoint parish deacons and rectors of seminaries, to recruit students for the seminaries, to publish religious literature, or to admit other believers into the Catholic Church.

The oppression of the Catholic Church became more severe after the uprising of 1863. Public church processions were banned, the property and lands of the Catholic Church were confiscated, censorship of Catholic publications and sermons was introduced, and the publication of religious literature and the teaching of religious subjects in schools was forbidden.

State and Church relations changed when Lithuania regained independence on 16 February 1918. The Constitution of 1922 restored to religious communities the right to administer their internal affairs following their own canons and statutes, and to carry out cultural, charitable, and educational activities. The State recognised church registrations of marriages and deaths. Religious communities were also granted the right to a legal personality.

However, the new Constitution of the Republic of Lithuania, adopted in 1938, limited some of the rights of religious communities. The Constitution did not acknowledge the right of religious communities to manage their affairs according to their own canons and statutes. It also restricted their public activities, and did not guarantee either the recognition of registration of deaths, marriages and births, or state financial support for private confessional schools.[4]

The status of religious communities was essentially changed again after the Soviet occupation on 15 June 1940. Restrictions to the rights of the Churches were accompanied by nationalisation of their property, and the persecution and deportation of priests and believers.

A new period in State and Church relations began only after Lithuania regained its independence on 11 March 1990.

On 30 August 1991 diplomatic relations between the Holy See and the Republic of Lithuania were re-established. One year later the Lithuanian ambassador to the Holy See, K. Lozoraitis, presented his credentials at the Vatican.

The second document relevant for development of the Church and State relations was the Act of Restitution of the Catholic Church's Status in Lithuania adopted on 12 June 1990. This Act did several things: it recognised the right of the Church to manage its affairs ac-

---

4   *Vardys V.* (1997), Christianity in Lithuania, Cikaga, p. 240-269.

cording to the norms of canon law; it provided a guarantee from the State to cover losses; according to a reciprocal agreement between the Church and the State it guaranteed not to restrict the educational activities of the Church; and it made explicit the collaboration between State and Church on a basis of parity.

Although this Act did not have the force of law, it was relevant to the situation in 1990. The Act expresses the State's stance on those questions and its obligation to pass a law regulating relations between the State and the Church. However, the Act of Restitution dealt only with the Catholic Church.

III. Basic Structures

1. Legal Sources

The fundamental legal act regulating State and Church relations is the Constitution of the Republic of Lithuania adopted on 25 October 1992. The Constitution defines the basis of State and Church relations and implements the main principles of human rights. It guarantees the freedom of the individual to choose and manifest his or her religion or faith in worship, practice, and teaching (Articles 25 and 26). The Constitution provides that convictions, professed religion or faith may not justify committing a crime or the violation of law; while exercising their rights and freedoms, persons must observe the Constitution and not impair the rights and freedoms of other persons (Art. 28).

The most comprehensive provisions dealing with State and Church relations are contained in the Law of 1995 on Religious Communities and Associations (LRCA).[5] This law guarantees the freedom of religion established by the Constitution of the Republic of Lithuania and international documents (Art. 2, 3, and 8); it lists the state-recognised traditional religious communities and associations (Art. 5); it defines the criteria and procedures for the state recognition of other religious associations (Art. 5 and 6); it provides procedures for conferring legal personality on state-recognised religious

---

5 Law on Religious Communities and Associations, adopted on 4 October 1995//Valstybės žinioss, 1995, No. 89-1985. Amendments are published in Valstybė sžinios 1997, No. 66-1618, 2000, No. 40-1115.

associations, and of registration for other religious communities and associations (Art. 5, 6, 10, 11 and 12). The procedure for the suspension or cessation of religious organisational activities is also set out in the LRCA.

The LRCA also regulates religious education in schools, the charitable, benevolent, and educational activities of the religious organisations (Art. 14), and their property rights, labour relations, taxation and social insurance issues (Art. 13, 16, 17, and 18).

The legal basis for the relationship between Church and State may also be found in the Civil Code of Lithuania,[6] the Law on Education,[7] and the Law on State Social Insurance Pensions,[8] which between them set out the main issues concerning State and Church relations.

In addition to the laws regulating Church-State relations in general, the legal framework for the relations between the State and the Catholic Church was established by three agreements signed by the Holy See and the Republic of Lithuania on 5 May 2000.

The first agreement is entitled On Co-operation in Education and Culture,[9] the second is Concerning the Pastoral Care of Catholics Serving in the Army,[10] and the last is Concerning Juridical Aspects of the Relations between the Catholic Church and the State.[11]

The opportunity to define the legal status of a religious body by mutual agreement between the State and the religious association concerned is provided by Article 43 of the Constitution of the Republic of Lithuania. Nevertheless, in recent times only the relationship between the Roman Catholic Church and the State is regulated by agreements.

---

6 Civil Code of the Republic of Lithuania//Valstybės žinios, 2000, No. 74-2262.
7 Law on Education of the Republic of Lithuania//Valstybės žinios, 2003, No. 63-2853.
8 Law on State Social Insurance Pensions of the Republic of Lithuania//Valstybės žinios, 1994, No. 59-1153; No. 113-3283; No. 41-1165; No. 92-2862.
9 The Agreement between the Government of the Republic of Lithuania and the Holy See On Co-operation in Education and Culture, Valstybės žinios, 2000, No. 67-2024.
10 The Agreement between the Government of the Republic of Lithuania and the Holy See Concerning the Pastoral Care of Catholics Serving in the Army, Valstybės žinios, 2000, No. 67-2023.
11 The Agreement between the Government of the Republic of Lithuania and the Holy See Concerning Juridical Aspects of the Relations between the Catholic Church and the State, Valstybės žinios, 2000, No. 67-2022.

2. Categories of System Approach

The system of Church and State relationship in Lithuania is characterised throughout as functioning under the middle road principle. The separateness of Church and State is declared by the Constitution of the Republic of Lithuania. Article 43 of the Constitution provides the right of religious organisations to function freely according to their canons and statutes, and proclaims that there is no state religion in Lithuania.[12]

More comprehensive regulations of State and Church relations are provided by the LRCA. Article 7 of this law states that "religious communities and associations shall not fulfil state functions, while the state shall not fulfil the functions of religious communities and associations".

The Constitutional statement on the absence of state religion in Lithuania is explained by the Ruling of the Constitutional Court of 13 June 2000.[13] According to the Ruling, the statement on the absence of state religion means State and Church separation and neutrality. The separation implements two main principles of State and Church relations. Firstly, that State activities are based on the principle of secularity and, secondly, that areas of State and Church activities and functioning are delimited. Therefore the separation means that on the one hand churches and religious organisations do not interfere in the official activities of the State and do not make State policy, and on the other hand the State does not interfere in the internal affairs of the churches, which function according to their own canons and statutes. However, the separation of the Church and the State does not mean that the Church and the State have nothing to do with each other. The term "separation" stresses the importance of both State and Church in social life of Lithuania rather than the absence of any contact between them. Neutrality means that the State and its institutions are neutral concerning world view and religion. Neutrality guarantees tolerance towards various religious world views and forbids discrimination against believers.

---

12   1. Constitution of the Republic of Lithuania.//Valstybės žinios, 1992, No. 33-1014.
13   Ruling of the Constitutional Court of the Republic of Lithuania on the compliance of Article 1(5), Article 10(3 and 4), Article 15(1), Article 20, Article 21(2), Article 32(2), Article 34(2, 3, and 4), Article 35(2 and 5), Article 37(2) and Article 38(2 and 3) of the Republic of Lithuania Law on Education with the Constitution of the Republic of Lithuania. 13 June 2000//Valstybės žinios, 2000, No. 49-1424.

IV. The Status of Religions

1. Legal Status of Religious Bodies

The main religious bodies are defined in the Constitution of the Republic of Lithuania and in the Law on Religious Communities and Associations. According to Article 2 of LRCA, a religious community is a unit comprising a group of individuals seeking to implement the aims of the same religion. An association has to be comprised of no fewer than two religious communities having a common leadership. A religious centre is the governing body of a religious association.
Defining the main concepts in this way, as a basic provision for the existence of different religious groups, the LRCA indicates that the aspiration of group members should be to put into practice their common religious aims. The registration of religious communities and associations is not compulsory, though unregistered religious communities are not subjects of law.
The LRCA identifies three different categories of religious communities and associations: "the traditional religious communities and associations", "state recognized religious communities and associations" and "other (non-traditional)" religious communities and associations.
The LRCA states that traditional religious communities and associations are those which are part of the historical, spiritual and social heritage of Lithuania. Article 5 lists the nine traditional churches in Lithuania: Roman Catholic, Greek Catholic, Evangelical Lutheran, Evangelical Reformed, Russian Orthodox, Old Believers, Jews, Sunni Muslim and Karaite.
Non-traditional religious communities and associations may be granted the status of a state-recognised religious community or association and be registered and acquire a legal personality.
LRCA Article 6 states that a religious community (association) may be recognised by the State if: it comprises a part of society's historical, spiritual and social heritage; it is approved by the State; and its teaching and rites do not conflict with laws and morality.
Consequently, according to the LRCA, both traditional and recognised religious communities and associations are considered to be part of Lithuanian cultural heritage. Nevertheless, to be recognised is not to be traditional. According to a Ruling of 13 June 2000 of the Constitutional Court of the Republic of Lithuania, "naming churches

and religious organisations as traditional is not an act establishing them as traditional organisations but an act stating both their traditional character and the status of their relations with society. Such an act reflects the development and the situation of the religious culture in society". Tradition is neither created nor abolished by an act of the will of the legislator. The effect of this is to close the list of traditional churches.[14]

Religious communities and associations may request state recognition not less than 25 years from the date of their initial registration in Lithuania. State recognition is granted by the Seimas of the Republic of Lithuania upon the receipt of a Opinion from the Ministry of Justice. If the request is denied, it may be resubmitted not less than 10 years from the day the original request was denied (Art. 6, LRCA).

On 1 July 2001 the Seimas granted the status of state-recognised religious community to the Union of Evangelical Baptist Communities of Lithuania.[15]

The procedure for acquisition of the status of a legal personality for both traditional and other religious communities and associations is established by the Constitution of the Republic of Lithuania, LRCA, and the Civil Code.

Article 43 of the Constitution provides that state-recognised religious communities enjoy legal personality, and the law does not require the registration of the statutes or documents corresponding to those of the traditional communities and associations.[16] Newly established (or re-established) traditional religious communities and associations acquire legal personality following a report by their authorities as to their establishment (or re-establishment) to the Ministry of Justice.

Non-traditional religious communities and associations acquire legal personality upon their registration in the legal persons' Register. The community can be registered provided it has at least 15 members who are adult citizens of the Republic of Lithuania. A religious association may be registered if it comprises at least two communities. A religious centre can be registered if it is established according to the statutes of the religious association or another corresponding document.

---

14 Ruling of the Constitutional Court of the Republic of Lithuania on the compliance of Article 1(5), Article 10(3 and 4), Article 15(1), Article 20, Article 21(2), Article 32(2), Article 34(2, 3, and 4), Article 35(2 and 5), Article 37(2) and Article 38(2 and 3) of the Republic of Lithuania Law on Education with the Constitution of the Republic of Lithuania. 13 June 2000//Valstybės žinios, 2000, No. 49-1424.
15 Decision No.9-464, Valstybės žinios, 2001, No. 62-2249.
16 The Ministry of Justice has already granted legal personality to 967 traditional religious communities, associations and centres. Source: www.religija.lt.

The religious body should submit documents to the Ministry of Justice as laid down by the LRCA and in the Civil Code. The Ministry checks that the documents comply with the LRCA and that the profession of this religion does not entail a violation of human rights, freedom and public order. The Statutes of a religious association may be registered within six months from the date of their submission.
The statutes or corresponding documents which are to be submitted must include the name of the community, its main office, legal form, objects and aims of the religion, organisational structure, and authorities of the community or association, procedure of management, procedures of amendment of the statute, methods of joining and resigning from the community, members' rights and duties, procedure for reorganisation, and distribution of its property following its liquidation.
Religious communities belonging to already registered non-traditional religious communities acquire legal personality when the authorities of the religious association acknowledge their existence and notify the Ministry of Justice of this in writing.[17]
The Ministry of Justice may refuse to register the statutes of religious communities and associations if "(1) necessary data are not provided; (2) the activity of religious community or association violates human rights and freedoms or public order; (3) when the statutes under the same name have already been registered" (Art. 12, LRCA).
According to the Civil Code Book Two, Chapter 4, Article 2(34) religious communities and associations are public (non-profit-making) legal persons.
Taking into account the recommendation "Concerning illegal activities of religious sects" of a committee of the European Parliament of 14 April 2000 the Government passed a decision on establishing a commission for co-ordinating the activities of various state institutions which, in accordance to their competence, resolve problems raised by the activities of religious, esoteric and spiritual groups. This Commission consists of representatives of the main Ministries – Justice, Internal Affairs, Education and Science, Health, Foreign Affairs, General Public Prosecutor's office, State Department, Committee of Human Rights, and the Centre for Religious Studies and Research. The main aims of this commission are as follows:

1) to co-ordinate the investigation on the compliance of activities of particular groups with the law;

---

17 140 non-traditional religious communities have been granted legal personality rights since 1988 in Lithuania.. Source:www.religija.lt

2) to guarantee exchange of information among State institutions and, if needed, to offer suggestions on urgent State action concerning the affairs of these groups. Every six months the Commission must present information on its work to the Government and the Committee on Human Rights.

2. The Meaning of Religious Community and the Right of Self-Determination

The right of self-determination is the main principle defining State and Church relations in Lithuania. The internal autonomy of religious communities is guaranteed by the Constitution. Article 43 stipulates that religious communities can function freely according to their canons and statutes and have the right freely to proclaim the teaching of their faith, perform the rituals of their belief, and have houses of prayer, and educational institutions for the training of priests in their faith insofar as they do not contravene Lithuanian law. In comparison with the Constitution the Law on RCA concerns the organisational structure of religious communities rather than their rights to perform religious activities. Article 7 states that religious communities and associations have a right freely to organise themselves in accordance with their hierarchical and institutional structure, and to manage their internal life according to their own canons, statutes and other norms.
The right of self-determination is also acknowledged in Lithuanian legislation by the provision of an option for religious communities and associations to organise and carry out social activities, participate in charitable activities, and to run general educational and other institutions of instruction. Religious communities and associations may engage in production and economic activity: publishing, establish medical, charitable institutions and organisations, and public information media (Art. 14, 15 LRCA). However, in performing these activities religious communities are bound by civil legislation, functioning as non-profit-making organisations.
The sovereignty of the Catholic Church is declared in the Agreement between the Holy See and the Republic of Lithuania concerning juridical aspects of the relations between the Catholic Church and the State. Though Article 1 provides for the independence and autonomy of the Catholic Church and the State (Art. 1(2)), it also stresses that in pursuit of its social, educational and cultural activities the Catholic Church must follow not only canon law but also procedures pre-

scribed by the laws of the State (Art. 4). Under Article 5 the State acknowledges the total competence of the Catholic Church in its own sphere.

V. Churches and Culture

Probably education is the area of the closest State and Church relations in Lithuania. The main provisions are declared in the Constitution, the Law on RCA and the Law on Education.
Article 40 of the Constitution lays down two principles. The first is that State and local government establishments for teaching and education must be secular, while the second principle is that at the request of the parents, local government establishments must offer classes in religious instruction.
According to the Ruling of the Constitutional Court, secular education means that all state and municipal educational establishments are tolerant, open, and available for people of all religions and none, and that the curriculum's world-view content is secular. There is no requirement concerning personal belief or religion for teachers, with the exception of teachers of religion.[18]
Although the LRCA and the Constitution differentiate between traditional and state-recognised religious communities, the previously adopted laws concerning State and Church relations provided equal rights for traditional and state recognised religious communities and associations in the area of religious instruction. For example, the original wording (4 October 1995) of the Law on Religious Communities and Associations stated that, upon the request of parents, religion of traditional and other state-recognised religious communities and associations may be taught in state educational establishments (Art. 9). However, subsequent documents showed a tendency to accord different rights to traditional and state-recognised religious communities. For example, Article 20 of the Law on Education and Article 9 of the amended LRCA stipulate that only the religion of traditional communities may be taught in the educational institutions of the State.
Classes in religious instruction of the traditional religious communities and associations are provided at all state and municipal schools.

---

18 Valstybes zinios, Nr. 49, 2000 birzelio 16 d. p. 17.

For those who do not attend classes in religious instruction, classes in ethics are offered. Attendance depends on the decision of parents or guardians. From the age of 15 years, pupils make the decision themselves (Art. 20, Law on Education). Children under State or municipal care may chose religious lessons conforming to the religion professed by their family (Art. 20, Law on Education).

Teachers of religious instruction are authorised by traditional religious communities and associations; however, they are required to have a teaching qualification. The teachers are trained at the State Higher Education establishments and their work in school is paid by the State.

According to the law, religious communities and associations have the right to establish and possess comprehensive schools, and training institutions for the clergy and teachers of religious instruction (Art. 40 of the Constitution, Art. 10 of the Law on Education, Art. 14 of the Law on RCA).

Article 10 of the Law on Education provides an opportunity at the request of parents for the creation of state and municipal educational establishments jointly with the traditional religious communities and associations. Nevertheless, according to the Ruling of the Constitutional Court, such schools are secular. Pupils at jointly established schools may attend religious classes only at the request of their parents. Traditional religious communities and associations may regulate only religious education. They have no right to set world-view or educational requirements for school personnel, for the assessment of teachers and other members of the staff, or to appoint the Principal of the school.[19]

The State's relations with the Catholic Church are also regulated by the Agreement on Co-operation in Education and Culture between the Holy See and the Republic of Lithuania. The main provisions in the area of education concern the process of teaching Catholic religion in general schools, the training of teachers in religious instruction, and the status and funding of faculties of Catholic theology and seminaries.

The State grants subsidies to schools preparing teachers of Catholic religion and to the public institutions of post-secondary education, including those where faculties of Catholic theology, centres for religious study and departments are established (Art. 10, Agreement on Education and Culture). According to Article 11 of this Agreement, the State must also provide financial support to Catholic seminaries.

---

19 Ruling of the Constitutional Court of 13 June 2000//Valstubes zinios, 2000, No. 49.

The amount is fixed by a separate agreement between the State and the Lithuanian Bishops' Conference. Recently there has been no such agreement in place. However, two seminaries (Kaunas and Vilkaviškis) have the status of higher schools (they are a part of Vytautas Magnus University) and full State support.

The Agreement states that professors of the theological faculty are State officials. Seminary professors and students have the same rights and duties as do professors and students of other educational institutions (Art. 11 of the Agreement on Education).

Diplomas of higher education granted by the seminaries are recognized by the State if the level of studies meets the qualification requirements for higher education (Art. 11 of the Agreement on Education). The State also recognises diplomas and academic qualifications granted by the Faculty of Theology which was in operation within the inter-diocesan Seminary in Kaunas between 1940 and 1991 (Art. 10 of the Agreement on Education).

State and the Church relations in the sphere of education are also regulated by the Decision on Confessional Education Establishments. According to this Decision, upon a request of the Ministry of Culture and Education, the Government may vote to reorganise the educational establishments of the State into confessional ones, and to grant on lease the buildings and equipment which belonged to the state school.

Relations between the Church and the media are regulated only by the Law on National Radio and Television.[20] According to this law, National Radio and Television has to provide air-time for the traditional and state-recognised religious communities to broadcast religious services following the procedure and conditions provided for in bilateral agreements. Other TV programmes are broadcast on National and commercial TV and radio in the same way as any other programmes. Probably the most influential means of the mass media is a daily programme "Mazoji studija" ("The small studio"), broadcast on National Radio. The authorities of the National Radio and Television stations do not influence the contents of the programme. Support for this radio programme comes from the Catholic Bishops' Conference and foreign Catholic funds.

The State did not provide any funds for the revival of the media of the Catholic or other religious communities.

---

20 Law on the National Radio and Television of the Republic of Lithuania//Valstybes zinios, 2000, No. 58-1712; 1996, No. 102-2319.

Special provisions are provided for the Catholic Church in the Agreement between the Holy See and the Republic of Lithuania on Co-operation in Education and Culture. It states that Catholic Church must have access to public mass media; however Catholic radio and television programmes are broadcast under a separate agreement between the Lithuanian Bishop' Conference and the authorised institution of the Republic of Lithuania (Art. 12 of the Agreement on Education).

VI. Labour Law within the Religious Communities

State and Church relations in the field of labour are regulated mainly by the Law on RCA and Law on the State Social Insurance Pensions. According to LRCA religious communities and associations in Lithuania have the right to employ individuals on work contracts. Most churches in Lithuania have employees who are considered to be civil servants. For the majority of the employees the normal labour laws apply (Art. 17).

Individuals, employed according to an employment contract with religious communities or associations have a right to social insurance and other guarantees established by law. For these purposes, religious organisations must contribute to the State Social Insurance Fund from their income the same amount as do State enterprises.

The Law on RCA states that members of clergy may be supported from their religious community or association funds, in accordance with established procedures. Members of the clergy and other individuals employed without labour contracts by religious organisations, may make their own private contributions to the State Social Insurance Fund according to the procedures established by the Law (Art. 18, LRCA). Clergy in paid work share the same social rights and benefits as other employees.

Since 1 January 2000 the clergy from traditional and other state-recognised religious communities, as well as monks working in monasteries have been compulsorily insured by the state social pension insurance. The State pays to National Budget all compulsory contributions for every notified person. Other persons working in religious organisations may be insured by a social insurance pension on a voluntary basis, by his or her own or the religious organisation's means. Clergy employed in secular establishments pay the same amount to the State Social Insurance Pension Fund as other persons.

VII. Financing of the Churches

State and Church financial relations include mainly state financial support and taxation policy. The main area for State financial support of churches is education.

An amendment to Article 14 of the LRCA (May, 2000) declares that educational establishments of traditional religious communities and associations providing education in compliance with the state standard are financed and maintained by the State.

From 1 September 2001 all comprehensive schools of traditional religious associations may be financed and supported by the Government, or by the institution authorised by the Government, in accordance with established procedure, by assigning them the same amount of budget funds as to the comparable state or local government establishments. The amount is determined by the level of expenses for one child or pupil in a similar state or local authority educational establishments.[21]

For the Catholic Church this option is defined more precisely in the above-mentioned Agreement. According to this Agreement, the State or municipal educational institutions established jointly with the Catholic Church, as well as programmes providing education of established public standard within non-State and non-municipal Catholic educational institutions, "are financed by the budgetary funds allotted thereto pursuant to the procedure prescribed by the Government of the Republic of Lithuania or its authorised institution to the same degree as the State or municipal institutions of a relevant type or level." Nevertheless, the founding institution must finance supplementary programmes of non-State Catholic educational institutions.

Private confessional schools of other religious communities and associations offering State-required education may also receive financial and other support from national and municipal budgets.

---

[21] Law on Amendment of Article 14 of the Law on Religious Communities and associations of the Republic of Lithuania. May 2000 No. VIII-1677//Valstybes zinios, 2000, No. 40-1115.

The main principles of the taxation policy are described in Article 16 of the Law on RCA. It stipulates that all religious communities, associations and centres are exempt from taxes on received contributions. According to the Law, income (ie contributions) from the sale of property acquired through charitable means is not taxable, if it is intended for the construction, repair or restoration of houses of prayer, charity, culture and education. The income received by the clergy, assistants at religious rites and service staff (except individuals performing construction, repair and restoration work) from the funds indicated above are not subject to personal income tax.

Charitable donations and support for religious development projects are also exempt from taxes.[22] Religious communities and associations must submit returns of the received charity and sponsorship funds both to the Tax Inspectorate and the Government Department of Statistics.

Religious supplies and literature brought across the border into Lithuania with the authorisation of religious communities with legal personality are not subject to customs duty.

Nevertheless, according to Article 16 of the Law on RCA, enterprises (organisations) established by religious communities are subject to taxation in accordance with the laws regulating the activities of an economic enterprise or organisation. Income tax must be paid on any income received from the commercial activities of the religious community or association. In cases where religious associations sell property received by way of restitution, they must pay a profit tax amounting to the sum of sales revenue minus the value of the property at the moment of restitution.[23]

Religious communities are exempt from real-estate tax when they use their buildings and facilities only for religious purposes or for the production of religious supplies. When religious communities lease a property or use it for other purposes, they must pay real-estate tax.[24]

Most of the above-mentioned taxes are not levied on the Catholic Church. The Agreement between the Holy See and Lithuania on the Legal Aspects of Relationships between the Catholic Church and the State specifies that the property of legal persons established in accordance with canon law and used for pastoral care, charitable, social, educational, and cultural purposes (including revenues from commercial activities) are not subject to State taxes.

---

22 The Law on Charity and Sponsorship Funds//Valstybes zinios, 2000, No. 61-1818.
23 Paper of the State Tax Inspectorate, 12 January 2000, No. 08-01-06/470.
24 *R. Ziliute, D. Gllodenis*, State and Church in Lithuania, in: *R. Balodis* (ed.), State and Church in the Baltic States: 2001, p. 83.

According to the paper of the State Tax Inspectorate, services provided by traditional religious communities are not subject to VAT provided the services are financed from donations.[25]

Article 7 of the LRCA states that all religious communities and associations possessing legal personality may obtain State support for cultural, educational and charitable work in accordance with the procedure established by law. It is important to stress that the Law enables, not obliges, the State to grant support. Although the Law provides this opportunity to all registered religious organisations, the traditional religious associations find it easier to obtain such support. For example, the Government of Lithuania by resolution annually appropriates from the State budget between 0.8 and 4 million LTL for traditional religious communities for the preservation of cultural monuments and other needs.[26] This sum is divided according to the membership of those communities, subject to a fixed minimum amount for each community. Targeted appropriations from the State and local authorities' budgets are also made for the restoration of churches, their charitable activities and the upkeep of seminaries. Local authorities also make small allowances for various needs and projects of churches and religious organisations.

The State's diverse financial relations with different religious communities permanently raise public awareness that the State does not provide sufficient protection for the equality of all religious groups.

Nevertheless, according to a Ruling of the Constitutional Court, some benefits gained by traditional religious communities are provided for by the Constitution. The grant of the name of 'traditional church' for a religious organisation is the special method of State recognition. The institution of traditional churches is recognised by the Constitution. Traditionality means the special recent state of the State and the Church relations, grounded in the meaning and influence of religious culture on the development of society. For this reason, traditional Churches may be granted rights which other churches do not have.[27]

The Law on the Restoration of Houses of Prayer and other Buildings regulates important issues of State and Church financial relations for religious communities. The Law was passed by Parliament in February 1990. This document repealed the Decree of the Lithuanian Supreme Soviet of 6 June 1948 concerning the nationalisation of prayer

---

25 Paper of the State Tax Inspectorate, 12 January 2000, No. 08-01-06/470.
26 For example, 2,879 mln. Lt. were allotted in 2002; 2,492 mln. Lt. in 2000; 1,783 mln. Lt. in 1998; 3,0 mln. Lt. in 1997.
27 Valstybes zinios, Nr. 49, 2000 birzelio 16 d. p. 16-17.

houses, church buildings, and other requisites; local government bodies were thereby obliged to sign an agreement with the religious communities either to define the terms for the restitution of nationalised buildings, or to provide financial compensation or other means which would enable the restitution of premises that had previously belonged to the Church.

VIII. Religious Assistance in Public Institutions

The Law on RCA establishes the legal grounds for religious assistance in public institutions. The Law states that at the request of believers religious rites may be performed in hospitals, social care facilities, places of detention and military units. The authorities must provide opportunities for the performance of religious rites and agree the time for religious rites and cult ceremonies to be held (Art. 8).

The pastoral care of Catholics serving in the army is regulated by an Agreement between the Holy See and the Republic of Lithuania. According to this document the Holy See must establish a Military Ordinariate responsible for the pastoral care of the Catholics serving in the Army (Art. 1). In co-operation with the Minister of Defence, the Military Ordinary appoints a Vicar General. The Vicar General is at the same time the Head Chaplain of the Army (Art. 3). Military Chaplains exercise pastoral ministry according to canon law, the ordinances of the Military Ordinary, and the rules and regulations of the Army. The duties of the Military Chaplain are to visit military units, celebrating Mass and presiding at other acts of worship, administering the sacraments, teaching religion and morals, to arrange talks on the topics of religion and morals, and to perform other pastoral work (Art. 8).

The Ministry of National Defence undertakes to provide relevant material support for the Army Ordinariate and the spiritual activities of military chaplains (Art. 7).

The Penitentiary Code of the Republic of Lithuania regulates religious services at detention establishments. It states "the administration of all penitentiary institutions should provide conditions for the performance of religious rituals for persons who are serving the penalty of deprivation of liberty. Clergy of all confessions should have the right to visit penitentiary institutions without any restrictions"

(Art. 60).[28] Clergy may visit the inmates at their request at times agreed with the administration. Representatives of religious communities and associations having legal personality may visit places of detention with the permission of the administration of the detention facility.[29]

IX. The Legal Status of Priests and Members of the Religious Orders

There are no special provisions in the Lithuanian legal system concerning the legal status of the clergy. Provisions of the Constitution and the LRCA are only indirectly related to this matter. According to the Constitution all citizens have the right to participate in the government of their State both directly and through elected representatives, and have equal opportunity to serve in a State office. Citizens who are 18 years of age or over have the right to vote in elections (Art. 33, 34). Provisions of the LRCA complement the Constitution stating that all individuals, regardless of the religion they profess, are equal before the law. It is forbidden to limit their rights and freedoms or to apply privileges.

X. Matrimonial and Family Law

Marriage in Lithuania is a concern of both State and Church. The Constitution of the Lithuanian Republic stipulates that the State registers marriages, births and deaths, and recognises marriages registered in Church (Art. 38).
The procedure for the registration of marriage is defined in the Civil Code. The church (confessional) marriage has civil effect as a legal act of the State from the moment of its religious celebration if it fulfils the following requirements:

---

[28] Internal Rules of the Penitentiary Establishments, approved by order of the Minister of Justice No.172, 16 August 2000//Valstybes zinios, 2000, No. 72.

[29] Internal Rules of the Penitentiary Establishments, approved by order of the Minister of Justice No.172, 16 August 2001//Valstybes zinios, 2001, No. 72.

a) there are no impediments to the requirements of Article 3.12-3.17 of the Civil Code concerning the spouses' age and free will;
b) the marriage has been celebrated according to the order established by the canons of religious organisations registered and recognised by the Lithuanian State;
c) the church (confessional) marriage has been recorded in the civil register (Art. 13, Agreement on Juridical Aspects).

A church marriage must be recorded in the civil register. The religious organisation must present the report in a special form (established by the Ministry of Justice) to the civil register office within ten days of the marriage ceremony. The civil register office registers the marriage and issues a marriage certificate. The date of marriage registration is that of its celebration in church. If the report is not presented to the civil register office within ten days the date of registration is that of its registration in the civil registration office (Art 3(304) of the Civil Code).
Decisions of ecclesiastical tribunals on the nullity of a marriage and decrees of the Supreme Authority of the Church on the dissolution of the marriage bond are to be reported to the competent authorities of the Republic of Lithuania with the aim of regulating the legal consequences of such decisions in accordance with the State legislation (Art. 13 of the Agreement on Juridical Aspects).

XI. Criminal Law

Article 171 of the Penal Code penalises interference with religious rituals or solemnities. A person who disrupts services or other ceremonies of a state-recognised religious community by insolent actions, threats, sneering or any other loose behaviour is guilty of a misdemeanour and is punished by public labour, or fine, or restriction of freedom.

XII. Bibliography

J. Kuznecoviene, Church and State in Lithuania, European Journal for Church and State Research, 1999-Volume 6, p. 205-217.
Religijos Lietuvoje, Siauliai, Nova Vita, 1999.
Žiliūtė R., Glodenis D. (2001), State and Church in Lithuania /Church and State in the Baltic States: 2001, Riga, Religijas Brivibas Asociacija, 2001.
Religija ir teisė pilietinėje visuomenėje. Tarptautinės konferencijos medžiaga. Vilnius, Justitia, 2001.
Matulionis A. (ed.) (2001), Europa ir mes. Vilnius, Gervelė, p. 129, 139.

Alexis Pauly
State and Church in Luxembourg

I. Social Facts

The Grand Duchy of Luxembourg lies between Germany, Belgium and France: the smallest Member State of the European Union. Luxembourg encompasses an area of 2,586.36 square kilometres and has a population of over 450,000. Of the total population, about 40 % are foreign nationals resident in Luxembourg.
Since the enactment of a law in 1979 the State has been precluded from collecting data concerning an individual's confession or membership of a religious group. However, one may assume that the majority of the population consider themselves to be Catholic. There are a few thousand Protestants, Lutherans, Calvinists and members of Free Churches; about 1,000 are of the Jewish faith; there are also groups of Orthodox and Anglicans. The Muslims are for the most part refugees from the Balkans. In the Portuguese sector there is a large number of persons who consider themselves as belonging to the Jehovah's Witnesses. Several thousand people are considered to be of no denomination, and the remainder of the population belongs to other non-formally-recognised religious groups. It must also be noted that it is rather difficult to estimate the strengths of the various confessions in the population due to the large number of foreigners living in Luxembourg.
From these statistics one can see that religion still plays an important role in Luxembourg. The current situation must nevertheless be examined from a historical aspect in order to be fully understood.

II. Historical Background

In the seventeenth century the Duchy of Luxembourg was divided between six Catholic dioceses: Trier, Liège, Metz, Verdun, Reims and Cologne. This fragmentation had serious consequences, particularly in the realm of Church discipline. The religious history of Luxembourg is thus partly intertwined with the history of foreign dioceses.

Given a rather powerless Church, the State's power was largely unimpeded and thus able to flower. Under Burgundian rule the State managed to retain a large measure of official control over the Church. The Spanish king acted in a similar way, so consequently the Austrian rulers found during their time of power that the circumstances regarding Church control were indeed favourable. Carl VI intervened in Church affairs only rarely while, in contrast, Maria-Theresa and Joseph II intervened on behalf of the State so regularly and systematically that one can properly speak of "Josephism". Measures taken by the various rulers included attempts to control certain forms of popular beliefs, and attempts to regulate religious communities; under Joseph II they went so far as to interfere with and control the training of the clergy.

The time of the French Revolution was clearly marked by the resistance and opposition of both clergy and people of Luxembourg to the republican laws. Essential to the understanding and interpretation of Church and State relations in Luxembourg is the Concordat of 1801. Luxembourg was at this time a French Department. Supplementary treaties and laws date from the year 1998.

III. The Concordat: Application and Resistance

From the moment that the Concordat of 1801 had been concluded, and especially after the unilateral enactment of the articles organiques (organic articles) by Bonaparte, it faced condemnation and rejection by the Church hierarchy. In Luxembourg there were many disputes concerning the Concordat. At first, there was criticism of certain sections of it, and after the independence of Luxembourg the legal force of the whole Concordat was called into question. Some organic articles were repealed *expressis verbis* by the legislature in 1998.

1. *The Application of the Concordat before the Independence of the Country*

a) *The French period*

According to the provisions of the Concordat of 1801, the majority of Luxembourg was to belong to the Diocese of Metz, which was at that time the largest diocese in France. Church life was for the most part peaceful even though two new sets of parish boundaries ran into opposition. The majority of the clergy and the faithful accepted the new law and remained loyal to the newly appointed bishop. The few priests who refused to accept the authority of the Concordat and their small band of followers were for the most part resident in the Francophone part of the country.

b) *The period during which the Grand Duchy of Luxembourg was under Dutch sovereignty*

Between 1814 and 1815 there was reluctance on the part of King and Church alike – although for quite different reasons – to apply the Concordat of 1801. The King believed that the Constitution of 1815 provided sufficient means to keep the Church in check. He attempted, for his own advantage as successor to the former Dutch rulers, to re-institute the *indult* that Pope Paul IV had granted in 1559 to Philip II and his successors, allowing them the right to appoint the bishops. According to Article 17 of the Concordat of 1801 which envisaged a special treaty should a successor to the head of State not be a Catholic, a Concordat between the King and the Holy See was concluded in 1827. It reaffirmed the validity of the Concordat of 1801. It further stated that the nominees for the office of bishop were to be put forward by the Diocesan Chapter. The King would be able to strike from the list those of whom he did not approve. The Diocesan Chapter would then elect the future bishop from the candidates already approved by the king. The Pope, for his part, would make the appointment, provided that the nominee fulfilled the criteria for a bishop as prescribed by Canon Law. The Concordat of 1827 was never put to practice, and in 1852 it was repealed by both sides. In 1823 Luxembourg was withdrawn from the Diocese of Metz and placed under the control of the diocese of Namur.

c) Luxembourg during the Belgian Revolution

Between 1830 and 1839, with the exception of the fortified city of Luxembourg, the country belonged to Belgium. This brought about a dual legal system with regard to religious matters. The relationship between the city of Luxembourg and the Diocese of Namur rapidly deteriorated, and in 1833 the Pope was forced to withdraw the city of Luxembourg from the diocese of Namur and appoint an Apostolic Vicar for the city. Since such a post was not provided for in the then current Concordat, the appointment was used as a means and as a piece of evidence to invalidate the Concordat. For the rest of the country, the Constitution of Belgium was in force; this was later to serve as a model for that of the State of Luxembourg.

2. The Concordat during the Time of Independence

a) Luxembourg under William I

The unification of the remainder of Luxembourg with the capital city occurred under rather poor circumstances. To avoid dislocation in the administrative structure, the former laws were provisionally to remain in force. As a result, many took the position that the Belgian Concordat system was now valid for the whole of Luxembourg. This point was, however, contested by others who argued that the system had been nullified by the Treaties of London. The Grand Duchy with its new borders was withdrawn from the Diocese of Namur and integrated into the apostolic vicariate of the city of Luxembourg.

b) The Constitution of 1848

The Belgian Constitution of 1831 served as a model for those who drew up the Luxembourg Constitution. However, on the subject of religious freedom, the Luxembourg Constitution was far more restrictive. One can see in it the powerful influence of the liberals. Without wanting to free themselves completely from the 1801 Concordat, the authors of the Constitution took the position that a new Concordat would be worked out and that, in the meantime, the terms of the current Concordat were to remain in force. This may be seen from a fairly dubious and relatively unclear compromise. Article 23 of the Constitution of 1848 (Art. 22 of the current Constitution) states that "the interference in the nomination and appointment of the *chefs des cultes* in the Grand Duchy, the method of nomination and suspension of the remaining clergy, their ability to correspond with their superiors and to report publicly about their activity insofar as they concern the relationship between the Church and the State are matters for treaties, which are to be submitted to the Chamber of Deputies, when provisions for intervention become necessary".

In the transitional conditions, an Article 125 was added which stated that until the treaties foreseen in Article 23(22) were concluded, the prevailing provisions concerning the churches were to remain in force.

3. The Practical Application of the Concordat

It is not easy to analyse the current application of the Concordat. Many of its provisions are too abstract and general to be applied either directly or indirectly. Measures to complete and amend the original text need to be taken. Often, however, the Concordat still gives the framework within which problems can be tackled.

In the Concordat of 1801 the Catholic Church as such was not recognised, but only certain structures necessary for its operation. So, a Decree of 1809 concerned the *conseils des fabriques d'Eglise* (church councils). This recognised the legal capacity of these bodies and regulated the administration of their property by the creation of administrative and supervisory authorities.

IV. The Luxembourg Concordat Model in Practice

1. The Luxembourg Concordat Model

Thus far, the aim of this essay has been to describe the establishment of the relationship between Church and State since the French Revolution, by reference to the Concordat of 1801. Maintaining the Concordat gave rise to numerous discussions. For some, particularly the 19th century liberals, it was considered to be not only still in force, but a valid device to control and keep the Church within certain defined boundaries. For others, above all the Catholics, either it was considered to have been dissolved or it was judged that it should be dissolved because it seriously impeded the freedom of the Church.

My opinion is that the Concordat was never formally nullified, but that its operation was certainly enlarged and modified. It is however unnecessary to determine which of the provisions of the organic laws of the Concordat are still in force, which have been expressly removed, or which have simply passed into obscurity with the passage of time. There were also certain articles that were originally applied, but which ceased to be operative at a time that cannot precisely be determined.

Behind the Concordat of 1801, it is possible to speak of a Luxembourg Concordat-model. That is, the intention of the Church and State to solve jointly any problems that arise, and to give mutual support to one another should there be any difficulties. The State grants the Church a measure of protection, and in particular cases financial means at its disposal. The Church, on the other hand, gives a measure of moral support to the State and is partly used to legitimise the State. Luxembourg, being a small, easily violable State, would be unable to sustain any major internal crisis, and the Church and the trades unions take this into consideration.

2. The Adaptability of the Concordat Model

The adaptability of the Concordat model is astounding. It would be wrong, though, to consider the Concordat of 1801 as a cast-iron arrangement; in the hundred years that it was in force in France, it also had changes made to it. There are, furthermore, certain reasons why in Luxembourg its adaptability was encouraged. For example, in Luxembourg there has never been specific secular legislation. Without a doubt, the anticlerical movement of the 19th century wanted to make certain that the power of the Church was kept tightly within its well-defined boundaries. In addition, the Constitution of Luxembourg is less advantageous to the Church than is the Belgian Constitution. Since the end of World War I, however, the Catholics have enjoyed political dominance.

Even more important, though, is the suppleness of the administrative system of Luxembourg. Everyone knows everyone else and it is therefore easy to find solutions... One has the impression that there exists a slight reluctance to regulate the status of the Church. Attempts are made to find solutions to problems by, for example, adapting the budgetary laws, through laws concerning the civil service, or simply through tacit administrative agreements. Beyond these methods of reaching legal solutions, there seems currently to be substantial support for this method, and a consensus throughout Luxembourg society. It might perhaps be easier to change a written law than to change a firmly entrenched convention. It is certainly not clear that it would be in the interest of the Church to demand rigid legislation.

The Church finds fault with the fact that certain organs of the Church, such as the dioceses or parishes, are not recognised by the State. Church and State laws are in opposition to one another in this respect.

As a result it can be said that the relationship between the Church and State in Luxembourg is determined by a Concordat system, which is eased by the Constitution and above all by reaching practical arrangements and agreements.

3. Systematics of Luxembourg Ecclesiastical Law

The Catholic Church indeed has extraordinary significance in Luxembourg. Religious freedom and freedom of worship are completely guaranteed by article 19 of the Constitution.

V. The Legal Status of Religious Bodies

1. Treaties and Agreements with Religious Communities

In 1998 Agreements were concluded with the following: Catholic Church, Protestant Church (the Reformed Church has had an Agreement since 1982), the Jews, the Greek Orthodox. In 2004 three further agreements were on the agenda: with the Anglicans, the Rumanian Orthodox and the Serbo/Croatian Orthodox. However, the Council of State has come up with serious objections to these.

The churches that are recognised as public corporations often set up associations and companies, as regulated by civil law, for administering their property and goods.

In the case of Muslims, the government has not yet found a representative partner who is accepted by all Muslims and the government.

Political pressure also comes from the U.S. Other religious communities are not yet recognised as public corporations in Luxembourg. Religious communities which are not officially recognised as such may, however, take advantage of all legal rights under private law, in particular the right to create a foundation. Such foundations have almost the same rights as are enjoyed by recognised religious communities.

2. *The Diocese*

Despite plans being put forward in the 16th century, it was only in 1870 through a unilateral act of the Pope that the Diocese of Luxembourg was established. The State was annoyed that it was not consulted beforehand, and thus refused to recognise the diocese immediately. A law passed on 30 April 1873 recognised the foundation of a diocese in Luxembourg under the condition that "the current relationship within the Church leadership was not to be changed and its rights and duties would furthermore be continued to be regulated by the provisions in operation". Two conclusions may be reached from these conditions. The diocese would not be recognised as an organ with legal capacity. Second, the legislator did not want to call the Concordat into question nor to touch the relationship between Church and State. The law stipulates the oath that the Bishop is to take and it also regulates his income. Only a Luxembourg national may be appointed as Bishop. Lastly, the appointment is valid only after the State has given its own consent. This means in practice that a nominee of the Pope who was not approved by the government could do nothing for which the approval of the State was required. The Bishop would also have no power to confer Church offices and he himself would receive no salary.

On the basis of a law passed in 1981, the bishopric is now a person under public law. This provision, similar in general to the status of religious communities regulated by public law in Germany, appears in the Luxembourg system like a transplant. Above all, the tax advantages of this law are similar to those granted to non-profit-making organisations and institutions of public interest.

In 1988, through a unilateral act of the Pope, the Diocese of Luxembourg was granted the status of archdiocese.

3. Church Autonomy in the Public Sphere, particularly the Social Services

Formerly, there was a large number of religious social service institutions in Luxembourg. This was particularly so in regard to hospitals and retirement homes, where the majority were run by women's religious orders. In both these cases there has been a steady increase in the number of such institutions provided through public funds. In addition, the State allots public funding for those hospitals and retirement homes run by nuns.

Generally, those social services which are still operated by the Church choose to be regulated by private law. This is true for hospitals, retirement homes, and also for schools, which will now be described in detail.

VI. Churches and Culture

1. Schools

In neither the Concordat of 1801 nor in the *articles organiques* are there specific arrangements for schools or religious instruction.

a) The provisions of the Constitution

The subject of schools is dealt with only briefly in the Constitution of Luxembourg. The text of Article 23 reads as follows: "The State is responsible for providing every Luxembourgian with an elementary education... The State is responsible for the creation of the necessary secondary schools and colleges... The funding of the public education system and the supervision of schools by the government and the local authorities are to be regulated by laws; furthermore all questions related to the education system are to be regulated by the law... All Luxembourgians are free to study at the university of their choice, either in the Grand Duchy or abroad, subject to the legal regulations concerning their terms of admission to the particular place of work and the exercise of the particular occupation."

The Constitution takes no particular stance on religion or religious instruction within the education system, but neither does it rule out its possibility. The private school system is not specifically protected by the Constitution; a citizen of Luxembourg, however, is free to attend either domestic or foreign schools. Since the 19th century there have been legislative provisions regulating religious instruction in the State school system; these laws have also been used to regulate private schools. Private schools, however, have never played a significant role in Luxembourg. The Church has instead attempted to influence the State school system, not to create its own guidelines for instruction.

b) The church and the private schools

aa) The legal framework

A law passed on 31 May 1982 governs the relationship between the State and private secondary schools. For approximately ten years before then, politicians had attempted to solve the problem of private schools by proposing that those schools which so desired could be integrated into the State school system. One such draft law was proposed in 1974. The 1982 legislation, however, goes in the opposite direction by acknowledging the existence of private schools, thus regulating and standardising their control and inspection. The directors and teachers of these schools are required to have the necessary professional qualifications. In the case of a refusal to allow such a school to open, it is possible to appeal to the administrative courts (first and second instance).

bb) The financial framework

The new law of 1982 allows for the possibility of contractual terms with private schools. Under such terms, instruction at secondary level must be comparable with the State school system, the lesson structure of State schools must be followed, and at each level private schools must make use of the State school curriculum; the content of three lessons per week may, however, be determined by the school itself. Private schools must also apply the same criteria for admission and transfer as State schools. If all these conditions are met, the State will take on 80 % of the costs of lessons following the State pattern; if the school fails to meet all the conditions, the State will finance only 40 % of these costs. The status of teachers in secular private schools is as a general rule regulated by the current labour law applicable to private sector employment. So the teachers' status must necessarily be seen as insecure. A socialist proposal that would have guaranteed such teachers privacy outside the workplace and their work duties was rejected. The schools may also receive State subventions for building and maintaining school premises (Law of 2003).

2. The Seminary

Luxembourg has its own Catholic seminary, founded for the training of ordinands; it is not part of a university, though, as Luxembourg has no truly fully-fledged State university. The seminary is therefore a self-supporting religious establishment.
The seminary was established in 1842 through a royal decree and has legal capacity (Art. 11 of the Concordat of 1801, Art. 113 of the Enactment of 1809, and Section IV of the Enactment of 1813). The director and professors are paid out of public funds. But as a result of the very small number of available clergy posts, the few ordinands from Luxembourg study abroad. So the seminary has diversified its curriculum and now trains lay religious teachers.

3. Mass Media

The daily newspaper with the largest circulation in Luxembourg is the "Luxemburger Wort" with a circulation of 80,000 copies per day; the paper belongs to the Archdiocese. Through the "Luxemburger Wort", the Archdiocese also owns a controlling interest in a radio station with the name of "De Neie Radio" (D.N.R.).

VII. Labour Law within the Church

1. Priests and other Ministers

The Constitution ensures that the stipends and pensions of priests and other ministers of religion are paid by the State and governed by law (Art. 106 of the Constitution of 1868). In 1848 the meaning of the text was clear to those who drew up the Constitution, as there was only one recognised religious community: the Catholic Church.

Today the situation is no longer clear-cut: the functions undertaken within the Church have become more complex and multi-faceted. Furthermore, the Protestant Churches, the Greek-Orthodox, and the Jewish community have become formally recognised by the State.

The laity have also taken on a much greater role within the Church, particularly in acting as catechists. Do these individuals also fall under the legislators' intentions and within the meaning of "priests and other ministers"? Since the Agreement of 1998 there has been hardly any doubt. The Churches and the Jewish Community may now organise their internal structures according to their own self-understanding.

2. A Special Status

The Concordat was supposed to re-establish the right to the performance of religious observances within France. In the 19th century the liberals in Luxembourg also wanted to integrate the clergy into the structural mechanisms of the State. This was done with the deliberate intention of favouring "lower clergy", whereby the prerogatives of the "higher clergy" would become restricted. The result was advantages and disadvantages for the entire clergy.

a) The advantages

Since 1842, appointments to the priesthood have been freely made by the Church without the need for State approval. Today, appointments and transfers within the priesthood are made solely by the Archbishop. The clergy are not part of public administration.

In the sphere of the right to religious freedom, the protection of churchly functions and dignitaries is clearly defined (Art. 145 of the Luxembourg Criminal Code).

The principle of clergy pay is guaranteed by the Constitution (Art. 126). However, the majority of legal conditions relating to the priesthood are to be found in the provisions of the Concordat.

There is now no difference between Luxemburgian or foreign clergy. There is a particular debate concerning who is able to exercise disciplinary action over priests and other clergy. The State is in any case allowed to suspend or take disciplinary action against such individu-

als when a criminal case is brought involving serious criminal actions or when imprisonment is a possible outcome of a trial.
What is the situation, then, when the Bishop exercises disciplinary action against the clergy? There seems to be no clear judicial answer. The Bishop is responsible for oversight of belief and morals, and the State for the maintenance of public order. State Labour Courts are competent for the clergy.

b) *The disadvantages*

For the those in the priesthood there are, nevertheless, certain disadvantages.
According to Article 268 of the Luxembourg Criminal Code, priests owe a duty of restraint when delivering a sermon. A priest who preached a sermon describing civil marriage as cohabitation, supporting his point of view by using obscene remarks, has been prosecuted under this provision of the Criminal Code.
Furthermore, priests are not allowed to become public officials, members of Parliament, members of the European Parliament, Mayors, or Deputy-Mayors. Finally, on the ground that he was under the authority of his Church superiors and was thus not qualified to act as an independent officer in the judicial system, a priest has been refused admission as an attorney.

3. *Social Security*

Priests and other clergy in a salaried occupation enjoy the same social rights and benefits as their secular colleagues. As teachers, hospital staff, or as professors, they will be treated in exactly the same way as any other employed individual.
For an analysis of the position in social security law of the clergy in Church posts, one must distinguish between the priesthood and ministers on one hand and the other employees of the Church on the other.

a) *Priests and other ministers*

According to the laws dealing with social security, priests and other ministers are on the same legal footing as civic officials and members of the civil service. In cases of illness or incapacity, they enjoy the same insurance protection as any other civic official. Clergy pensions are guaranteed by Article 106 of the Luxembourg Constitution. The standard age for retirement, at which pension benefits may be enjoyed, is 65 years. Priests are, however, free to continue working beyond this age.

Those priests or clergy who give up their church or religious office are entitled to a portion of their pension, which is assessed according to the duration of their tenure in office.

Lastly, priests and clergy are protected by social security laws in the case of injury while performing their duties.

b) *Other employees of the Church*

A law passed in 1974 integrated non-clerical employees of the Church into social security law.

The criteria for qualification of being a member of a religious order have been interpreted very broadly and go beyond the canonical requirements. Other non-clerical employees of the Church are subject to rules under private law in the same way as any other privately employed individual, both in respect of their pension and for accident and health insurance.

4. The Laity as Employees of the Church

As a result of the declining numbers of ordained priests, lay people are bolstering the Church by being increasingly entrusted with the performance of religious duties and functions.

The Concordat, though, makes no mention of regulations concerning the laity. The lack of legislative provisions and pertinent case-law hampers the understanding of the exact terms of the legal position of the laity as employees of the Church. Many lay teachers of religion are bound by labour contracts governed by private law. The Archbishop proposes catechists for employment to the Minister of Education and then after they are successfully employed, he bestows upon them the *missio canonica*.

It seems that employees under private law terms are employed under the standard of the *missio canonica*.

VIII. Financing of Churches

In contrast with the position in Germany, the Church in Luxembourg is not supported by a Church tax. Instead, its funding is found from the State budget. The officeholders of the Church, that is the Bishop, the clergy, and also some of the employed laity, are paid out of funds in the general State budget.
The publicly acknowledged Churches, moreover, enjoy as corporations under public law the same tax-exemption as private law foundations.

IX. Religious Assistance in Public Institutions

1. Military and Hospital Chaplains

In Luxembourg, military personnel and the police force are under the pastoral care of military chaplains. The legal status of the chaplains is dealt with and governed by military law. In public hospitals, hospital chaplains have the right to visit patients, but there are no specific legislative arrangements concerning the pastoral care of patients in hospitals or nursing institutions.

2. The Church and the State School System

Under a law of 1843 concerning primary-school instruction, the Church was allowed to wield considerable power. The Church in general had oversight of public elementary schools, had a right of co-determination concerning the textbooks to be used, and also had the opportunity of making religious education a mandatory subject. In 1912 a socio-liberal coalition instituted a law which demanded that elementary schools be neutral with regard to religion. Although the Church lost its power over the school system, priests were still allowed to give one hour of religious instruction. The Bishop boycotted this law until 1921, when a *modus vivendi* was found, granting freedom not only to the teachers, but also for the Church. The pupils (primary school, secondary school or vocational school) have a right to choose between taking part in Christian religious education or courses in world ethics.

X. The Legal Status of Priests and Religious: Especially Eligibility for Elections

In Luxembourg, priests and other paid members of the clergy may not be elected to Parliament or local councils; judges have the same restrictions upon them. Technically, this result has been reached because neither the priests nor judges may take leave in order to fulfil a political mandate.
Non-stipendiary clergy, on the other hand, are free to enjoy the right to stand for political office.

XI. Matrimonial and Family Law

In this area of law there are no features peculiar to Luxembourg: the legal principle of universal civil marriage is in force.

XII. Bibliography

E. *Donckel,* Die Kirche in Luxemburg von den Anfängen bis zur Gegenwart, Luxembourg, Sankt-Paulus-Druckerei, 1950.

P. *Eyschen,* Das Staatsrecht in Luxemburg, in: Marquadsens Handbuch des öffentlichen Rechts IV, I.H.II, Freiburg, J.C.B. Mohr, 1890.

P. *Eyschen,* Das Staatsrecht in Luxemburg, in: Das öffentliche Recht der Gegenwart, Tübingen, J.C.B. Mohr, 1910.

A. *Heiderscheid,* Aspects de sociologie religieuse du diocèse de Luxembourg, Luxembourg, Imprimerie St. Paul, t. 1 (1961); t. 2 (1962).

L. *Held,* (FIDELIS Catholicus), Staatsrecht und Kirchenrecht im Grossherzogtum Luxemburg, Sankt-Paulus-Druckerei, 1984.

G. *Hellinghausen,* Kampf um die Apostolischen Vikare des Nordens, *J.-Th.*

Laurent and *C.A. Luepke*, Roma, Editrice Pontificia Università Gregoriana, 1987.
N. Majerus, La situation légale de l'Eglise catholique au Grand-Duché de Luxembourg, Luxembourg, Imprimerie St. Paul, 1926.
N. Majerus, L'Administration des Biens d'Eglise dans le Grand-Duché de Luxembourg, Luxembourg, Imprimerie St. Paul, 1937.
A. Pauly, Stato e Chiesa in Lussemburgo, Città e Regione, no. 6, Dicembre 1982, p. 185-195.
A. Pauly, Eglise et Etat dans le Grand-Duché de Luxembourg, un modèle concordataire original, in: Conscience et Liberté, 32, 1986, p. 114-122.
A. Pauly, Kirche und Staat im Grossherzogtum Luxemburg, in: Gewissen und Freiheit, 27, 1986, p. 77-84.
A. Pauly, Les Cultes au Luxembourg, Un modèle concordataire, Luxembourg, forum, 1989.
A. Pauly, Eglise et Etat au Grand-Duché de Luxembourg 1992, in: European Consortium for Church-State Research, Newsletter, November 1993, p. 44-46.
A. Pauly, Eglises et droit du travail au Grand-Duché de Luxembourg, in: Churches and Labour Law in the EC Countries, European Consortium for Church and State Research, Pubblicazioni di diritto ecclesiastico, no.9, Università degli studi di Milano, Milano 1933, p. 173-194.
A. Pauly, Nouveaux droits et relations Eglises-Etat au Luxembourg, p. 267-285.
A. Pauly, Religions et État au Grand-Duché de Luxembourg en 2000, p. 217-218.
A. Pauly, Religions et État au Grand-Duché de Luxembourg en 1999, p. 179-188.
A. Pauly, Religions et Etat au Grand-Duché de Luxembourg en 1998, p. 145-147.
A. Pauly, Religions et Etat au Grand-Duché de Luxembourg en 1997, p. 93-98.
A. Pauly, Religions et Etat au Grand-Duché de Luxembourg en 1996, p. 91-109.
A. Pauly, Eglises et Etat au Grand-Duché de Luxembourg en 1995, p. 69-75.
A. Pauly, Eglises et Etat au Grand-Duché de Luxembourg en 1994, p. 67-71.
A. Pauly, Eglise et état au Grand-Duché de Luxembourg en 1993, p. 67-73.
A. Pauly, Rapport luxembourgeois, p. 133-136.
A. Pauly, Le régime constitutionnel des cultes au Luxembourg, p. 191-202.
M. Pauly, Von der staatlichen Kontrolle zur Partnerschaft, in: Landeskundliche Vierteljahresblätter, 28, 1982, Heft 1, p. 14-27.
M. Schiltz, A. Pauly, Les nouveaux mouvements religieux au Grand-Duché de Luxembourg, p. 239-255.
A. Thill, L'assujettissement du clergé à la Sécurité Sociale, in: Questions Sociales, no. 3, 1971, p. 106-116.
G. Trausch, Le Luxembourg à l'époque contemporaine, Luxembourg, Bourg-Bourger 1973.
G. Trausch, Le Luxembourg sous l'Ancien Régime, Luxembourg, Bourg-Bourger, 1975.

G. *Vuillermoz,* Das luxemburgische Primärschulgesetz. Eine rechtsgeschichtliche und kirchenrechtliche Untersuchung, Thèse de Droit canonique, Pontificia Universitas Gregoriana, 1955, (Manuscrit).

P. *Weber,* (Abbé), La Condition Juridique de l'Eglise Catholique au Grand-Duché de Luxembourg, in: Feuilles de Liaison de la Conférence Saint-Yves, mai 1977, no. 38, p. 3-17.

P. *Weber,* (Abbé), La nomination des évêques au Grand-Duché de Luxembourg, in: Feuilles de Liaison de la Conférence Saint-Yves, 1968, no. 29-30, p. 12-1

Balázs Schanda
State and Church in Hungary

I. Social Facts

Religious affiliation qualifies as sensitive data that cannot be registered by the Hungarian State.[1] Consequently there are no full official statistics on adherence to religious communities in Hungary. Sociological surveys show that most of the population have a denominational identity and consider themselves to be believers. However, only about 15 % of Hungarians are regular churchgoers. Around half of the population of Hungary describe themselves as "believing in their own way". After rapid and enforced secularisation in the 1960s, there has been since the late 1970s an increasing trend towards religiosity.[2] For the census conducted in 2001, a question on religion were included. The question was formulated in an open way (there were no predefined answers); response was optional and anonymous, for reasons of data protection. The results of the census are as follows:

Catholic	5,558,961	54.5 %
- Roman Catholic	5,289,521	51.9 %
- Greek Catholic	268,935	2.6 %
Reformed (Calvinist)	1,622,796	15.9 %
Lutheran	303,864	3.0 %
Jewish	12,871	0.1 %
Other	112,121	1.1 %
- Orthodox	15,298	0.2 %
- Baptist	17,705	0.2 %
- Adventist	5,840	0.1 %
- Other Christians	24,340	0.2 %
No denomination	1,483,369	14.5 %
No answer	1,034,767	10.1 %
No data	69,566	0.7 %
Total population	10,198,315	100 %

---

1 Act IV/1990, section 3 (4).
2 For a comparative overview of attitudes see *Tomka, M./Zulehner, P.*, Religion in den Reformländern Ost(Mittel) Europas, Ostfildern 1999.

It can be said that the proportion of those having a religious affiliation generally increases with the age of respondents. The average age of the population is 39.22 years, the same as the average age of Greek Catholics and those belonging to "other" denominations. The average age of Roman Catholics is 41.69, Calvinists 42.49, Lutherans 44.79; that of those having no affiliation is only 28.85, while the average age of those not responding is 34.61. Generally a higher proportion of women declared affiliation to churches than men. Data also proved the shift in the relative numbers in each denomination: the century-long decline of Protestants (especially that of Lutherans, who live in diasporas with a consequently high proportion of mixed marriages) compared with the Catholic population (especially the Greek Catholic minority) continued during the decades of communism. Affiliation to mainstream Christian denominations is stronger in rural areas than in towns. The proportion of people having no denomination or not responding to the census question was highest in Budapest, whereas the smaller a settlement becomes, the lower is this percentage. Most religions have more female adherents than males; consequently men constitute the majority of those having no denomination or not responding. Presumably Jews and adherents of some "new religious movements" are over-represented among those declaring no religion: some estimates put the number of Jews ten times higher than the census results.

According to the 2001 Census the largest Orthodox church in Hungary is the Romanian Orthodox Church with 5,598 adherents. 3,502 people belong to a diocese under the jurisdiction of the Moscow Patriarchate, and 2,472 belong to the Exarchate of the Ecumenical Patriarchate of Constantinople. 1,914 stated that they were Serb Orthodox and 508 that they belonged to the Bulgarian Orthodox Church. Some further interesting data: 21,688 declared membership of the Jehovah's Witnesses, 6,541 the Unitarian Church; there were 7,408 Pentecostals, and 2,907 Muslims. Altogether the population claimed affiliation to 260 different religious communities and beliefs.[3]

---

3 Data were published indicating regions, settlements, correlation to marital status and age. Központi Statisztikai Hivatal, 2001, évi népszámlálás, 5. Vallás, felekezet. Budapest, Központi Statisztikai Hivatal 2002; Hungarian Central Statistical Office, Population census 2001, 5. Religion, denomination, Budapest, Hungarian Central Statistical Office, 2002; http://www.nepszamlalas2001.hu/dokumentumok/pdfs/vallas.pdf.

II. Historical Background

Hungary is a country that emerged to statehood by its adoption of western Christianity in the first millennium. The foundations of the structure of the Catholic Church were laid by St Stephen (997-1038), the first king of Hungary, who founded ten dioceses. The claim of the "patronate", the royal (state) care of spiritual issues, remained firm throughout the 20th century. Whereas Hungarian history is determined by adherence to western Christianity, Orthodox minorities have been present in Hungary throughout the country's history.

The Reformation reached the country when the central state power was weak, so it was highly successful in the 16th century. The Reformed (Calvinist-Presbyterian) Church became the birthplace of national culture in respect of Bible translation, schools, and so on. The Counter-Reformation also achieved success, but the country has preserved a high level of denominational pluralism. A generally tolerant approach to religious issues is deeply rooted in Hungarian society. The coexistence of Catholics and Protestants (mainly Calvinists who often regard themselves as the "Church of the nation") has not always been free of conflict but it proved to be a fruitful tension enriching both national and local culture. After the Turkish wars at the end of the 17th century, ethnic Hungarians became a minority in the Kingdom of Hungary. While the Serbs in the south remained Orthodox, large numbers of Romanians in Transylvania and Ruthenians in the Carpathians entered into union with the Catholic Church, favoured by the Habsburgs.

By the end of the 19th century, the Jewish population had risen to over 5 %. The liberal era of the late 19th century enhanced the rapid assimilation of the Hungarian Jewry. This era produced the Law No. 43 of the year 1895, which proclaimed religious freedom for all, restricting, however, a right of public worship to the communities that were acknowledged (either incorporated or recognised). The law established a de facto two tier system of religious communities: it upheld the legal framework that had emerged in the course of history concerning the status of the Catholic Church, the Reformed (Calvinist) and the Lutheran Churches, the Orthodox, Unitarians and Jews (the latter having just become an "incorporated" religion); but the law also opened up the possibility of setting up "recognised" denominations. The mainstream churches remained part of the establishment, not only in a legal, but also in a social sense – for example, until 1945 the Catholic Church was the largest landowner, and until

1948 two thirds of elementary schools were run by churches. After the trauma of the secession of Hungary that took place after World War I, national conservative forces dominated the political and the cultural landscape, cutting back some of the liberal legislation of the late 1800s. Hungary became a small country surrounded by her former self – and large ethnic Hungarian minorities. The country became involved in World War II and came under German occupation on the 19th of March 1944. In the following few months three-quarters of the Hungarian Jewry – who had suffered massive discrimination, but had enjoyed relative security until then – were deported and killed.

After World War II the Communists came into power with Soviet assistance and abolished the democratic structures – human rights as well as the rule of law. The Communist authorities systematically harassed clergy and lay believers. Religious freedom was a dead letter, remaining only on the paper on which the Constitution had been written. The "separation" imposed was nothing else but strict state control and persecution. As the control over the churches became almost total, open persecution got somewhat milder ("goulash communism"), but the guiding principles did not change until 1989. In the 1970s and 1980s churches were relatively free to worship within their own church buildings, but there was no space for any kind of social activity – no communication, charitable organisations, institutions, or religious orders. Hungary played a notable role in the *Ostpolitik* of the Holy See as an experimental test case; the detente between church and State did have beneficial effects but it also meant painful compromises: the Holy See and the Peoples' Republic of Hungary concluded a partial agreement in 1964. The first three decades of communist rule brought a massive and forceful secularisation of Hungarian society. Communism has left Hungary an atomised society in a moral vacuum. Ironically, the churches – hit so hard by the regime – turned out to be the greatest forces of civic society. The collapse of communism brought a new freedom and new challenges. Never before in Hungarian history have the churches had their present independence of the state – lacking on the one hand state control, and on the other the means they enjoyed prior to World War II. Finding their new role in society is proving to be a difficult and complex process.

III. Basic Structure

1. Legal Sources

The sources of ecclesiastical law are basically the generally applicable sources of law: the Constitution, Acts of Parliament, Decrees of the Government and of Government Ministers.
According to Section 60 of the Constitution of the Republic of Hungary:

> (1) In the Republic of Hungary everyone has the right to the freedom of thought, conscience and religion.
> (2) This right includes free choice or acceptance of religion or other conviction and the liberty to publicly or privately express or decline to express, exercise and teach such religions and convictions by the way of religious actions, rites or in any other way, either individually or in a group.
> (3) In the Republic of Hungary the Church functions in separation from the State.
> (4) The ratification of the law on the freedom of conscience and of religion requires the votes of two thirds of the MPs present.

The Act on the Freedom of Conscience and Religion and the Churches provides for the legal status of religious communities, and sets out a detailed framework for their independent operation (Act 4/1990). The Act on the Settlement of Ownership of the Former Real Estates of the Churches (Act 32/1991) provides for the restitution of church property that was formerly and is in the future to be used for cult or public benefit purposes. The Act on the Financial Conditions of Religious and Public Activities of Churches (Act 124/1997) sets out a framework of public subsidies for churches. Other Acts have relevance to church activities (education, higher education, taxation etc.) in addition to a number of Government decrees which relate to certain specific issues in the life of the churches.
Hungary is party to a number of international agreements that are of significance to matters of religious freedom. Hungary signed and ratified the International Covenant on Civil and Political Rights,[4] and the Convention of the Rights of the Child,[5] as well as the European Convention for the Protection of Human Rights and Fundamental Freedoms[6] with its additional protocols.

---

4 Ratified by the law decree 8/1976.
5 Ratified by Act 94/1991.
6 Ratified by Act 31/1993.

On 9th February 1990 – a few days after Parliament had passed the new law on the freedom of religions, but before it was promulgated – the Holy See and Hungary re-established diplomatic relations at the highest level. The accord signed in Budapest states that issues relating to the church are to be settled by the new CIC and the new law on religious freedom.[7] This means on the one hand that the Hungarian law on churches is primarily not based on agreements but on the law,[8] on the other hand the law enjoys the positive acknowledgment of the Catholic Church. Two further agreements have been concluded with the Holy See. On 10th January 1994 an agreement was signed on the military ordinariate[9] as this was a precondition for the Government to set up an army chaplaincy. On 20th June 1997 an third accord was solemnly signed in the Vatican on the financial issues concerning the Catholic Church.[10] It is to be noted that the agreements between Hungary and the Holy See are of a highly technical nature, lacking the kind of general statements well known from concordat-type agreements. Hungary has no general agreement with the Holy See; neither a concordat nor a basic agreement providing a comprehensive set of rules.

Other churches have entered into contractual relations with the government, though without any international dimension. Contracts were signed on the army chaplaincies as well as on financial issues, the latter – especially the agreements with the Reformed Church and the Alliance of Jewish Communities – containing fundamental regulations on co-operation between state and church. The status of these agreements is however disputed.

Freedom of conscience enjoys a similar protection to that of freedom of religion. The accomodation of claims to religious freedom is generally done on the level of the individual, rather than by granting privileges to certain groups. For example, in the case of conscientious objection to the military service it is the individual conscientious conviction which is to be invoked and not the person's membership of a particular religious community. Freedom of conscience cases do emerge in labour law, but the relevant case law is not especially rich.

---

7 Published in the official gazette Magyar Közlöny 1990/35.
8 *Erdő, P.*, Aktuelle staatskirchenrechtliche Fragen in Ungarn, ÖArchKR 40 (1991), 390.
9 AAS 86 (1994) 574-579, 19/1994 international agreement from the Minister of Defence; *Baura, E.*, L'Accordo tra la Santa Sede a la Republica di Ungheria sull'assitenza religiosa alle Forze Armate e di Polizia di Frontiera, in Ius Ecclesiae, 7 (1995), 374-381.
10 Ratified by the decree of the Parliament: Act 70X/1999; AAS 90 (1998), 330-341.

Freedom of religion is regarded as one of the fundamental rights of communication. The limitations on the free exercise of these rights are subject to a narrow interpretation. Generally, the limitations of fundamental rights are to be scrutinised on criteria of necessity and proportionality. Limitations must be prescribed by Acts of Parliament; they have to be necessary in order to ensure another constitutional right or constitutional value; and they have to be proportionate to the goal of the limitation. The essential content of fundamental rights must not be limited. Litigation on religious freedom issues is rare.

2. Categories of System: Neutrality, Separation, Co-operation

Neutrality may be seen as the most important principle governing the State in its relationship with the religious communities as well as with other ideologies. The State should remain neutral in matters concerning ideology: there should be no official ideology, be it religious or secular. Neutrality means that the State should not identify with any ideology (or religion); consequently it must not be institutionally attached to a number of churches or to any one single church. This shows that the underlying doctrine behind the principle of separation (as explicitly stated in the Constitution) is the neutrality of the State. It is to be noted that neutrality has to be distinguished from indifference which is not what the Constitution implies – as follows from the concept of neutrality elaborated by the Constitutional Court. Neither is neutrality "laicism": the State may have an active role in providing an institutional legal framework as well as funds for the churches to ensure the free exercise of religion in practice; *"from the right to freedom of religion, follows the State's duty to ensure the possibility of free formation of personal convictions"*.[11] The State should not enter into institutional involvement with any organisation that is based on an ideology, either religious or secular. Freedom of religion and freedom from religion are equally protected – neither case should be treated as an exception. All public institutions are bound by the principle of neutrality: the State must

---

11 Decision 4/1993 (II. 12.) AB (commentary and text in English: *Sólyom, L./Brunner, G.* (eds.), Constitutional Jurisdiction in a New Democracy. The Hungarian Constitutional Court, The University of Michigan Press 2000, 246-266; in German: *Brunner, G./Sólyom, L.* (eds.), Verfassungsgerichtsbarkeit in Ungarn. Analysen und Entscheidungssammlung 1990-1993, Baden-Baden 1995, 421-468).

not maintain non-neutral institutions such as schools or theological faculties; church institutions, however, do enjoy public funding.

The meaning of separation may be defined on the one hand by respecting the autonomy (or self-determination) of the churches ("*the State must not interfere with the internal workings of any church*"), and, on the other hand, by the principle stated in the law on religious freedom: "*No State pressure may be applied in the interest of enforcing the internal laws and rules of a church*".[12] Religious communities are not allowed to make use of State power. In the relationship between the individual and his or her church, the State plays no role.

In comparison with other European countries, the Hungarian system seems to be closest to the Italian-Spanish pattern. The separation – especially institutional separation – between church and State in Hungary is definitely stricter than in the "co-ordination model" of Germany, but the Hungarian State provides favourable conditions for church activities and public funds to a much greater degree than is the case in "laïque" France. The Hungarian model that emerged in the 1990s may be described as a benevolent separation, respecting religious freedom and the freedom of the Churches, enhancing their activities and open to co-operation for the common good – especially in the field of public services.

IV. Legal Status of Religious Bodies

1. Legal Status of Religious Communities

The Law on the Freedom of Conscience and Religion and the Churches was passed in 1990. According to this Law,

> Those following the same religious beliefs may, for the purpose of exercising their religion, set up a religious community, religious denomination or Church (hereinafter together referred to as "Church") with self-government. (...) Churches may be founded for the pursuance of all religious activities which are not contrary to the Constitution and do not violate the law.

---

12 Act 4/1990, Section 15.

The registration of churches is done by the county courts in the same way as associations, political parties or foundations are registered. The requirements are highly formal: churches registered prior to 1990 were re-registered automatically; other religious communities wishing to be registered need to submit the names of 100 private individuals as founder members, and a charter containing at least the name of the religion, its headquarters address, and its internal organisational structure, and specifying those internal units of the church that enjoy legal personality; it also has to have an elected system of administration and representation. The founders must further submit a declaration that the organisation they have set up has a religious character and that its activities comply with the Constitution and the law (sections 8-9).

All Churches that are registered have the same rights and obligations. Equality, however, is a matter of legal status and not of social significance. As the Constitutional Court stated:

> "Also, treating the Churches equally does not exclude taking the actual social roles of the individual Churches into account."[13]

Consequently external, social differences between religious communities may be taken into account by the legislator if these are of relevance in the given issue.

The status of "churches" is neither that of a public law corporation nor that of an association. Churches enjoy legal personality as sui generis entities. Their internal organisational units, such as institutions or parishes, are also legal entities if the "charter" of the church so provides. This means that the internal law of each religious community determines whether legal persons acknowledged by the State come into existence or not – no further State registration of these persons is required. In the case of the Catholic Church the Code of Canon Law and the Code of Canons of the Eastern Churches determine which church entities have legal personality in the Hungarian legal system. "Independent organisations of churches set up for religious purposes" (such as religious orders) are also legal entities, but they need to be registered by the court.

As the legal system is very generous concerning registration and providing legal personality, "new religious movements" and splinter groups can easily make use of the same legal regimes as traditional

---

13 Decision No. 4/1993 (II. 12.) AB.

churches. The number of registered religious communities is currently about 150.

2. The Meaning of Religious Community and the Right of Self-Determination

Church autonomy may be seen as the most important difference between entities registered as churches and other registered legal entities,[14] such as associations, political parties or trades unions. Autonomy in the strict legal sense means that the internal actions of organisations registered as "churches" are not subject to any kind of state interference. Whereas a resolution of an association can be brought before the court (and courts have the power to close it down if these internal actions are unlawful or violate the charter of the association), no resolution of a bishop or a synod may be challenged before State courts. Neither are churches bound by the principle of democratic internal structure; associations, on the other hand, do have to be democratic. If a church violates the law, the public prosecutor has the right to sue the church. The court has to call upon the church to restore the legality of its operation. If the church does not comply with the court order it will be struck off the register of churches. This means the loss of the status of being a "church" but there is no ban on its activities. Unlawful actions themselves cannot be challenged, but they may lead to the removal of the church from the register. Churches determine their structure independent of the State: neither consent nor notification is required, for example in the case of creating new dioceses. The appointment of church officials is exclusively determined by the church concerned – only the nomination of the Catholic military Ordinary is subject to prior communication to the Government.

Churches – as well as other non-public entities – may maintain all kinds of schools, institutions of higher education, health or social care; they may also engage in economic activities, under special funding and taxation arrangements.

---

14 Decision 8/1990 (II. 27.).

3. Churches and Religious Communities within the Political System

There are no legal limitations on the political involvement of churches. The strict interpretation of the principle of separation rules out the possibility of any imposition of bans or limitations on clergy or churches concerning their political activities. Church practices differ on this issue. Mainstream churches prefer not to become involved in partisan politics; this, however, is a self-limitation, not one imposed by public authorities. The self-restraint of churches is often urged by certain actors in the political arena, fearing church involvement in partisan politics, or the instrumentalisation of churches. Moral statements, however, are generally welcome, if heard; the Catholic Bishops' Conference has issued significant documents on social issues, the family, and bio-ethics.

V. Church and Culture

Parents with the constitutional right to decide on the education of their children[15] also have the right to set up non-neutral schools. 'Church schools' are classed as neither public nor private. After public schools run by the municipalities, most schools are run by churches: at the level of secondary education the proportion of church schools is over 10 %. In Hungary all schools are bound by a national core curriculum. This, however, allows each school to establish its own teaching programme. A large variety of school-books is being published; there are no compulsory school textbooks. Church schools are not bound by the principle of ideological neutrality. This means that such schools can identify themselves with a particular religion. Religious symbols are allowed on the building as well as in the classrooms. Religious instruction may be part of the curriculum, and the marks gained are shown in the school report. The church schools are allowed to select not only their staff but also their pupils according to religious principles – none of this is allowed in public schools. It is to be noted that the State budget grants equal funding for church schools formally the school is maintained by the church, but the State provides the necessary funds – the enjoyment of equal

---

15 Constitution, section 67 (2).

public subsidies, however, precludes the right to collect tuition fees. Equal funding is guaranteed by the law[16] and was reaffirmed as a principle deduced from the Constitution, guaranteeing religious freedom, parental rights and non-discrimination.[17] Most church schools function in buildings that used to be church schools prior to their nationalisation in 1948, but churches are also engaged in the construction of new schools, and in some cases have taken over public schools from municipalities on a contractual basis.

Churches also have the right to provide religious education in public schools at the request of students or their parents.[18] Non-public schools are not obliged to provide religious education. Public schools must be of a neutral character and should be accessible to everyone, without an "undue burden". Neutral public schools should not endorse any religion or ideology, but must provide objective information about religions and philosophical convictions. Teachers at public schools should teach on a neutral basis; they have the right to express their opinion or belief, but they should not indoctrinate their students (headscarves have not yet become an issue in Hungary, but there is no dress code that would rule them out). Schools should provide fundamental information on ethics.[19] Public education on religion, and church education in religion are not the same. Church religious instruction in public schools is not a part of the school curriculum, the teacher of religion is not a member of the school staff, grades are not given in school reports, the churches decide freely on the content of the religion classes as well as on their supervision. Teachers of religion are in church employment; however, the State provides funding for the churches to pay the teachers. The school has only to provide an appropriate time for religious classes (this is a difficult issue in many cases) as well as teaching facilities. Churches are free to expound their beliefs during the religious classes: they do not have to restrict themselves to providing neutral education, merely giving information about religion, as do the public schools otherwise. Religious education is not part of the public school's task; it is a form of introduction into the life and doctrines of a given religious community at the request of students and parents.

There are no theological faculties at State universities in Hungary. The interpretation of separation and neutrality rules out the possibility of a religion-affiliated institution maintained by or linked with the

---

16 Act 4/1990, section 19 (1).
17 Decision No. 22/1997 (4. 25.) AB.
18 Act 4/1990, section 17 (2), Act 79/1993 (on education), sections 4 (4), 10 (3) d), 13 (3).
19 Act 79/1993, section 4 (2)-(3).

State. Certainly courses *on* religion may be delivered at State institutions, but courses *of* religion may not. Churches also have the right to maintain universities and other institutions of higher education that provide training in fields other than theology. Training in secular professions is subject to the same scrutiny of the procedures towards accreditation as at public universities; degrees have the same value, and the institutions are funded to the same extent as public institutions. The number of subsidised student places is set each year within the framework of agreements concluded between the maintaining church and the Government. After the Reformed Church set up a teacher training college, the Catholic Theological University in Budapest was extended to become the "Péter Pázmány Catholic University" that has, besides a Faculty of Theology, a Faculty of Humanities, a Faculty of Information Technology and a Faculty of Law and Political Science as well as an Institute of Canon Law. A few months after the Catholic University was founded, the Reformed Church also founded a university, adding to its Faculty of Theology in Budapest a Faculty of Humanities and a Law Faculty; a teacher training college was also integrated with it.

Institutions of theological higher education are acknowledged as colleges while existing theological faculties qualify as "theological universities". This, however, does not affect the purely ecclesiastical nature of these institutions. A list of the theological institutions – extended several times – is annexed to the Act on higher education.[20] The law on higher education requires the accreditation of theological institutions, but the content of theological courses is not subject to scrutiny.[21] Degrees are recognised by the State. The law has detailed provisions which provide exemption for church institutions from various obligations, while in other cases no distinctions are made. Professors of church universities are appointed by the President of the Republic as are other university professors, but in their case the nomination is not made exclusively by the Minister of Education but jointly by the maintaining church and the Minister. Besides the training of the clergy, the training of teachers of religion has become a major activity of church institutions.

---

20 Act 80/1993 (on higher education); at present there are five "church universities" (a Catholic, a Lutheran, a Jewish and two Calvinist), as well as 23 other institutions of higher education, 13 of which are Catholic (one Greek Catholic), while a number of religious communities that are not large in Hungary maintain such institutions (Baptists, Adventists, Pentecostals, Buddhists etc.).

21 Act 80/1993, section 114.

Churches may provide mass media as may other bodies. In fact, there are some local radio stations run by the Catholic Church. There are both religious and church programmes in the public media: religious programmes are on general religion (on a neutral base), whereas church programmes reflect the beliefs of their respective community. The public media allocate air time (not to be interrupted by commercials) to eight religious communities. The public media boards have two seats each for religious communities: one seat is occupied by the representatives of the four large religious communities by rotation (Catholic Church, Reformed Church, Lutheran Church, Alliance of Jewish Communities), whereas all other registered religious communities may apply for the second seat, the holder of which is determined by lot.[22]

VI. Labour Law within the Religious Communities

Labour law and social security law provide particular schemes for the persons defined by the internal law of a church and who are in a special "ecclesiastical labour regime" with a church.[23] The relationship between clergy and church does not generally fall under labour law, but is exclusively regulated by internal church law.
Discrimination, inter alia on the basis of religion, is prohibited by the Labour Code.[24] Distinctions set by the requirements of the job are not considered as discriminative. That is an exemption concerning the nature of the work, not that of the employer. This could suggest that different standards should be applied to teachers in church schools and school cleaners, for example. There is no established court practice concerning how far ecclesiastical employers can go in requiring belief, membership, or loyalty in the selection of their employees. The general legislation on non-discrimination allows for an exception for organisations based on a particular religion or belief relating to religion or belief if this aspect is directly relevant.[25] Employees in the institutions of churches that serve the public (schools, hospitals etc.) are not public employees: they are under the labour code regime

---

22 Act 1/1996 (on the media), sections 5, 10, 17, 23, 25, 56.
23 Act 80/1997 (on social security and private pensions), section 26 (3).
24 Act 22/1992 (Labour code), section 5.
25 Act 125/2003 (on equal treatment), section 6 (1)(c).

and not under the Civil Service regime as are their colleagues in municipal institutions. In practice, churches provide a quasi civil service regime in framing their labour contracts.

VII. Matrimonial and Family Law

Since 1895 Hungary has had an obligatory civil marriage regime.[26] Under legislation dating from 1962, a church wedding does not have to be preceded by a civil wedding. It follows that one can enter into marriage in church without any consequences under State law (however, in State law such couples are regarded as non-marital cohabitants).

VIII. Finances of the Churches

1. Restitution of Nationalised Property

In Hungary there was no re-privatisation after the collapse of communism. Nationalisation was regarded as harmful, unjust, and also illegal, but not invalid. The economic situation, which the "real socialism" left behind, did not allow for full restitution or full compensation. Private individuals who lost their property received partial compensation in the form of vouchers that they could use in the course of the privatisation process. Political parties and NGOs were granted office space – usually that of the former communist party – to facilitate their activities. Churches were compensated on the basis of a special law,[27] under which they could reclaim buildings appropriated after 1948 and originally used for specific purposes in so far as these properties were – at the time the Act came into force – the property of the State or a local municipality. These specific purposes did not cover economic utilisation, but they did cover a wide range of religious and non-profit-making activities such as reli-

---

26 Act 31/1894 (on marriage law).
27 Act 32/1991.

gious life, education, culture, health care institutions, and houses of religious orders. The building thus reclaimed is to be used for one of these purposes. In a strict legal sense this is not re-privatisation but the transfer of a building that is in public property that used to be as church property to a church. The nationalisation is not annulled, but a new transfer is made. The guiding principle of the Act was that churches should be helped to re-establish their functions: this was regarded as constitutional as it was inevitable to ensure religious freedom.[28] Furthermore, the legislator tried to avoid the creation of new injustices and uncertain legal circumstances. A joint committee, consisting of representatives of the church and the government, was established for each denomination and drew up proposals for the transfer of properties. The government makes the final decisions on these proposals. The law took into consideration compensation to the current owner of the property – in most cases the municipality.

As this financial burden made the procedure much slower than anticipated, in 1997 the deadline for the settlement was changed from the original 10 years to 20 years. Following a financial agreement with the Holy See on 20th June, 1997, a new law[29] passed in 1997 provided for the possibility of turning the value of non-restituted property into a virtual fund that grants a sum every year to the church concerned. Besides the accord with the Holy See, similar agreements were concluded with the Alliance of Jewish Communities, the Lutheran Church, the Reformed Church, the Baptist Church and the Serb Orthodox Diocese. Claims falling under the Act can be settled in four different ways:
- Direct agreement between the owner (the municipality) and the church on the transfer of the property. In most of these cases the building was not in public but in church use even before, such as places of worship or parish buildings; the transfer in these cases affects ownership rather than factual reality, and no financial compensation is invoked.
- Transfer of the building by resolution of the Government, with compensation for the owner. In these cases the central budget provides funds for the municipality that leaves the building in order to give it back to the church, and receives compensation to move the public institution (e.g. a school) to a new location.
- Financial compensation by the Government instead of taking over the same building. This option is chosen by churches when they

---

28 Decision 4/1993 (II. 12.) AB.
29 Act 124/1997.

have less interest in taking possession of the actual building, but prefer to invest in a new construction.
- Transfer of property claims into a fund that pays a fixed dividend for an unlimited time.

2. Funding of Public Activities

Churches are free to perform any public activity that is not reserved to the state. Churches performing public activities (maintaining schools or engaging in social service) are granted support from a budget that is supposed to equal the support received by public institutions that serve the same purpose.[30] Taking education as the most important activity as an example, the budget grants the same subsidy to churches maintaining schools on a per capita (per student) basis, that municipalities spend on education, based on a national average. In the case of a church-owned hospital the social security system provides the same fees as to public general hospitals. The principle of equal funding of public activities is guaranteed by law and was reinforced by a Constitutional Court case that stated that the equal funding was required by the Constitution as a consequence of religious freedom and the principle of non-discrimination.[31] The accord with the Holy See and agreements with other major churches also reinforced this principle, that can be regarded as a characteristic, and (by now) undisputed achievement of church-state relations in Hungary. It is to be noted that under the given social and financial circumstances only this principle allows the actual presence of church institutions in public services. As the funding is guaranteed in many ways and flows automatically, it does not infringe the independence of church-maintained public institutions.

3. Funding of Religious Activities – Tax Assignment (1 %)

Until 1998 the churches had direct state funding. Beginning with the tax return for the year 1997 (due in March 1998) taxpayers were given an option to assign 1 % of their income tax and could direct this sum to a church of their choice or to a public fund (a further 1 % may be directed to NGOs, museums, theatres, and other public insti-

---

30 Act 4/1990, section 19 (1).
31 Decision 22/1997 (IV. 25.) AB.

tutions).³² Until 2002, the State guaranteed to add to this amount up to 0.5 % of the income tax revenue according to the proportion of the declarations in favour of the churches. Beginning in 2003, the sum resulting from the declarations was supplemented by 0.8 % of the total state revenue from income tax and from 2004 on to 0.9%. The system is fairly complicated (partly due to a need for data protection) so churches were given a so-called technical number that is to be written in a special form that has to be attached to the tax return in a closed envelope or to be handed over to the employer if the employee has income only from that one employer so that he or she does not need to fill in a tax return. As a result, in the first year only about 10 % of the taxpayers (practically only regular churchgoers) filled in the declaration – this percentage has now risen to about 15 %. One of the difficulties of the system is that – contrary to the Italian model – Hungarian taxpayers assign 1 % of their own income tax, so those with a larger income and paying more income tax (on a progressive basis) have a larger say in distributing this sum. Another unfortunate aspect is that pensioners (who pay no income tax in Hungary if their only income is a pension) and low income taxpayers are excluded from the scheme. This has the consequence that only a small part of the active population, not the whole community of citizens, decides on the distribution of these funds. The denominational proportions are not surprising: about 65 % of the declarations were made for the benefit of the Catholic Church, about 20 % for the Reformed Church, and 5.7 % for the Lutheran Church. According to the proportion of the declarations, the Faith Church (a charismatic-evangelical congregation) has become the fourth biggest religious community, followed by the Jewish Community. Altogether about 100 religious communities now make use of this system of funding.

4. Other Channels of Funding

Churches can receive subsidies from the central budget for the maintenance of religious and cultural heritage, historic buildings, archives, libraries, and museums.³³ Some municipalities also contribute to reconstruction projects.

---

32 Act 129/1996 (on the use of a specified amount of personal income tax in accordance with the taxpayer's instruction).
33 Act 124/1997, section 7 (1).

Churches are free to receive donations (with limited tax-deductibility). Churches also have the right to act as entrepreneurs enjoying some benefits. In practice, the business activities of churches is insignificant – except for some "new religious movements". Churches enjoy benefits of various kinds, similar to those of non-profit-making organisations: for example they are exempt from local taxes[34] and fees.[35]

Since 2002 churches have received special contributions towards the salaries of their staff (clergy and other full time church employees) serving and living in rural settlements of less than 5,000 inhabitants. With these grants the government acknowledges that churches have a vital role in keeping the rural areas alive. Individual clergy do not receive state stipends, but it is the church that receives a public fund to assist their staff who – besides their genuine religious duties – also contribute to the welfare of villages.

Besides this complex of public subsidies it is to be noted that – especially at the local level – churches are basically maintained by the voluntary donations of their faithful.

IX. Religious Assistance in Public Institutions

Individual and collective worship is facilitated in social and health care institutions[36] as well as in penal institutions.[37] Chaplains of the mainstream denominations in penitentiaries may become civil servants, but free access to pastors of all denominations is guaranteed.

For those serving in the army, a military chaplaincy was set up[38] for the denominations that could provide a minimum level of religious service within the army (Catholic Church, Reformed Church, Lutheran Church, Alliance of Jewish Communities). All other religious communities are free to operate within the military organisation in accordance with the rules and regulations of the army. Due to the special nature of the military, the army chaplaincy was not regarded as unconstitutional; the Constitutional Court also accepted a margin of interpretation on the part of the State in dealing differently with

---

34 Act 100/1990 (on local taxes), section 3 (2).
35 Act 93/1990 (on duties), section 5.
36 Act 4/1990, section 6; Act CLIV/1997 (on health care), section 11 (6).
37 6/1996 (VII. 12.) IM, sections 93-99; 13/2000 (VII. 14.) IM.
38 Government Decree 61/1994 (IV. 20.) Korm.

religious communities that show significant differences in practice. As the Constitutional Court stated, the Chaplaincy did not lead to an unconstitutional entanglement as it did not become an institutional part of the military, but works alongside it.[39] Army chaplains are nominated by their church and they are appointed as officers with a military rank. They must comply with military orders, but their religious activities are not subordinated to the hierarchy of the army. The Chaplaincy is financed by the State. According to the relevant agreement with the Holy See, the Military Ordinariate operates according to the apostolic constitution *"Spirituali Militum Curae"*. The Ordinary is appointed by the Holy See, after notifying the Hungarian Government, taking military requirements into consideration. The Government has the right to raise political objections within 15 days, but these do not bind the Holy See. The Ordinary may be a diocesan bishop at the same time. The Military Ordinary and the chaplains have different positions. As officers of the army and as priests of the Ordinariate, their liabilities are rigorously distinct. Similar requirements apply to the Protestant pastors in the army as well as to the rabbi of the army.

X. Criminal Law and Religion

The Criminal Code has a provision on the *"Violation of the Freedom of Conscience and Religion"*,[40] that was incorporated into the Code by Act 4/1990. According to that provision:

> Whoever
> a) restricts another person by violence or by threats in his freedom of conscience,
> b) prevents another person from freely exercising his religion by violence or by threats,
> commits a crime, and is punishable by imprisonment extending to three years.

The abuse of someone because of his or her actual or assumed membership of a national, ethnic, race or religious group is punishable by five years' imprisonment. However, it is difficult to prove that a per-

---

39 Decision No. 970/B/1994, AB, ABH 1995, 739.
40 Act 4/1978 (Criminal Code), section 174/A.

son was attacked because of his or her membership of a religious group.

Clergy enjoy protection under criminal law as persons "performing public duties", such as lawyers, teachers, medical doctors on duty, or firemen.[41]

As a misdemeanour, the "*Violation of the Right of Worship*" is penalised. According to this:

> "A fine not exceeding HUF one hundred thousand may be imposed on whoever causes a public scandal on premises designated for the purposes of the ceremonies of a registered church or desecrates the object of religious worship or an object used for conducting the ceremonies on or outside the premises designated for the purposes of ceremonies."[42]

In a sense this provision protects the institution: the religious community itself, not merely the beliefs and feelings of the individual members or those of the community.

XI. The Legal Status of Clergy

There are no limitations on the political or public activities of the clergy; mainstream churches, however, practise self-restraint in this respect.

Clergy enjoy privileges concerning military service. National Service was abolished in 2004, but even before thet clergy could not be drafted in peace time.

In civil and administrative procedures, clergy may make use of a provision that allows for a refusal to testify in the case of "professional" secrets. The confessional secret is protected in the same way that medical doctors or advocates enjoy protection concerning the secrets with which they are entrusted in the practice of their profession. According to the new criminal procedure code, clergy enjoy a qualified protection, as they may not be questioned about issues in which they invoke the seal of confession.[43] This means that it is not for the clergy to refuse to testify but the court and the public prosecutor must not cross-examine them.

---

41 Act 4/1978, 137, 2. j).
42 Act 69/1999 (on misdemeanours), section 150.
43 Act XIX/1998 (on criminal procedure), section 81 (1) a)

XII. Particular Questions of Civil Ecclesiastical Law and Developments

The principles and the basic structure of church-state relations seem to enjoy a social consensus. But this consensus does not mean that that there is no discussion of particular issues. Many regard the easy registration of religious communities and the formal equality of all registered communities as over-generous towards new religious movements and splinter-groups. Some groups registered as "churches" may have no religious ethos at all: they may be registered as churches merely in order to enjoy the special benefits. There is no effective procedure to prevent abuse of the system, or to challenge the abusers. Other people submit that the formal equality of churches has been overwritten step by step by a de facto stronger co-operation between the State and the mainstream or historic churches. Whereas some would be in favour of a two-tier system, others regard the equality of all religious communities as the cornerstone of religious freedom. Some support a stronger position for religious education in public schools. The optional character of religious education is not a matter for debate, but the issue of whether it could become more integrated into the public school curriculum is being considered: if the State introduced courses of ethics, those participating in religious education at schools could eventually opt out of ethics. Data protection, parents' rights, and the respect of church autonomy need to be considered at the same time. There are also voices that regard obligatory civil marriage as outmoded, and seek civil recognition for church weddings.

After some hectic disputes in the early 1990s the basis of the system is now firmly established. The foundations are based on respect for the individual, as well as on respect of the self-governance of religious communities, on a positive neutrality of the State, and on a strict institutional separation between church and state that is open to co-operation.

XIII. Literature

Ádám, Antal, La liberté religieuse en Hongrie, in Il diritto ecclesiastico XI (1995), p. 283-309.

Boleratzky Lóránd, Neues Gesetz über die Gewissens- und Religionsfreiheit und die Kirchen in Ungarn, in Zeitschrift für Evangelisches Kirchenrecht 35 (1990), p. 323-331

Erdő, Péter, Aktuelle staatskirchenrechtliche Fragen in Ungarn, in Österreichisches Archiv für Kirchenrecht 40 (1991), p. 387-397.

Erdő, Péter, Die gegenwärtige Lage des Staat-Kirche-Verhältnisses in Ungarn – Staatskirchenrechtliche und kanonistische Aspekte, in Essener Gespräche zum Thema Staat und Kirche 29 (1995), p. 134-150.

Erdő, Péter, Libéralisation de la societé civile et responsabilité de l'Église catholique en Hongrie, in Folia Theologica 7 (1996), p. 5-20.

Erdő, Péter, Das Verhältnis von Staat und Kirche in Ungarn nach Beendigung der kommunistischen Ära, in La libertad religiosa. Memoria del IX Congreso Internacional de Derecho Canónico, México 1996, p. 621-638.

Erdő, Péter, Accordo tra la Santa Sede e la Repubblica d'Ungheria, in Anuario de Derecho Eclesiástico del Estado XIV (1998) 721-728; Ius Ecclesiae 10 (1998), p. 652-659.

Erdő, Péter – Schanda, Balázs, Church and State in Hungary. An Overview of Legal Questions, in European Journal for Church and State Research 6 (1999), p. 219-231.

Schanda, Balázs, Freedom of Religion and Minority Religions in Hungary, in Social Justice Research 12/4 (1999), p. 297-313.

Schanda, Balázs, Church and State in Hungary in 1999. The Funding of the Churches in Hungary, in European Journal for Church and State Research 7 (2000), p. 259-278.

Schanda, Balázs, Church Autonomy and Religious Liberty – National Report on Hungary, in *Robbers, Gerhard* (ed.), Church Autonomy. A Comparative Study, Frankfurt am Main 2001, p. 541-560.

Schanda, Balázs (ed.), Legislation on Church-State Relations in Hungary, Budapest 2002.

Schanda, Balázs, Magyar állami egyházjog (Hungarian ecclesiastical law), 2nd edition, Budapest 2003.

Tomka, Miklós, Changes in the Structure of Denominations in East and Central Europe, in Review of Sociology (Special Issue) 1996, p. 88-103.

Ugo Mifsud Bonnici
State and Church in Malta

I. Social Facts

At 1st October 2003 the population of the Maltese Islands was 398,985. With an area of 316 square kilometres, the islands have the highest population density in Europe: 1,263 persons per square kilometre. The age-child ratio in 2002 was 68 old persons to one hundred children, whereas the total dependency ratio was 46.09. The crude birth rate was 9.86 in 2002 (compared with 17.6 in 1970), births outside marriage 14.95. The crude death rate was 7.85; the life expectancy rates were 75.78 years for males and 80.48 years for females. The crude marriage rate was 5.80. Out of the 2,240 marriages registered in 2002, 575 were civil marriages whilst the rest were celebrated according to a religious (mainly Catholic) rite. Marriages with a non-Maltese partner totalled 500. The total fertility rate for 2002 was 1.46.

The genetic mix is derived from mainly Mediterranean, predominantly southern European, stock with some British genes imported through intermarriage during the last two centuries. Though their physical features can be diverse, the population is very homogeneous in culture and outlook. The last Census returns (1995) show that though a high proportion have a second language (English) and other languages (Italian, French, German), almost all Maltese know the Maltese language, which is widely used in social life, in the Courts of Law, in the churches, and in Parliament; English is also a second official Language, used for administration. Maltese is a complex language with a Semitic base, a large and predominant Romance element in its lexicon and sentence structure, and with a good sprinkling of English terms.

Traditionally, the Census Questionnaire has no question concerning religious faith, but almost all Maltese are baptised Catholics, and the attendance at Sunday Mass varies in percentage terms from a low of 48 % in some towns and villages in the South East to a high of 79 % in parts of Gozo, with an average of 61 %. There is a number of Protestant Churches: Anglican, Presbyterian, and Baptist, which cater for foreign residents; and nuclei of Jehovah's Witnesses and Unification Church followers, mainly composed of repatriated Maltese emigrants from the United States and Australia. There is a mosque, attended mostly by foreign Muslims and a small number of Maltese wives of Moslem husbands.

The social life of the country shows evidence of a Catholic tradition, with Sundays, feasts of patron saints, and the liturgical calendar providing the rhythm of the Maltese week and year. However life-styles are moving towards more of a Mid-European way of life as the statistics amply demonstrate by the fall of birth and marriage rates.[1]

II. Historical Background

The *reconquista* of Malta and Gozo from Arab domination by Roger the Norman in 1090 established a very close relationship between the civil and religious authorities. Count Roger and his successors, the Norman Kings, saw themselves as the patrons and benefactors of the Church, and subsequently were given by the Papacy the right of nomination to the bishoprics within their realm. Even today, the Cathedral in the old capital of Mdina recalls the endowment supposedly received from the Norman liberator. During the Middle Ages the Maltese Università[2] ran the Island under the privileges received from Kings and Emperors, be they Norman, Angevin, Suabian, Aragonese or Spanish, under the shadow of the Cathedral which was administered by the Chapter in the absence of the mostly foreign-born bishop. The priests never formed part of this body, but occupied themselves in running the grammar school or the hospital with financial contributions from both Università and Cathedral (and occasionally from the absent bishop's rents).

When the Emperor Charles V granted Malta on fief to the Order of St. John in 1530, the civil and religious affairs of these islands became further entwined. The Hospitallers were a religious order responsible directly to the Pope, but they were put in charge of the defence of the country, and became *de facto* the government of Malta

---

1 Sources: Period Demographic Indicators issued by the National Statistics Office of Malta, and the Demographic Review of 2002 as well as Malta's Demography within a European Perspective 2002, both published by the National Statistics Office of Malta.
2 The Commonwealth or Municipal Authority which was the permanent government of the country.

even though they were supposedly bound to respect the *franchigie* of the Università. Thereafter the Grand Master of the Order ruled and the Order provided all the services of Government except for some judicial functions retained by the Università's civil and criminal courts at Mdina. The Grand Master's absolute rule was at times compromised by the presence of the Bishop and later by the Roman Inquisition: that is, there were three religious authorities holding sway over the country. Over the centuries, the Church, collegiate chapters, and convents received bequests and pious foundations from knights, from the nobility and from all classes of what was a pious population, so that by the end of the eighteenth century a significant proportion of the immovable property in both islands was in ecclesiastical hands.

When General Napoleon Bonaparte, commanding an army of the French Republic bound for Egypt, landed in June 1798, the position changed: the Order of St. John was disbanded and all its property (including its thirty-eight churches and chapels together with their treasures) became State property. The other religious Orders had to restrict their presence to only one of their convents in Malta and Gozo. The sale, by public auction, of the sacred vestments and silver of the Carmelite Church and convent at Imdina, one intended for suppression, triggered the Maltese counter-revolution and the ensuing liberation of the Islands from French Republican troops with the help of the British Forces and those of their allies, the Portuguese.

The British Government, which had assisted the Maltese insurgents, was tempted into staying, and the Islanders issued them with an invitation to continue to "protect" them. However, the Declaration of Rights of 1802 made by the Representatives of the Maltese expressly stipulated respect for the status of the Catholic Church. The French experience, together with the British colonial principle of non-interference with the religious beliefs of the inhabitants, meant that throughout the whole period of colonial rule (informally from 1800 and formally between 1814 and 1964) the position of the Catholic Church was in general guaranteed. This did not mean that no changes were made. When the position of Great Britain in these Islands was further assured, a series of Proclamations and Ordinances was issued, the effect of which was to remove some of the privileges hitherto enjoyed by the Church.[3]

---

3 By Proclamation XXIII of 1822 a Law of Mortmain was enacted whereby the position of ownership of immovable property by the Church and its entities was frozen. The Church and its Orders, Chapters, Foundations and other entities could not acquire new property by any transaction inter vivos, except by Government dispensation, and had to sell within one

We now know from the discovery of secret files[4] that the British Governors were extremely jealous of the position enjoyed by the diocesan bishop and of the revenues due to his *mensa*, but they were more concerned by the fact that the King of the Two Sicilies had exercised the right of presentation of three names to the Holy See when the Bishopric became vacant. Furthermore, this right of presentation, which went back to the Normans, was entertained by the Pope for the vacancy which occurred in 1807 with the death of Bishop Labini. The Vatican was naturally happy to see this anachronistic right discontinued, and when the succeeding bishop, Mattei, died, it resisted an attempt by the British Government to impose Francesco Saverio Caruana as the next Bishop. The ban was finally lifted when the new Pope Pius IX opted for a loose arrangement of "consultation" before every new appointment; this was put in place after Caruana's death. Throughout the whole period of British sovereignty, both the British Imperial Government and the Vatican avoided confrontation.[5] Great

---

year, on pain of forfeiture, any immovable property bequeathed to them causa mortis. This Mortmain principle, although rendered much more flexible by the Mortmain Law of 1967, in fact remained operative in Maltese legislation until 1992. The British Colonial Authorities through Governor Maitland justified the introduction of Mortmain by invoking the principles of free trade. Property in the hands of Ecclesiastical entities, it was said, in fact became extra commercium. This was however not the only reason. Also curbing the economic relevance of the Church was Proclamation V of 1828, which is still on the Statute Books as Chapter I of the Laws of Malta, and which provided that the decisions of the Ecclesiastical Court would henceforth have no binding effect at Civil Law except where a special Law so provides. The Acts and documents of these Courts, properly authenticated, can be produced in evidence in the Civil Courts only when relevant under the special Law. Proclamation VI of the same year (still in force as Chapter II) abolished the right of sanctuary whereby persons fearing arrest for a crime or a civil debt could take refuge in certain churches. A Law of 1831 (now Chapter III) provided that the Curia Deputation, deciding on the bestowal of Marriage Legacies administered by the Church, had to be appointed in consultation with the Governor. A Law of 1834 (now Chapter V) limits the effects of a promise of marriage to an action for damages in certain cases, solely in the Civil Courts. A Law promulgated through Proclamation VI of 1838 (now Chapter VI) provided for the appointment to Ecclesiastical positions or benefices of persons nominated by a foreign power, in the sense that such an appointment had to be approved by the Government and the appointment of an administrator to a vacant position or benefice when it had, according to custom or inveterate right, to be made by a foreign power, had henceforth to be made by the Archbishop of Malta or if the Archbishop made no such appointment within fifteen days, by the Governor.

4   Extant in the National Archives and now open to inspection and study.
5   As an example: At one time a decision was taken to revise the Laws of Malta and a Commission was appointed, composed mainly of judges from the United Kingdom. However it soon became apparent that as the Maltese legal profession including the minority on the Commission had a continental legal culture with a basis in Roman Law, and had practised for centuries in the Italian Language, the only tenable and acceptable way to modernise would be to continue within that cultural environment without trying to impose Common Law. Eventually, a new Commission was formed, composed totally of Maltese Judges, and

respect was shown and precedence given by the colonial authorities to the Bishop of Malta and to visiting Cardinals and prelates. The Bishop of Malta and later, when the Bishopric of Gozo was instituted as a separate See, the Bishop of Gozo, were exempt from any criminal action in the ordinary Courts.

With the advent of self-Government in 1921, complications of a local political nature found both the Government at Westminster and the Vatican again involved, albeit involuntarily. When the first Self Government Constitution was brought into force by the British Imperial Government in 1921, there was no religious clause in the document, but the first Act passed by the Maltese Legislative Assembly proclaimed the Catholic faith as the religion of Malta. For a time matters proceeded smoothly. However in the years 1928-32, the Government of Lord Strickland, formed by a compact between the Constitutional[6] Party and the Labour Party came into collision with the Catholic Hierarchy of Malta and Gozo over a matter of Church discipline.[7]

---

the Commission adopted the Code Napoleon. However, not only was any reference to divorce expunged, but the undeclared, though very much implied, premise that Canon Law was the only law regulating marriage between Catholics in Malta, meant that there was no provision for any other kind of marriage. British Protestants were married first in the Governor's private chapel at the Palace and thereafter in the newly erected Anglican Cathedral and various Protestant Churches. A problem arose concerning mixed marriages and especially the validity of marriages contracted by ex-Catholic priests in Protestant Churches. These problems gave rise, in time, to protracted negotiations at the Vatican between Cardinal Rampolla, the Secretary of State, and the Governor of Malta, Lintorn Simmons, who represented the British Government. No legislative solution was found, but both parties felt they could rely on the written advice of Sir Hadrian Dingli, ex-Chief Justice of Malta, in the sense that by inveterata consuetudo all marriages contracted in the Churches or places of worship belonging to the various denominations and religions were valid according to the Law of Malta, and the parties were bound as regards questions of validity by the Canon laws of their faith. This was substantially the law prior to the arrival of Napoleon. Jewish and Muslim marriages had always been recognised as valid in Malta from time immemorial. The matter of the validity of a 'mixed' marriage, not celebrated according to the decrees of the Council of Trent, when one party was a Catholic, even a lapsed one, was not legally addressed until 1974.

6   The most decidedly pro-British Party.
7   A Maltese Friar too friendly with the Constitutional Club in Valletta was transferred to an Italian Convent by his Provincial who was an Italian national. Whereupon the Compact Government intervened by withdrawing the Maltese Friar's passport and declaring the Italian Provincial Father Carta, persona non grata. Tempers flared, and following the issue of a Pastoral Letter enjoining the faithful, under the pain of Church sanctions, not to vote for Lord Strickland and his supporters, the 1930 elections were suspended during the actual voting, and the Constitution was partially suspended. Before its restoration, the Vatican sent to Malta a prominent ecclesiastic, Monsignor Robinson, who reported against Lord Strickland, in effect forcing him to ask to be reconciled in time for the 1932 elections, which, nevertheless, he lost. This did not deter him from putting all possible spokes in the wheels when the Bishop of Gozo, Monsignor Gonzi, whom Strickland suspected to be the

After the 1939-45 war, self-government was restored in 1947. No church-state difficulties were encountered until 1955, under the first Labour Prime Minister and subsequently with the Nationalist and coalition Governments. A number of crises occurred when the second Labour Prime Minister, Dom Mintoff, acted somewhat high-handedly in clashes with the church hierarchy led by Archbishop Gonzi in 1958[8] and between 1962 and 1967.[9] Mintoff had suspected collusion between the British Government, the Nationalist Party in Government locally, and the Church headed by Gonzi, during the negotiations concerning the framing of the 1964 Independence Constitution. In fact Dom Mintoff had emphasized the need to include six points, which would guarantee a more clear cut division between State and Church. The quarrel was patched up in 1967, after the achievement of Independence, but the six points were to continue to trouble Labour Party-Catholic Church relations for a number of years, until the 1974 Constitutional Amendments and beyond.

Mintoff was re-elected Prime Minister in 1971 and set about a course that would ensure a removal of what he deemed was the undue influence of the Catholic Church in Malta's political, social, cultural and even economic life. In 1974, whilst the negotiations with the Nationalist Party Opposition for the amendment of the 1964 Constitution were being conducted, the Labour Government took the opportunity of trying to arrive at an accommodation on certain matters with the Vatican directly. As regards direct political influence, the Labour Party insisted on a clearer description as a "corrupt practice" of the imposition of Church moral sanctions during elections. The Constitution was amended to specify in a more precise way that freedom of conscience had as a corollary the consequence that no adherence to a religious creed should be a requirement for state positions or state examinations. All supposed or real[10] privileges enjoyed by the Bishops were suppressed.

In addition the 1971-76, 1976-81 and 1981-87 Labour Governments took a number of steps to try to diminish the Catholic Church's influence. The Theological Faculty at the University, which had been the

---

real instigator of the Pastoral Letter, was mooted as successor to the Bishop of Malta, Monsignor Caruana. Gonzi only became Bishop of Malta in 1943, when Strickland had been dead for three years.

8 In the matter of the return to St. John's Co-Cathedral of the Caravaggio masterpiece showing the beheading of that Saint; as well as regarding Gonzi's allegedly pro-British attitude when the Constitution was suspended.

9 In the matter of the then Leader of the Opposition, Mintoff's alleged extreme leftist views and laicist policies and Gonzi's supposed leanings towards the Nationalist Party.

10 Such as immunity from criminal action in State Courts.

senior Faculty, present from its foundation in 1592, was abolished and the Church had to reconstitute it outside the University. Catholic schools which catered for a third of Maltese students were hamstrung by the imposition of "gratuity": to continue the schools' existence, tuition would have to be provided free of charge, and the Church had to fund the schools out of income from Church property. Without some kind of supplementary Government funding this was impossible in practical terms, and the schools were kept forcibly closed, with police stationed outside their doors. Help to Church schools was given, paradoxically in a wider context, but understandably in Catholic Malta, by a teachers' general strike proclaimed and maintained by the teachers of Government schools. To add to all this the Labour Government also sought to divest the Church and its institutions of all immovable property for which it had no written record of acquisition of ownership. Understandably the Courts of Malta declared this law (the so-called Devolution Act) unconstitutional as it concerned property which had been in the hands of the Church in some instances for over nine hundred years, some supposedly having been given as endowment to the Cathedral by Count Roger the Norman in 1090. Church hospitals were forced to close because the Government imposed as a condition for the renewal of their licence that they should offer to the Government half their beds free of charge, without receiving any supplementary subvention. The Marriage Law of 1974 turned the wheel full circle: canon law was declared no longer of any effect at civil law, and all declarations by the Roman Rota as to the nullity of a Catholic marriage were not to be recognised. Foreign sentences pronouncing divorce were, on the contrary, to be given recognition. The conditions for the declaration of nullity by the civil courts of Malta were not aligned with those of canon law. This was partially rectified in 1981. Marriage according to the Tridentine Rite was not deemed to be a valid marriage if unaccompanied by registration by a government official in the church. In effect not only was a form of civil marriage provided for, a measure which was unanimously agreed upon in Parliament, but all marriages had to be "civil" marriages.

As a result of the crisis provoked by the schools and devolution issue, but not before a demonstration by Labour sympathizers had stormed into the Law Courts and the Curia, in the aftermath of the Court judgment declaring the Devolution Law unconstitutional, negotiations were initiated at the Vatican for some kind of settlement of the then current issues. Church schools had to be non-fee-paying, a *desideratum* for the Church, but the Government agreed to provide a partial subvention. The number and size of Church Schools had to be frozen. The Government repealed the Devolution Law. Church Hospitals never reopened as hospitals though some Religious Orders converted them into Old People's homes.

The Vatican sent to Malta as Nuncio a diplomat of the circle of Cardinal Casaroli, Monsignor Luigi Celata, and some compromise solutions were negotiated, such as the gradual introduction of Government subventions. With a change of Government in May 1987, church-state relations improved considerably and the *contentieux* were tackled systematically and radically. Thus it was agreed that all immovable property held by the Church which was not required for pastoral, educational or social welfare purposes, was transferred to the State at an equitable "social" price. The property which had been targeted under the Devolution Law was also transferred, and the appeal lodged against the Court judgment which had declared that law unconstitutional was abandoned. The Mortmain Law dating back to 1822, as amended in 1967, was repealed so as to remove any obstacle to the acquisition of property which could be deemed discriminatory in the context of the European Human Rights Convention. The Nationalist Government took the step, immediately on its return to office in 1987, of rendering the Convention directly enforceable. Special Accords were agreed with regard to the subvention to be given by the State so that Church Schools could continue to be free of charge, as well as concerning the teaching of Catholic religious principles in State Schools. The Theological Faculty returned to the University. Agreement was also reached on the appointment by the Bishops in consultation with government of religious "Animators", as spiritual directors in the State schools.[11] Some of the difficulties in the Marriage Law of 1974 as amended in 1980 were rendered more acceptable.

---

11 The author of this contribution was then the Minister of Education delegated by the Nationalist Government to negotiate and arrive at a conclusion of these agreements and accords.

III. The Present Position at Law

1. In the Constitution

I. Article 2 of the Constitution deals specifically with and is entitled in its marginal note 'Religion'. The text runs as follows:

> (1) The Religion of Malta is the Roman Catholic Apostolic Religion.
> (2) The authorities of the Roman Catholic Church have the duty and the right to teach which principles are right and which are wrong.
> (3) Religious teaching of the Roman Catholic Apostolic Faith shall be provided in all State Schools as part of compulsory education.

This is not the original text of the 1964 Constitution. It is the text negotiated with the Vatican in 1974 to which the Nationalist Opposition in Parliament gave its assent, even though it criticised the text as not clear and not precisely worded in its second sub-article. The substitution was effected by Act LVIII of 1974.

It was explained that sub-article (1) should not be deemed prescriptive but only descriptive. In fact sub-articles (1) and (3) were not entrenched by Article 66, which establishes the special conditions for the amendment of certain articles of the Constitution, whilst sub-article (2) recognising the Church's right to teach was so entrenched. It was argued that the right to teach should be recognised even if or when the Church was no longer the church of the majority.

Notwithstanding the partial non-entrenchment, Article 2 is of great importance in that it provides the legal foundation for the practice of having the crucifix displayed in Parliament, in the courts of Law, in State schools and hospitals, and in public buildings and offices. The prayer which is recited by the Clerk of the House before every parliamentary sitting is a Catholic prayer and every session of Parliament begins with a Mass of the Holy Spirit in St. John's Co-Cathedral, considered as State co-owned at least. The form of oath administered to holders of office is assumed to be in the usual Catholic form, but the law provides for a solemn affirmation without any religious connotation. Under the umbrella of this provision the State pays for chaplains in hospitals, schools, prisons and the Police and Armed Forces.

Sub-article (3) was drafted when the Constitution mentioned, as it still does in Article 10, that Primary education had to be free and compulsory, but as from 1974 the age of compulsory education was raised to sixteen, and therefore as a matter of fact religious instruction in the Catholic Faith is provided in all State Primary and Secondary Schools. This does not mean that it is compulsory for students to receive it. The obligation is on the State to provide it, and to pay for it.

II. Article 32, which is an original 1964 provision, deals with the Fundamental Rights and Freedoms of the Individual, and is the first of a series of articles grouped under Chapter IV with the same description. The text reads:

> Whereas every person in Malta is entitled to the Fundamental Rights and Freedoms of the individual that is to say the right, whatever his race, place of origin, political opinions, colour, creed, or sex, but subject to the respect for the rights and freedoms of others and for the public interest, to each and all of the following, namely:
> (a) life, liberty and security of the person, the enjoyment of property and the protection of the law;
> (b) freedom of conscience, of expression and of peaceful assembly and association; and
> (c) respect for his private and family life,
> the subsequent provisions of this Chapter shall have effect for the purpose of affording protection for the aforesaid rights and freedoms, subject to such limitations of that protection as are contained in these provisions, being limitations designed to ensure that the enjoyment of said rights and freedoms by any individual does not prejudice the rights and freedoms of others or the public interest.

Malta has a long tradition of being hospitable to people of a variety of races and creeds. With the British colonial presence the number of protestants of all denominations occupying high positions in the State was a frequent occurrence, and the islands have had a small Jewish community as well as a small number of Moslem traders for centuries. In fact in the 1860s a number of cemeteries to cater for the burial of non-Catholics were built at Government expense concurrently with the building of a Roman Catholic cemetery. The practice of non-discrimination continued during self-government, after Independence, and continues to date.

Within the same Chapter, Article 40 expressly provides for the protection of the freedom of conscience and worship in these terms:

> (1) All persons in Malta shall have full freedom of conscience and enjoy the full exercise of their respective mode of religious worship.

(2) No person shall be required to receive instruction in religion or to show knowledge or proficiency in religion, if, in the case of a person who has not attained the age of sixteen years, objection to such requirement is made by the person who according to law has authority over him and, in any other case, if the person so required objects thereto;
Provided that no such requirement shall be held to be inconsistent with or in contravention of this section to the extent that the knowledge of, or the proficiency or instruction in, religion is required for the teaching of such religion, or for admission to the priesthood or to a religious order or for other religious purposes, and except so far as that requirement is shown not to be justifiable in a democratic society.
(3) Nothing contained in or done under the authority of any law shall be held to be inconsistent with or in contravention of subsection (1) to the extent that the law in question makes provision that is reasonably required in the interest of public safety, public order, public morality or decency, public health, or the protection of the rights and freedoms of others, and except in so far as that provision or, as the case may be, the thing done under the authority thereof is shown to be not reasonably justifiable in a democratic society.

This was not the original text in the 1964 Constitution, nor can it be said to have been very elegantly phrased and drafted. It seems to have been the result of compromise not only between the Maltese Government's position and that of the Vatican, but also of considerable cobbling with the words. However it satisfied at the lowest technical mean the compromise needs of that moment and has not caused any difficulty of interpretation since then, as it is sufficiently clear notwithstanding the abundant verbiage.
Article 45, within the same Chapter IV, provides for the remedies and the means of redress in the case of discrimination on various grounds. As a further note of clarification, sub-article (9) provides expressly:

A requirement, however made, that the Roman Catholic Religion be taught by a person professing that Religion shall not be held to be inconsistent with or in contravention of this section.

2. In the Education Act (Act XXIV of 1988, Chap. 327 of the Laws of Malta)

The Act was conceived when the problems which had arisen between the Church and the Labour Government in the 1970s and early 1980s were still very vivid memories. Article 3 safeguards the right of every citizen to education, and the following articles recognise the rights and duties of the parents (Articles 5 and 6), the State (Articles 4 and 7), and other entities (Article 8) amongst which the Roman Catholic Church is specifically mentioned. Sub-article (2) of that Article provides that when the Church [specifically mentioned but in common with other moral entities which do not have a profit motive] applies for a licence to open a school [provided that such application is signed by the Bishop in Ordinary] the Minister of Education [provided also that the proposed school abides by the Minimum Conditions] cannot refuse the application. In effect the Act recognises the right of every citizen, and his or her parents or guardians when still a minor, to choose the schools to attend. It also obliges the State to give proper space to schools with different cultures, *charismae* and characteristics, so that a proper choice is available.

There is a Scholastic Tribunal to which recourse may be made in the case of an institution deeming itself aggrieved were the Minister to refuse a licence on the basis of alleged non-conformity with the National Minimum Conditions.

3. In the Criminal Code (Chap. 9 of the Laws of Malta)

Under Title IV, Articles 163-165 of the Criminal Code provide for sanctions against crimes which offend the religious sentiment of others. Articles 163 and 164 deal with publicly "vilifying" by means of words, gestures, written matter, whether printed or not, or pictures or by other visible means, the Roman Catholic religion (163) or any other religion [the words used are "cult tolerated by the State", which are a leftover from previous times] (164). There is a differentiation between punishments, which was justified by the fact that public vilification of the Catholic Church could and did produce civil commotion when, though rarely, such incidents occurred.

Article 165 punishes "whosoever impedes or disturbs the performance of any function, ceremony, or religious service of the Roman Catholic Apostolic Religion or of any other Religion" with a term not exceeding one year's imprisonment, which was to be deemed aggravated if the act amounted to threats or violence against the person, and the punishment raised to two years. Article 165 does not discriminate in any way between religions.

4. In Fiscal Law

The Church as such enjoys no sort of exemption from Income Tax, from Value Added Tax, from Customs Duty or from any other tax. There are exemptions from which the Church and church entities benefit in the same way as other philanthropic or charitable organisations, and there are goods, such as those which are educational or related to an educational purpose, which do not attract any tax. There are cases where the Minister of Finance can, in his discretion, recognise an institution or an initiative as philanthropic or charitable, and in the great majority of cases Church institutions and initiatives are so classified.

Malta does not have any means by which a citizen can devolve part of his or her tax payments to the Church. The Church is financed principally from the income deriving from the Government Bonds transferred in payment of its former immovable property, contributions by the faithful, and other monies and bequests.

5. According to the Marriage Act (Act XXXVII of 1975 as subsequently amended, Chap. 255 of the Laws of Malta)

The Marriage Act of 1975 sought first of all to provide a form of civil marriage, as before that date only marriages performed according to some religious rite were considered to be legally valid, and a marriage between Maltese Roman Catholics or in which one of the parties was a Maltese Roman Catholic was deemed valid only if it conformed to Canon Law and the norms of the Council of Trent. Prior to 1975, Canon Law was regarded as part of the *jus comune,* applied in Malta from time immemorial in matters of marriage, in the absence of any municipal legislation. It was assumed that all Maltese were Catholics and that for Catholics there could be no marriage which was not, of itself, a sacrament. The 1975 Act specifically declared (Article 35) that Canon Law would no longer be a part of the law of Malta.

That Act as originally enacted changed completely the way in which marriage was deemed to exist in Maltese law. Thereafter all marriages had to be registered in the same way and subject to the same procedures in the Public Registry. If the parties chose to marry in Church, as most did, they had to pay a fee to an official appointed to be present and then register their marriage in the sacristy or on a side table. Without this registration the marriage would have no civil effect.

The Act moreover legislated for the essential ingredients for validity, and for the required formalities as well as the grounds for nullity. The decisions of the Ecclesiastical Courts on the existence or non-existence of a marriage were no longer recognised. On the other hand, though divorce was not introduced, the decisions of foreign courts declaring a marriage dissolved, when the foreign Court was deemed to have had jurisdiction to pronounce on the marriage bond, were henceforth to be recognised, and if registered with the proper procedure, be taken as proof of the status of liberty to marry.

The grounds for nullity were not perfectly aligned with those of Canon Law. After 1975 a state of affairs came into being whereby persons who sought to have their marriage declared null and void had not only to sue before the civil courts for the annulment to have its civil effects but, if they wished to remarry in Church, as many would for obvious reasons in a predominantly Catholic community, had also to seek a similar declaration from the Church Tribunal. Sometimes these parallel procedures produced dissimilar results. As the civil courts were now competent to examine the validity of Catholic marriages contracted before 1975, the civil judges found themselves analysing purely canon law points. In addition to the variations in the grounds for annulment, there was considerable dissimilarity in the nature of the court procedures. One advantage, amongst a number of disadvantages, of this duality was the fact that as it was possible to produce in the ecclesiastical Tribunal the evidence collected in the civil courts, a number of cases in which the respondent in a case before the Tribunal refused to appear (and could not be compelled to appear) could be resolved, as that side of the story was obtained *in subizione.*

In 1981 the then Labour Minister of Justice, Joseph Brincat, took into law some amendments which narrowed the gap between the grounds for annulment at Canon Law and those in the Marriage Act. However the Church continued to nurse misgivings concerning the Act inasmuch as it did not recognise the validity of the judgments of the ecclesiastical Tribunals and in fact subjected the marriage of Catholics in church to a purely civil law registration. The Church, which had always asserted an exclusive jurisdiction over the marriage bond of Catholics, considering that for Catholics the sacrament and the marriage were one and indivisible, could not countenance a situation in which it was denied recognition of its decision on matters of Canon Law.

After the change of Government in 1987, protracted negotiations finally led to a settlement on the matter by means of two agreements entered into on the 3rd February 1993 and 6th January 1995, which later were attached to the Marriage Law Amendment Act (Act I of 1995). Canon Law marriage was given recognition at civil law and the exclusive jurisdiction of ecclesiastical Tribunals with regard to Catholic marriages was restored, however with the proviso that should neither of the parties seise the Tribunal, or if having begun a case before the Tribunal a party were to discontinue it, the civil court would exercise jurisdiction. Although this amendment resolved the dispute, it had the undesirable effect of making a purely civil marriage more attractive as, when the marriage was celebrated in church, the Tribunals had a prior claim to jurisdiction, and it was known that procedures in the church Tribunals were lengthier and the judges more reluctant to declare the nullity of a marriage. A purely civil law marriage presented no such complications and the more lukewarm of the faithful opted for this. Whilst for many years civil marriages were few in number, since 1996 there has been a dramatic increase.

6. *Under the Cultural Heritage Act (Act VI of 2002)*

As in the previous Act of 1925, a special position at law was granted by the 2002 Act to cultural property belonging to the Catholic Church and to Catholic religious orders and "destined or used" for religious purposes, in that they were deemed to fall (Article 52) under the exclusive regulation and superintendence of the Catholic Cultural Heritage Commission. A similar exemption was given to cultural property belonging to other Churches or religious communities. However, should no such Commissions be appointed, the regulation and superintendence falls to the Superintendence of Cultural Heritage constituted under Article 7 of the Act.
When Napoleon Bonaparte conquered Malta and abolished the Order of Saint John, all the property belonging to the Order was declared Government property, including not only the palaces and auberges, but also the churches and chapels. Foremost amongst these churches was the Conventual Church which contained perhaps some of the most important cultural treasures of Malta, including paintings by Caravaggio and Mattia Preti. Napoleon gave permission to the Bishop to use the church as co-cathedral by a note from his own hand, which is still extant. The Catholic Church has always contended that St. John's Co-Cathedral and all the other churches and

chapels which belonged to the Order – which was a religious order owing direct allegiance to the Pope – could not be taken over by Government. Every year since 1798 has seen St. John's used by the Cathedral Chapter and the Bishop, and also serving the State as the "Official" Church for public thanksgiving services. The expenses of its upkeep were defrayed by the Government but at one time problems arose as to its being visited as a tourist attraction and for its proper safeguard. A Foundation was set up to administer this important monument through a Board on which both the Government and the Church appointed Trustees.

7. The Public Meetings Ordinance (Chapter 68)

Under Section 7 of this Law, the Commissioner of Police may order that a public (including a political) meeting be not held on any day, in any town or village where the meeting was intended to be held, on which a public solemnity or festival is to be celebrated. Sub-section (2) states that for the purpose of that Section "public solemnity" includes solemn functions held inside any church building, which it is reasonable to think might be interfered with by speeches delivered at, or the commotion caused by, a public meeting held in the vicinity of that church.

IV. The Present Position in the Cultural, Social, Political and Economic Life of Malta

The Church has a Radio Station (*Radju ta' kulħadd [RTK]* literally Everybody's Radio) which is one of the most popular and which enjoys considerable prestige because of its unbiased reporting of political events. Two weeklies (*Leħen is-Sewwa*, [literally the Voice of Truth] founded in the late twenties, and *Il-Ġens* [literally the old Latin meaning the people]), and a good number of other publications mostly devotional or sectoral, provide ample space for disseminating a broad mixture of Catholic opinion. In addition, most of the other secular dailies [three privately owned English language and two in Maltese, one owned by the Nationalist Party and one by the General

Workers' Union] or weeklies have pages allotted to church news or opinion.

The religious feasts of the country, national or local, are very closely followed by the general public. Church attendance on Sundays is high by most standards. There has not been a generalised apostasy of the working class or of the bourgeoisie. The Church also takes part in the cultural life of the country especially through its patronage of the arts, mostly painting and music in the churches.

There are sixty church schools across the whole range from kindergarten to sixth form, and about a quarter of all Maltese students of the relevant age groups attend these schools. These schools are free of charge and are heavily subsidised by Government. Admission to the boys' secondary schools is mostly through passing a common entrance examination.

The Church runs a crêche, a number of orphanages, as well as a home for the disabled which is in fact the only one catering for this need in Malta. In addition there are various old peoples homes run by religious orders and by Catholic Action. The Emigrants' Commission runs welfare services for Maltese migrants, and as these have become progressively less in need of help it has taken on the care of refugees coming to Malta from the Third World often in very difficult circumstances. There is also a Jesuits' Justice Commission championing the cause of dignified treatment of illegal immigrants.

The Church hierarchy generally tries to maintain a strictly neutral stance in matters of political controversy, even in the case of major national choices such as the Independence Referendum in 1964 and the very recent 2003 Referendum concerning the European Union Accession Treaty. Nevertheless the Church's teachings influence public opinion and have an indirect, and sometimes a very direct, influence on the country's political choices.

The Church owns a bank, the APS Bank, formerly bearing the full name of Apostleship of Prayer Savings Bank, which is no longer merely a savings bank but performs a number of banking services, and is the third in importance, albeit a distant third, in Malta. It also has other investments, but conducts its activities in the economic field with the greatest possible discretion. When the bulk of church immovable property, that which was not in use or intended for pastoral or social work, was transferred to Government, by agreement and under the terms of Act IV of 1992, the price, amounting to 29,000,000 Maltese pounds was paid in Government Bonds which provide a substantial yield. The Dioceses of Malta and Gozo publish yearly statements of account concerning the administration of Church finances.

The State pays for Catholic chaplaincy services in public hospitals and old people's homes, in the prisons, in the public cemetery, as well as in the armed forces and police.

The Anglican Church has a beautiful cathedral at Valletta and another church in Sliema, there are also churches of other Protestant denominations (Church of Scotland, Baptist, etc) mostly serving the expatriate community. There are some Maltese Jehovah's Witnesses and members of the Unification Church, though the numbers are small. There is a mosque attended mostly by foreign residents or workers from Moslem countries and some Maltese wives and the offspring of mixed marriages.

V. Concluding Note

Relations between the Holy See and the Government of Malta have returned to normal after a period of some tension in the 1970s and early 1980s. There has been no confrontation between the Catholic Hierarchy and political leaders for quite some time. Though the Labour Leader Dr. Alfred Sant has occasionally thrown a *ballon d'essai* concerning the introduction of divorce which the Church opposes, the issue has not been presented to the electorate for an expression of opinion. There is a general consensus in both major parties that abortion should continue to be considered a crime. Neither the introduction of gay marriages nor the decriminalisation of euthanasia has been formally proposed by any political party, not even by the small Green Party which is not represented in Parliament.

Though social mores have been influenced by more liberal life styles, the general ethical tone of Maltese society can be seen to be firmly rooted in the Catholic tradition. This notwithstanding, there is a general feeling that the State should guarantee non-discrimination against people for their faith or lack of it. It is a generally held view that the State should be strictly lay and that the Catholic Church should continue to enjoy the utmost liberty but that there should be no trace of imposition through social censure or in any other way of any religious faith.

VI. Bibliography

P. Debono, *Storia della Legislazione in Malta*, Edizioni Malta, Malta 1903.
A. V. Laferla, *British Malta*, 2 vols., Aquiline & Co., Malta 1938.
A. Bonnici, *History of the Church in Malta*, Vol. III, Period IV – 1800-1975, Veritas Press, Malta 1975, p. 285 + (17).
Esposizione Documentata della Questione Maltese (February 1929-June 1930), The Vatican Polyglot Press, Vatican 1930.
J. M. Pirotta, *Fortress Colony: The Final Act 1945-64*, Studia Editions 1986.

Sophie C. van Bijsterveld
State and Church in the Netherlands

I. Social Facts

The law and the current situation in the Netherlands are a vast departure from the days of the Constitution of 1801, one of the Constitutions of the turbulent period of 1795-1814, which stated that every head of family or independent person of either sex must, upon reaching the age of fourteen, register with a church denomination. Changing denominations at a later date was allowed.[1] Currently, both the obligation of church membership as a principle and also the assumption that everyone belongs to a church are obsolete. Insofar as the provision reflects the expression of free choice of religion, and makes an implicit reference to the existence of a variety of religious denominations, it still has a bearing on the present.
In the Netherlands, pluralism is a basic characteristic of religious life. Even in the days of the Republic of the United Netherlands, with its established Reformed Church and privileges for its adherents, a variety of denominations existed. The Union of Utrecht of 1579, the basis of the Confederacy, guaranteed freedom of religious conviction and outlawed inquisition. Public worship was restricted, though in the course of time it was practised with an increasing openness. An atmosphere of toleration was fostered. Even in the early days of the nation's history minority religions were a part of the societal pattern.
Religious variety continued and increased after the Kingdom of the Netherlands was founded in 1814, though in a different legal context. Separations from the Reformed Church and later on from its newer branches took place, resulting in a wide variety of Reformed denominations. From the late 19th century onwards, new church denominations emerged, including Pentecostal churches, Evangelical churches and the Salvation Army. Philosophical movements based on non-religious spiritual belief became structured organisations, most notably following the Second World War. Immigration has led to an

---

[1] Art. 12 Staatsregeling des Bataafschen Volks 1801.

influx of adherents of Christian churches organised on a national or ethnic basis, as well as adherents of non-Christian religions.

In addition to religious diversification, secularisation has also become entrenched in society. Over the years, a distinct decline in church membership has become apparent. This phenomenon first became noticeable in the 1880s. It halted after the 1930s.[2] The period of the 1960s once again showed a further decline in church adherence. Initially, the large churches suffered from loss of membership. The main Reformed Church was confronted with this development early on. The Roman Catholic Church followed somewhat later. The extent to which smaller Christian denominations were affected by decline in membership varied. It seems that the traditional Christian denominations encountered membership decline, whereas the relatively new branches of the Reformed Church remained fairly stable.

Until recently, the demographic spread of religious denominations within the country was a stable one. Notoriously non-religious areas in the country could also be outlined. Increased mobility and the general decline in church adherence have profoundly altered the picture.[3]

The total population in the Netherlands numbers over 16 million. Out of the population aged 18 and older, the percentage of members of the Roman Catholic Church is estimated at 31 %.[4] For the two main Reformed Churches, these figures are 14 % and 7 %, respectively.[5] In 2002, the number of adherents of Islam with various national backgrounds was estimated at 886,000, a number equalling 5,5 % of the total population. The Hindu population was estimated at about 95,000.[6]

---

2   H. Knippenberg, De religieuze kaart van Nederland, Assen 1992, p. 227, p.230.
3   Although the degree of secularization in the Netherlands is high compared to other Western European countries, the degree of active participation of church members in their church is also comparatively high: H. Knippenberg, op cit, p. 247-248; M.M.J. van Hemert, Godsdienst in cijfers, in: H. Schaeffer et.al. (ed.), Handboek Godsdienst in Nederland, Amersfoort 1992, p. 182. See also J.W. Becker, R. Vink, Secularisatie in Nederland, 1966-1991, Sociaal en Cultureel Planbureau, Rijswijk 1994; Gerard Dekker, Joep de Hart, Jan Peters, God in Nederland, 1966-1996, Amsterdam 1997.
4   These figures date from 2002. Source: Central Bureau of Statistics [Centraal Bureau voor de Statistiek] www.cbs.nl; more specifically, http://www.cbs.nl/nl/cijfers/themapagina/leefsituatie/1-cijfers.htm.
5   The two main Reformed Churches and the Evangelical Lutheran Church are united, with effect from May 2004, to form the Protestant Church in the Netherlands (Protestantse Kerk in Nederland).
6   These figures date from January 1, 2002. Source: Central Bureau of Statistics.

II. Historical Background

The Constitution of 1814 established the Kingdom of the Netherlands, a decentralised unitary state. This Constitution formed a renewed starting point for church and state relationships. At the time of its enactment, it was clear that the idea of an established church belonged to the past. Nevertheless, the 1814 Constitution did not contain all the prerequisites for separation.[7] In its general realisation of democratic principles and the rule of law, the 1814 Constitution was bleak compared to its more progressive predecessors. Subsequent Constitutions, starting with that of 1815, further continued in the line of development that had already been established. Although there are some clear break-points, the overall constitutional development has been an evolutionary one, and this is true also with respect to church and state relationships.

The chapter on religion in the 1814 Constitution was concerned with church and state, rather than with the individual's freedom of religion. The Constitution, and even more so its 1815 successor, did in essence contain the idea that the state should not interfere with church organisation. In practice, however, the Crown was still actively involved in church matters. This situation would change in the latter part of the century.

The revision of the Constitution of 1848, initiated under the pressure of the revolutionary developments abroad, further shaped constitutional government. Various new fundamental rights were adopted, such as freedom of association and education. The chapter on religion was modernised. The 1848 revision prompted the Roman Catholic Church to restore its hierarchy in the Netherlands. This was effected in 1853. In that same year the Religious Bodies Act [*Wet op de kerkgenootschappen*] was enacted. Its main merit was the explicit formulation of freedom of internal organisation of the churches. This Act remained to be in force until 1988.

At one point the 1848 Constitution proved to be restrictive. A new article was adopted which allowed religious processions only in situations where express permission had been given. As such permission was rarely granted, the result was a de facto ban on processions. The arrangement is illustrative of the somewhat tense relationships between the adherents of the various religious denominations at the

---

7 *S.C. van Bijsterveld*, Godsdienstvrijheid in Europees perspectief, Deventer: W.E.J. Tjeenk Willink.

time. It must be realised, however, that the general law with respect to meetings in the open air at that time was limited even by modern standards.

The period which followed was basically one of consolidation as far as institutional relationships between church and state were concerned. Major issues in the debate between church and state concerned the system of poor relief and that of education. A milestone was the revision of 1917 which prescribed full government funding for private elementary schools which met set educational standards and complied with given financing conditions.

From 1848 till 1972 the chapter on religion remained unchanged. The 1972 revision enabled the government to buy off its traditional obligations with respect to salaries and pensions for church ministers. This was realised in 1983. These obligations went back to the late 18th century and originally served as compensation for the loss of church property through government expropriation.

The year 1983 saw a general revision of the Constitution. The revised Constitution incorporated new fundamental rights including a wide range of social rights. It provided a renewed formulation of fundamental rights which were already protected. Fundamental rights are contained in the first chapter of the Constitution. In order to guarantee optimum freedom, a strict and quite clearly defined system of restrictions of fundamental rights was introduced. The 1983 Constitution brought a new formulation of freedom of religion. As of 1983, freedom of non-religious belief is also protected by the Constitution.

Religious denomination – together with political persuasion – have been a driving force for the organisation of social activities. Schools, hospitals, trade unions, employers' organisations, broadcasting companies and other social institutions were and are organised on a denominational basis.[8] In the early process of development of political parties, religion played a role as a basis of organisation.[9]

---

8   On this process, its origins and significance, see *A. Lijphart*, The politics of accommodation. Pluralism and democracy in the Netherlands, Berkeley/Los Angeles/London 1975.
9   *A. Hoogerwerf*, Godsdienst en politiek, in: *H. Schaeffer et.al.* (ed.), Handboek Godsdienst in Nederland, Amersfoort 1992, p.303-312.

III. Basic Structure

a) Legal sources

Sources of (constitutional) law in the Netherlands are the Statute of the Kingdom, the Constitution, further legislation, court decisions, legal custom or precedent, and European and international law. For the determination of legal relationships between church and state, each of these sources has its significance, albeit to a varying degree.[10] The most significant sources of law for church and state relationships will be highlighted below.

The basis of church and state relations in the Netherlands is found in the Constitution of 1983. The 1983 Constitution replaced the former chapter on religion by one article. This article guarantees freedom of religious belief as well as freedom of non-religious belief. Article 6, section 1, of the Constitution states that "(e)veryone shall have the right to manifest freely his religion or belief, either individually or in community with others, without prejudice to his responsibility under the law". The second section adds that "(r)ules concerning the exercise of this right other than in buildings and enclosed places may be laid down by Act of Parliament for the protection of health, in the interest of traffic and to combat or prevent disorders".

Although Article 6 does refer to various manifestations of religious freedom, it is not very specific about the subject matter of its guarantee. Nevertheless, the guarantee in Article 6 is meant to be wide-ranging.[11] At the time of the revision, it was accepted that Article 6 not only protects the freedom to have a religious or non-religious belief, but also the freedom to act according to that belief.

The clause "without prejudice to his responsibility under the law" of the first section means that only the national Legislature is competent to restrict the guaranteed right. It gives, however, no clear indication of the concrete criteria to be met. The purpose of the second section is to allow delegation by the national Legislature of the power to restrict the guaranteed right in so far as it concerns the exercise of re-

---

10 The Statute of the Kingdom, which is concerned with the relationship between the Netherlands, the Netherlands Antilles and Aruba, may be disregarded in this respect.
11 See *S.C. van Bijsterveld*, op cit; *B.P. Vermeulen*, Artikel 6, in: *A.K. Koekkoek* (ed.), De Grondwet. En systematisch en artikelsgewijs commentaar, Deventer 2000, p. 93-109; *M.M. den Boer*, Artikel 6 Grondwet: vrijheid van godsdienst en levensovertuiging, in: NJCM-Bulletin 1987, p. 110-127.

ligion or non-religious belief other than in buildings and enclosed places, and only for the purposes mentioned.

The courts have slightly modified the strict system that the Constitution introduced concerning the competent authority for restricting fundamental rights. The way this is done is, generally speaking, satisfactory.

On the basis of Article 6 (and 9) of the Constitution, the Public Manifestations Act [*Wet Openbare Manifestaties*] was enacted. This Act regulates, among other things, religious manifestations outside buildings and enclosed places, including religious processions.

Apart from Article 6, other articles refer to religion. Article 1 of the Constitution states that all persons in the Netherlands shall be treated equally in equal circumstances. Furthermore, it does not permit discrimination on the grounds of religion, belief, political opinion, race or sex or on any other grounds whatsoever. A specific reference to religion can be found in Article 23 which relates to education. It guarantees freedom of (denominational) education. With respect to public-authority education, it prescribes equal treatment and respect for everyone's religion or belief. The Constitution entails no general guarantee of freedom of conscience.[12]

Although the Constitution is higher in the hierarchy than parliamentary legislation, the courts are denied the power of review.[13] In interpreting the constitutionality of parliamentary legislation, the Legislature itself has the final word. The Courts only have the right to review legislation other than parliamentary legislation as to its compatibility with the Constitution. However, the Constitution prescribes that the courts may review the compatibility of any legislation – including parliamentary legislation and even the Constitution itself – with provisions of treaties that are binding on all persons or of resolutions by international institutions.[14]

Thus, Article 9 of the European Convention on Human Rights (ECHR) and Article 18 of the Covenant on Civil and Political Rights (CCPR) may be invoked in court procedures relating to religion. The courts, notably the Supreme Court (Hoge Raad), however, are reluctant to uphold challenges. In a remarkable ruling in 1962, the Supreme Court held that the – then still existing – constitutional ban on religious processions was compatible with Article 9 ECHR.[15] The

---

12 Art. 99 Const. provides the basis for acknowledgment of conscientious objection against military service. This has lost practical meaning as drafting no longer takes place.
13 Art. 120 Const.
14 Art. 94 Const.
15 HR 19 January 1962, NJ 1962, 107.

Supreme Court interpreted its power of review in a restrictive way. The same was true of its interpretation of Article 9 ECHR itself. Recently, the Supreme Court has adopted a more active approach in reviewing legislation. The cases concerned did not involve religion. The general administrative court seems to have taken a more liberal view from the start.[16]

In the present Constitution, the church as an organisation is no longer mentioned. Likewise, financial relationships between church and state find no explicit basis in the Constitution. But it should not be concluded from this that the Constitution has no relevance in these areas. On the contrary, freedom of church organisation is an essential element of the guarantee of freedom of religion. The Constitution does provide a framework for appreciating financial relationships between church and state. Further institutional guarantees are necessary. The same is true for ensuring the free exercise of religion individually or in community with others. Exposition of these freedoms by the Legislature is required to secure the guarantees in the various specific areas of the law.

Treaties between church and state are not a normal feature of the law. A special event was the agreement reached in 1983 between the state and the respective churches concerning the termination of the traditional government obligations with respect to salaries and pensions of church ministers. This agreement was subsequently confirmed by Act of Parliament. Legal doctrine is relevant for the development of church and state relationships, though in itself it is not a source of law.

Religion may play a role in legal relations between private individuals. The law is responsive to this. At the time of the general revision of the Constitution, it was explicitly acknowledged that fundamental rights not only function in relation to public authorities, but that they may have relevance for legal relationships between private individuals as well. Aspects of these relations may be determined in general by the intervention of the Legislature. More often, the courts have to balance interests in concrete cases on the basis of an interpretation of general concepts of civil law.

b) *Categories of system approach*

The system of church and state relationships is characterised throughout as one of separation of church and state. This principle

---

16 Vz.ARRvS 1 May 1981, AB 1982, 28; ARRvS 20 December 1981, AB 1983, 243.

has never been formulated in the Constitution or in any further legislation. Nevertheless, it does play a role and is referred to in the legislative process, in administration and in court decisions. The principle has a clear significance in the organisational independence of the church and has relevance for the financial relationship between church and state. Likewise, it has implications for the equal position under the law of the various denominations and for the attitudes towards denominational and non-denominational movements. Its precise meaning, however, is not easy to define.

The separation of church and state is not a "strict separation" in the sense that church and state should have nothing to do with each other. Such an idea would not be in keeping with social and political realities either. Nor is it to be understood as a church-hostile principle. In its actual functioning it is best understood by the interpretation of the constitutional provisions in which the principle is embedded as current law against a background of the historic development.

This means that the principle of separation of church and state must be interpreted in harmony with the principle of state neutrality and of freedom of religion or belief as reflected in the Articles 1 and 6 of the Constitution, separately and taken together.

In this instance, it is also interesting to notice that current fundamental-rights doctrine acknowledges that classic liberal rights may induce positive government action under certain circumstances in order to secure the actual functioning of that right. This applies equally to freedom of religion.

Neither the principle of separation of church and state nor its constitutional expression gives a blueprint for the precise relationship between church and state. It must also be realised that guarantees which in a given period may be seen as necessary for ensuring separation, whether on the side of the church or on the side of the state, may eventually become unnecessary.[17] With the development of law and society, new safeguards may, however, become necessary. Thus, the fundamentals on which the relationship between church and state are based need continuous interpretation and explication.

---

17 See *S.C. van Bijsterveld*, Kerk en staat. Vrijheid en verantwoordelijkheid, in: *H. Schaeffer, et.al.* (ed.), Handboek Godsdienst in Nederland, Amersfoort 1992, p. 292-302.

IV. Legal Status of Religious Bodies

a) Legal status of religious bodies

The church as an organisation is no longer mentioned in the Constitution. Nevertheless, the church is protected under the Constitution, as is its freedom to organise itself. Obviously, freedom of church organisation needs explication within the framework of law. The basic expression of the status of the church as an organisation is to be found in the law relating to legal entities.

Churches are legal entities of civil law. The Civil Code recognises churches as legal entities *sui generis*. Thus, their status as legal entities is distinct from that of other legal entities such as associations or foundations. Whereas the Civil Code defines the structures of the various types of legal entities, shaping their internal legal order is the sole province of the churches themselves. The Civil Code merely states that churches are governed by their own statutes in so far as they do not conflict with the law.[18]

As a consequence of the autonomy of the church with respect to its organisation, the Civil Code also exempts the churches from its general provisions which are applicable to all types of legal entities. Analogous application of these provisions is allowed, in so far as this does not conflict with the churches' statutes or with the nature of their internal relations.[19] Although the latter clause is not clear-cut, it does express the priority of church law over the civil law in this field. The current tendency in favour of analogous application is best illustrated by the decision of the Supreme Court which held that analogous application should be the starting point for rulings in this field.[20]

Neither the Civil Code nor any other piece of legislation provides a definition of a "church". It is the organisation that constitutes itself as a church which determines this. In concrete cases, the administration may have to decide on this issue, and, in cases of conflict, the court may have to do so. In a case which did involve a dispute on the nature of the organisation, the court formulated the minimal requirements that there must be a "structured organisation" and that "relig-

---

18 Art.2:2 Civil Code [Burgerlijk Wetboek]. The precise content of the clause is debated. See J.J.M. *Maeijer*, Rechtspersoon, godsdienst en levensovertuiging, Mededelingen der KNAW, Afd. Letterkunde, Amsterdam 1986.
19 Art.2:2, section 2, Civil Code.
20 HR 15 March 1985, NJ 1986, 191.

ion must be involved".[21] There is no system of prior recognition of churches.
Religious communities may organise themselves differently from a church, notably as an association or foundation under civil law, in which case the normal civil law regulations apply. Non-Christian religious communities often choose these forms of organisation.[22]

b) The concept of Church in law and the right to self-determination

The legal status of the church as described above also applies *mutatis mutandis* to independent units within churches as well as bodies in which churches are united.[23] Thus, the law is equally receptive to church structures based on a central, hierarchical church concept, and to decentralised church models.
Neither of these categories is defined by the law. As to bodies in which churches are united, the requirement of a "distinctive incorporation in church law" was formulated during the process of enactment.[24] Furthermore, the will to constitute a legal entity of that type is an essential condition. Councils of churches and other forms of co-operation between churches will usually not be regarded as such.
As to independent units of churches, the intent of the church is a formative condition. The way in which the intent should be expressed is not completely clear. Material criteria (what is the organisation occupied with, religious, social, economic activities) as well as formal criteria (what is the formal influence of the church within the organisation) have been suggested as elements which may play a role in determining whether or not an organisation should be qualified as an independent unit of a church.[25] In the light of the freedom of church organisation, notably the self-determination of churches, it is important, however, not to set strict criteria. The open character of the legal system itself does not justify strict criteria either.
Though churches are free to organise certain areas of their activities as independent units, there is in fact a long tradition of organising

---

21 HR 31 October 1986, NJ 1987, 173.
22 See *S.C. van Bijsterveld*, Religious minorities and minority churches in the Netherlands, the legal context, in: *European Consortium for Church and State Research*, The Legal Status of Religious Minorities in the Countries of the European Union, Thessaloniki/Milano 1994, p. 277-298.
23 The latter category has been added in 1992, but in fact it was already recognized.
24 Kamerstukken II, 1982-1983, 17 725, no. 3, p. 53.
25 See e.g. *F.T. Oldenhuis*, Kerkgenootschappen en hun zelfstandige onderdelen, in: WPNR 5865 (1988), p. 155-159.

activities in the field of social, cultural and educational matters as normal associations or foundations on the basis of a religion or belief.[26] These organisations may to a greater or lesser extent be linked to a church, which link may be formalised in terms of statutes and regulations. The denominational identity of such organisations is, in general terms, protected by the Civil Code. These organisations are subject to legislation governing their field of activity.[27] Within the framework of this legislation, special provisions may be needed to take the denominational aspect into account.

The preceding material shows that in its basic arrangement, freedom of church organisation and freedom of organisation on the basis of a religion is respected by the law. Occasionally, however, problems may arise. This is notably the case in relation to legislation which itself is not pertinent to church or religion but which may nevertheless affect churches and religion, for example, legislation prescribing democratisation of organisations, data protection legislation or equal treatment legislation.

The result for either type of legal entity may not always be satisfactory. In any case, the freedom of the denominational organisations is usually respected to a lesser extent than that of the church as a legal entity – including the independent units and structures in which churches are united. The discussion on the criteria for independent units gains an extra dimension in view of the legal consequences which may thus evolve.

c) Churches and the political system

No statutes or case law exist regarding the involvement of churches or members of the clergy in political life.[28] Therefore, there is no obstacle to members of the clergy participating in politics or holding

---

26 *Sophie C. van Bijsterveld*, Church-related, Charitable, Non-Profitmaking Institutions and their Relations to Church, State, Civil Society and the Market. The Dutch Experience, European Consortium for Church and State Research, in: *Inger Dübeck, Frands Ole Overgaard* (ed.), Social Welfare, Religious Organizations and the State, European Consortium for Church and State Research, Proceedings of the Sandjerg Meeting, November 18-20, 1999, Milan 2003, p.137-155. For the relationship between ecclesiastical proceedings and civil court proceedings, *Sophie C. van Bijsterveld*, Church Autonomy in the Netherlands. The Distinctiveness of the Church. The Interplay between Legal, Popular, and Ecclesiastical Perspectives. Church Autonomy as a 'Test Case, in: *Hildegard Warnink* (ed.), Legal Position of Churches and Church Autonomy, Leuven: Peeters, 2001, p. 147-163; *A.H. Santing-Wubs*, Kerken in geding: de burgerlijke rechter en kerkelijke geschillen, Den Haag: Bju 2002.
27 See also below, section VIII.
28 See below, section XI.

public office. Similarly, churches can and do participate in public debate; the extent to which (representatives of) various religious or religious denominations feel inclined to do so varies.[29] This is also true for the way in which such participation takes place.

In the Netherlands, the churches also cooperate as far as their activities in the public domain is concerned. The Council of Churches in the Netherlands is a forum on which Christian Churches of a wide variety of denominations cooperate with a view of developing joint statements and on public policy issues and commenting on public policy. For their joint legal interests, that is, for legal issues with a church-state dimension, including issues of freedom of religion, Jewish communities and Christian Churches cooperate in the Interchurch Contact in Government Affairs [*Interkerkelijk Contact in Overheiszaken – CIO*] and, for purpose, maintain contact with public authorities at the national level. These forms of cooperation do not preclude churches from acting on their own behalf in these areas as well. Islamic believers are still in a process of setting up a joint organisation, representative of the various Islamic communities in the Netherlands, for maintaining contact with the state authorities. In addition to this, it is worth noting that various political parties represented in (both chambers of) Parliament have a confessional basis. The most significant of these, that of the Christian Democrats [*CDA*] is a constant factor in Dutch politics. Apart from the *CDA*, there are currently, at the national level, two (small) reformed parties.

V. Churches and Culture

At the beginning of the last century, the basis was laid for a distinction between public(-authority) education and private education. On the basis of this distinction free private education was advocated as the Constitution gave the government responsibility for public education alone. Freedom of education was subsequently guaranteed in the Constitution of 1848. In the following period, the discussion concentrated on the character of public-authority schools – notably the place of religion in those schools – and on the (financial) position of private schools. The development with respect to elementary education was trend-setting for other areas of education.

---

29 *Henk Vroom, Henk Woldring* (eds.), Religies in het publieke domein, Zoetermeer 2002.

The prescription that public-authority education be given "with respect to everyone's religion or belief"[30] is to be interpreted as a neutrality clause which requires a positive attitude towards religion. The various education Acts provide that attention must be paid to the different religious values and traditions. Provision is made for religious education in public-authority schools. This instruction is offered on a voluntary basis. A whole series of court rulings established that instruction in non-religious (humanist) belief should be offered and subsidised on the same basis as religious instruction.

Freedom of education comprises freedom to found a school, freedom of denomination and freedom to administer a school.[31] Private schools are financed by the state under the condition that they meet certain educational standards and comply with the financial conditions. This was laid down in the Constitution of 1917 for general elementary schools.[32] Among other things, the Legislature specifies numerical criteria for the foundation of a school. In setting up standards and conditions, the Legislature must respect freedom of denomination and freedom to administer the school.[33] The precise range of these freedoms and the powers of the Legislature with respect to these freedoms are subjects of ongoing discussion. Private (denominational) schools may set loyalty conditions for their staff with regard to denominational views. Admission of pupils may be subject to such conditions as well.[34]

In the field of higher education also, a distinction must be made between private universities and public-authority universities. Private (denominational) universities originated at the end of the last century. These universities are financed by the state, again subject to the condition that they meet certain educational standards and comply with financial regulations.

The faculties of theology of private universities may offer programmes leading to an academic degree as well as programmes for the education of church ministers.[35] Apart from these institutions, churches run education centres which are under the financial and administrative control of the church itself.

---

30 Art.23, section 3, Const.
31 The so-called freedoms of "stichting, richting, inrichting". They are hard to translate.
32 For other schools this finds application too.
33 See *A.K. Koekkoek*, State Control of Education in the Netherlands, in: *E.H. Hondius, G.J.W. Steenhoff* (eds.), Netherlands reports to the thirteenth international congress of comparative law (Montreal 1990), The Hague 1990.
34 Under the General Equal Treatment Act (Act of 2 March 1994, Stb. 230), these powers are to some extent restricted. See below.
35 Some of these universities have only the one faculty of theology.

Theological faculties at state universities do not prepare students for the office of church minister as was the case for the ministers in the previously established Reformed Church until 1876. Education for the office of church minister rested with the state university and was financed by the state. Other churches established colleges at state universities too, which were also were financed by the state.

Religion is also a relevant factor in the field of mass media. Broadcasting time is allotted to broadcasting companies. According to the Mass Media Act, these companies – associations under civil law – represent a specific societal, cultural, religious or spiritual tendency and focus on the satisfaction of the corresponding needs of the population. The amount of time allotted to each company is dependent on the number of members it has. Several of these broadcasting companies have a denominational background.

Churches are allotted broadcasting time as well. A considerable number of churches, in fact, broadcast on television and radio. For this purpose churches may work together. They may work together with the broadcasting company of their religious persuasion. They may also broadcast under their own name. The mass media legislation specifies, among other things, the percentage of broadcasting time as well as the financial arrangements.

The churches are usually not represented as such in public boards and official advisory committees. In the composition of such boards, a balance is sought with regard to characteristics such as the political and denominational backgrounds of its members.

VI. Labour Law within the Churches

In the field of labour law, religion and the freedom of church organisation is taken into account in various ways. The Labour Relations Act, for instance, exempts spiritual offices from the obligation of a public-authority permit in the case of the dismissal of the office-holder. The relevance of this provision to church and state relations has been clearly demonstrated in a ruling of the Supreme Court. Initially, an Islamic imam was not regarded as having a religious office. A relevant consideration in reaching this conclusion was the fact that he would otherwise not enjoy dismissal protection. The Supreme Court came to the opposite conclusion and stressed the importance of the provision in terms of church and state relationships.[36] The General Equal Treatment Act exempts churches, their independent units as well as the spiritual office, from its application.[37]

This does not mean that the state exercises no control over labour relations within the church. As was mentioned above, the Civil Code does not prevent courts from applying to churches the general provisions relating to legal entities "in as far as this does not conflict with the churches' statutes and the nature of their internal relations". These general provisions include the right of the court to declare void a decision of a legal entity which is taken contrary to "good faith". The specific case in which the Supreme Court accepted this analogous application dealt with a church minister who challenged his dismissal.[38]

Traditionally, the labour relationship between a church minister and a church is not regarded as a contract of employment under civil law.[39] In the field of social security law, a marked change in approach became apparent in a series of rulings by the social security court in 1977. Until then, holders of a spiritual office were not subject to social security legislation as the element of subordination necessary for the application of the law was considered absent. In 1977 it was decided that the fact that the work performed was of a spiritual nature did not in itself exclude the possibility of a contract of employment. The change of opinion resulted in detailed case law which is not always easily accessible. In concrete cases, it has to be decided whether the official performs his work in "subordination", an essential requirement for a contract of employment. Traditional ministries in the church will usually not be regarded as meeting this criterion.

In the ordinary civil courts, where dismissals are usually dealt with, categorisations may differ from those in the field of social security law. The Supreme Court concluded with respect to a church minister that he did not have a contract of employment. The perspective of church and state relationships and freedom of church organisation

---

36 HR 30 May 1986, NJ 1986, 702; see also in this respect – with application of church statutes – Rb. Groningen, 21 December 1990, KG 1991, 90.
37 See also *Rb.Den Bosch* 11 December 1992 (unpublished).
38 HR 15 March 1985, NJ 1986, 191.
39 See *J.J. Oostenbrink*, Een relativering van "godsdienstig karakter", in: Een stellig karakter, Zwolle 1982, p. 73-87; and *A. Jacobs*, Labour and social security law and the churches in the Netherlands, in: Churches and Labour Law in the EC Countries, European Consortium for Church and State research, Proceedings of the meeting Madrid, November 27-28, 1992, Milan/Madrid 1993, p. 215-230.

played a prominent role in this decision.[40] A test as to whether the work was conducted in subordination, however, was applied. In a more recent decision of the Court concerning an Imam it was decided on the basis that a contract of employment existed.[41]

Labour relations which seemingly take place in an ordinary setting, but in which the church exercises influence in one way or other, such as church ministers working in hospitals or homes for the elderly or other social institutions, whether denominational or not, are usually classed as contracts of employment by the ordinary civil courts. The essence of the employment is the church mission. When the requirements for the spiritual office no longer are fulfilled, which is a matter for the judgement of the church, the basis of the contract of employment is gone. Problems do arise when the reason for the church's action is based on grounds applicable to the clergy which would ordinarily not be valid a reason for dismissal, such as (a second) marriage.

A similar situation is found in public institutions such as the armed forces and penal institutions. The difference is that in such cases the church minister will have the status of a military or civil servant. In a court ruling concerning a spiritual assistant in a penal institution, it was acknowledged that the church and state aspect played a role in interpreting the applicable civil servant law.[42]

Denominational institutions with personnel in non-religious functions apply normal contracts of employment. The identity of the institution may justify specific loyalty requirements. The question is how far can they go. This is mainly a matter of case law, in which the courts balance the interests. The General Equal Treatment Act sharpens the scrutiny of the courts. Schools have somewhat more freedom under the Act.

Collective labour relations within churches are not well developed.[43] Labour conditions are fixed unilaterally. Trade unions in the classic sense of the term hardly exist; various professional groups within the church, however, have organised themselves and are taking part in discussions on labour conditions. Their status in regard to the church authorities varies.

---

40 HR 14 June 1991, NJ 1992, 173; the decision was in contrast to the court of first instance and the court of appeal. Lower courts, however, may conclude that a contract of employment exists, e.g. Rb. Breda 3 February 1987, KG 1987, 103; Ktr.Den Bosch 2 February 1988, NJ 1992, 173.
41 HR 17 June 1994, RvdW. 136.
42 Rb. Assen 23 March 1993, (unpublished).
43 See *A. Jacobs*, op.cit., p. 225.

VII. Matrimonial and Family Law

Just as religion may play a role in relationships between private individuals in general, religion may be a factor of legal relevance within family relations as well. As the legislation which deals with family matters is not specific with regard to religion, the courts decide upon family issues involving religion in concrete cases. In interpreting open legal concepts, courts can take the religious factor into account, without showing a preference for a particular denomination.

Legislation does specify the relation between civil marriage and "religious marriage". The institution of marriage is clearly defined by the Civil Code and outlined in relation to religious procedures. The Civil Code states that it regards marriage only in its civil aspects. Religious ceremonies with regard to marriage[44] are not legally binding and cannot take place prior to the performance of a legally valid marriage. Thus, the Civil Code leaves no doubt as to the primacy of civil marriage over religious marriage. The church minister who performs a religious wedding ceremony without having verified the existence of a legally binding marriage is liable to prosecution.[45] Discussions in recent years about the abolition of the requirement of a prior civil marriage before a religious ceremony with respect to the marriage have not led to any change in the law.

Denying legal validity to church marriages is seen as a consequence of the separation of church and state. The justification of the priority in time of civil marriage is to allow no misunderstanding of the legal consequences. The arrangement has been challenged under Article 9 ECHR. In 1971, the Netherlands Supreme Court upheld this system as a justified restriction of religious freedom.[46]

As of 2002, persons of the same sex can also marry.[47] Not all Churches regard same-sex marriages as a marriage in the religious sense and some therefore they do not allow the performance of religious marriage ceremonies for such relationships. Prior to 2002, the so-called "registered partnership" was introduced in the Civil Code.[48] The Roman Catholic Bishops' Conference has determined that the prohibition to marry for its clergy also extends to registered partnerships.

---

44 Art.1:68 Civil Code.
45 Art. 449 Criminal Code.
46 HR 22 June 1971, NJ 1972, 31.
47 See Article 1: 30 Civil Code.
48 See Article 1: 80 ff. Civil Code.

Within family relations, conflicts may arise which find their roots in religion; conflicts between spouses or between parents and children. The courts acknowledge, for instance, that religious differences may lead to such estrangement between spouses that divorce is justified. In relations between parents and children, it has been decided that a parental refusal of marriage consent on religious grounds is not acceptable. On the other hand, parents are entitled to deny permission for a passport for their daughter to travel abroad with a boy friend. Religious convictions or church membership may not be a condition for inheritance.

Even when religion itself is not at the root of the conflict, religion can be taken into account. In cases of guardianship, the religious background will be taken into account, especially if so desired. The area is primarily shaped and influenced by case law. The courts deal with these cases in a satisfactory way.[49]

VIII. Finances of the Churches

No general state support to churches exists. Nevertheless, financial support to church and religion has been granted over the years in various forms and for various causes. These ways of support are of a limited nature. Their legal basis varies. Financial relationships are not mentioned in the Constitution.[50]

Financial relationships between church and state have been a subject of serious discussion in the 1980s and 1990s. The conclusion of this discussion was that financial support to churches and religion is allowed under special circumstances in order to prevent the free exercise of religion from becoming illusory.[51] Thus, the Cabinet has left open the possibility of financing buildings for non-Christian minorities, though no need is seen at present. Sometimes arrangements with

---

49 A more difficult and controversial issue relating to families is the way in which the state may interfere in cases of adoption or refusal of certain medical treatment.
50 Previously, the Constitution did contain a specific article on the subject (see above). Only in the additional articles to the Constitution is there a relic which has lost its force. It is expected to be eliminated in the current revision.
51 Kamerstukken II, 1989-1990, 20 868, no. 2; Kamerstukken II, 1990-1991, 20 868, no. 3; UCV 47, 22 june 1992, Handelingen II, 1991-1992. Committee report, Overheid, godsdienst en levensovertuiging, eindrapport van de Commissie van advies inzake de criteria voor steunverlening door de overheid aan kerkgenootschappen en andere genootschappen op geestelijke grondslag, 's-Gravenhage 1988.

financial consequences are made in the process of setting up urban renewal projects.

Financial support is given to specialised church ministries, i.e., for religious care in institutions like military institutions and penal institutions. Currently, the basis of this support is the right to the free exercise of religion by persons in such institutions. For the armed forces, a special consideration is the element of ethical conflict which plays a role in the justification as well.

In institutions such as hospitals and homes for the elderly specialised religious care also takes place. This is financed by the general funds of such institutions. Spiritual care is regarded as an essential element in the overall care which is provided. The organisation of the care in special institutions has consequences for the provision of religious care.

Apart from these specific areas, financial support exists which is not exclusively aimed at church and religion, but focuses on other causes. Tax exemptions exist in various forms. Donations to churches as well as to a wide variety of charitable institutions are exempt from taxation. This holds for both private individuals and for corporations or institutions. In this way, donations are encouraged.

Ancient church monuments like other ancient monuments share in public subsidies for repair and maintenance. Apart from central government funds, there are local and provincial monument lists and subsidies. These subsidies are partial and church communities which use ancient monuments still have a lot of costs. Church buildings, i.e. buildings used predominantly for worship, are excluded from local rates.

(Local) governments subsidise a whole range of social activities. They are not obliged to do so, but if they do, denominational activities should not be excluded. Only if the denominational background leads to objective differences in terms of the activity to be subsidised may it be taken into account. As to key areas of social work such as health care, financing structures are quite complex. Denominational institutions, however, participate in the same way as do other institutions.[52]

---

[52] Problems arise in the case of budget cuts, and forced consolidations. For schooling, see above.

IX. Religious Assistance in Public Institutions

Specialised religious care takes place in various types of institutions, such as the armed forces, penal institutions, health care institutions, institutions for young people, and homes for the elderly. The church sees it as part of its task availability to people in unusual circumstances. The history of specialised religious care in various institutions, its structures, its financing, and its specific legal basis are varied, though certain similarities do exist.

From the perspective of church and state relationships, these forms of spiritual care hold a special position. Although providing spiritual care is the province and responsibility of the church itself, the state has a responsibility as well. This responsibility varies according to the circumstances under which the spiritual care takes place.

At present, it is accepted that the government must take action when fundamental freedoms are threatened. Depending on the nature of government involvement with these institutions as a whole, the necessary involvement with regard to the conditions of providing spiritual care needs to be specified. In institutions which are fully controlled and financed by the state, such as penal institutions, government responsibility with regard to the availability of spiritual care is substantial. In social institutions for which the government merely prescribes the organisational structure, government responsibility takes a different shape.

The justification of government involvement can be further outlined for every specific type of institution. Elements of relevance are involuntary presence (e.g. penal institutions), confrontation with ethical conflicts (armed forces), and reduced accessibility for regular spiritual care due to structures of organisation (hospitals).

It is clear that spiritual care cannot be provided on the basis of strict proportionality of denominational preference. Co-operation between denominations is necessary.[53] In public institutions, the responsible government minister appoints the church minister on the basis of nominations by the churches.

The legal basis varies to a large extent.[54] In penal institutions, the basis is an Act of Parliament. For the armed forces funds are set aside in the budget. The specific services make the more precise arrangements on their own. There is no Act of Parliament pertinent to spiri-

---

53 Also non-christian religion, and non-religious belief.
54 See *Overheid, godsdienst en levensovertuiging*, op cit.

tual care within health care institutions. In ministerial subsidy and acknowledgement regulations religious care is mentioned. The same is true for the institutions for young people and homes for the elderly.

The desirability of a clear legal basis does not exist solely in the realm of theory. In practice, such a legal basis is a necessary guarantee, as major changes are pending in the structures of organisation and financing of the above-mentioned institutions. Key words in this process are "decentralisation" and "budget financing". Availability of religious care in the institutions other than the armed forces is secured by Act of Parliament.

X. *Criminal Law and Religion*

The Criminal Code contains a few provisions regarding religion. Specific types of public blasphemy are penalised by Article 147 a. It must be noted that convictions on the grounds of these articles are highly unlikely. Public blasphemy is penalised as a misdemeanour by Article 429 b.

Articles 137 c-e of the Criminal Code recognise as felonies public oral expressions or expressions in writing which are offensive to people on grounds of their religion, belief or race, or which incite to hatred against or discrimination of people. Convictions on the basis of these articles do take place from time to time.[55]

Expressions regarding religion or religiously inspired expressions which are not pertinent to religion can and do give rise to civil lawsuits. In these cases, courts usually balance the interests of the parties involved, taking into account fundamental principles such as freedom of religion or belief, freedom of expression, and the principle of non-discrimination. In a civil lawsuit, an expression may be regarded as wrongful vis-à-vis another party, even if that same expression would not lead to a criminal conviction.

Another example of the way criminal law and religion are connected is the protection of the secrets of the confessional which falls under the generally worded Article 218 of the Criminal Procedure Code.[56]

---

55 See *S.C. van Bijsterveld*, 'De controversiële godsdienst – en meningsuiting', in: Ars Aequi juli/augustus 2003, p. 533-540.
56 See also Article 272 of the Criminal Code on professional secrets.

XI. Legal Status of Holders of a Spiritual Office

It would be inaccurate to claim that holders of a spiritual office have a special legal status. Specific fields of law, however, do mention the spiritual office. In the field of labour law, for instance, exceptions to the general rules are made with regard to holders of a spiritual office, and by means of interpretation, courts may regard the employment relation within a church as other than a labour contract.[57]
Another area which should be mentioned is that of military service. The Military Conscription Act provides the basis for the exclusion of holders of a spiritual office from military service. The same arrangement has been made for ordinands. For this purpose, secondary legislation covers in detail the specific church offices in specific churches. This list, however, is not exhaustive.
The Criminal Code makes it a crime to insult a cleric during the lawful execution of his vocation.[58] Apart from this, other hate crimes against religions are also dealt with.[59] Convictions on the basis of these articles are highly unlikely.[60] In regulations concerning specialised religious care, the office of church minister is, likewise, sometimes dealt with, as well as in the legislation concerning religious and civil marriage.[61]
In the past, provisions existed which excluded holders of a spiritual office from representative councils of government. From 1848 to 1887, the Constitution stated that holders of a spiritual office were not eligible to be elected and sit in the national parliament. Until 1931, a similar provision existed in the Local Communities Act for the municipal councils. Such impediments no longer exist.

---

57 See above, section VI.
58 Art.147, introduction and sub 2, Criminal Code.
59 See other sections of Art.147, as well as Art.147a Criminal Code.
60 Article 429 bis and Articles 137 c-e Criminal Code (discrimination) play a more substantial role; these articles are not specifically pertinent to holders of a religious office. See also Art.145, 146 Criminal Code on disturbing ceremonies.
61 See above, section VII.

XII. Developments

Major general developments in law and society are likely to influence (debates on) church and state relationships and freedom of religion or belief in the Netherlands. Even if these developments may not lead to radical legal change in these fields, they will certainly influence the context in which (debates on) church and state relationships and freedom of religion or belief are set.
One of these developments is that of immigration and the presence of a large number of adherents of Islam. Although this development is not new in itself, societal issues related to it have become more pressing over the last few years. This is reflected in debates on integration policies and, in part, also on "values and norms"-debates, and a renewed orientation on the relationship between Islam and Christianity. In a wider context, developments in and debates on the ways in which law and morality are relevant.[62]

XIII. Bibliography

S.C. van Bijsterveld, Church Autonomy in the Netherlands. The Distinctiveness of the Church. The Interplay between Legal, Popular, and Ecclesiastical Perspectives. Church Autonomy as a 'Test Case', in: *Hildegard Warnink* (ed.), Legal Position of Churches and Church Autonomy, Leuven 2001, p. 147-163.

S.C. van Bijsterveld, 'De controversiële godsdienst- en meningsuiting', in: Ars Aequi juli/augustus 2003, p. 533-540.

S.C. van Bijsterveld, 'Freedom of Religion: Legal Perspectives', in: *Richard O'Dair, Andrew Lewis* (eds.), Law and Religion. Current Legal Issues 2001 (Vol. 3), Oxford, p. 299-309.

S.C. van Bijsterveld, Godsdienstvrijheid in Europees perspectief, Deventer 1998.

S.C. van Bijsterveld, Religious Liberty and Church Autonomy in the Netherlands, in: *Gerhard Robbers* (ed.), Church Autonomy: A Comparative Survey, Frankfurt am Main, 2001, p. 59-75.

Gerard Dekker, Joep de Hart, Jan Peters, God in Nederland, 1966-1996, Amsterdam 1997.

---

62 See also *Sophie van Bijsterveld*, The Empty Throne: Democracy and the Rule of Law in Transition, Utrecht 2002.

E.M.H. Hirsch Ballin et.al., Kerk en Staat. Hun onderlinge verhouding binnen de Nederlandse samenleving, Baarn 1987.

A. Jacobs, Labour and social security law and the churches in the Netherlands, in: Churches and Labour Law in the EC Countries, European Consortium for Church and State Research, Proceedings of the meeting Madrid, November 27-28, 1992, Milan/Madrid 1993, p. 215-230.

H. Knippenberg, De religieuze kaart van Nederland, Assen 1992.

B.C. Labuschagne, Godsdienstvrijheid en niet-gevestigde minderheden. Een grondrechtelijk-rechtsfilosofische studie naar de betekenis en grenzen van religieuze tolerantie, Groningen 1994.

J.J.M. Maeijer, Rechtspersoon, godsdienst en levensovertuiging, Mededelingen der KNAW, Afd. Letterkunde, Amsterdam 1986.

J.J. Oostenbrink, Een relativering van "godsdienstig karakter", in: Een stellig annotator, Zwolle 1982.

Overheid, godsdienst en levensovertuiging, eindrapport van de Commissie van advies inzake de criteria voor steunverlening door de overheid aan kerkgenootschappen en andere genootschappen op geestelijke grondslag (Commissie-Hirsch Ballin), 's-Gravenhage 1988.

J.A.F. Peters, (ed.), Kerk en Staat. Actuele ontwikkelingen belicht, Zwolle 1989.

A.H. Santing-Wubs, Kerken in geding: de burgerlijke rechter en kerkelijke geschillen, Den Haag 2002.

H. Schaeffer et.al. (ed.), Handboek Godsdienst in Nederland, Amersfoort 1992.

B.P. Vermeulen, 'Artikel 6', in: *A.K. Koekkoek* (ed.), De Grondwet. Een systematisch en artikelsgewijs commentaar, Deventer 2000, p. 93-108.

Henk Vroom, Henk Woldring (eds.), Religies in het publieke domein, Zoetermeer 2002.

Annual publications:
The annual proceedings of the European Consortium for Church and State Research.
The European Journal for Church and State Research, with an annual review of developments in the Netherlands.

Richard Potz
State and Church in Austria

I. Social Facts

According to the 2001 Census the religious and denominational structure of the population of Austria presents the following picture:

Roman Catholic	73.66 %
Protestant	4.68 %
Islamic	4.30 %
Orthodox	2.17 %
Jehovah's Witnesses	0.29 %
Old Catholic	0.18 %
Buddhist	0.13 %
Jewish	0.10 %
Pentecostal	0.09 %
Oriental-Orthodox	0.06 %
Evangelical	0.06 %
Seventh Day Adventist	0.05 %
New Apostolic	0.05 %
Belonging to no denomination	11.99 %

II. Historical Background

The roots of the socio-cultural and psychological factors determining Austrian law on religion go back to the Habsburg Counter-Reformation and the enlightened church establishment of Joseph II., some of which remained influential until the 19th or 20th century. A systematic understanding of the law on religion is difficult to achieve because the ecclesiastical legislation currently in force emanates from the various political systems operating in Austria since the beginning of the 19th century, reflecting the state of religious policies of their time..

The 1867 Staatsgrundgesetz (StGG: Constitutional Act on the Fundamental Rights of Citizens) is still in force. It signalled a reduction of the denominational bias of the State and the introduction of a denominationally neutral system in ecclesiastical matters; in practice, however, the State administration continued to favour the Church. In the Bundesverfassungsgesetz (B-VG: Federal Constitution of the Austrian Republic) of 1920, the StGG was retained in principle due to a failure to agree on a new set of fundamental rights. The revision of the law on religion that was felt to be necessary initially affected only the Catholic Church.

After lengthy negotiations a Concordat was concluded which came into force on 1 May 1934 together with a corporative-authoritarian Constitution.

The "Anschluss" to Nazi Germany on 13 March 1938 brought an end to the denominational structure of Austria. The Concordat of 1934 was declared invalid, but the Concordat of the German Reich was not extended, so there was no concordat applicable to Austria.

After the reconstitution of Austria in 1945 several laws relating to religion were transferred almost en bloc to the legal system of the Republic.[1]

Initially, the validity of the 1934 Concordat in domestic and in international law was unclear. In 1957 the Federal Government expressly recognised the validity of the Concordat and an active period of legislation on religion was initiated which in particular brought about a renewal of the law for specific recognised churches and religious communities.[2] A further tranche of legislation on religion has been introduced in more recent years, with the specific aim of coping with the problems related to the emergence of new religious movements.[3]

---

1 Especially the law of 6 July 1938 on Matrimony and Divorce, Gesetz vom 6. Juli 1938 zur Vereinheitlichung des Rechts der Eheschließung und Ehescheidung (im Land Österreich und im übrigen Reichsgebiet). See infra, and the Law on church contribution, Gesetz über die Erhebung von Kirchenbeiträgen im Lande Österreich.
2 Especially the partial treaties with the Holy See in the 1960s, the Protestants-Act (ProtestantenG) 1961 and the Orthodox-Act (OrthodoxenG) 1967. Within this period also the Islam-Recognition-Ordinance (Islam-AnerkennungsVO) 1982 and the Israelites-Amendment-Act (IsraelitenG) 1984 count.
3 Especially the BekGG 1998 and the SektenstellenG 1998.

III. Constitutional Guarantees

1. Principles

The most important constitutional provisions in Austrian law relating to religion are contained in the *Staatsgrundgesetz* (StGG) of 21 December 1867, which was declared a constitutional law of the Federal State by Article 149(1) of the Austrian *Bundes-Verfassungsgesetz* (B-VG) of 1920. Guarantees of individual religious rights are contained in Article 14,[4] the institutional guarantees in Article 15. The legal provisions on religion in the Treaty of St. Germain of 10 September 1919,[5] and Article 9 of the European Convention on Human Rights (ECHR) which has constitutional status, are also of importance. There are also guarantees in constitutional and international law intended to protect religious freedom; these include general rules of non-discrimination relating, among other things, to differences in denomination.

2. Comprehensive Protection of Freedom of Religion

The constitutional norm of the European Convention on Human Rights overlays the older specific guarantees (freedom of belief, freedom of conscience, freedom of cult, freedom of confession) and summarises them in one "aggregated law on human rights"[6] in which the separate guarantees come together. This comprehensive idea of religious freedom also makes it clear once and for all that not only is religious confession protected by the constitutional order but a Weltanschauung (world view) which is not religion-related is similarly protected.

At the heart of the concept of freedom of religion lies respect of convictions of conscience. The State guarantees their free development

---

4 Especially Art. 14 StGG: (1) full freedom of belief and conscience is guaranteed for everybody. (2).
5 Section V (Protection of Minorities) of Part III of the Treaty of St. Germain is to be seen as constitutional law according to Art. 149 B-VG 1920: Of importance is especially Art. 63(2): "All inhabitants of Austria have the right to exercise in public or private every kind of belief, religion or confession freely, insofar as their exercise is not incompatible with public order or good morals."
6 W. Berka, Die Europäische Menschenrechtskonvention und die Österreichische Grundrechtstradition, in: ÖJZ 34/1979, p. 428.

in the field of education and their free exercise, if necessary by offering alternatives modes of action, as long as basic principles of the rule of law are not compromised.[7]

A particularly important expression of freedom of conscience is to be found in the law on defence. If a person liable for military service expressly declares that he or she cannot fulfil military service because – except in cases of individual self-defence or defence of another from imminent attack – of an objection to using force of arms against other human beings for reasons of conscience. They would be subject to moral conflict if forced to do military service; this person has to do alternative social service (ZivildienstG Section 2(1)[8]).

In education law, freedom of conscience is given concrete expression in the opportunity to opt out of religious instruction in school (ReIUG Section 1(2)), and in the right of the teacher to refuse to teach in a denominational private school (PrivSchG Section 20). At university level, staff and students have the right not to participate in scientific and artistic tasks for reasons of conscience (UniversitätsG Section 105)

In the law of medicine, there must be no discrimination against those who for reasons of conscience either will or will not participate in performing a legal abortion (Strafgesetzbuch Sections 97(2) and (3)) or in medically assisted procreation (FortpflanzungsG Section 6).

Freedom of belief encompasses the right to have any belief, to change this belief or to have no belief, without interference from the state or groups in society. This fundamental right has been shaped by the provisions on secession, which in the case of a recognised church or religious community must be declared before a state administration office to take effect (InterkonfG 1868, Section 6). In case of a registered religious community, even though a formal provision on secession is not statutorily necessary (BekGG Section 4(1)(4)), termination of membership may be declared before a district administration office (BekGG Section 8(1)).

3. Protection of Fundamental Rights

As they are fundamental rights, the rights to freedom of religion are part of subjective public rights, the infringement of which can be

---

7   See E.W. Böckenförde, Das Grundrecht der Gewissensfreiheit, in: Staat-Gesellschaft-Freiheit, Frankfurt/Main 1976, 287.
8   As amended by the Act of 1990.

brought before the Constitutional Court or the Supreme Administrative Court. The Constitutional Court has (B-VG Art. 144(1)) the task of protecting fundamental rights by deciding on complaints against decisions of the administrative authorities, if the complainant claims that one of his or her fundamental rights has been violated by such a decision, either by a decision or an unconstitutional ordinance or law (Sonderverwaltungsgerichtshof). The Supreme Administration Court exercises its control of the law by deciding on appeals against decisions of the administrative authorities after all other legal remedies have been exhausted (B-VG Art. 131(1)).

4. Provisions of Ordinary Law

State law which is relevant to religion comes in two categories: the first deals with questions of the law on religion as, for example, the Recognition Act (AnerkennungsG) 1874, the Act on Confessional Communities (BeKGG) 1998 and the Act on Interconfessional Relations (Gesetz über interkonfessionelle Verhältnisse) 1868; the second relates to the legal status of specifically recognised churches and religious communities. The special church-state law of the Catholic Church in Austria is traditionally made by treaties with the Holy See; these are recognised as international public law treaties sui generis and are subject to the procedure of transposition (B-VG Art. 50).
According to current Austrian constitutional law there is no further legal basis for church-state law by way of agreements.
With the many different shades of relationship between state and church, ecclesiastical law has over the course of time permeated the entire legal order; thus it cuts across all fields, defined only by relevance to religion.

5. Basic Categories of the Austrian System

The legal system of the relations between State and Church in Austria is based on two main principles: the fundamental right to individual freedom of religious and philosophical beliefs; and the guarantee through fundamental rights of the corporate activities of religious communities in public. In Austria there is no established church: at the institutional level, State and religious communities are separate. The State accepts, however, the activity of churches and religious communities in the public arena. The basic idea of this system is to provide the relevant legal framework for the incorporation of pluralistic religion into society in a context in which, as a matter of principle, the State does not exercise its sovereignty.

IV. Ordinary (State) Law

1. The Legal Status of Religious Communities

a) Recognised churches and religious associations

The constitutional basis of the legal status of recognised churches and religious communities is found in StGG Article 15:

> Every Church and religious society recognised by the law has the right to joint public religious practice, to arrange and administer its internal affairs autonomously, and to retain possession and enjoyment of its institutions, endowments and funds devoted to worship, instruction and welfare, but is like every society subject to the general laws of the land.

The treatment of churches and religious communities as corporations under public law sui generis carries less positive legal substance than the qualification that the State does not see religion as a private matter. The churches are generally included whenever state legislation relates to corporations under public law, except when the law expressly excludes them.[9] The way in which the followers of a denomination can obtain legal recognition was established by the Recognition Act (AnerkennungsG) 1874. According to Section 1 of that Act recognition as a religious association will be granted to the followers of a previously legally unrecognised denomination under the condition, "that (1) religious teaching, service, statutes, and chosen names do not contain anything illegal or morally offensive and (2) the creation and existence of at least one cult community created according to the requirements of this law is guaranteed."

This provision has been given expression and complemented by Section 11 of the BeKGG 1998. Of the conditions required for recogni-

---

9 E.g. in the law on private radio broadcasting and in the law concerning subsidising print media, see infra.

tion, the demographic condition in particular is so prohibitive that for a long time only Jehovah's Witnesses will be able to meet it. It requires a minimum number of believers of 2% of the Austrian population according to the latest census (2001 Census: 16,066).

Recognition according to the Recognition Act is granted by ordinance.[10] Since 1988 the Constitutional Court has acknowledged a legally enforceable right to recognition. Although the recognition is to be granted by way of ordinance, official notice must be given in a case of non-recognition to make possible an appeal to the Supreme Administration Court.[11] The Supreme Administration Court followed this legal opinion in 1997.[12]

The provisions concerning the churches and religious communities recognised by the Recognition Act are to be found in this Act. However, the law on religion concerning the "historically recognised" churches and religious communities is developed by way of special laws.

An example of this relates to the Catholic Church in the Concordat between the Holy See and the Republic of Austria with the Additional Protocol of 5 June 1933 and additional and complementary treaties.[13]

According to the Concordat, the State gives the Church a guarantee that it may make laws, decrees and orders within its own field of competence without hindrance (Art. 1(2)). The institutions of the Catholic Church with legal personality according to Canon Law also enjoy public law status in the sphere of State Law. Institutions that are to be founded in the future obtain the status of State institutions as soon as the notice of foundation is lodged with the competent Federal ministry (Art. 2). The foundation of Church provinces and

---

10 On the basis of the Recognition Act the following are recognised by ordinance today: The Old Catholic church (1877), the Methodist Church (1951), the Church of Jesus Christ of the Latter Day Saints (Mormons) (1955), The New Apostolic Church in Austria (1975), the Austrian Buddhist Religious Association (1983).

11 VfSlg 11.931/1988. If one follows the opposite legal opinion, according to which the Recognition Act does not give an enforceable right, no legal consequences could follow from the constitutional difference between recognised and non-recognised religious associations. Otherwise there would be a violation of the equal treatment principle (requirement of reasonableness), and also a violation of the principle of rule of law which implies that a right given by law must also be enforceable.

12 By a decision of 28 April 1997, 96/10/0049.

13 Treaty concerning the Regulation of Proprietary Relations 1960 as amended by 5. Additional Treaty 1996; Treaty concerning the Regulation of Questions relating to the School System and Concluding Protocol 1962, and the Treaties on constituting Dioceses concerning the Elevation of the Apostolic Administrative Burgenland to a Diocese 1960, concerning the elevation of the Apostolic Administrative Innsbruck-Feldkirch to a diocese 1964, and concerning the establishment of a diocese of Feldkirch 1968.

dioceses as well as important boundary changes must be the subject of a treaty with the Federal government (Art. 3).[14] There is no State participation in appointment to church offices, with the exception of the operation of the Political Clause in the case of bishoprics (Art. 4).[15] The Concordat contains rules dealing with the theological faculties, religious orders, the law on church property, and pastoral care in institutions. In the case of difficulties in the interpretation of the Concordat or the occurrence of problems not yet treated which affect State and Church, an amicable solution is reached (Clause of Amicability) or a ruling arrived at by mutual consent.

The ProtestantenG 1961 represents the conclusion of a process leading to the equal treatment of the Protestant and the Catholic Churches. In comparison with the Concordat this more recent law guarantees greater religious freedom. ProtestantenG Section 1(1) gives separate legal recognition to the Church of the Augsburg Confession and the Church of the Helvetic Confession, in addition to the Church of the Augsburg and Helvetic Confessions, at their express request.

The Protestant Church is completely independent of the State in the appointment of all its functionaries. It is, however, obliged to name legal representatives for all its institutions possessing legal capacity and to inform the State of their names, in addition to the names of the members of the governing body of the Protestant Church.

OrthodoxenG 1967 first recognised the Greek Orthodox Church in Austria in addition to the existing communities. For the purposes of State law, membership results directly from the law for all persons of Orthodox faith who have their permanent address (or in the case of those with no fixed address, have their habitual residence) on federal territory. Because of the internal structures of the Orthodox Church, which are liable to lead to conflict, the State felt called upon to include in the Law provisions as to rights of supervision; this lead to comments that it was incompatible with the Constitution.

IsraelitenG 1890 was based on the concept of the uniform religious community: every Jew belonged to the religious community in the catchment area in which he or she had a permanent address. This rule was modified by an amendment of 1984. Now every Jewish commu-

---

14 See treaties on Diocesan Establishment in the preceding note.
15 According to this clause the Austrian Federal Government is informed of the name of the person chosen. The Government can then impose conditions of a general political nature. If no agreement is reached, the Holy See is free to appoint the candidate of its choice. The political clause is of little practical relevance nowadays; however, it may encourage the Holy See to consult the Government at an early stage if the candidate is likely to cause controversy.

nity has the option of gaining recognition as an independent religious community because of a pre-existing difference in position according to the Recognition Act.[16] Reflecting the date at which it came into being, the IsraelitenG is characterised by State sovereignty over ecclesiastical law and contains a number of State rights of supervision; these, however, are no longer exercised in their original form.

Muslims were initially given only the status of adherents of a recognised religious community by IslamG 1912 because institutional recognition of Islam by the procedure set out in AnnerkennungsG was not possible,. The institutional recognition of the Islamic Religious Community took place by way of an ordinance in 1988, which summarises in seven points the elements that must be contained "in particular" in the constitution of the Religious Community with respect to its external legal circumstances.

Legal questions relating to Muslim exercise of religion have found a fundamentally liberal solution in Austria, not least because of the public law status of that religious community. Ritual slaughter does not constitute a contradiction either to "good morals" or to "public order" if it is performed lege artis, This opinion has been held by the Supreme Administrative Court since the end of the 19th century and was confirmed recently by the Constitutional Court and the Supreme Court.[17] With regard to the hierarchy of values within the fundamental rights, and in view of all other circumstances, the protection of animals is less important than the freedom to exercise one's religion.

Up to now there has been no case in Austria concerning the Muslim headscarf. In both theory and practice, the wearing of a Muslim headscarf does not of itself carry significance in terms of identification, proselytising, or indoctrination. Someone wearing a Muslim headscarf, therefore, would not necessarily be barred from teaching.

OrientalenG 2003 put an end to the unequitable treatment between the Coptic-Orthodox Church and the two other Oriental-Orthodox churches which were already recognised – the Armenian-Apostolic Church since 1973 and the Syrian-Orthodox Church since 1985. These churches do not differ doctrinally, notwithstanding their canonical independence. The aim of this law was to create a legal situation which not only respected the internal constitution of the Oriental-Orthodox churches but also created a specific and homogeneous civil ecclesiastical law for them.

---

[16] This provision needs a purposive interpretation in view of BekGG Section 11 concerning the minimum number of believers required for recognition.
[17] VwSlg 10666/1897; VwSlg 5248 A/1907; OGH 28.3.1996, 15 Os 27, 28/96; VfSlg 15394/1998.

b) Registered religious communities

The Act on the Legal Status of Religious Communities (BeKGG) 1998 created a legal basis for religious communities to obtain legal personality without at the same time giving them the status of a public law corporation.[18]

This law does not apply to philosophical communities as being "non religious belief communities"; there are problems associated with this, however, when viewed from a fundamental rights perspective.

The provisions on obtaining legal personality by religious communities were in many ways drafted according to association law Registration being obtained on application, subject to the possibility of rejection on specified grounds. A legal personality in private law is created at the point of registration,. As part of the application, the applicant must prove that at least 300 persons resident in Austria belong to the religious community; these persons must not belong to another religious community or legally recognised church or religious community (Section 3(3)).

According to Section 5, the authorities must reject the application if the community's statutes do not meet the legal formal requirements, or if this is necessary in view of its teaching or practice to protect the interests in a democratic society of public order, health, and morals, or to protect the rights and freedoms of others. This is a necessary safeguard particularly in the areas of inciting the commission of crime, impeding the psychological development of minors, injuring members' psychological integrity, or the application of psycho-therapeutical methods in order to win converts.

The religious communities obtain with registration a sort of seal of approval. This has legal relevance beyond the grant of legal personality as, for example, where the legal order draws legal consequences from the religious dimension as such and not merely from the status of recognition.

---

18 Registered as religious communities are: Bahá'i-Religion, Federation of Baptist Communities in Austria, Federation of Evangelical Communities of Austria, Christian Community-Movement for Religious Revival in Austria, Free Christian Community/Pentecostal Community, Hindu Mandi (?) Society, Jehovah's Witnesses, Church of Seventh Day Adventists, Mennonite Free Church of Austria, Pentecostal Church-Community of God in Austria. The Church of Scientology of Austria has withdrawn its application; the registration of Jahaja Yoga has been rejected (BeKGG Section 5(2))

c) Religious communities as associations

According to VereinsG 2002 Section 1(2) this law does not apply to those associations constituted under other legal provisions or which have adopted a different legal form under other appropriate legislation. Religious communities now can obtain legal personality by the association route, which is not possible under the previous law. The religious communities constituted according to the VereinsG have equal status with other ideological associations.

2. The Notion of Freedom of Religious Communities

The term "internal affairs" (StGG Art. 15) as applied to the recognised churches and religious communities is a constitutional term restricting the State's freedom of action. In these affairs the activity of the Church is not State activity: its general and individual acts are not administrative acts within the meaning of the Federal Constitution, so they are not submitted to the control of the Administrative or Constitutional Court.

What the term means for a particular church or religious community must be derived from the scope of the functions of that body and must be defined primarily by the holder of the fundamental right, as it may be understood only within the self-understanding of the church or religious community. Ordinary State legislation may not impose a restriction on church action; it must respect the inherent distinctions just drawn and consider other fundamental rights. This opinion developed in the literature has been accepted by the Constitutional Court.[19]

The Constitutional Court recognises the right of legally recognised churches and religious communities to the full regulation and administration of their internal affairs without state interference and supervision (StGG Art. 15 (VfSlg. 6102/2001)). This is open to criticism, as the right has to be seen as a consequence of the fundamental right to religious freedom and thus should in general be guaranteed regardless of specific legal status.

---

[19] See VfSlg. 3657/1959 (ÖAKR 32/1981, p. 426), VfSlg. 7801/1976 (ÖAKR 32/1981, p. 556), VfSlg. 7982/1977 (ÖAKR 32/1981, p. 559), VfSlg. 11574/1987 (ÖAKR 37/1987/88, p. 353).

3. Organisation of Religious Communities

a) Legal status of church institutions in general

The institutions of the Catholic Church which possess legal personality according to Canon Law also enjoy public law status in the sphere of State legislation. They are granted this status as soon as the notice of foundation is lodged with the responsible ministry (Concordat Art. 2 and 10). The institutions of the Protestant Church possessing legal personality become public law entities from the date of the lodging of the notice by the Protestant Church with the responsible ministry (ProtestantenG Section 4(1)). With regard to all other recognised churches and religious communities, only religious communities and their associations may in principle attain legal personality. Furthermore, institutions of religious communities may make use of all other legal forms permitted in State legislation.

b) Educational institutions: see below, Section VI)

c) Welfare organisations financed (supported) by churches

The increasing regulation of social and welfare tasks normally provides for the integration of non-State sponsors of such work into the welfare system. Traditionally church institutions have played an important part in many areas. The State has taken this into consideration by expressly mentioning church institutions in several cases, for example in providing aid for asylum-seekers (AsylG Section 4(2)) and in the field of development (EntwicklungszusammenarbeitsG 2002 Section 2(3)).

V. Churches and Religious Communities in the Political System

After the Second World War, the religious communities were assigned the "office of custodian" over the ordering of fundamental rights and democracy. There is now, however, broad political acceptance that they carry out an important function in society as expressed in the conferring of public law status on recognised churches and religious communities. Religious communities belong to those social associations which establish contexts for communication in society and politics. They are important participants in that public dialogue by which citizens are motivated to act responsibly. This leads to the fact that the religious communities are not only integrated in the process of opinion-making concerning the formulation of State legislation which is relevant for them in a broad sense, but that they also are represented on many advisory bodies and committees.

VI. Religious Communities in State Law on Culture

1. Private Schools

State schools financed by the Federal Republic, Federal States, and local authorities are open to everyone, regardless, among other things, of denomination. Private schools are granted public status if their governors, heads and teachers can guarantee proper and regular instruction in accordance with the aims of Austrian schooling. In the case of legally prescribed types of schools the results achieved in class must be equivalent to those at a State school of the same type. The fulfilment of these conditions is a legal presumption in the case of recognised churches and religious communities.[20] As a result of their public status the reports issued by their schools have the same legal force as those issued by State schools.

Recognised churches and religious communities are granted subsidies towards the costs of personnel for denominational private schools with public status (*PrivatschulG* Section 17).[21] This subsidy must be given as a "living subsidy" by means of the appointment of teachers employed by the Federation or the Federal States to the private schools. If this is not possible, an equivalent financial subsidy is granted (Section 19). Only teachers who agree to the appointment

---

20 The Constitutional Court has no reservations as to this ruling with reference to the principle of equal rights because of the experience of the recognised churches and religious communities which has been gathered down the centuries (see coll 5063/1965 in ÖAKR 32/1981, pp 482).

21 On the contrary, private schools run by unrecognised religious communities have no legal claim to financial assistance; this seems questionable on constitutional grounds especially with respect to Article 2 of the first supplementary protocol of the ECHR.

and to whose appointment the governing body of the church or religious community also agrees, may be appointed to denominational schools. The appointment must be terminated if the teacher so requests or if the church's governing body declares further employment of the teacher to be intolerable for religious reasons (Section 20).

2. Religious Instruction

Religious instruction is guaranteed by Article 17(4) StGG, which provides that the respective churches or religious communities are responsible for classes in religious instruction in school. Viewed systematically, this Article elaborates the religious freedom of pupils and parents and of the parents' right to the religious or philosophical education of their children.
According to *SchulorganisationsG* 1962 Section 2(1) the aim of Austrian schooling is to co-operate in the development of the young people's aptitudes according – amongst other things – to religious values by way of appropriate instruction. The inclusion of religious values in an Article describing the aims of education is due to the aim of making education comprehensive, giving a choice relevant to persons open to religious education and development. Accordingly Section 2(b)(1) of the ReligionsunterrichtsG (RelUG 1949) prescribes that in classrooms of public schools and of schools with public status in which religious instruction is a compulsory subject the school must exhibit a cross if the majority of the pupils belong to a Christian denomination. The legitimation of religious instruction in fundamental rights would suggest the introduction of ethics as a compulsory subject, that is instruction in ethics for these pupils who do not belong to a legally recognised church or religious community or who have opted out of religious instruction. The school experiment in "Ethics" which began in 1997 was carried out in over 100 schools during the school year of 2003/04. Whether the scheme will be introduced into the whole school system is as yet unclear.
The organisation, implementation and direct control of classes in religious education is left to the respective church or religious community. The State has the right to supervise religious instruction by way of its school supervisory bodies for organisation and disciplinary measures (RelUG Section 2). Therefore it is the religious communities and not the State which organise religious instruction classes, despite the fact that as a compulsory subject religious instruction enjoys equal standing with other subjects.

For all pupils who are members of a legally recognised church or religious community,[22] religious instruction in their denomination is a compulsory subject in primary schools, secondary schools, colleges of education, agricultural colleges and colleges of forestry, as well as at all vocational colleges in Tyrol and Vorarlberg. At other schools religious instruction is an optional subject.

Pupils under fourteen years old may be withdrawn from religious education by their parents making a request in writing to the Head of the school during the first ten days of every school year. Pupils over fourteen may effect such a withdrawal by writing themselves.

The curricula for religious education are adopted by the churches and religious communities; the Ministry of Education must be informed of them and publish them, though this is of merely declaratory significance. State approval is not necessary. One restriction is the requirement that only such books and teaching materials may be used as are not in conflict with the aim of educating responsible citizens (RelUG Section 2(3)). Textbooks for religious instruction classes are included in the school book programme according to *Familienlasten-AusgleichsG* 1967, and are financed by the State.

Pupils and teachers are free to participate in religious devotions and ceremonies (primarily, school Mass). Teachers of religious instruction at State schools are appointed either by the Federation or the State or by the churches and religious communities. Only persons who have been qualified and approved as such by the competent church or religious community may be appointed as teachers of religious instruction.

3. *Academies of Religious Education*

According to the AkademienStudienG (AStG) 1999 the Academies of Education which were up to then organised according to the PrivatschulG are to be changed into "Universities for Pedagogical Professions". The assignment of the academies of religious instruction to the AStG has a number of consequences which are especially rele-

---

[22] In view of the systematic justification of religious instruction in religious freedom and the parent's right, it is constitutionally problematic to bind the right of giving religious instruction to the fact of legal recognition. On the other hand one has to ask whether in such an important area as the public school system a certain degree of willingness to co-operate on the part of the recognised churches and religious communities can be required, and that thus the "institutionalised constitutional expectation of the state" which is expressed in the act of recognition does in fact even imply a duty to give religious instruction.

vant for the Islamic Academies. The orientation to ideas and values required as a leading principle in AStG Section 5(2)(4) which has to be seen in relation to the tasks of the Austrian schools poses a challenge to Islam, as do the three other leading principles: the range and freedom of scientific theories and opinions; the interconnection between research and teaching; and the equal treatment of women and men. By way of this Islam has for the first time experienced integration into State legislation on universities.

4. Theological Faculties at State Universities

a) Faculties of Catholic Theology

There are Faculties of Catholic Theology at the Universities of Vienna, Graz, Innsbruck and Salzburg. Article 5 of the Concordat guarantees the continued existence of these faculties, financed by the State, for the purpose of the academic education of the clergy. Their internal organisation and educational practice is regulated by the State according to the law on universities. The term "internal organisation" in this context refers to the organisational provisions of the *UniversitätsG* (UnivG) 2002; the term "educational practice" refers to the provisions on academic studies of this law. There is also an explicit proviso in favour of the terms of the Concordat (UnivG Section 38(1)).

Academic degrees in theology awarded by a papal academy in Rome or any other papal academy are recognised as having the legal status of State degrees in Austria.

The appointment or admission of professors and lecturers must be agreed by the competent church authority. If church authorisation is withdrawn, the teacher must be excluded from exercising the teaching activity concerned.

The majority opinion is that the disciplinary measure of the compulsory redundancy of a theology professor whose authorisation has been withdrawn according to Article 5(4) of the Concordat does not violate the rights of freedom of religion and conscience, opinion, or academic teaching and research, since the aim is to educate pastors and teachers of religious education.[23]

---

23 See Constitutional Court VfSlg. 6998/1973, VwSlg. 8419 A/1973.

On the basis of Article 5 of the Concordat, theology may also be studied at theological colleges established by the competent church authorities.

b) Faculty of Protestant Theology

The Federal State is obliged to maintain a Faculty of Protestant Theology with at least six permanent chairs at Vienna University to guarantee the academic education of ordinands, and theological research and teaching (*ProtestantenG* Section 15). Teachers in the faculty must be members of the Protestant Church. When appointing a professor to a chair, the commission charged with the appointment must consult the Protestant Church authorities.

5. Church Private Universities

The Universitäts-AkkreditierungsG 1999 put an end to the State monopoly in Austria and made it possible to organise private universities. In 2000 the Catholic Theological Private University of Linz made use of this provision.

6. Mass Media

a) Broadcasting legislation

A law of 2001 created a public law foundation with the aim of fulfilling the public service role of Austrian Radio. It must have "adequate regard to the importance of the legally recognised churches and religious communities" within the framework of broadcasting (Section 4(1)(12)). On the foundation council of 35 members there must be at least one representing the legally recognised churches and religious communities. The Catholic Church and the Protestant Church appoint one member each of the audience council which also has 35 members (Section 28(3)(3) and (4)). According to Programme Directives 1.2.2., not only must events involving churches and religious communities be represented in their social context, but also the belief-systems of the churches and religious communities.
The Privatfernsehgesetz 2001 regulates private broadcasting on terrestrial television as well as radio and television on cable networks

and via satellite. Churches and religious communities are expressly not excluded from broadcasting as they are "legal persons of public law" (Section 10(2)(1)).

b) Print media

The legally recognised churches and religious communities explicitly do not fall under the exclusion of subsidies for print media on which legal persons of public law participate as owner, editors, or publishers (PublizistikförderungsG 1984 Section 7(3)). The subsidies are distributed by a council, one of whose members is a representative of the legally recognised churches or religious communities (Section 9(1)(6)).

7. Protection of Historic Monuments

Section 2(1) of the DenkmalschutzG (DMSG) 2001 states that a legal presumption of protection in the case of monuments in the ownership of recognised churches or religious communities will expire on 31 December 2009 (Section 2(4)). Thereafter only such monuments will be protected for which a decision has been taken declaring a public interest in its preservation.

No alterations to or destruction of monuments are allowed without the consent of the Federal Authority for Monuments (DMSG Section 5(1)). Notwithstanding this provision, consent must be given to an application for alteration if the monument is used for worship and the alteration is necessary for the exercise of worship on the basis of compelling liturgical considerations.

A Council for Historic Monuments has been established, whose responsibility it is to represent specialist expertise. One representative of the church or religious community concerned takes part in meetings of the Council as an ad hoc member if a monument in majority church ownership is affected or if general problems of sacred or other church monuments are being examined (*Denkmalbeirat-VO* 1979 Section 5).

VII. Labour and Social Law

1. Collective Labour Law

The churches and religious communities are subsidiarily empowered to conclude collective agreements by reason of their status as public-law corporations as set out in Section 7 of the *Arbeitsverfassungsgesetz* (ArbVG) 1974. However, this opportunity has rarely been used up to now. At the level of businesses and enterprises there are usually company agreements.
According to ArbVG Section 132(1), some provisions are wholly or partially non-applicable to businesses and enterprises which directly serve political purposes and purposes of coalitional politics, denominational, scientific, educational, or welfare purposes. The aim of this arrangement is to prevent the participation of a works council in the making of economic decisions that would lead to a weakening of the specific purpose of the institution. The general exemption from co-determination by employees is not limited to the denominational purposes of recognised churches and religious communities. The first sentence of ArbVG Section 132(4) makes it clear that the provisions regarding the organisation of industrial relations are not applicable to businesses and enterprises which serve the denominational aims of a recognised church or religious community insofar as such provisions are in conflict with the specific nature of the business or enterprise. For this reason each case must be examined in order to determine whether the provision is compatible with the specific nature resulting from the right to self-determination.
According to the second sentence of ArbVG Section 132(4), provisions on company agreements in certain matters and some further provisions, are not applicable in any case to enterprises and administrative organisations charged with the administration of the internal affairs of legally recognised churches and religious communities.

2. Individual Labour Law

Church employment is part of civil law. An internal church statute on employment and remuneration is a matter of contract law adopted by the churches and religious communities as holders of private law rights. This law is in principle variable within the legal limits of the free elaboration of employment contracts.[24]

Persons whose activity is characterised mainly by religious, welfare, or social purposes do not count as employees if they are not employed on the basis of a labour contract (ArbVG Section 36(2)(6).

A special relationship with the church or religious community as employer results from direct participation in the pursuit of denominational aims. This expresses itself in a special sort of allegiance: acceptance of the teaching of the church or religious community and an appropriate way of life, as well as in a special duty of care by the church employer. This allegiance may vary with the importance of a person's work to the church's spiritual mission.

3. Welfare Law

Among the persons exempt from full insurance according to the *Allgemeines SozialversicherungsG* (ASVG-Social Security Act) 1955, Section 5(1)(7), are priests of the Catholic Church, and members of religious orders and similar institutions of the Catholic Church[25] if they do not have contractual relations with other corporations apart from their church or its institutions. Some of these persons have partial insurance which covers only illness, accident or retirement.

If a person who is exempt from full insurance in this way ceases to be a member of the clergy, an order, or similar institution, then a certain sum is payable to the new pension insurance institution on transfer (ASVG Section 314).

The BundespflegegeldG (Federal Care Constitution Act) 1993 introduced a nationwide (and in principle homogenous) reorganisation of payments to persons who need care. Priests and members of religious orders who are not covered by ASVG Section 3(1) are not included in the range of persons entitled, because they do not receive "basic payment by federal law". By way of ordinance of the competent fed-

---

24 See especially OGH Arb coll 9490/1976, OGH 16.9.1987, 9 Ob A 71/87 (ÖAKR 37/1987/88), p. 36). Conflicts between a church or religious community and its officials in matters of private law employment contracts may in principle be taken to court; however all preliminary questions of e.g. the validity of the removal from office, the retirement, the disciplinary measure, the transfer to another post etc., are excluded from the court's decision. See OGH SZ 47/135/1974, SZ 60/80/1987 (ÖAKR 37/1987/88, pp 371, SZ 60/173/1987 (ÖAKR 37/1987/88, p. 376).

25 Holders of spiritual office in the Protestant churches, who were also previously exempt, were included in full insurance by the ASVG amendment 1980 and the Sozialrechts-ÄnderungsG 1996.

eral ministry, however, persons who are excluded from pension insurance may be included in the range of persons entitled to care allowances. This has been done for secular priests (BGBl II 2002/72), though not yet for members of religious orders.

VIII. Financing of Churches

1. The State Guarantee of Church Property

The possession and enjoyment of church special-purpose funds is guaranteed by StGG Article 15: this is a specific application of the general fundamental guarantee of property. Additionally, Article 13 of the Concordat ensures that the property of the Catholic Church will not be violated and that the church is free to acquire property within the limits of the general laws. According to the unanimous opinion of courts and commentators, the independent administration of property is an internal matter for the churches and religious communities.

2. State Payments and Reserve Rights

State payments to religious communities exist only in relation to indemnity for financial losses caused during the Nazi occupation. According to the Treaty of Vienna of 1955 (Art. 26), Austria is obliged to indemnify those suffering financial losses resulting from Nazi legislation or rioting during the time of Nazi occupation. To enable this, international law agreements were concluded with the Catholic Church and legal settlements adopted with respect to the Protestant and Old Catholic Churches as well as with the Hebrew Religious Community.[26]

A special problem was and is posed by the rights to restitution and indemnity of the Hebrew community and its institutions. The necessary proofs required by law are often difficult to give and implemen-

---

[26] For this reason the Catholic Church at present receives 192m Schillings, the Protestant Church 12,351m Schillings, the Old Catholic Church 0.570m Schillings, the Hebrew Community 3,420m Schillings: the equivalent of the salaries of a number of state employees on the basis of an average salary.

tation of these laws has been very slow. The 2. RückstellungsanspruchsG (Reserve Rights Act) 1951 gave the Hebrew communities the right to raise claims of legal persons who had served religious, cultural, welfare or social aims of the Hebrew Community including Hebrew foundations and funds. Finally the Federation established a general compensation fund based on a 2001 treaty for Jewish property which was confiscated or destroyed during the Nazi period which can also serve for claims of the cult communities and other Hebrew institutions (EntschädigungsfondsG 2001 – Compensation Funds Act).

3. Church Contributions and Taxes

The collection of church contributions and assessments for financing its material and staffing needs is an internal matter for a legally recognised church or religious community, but one for which the right to State legal guarantee may be used.

A Law on Church Contributions came into force for the Catholic, Protestant, and Old Catholic Churches on 1 May 1939. Adult members are liable for contributions, whether or not they avail themselves of church services. The decision on and collection of the contributions takes place in accordance with an ordinance on church contributions which has been adopted by the churches. The binding character of the ordinance for the members of the church is part of internal church law. Non-payment of contributions may be the subject of a civil court action.

For those churches and religious communities not subject to the Law on Church Contributions there is the option of raising contributions by way of administrative enforcement. At present none of these churches and religious communities makes use of this provision.

IX. Status of the Recognised Churches and Religious Communities in Taxation Law

The provisions of tax law which are relevant to religion are based partly on the consequences in revenue law resulting from the public law status of churches and religious communities. Also relevant are

the conditions which must be met if the revenue law attributes benefits (reductions, exemptions) to corporations which display ecclesiastical aims in addition to those with public utility or charitable purposes.[27] (Section 34 Bundesabgabenordnung 1961 – Federal Revenue Act).
Donations in memory or for the spiritual welfare of the donor or his relatives are exempt from inheritance and gift tax regardless of whether those donations have been given while living or after death. Gifts of movable property and money from living persons to national institutions of legally recognised churches or religious communities serving church purposes are completely exempt from inheritance and gift tax (Sections 15(1)(13) and (14)(a) and (b) of the *Erbschafts- und Schenkungssteuergesetz* - Law on Inheritance and Gift Tax).

X. *Access of the Religious Communities to Public Institutions*

1. *Religious Assistance in the Armed Forces and in the Police*

The organisation of Catholic pastoral care in the armed forces is the task of the Bishop for the Armed Forces. He is appointed solely by the Pope on the non-binding suggestion of the Federal Government or according to the process envisaged in the political clause. Service chaplains are chosen by the bishop with the consent of the Defence Ministry and appointed by the State; they must be authorised by the Church to give pastoral care to the general public (Concordat Art. 8).
The Protestant Military Superintendent is charged with the organisation of Protestant pastoral care in the armed forces. He is nominated by the Protestant Church Council and appointed by the Defence Secretary. In spiritual matters he is subordinate to the governing body of the Protestant Church, in all other matters to the competent commanders of the Federal Army. The chaplains are appointed by the State, but they must be authorised by the Church (*ProtestantenG* Section 17).
The organisation of Islamic pastoral care is currently under discussion.

---

27 The analogous (and because of equal treatment reasons probably necessary) extension of the benefits in revenue law resulting from "ecclesiastical aims" to other religious communities has not yet been put into practice.

In relation to religious assistance in the police an agreement between the Austrian Bishops' Conference and the Federal Ministry of the Interior on Catholic religious assistance for executive officers has been in force since December 2002.

2. Religious Assistance in Institutions

Special pastoral care may be organised for public hospitals, medical institutions, nursing homes, prisons,[28] and community homes with the consent of the competent church authority (the Catholic diocesan bishop; the governing body of the Protestant Church). In addition the local pastors of all denominations - including those not legally recognised - or their representatives have the right of free access to members of their denomination in institutions which do not have independent pastoral care.

XI. Clergy and Members of Religious Orders in State Law

In principle it is the self-understanding of the relevant religious community which decides who is to be regarded as clergy in State law.[29] With respect to political rights, especially concerning the right to be voted into public office, there are no restrictions in State law.

1. Special Procedural Status

The clergy may not be summoned to give evidence in criminal, civil or administrative legal proceedings[30] on matters entrusted to them

---

28 Section 85 *StrafvollzugsG* 1969 (Punishment Act), contains provisions on the religious activities of prisoners.
29 According to a typological description of the VwGH (Slg 9491/1913), if there is any doubt, a "person who is a teacher of the religious doctrine and advisor in religious matters, who supervises the service and the ritual institutions, who is entrusted with the office of preaching, the administration of the service and the decision in ritual questions, and who finally has to administer the register, is to be regarded as clergy".
30 Section 151(1) *Strafprozeßordnung* 1975 (Criminal Procedure Law), Section 320(2) *Zivilprozeßordnung* 1895 (Civil Procedure Law), Section 48(2) *Allgemeines VerwaltungsverfahrensG* 1991 (General Administration Procedure Law).

during confession or under the obligation of confidentiality resulting from their pastoral office. As this provision protects individual freedom of religion, it also applies to pastors of denominations not legally recognised.

2. Special Status in Military Law

The following persons are exempt from military service or social service for conscientious objectors, if they belong to a legally recognised church or religious community: priests; persons who work in pastoral care or religious teaching on the basis of a completed course of theological studies; members of religious orders after taking life-long vows; students of theology who are preparing for spiritual office (Section 18(3) *WehrG* 1990 (Defence Act), Section 13(a)(1) *ZivildienstG* 1986 (Civilian Service Act).

XII. Matrimonial and Family Law

1. Religious Upbringing of Children[31]

The parents of children who have not yet attained majority in religious matters may for as long as the marriage continues freely agree on the denomination or philosophy according to which they wish to bring up their children. The agreement ends with the death of either spouse. If one person has sole custody of a child he may decide on the nature of his or her religious upbringing. Guardians and trustees, however, require the authorisation of the guardianship court. After divorce the parent not entrusted with the child's upbringing merely has a right of comment in the case of a change of religion.[32] It is al-

---

[31] Sections 1 to 3 BundesG über die religiöse Kindererziehung 1985 (Federal Law Concerning Religious Upbringing of Children).

[32] In a decision on the granting of parental custody, the Supreme Court decided that if a child is forced into the role of an outsider in society because of his or her upbringing according to the beliefs of Jehovah's Witnesses or runs health risks (prohibition of blood transfusions), this must be considered as a relevant factor: OGH 3.9.1986, 1 Ob 586/86 (ÖAKR 37/1987/88, pp 104), and OGH 12.5.1993, 3 Ob 521/93 (ÖAKR 42/1993). In the first case the matter was taken to the Court of Human Rights in Strasbourg which found that there

ways possible to reverse the decision. For children of twelve or over, their consent is necessary. If the parents cannot reach agreement, a decision may be sought from the guardianship court. This must grant a hearing to children of ten or over. From the age of fourteen every person has the right freely to choose a religious denomination according to his or her own conviction and if necessary must be protected in that choice by the authorities.[33]

2. Church and State Matrimonial Law

In Austria it is in principle possible to be married only by Canon Law without legal recognition in State legislation. This alternative is often chosen for economic reasons, for instance because of the higher maternity grant for single mothers. The church is here faced with the dilemma of insuring the continued significance of its concept of marriage in society by encouraging the adoption of the appropriate laws. On one hand it demands the support of marriage and the family, on the other it risks participating in the exploitation of social welfare institutions by allowing a Church wedding without a State marriage.

XIII. Sect Office

By way of the controversial BundesG über die Einrichtung einer Dokumentations- und Informationsstelle für Sektenfragen 1998 (Federal Act on the Establishment of an Office on Documentation and Information about Sects) a legal basis for state informative action was created in relation to new religious movements. The law does not apply to recognised churches and religious communities nor to their institutions (Section 1(2)).
The "Bundesstelle für Sektenfragen" (Federal Office for Sect Issues) is structured as an independent institution of public law. Its tasks comprise the documentation and information about dangers that can come from programmes or activities of sects or sect-like activities.

---

had been a violation of the right to family life according to Art. 8 ECHR and Art. 14 ECHR (22.6.1993, Nr 15/1992/360/434, ÖAKR 42/1993).
33 Section 4 BundesG über die religiöse Kindererziehung; Section 4 InterkonfG 1868.

There must be a well founded suspicion and a danger to certain legal values. The range of tasks of the Federal Office for Sect Issues is equivalent to the limits stated in the ECHR (Art. 8(2) and Art. 9(2)). Protected values to which these dangers can be related to are explicitly mentioned: life or physical or psychological well-being of human beings; the free unfolding of human personality including the freedom to enter or leave religious or philosophical communities; integrity of family life; property, financial independence of people; and the free mental and physical development of children and juveniles (Section 4(1)). To fulfil its tasks the Federal Office is especially entitled to collect; analyse and forward information; advise persons affected; co-operate and exchange information with internal and foreign authorities; and to develop, supervise and co-ordinate research projects.

XIV. Provisions in Criminal Law

The classification of certain acts as religious offences is essentially to protect the religious peace and people's religious convictions against disparagement or violation. For this reason the StGB does not apply only to legally recognised churches or religious communities, but to all those with a permanent community situated within the national territory.
As religious offences in the narrower sense, the StGB cites the disparagement of religious doctrines[34] and the disturbance of a religious worship.[35] In addition, the religious dimension forms a qualifying characteristic in the case of certain other offences, for instance in the case of the defamation of a member of the clergy in the exercise of his or her office, or damage to or theft of objects used for the pur-

---

34 According to Section 188: a person who derides or disparages a person or an object worshipped by a church or religious community on Austrian territory, or a religious doctrine, a legally permitted tradition or a legally permitted institution of such a church or religious community in circumstances in which such behaviour is apt to cause a breach of the peace, is punishable with a prison sentence up to six months or a fine of up to 360 daily instalments.

35 According to Section 189(1), a person who prevents or disrupts a legally permissible church service or a similar form of religious ceremony or worship of a church or religious community on Austrian territory by violence or the threat of violence is punishable with a prison sentence of 2 years. Sect 2 contains less serious disruptions of religious worship by mischief.

poses of worship or devotion, or damage to property or theft in rooms serving for worship (StGB Sections 126 and 128).

XV. Bibliography

Collection of Laws
I. Gampl/R. Potz/B. Schinkele, Österreichisches Staatskirchenrecht. Gesetze, Materialien, Rechtsprechung. Vol. 1, Wien 1990, Vol. 2, Vienna 1993.

Studies and reference books
H. Kalb/R. Potz/B. Schinkele, Religionsrecht, Vienna 2003.
H. Schwendenwein, Österreichisches Staatskirchenrecht, Graz 1992.
H. Pree, Österreichisches Staatskirchenrecht, Vienna-New York 1984.
I. Gampl, Österreichisches Staatskirchenrecht, Vienna 1971.

Periodical
Österreichisches Archiv für Recht und Religion (öarr), formerly Österreichisches Archiv für Kirchenrecht (ÖAKR), three issues per year, since 1950.

Michał Rynkowski[*]
State and Church in Poland

I. Social Facts

Throughout Europe, Poland is generally regarded as a Catholic State, a view which is confirmed by the statistical data. Unlike some other States the exact number of followers of the various confessions is not known in Poland, since adherence to a religion is not included in any official documents – not even school reports which give the grades obtained in religious instruction. This situation is legally provided for by the Constitution.[1] Moreover, in the 2002 Census there was no question as to membership of churches and faith communities. Therefore the figures in the table below are only estimates, according to the number of baptisms or according to the data given by each community itself. The estimates are as follows:[2]

Church or Religious Community	Number of parishes or respective entities	Number of clergy	Number of members
Catholic Church/Latin Rite	10,018	28,259	34,498,271
Orthodox Church	223	296	509,500
Catholic Church/Byz.-Ukr. Rite	137	71	123,000
Jehovah's Witnesses	1,769		123,034
Augsburg Confession (Lutheran) Church	292	175	86,880
Old-Catholic Church of the Mariavites	37	27	24,288
Polish-Catholic Church	83	106	22,422
Pentecostal Church	186	324	20,027

---

* The author thanks Dr. Maciej Lis from the Lutheran Church in Poland for his valuable advice while writing this paper.
1 No one may be compelled by organs of public authority to disclose his philosophy of life, religious convictions or belief – Constitution, Art. 53(7).
2 Only churches and faith communities with a minimum of 5,000 baptised/members are included. The number of members of the Jewish Cult Community is about 1,250. Complete data can be found in: Maly rocznik statystyczny, GUS, Warszawa 2003, str. 135-137.

Church or Religious Community	Number of parishes or respective entities	Number of clergy	Number of members
Seventh Day Adventist Church	151	69	9,492
Catholic Church/Armenian Rite			8,000
New Apostolic Church	52	50	5,433
Islamic Religious Community	6	5	5,123
International Society for Krishna-Consciousness	5	275	5,043
Christian Church of the Preachers of the Gospel	43	43	5,000

The following should be noted with regard to this table:

1) The numbers given above represent the numbers of baptised/members, which are not the same as the number of a people attending religious ceremonies: in the Catholic Church about 40 % of the baptised attend Sunday services, depending on the region of Poland and the size of the town; in the Lutheran Church the average attendance is 85 % of the baptised.
2) The Catholic Church in Poland comprises four rites: Latin (normally called Roman Catholic), Armenian, Byzantine-Slavic (with only one parish Kostomłoty near Terespol) and Byzantine-Ukrainian (normally called Greek-Catholic). All these rites acknowledge the Pope as head of the Catholic Church. The Law of 1989 governing the relationship between the State and the Catholic Church applies to all four rites.
3) Contrary to that, the Polish-Catholic Church was created in the USA in the 19th century; their members came to Poland only after 1918. This church is registered in the official register of churches and religious communities (see (4) below) separately from the Catholic Church. The Church is a member of the Union of Utrecht of the Old Catholic Churches and does not recognise the Pope as head of the Church.
4) The data of the first Census (1921) after the rebirth of Poland may be taken as a comparison:[3] at that time 63.8 % of the population declared themselves to be Roman Catholic, 11.2 % Greek Catho-

---

[3] Historia Polski w liczbach (The History of Poland in data), GUS, Warszawa 2003, p. 385.

lic, 10.5 % Orthodox, 10.5 % were of Jewish belief, 3.7 % Protestant, and 0.3 % belonged to other faith communities.

The number of those attending Mass declined shortly after 1989, but has remained relatively stable since. Many Catholic University churches in university towns are well attended by students and non-students alike.

II. Historical Background

The year 966, during which Duke Mieszko was baptised on the occasion of his marriage with the Bohemian princess Dąbrówka (Dobrava), is regarded as the foundation year of the Polish State and the birth of Christianity on Polish soil. In 968 the first diocese was founded in Poznan; this was followed in the year 1000 by the Archbishopric of Gniezno and dioceses in Krakow, Kolobrzeg and Wroclaw. From the beginning, Poland was part of Western Christendom. In 1385 Lithuania was christianised as a consequence of a spectacular marriage: the Polish King [sic], Saint Jadwiga (Hedwig from the House of Anjou), married the Lithuanian Grand Duke Jagello. A final union between the two States was established only in 1569 in Lublin. Thus was created a republic consisting of both nations (Rzeczpospolita Obojga Narodów): a multinational and multi-religious state, in which each noble had a passive and active right: either to elect the king or to be elected as king. This period, which lasted until the third partition of Poland in 1795, is known as the First Republic and existed as a republic of the nobles.
In the first half of the 16th century relatively large numbers of the richer strata of society followed Lutheranism, Calvinism, and the "Polish brothers" (the so-called Arians, who opposed the doctrine of the Trinity). During the course of the Counter-Reformation many returned to Catholicism, but in the 16th century Poland experienced relative religious freedom compared with other European States. In the time between the death of one king and the election of the next, the Primate, the Archbishop of Gniezno, was ex officio the Interrex. Of particular importance was the Confederation of Warsaw of 1573, which introduced the principle of the equal treatment of religions. In 1596 an agreement was concluded between the Catholics and that

part of the Orthodox Church which had kept to their customs but which recognised the Pope as head of the church: this was the foundation of the Byzantine-Ukrainian rite. In 1668 a law was adopted according to which a change from Catholic belief to any other should incur the death penalty. In the Kingdom of Poland there was very little persecution of Protestants, however, and only a limited number of witch trials took place. Only as late as 1716 was the building of Protestant churches prohibited. In 1768 religious tolerance was once again recognised in law. The Polish Constitution adopted on 3 May 1792 was the first modern constitution in Europe; it contained some provisions relevant to religion. Even in the Preamble it was stated: "In the name of God within the Trinity", and in Article 1 it was established that "The dominant national religion is and will be the holy religious faith with all its rights. The change from the ruling religion to any other confession will be punished as Apostasy. Yet, because our same belief orders us to love other brothers we shall offer all people of any confession religious peace and government protection, and we guarantee the freedom of all rites and religions in Polish territories according to the laws".

The Constitution was, however, not able to prevent the end of the First Republic, and so came the complete partition of Poland in the years 1772, 1793 and 1795. During this time the church played a special role in preserving Polish identity, culture, and language, a fact which Cardinal Mieczysław Ledóchowski, Archbishop of Gniezno, confirmed during his imprisonment in the Prussian prison. In 1916 a Regency Council of three members was constituted in which the Archbishop of Warsaw, Cardinal Kakowski, played a leading role. The first constitution after the partitions, the Constitution of March 1921, contained only a short Invocatio Dei: "In the name of the almighty God", by way of a compromise in recognition of the Jewish and Muslim communities. The first Concordat with the Holy See was concluded in the year 1925.[4]

The war and post-war periods were characterised by the great personalities of three cardinals: Adam Stefan Sapieha, Stefan Wyszyński, and Karol Wojtyła. The Archbishop of Krakow, Adam Stefan Sapieha, offered unprecedented resistance against the occupying powers of the First and Second World Wars, especially against the Governor General H. Frank. The two heroes of the second half of the 20th century – Cardinals Stefan Wyszyński and Karol Wojtyła (the

---

[4] The historical development, especially during the years 1921-1989, is described by W. Wysoczański in his contribution: Beziehungen zwischen Kirche und Staat in Polen unter besonderer Berücksichtigung der Rechtslage, in: ÖAfKR, 1991, issue 1, p. 145.

latter elected as Pope John Paul II in 1978) successfully challenged the communist regime. Ostensibly favourable laws (such as that introducing the church fund which only existed on paper), violations of existing laws (expropriation of the property against the provisions of this law), and numerous mysterious deaths of clergy – always caused by "unknown delinquents" – were permanent features of the anti-church policy of the communist regime.

The majority of the norms that are in force today were adopted shortly before or after the political changes that came about in 1989. An important change was brought about by the Law of 1989 guaranteeing the freedoms of conscience and confession, which was negotiated with the (Catholic) Bishops' Conference. Recent steps in the history of Polish civil ecclesiastical law are marked by the Concordat of 1993[5] and by the Constitution of 1997, which are discussed below.

III. Legal Sources

1. First, two important points about terminology: the Polish legislator uses the term "Kościoły i inne związki wyznaniowe", which is correctly translated as "Churches and other faith communities". In foreign publications they usually are called "Churches and religious communities". The predominantly German term "Staatskirchenrecht" (Civil ecclesiastical law or state church law), although known in Polish legal writing, is not used in relation to Poland. The field of law governing these questions is usually called "prawo wyznaniowe" (confessional law).[6] In the Constitution and in the law generally the terms "wolność religii" (freedom of religion) or "wolność wyznania" (freedom of confession) are used. The predominant opinion holds that in practice no significance should be attributed to this difference in mere language.

The provisions of civil ecclesiastical law may be distinguished in two ways: those which relate to all churches and religious communities (general confessional law) and those provisions which relate to specific churches and religious communities (specific confessional law).

---

5 Information about the history and contents of the current Concordat may be found in: B. W. Zubert: Kirche und Staat in Polen im Rahmen des neuen Konkordats, ÖAfKR, 1995/1997, issue 2, p. 491-513.
6 All the handbooks in Poland bear such titles, see literature section below.

In particular the Constitution of 1997 and the Law of 1989 on the guarantees of freedom of conscience and confession belong to the first group.

The most important source of Polish law on religion is the Constitution of the Republic of 2 April 1997. The Constitution – insofar it does not state otherwise – is directly applicable (Art. 8(2)), a fact that is relevant in relation to its provisions on religion. According to Article 87 the following categories of legal acts are general legal sources of the Republic: the Constitution, ratified international treaties, laws and ordinances. In all these categories of legal acts one can, to various degrees, find elements of the law on religion. Hence it is necessary to deal with them here.

The Constitution itself contains some provisions relevant to religion: on the legal status of churches and other religious communities (Art. 25), the right of national and ethnical minorities to the preservation of their religious identity (Art. 35), religious instruction in schools (Art. 48), freedom of religion (Art. 53), and freedom of assembly (Art. 57). The Preamble to the Constitution is remarkable in that it contains an Invocatio Dei that was the result of difficult negotiations: "...the Polish Nation - all citizens of the Republic, both those who believe in God as the source of truth, justice, good and beauty, as well as those not sharing such faith but respecting those universal values as arising from other sources". This preamble was presented to the European Convention as a possible solution of the issue for the Constitution for Europe.

In relation to the legal status of churches and religious communities Article 25 is of fundamental significance. It reads as follows:[7]

> 1. Churches and other religious organizations shall have equal rights.
> 2. Public authorities in the Republic of Poland shall be impartial in matters of personal conviction, whether religious or philosophical, or in relation to outlooks on life, and shall ensure their freedom of expression within public life.
> 3. The relationship between the State and churches and other religious organizations shall be based on the principle of respect for their autonomy and the mutual independence of each in its own sphere, as well as on the principle of cooperation for the individual and the common good.
> 4. The relations between the Republic of Poland and the Roman Catholic Church shall be determined by international treaty concluded with the Holy See, and by statute.
> 5. The relations between the Republic of Poland and other churches and religious organizations shall be determined by statutes adopted pursuant

---

[7] Translation: Chancellery of the Sejm, Warsaw 1999.

to agreements concluded between their appropriate representatives and the Council of Ministers.

Sections 1 to 4 raise no specific controversies. In relation to Section 5, representatives of churches and religious communities note that at the time of writing the treaties promised in the Constitution have not been concluded; indeed, negotiations have scarcely begun. The current laws on the relationship of the State with the various churches and religious communities are unilateral acts of the State, not treaties or agreements comparable to treaties. From a legal point of view churches and religious communities have, in theory, the same rights. In practice there are some inequalities in view of the greater presence and influence of Roman Catholic clergy compared with clergy of other denominations, which makes it difficult to avoid taking into account the overwhelming majority of Catholics.

Article 53 of the Constitution is also comprehensive, and it is made up of seven sections. According to its Section 1, freedom of conscience and religion is guaranteed to everybody. This freedom comprises (Sect. 2) various forms of the exercise of this right, among them the right of parents to secure the moral and religious education and teaching of their children. The limits to religious freedom in Section 5 are similar to the principles in the European Convention on Human Rights; limitations must be necessary for the protection of the security of the State, public order, health, morals, and freedoms and rights of others. According to Article 85(3) civilian service is a possible alternative to military service on the grounds of religious attitudes and moral convictions.

Alongside the Constitution, the Law on the guarantees of freedom of conscience and confession of 17 May 1989 (referred to below as the Law of 1989) is the basis of the whole system of civil ecclesiastical law in Poland.[8] This law was introduced two weeks before the historic elections of 4 June 1989, that is before the change of the political system. It has the legal character of a lex generalis, from which a lex specialis can deviate. Article 7 of the Law states that aliens in the territory of the republic enjoy the same freedom of confession as Polish citizens.

2. Commentaries and handbooks insist that the term or the idea of separation of state and church has been expressed only very rarely since 1989 for historical reasons. Article 10 of the Law of 1989 says

---

8   Dz. U. (Polish Official Journal) 1989 No. 29, Item 155, important changes were introduced especially by the amendment of 30.05.1998, Dz. U. 98, No 59, Item 375.

that the Republic of Poland is a State which is secular and neutral in questions of religion and Weltanschauung. According to Article 16 of the same Law the State co-operates with churches and religious communities in preserving peace, framing the terms of development of the State, and in fighting malaise in society. This co-operation also exists in relation to the protection, restoration, and extension of monuments of architecture, arts, and religious literature that form part of Poland's cultural heritage (Art. 17). Co-operation is a term also used in the Concordat and other laws.

IV. Legal Status of Churches and Religious Communities

1. The legal status of a corporation under public law is not recognised in relation to churches and faith communities in current Polish law.[9] Today, such a status is given only to territorial entities of the State. The differences between churches and faith communities are marked by the method of registration, but all subjects lawfully registered enjoy the same rights from a legal perspective. Churches and faith communities can be distinguished as forming two groups according to their recognition or registration:
1) Those which function according to a special law that governs the relations between a specific church or religious community and the State, or
2) Those that function on the basis of the law on the guarantees of the freedom of conscience and confession of 1989 which created a general framework for all churches and religious communities in Poland.

Only 14 of the more than 150 recognised or registered churches and religious communities belong to the first group, but this group comprises all of the large and, at the same time oldest, religious communities (with the exception of Jehovah's Witnesses which, though being the fourth largest community, does not operate on the basis of a special law, but on the basis of the Law of 1989). To the first group belong the following churches and religious communities, in chronological order (with the date of the relevant law in brackets): Eastern Old Rites Church (Ordinance [sic] of the President of the Republic,

---

9 Some churches and religious communities had enjoyed such a status to a certain extent before the Second World War.

22 March 1928), Islamic Religious Community (21 April 19 36), Karaim Religious Community (21 April 19 36), Catholic Church (17 May 1989), Polish Autocephalous Orthodox Church (4 July 1991), the Augsburg-Confession Church in the Republic of Poland (henceforth referred to as the Lutheran Church) (13 May 1994), Protestant Reformed Church (13 May 1994), Protestant Methodist Church (30 June 1995), Baptist Christians Church (30 June 1995), Seventh Day Adventists Church (30 June 1995) Polish-Catholic Church (30 June 1995), Union of Jewish Confessional Communities (20 February 1997), Catholic Church of the Mariavites (20 February 1997), Old Catholic Church of the Mariavites (20 February 1997), Pentecostal Church (20 February 1997).

The civil legal personality of the various confessional entities or institutions was granted in the above-mentioned laws by recognising the different levels and kinds of church institutions as having legal capacity. The Concordat explicitly recognised the legal personality of the Catholic Church entities if they acquired this status according to canon law. In rare cases, legal personality is granted by way of an Ordinance of the Minister for the Interior and Administration: such cases include the foundation of the Catholic "Caritas", the Protestant "Diaconic Work" or the broadcasting institution "Orthodoxia".

Since 1998 it has been possible for a group of at least 100 Polish citizens with full legal capacity to apply for the registration of a church or religious community. In the first version of the Law of 1989, 15 persons were needed as the minimum number of members; this led to some misuse of the right especially in relation to exemption from military service, taxation benefits, and duty-free imports. The Minister for the Interior and Administration is competent to enter communities in the register. According to the Law of 1989 and the Ordinance of 31 March 1999 on the registration of churches and religious communities, the application must contain the following: a list of members, information about the general aims, principles of doctrine and ritual practice, location and subordinate bodies, and statutes. Since 1989 about 150 churches and religious communities have been registered; 48 applications were refused – in relation to some churches and religious communities the application has been refused repeatedly because of formal criteria. The criteria are equivalent to those of Article 9(2) of the European Convention on Human Rights, and the Minister checks, inter alia, on whether the aims and the doctrines of a church or religious community are likely to endanger public order or security, or are contrary to the right to life, morals, or the rights of parents. Because of this, the Raelians who were the first to claim the cloning of a human being in 2002 were not registered in the Polish register[10] as early as 1998. The refusal by the Minister was upheld by the Main Administrative Court (NSA) in a decision of 22 January 1999.

In the year 1997 the Prime Minister set up an inter-ministerial committee on new religious movements[11] which published in 2000 a "Report About Some Phenomena Related to the Activities of Sects". The information contained in the report was of a general nature; a special institution to monitor sects was not established. The committee was dissolved in 2002 (Order of 22 March 2002). The Dominicans in particular have been very active in Poland, monitoring and fighting sects by establishing so-called sect-centres in their monasteries in which information is gathered about the activities of sects and help offered to victims and their families.[12]

V. Churches and Culture

1. Churches and religious communities have the right to establish and operate schools, kindergartens, and other educational institutions (Art. 21, Law of 1989). The proportion of confessional schools, however, is relatively small, and they educate only about 1 % of the total number of pupils. Non-Catholic educational institutions have also been established. For example, the Lutheran Church in Poland runs three kindergartens, two primary schools, one bilingual Polish-German primary school, five secondary schools, and one bible school. Moreover, the Diaconic Work in Wrocław runs a training and rehabilitation centre for disabled people (CeKiRON).

2. Religious instruction was abolished shortly after the Second World War in all schools. Since confessional schools had also been abolished, religious instruction took place in parish houses throughout Poland. Only in 1990 – by way of an Order by the Government Minister that was intensively discussed in legal circles – did religion return to the school curriculum. Later, this was settled by an Ordinance of the Minister for National Education of 1992. According to the Or-

---

10 Cf. the list of registered churches and religious communities: www.mswia.gov.pl/index1_s.html.
11 Order of 25 August 1997, Monitor Polski No 54, Item 513.
12 Cf. internet: www.dominikanie.pl.

dinance the desire of the parents for their child to take part in religious instruction courses may be "declared in a most simple way". In practical terms, it is assumed that children take part in these courses. If the parents (and in secondary schools, the pupils themselves) want it, instruction in ethics may be offered as an alternative. If seven or more pupils, or their parents, of any given confession request it, religious instruction should be offered. If the number of children of a specific confession is between three and seven, religious instruction should be offered in co-operation between the school and the religious community. If the number of children is smaller, religious instruction is given in the respective church institutions. In all cases the teacher of religion must have a teaching qualification as stated in the Agreement between the Minister of National Education, the Bishops' Conference, and the Polish Ecumenical Council (see section XII, below).

3. Theological faculties returned to State Universities only in the 1990s, after over 40 years' prohibition. The Catholic University in Lublin (KUL) always had a theological faculty, but the KUL was a really special case in the whole Eastern bloc; between the war and 1989 it was maintained as a non-State university and run exclusively on private donations. After the end of communist rule some changes took place: the KUL is now financed according to the Law of 14 June 1991 from the State budget; this is also the case for the pontifical theological faculty in Krakow (Law of 26 June 1997), and for the Kardynał-Wyszyński University in Warsaw which was founded in 1999 and which evolved from the Academy of Catholic Theology (Law of 3 September 1999).

Currently, there are theological faculties in the State Universities in Katowice, Toruń, Poznań, Opole, Olsztyn. In the two latter cases the faculties were established together with the creation of the universities in the 1990s. In the University of Białystok there is a faculty in which Catholic as well as Orthodox theology is taught. In Wrocław and Gdańsk the University Senates have voted against the establishment of theological faculties.

In addition to the Catholic institutions there is in Warsaw the "Christian Theological Academy", which takes care of the training of the non-Roman Catholic clergy and theologians. It emerged from the Evangelical-theological Faculty of the University of Warsaw which was dissolved in 1954. The Christian Theological Academy has been in existence ever since – even between 1954 and 1989 – but only in the year 2000 was funding by the State budget secured by law. In addition to the Academy there is a bible seminary in Wrocław with a right to award degrees, which is run in co-operation with the American Baptist Church.

4. Churches and religious communities are active in the field of the media in different ways. On public television they broadcast religious programmes explicitly provided for in the Concordat and laws. According to the agreement between the Polish Ecumenical Council and the public television providers there is an editorial committee responsible for ecumenical religious programmes. There are, however, no official representatives serving ex officio on supervisory or advisory councils. Some churches and religious communities also have their own broadcasting stations: there are both national and regional Catholic radio stations, and in addition there is Radio "Orthodoxia". With State permission equivalent to a law there is even a confessional television station: "Trwam".

According to Article 25 of the Law of 1989, churches and religious communities may operate publishing houses and edit journals and books, provided that they observe the general law in this field. For this purpose they may receive paper, machinery, and relevant equipment as donations from abroad. The import of objects serving cult and charity is duty-free (Art. 13(7), Law of 1989)

VI. Labour Law

A person's religious affiliation is not stated in any official document and must not be inquired about for employment purposes.

The terms of work for clergy are laid out in the internal statutes of each respective church or religious community. This applies especially to the formal requirements, the hierarchy and routine of office, compensation for torts committed by clergy, and terms of responsibility. In the Lutheran Church, for example, "vocation" is the term for an agreement between the pastor and the parish. This agreement must meet certain standards relating to the pay within the group of clergymen (deacon, pastor, bishop, etc.) or to their rights after retirement. The same rules of employment law apply to laypeople employed in confessional institutions as to any other persons. A certain degree of loyalty is expected from those lay employees, however, according to the ethos of the religion.

Work-free holidays for the Catholics have been defined in Article 9 of the Concordat, making those days State holidays. In relation to other churches and religious communities the law has defined work-free days with the provision that the members of the respective confession have the right to a work-free, but unpaid, day.

VII. Marriage and Family Law

"From the time on in which a canonical marriage is concluded it has the same effect as has a marriage concluded according to Polish law", according to Article 10 of the Concordat. This provision was one of the reasons for the long delay in the ratification of the Concordat by Parliament: representatives of the left wing SLD-Party feared that the clergy would not fulfil their duty to notify the registrar's office in time or in the correct manner. So-called "concordat marriages" have been possible since November 1998, that is since the ratification and coming into force of the Concordat and after the amendment of the family code by the Law of 24 July 1998. Marriages that have been solemnised according to the confessional provisions of the following churches and religious communities have effect in civil law: the Catholic Church, Orthodox Church, Lutheran Church, Reformed Church, Methodist Church, the Baptist Christians, Seventh Day Adventists, the Polish Catholic Church, the Union of the Jewish Confessional Communities, the Old-Catholic Mariavites and the Pentecostal Church. Marriages conducted by the following religious communities whose relations with the State are governed by a special law are not recognised: the Catholic Church of the Mariavites, the Eastern Old-Rites Church, the Islamic Religious Union and the Karaim Religious Union. According to commentators, the latter churches and religious communities declared no interest in the so-called concordat marriage.
The provisions in the field of marriage law were the basis for a statement by the Catholic Church that the Concordat also privileged other churches and religious communities because, following the Concordat, provisions were made which gave equal status to these bodies or to their members.
A confessional marriage may be concluded only after confirmation from the registrar's office that a marriage between the parties is legally possible (to guard against bigamy). It should be stated at this point that according to Article 18 of the Polish Constitution a mar-

riage "as a union of a man and a woman...shall be placed under the protection and care of the Republic of Poland".

An amendment to the Constitution would be necessary to introduce same-sex marriage, but this is not on the agenda despite some voices being raised in political debate. Article 18 is part of Chapter I; this is relevant insofar as chapter XII of the Constitution provides for a more difficult amendment procedure for chapters I, II (Fundamental Rights), and XII. An important condition for a confessional marriage to have civil effect is that the minister has to notify the local registrar's office of the marriage within five days. In addition to that, a new legal procedure was introduced in 1999, called Separation, which in principle is equal to divorce; however, even after this, a subsequent marriage is not possible.
Divorce with civil effects (including re-marriage) is only possible by way of a court procedure before a State court. In order to protect the family, only the circuit court (sąd okręgowy) is competent in marriage cases, not the more local municipal court (sąd rejonowy).

VIII. Financing of Churches

Article 10 of the Law of 1989 says that the State and its entities may not provide financial assistance to churches and other religious communities. Exceptions are provided for by law or by provisions passed on the basis of a law. The churches and religious communities exist and operate thanks to the voluntary donations of believers. There is no tradition of a church tax in Poland, though in recent years there has been public discussion about the introduction of such a tax.[13] The most important financial sources for all churches and religious communities are: Sunday collections, donations (in most cases quasi fees) for baptism, marriage, and burial, and donations on the occasion of the annual "pastoral visit", normally called "kolęda". This takes place in the Catholic Church all over Poland at around Christmas time, usually in January: a priest or some other cleric pays home visits to all the inhabitants of the parish who so wish, and dis-

---

13 The Lutheran Church in Poland has introduced internally a kind of church-tax (1 % of the income), which is however not comparable with the German system. Above all, there is no provision for the levy of the tax through State authorities.

cusses with them any questions concerning their religious or societal life.

Church property and income are subject to general tax provisions, as stated by law. There are, however, many legal exemptions with the consequence that churches and religious communities pay hardly any tax for their non-economic activity. In the field of economic activities the confessional entities are liable to consumption tax and local taxes. They are liable to income tax for that part of their income which is not intended to be used for the purposes of religious observances or the renovation of buildings. The clergy of all churches and religious communities are, according to the Law of 20 November 1998, liable to a quarterly over-all tax based on the size of the parish for pastors (between 319 PLN and 1136 PLN) and the size of the parish plus the size of the town for vicars.

The current left-wing government has it in mind to introduce a change in this field: today, taxpayers can deduct from their tax liability donations to churches and religious communities up to 10 % of their income. The government plans to cut this sum to 350 PLN (about 80 €) per year which is less than 1 % of average income. In addition, money given for public elections should also be liable to taxation at a rate of 19 %. In this way churches and religious communities would be treated equally with other legal persons of normal law, a fact that would go against Polish tradition.

The clergy do not receive payment from the State for carrying out their priestly duties. They do, however, receive a remuneration when they work as teachers of religion in schools. In the school year 1990/1 when religious instruction was reintroduced after many years, the church waived the payment of the teachers of religion in view of the crisis in State finances (immediately after the breakdown of the communist regime this applied especially to priests and nuns; in the ensuing years the number of lay persons as teachers of religion has continued to increase). It has turned out, though, that this was inconsistent with Polish labour law, because the person affected cannot waive his or her pay.

As far as social insurance is concerned, individual clergy are responsible for their own contributions; superiors of religious orders are responsible for the contributions of the members of that order. The clergy pay 20 % of the sum themselves; the rest is paid from the church fund. The church fund was created in 1950 after the expropriation of the property of various churches and religious communities. In the beginning it existed only on paper; it took up its proper function as recently as the 1990s.

A question of current importance is the restitution of church property, the so-called "regulation process". The churches in Poland, among them the Catholic Church, never were big land-owners (in total they owned 150,000 hectares) but, nevertheless, the main part of their property was expropriated after the war. The restitution process takes place on the basis of several laws and it amounts to a complex problem. In charge of the process are so-called "regulation committees" – mixed committees made up of representatives of the Ministry of the Interior and of the churches and religious communities. They function as a kind of arbitration court. In total there are five committees: committees for specific religious communities (i.e. the Catholic Church, the Lutheran Church, the Orthodox Church and the Jewish Religious Communities), and a general committee, which was appointed on the basis of an amendment to the Law of 1989; the procedure of this general committee is laid down in an Ordinance of the Minister of the Interior and Administration of 9 February 2000. This committee dealing with the claims of the other entitled churches and religious communities (Reformed Church, Methodist Church, Christ-Baptist Church, Adventist Church) is made up of 22 members: the Minister appoints four representatives, and the churches and religious communities appoint a further 18 members. The decisions of all these committees have the legal effect of a court decision. Due to obvious historical and statistical considerations, this process is particularly relevant to the Catholic Church and the Lutheran Church in West Poland. The claims of the Jewish cult communities are a special case, because their claims mostly refer to the restitution of property that had been taken away by the German Reich between 1933 and 1945. It is remarkable that the settlement of the restitution of church property is really a special case in the Polish legal system, since up to now no "law on re-privatisation" has been drafted.

IX. *Pastoral Care in Public Institutions*

The pastoral care in the armed forces, the police, in hospitals, in medical, charitable, or care institutions, as well as in prisons, is governed by the Law of 1989, by further laws on the relationship of the State with various churches and religious communities, and by Ordinances. Up to now, no specific controversies have emerged in this respect. There are three dioceses in the military forces: a Catholic, an

Orthodox, and a Lutheran. The Catholic military bishop (more specifically: biskup polowy – field bishop) is at the same time a General of second degree (generał dywizji), the bishops of other denominations have the rank of Colonel up to General first degree (generał brygady).

X. *Criminal Law and Religions*

A general prohibition on discrimination has been incorporated in Article 32 of the Constitution of the Republic. Further provisions can be found in the Criminal Code of 1997, Chapter XXIV, Articles 194-196. The Criminal Code provides in each case for three different kinds of possible sanctions: a fine, the restriction of liberty, and imprisonment for up to two years. Liable to punishment are all actions by which a person is restricted or impaired in his or her rights because of adherence or non-adherence to a belief; it is also an offence to disturb the public worship of a church or religious community that enjoys legally recognised status – it is to be noted that the term "public worship" can be interpreted extensively, and it is certainly not limited to Catholic Mass or other Christian services. The same punishment applies to a person who disturbs the ceremony of burial or marriage. A person is also liable who injures the religious feelings of another person or who publicly shows disrespect for an object of religious cult or a place destined for the public exercise of religious rites.

The Law on the execution of punishments provides in its Article 107 that a person who has committed a crime for political or religious reasons must not be imprisoned together with a 'normal' criminal; he or she has the right to own clothing and shoes, and is not obliged to work. These privileges do not apply when the crime has been committed by force.

XI. Legal Status of Clergy

The clergy enjoy the same rights and have the same duties as all other citizens in all fields of state, political, economic, societal and cultural life. They are exempt from those duties that contradict the functions of a minister (Art. 12, Law of 1989). This applies especially to exemption from military service; in this case the statute of the religious community must explicitly state who is a minister of the community, the method of their election or appointment, and the ministerial tasks. The necessary conditions for exemption from military service are stated by the Main Administrative Court in a judgment of 19 September 2000.[14] The laws on election to the Sejm, to the Senate or to the organs of local self-administration do not provide for any restrictions for clergy, but because of tradition or of internal church provisions (as for example in the Lutheran Church) clergy do not run for public office. Shortly after 1989 clergy tried to bring political influence to bear on believers during the elections, but this turned out to be in vain; since then, clergy have merely stressed the civil obligation to participate in elections, without mentioning the names of parties or of their candidates.

The secret of the confessional is protected in the Civil Procedure Code of 1964 (Art. 261(2)(2)) as well as in the Criminal Procedure Code of 1997 (Art. 178).

XII. Final Remarks

Though the number those attending Mass is not nearly as high as the number of its baptised members, the Catholic Church with its three cardinals (the Archbishops of Warsaw, Krakow and Wroclaw), 121 bishops, and almost 30,000 priests is without any doubt the most important and most influential religious community in Poland. Seven other big churches (Lutherans, Methodists, Baptists, Mariavites, Orthodox, Reformed and Polish-Catholic) founded the Polish Ecumenical Council (Polska Rada Ekumeniczna) in 1989; although the Catholic Church is not its member, it works together with the PRE. A certain new spirit may be seen in the establishment of church build-

---

14 NSA sygn. III S.A. 1411/00.

ings that are used by two denominations or that have even been consecrated by bishops of two different denominations, as happened in Wroclaw in 2000. Caritas, Diaconic Work and the Orthodox Eleos sell candles together before Christmas; the proceeds are used for the support of children in need. The churches and religious communities make common statements in relation to draft laws and draft ordinances that relate to their social and charitable activities, and they organise joint conferences to discuss such questions.

The most important sign of ecumenical co-operation was the Common Declaration of seven churches (Catholic, Lutheran, Orthodox, Methodist, Polish-Catholic and Old-Catholic Church of the Mariavites) of 23 January 2000, in which they mutually recognised each others' baptisms. A special example can be found in Wroclaw, where bishops of five denominations have their seat: Roman-Catholic, Greek-Catholic, Polish-Catholic, Lutheran, and Orthodox. Here, a "quarter of mutual respect" can be found, in which within a range of about 1,000 metres there are Roman-Catholic, Lutheran, and Orthodox churches, and a Jewish synagogue. The city of Wroclaw has recognised this example of practical cooperation, including co-operation in religious instruction in schools, by a City Award.

XIII. Literature

Basic reference books in the Polish language:

J. *Krukowski, K.Warchałowski*, Polskie prawo wyznaniowe [Polish Confessional Law], Warszawa 2000.

H. *Misztal*, Prawo wyznaniowe [Confessional Law], Lublin 2000.

M. *Pietrzak*, Prawo wyznaniowe [Confessional Law], Warszawa 1999.

W. *Uruszczak, Z. Zarzycki*, Prawo wyznaniowe. Zbiór przepisów [Confessional Law, Collection of Texts], Kraków 2003.

M. *Winiarczyk-Kossakowska*: Państwowe prawo wyznaniowe w praktyce administracyjnej [State Confessional Law in Administrative Practice], Warszawa 1994.

W. *Wysoczański, M. Pietrzak*, Prawo kościołów i związków wyznaniowych niekatolickich w Polsce [The Law of Non-Catholic Churches and Religious Communities], Warszawa 1997.

M. *Libichowska-Żółtowska*: Kościoły i związek wyznaniowe w Polsce [Churches and Religious Communities in Poland], Warszawa 2001.

Contributions and articles in foreign languages:

M. Lis, Die Kirchen als Arbeitgeber. Tendenzschutz, Nichtdiskriminierung und Anerkennung von Schul- und Berufsausbildungen, in: Österreichisches Archiv für Recht und Religion, 2003, issue 1, p. 76-84.

A. Orszulik, Bericht über Polen, in: Essener Gespräche 29, p. 90.

M. Pietrzak, La situation juridique des communatés religieuses en Pologne contemporaine, in: European Journal for Church-State Research, vol. 6, 1999, p. 233.

M. Rynkowski, Church and State in Poland in 2000 and in 2001, in: European Journal for Church-State Research, vol. 9, 2002, p. 279-290.

R. Sobański, Das Verhältnis von Gesellschaft, Staat und Kirche in Polen, in: B. Kämper, M. Schlagheck (Hrsg.) Zwischen nationaler Identität und europäischer Harmonisierung, Berlin 2002, p. 25.

W. Wysoczański, Beziehungen zwischen Kirche und Staat in Polen unter besonderer Berücksichtigung der Rechtslage, Österreichisches Archiv für Kirchenrecht, 1991/1.

B. W. Zubert, Kirche und Staat im Rahmen des neuen Konkordats, Österreichisches Archiv für Kirchenrecht, 1995/97, Heft 2, p. 491-513.

Vitalino Canas
State and Church in Portugal

I. Social Facts

According to official figures (the 2001 Census in Portugal), 85 % of Portuguese aged over 15 years still reckon themselves to be Roman Catholics,[1] despite an obvious decrease in actual attendance at and participation in religious ceremonies and events.[2] There are a few other religious groups with some social importance and organisation, especially in urban centres (Lisbon, Oporto, Setúbal, Braga): Orthodox, Jehovah's Witnesses, several Protestant churches, Muslims (mainly Shia Ismailis and Sunnis), Jews, Hindus and a number of newcomers such as the Maná Church and the Universal Church of God's Kingdom.[3] However, some of them, particularly the less traditional, are seen as sects rather than alternatives challenging the majority religious groups. They face indifference and in many fields they are not yet treated as equals by either State or private entities, although constitution and law now demand their equal treatment. This situation derives from the historical development of religion in Portugal.

---

1 The highest concentration of Catholics is in the Azores, with 94 % of the population; the lowest concentration is in the Lisbon region (73 %).
2 E.g., according to Catholic Church statistics the number of practising Catholics in the district of Lisbon decreased by 9 % between 1991 and 2001; further churches have been closed and the number of masses has been reduced: see *Prática Dominical no Patriarcado de Lisboa. Resultados do Recenseamento de 2001* at http://www.patriarcado-lisboa.pt.
3 Some figures from the 2001 Census: Orthodox: 17,443; Protestants: 48,301; Muslims (Shia and Sunni) 12,014; Jews: 1,773; Maná and Universal Church of God's Kingdom probably account for most of the 135, 000 members of other Christian denominations.

II. Historical Background

The assertion by the Portuguese of independence from their neighbours in the twelfth century (1143) was of course decisive for the creation of a new political body. But without recognition by the Pope in Rome, Portugal could not be considered to have a real independent existence. Over approximately the first two centuries of its existence as a new State, Portuguese sovereigns were vassals of the Catholic Popes. And the latter used their prerogatives more than once, even to excommunicate and replace kings. However, throughout the following centuries the relative positions changed (into the so-called *jurisdicionalismo*, or control of local Church institutions by the King).

By the end of the Middle Ages we still find the State and the Catholic Church intertwined. However, these two powers tried to balance the mutual benefits they could achieve. The State would use religion as legitimation and a social control device; the Church would use State power as a secular arm for the propagation of the Faith and for facilitating its mission.

The Reformation and the conflicts between Catholics and Protestants hardly reached Portugal. The ideas of Luther, Calvin, and others were not popular either at the Court or among the general population. Hence, when we arrive at the first liberal revolution and to the enactment of a Constitution based on liberal ideals (1822) we cannot be surprised at the statement in Article 25 of the first Portuguese Constitution: "the religion of the Portuguese nation is the Roman Catholic".[4][5] Other religions were allowed only to foreigners. Furthermore, their cult could not be exercised in public places or in public temples.

---

4 For the Portuguese Constitutions see *Jorge Miranda*, As Constituições Portuguesas. De 1822 ao texto actual da Constituição, 3rd ed., Lisbon, 1992.

5 For an account of religion in Portuguese constitutionalism, *Lopes Praça*, Estudos sobre a Carta Constitucional e o Acto Adicional de 1852, I, Coimbra 1878, p. 57 ff; *Marnoco e Sousa*, A Constituição Política da República Portuguesa. Comentário, Coimbra, 1913, p. 59 ff; *Marcello Caetano*, Curso de Ciência Política e Direito Constitucional, (3rd ed.), vol. II, Lisbon, 1961; Manual de Direito Administrativo, vol. I, Coimbra, 1973 (10 ed.), p. 403; *António Leite*, "A religião no Direito Constitucional Português", in Estudos sobre a Constituição, vol. III, ed. *J. Miranda*, Lisbon, 1978, p. 279; *J. Miranda*, Manual de Direito Constitucional, IV vol, 3.ª edição, Lisboa, 2000, 410-16; *Jónatas Eduardo Mendes Machado*, Liberdade Religiosa numa Comunidade Constitucional Inclusiva. Dos Direitos da Verdade aos Direitos dos Cidadãos, Coimbra, 1996, 103-26; *Antunes Varela*, Lei da liberdade religiosa e Lei de imprensa, revista e anotada, Coimbra, 1972; judgment 423/87 of the Constitutional Court in Acórdãos do Tribunal Constitucional, vol. 10 (1987), p. 77 to 160; *Sousa e Brito*, dissenting opinion to the judgment 174/93 of the Constitutional Court

During the last eighty-four years of the Monarchy, two further Constitutions were enacted: one in 1826 which, with some interruptions, was to remain in force for most of the time until the Republican revolution (October, 1910); the other in 1838 which was in force for a mere couple of years. They were both emphatic: the Catholic religion was the official religion of the State. However the author of the Constitution of 1826 (King Pedro IV himself) for the first time in Portugal granted to all the right of not "being persecuted for religious motives provided the State religion is respected and morality is not offended" (Art. 145(4)).

During the final decades of the nineteenth century, legal concessions to the freedom of religion and conscience were few despite the de facto liberalisation.

The Republican revolution (1910) was also a religious revolution. One of the most significant decisions of the new republican authorities was the proclamation of the principle of separation of Church and State (Decree of 20 April 1911, "Law of Separation"), obviously inspired by the homologous French Law of 1905. The Constitution of 1911 confirmed this principle.

Due to some radical Jacobin pressures and probably also to the conservatism of the Catholic Church, the principle of separation was not interpreted as prescribing the neutrality of State institutions towards the Church. Separation in many instances simply meant opposition.[6] Instead of being neutral, the State often adopted a negative position on religion and on the existence of God, and became involved in a permanent feud with the Catholic Church.[7] But despite some lack of moderation, this was the beginning of a long process leading to a civil rights approach.[8] Freedom of religion and conscience began to be recognised as a fundamental aspect of human dignity.

On 28 May 1926 an authoritarian uprising put an end to the liberal-republican regime. The Constitution of 1933 was a creation of Salazar. His connections with the Church hierarchy and the Catholic

---

of 17 February 1993, in Diário da República 127, of 1 June 1993; *Paulo Pulido Adragão*, A Liberdade Religiosa e o Estado, Coimbra, 2002, 279 e segs.; *Manuel Braga da Cruz*, O Estado Novo e a Igreja Católica, Lisboa, 1998.

6 See however a moderate interpretation in *João T. Magalhães Collaço*, "O regimen de separação", in Boletim da Faculdade de Direito da Universidade de Coimbra, n 31/40, 1917-18, p. 654.

7 This feud was attenuated after 1918: legislation such as Decree 3856, of 22 February 1918, encouraged the détente. Almost a century later, the debate on the "Law of Separation" (Decree of 20 April 1911) remains emotional. See the position of the Catholic Church described in *Mário Bigotte Chorão*, "Formação eclesiástica e educação católica", in A Concordata de 1940 Portugal – Santa Sé, Lisbon, 1993, p. 249.

8 Disagreeing, *Paulo Adragão*, A liberdade..., p. 322.

movement were obvious. However his Constitution was cautious in religious matters and the previous liberal-republican achievements were not completely forgotten. Article 46 of the Constitution stated that the State remained separate from the Catholic Church and any other religion. And Article 45 stressed the principle of equal treatment of the different denominations, freedom of organisation and worship, and the neutrality of teaching in State schools.

This constitutional balance was soon disrupted. Through consecutive constitutional amendments, from 1935 (Law 1910) to 1971, the Roman Catholic religion recovered its position as "the religion of the Portuguese nation" (amendment of 1951, Law 2048) or "as the traditional religion of the Portuguese nation" (amendment of 1971, Law 3/71).[9]

But the verbal changes in the Constitution were strictly semantic[10] as they were not really important. This is because the relations between State and Catholic Church were set out in the Concordat agreed between Portugal and the Holy See (as two subjects of public international law[11]) in 1940.[12] This Concordat was partially in force until December 2004.

The Concordat system was unquestionably a system of inequality. In 1971, during the "liberal phase" of the régime, Law 4/71 tried to mitigate these inequalities by acknowledging in general terms some institutional rights to be enjoyed by other denominations and some civil rights by their believers, though not equal rights compared with those enjoyed by the Catholic Church.

Nearly equal treatment was only achieved by the Constitution of 1976, further especially by Law 16/2001 of 22 June (Law of Religious Liberty). Another step towards this aim was taken with the new Concordat between the Portuguese State and the Holy See, which was signed on 18 March 2004.

---

9 Disagreeing with *Paulo Adragão*, A Liberdade..., p. 357, who argues that "the constitutional revisions were never more than a mere description of the sociological facts".
10 See the concept in *Karl Löwenstein*, Teoria de la Constitución, reprint 1982, Barcelona, p. 218.
11 Consequently the Concordat is almost unanimously taken as a treaty under international law. Cf. the examination of some difficulties in this assumption in *Jónatas Eduardo Mendes Machado*, O regime concordatário entre a *"libertas ecclesiae"* e a liberdade religiosa. Liberdade de religião ou liberdade da Igreja, Coimbra, 1993, p. 87.
12 This Concordat is just one of a long series of agreements between the Holy See and Portugal. For an account of those that are especially relevant, see *António Leite*, "Acordos entre a Santa Sé e Portugal anteriores à Concordata de 1940", in A Concordata de 1940, p. 11, and in Brotéria, n. 132, p. 493.

III. Basic Structure

1. Legal Sources

For an overview of the status of the relations between State and Church in Portugal after 1976 the relevant legal sources are:[13]
- The Constitution of the Portuguese Republic of 1976 (cited hereinafter as CPR), Articles 13, 19(6), 35(3), 41, 43(2), 51(3), 55(4), 59(1), and 288(c);
- Law 16/2001 of 22 June, Law of Religious Liberty (cited hereinafter as LRL), complemented by Decree-Law 134/2003 of 28 June, on the registration of religious legal entities; by Decree-Law 194/2003 of 23 August, regarding fees; by Decree-Law 308/2003 of 10 December, on the Commission for Religious Liberty (CRL);
- The Concordat of 7 May 1940, amended and confirmed by the Protocol of 15 February 1975 (Conc. 1940); the Concordat of 18 May 2004 (Conc. 2004)[14];
- Missionary agreement of 1940 between the Holy See and Portugal;
- Decree-Law 323/83 of 5 July, Ordinance (*Portaria*) 333/86 of 2 July, Law 46/86 of 14 October (especially Art. 47), Ordinance (*Portaria*) 831/87 of 16 October, Ordinance (*Portaria*) 344-A/88 of 31 May, Decree-Law 286/89 of 29 August (especially Art. 7), Decree-Law 407/89 of 16 November, Decree-Law 329/98, of 2 November (all relating to the teaching of religion in State schools); Decree-Law 79/83 of 9 February, and Decree-Law 345/85 of 23 August, on chaplaincy work in prisons and young people's homes.
- Decree-Law 34-A/90 of 24 January, Decree-Law 93/91 of 26 February, amended by Decree-Law 54/97 of 3 March, and Ordinance (*Portaria*) 302/91 of 18 September (on military chap-

---

[13] See *Jorge Miranda*, Manual de Direito Constitucional..., 425-8; *Vinicio Ribeiro*, Constituição da República Portuguesa, Coimbra, 1993, p. 75-76 (the latter quoting legislation, case-law and other sources); *David Valente e Alberto Franco*, Liberdade Religiosa. Nova Lei anotada e comentada, Lisboa, 2002.

[14] The Concordat of 1940 was still in force at the time of writing of this paper. Latter on it was replaced by the new Concordat which was signed by the Portugueseportuguese prime minister and the permanent secretary of the Holy See on 18 May 2004 in the Vatican and ratified on 16 November 2004. It is in force since December 2004. The present text will refer both to the content of the old Concordat and the new Concordat.

laincy);
- Regulational Decree 58/80 of 10 October, Ordinance 603/82 of 18 June, and Regulational Decree 22/90 of 3 August (on hospital chaplaincy);
- Law 31-A/98 of 14 July (Art. 45(c)), concerning the amount of broadcasting time for each denomination on State TV);
- Law 7/92 of 12 May (on objection to military service for religious reasons).
- Several scattered provisions on the ineligibility of the ministers of religion for election to Parliament and other State and municipal functions: Decree-Law 701-B/76 of 29 September (Art. 4, Municipalities), Law 14/79 of 16 May (Art. 6(1), *Assembleia da República* and regional parliaments);
- As important precedents, decisions of the Constitutional Court 92/84 of 7 November; 423/87 of 26 November, and 174/93 of 17 February.

2. System Approach

Freedom of conscience and religion are inalienable rights of all citizens of all denominations. Citizens without religious convictions[15] should be treated equally. State bodies must remain neutral on the question of God and his dignitaries on earth. The system established by the CPR is therefore a system of equality and separation between the State and the denominations (Art. 41 CPR, especially para. 4).[16] Even the sociological concept of "the traditional religion of the nation" which could be found in previous constitutions was abandoned by the CPR. As we have seen, the CPR approach is completely new

---

15 There is the challenge of facilitating or extending some rights traditionally enjoyed specifically by the churches to those citizens who do not have religious convictions, or are agnostic about religion and God. For instance the right to maintain classes in State schools based on humanist views. The situation of unequal consideration of students and parents who choose to abstain from enrolling in any religious classes at State schools has an obvious expression in Art. 11 of Ordinance (Portaria) 333/86 (on the teaching of the Catholic religion and morals at State schools): for those students and parents the option during religious classes is either to participate in some unspecified activities at school or, if that is not possible, to arrange their own occupation in or outside the school. See further argument in the dissenting opinions of judges *Luis Nunes de Almeida, Armindo Ribeiro Mendes and António Vitorino* to sentence 174/93 of CC. Disagreeing *Paulo P. Adragão*, A Liberdade..., p. 427.

16 This principle is even a material limit to constitutional revision: Art. 288(c), CPR.

in the historical context of Portuguese constitutionalism.[17] The novelty of this approach was mainly responsible for the slow effectiveness of the principles of equality and neutrality. Besides, there were still sharp differences regarding the scope of its possible application, especially concerning the relationship between the State and the Catholic Church. In theory as well as in practice a position prevails that can be summarised by the phrase 'neither complete equality nor full separation'.

IV. Legal Status of Religious Bodies – General Principles

In fact, despite the constitutional progress towards equality and separation, the combination of sociological factors, history and some legislation lead us to two propositions: (a) the principle of equal treatment is not entirely enforced; (b) the principle of separation is interpreted in a way that is not entirely strict.

The LRL of 2001 was a milestone on the way to equal treatment: it grants to *all* religious denominations a number of rights and privileges which were formerly given only to the Catholic Church by the Concordat of 1940.[18]

The LRL may be supplemented by Concordats with the Catholic Church and agreements between the State and non-Catholic churches or religious communities.

As the Concordat is an international treaty that takes precedes over national law it does not have to correspond to the LRL. Nevertheless the Concordat must agree with the Constitution. Therefore the status of the Catholic Church need not be completely identical to the status

---

17 *Jónatas Eduardo Mendes Machado*, O regime concordatário, n.3, above, p. 41, uses the apt expression "new paradigm of the Portuguese constitutionalism". See also Liberdade Religiosa…, 183 e segs.

18 In the first edition of this text it was written "assuming it is neither practically feasible nor politically possible that the Catholic Church should have its historically-based rights and privileges diminished, the strategy for equalisation would be to extend most of those rights and privileges to other denominations". And as a way to reach equality between the various denominations was proposed "the best option might be to enact a general law (or to amend thoroughly the existing Law 4/71) accepting concomitantly a dramatic contractualisation of the procedure for the preparation of that law. The Concordat and other Church agreements would take care of the specific features of each denomination. But the general principles and the major rights and privileges would emerge directly from the Constitution and the law." This was, basically, the method used in 2001 by the legislator.

of other denominations, but the differences may not be bigger than is justified by the fact that the Catholic Church is the predominant religion. A reasonable level of equal treatment has been achieved between the various denominations by means of the LRL. The Concordat of 2004 heads into the same direction, although the Catholic Church still claims a certain amount of privileges.

An important role in the development of all these matters will be played by the Commission of Religious Liberty, created by the LRL and regulated by Decree-Law 308/2003 of 10 December.

In what follows, the most important aspects of the laws (LRL and Constitution) concerning the various denominations will be presented. Then the special status of the Catholic Church based on the Conc. of 1940 and 2004 will be explained.

1. Rights of all Denominations

The Portuguese law distinguishes three categories of churches and religious communities:
- churches and religious communities without legal personality for they are not enrolled in the registry of the religious collective persons;
- churches and religious communities enrolled in the register of religious collective persons, and therefore with legal personality as religious collective persons;
- settled or rooted churches and religious communities.

The constitutional principles and the LRL involve as necessary and direct consequences for all these churches and religious communities
- The right to equal treatment and to treatment as equals;
- The right to acquire the status of a legal entity by means of special registration;
- Freedom of organisation, disposing on the training, composition, competence and functioning of its organs, the designation, functions and powers of its representatives, ministers, missionaries and religious auxiliaries and on whether to join or participate in the establishment of federations or interdenominational associations;
- The right of creating places of worship or locations for meetings with religious aims and the exercise of their functions, including all religious observances, both in private and public places (e.g. streets, squares);

- The right to assist religiously its members;
- The right to non-interference by the State in the religious field, and the right to the neutrality of State institutions;
- The disability of the State to perform any religious act, function, or ceremony or governmental act that follows religious rules;
- The right to receive services and donations of believers and to carry out collections;
- The right of churches and religious communities to co-operation by the State, according to their respective importance;
- Freedom to establish seminaries and other training centres and schools of Church culture, without supervision or control by the State;[19] [20]
- Freedom to establish and operate private or co-operative schools, under the supervision of the State; the right to teach religion in those schools;[21]
- The right to non-confessional teaching in State schools;
- Freedom to proselytise;
- The right to promote and spread their faith through their own papers, radio stations and TV networks;
- General recognition of the ownership of real estate and of being consulted when the State plans to demolish or to give another use to a building hitherto reserved for public worship;[22]
- The disability of the churches and religious communities to interfere in the organisation or government of the State; the ineligibility of ministers of religion for political appointments (e.g. Law 14/79 of 16 May, Art. 6(1); Decree-Law 701-B/76, 20 September[23]);
- The disability of ministers of churches and religious communities to become civil servants, by reason simply of their ecclesiastical

---

19 This is an exception to the general régime of CPR Art. 75(2): see *Canotilho/Moreira*, Constituição da República Portuguesa anotada, p. 245.
20 For the Catholic Church, see specific provisions in Conc. (Art. XX), new Conc. (Art. 20) and *Mário Bigotte Chorão*, "Formação eclesiástica e educação catélica", in A Concordata de 1940, p. 239. I must dissociate myself from the premises on which the author has based his argument.
21 *M. B. Chorão*, Id.
22 On the issue, see *Vasco Vieira da Silva*, Património..., p. 135.
23 The ineligibility of ministers of religion has been discussed within the Constitutional Court. Up to the present, the CC has not declared the unconstitutionality of the legal provisions quoted in the text. But it has expressed doubts: see judgment 602/89, in Acordãos do Tribunal Constitucional, vol. 14 (1989), p. 561. See also for hesitations (since 1974) on the justification of these restrictions on the rights of ministers of religion, *J. Miranda*, Manual..., IV, q., p. 428.

status;
- The privilege of ministers of churches and religious communities not to be cross-examined on facts known through confession;[24]
- The Catholic Church, the churches and religious communities enrolled in the register of religious collective persons and the settled churches and religious communities have further rights.

2. *Special Status of the Catholic Church*

The LRL contains a reservation (Art. 58) which guarantees that the Concordat between Portugal and the Holy See remains in force in addition to other laws concerning the Catholic Church. Apart from this the LRL clarifies that its provisions concerning churches or religious communities are not applicable to the Catholic Church.
This causes difficulties in interpretation, especially with regard to the delimitation of the laws applicable to the Catholic Church. There is no doubt that the regulations regarding the principles (Chapter I/LRL) and the rights of the individual concerning religious liberty (Chap. II/LRL) may be applied to the practice of the Catholic faith. Further there are provisions in Chapter III of LRL which could also be applicable to the Catholic Church: for example, the regulation on the religious killing of animals (Art. 26), the right of being heard in the process of making development plans so the Catholic Church can give its opinion regarding the dedication of certain areas to religious aims (Art. 28), the provisions concerning tax benefits (Arts 31, 32), etc.
However, the Concordat of 2004 does not support the notion of the application of chapter III. Instead, it specifically regulates these aspects, even though in a way which is quite similar to the LRL approach. The Concordat of 2004 explicitly regulates the right of the Catholic Church to be heard on the dedication of certain areas to religious aims (Art. 25), and awards the Bishops' Conference the right to include the Catholic Church in the system of collection of revenues from taxation. The conditions of such an inclusion are then determined in a special agreement (Art. 27). Therefore it may be concluded that the provisions of the LRL are not directly applicable.

---

24 *Paulo P. Adragão*, A Liberdade..., 357, critisises the use of the term "privilege" in this context. Nevertheless it is impotant to note that the term here is used in the classical sense of *Wesley Newcomb Hohfeld*, Fundamental legal conceptions as applied in judicial reasoning, Westport, 1919, being used equivalently to "liberty". On this, see *Vitalino Canas*, Relação Jurídico-Pública, in Dicionário Jurídico da Administração Pública, VII, 207-234.

The most important aspect of Article 58 of the LRL is the fact that the LRL strengthens the claim of the Catholic Church to maintain its special status. Although the Constitution does not mention any specific religion – contrary to other constitutions in Europe – the legislator decided to award a special status to the Catholic Church, further characterised by its origin as an international treaty and not merely a national law.

The Law of Religious Liberty of 2001 approximated the status of the other denominations to that of the Catholic Church. Therefore some of the provisions of the Concordat of 1940 which formerly had been unconstitutional ceased to be so as the principle of equal treatment was no longer violated. But there were other provisions of the Concordat.of 1940, confirmed or amended in 1975, which were not extended to the other denominations by the LRL. These provisions were null and void due to their violation of constitutional rules and principles. This applies to the following provisions:[25] (i) Article IX (obligation for most of the dignitaries of the Church in Portugal to have Portuguese nationality); (ii) Article X (power of the Portuguese Government to object to the appointment of archbishops and bishops); (iii) Articles XI and XV (protection by the State of the clergy as if they were public officials); (iv) Article XXI (teaching in State schools must be guided by Catholic principles and all pupils whose parents do not ask for exemption must attend regular classes in religion in those schools; the State is bound to teach religion in some institutions).[26] The tax exemption for priests, namely from the income tax (Art. VIII), was also unconstitutional: it violated the principle of equal treatment as other denominations had not been granted comparable advantages. All these provisions were null and void.[27] [28] They were revoked by the Concordat of 2004.

Some other provisions of the Concordat of 1940 were only partially unconstitutional, such as Article XVIII (duty of the Portuguese Re-

---

25 For a different view on some of these aspects, see *Paulo P.Adragão*, A Liberdade..., p. 378-385.
26 See section V, 3, below, for the current situation.
27 In its original form Article XXIV (prohibition of divorce in case of Catholic marriage) was also void; this Article was amended in 1975. Divorce is now permitted by civil law in all cases notwithstanding the opposition of the Church, which was forced to accept revision of the Concordat of 1940 accordingly. See a report in *António Leite*, "A Concordata e o casamento", in A Concordata, p. 293.
28 For *Canotilho/Moreira*, Constituição, p. 221, Art. XXV Conc. 1940, in connection with Art. 1625 of the *Codigo Civil* [Civil Code] would be void as well. Art. XXV submited some issues concerning the validity of Catholic marriage to ecclesiastical courts. For a different approach, see *António Leite*, "A Concordata e o casamento", in A Concordata, p. 299, and *J. Miranda*, Manual... IV, p. 424.

public to provide Catholic chaplaincy to the members of the Army). This duty of the Portuguese Republic is also abolished by the Concordat of 2004. .

V. Legal Status of Religious Bodies

1. Definition, Registration, and Juridical Classification of Churches and Religious Communities

The law defines churches and religious communities as "organized social communities that promise a lasting existence in which the believers can pursue the religious aims which their religion dictates" (Art. 20 LRL).
As a result of the fact that the Catholic Church and the other denominations are subject to different legal systems, the method of acquiring the status of a legal entity differs. The status of the Catholic Church as a legal entity is acknowledged by the signing of a treaty under international law. (Art. 1 of the Concordat of 1940 and of the new Concordat of 2004[29]).
Other churches and religious communities acquire the status of a collective religious body and thereby of a legal entity through registration (and not acknowledgement) in, the register of collective religious bodies, a special register created by Decree-Law 134/2003 of 28 June. Registration is not obligatory. However, those churches and religious communities which want to acquire the status of a collective religious body have to register.
Either international or national or regional and local churches and religious communities, may opt for registration.
International churches and religious communities (such as *shia ismaili*) can choose whether to register a separate organisation which represents their believers in Portugal or to register simply that part of their church (or religious community) which exists in Portugal.

---

[29] There is some ambiguity as to the kind of legal person: the best understanding of Art. I is that the Catholic Church (such as the Vatican and the Holy See?) is a legal person under international law and as such can act as a domestic legal person. Is this theory applicable to the organisations and associations created by the Catholic Church in Portugal according to Canon Law? At least some of them (if not all) seem to be exclusively domestic legal persons.

If churches and religious communities choose to register they receive additional rights: the right to teach Religion and Moral Education in public schools (primary and secondary), the lessons being non compulsory; the right to broadcasting time on State TV and radio; the right to be heard in the process of making development plans; the right to special tax benefits. Also, their believers and clergymen have some additional rights.

Within the registered churches and religious communities the law distinguishes between *settled* and *non- settled* ones.

A church or religious community is *settled (or rooted)* if it has been present in Portugal in an organised form for at least 30 years and is expected to be permanent, taking into account the number of believers and its history in Portugal. The requirement of 30 years of existence in Portugal may be ignored if the church or religious community can prove that it was founded abroad more than 60 years ago. The status *of settled church* is awarded by the Government, after obtaining an opinion from the Commission for Religious Liberty.

Other churches and religious communities are *non-settled*.

The status of a church or religious community as *settled* is of importance because there are certain rights and privileges available only to this group: (i) the power to perform valid wedding ceremonies conforming to the rules of the respective religion; (ii) the power to conclude agreements with the Government regarding questions of common interest; (iii) the right to participate in the Commission for Religious Liberty and in the Commission for Broadcasting Time for Religious Communities; (iv) the opportunity of receiving 0.5 % of the income tax of their believers; (v) the right to be repaid the VAT in certain circumstances.

By means of the "*settled*" criterion the law prevents new religious groups whose aims and intentions are doubtful having access to various privileges and rights – the absence of this measure could cause the appearance of a multitude of artificial "religious" groups.

On the other hand, this system leaves the decision as to whether a church or religious community is registered as *settled* or only as non-*settled* to the older and established – more trustworthy – churches and religious communities as registration as *settled* depends on the opinion of the Commission of Religious Liberty which is composed of representatives of the government, the Catholic Church and the already *settled* churches and religious communities (Art. 54 LRL). This avoids the possibility of embarrassment for the Government because its duty of absolute neutrality basically prevents it from defining what "religion" means. In a liberal interpretation of neutrality, defining what is a church or a denomination and what is "religion" is to be dealt with by the State only subsidiarily and occasionally. Therefore the risky operation of classification involved in a decision whether, for instance, the Moonies and Scientology are eligible for tax exemption, access to the State schools, and so on, is not the task of the Government.

2. Concordats and Agreements

As mentioned above the LRL confirms the exclusive privilege of the Catholic Church, i.e. the Holy See, to conclude concordats with the State of Portugal. Thus, the Catholic Church is the only denomination formally recognised by the Portuguese State as a subject of international law with the ability to conclude international conventions. with the State. Further, the Holy See is represented in Portugal by an apostolic nuncio, while the Portuguese Republic has an ambassador to the Holy See.
In place of this, the other rooted denominations were granted a different power, which had not previously existed in Portuguese law: the power to conclude agreements with the Portuguese State (Art. 45-51 LRL). These are agreements under internal law with atypical structure and form. Only *settled* churches and religious communities may enter into negotiations for such agreements; the Government itself may not open such negotiations. Once negotiations have been opened by an offer of the church or religious community and once the Government has agreed to negotiate (it may refuse only for certain reasons), the negotiations are led by a "Negotiation Commission" appointed by the Minister of Justice. After the negotiations any agreement is approved by the Council of Ministers and signed by the Prime Minister and other Ministers. Next it is presented to Parliament, together with a proposal for a ratification law. The Parliament may neither alter the agreement unilaterally nor negotiate modifications to it. Nevertheless, the agreement may be changed before ratification if both parties concur. Therefore, Parliament may ask the Government to renegotiate the agreement if it wants changes to be made. The agreement comes into force only after its ratification by Parliament.
Obviously, these agreements are a dramatic innovation from the Constitucional Law theory point of view. For the first time it is admitted that a law can be the direct outcome of a formal negotiation

between the Parliament, the Government and a private person, the *settled* collective religious body.

The collective religious body – *settled* or non-*settled* – may also conclude agreements with the Government, autonomous regions or municipalities in order to realise aims which do not require approval by law (Art. 51 LRL).

3. Religious Education

The Constitution expressly guarantees the right to religious education to every denomination (Art. 41(5)). This includes the foundation of seminaries or other establishments for formation or religious culture (Art. 23(i) of the LRL; Art. 19(1) of the Conc. 2004).

Although this right does not derive from the Constitution, the Catholic Church (Art. 20 of the Conc. 1940; Art. 21 of the Conc. 2004) as well as other churches or religious communities (Art. 27(a)) of the LRL) may further found *private or co-operative* schools which children may attend as an alternative to public schools. This is uncontroversial.

However, religious education in *public schools* has been the subject of controversy.

Over the last 25 years in Portugal the touchstone of the relationship between the State and the churches (especially the Catholic Church) has been mainly the question of teaching religion in State schools. Until 1976 (or 1974) the State had the obligation of teaching Catholic morals and religion at some levels in school. Since the Constitution of 1976 there has been an impassioned debate as to whether the State is still so obliged.

A preliminary consensus was reached: the principle of separation precludes such an obligation. This is virtually unanimously agreed.

But the debate was not over. Another topic was raised: could the State allow the Catholic Church to teach its religion and morals in State schools? The legislator agreed that it could, and the Constitutional Court was asked to decide the constitutionality of the legislator's decision. A judgment of 1987 (*acórdão* 423/87) declared the authorisation of religious classes at these schools not to be against the constitutional principles of separation (Art. 41(4), CPR) and non-confessional nature of teaching in State schools (Art. 43(3), CPR).

For the Court such authorisation is not only allowed but also mandatory since the Constitution deals with the freedom of religion as something demanding the creation by the State of real conditions for the exercise of religion by all. Consequently the State must give the opportunity to the Catholic Church as the major Church[30] in Portugal to teach morals and religion in State schools.

Respect for the principles of separation and non-confessionality would require only that religious classes were the sole responsibility of the Catholic Church, and also that they were given only to the students whose parents formally requested attendance at those classes.

Furthermore the principle of equal treatment was not damaged by the fact that these facilities were given *in casu* uniquely to the Catholic Church. The principle is damaged only by the fact that the legislator omitted to grant the same facilities to the other denominations.[31]

This judgment of the Constitutional Court did not settle the matter. Of the ten voting members of the Court no fewer than nine indicated partially dissenting opinions. In fact the judgment tried to strike a balance between a radical and a soft approach to the principles of separation, non-confessionality and equal treatment. At the end of the day neither of these two tendencies was satisfied with the legal reasoning adopted by the Court.

Subsequently a further opportunity for discussion was provided by a new case. But on this occasion the soft approach prevailed. Using some arguments (and forgetting others) already developed in judgment 423/87, the new judgment 174/93 of the Constitutional Court rested upon a most unconvincing interpretation of the principles of separation, non-confessionality and equal treatment, and came to the conclusion that from the constitutional point of view there is nothing wrong with provisions which, taken together, would allow: (i) the teaching of Catholic morals and religion; (ii) as a regular curricular subject; (iii) by civil servants (the regular teachers) or others; (iv) properly trained, funded, and appointed by the State (on the nomination of the Church); (v) in State schools; (vi) during the regular school day; (vii) and using teaching materials and textbooks prepared by the Church but adopted by the State. For the Constitutional Court this is teaching of religion *in school* and not *by the school* (or by the

---

30 In the dissenting opinions of judges *Luis Nunes de Almeida, Armindo Ribeiro Mendes and António Vitorino* to judgment 174/93 of the Constitutional Court, there is a vehement attack on the assumption (apparently adopted in the judgment) that the major denomination in Portugal, simply on the ground of its being the most popular, has a right to special consideration. They stress that the equal treatment principle should be used to protect minorities against the majority rather than the other way round; cf. *Jónatas E. M. Machado*, O regime concordatário..., p. 45.

31 Judgment 423/87, p. 115-6. The sentence quotes *J. Miranda*, Manual... IV, 2nd ed. p. 375-6.

State). For the Court, teaching of religion *in State schools* would be tolerable; teaching of religion *by State schools* is not.

The Constitutional Court stated clearly that attendance of pupils at Religious or Moral Education depends on a positive declaration of each pupil or his or her legal guardian. Therefore must attend the lessons only those who have expressly chosen to do so. While it was not considered a violation of the Constitution to teach Catholic Religion in public schools, what was reprehensible was that this was allowed only to Catholics.

Since then, Catholic Religious and Moral Education has not been subject to relevant juridical controversy and the legislation has built on and developed the judgment of the Constitutional Court. The new Concordat of 2004 also tries to adapt to this jurisprudence. (Art. 19(2)).

Immediately after the verdict of the Constitutional Court in 1987, laws were enacted in order to realise the principle that must attend the lessons only those pupils who have expressly agreed (see Ordinance no. 344/88 of 31 May).

However, the principle that established that non-Catholic denominations have the right to the same educational possibilities as Catholics has been put into effect but gradually. Yet the extent of those rights depends on the social importance of the respective denominations. Thus the decree (Despacho Normativo) no. 104/89 of 16 November experimentally permitted the teaching of Religious and Moral Education in primary and secondary schools by established non-Catholic denominations. In 1998, Decree-Law no. 329/98 of 2 November abolished the experimental character of this permission and extended it permanently to all primary and secondary schools (Art. 2 of the aforementioned Decree-Law). Though these lessons are subject to conditions and provisions which do not apply to Catholic Religious and Moral Education, there has unquestionably been a gradual approximation which ended the unconstitutional violation of the principle of equal treatment.

The LRL (Art. 24) consolidates this development regarding the non-catholic denominations by uniting the fundamental aspects of the current laws: (i) Churches and religious communities may demand permission to teach Religious Education in public primary and secondary schools; (ii) lessons of Moral and Religious Education are optional; (iii) in order to guarantee the running of lessons there have to be at least 10 pupils (this minimum number has been fixed in another law); (iv) the pupils or their legal guardians must state expressly their wish to participate in the lessons; (v) teachers of religious education may not teach other subjects to those pupils who participate in religious education – except in special circumstances; (vi) teachers are nominated and engaged by the State in agreement with the church or religious community – teachers who are not considered suitable by them may not be engaged; (vii) the churches and religious communities train the teachers, develop the curriculum, and must approve the teaching materials.[32]

4. Church and Culture

For centuries the Catholic Church has been one of the most important centres of culture – and until the last century probably the major centre – in Portugal. Today, besides the confessional schools of theology, which face serious problems due to a lack of people with the necessary vocation, the Catholic Church is the owner of a prestigious university (*Universidade Católica*[33]) with branches in different cities. It also runs many colleges and private schools. In State schools, including universities, there is a good number of teachers coming from the staff of the Catholic Church.

This educational and cultural influence is reinforced by the Church's ownership of a national radio-broadcasting channel (*Rádio Renascença*). The Catholic Church even owned a private television channel (channel 4),[34] which has been sold mainly because of its high running costs.

The influence of other denominations is minor, despite their militancy. A few of them are now seeking to gain a position within the mass media through their social and cultural activities.

Noteworthy is the fact that the LRL grants to registered churches and religious communities the right to broadcasting time on radio and TV for religious programmes so they may broadcast their religious aims

---

[32] The laws that preceded the LRL granted the right to teach their religion only to denominations who do not profess "moral and religious orientations which damage fundamental principles of the Portuguese society". This last formulation was too broad: it left to the administrative agencies excessive opportunities to prevent any denomination which does not profess moral and religious values consistent with the sociologically dominant moral and religious values from using the right to teach religion in State schools. This restriction is not part of the LRL.

[33] On the legal status of this University, see Decree-Law 128/90 of 17 April. This regulation has not been changed by the Concordat of 2004 (Art. 21(3)).

[34] On the constitutional basis for granting concessions for the operation of TV channels to denominations, see *J. Miranda*, "Televisão e confissões religiosas. Dois pareceres", in O Direito, 1990, 1 (Jan-Mar), p. 205.

(Art. 25). The assignment and distribution of broadcasting time is determined according to the social importance of the denomination concerned.

A critical point concerns the ownership of historic buildings. In many aspects the history of Portugal and the history of the Catholic Church are inextricably connected. Hence many historically significant buildings initially belonging to the Church are constantly in danger of being declared national monuments or national buildings and consequently expropriated by the State. This is a delicate matter. Many of the conflicts of the liberal (1820) and the republican (1910) revolutions were induced by the expropriation of Catholic Church property. This experience prompts the need for a careful balance between public interests and Church interests through a system of fair "separation of rights and duties".

In general, the Church keeps the right to permanent use of the buildings even when they are classified as "national monuments" or "of national interest". The State is the owner and is in charge of all works of conservation and repair (Art. VI of the Concordat of 1940; Art. 22(1) of the new Concordat.).[35] This *modus vivendi* was laid down in Law no. 107/2001 of 8 September (basics of the politics and provisions concerning protection and preservation of Portuguese cultural possessions), which further strengthens the principle of contract with regard to the protection of cultural possessions owned by the Catholic Church and other denominations (Art. 4 of the aforementioned Law).

5. Labour Law

From the Constitution derives a duty of the employer to reconcile the religious liberty of the employee with his or her own rights as an employer, by means of the principle of practical concordance.[36] Labour Law in general (Law 99/2003 of 27 August, Código do Trabalho *[Code of Labour Law]*) contains no special provisions concerning the consequences of the practice of religious liberty or functions. The Code only protects the freedom of the workers to choose their religion (Art. 16); prohibits privilege or discrimination on reli-

---

35 Details in *Vasco Vieira da Silva*, Património e regime fiscal da Igreja na Concordata, supra, p. 139.
36 Agreeing, *Jónatas Machado*, Liberdade Religiosa..., p. 269.

gious grounds (Art. 22 and 23); and forbids dismissal on religious grounds (Art. 429(b) and 438(4)).

Unsurprisingly, the weekly rest-day coincides with that determined by tradition and Catholic culture. Some of the more important days with religious significance for the Catholic Church are also official holidays (Art. 208 of the *Code of Labour Law*).

In this regard, the LRL introduced some significant innovations for members of other denominations. Article 14 grants to civil servants and representatives of the State or other public legal entities, and to contracted workers, the right to claim exemption from work on the weekly rest-day, holidays, and special hours prescribed by their religion.

These rights, however, depend on certain conditions. The employee must: (i) have flexible working time; (ii) be a member of a registered church or religious community which has submitted to the Government a list of their days and hours of religious importance; (iii) make up in full the time during which he or she has not worked.

6. Matrimonial and Family Law

The Concordat confers on the Catholic Church power to solemnise marriages under Canon Law to which the civil law assigns full legal force (Conc. 1940, Art. XXII, XXIII; Conc. 2004, Art. 13, 14). Since the revision of 1975 which changed Article XXIV of the Concordat of 1940, it has been possible for such marriages to be dissolved under civil law.

The Concordat of 2004 recognises the rights of the ecclesiastical authorities to determine whether a marriage is null and void and to give dispensation from a marriage that has not yet been consummated. In contrast with Article XXV of the Concordat of 1940, the decisions of these authorities take effect only after being examined and confirmed by the competent court of the Portuguese Republic (Art. 16).

Until 2001 other denominations were, however, prohibited by law from solemnising marriages. The LRL substantially changed this situation by acknowledging the legal force in civil law of such marriages (Art. 19). Requirements for this acknowledgement are: that the marriage has been carried out by an office-holder of a *settled* church or religious community; that a certain procedure has been observed; and that the office-holder fulfils certain conditions.[37]

7. Finances and Tax Regime

Portugal has no system of public financing of the churches. However, there are some indirect funding mechanisms, by means of a generous exemption from major taxes. And occasionally the State agrees to endorse and fund some specific initiatives with a social impact, mainly those of the Catholic Church, such as providing funds for the construction of important church buildings.

The Concordat of 1940 granted the Catholic Church a general exemption from taxes, both local and national, including the taxes on income and consumption, stamp duty, taxes on real estate, and so on. The most delicate aspect of these provisions concerns VAT because of European rules on this tax. In order to circumvent a substantial change in the tax benefits to the Church, a special mechanism was created after Portugal introduced VAT to repay the amount of this tax which is raised at the time of the acquisition and import of goods by the Catholic Church and its connected institutions (Decree-Law no. 20/90 of 13 January, with many amendments since that date). Compared with the Concordat of 1940 the Concordat of 2004 leaves the tax provisions for the Catholic Church practically unchanged (Art. 26).[38]

Meanwhile the LRL extended these tax provisions to the other churches and religious communities, though it reserved some of the tax exemptions for registered and *settled* churches and religious communities.

Thus, all churches and religious communities, whatever their status, are exempted from all taxes if they receive services or donations from their believers for the pursuit of their religious aims, or if they make collections (Art. 31(1)). The law, however, contains an exception: tax is levied on services with a business-like character such as formation, therapy, or spiritual advice (Art. 31(2)).

Article 32(1) of the LRL further exempts *registered* collective religious bodies from taxes regarding locations and buildings which are mainly or partially used for ritual acts or religious aims (e.g. exemp-

---

37 As *José Vera Jardim*, the principal mentor of the LRL and member of Government and Parliament points out in "Sobre a Lei da Liberdade Religiosa", Finisterra, n.ºs 42/43, 2002, p. 70, the exercise of this right still requires some previous regulation.
38 However, as mentioned above, clergy are now taxed according to general provisions.

tion from municipal tax). Moreover Article 32(2) of the LRL exempts them from taxes concerning transaction of property both in life and due to death.

Furthermore, *settled* churches and religious communities are refunded VAT (a privilege that was granted, as previously mentioned, to the Catholic Church in 1990) in some cases (Art. 65(1) of the LRL). Alternatively these *settled* churches and religious communities may use another innovative tax privilege provided for in Article 32(4) of the LRL: annually they may receive a share of 0.5 % of the income tax of natural persons (fiscal remittance). This privilege of settled churches depends upon various conditions:

(i) the church or religious community must have applied for this tax benefit, forfeiting the above-mentioned repayment of VAT; (ii) the taxpayers must declare expressly that this part of their tax will be used for religious aims or charity (if they do not make this declaration, the State will receive the whole tax); (iii) the taxpayer has to choose a particular church or religious community which will receive only the tax shares which were expressly designated to them.

The amounts designated by the taxpayers to each church or religious community are raised by the State, which pays them to the chosen church or religious community.

It is worth noting that the taxpayers may as an alternative choose not to make this declaration or to make it in favour of legal entities of benefit to the public with charitable, pastoral or humanitarian character, or to private institutions with social aims (Art. 32(6) of the LRL). Two final points: first, it is important not to confuse this mechanism with the church tax existing in other systems of law; second, the Concordat of 2004 allows the interpretation that this new mechanism is not directly applicable to the Catholic Church, but that a subsequent agreement between the State and the Church concerning this pointis necessary (see article 27 of Conc. 2004).

8. *Religious Assistance in Public Institutions*

The spiritual welfare of the Catholic Church in public institutions was subject to various rules of the Concordat of 1940, some of which conflicted with provisions in the Constitution.

In general the Concordat of 1940 granted free access to clergy of the Catholic Church to hospitals, State schools, asylums, prisons, and the like in order to supply spiritual assistance (Conc. 1940, Art. XVII). Moreover, the Concordat of 1940 was highly detailed regarding chaplaincy work for the military, *guaranteeing* it in the field (Conc.1940, Art. XVIII).This provision was connected to Article XIV of the Concordat of 1940 which provided that ministers of the churches were exempted from some military duties, and that such duties were replaced by the obligation to do chaplaincy work for the Army (Conc. 1940 Art. XIV).[39]

As explained earlier (Section III. 1.), chaplaincy work in these institutions is still regulated by various laws and provisions. The following aspects are worthy of mention: (i) hospitals employ Catholic chaplains (Ordinance no. 603/82 of 18 June); (ii) in the military there is a Catholic pastoral care service, the structure of which is embedded in the military structure itself (Decree-Law no. 93/91 of 26 February), and the staff of which is paid by the State (Ordinance no. 204/99 of 25 March); (iii) in prison there are pastors, subordinated to the governor of the respective prison, integrated into the public staff, and on a public payroll (Decree-Law no. 79/83 of 9 February).

The integration of spiritual welfare by the Catholic Church in public institutions is to undergo major change with the Concordat of 2004. As to spiritual welfare in public institutions concerning health, care, education, etc., or imprisonment, Article 18 grants only the *unlimited performance* of Catholic spiritual welfare, and no longer *free access*. The underlying philosophy of the new Concordat will certainly require important additional changes to internal provisions concerning spiritual welfare.

Concerning the Catholic spiritual welfare for members of the armed forces the changes will be even more substantial. According to Article 17 of the new Concordat, the State no longer grants either Catholic spiritual welfare, nor is it obliged to provide a corps of chaplains. The possibilities to nominate an army chaplain and vicar general by way of an agreement between Government and organs of the Catholic Church has been abolished. The State restricts itself to granting to the members of the armed forces – and to the members of the security forces – the right of free exercise of religious liberty by means of Catholic spiritual welfare; the spiritual welfare is provided and guaranteed by the Catholic Church. Only those who wish to have such spiritual welfare will receive it. The specific conditions of the implementation of the above-mentioned provisions depend on further agreements and regulations.

---

39 See *Miguel Falcão*, "A Concordata de 1940 e a assistência religiosa às Forças Armadas", in A Concordata..., p. 197.

These changes, in addition to the ones already introduced by the LRL, achieve a more equal treatment of the confessions regarding spiritual welfare.

In a provision of the LRL (Art. 13), inserted in the chapter on individual rights and religious liberty and not in that dealing with collective rights, the right of the members of the various denominations to spiritual welfare and the celebration of religious acts in special situations is granted to: members of the military, security forces (*forças de segurança*), and the police; and during military service or community service, or a stay in hospital, a hostel, college, institutions for health care, locations for detention, and so on. The State is obliged to "create adequate conditions for the pastoral care", but this obligation may be waived for security or functionality reasons. However, this cannot happen until after the minister of the respective church has had the opportunity to appeal against the decision.

The LRL does not say what is understood by the term "to create adequate conditions for the pastoral care". This phrase could be understood in the sense that equal treatment requires a system identical to the one that will be applied to the Catholic Church after the ratification and implementation of the new Concordat.

But it is doubtful whether it is possible (or even necessary under the guise of equality) to copy this system to all the other denominations.

9. *Criminal Law and Religion*

In the Penal Code (*Código Penal*) of 1982, after a thorough revision in 1995, there is a chapter in the "special part" concerning crimes against the family, religious sentiments, and due respect for the dead. In this chapter crimes of religious coercion and discrimination are penalised. However, these crimes are not mentioned specifically, but are part of more general crimes, namely *coercion* (Art. 154) and *religious/racial discrimination* (Art. 240). Additionally, the Penal Code cites two crimes that are directed specifically against religious sentiments: insult because of religious beliefs (Art. 251) and the prevention, disturbance or insult (by belittling) of ritual acts (Art. 252).[40]

---

[40] On this, see in particular *José J. A. Lopes*, "Os crimes contra a liberdade religiosa", in Liberdade Religiosa. Realidades e Perspectivas, , Lisboa, 1998, p. 177-237.

10. The Legal Status of Clergy

The Concordat of 1940 contained numerous provisions about the status of the clergy. Some of these have not been carried over into the Concordat of 2004, probably because they were unconstitutional or because it was not possible to reach agreement about them. They are: (i) tax exemption for the practice of their office (Art. VIII); (ii) the obligation to have Portuguese nationality (Art. IX); (iii) the requirement to have governmental approval for nominations (Art. X); (iv) the right to the same protection by the State as is guaranteed to public legal entities (Art. XI); (v) the misuse of vestments being punishable in the same way as the misuse of uniforms of public employees (Art. XV).

Other provisions of the Concordat of 1940 were maintained by the Concordat of 2004, some with minor changes. This applies to the following provisions: (i) the right to maintain the seal of the confessional before judges or other public entities about facts which came to be known through their office (Conc. 1940, Art. XII; Conc. 2004, Art. 5); (ii) exemption from jury service and other comparable duties (Conc. 1940, Art. XIII; Conc. 2004, Art. 6); (iii) substitution of military service by chaplaincy work in the army (Conc. 1940, Art. XIV; Conc. 2004, Art. 17(4), being allowed only for conscientious reasons). These provisions are supplemented by others laid down in documents of national law, as, for example, those granting to clergy the privilege of social security benefits (see Regulational-Decree no. 5/83 of 31 January).

With these changes introduced by the new Concordat of 2004, the position of Catholic clergy will become quite similar to the position of the clergy of other denominations, as prescribed by the LRL.

The LRL prescribes that *all* ministers of *all* denominations have the right to: (i) refuse to give evidence to judges or other authorities about facts they have come to know solely in the exercise of their office (Art. 16(2)); (ii) social security payments (Art. 16(4)); (iii) substitution of military service by chaplaincy work in the army (Art. 17(1)); (iv) exemption from jury service (Art. 18).

11. Developments of Ecclesiastical Law: the Committee of Religious Liberty

The Decree-Law no. 308/2003 of 10 December completed the most important phase in the development of the LRL. It introduced the statutes of the Committee of Religious Liberty (CRL). This Committee is independent from the Government and it is composed of five members chosen by the denominations (two of these are nominated by the Catholic Church) and five chosen by Government, who must be people of acknowledged scientific competence. The President is chosen and appointed by the Government. The Committee (CRL) has recently been constituted.

All developments in the fields of ecclesiastical law and exercise of religious liberty will come from the CRL. Under its remit the CRL has to: (i) control the application, development and revision of the LRL; (ii) give opinions on the legal status of denominations; (iii) promote the study and scientific research on churches, religious communities and movements in Portugal. This includes, for example, that the CRL gives its opinion on planned agreements between churches/religious communities and the Government, on the question of whether a church or religious community is settled in Portugal and about the registration of these churches/religious communities in the register for religious legal entities. Among other duties, the CRL is obliged to report to the appropriate authorities any possible violations of or attacks on religious liberty or religious discrimination (see for other competences of the CRL Art. 2 of Decree-Law no. 308/2003).

VI. Conclusion

Summing up the relevant provisions of the Portuguese Constitution of 1976 we conclude that the involvement of the State in the area of religion is limited. Principles of (i) separation between State and denominations, (ii) neutrality, and (iii) equal treatment (or treatment as equals) are duly defined and adopted. Unlike the Constitution of 1911, the Constitution of 1976 avoids radicalism and hostility to religion and religious institutions. And unlike the Constitutions of 1822, 1826, 1838 and 1933, it avoids any reference to whatever religion, church or confession. Hence, sympathy towards religion as a socially beneficial phenomenon is coupled with complete neutrality towards the churches as such.

However, the social-factual weight of the Roman Catholic religion has been enough to warrant the Catholic Church enjoying a special status based on instruments and provisions on a level different to that

of the Constitution. The combined effect of these instruments and provisions has led to a situation of *de facto* inequality in a number of respects, and to a somewhat inconsistent interpretation of the principle of separation. This situation of *de facto* inequality – which some consider to be, after all, the very expression of the principle of equality because it corresponds to the social importance of the Catholic Church in Portugal – was significantly mitigated by the Law of Religious Liberty of 2001 and by the new Concordat of 18 May 2004.
As a general conclusion, it seems appropriate to describe the current system of relations between State and Church in Portugal as a mitigated *separation system*.

VII. Bibliography

Paulo Pulido Adragão, A Liberdade Religiosa e o Estado, Coimbra, 2002.

Pedro Amaral e Almeida, As seitas e a liberdade religiosa, in O Direito, January-June,1998, . p. 105-130.

Miguel Almeida Andrade, La Liberté Religieuse, in Boletim do Ministério da Justiça, January-June 1994, n. 57-58, p. 205-230.

José de Sousa Brito, La Jurisprudence Constitutionnelle en Matiére de Liberte Confessionelle au Portugal, texto apresentado na XI ème Conference des Cours Constitutionnelles Européennes, Varsóvia, 17-21, May 1999.

Cabral/Vala/Pais/Ramos (org.), Atitudes e Práticas Religiosas dos Portugueses, Lisboa, 2000

J.J. Gomes Canotilho, – Anotação ao acordão 423/87, in Revista de Legislação e de Jurisprudência, 126, n. 3832-3834, p. 271.

J.J. Gomes Canotilho, / Vital Moreira, – Constituição da República Portuguesa anotada, 3rd. ed., Coimbra, 1993.

J.J. Gomes Canotilho, / Jónatas Machado, Bens culturais, propriedade privada e liberdade religiosa, in Revista do Ministério Público, October-December 1995, n. 64.

Mário Bigotte Chorão, – Formação eclesiástica e educação católica segundo a Concordata de 1940 (artigos XX e XXI), in O Direito, y. 123, 1991, p. 387; also in A Concordata de 1940 (col.),. p. 233-70.

Magalhães Colaço, – O regime de separação in BFDUC, y. IV, n. 39 and 40, 1918, p. 654.

Manuel Braga da Cruz, O Estado Novo e a Igreja Católica, Lisboa, 1998.

Miguel Falcão, – A Concordata de 1940 e a assistência religiosa às Forças Armadas, in A Concordata..., (ob. col.), p. 195-231.

António de Sousa Franco, La Iglesia y el poder (1974-1987), in Revista de Estudios Politicos, 1988, n. 60/61.

António Leite, – A religião no Direito Constitucional português, in Estudos sobre a Constituição, vol. II, Lisboa, 1978, p. 265.

António Leite, – Acordos entre a Santa Sé e Portugal anteriores à Concordata de 1940, in Brotéria, 132, p. 493, and A Concordata de 1940 (col.) p. 11-27.

António Leite, – A Concordata e o casamento, in A Concordata de 1940 (col.), p. 271-305.

Jónatas Eduardo Mendes Machado, – O regime concordatário entre a "libertas ecclesiae" e a liberdade religiosa. Liberdade de religião ou liberdade da Igreja, Coimbra, 1993.
- A Constituição e os Movimentos Religiosos Minoritários, in BFDUC, 1996, vol. LXXII, p. 193-271.
- Liberdade Religiosa numa Comunidade Constitucional Inclusiva. Dos Direitos da Verdade aos Direitos dos Cidadãos, Coimbra, 1996.

Jorge Miranda, Manual de Direito Constitucional, IV volume, 3.rd. ed., Coimbra, 2000
- Direitos fundamentais: liberdade religiosa e liberdade de aprender e ensinar, in Direito e Justiça, vol. III, 1987/8.
- Televisão e confissões religiosas. Dois pareceres, in O Direito, 1990, 1 (Jan-Mar), p. 205.
- A Concordata e a ordem constitucional portuguesa, in Direito e Justiça, vol. V, 1991, p. 154; also in A Concordata de 1940, col., Lisboa, 1993, 69 ff..
- A liberdade religiosa em Portugal e o ante-projecto de 1997, in Direito e Justiça, 1998, vol. XII, 2, p.. 3-24.

J. A. Teles Pereira, A liberdade religiosa e as relações Igreja-Estado em Portugal nos anos noventa, in Revista do Ministério Público, January-March 1996, n. 65, p.. 77-96.

David Valente e Alberto Franco, Liberdade Religiosa. Nova Lei anotada e comentada, Lisboa, 2002.

António Marques dos Santos, Citoyens et Fideles dans les Pays de L'Union Europeenne: Rapport Portugais, in *Consorzio Europeo di Ricerca tra Stati e Confessioni Religiose* (org.), Cittadini e Fedeli nei Paesi dell'Unione Europea, Reggio Calabria, 1998.

Paula Costa e Silva, A jurisdição nas relacões entre Portugal e a Santa Sé, Coimbra, 2004

Vasco Vieira da Silva, – Património e regime fiscal da Igreja na Concordata, in A Concordata de 1940 (col), p. 133-163.

Antunes Varela, – Lei da liberdade religiosa e Lei de imprensa, revista e anotada, Coimbra, 1972.
A Concordata de 1940 Portugal-Santa Sé (col.), Lisboa, 1993.
Liberdade Religiosa. Realidades e Perspectivas (ob. Col.), Centro de Estudos de Direito Canónico da Universidade Católica Portuguesa, Lisboa, 1998.

Lovro Šturm
State and Church in Slovenia

I. Social Facts

Compared with other religious communities in Slovenia, the Roman Catholic (hereinafter: Catholic) Church occupies a special position. Both historical development and the current number of members support the claim of Catholicism to be the main religion of the nation. In all, there are 36 religious communities registered in Slovenia.

Table 1: Slovenian religious demographics according to the 1991 census

Confession	Percentage of Population
Catholics	71.40 %
Orthodox Christians	2.40 %
Muslims	1.50 %
Protestants	1.00 %
Other religions	0.30 %
Atheists	4.20 %
Response denied	4.20 %
No response known	15.00 %

Table 2: Slovenian religious demographics according to the 2002 census

Confession	Percentage of Population
Catholics	57.80 %
Muslims	2.40 %
Orthodox Christians	2.30 %
Protestants	0.80 %
Other religions	0.30 %
Believers without specific religion	3.50 %
Atheists	10.10 %
Response denied	15.70 %
No response known	7.10 %

II. Historical Background

Within the boundaries of the Habsburg Empire, which included Slovenia, Catholicism was for a long time considered to be the state church. By the end of the 18th century, the state had become secularized (Josephinism), but the Church retained a special position in society long after that – educational and charitable activities, for example, have remained almost completely in its hands. After World War II, the Catholic Church in the Socialist Federal Republic of Yugoslavia (hereinafter: SFRY) was heavily persecuted by the State, and relations between Church and State did not improve until the Holy See and Yugoslavia re-established diplomatic relations in 1966.

Despite the declared principle of separation between church and state, from 1945 to 1990 every church in Slovenia was actually under strict state control. The legal status and the actual position of religious communities in the former Yugoslav communist régime were not solely determined by generally known and published legal rules. They were, in fact, primarily determined – especially in the case of the Catholic Church – by strictly confidential legal rules which, together with other confidential regulations, formed a parallel secret legal system. For instance, National Security Service documents from 1967, 1970, 1982, and 1985 dealt extensively with the Catholic Church. The common idea binding these secret internal rules together is that the Catholic Church is a "permanent internal enemy," that – after the signed protocol between the SFRY and the Holy See – renounced the idea of directly opposing socialism, yet also "opened an ideological confrontation with then current socio-political conceptions".[1] Even though free profession of religion was constitutionally guaranteed, the Catholic Church and other religions were not allowed to play a part in public life.

From 1945, the former Yugoslavia prohibited the operation of any kind of private school. Many private schools that had operated before this time were nationalized at the time of prohibition. This prohibition lasted until 1991 in the territory of present day Slovenia. Religious communities could establish religious schools only to train ordinands. Diplomas from these religious schools were not publicly recognized. Between 1945 and 1991 religious communities were forbidden to engage in "activities of a general or social significance." Forbidden activities included educational activities. Atheism was the

---

1   see OdIUS VI, 69, p. 390.

privileged ideology in Slovenia for almost half a century and was encouraged throughout the educational system.

III. Legal Sources

The Constitution of the Republic of Slovenia (passed in December 1991) regulates in Article 7 the relations between the state and religious communities. The legal position of religious communities is based on the following fundamental principles: (1) separation of the state and religious communities, (2) equality of religious communities and (3) free activity of religious communities within the legal order.
In the Slovenian legal system, freedom of conscience and belief is provided for under Article 41 of the Constitution and is entitled "freedom of conscience." This provision broadly protects the freedom of self-definition; it refers not only to religious beliefs but also to moral, philosophical and other views of life. The Article comprises three provisions: the assurance of freedom of conscience or the positive entitlement, the right for a person not to have any religious or other beliefs, or to not manifest such, or the negative entitlement, and the right of parents to determine their children's upbringing in the area of freedom of conscience. The first provision protects the particular right of every individual to profess freely his or her religion and other self-definitions in his or her private and public life. The Constitution does not define in more detail which activities are embraced by freedom of conscience. The individual's freedom of conscience implies both the positive entitlement – the opportunity for individuals to have, change and manifest their optional religious and other beliefs – and also the negative entitlement – the right for a person not to have any religious or other beliefs, or to not manifest them. The Constitution formulates this negative entitlement in such a manner that no individual is obliged to admit to religious or other beliefs.
As a special aspect of freedom of conscience, the Constitution provides for the right of parents to give their children a moral and religious upbringing in accordance with their beliefs. Religious and moral guidance given to a child must be appropriate to his or her age and maturity. The guidance must also be consistent with the child's free conscience and religious and other beliefs or convictions.

According to the explicit provisions of Article 16 of the Constitution, freedom of conscience is one of seven special constitutional rights and freedoms that can never be temporarily suspended, not even in war.

The right of conscientious objection is also protected by the Constitution under Article 46. This right is permitted in such circumstances as are determined by statute, to the extent that the rights and freedoms of others are not adversely affected. Conscientious objection is allowed only in two areas: state defence and medical operations. More precisely, citizens who, because of their religious, philosophical or humanitarian beliefs, are not willing to perform military duty are assured the opportunity of participating in the defence of the state in some other manner. In deciding whether to accept claims of conscientious objection, one of the factors that must be considered is religious belief. The right to conscientious objection is given to everyone who is obliged to participate in performing military duties: recruits, soldiers during their military service, and commissioned officers. Doctors may refuse to operate on patients, except in emergencies, if the operation is contrary to their conscience and to the international rules of medical ethics. In order to exercise this right, they must first inform the medical facility concerned of their objection. That facility must respect their decision and, at the same time, ensure that its patients can exercise their health care rights.[2]

Further Constitutional provisions regulate not only the relations between individuals and the state but also the religious relations among individuals. Under the provision of Article 63, inciting religious discrimination and inflaming religious hatred and intolerance are prohibited. The provisions of Article 14, as a reflection of the principle of equality before the law, prohibit discrimination on the basis of religion or other belief. The violation of this principle of equality and the prohibition of discrimination in the area of freedom of religion have been criminalised under the Penal Code of the Republic of Slovenia because they violate human rights and freedoms.

The Slovenian legal system addresses the churches and religious communities only in general; it does not include statutes regulating individual churches or religious communities. However, following negotiations, the Government of Slovenia signed mutual agreements on legal questions with the Catholic Church in 1999 and the Protestant Church in 2000. There are currently negotiations in progress with the Serbian Orthodox Church, the Seventh Day Adventist

---

[2] These rights are further detailed in the Health Services Act (1992).

Church and the Islamic Religious Community in Slovenia. The first international agreement between the Government of Slovenia and the Holy See was signed in 2001. The Agreement was under constitutional review till 19 November 2003 when the Constitutional Court declared it in accordance with the Constitution.[3]

The Act on the Legal Position of Religious Communities (hereinafter: RCLPAct)[4] provides more detailed regulations concerning the legal position of religious communities. The RCLPAct was adopted in 1976 and is still in force. As time passes, deficiencies in the Act are becoming more and more evident. Nowadays, not only has an evolving society rendered the Act obsolete, the Act is also inconsistent with the new Constitution and free democracy. The RCLPAct has been amended twice: amendments in 1986 included penal provisions, and important amendments were adopted in 1991 authorizing for the first time the establishment and operation of private religious schools in Slovenia.

The basic principle of the RCLPAct is to ensure the freedom of individuals to profess their religion. This Act defines that freedom as an individual's private concern. When the law was enacted, this provision meant that everything pertaining to religion should be relegated to the private sphere. Religion as such had no place in the media, in the professional life of an individual, or in schools. The educational system, as previously mentioned, was not only secular and neutral but emphatically actively atheistic. The Constitution declared atheism the state ideology.[5]

That type of provision is unconstitutional under Article 41 of the Constitution which provides for the freedom to profess religious or other beliefs within public life.

Furthermore, the RCLPAct provides for the freedom to establish religious communities. All religious communities have an equal position, are separate from the state, and are free to attend to their religious matters within the framework of the legal system. Additionally, they are legal entities under civil law, obtaining legal status through registration with the Office for Religious Communities. The RCLPAct also contains a series of other provisions that cover the religious press, the performance of services, the establishment of religious schools and religious teaching, the pastoral activity of reli-

---

3 Decision No. Rm-1/02-21 dated 19 Nov 2003.
4 Official Gazette SRS, Nos. 15/76 and 42/86, and Official Gazette RS, No. 22/91.
5 See Constitution of the Socialist Federative Republic of Yugoslavia, Part V (February 1974), which provided for upbringing and education to be based on the achievements of contemporary science and especially on Marxism.

gious communities, the financial and other property rights of religious communities, and also the prescription of criminal sanctions for violations.

In addition to the RCLPAct, a series of statutes dealing with different areas of law also defines the legal position of religious communities in the Republic of Slovenia.[6]

Discrimination on the basis of religious belief is prohibited by the Constitution and defined as a criminal offence under Article 141 of the Penal Code. This article provides that any individual who, because of a difference in religious beliefs, deprives another individual of any human right or fundamental freedom recognized by the international community or determined by the Constitution and Statutes, or who restricts such a right or freedom, or who grants someone some special right or benefit on the basis of discrimination, violates the principle of equality. A fine or imprisonment for up to one year is prescribed for such an offence. If the offence is committed by an official abusing his or her official position or the rights associated with it, the penalty is imprisonment for up to three years.

---

6 In their provisions, these Statutes explicitly mention religious communities, and protect the freedom of religious belief, e.g. some protect certain religious values (The Media Act, The Film Fund Act, The Penal Code, The Military Service Act, The Health Activities Act); some protect the confidential relation between an individual and his or her confessor (The Criminal Procedure Act, The Civil Procedure Act, The General Administrative Procedure Act); some enable the implementation of freedom of religion in various areas (The Public Meetings and Performances Act, The Act on Graveyard and Burial Activities and on the Arrangement of Graveyards); some make possible and restrict the participation of religious communities in certain activities and in public life (The Act on the Organization and Financing of Child Rearing and Education, The Radio-Television of Slovenia Act, The Election Campaign Act, The Political Parties Act, The Institutes Act); some determine the special tax status of religious communities or priests (The Tax on Legal Entities' Profits, The Sales Tax Act, The Building Lands Act, The Foreign Trade Act, The Income Tax Act) and a special system for priests' insurance (The Social Protection Act, The Retirement Pension and Disability Insurance Act); and some regulate the return of property in denationalization proceedings and to religious communities (The Denationalization Act). Also relevant are all those general legal acts which apply to a generic legal entity or a legal entity under civil law.

IV. Basic Categories of the System

1. General Perspectives

Article 7 of the Constitution provides for the separation of the state and religious communities. The RCLPAct contains an almost identical provision. This provision has been interpreted as meaning that the state remains neutral to all religions, that it does not take a position concerning world views, and that it does not identify itself with any one religion or religious community. Thus there is no state church. Additionally, both discrimination against and privileges for members of a religious community are prohibited; members do not have special status under public law, and are not allowed to discharge any authoritative public functions. Accordingly, the Act explicitly provides that religious communities and their appropriate organs are legal entities under private law and that their acts are not binding. The only acts of religious communities that are publicly recognized are the certificates and diplomas of private religious schools.[7]

The principle of church-state separation means not only that religious communities are autonomous in their internal affairs, but also that public life is secular. While religious communities have some degree of autonomy, they must conform to the Constitution, Statutes, and other regulations. Accordingly, the state imposes on them certain duties and grants them certain rights, including the opportunity of free establishment, but does not become involved with either religious questions and disputes or with the content of their religious beliefs.

A special document of the Joint Commission of the Catholic Church and the Government of Slovenia, dated 1994, establishes *inter alia* that the democratic State of Slovenia does not take sides with religiosity or non-religiosity as such, but respects the right of citizens to the free, personal and collective, ideological or practical, profession of their religion or their non-religious persuasion. Thus, it understands that citizens have different religious or non-religious persuasions, and that it is has a responsibility to respect the freedom of all.

The interpretation of the separation principle – in the media, in governmental understanding and in the post-1999 decisions of the Constitutional Court – has established Slovenia as a country with an ultra-strict model of separation.

---

7   The accreditation standards are the same for religious and non-religious private schools.

2. Constitutional Review

The initial statements of the Constitutional Court were favourable towards religious communities:
The Military Service Act was not consistent with the Constitution insofar as the Act allowed one to claim the right of conscientious objection at conscription but not at a later date[8].
Church organizations and institutions are bound by State law and also depend, in the matter of their legal status, upon State regulations. These bodies are treated as domestic legal entities, and are as such also governed by positive law.[9]
Churches and religious communities are universally beneficent institutions.[10]
Churches and religious communities perform an important function in society.[11]
After 1999 the Constitutional Court dealt in more detail with the principle of the separation of the state and religious communities and demanded an ultra-strict separation.
The prohibition under the Education Act of religious activities in private kindergartens and schools that have been granted state licenses is unconstitutional.[12] However the Constitutional Court confirmed the validity of the existing enactment that prohibits all religious activity in public kindergartens and schools. The Court's reasoning was that the rights of the non-believers and the principle of the separation made it necessary in a democratic society to ban religion completely from public educational institutions, not only from the curriculum, but also from school premises.
The 2001 Census Act ensures that the person counted has the freedom to declare their religion and, indeed, whether or not they are willing to answer that question at all. Collecting data by the state on the religious belief of its inhabitants is not contrary to the principle of the separation of religious communities and the state.[13]
The Constitutional Court declared in its interpretative decision the Agreement between the Government of Slovenia and the Holy See to be in accordance with the Constitution insofar as the court's recent interpretation of the principle of separation is obligatory for all state

---

8   OdlUS IV, 50 (Decision No. U-I-48/94 dated 25 May 1995).
9   OdlUS II, 23 (Decision No. U-I-25/95 dated 4 March 1993).
10 OdlUS V, 174 (Decision No. U-I-107/96 dated 5 Dec 1996).
11 OdlUS VII, 190 (Decision No. U-I-326/98 dated 14 Oct 1998).
12 OdlUS X, 192 (Decision No.U-I-68/98 dated 22 Nov 2001).
13 OdlUS XI, 25 (Decision No. U-I-92/01 dated 28 Feb 2002).

organs not only in implementing that agreement but also for all future agreements.[14]

V. Legal Status of Religious Communities

The Slovenian legal system does not recognize a distinction between churches and religious communities but recognizes only a general concept of a religious community. While the legal system uses the term "church" in a few locations, it is only as part of a conventional phrase, such as "the separation of church and state". These phrases are used particularly in public discussions.

The RCLPAct governing the registration of religious communities provides that the establishment (or dissolution) of religious communities is to be reported to the Office for Religious Communities (hereinafter also: the Office). The Office is a special organ of the Slovenian Government. The Office issues a certificate on registration. A religious community does not obtain special recognition from the state, but the Office enters it into the register of religious communities operating in Slovenia. Registration entails merely an opportunity to carry out activities as a religious community, rather than gaining any special privileges. For example, registered religious communities may open a bank account and operate through it; it may apply for any state funds allocated to religious communities.

A similar system was also created for organizational units[15] within religious communities so that these units could have equal legal entity status. The RCLPAct does not definitively establish a registration system for these units: it provides for religious communities or their associated organs to be legal entities under civil law. As case-law has evolved, it has reached the point where it allows associated organs or

---

14 Decision No. Rm-1/02-21 dated 19 Nov 2003.
15 These organizational units can either be local congregations of a religious community, such as a parish of the Catholic Church, or organs of the religious community, such as a publishing company, but they cannot be either educational or charitable institutions. This limitation arises from the Decree on the Introduction and Use of the Standard Classification of Activities and states that independent religious legal entities cannot be registered educational or charitable institutes that are constituent parts of religious communities and operate externally (these will have to register as, for example, private institutes). Under this decree, educational and charitable activities must be separated from religious activities. An exception to this is Caritas, a charitable organization of the Catholic Church, which had already been registered before the Decree came into force.

institutions of religious communities to obtain legal entity status insofar as the organ or institution is not also being organized in some other existing legal form – such as an institute under the Institutes Act, as a society under the Societies Act, or as a company pursuant to the Companies Act. Currently, the Office issues certificates conferring legal status to representative constituent parts of religious communities if these constituent parts also receive a certificate issued by a competent organ of the religious community.[16] Thus, for example, parishes may be registered as independent legal entities, if the competent church organ approves the decision and issues a certificate.

No case-law yet exists on the resolution of disputes within religious communities. Such disputes are viewed as civil-law disputes between two civil-law subjects and not as an administrative issue. The competence of the internal organs of religious communities in resolving such disputes is regulated by their internal rules; the state does not interfere with these relations.

Registered religious communities are not under any special supervision of the state. They are, however, subject to the same general supervision as other legal entities because their activities must conform to the Constitution, Statutes and other regulations. For example, the registration of religious communities is intended to protect third parties, and religious communities must carry out financial transactions through banks and under the supervision of the Tax Authorities.

Generally, religious ceremonies must be performed inside church buildings; the only exception to this rule is burials at cemeteries. Such ceremonies performed during burials are subject to potential suspension by a competent state authority in order to protect public health and order. Any ceremony performed outside a church buildings requires permission from the Minister of Interior Affairs; however, no response to such a request may be held to be a grant of permission.

Slovenian legislation has no explicit mention of the right to observe and celebrate religious holidays. That right is encompassed by the right to profess one's religion privately and publicly. In fact, certain church holidays are also Slovenian national holidays: Christmas (December 25), Easter Monday, Whitsuntide, the Assumption of the Virgin Mary (August 15), and the Protestant Day of Reformation (October 31).

---

16 Internal law of the religious communities governs which community organs are competent to issue such certification.

VI. Culture

1. Education

The main Statute in this area is the Act on the Organization and Financing of Child Rearing and Education (hereinafter: Education Act). This Act established the separation of public and private educational institutions. Private institutions may perform educational programmes certified under the same standards as public programmes. Accordingly, the diplomas issued by private institutions are recognized as public documents if their conferring institutions fulfil the same standards as public schools. These statutory standards require certain minimum levels in the training and education of employees, upkeep of premises, and availability of equipment. In Slovenia, municipalities and local communities establish public kindergartens and elementary schools, while the state generally establishes and finances secondary schools. Urban municipalities may also establish general secondary schools by agreement with the state. Public schools (and kindergartens) must be neutral vis-à-vis religion. The Education Act, on the basis of the strict interpretation of the constitutional provision separating the state and religious communities explicitly prohibits religious activities. These prohibitions apply both to public kindergartens and schools, as well as private kindergartens and schools that have been granted state licences. The only exception to this is the private schools which were licensed prior to the coming into force of the Education Act. After the Constitutional Court held in 2001 that the prohibition concerning private kindergartens and schools that have been granted state licences was unconstitutional, the Education Act was consequently amended in 2002. However, certain restrictions remain. Religious activities in private schools must be extra-curricular. The regular programme must be interrupted neither in time nor in the premises.

The restrictions applicable to public schools prohibit:

- lessons in religion with the aim of educating children in a particular religion,
- lessons where religious communities decide on the content of the syllabus, textbooks, educational criteria of teachers, and the suitability of a particular teacher for teaching, and

- the organization of religious observances.[17]

In special cases, the Minister of Education may allow religious lessons on the premises of kindergartens and schools. Such lessons are allowed only if there are no other "appropriate premises" in the local community. Additionally, such religious instruction requires the headmaster's approval and must be given outside the regular curriculum and regular operation of the school. In practice, no other "appropriate premises" in the local community means that: no premises whatsoever are available in the local community; premises exist but their condition is bad enough to pose a health and security risk; the premises are more than four kilometres away from the kindergarten or the school; or if the premises are less than four kilometres away from the kindergarten or school but travel to those premises threatens the safety of the children.

The Education Act lists autonomy as one of the goals of child-rearing and education. Under the Act, this concern for autonomy is shown in extra-curricular "types and varieties of knowledge and persuasion," and by ensuring the optimal development of individuals irrespective of their religious belief. Accordingly, the Act requires that schools be religiously neutral and independent of religious communities. Additionally, this principle of autonomy prohibits discrimination against any religious belief and urges principled tolerance.

While the Constitution does not regulate religious lessons, the Education Act explicitly prohibits lessons whose aim is to teach children to follow a particular religion. This prohibition applies to public schools and kindergartens. One law, the Elementary School Act, obliges schools to provide non-religious lessons on religion and ethics within the framework of their elective courses.[18] All religious communities have the opportunity of organizing religious lessons on their premises at any time, but this is not a concern of the school or the state. The nub of this issue is that it is a private matter for students. Regarding religious lessons, the RCLP Act states that religious communities may hold them on premises designated for observances and other premises where a religious community permanently carries out its religious activities. Minors, however, can attend these lessons only if they consent and have the consent of their parents or guardian.

---

17 The Education Act (February 1996).
18 The Elementary Schools Act, Art. 17, para. 2.

As previously described, the Education Act prohibits lessons in public schools where religious communities decide on syllabus, the textbooks, the educational requirements of teachers, and the suitability of a particular teacher for teaching. Accordingly, this legislation prevents the churches from designing religious lessons for public schools and from nominating the teachers of these courses.

Religious lessons in public schools are prohibited. In unlicensed private (religious) schools, they may be, and usually are, a mandatory course. Statutes prohibit religious observances, such as prayer meetings, from being held in public schools and kindergartens. This prohibition, however, does not extend to private schools that were granted licences before the statute came into force. Among these private schools licensed before the statute entered into force are three Catholic general secondary schools. In these schools prayers are permitted but not mandatory.

While legislation does not explicitly prohibit or allow displaying a crucifix or the cross (there is no distinction between them) in schools, these symbols are prohibited in practice as violating the principle of separation of the state and religious communities. However, there is no information indicating that any public school has ever tried to hang a cross or a crucifix nor has the Constitutional Court yet adjudicated in such a case.

The Slovenian legal order envisages no difference between private religious kindergartens and schools and other private kindergartens and schools; the Education Act, for example, exclusively regulates private schools in general and does not mention religious schools. Religious communities may establish kindergartens and schools under the same conditions as other private-law subjects.

For the private religious schools that were granted licences before adoption of the Education Act, there are special transitional rules governing their funding.[19] These schools received licences that provided 100 % state funding. Under the new Act, the Education Act, they would be entitled to only 85 % funding.[20] Under the transitional provisions of the new Act, this more generous funding will end if the governors do not change their curriculum to comply with the religiously neutral provisions of the Education Act. Without such a transi-

---

19 These schools were organized and operate under the 1991 Act on the Organization and Financing of Child Rearing and Education. Their licences are dependent on meeting the state educational and instructional requirements that were in force before the Education Act.

20 The Education Act, Art. 86 (February 1996).

tional provision, pre-existing licensees[21] would either need to switch to the current system of financing in Article 86 of the Education Act (*i.e.* to 85 % funding), or follow only public educational programmes, in order to preserve their licences. If they followed public educational programmes, they would need to respect the prescribed autonomy of schools and would be prevented from carrying out their religious activities.

Private schools may be freely established. This means that on the basis of the Act on Establishment it is necessary to enter an educational organization into the court register or any other appropriate register. Private schools are free to follow their own educational programmes, unless they wish to obtain state licensing. In that case, they must obtain approval from the Government of Slovenia, or from its competent professional council, that their educational programme meets the same educational standard as the public educational programme. Founders of schools may be either domestic or foreign legal entities; however, only domestic natural persons or legal entities may establish elementary schools. In Slovenia there are no private elementary schools; there are 448 public elementary schools (with a nine year programme). Among 130 secondary schools there are four private religious general secondary schools (*i.e.* 3 % of secondary schools or 0.7 % of all schools).

The State supervises the registration of schools. It also supervises their educational programmes when schools are licensed, that is, when they want their diplomas to be recognized as public documents. The State does not, however, control the internal organization of schools, except when it grants licences, and then statutory provisions apply ex lege to licensees. If the State, on the basis of a public call for tenders, makes licence contracts with private educational institutions for operating public services, all the provisions of the Education Act apply to licensed public kindergartens and schools. The most significant of these provisions concern the equal rights and obligations of students and their parents; the same quality in implementing the programmes; the internal organization; the financing of programmes; and the educational conditions for professional employees.

Private schools have complete freedom in enrolling students and in determining admission criteria. According to current information, only one out of the four present private Catholic general secondary

---

21 These pre-existing licensees are three Catholic general secondary schools: the Bishop's Classical General Secondary School in Ljubljana, the Secondary Religious School in Vipava, and the Secondary Religious School in Želimlje.

schools requires a baptismal certificate and a priest's reference for a particular candidate. Others do not mention registration for either the followers of other religions or for atheists, yet their students must adjust themselves to the manner of work, orientation and programs of these schools, including religious lessons as a mandatory course. The certificates of the present religious private schools (general secondary schools) are recognized as public documents.

Private educational institutions may be financed in two ways: they are either granted licences or financed directly under statute. The receipt of a licence means that the purportedly private school or kindergarten is part of the public network. Consequently, all conditions that apply to public schools or kindergartens also apply equally to the licensed school – they must carry out the same educational programme and fulfil all other conditions (and equally regulate the rights and obligations of students and their parents, maintain the same quality in implementing programs, have equal internal organization and provide the equal financing of programs and educational conditions for professional employees).

According to the Statute itself, if private kindergartens, private elementary and music schools, and private general secondary schools (but not including professional schools) which carry out public programmes and are not licensees comply with statutory conditions, they have the right to public funds to a maximum of 85 % of the funds that the State or local community designate for salaries and material costs per student in public schools.[22] The only condition is that the existence of public elementary schools in the same area is

---

22 For schools, the following conditions are prescribed by Art. 86 of ZOFVI:
- that they carry out educational programmes from the first up to the final year of the school,
- that they provide or register at least two classes of the first year, or that the music school organizes in its educational music programme lessons in three orchestral instruments and registers at least 35 students,
- that they employ or in some other manner provide teachers or tutors necessary to implement the public programme in accordance with the Statute and other regulations.

The right of private schools to public funds also carries some restrictions concerning: the setting of tuition fees (for students who do not exceed the total for obtaining State scholarships, a maximum of 15 % of the funds which are granted by the State to public schools per student); the salaries of professional employees (which must not exceed the salaries of professional employees in public schools); the expenditure of public funds in private schools, which is supervised by the Court of Auditors of RS. The expenditure of funds and particularly the organization and implementation of public programmes according to Statute are however supervised by the schools inspectorate (the Inspectorate of RS for Education and Sport).

Concerning kindergartens, the salaries of teachers must not exceed the salaries of teachers in public kindergartens (Art. 23 of the Kindergartens Act).

not thereby threatened. In the transitional period of three years before the coming into force of the Statute (*i.e.* until 15 March 1999), such schools had the right to receive 100 % of funds from the state, in order to stimulate the establishment of private schools. Both of these financing provisions enable the financing of religious private schools. Indirect state financing, however, is not regulated by the Slovenian legal system.

The state has established a Schools Inspectorate to supervise the contents of the programmes of those schools which are publicly licensed. It has already begun supervising the first phase so that it can grant public recognition to educational programmes if the competent profession council of the Republic of Slovenia determines that these programmes meet the same standards as public educational programmes. The criteria used in this supervision are not statutorily defined. Private schools carrying out public programmes must comply with conditions prescribed for professional employees of schools. If teachers comply with the statutory conditions (particularly concerning their education), private schools are free to choose their own staff. Thus far, in Slovenia, there have been no cases concerning the possibility of terminating an employment contract because of the nature of the school.

2. *Media*

The Media Act, which regulates the manner of realizing the freedom of public information and the rights and duties of the media and journalists, explicitly exempts bulletins, press, and other forms of publishing information intended exclusively for use within Church organizations. A religious community can publish a public gazette, if this is related to its activities. Exceptions to this are radio and television programmes. Concerning observances, there is no so-called right to short reports, that is the right of every radio and television organization to brief (up to one and a half minutes) report on important performances and events which are accessible to the public and are of a general interest. A special permit from the corresponding religious community is necessary for such a report. Religious broadcasting must not be interrupted by advertisements.

The Radio-Television of Slovenia Act prohibits religious propaganda in programmes of RTV Slovenia. In creating and preparing programmes, RTV Slovenia must respect the principles of opinions, world views and religious pluralism. To the Council of RTV Slovenia, which is the managing organ of the public institute RTV Slovenia, religious communities directly appoint one member (out of thirty-six). RTV dedicates a few hours of its programming to religious content and has been broadcasting programmes with the religious content of various denominations.

If the contents of a particular film would lead to incitement to intolerance, the Minister of Culture is not permitted to issue a permit for the shooting of such a film in Slovenia.

The leading daily newspaper in Slovenia – Delo – where the majority of death notices are published, strictly rejects the inclusion of religious symbols (*e.g.* a cross) in the notice.

VII. Labour Law within the Religious Communities

There is no special regulation of labour law within churches. This may be difficult to understand, especially compared with other countries, but there is no such exemption for religious organizations to be able to hire or fire according to religious criteria. General labour law applies to the (very few) church employees; these are mainly in church-sponsored private schools.

VIII. Financing of the Religious Communities

The financing of religious communities by the state or local authorities may be direct, *i.e.* by grants, or indirect, *i.e.* by providing exemption from taxes. The state may restrict direct financing to a completely defined purpose, meaning that the religious community alone disposes of such funds; upon request, however, the religious community must report to the state or municipal organ the use of such specifically allocated funds. In fact, the state earmarks very little money for religious communities. In 2002 the total sum was 3,790,000 Sit (16,840 Euro). The government apportions this money to religious communities in proportion to the registered projects. A greater amount of aid is given in the form of social transfers to help cover a certain part of the cost of the health and pension insurance of priests which has been paid by the State since 1991. In 2002 the total sum was 282,020,000 Sit (1,253,422 Euro) for the 1116 priests (including members of religious orders), *i.e.* 1,123 Euro per priest per annum.

Funds earmarked by the state are generally used for (co-)financing (30 % – 50 %) the reconstruction of sacred objects that form part of the national cultural heritage. What is really involved here is not the financing of activities of religious communities as such, but rather the preservation of the objects of our cultural heritage whose appropriate condition is also (or particularly) in the interest of the state.

Indirect financing is represented by certain exemptions and reliefs in fiscal matters. For instance, religious communities are exempted from paying income tax. In practice this statute is usually interpreted to mean that while religious communities and societies as a rule do not pay taxes, since it is assumed that they were established with non-profit intentions, they must however pay taxes on all profit-generating activity, *e.g.* on publishing and selling books. They are also exempted from taxes on gifts received from individuals and legal entities. Additionally, the basis for personal income tax is reduced (by a maximum of 3 %) for voluntary contributions in money and gifts in kind; furthermore, the contributions of legal entities to religious communities are treated as business expenses, thereby reducing their taxable base. Religious communities are exempted from paying sales tax on their products for the protection of the old and handicapped people and children, and from paying sales tax on their religious services. Caritas is by statute a specified organization which does not pay sales tax on products obtained freely and used for the purpose for which it was established (*i.e.* for charitable activities), nor tax on the purchase of the products it distributes freely or sells within the framework of its activities (it may sell only badges, stamps and other graphic products which have its own symbol imprinted and whose content is limited to its own activity). Religious communities are also exempted from paying property tax on buildings used for their religious activities.[23] Furthermore, they are exempted from customs duty on the sending and receiving of goods and operating services with religious and other non-profit purposes.

Priests, as well as all other citizens, are bound to file their tax returns. However, they may, like other persons with the status of so-called independent professionals, request that their profit is determined by deducting 40 %, as business expenses, from their incomes.

---

23 The Act on the Land Designated for Construction.

In the area of property law, religious communities are, like all legal subjects in the state, equally guaranteed the constitutionally protected right under Article 33 to private property and inheritance. Generally, in participation in legal transactions and fiscal matters, everything that applies to legal entities under private law also applies to religious communities, especially the fact that they may participate in legal transactions independently within the framework of their activities, with all rights and obligations, on their own behalf.

The RCLPAct states that religious communities in Slovenia may independently dispose of the funds generated by income from their own property, from awards and contributions of believers for observances performed and services they offer to them, and from gifts, legacies and bequests of individuals and legal entities. There is no church tax in Slovenia. According to an express provision of statute, the contributions of believers are voluntary and are allowed to be collected in the premises intended for observances and other premises of religious communities, and outside these only with a permit issued by the competent state organ (*i.e.* the competent administrative unit of the Ministry of the Interior). For religious observances carried out at the request of individuals, priests may accept remuneration in money or in other kind (*e.g.* produce, etc.).

The property rights of religious communities also changed with the introduction of the restitution of seized property. According to the Denationalization Act which came into force in 1991, property seized by agrarian reform, nationalization, and confiscation, and by other regulations and in circumstances determined by the statute itself, is to be returned normally in kind, but if this is not possible compensation shall be given (*i.e.* as substitutive property, securities or money). Among the claimants to the return of property, the Denationalization Act expressly includes churches and religious communities, their institutes or orders operating within the territory of the Republic of Slovenia at the time of the statute's coming into force. Legal succession is considered pursuant to their autonomous law. The restitution of seized property is not proceeding without complications. The Constitutional Court has frequently decided in favour on the constitutionality of the provisions of the Denationalization Act.

IX. Religious Assistance in Public Institutions

After the Slovenian Government signed special agreements with the Catholic and the Protestant Church in October 2000, the Slovenian Military Service Rules were reformed in November 2000 so that Slovenian servicemen can now more easily fulfil their religious obligations. The amended rules make it possible for the practice of religious beliefs to be an integral part of the work and life in a military institution. The rules introduced military chaplaincies, led by military chaplains, and funded by the government. In addition, it is possible for military chaplains – in a state of emergency – to help to compose a testament for a military person, to give lectures with religious or moral content, and to conduct religious ceremonies in the event of solemn or funeral occasions.

In the Slovenian legal system, the right of national servicemen to profess their religion without interruption during military service was introduced in 2002. National servicemen may attend observances in their spare time when their military service duties do not prevent them from leaving their headquarters, unit or institution.

Religious Assistance in other public institutions is more limited and is not paid for by the state. People in hospitals, retirement and similar homes, who cannot attend services outside these institutions for health or other reasons, may be visited by clergy at their or their relatives' request. Clergy may also perform services in such institutions, and administer the sacraments but they must respect house regulations and must not interrupt persons who have not requested a visit of the clergy or their services.

Visiting persons in penal institutions, and closed wards of psychiatric hospitals, in which persons are placed involuntarily, is already an established practice; visiting prisoners is, however, possible only if they express such a wish.

There is no religious assistance in the police.

X. The Legal Status of Priests and Members of the Religious Orders

Priests and members of religious orders have no special legal status in comparison with other individuals. There are, however, some incompatibilities with various positions in public life, not in any statutory law, but established by custom.
To protect individual religious freedom and confidential relations between individuals and religious confessors, confidential religious communications are privileged in criminal, civil (litigious and non-litigious), and administrative procedures. Clergy are exempted from the duty to testify on what they have heard as the defendant's or party's confessor. It is left to religious confessors to decide for themselves whether to testify, but if they do testify they must tell the truth. Religious confessors are exempted from the general duty to report criminal offences or their perpetrators.
The crime of the unauthorized betrayal of a business secret may also be committed by priests, if they unauthorizedly betray a secret they heard while carrying out their profession, unless they do this for the general good or the good of an individual, this being greater than the good of keeping the secret. It is considered that they must keep such information confidential even after they cease to follow their profession. Prosecution in such cases is brought by a private action (Art. 153 of the Penal Code of the Republic of Slovenia).

XI. Matrimonial and Family Law

Article 53 of the Constitution provides for mandatory civil marriage. The state holds that religious communities cannot be granted any public authorization. Accordingly, they have no authority to conduct legally binding marriages. They may marry or divorce couples only according to their internal law, which has no civil-law consequences, *i.e.* from the state's position, these acts are not binding.
Registers concerning marital and family status are kept by the state. The archival material of the Catholic Church (historical documents, *e.g.* records of births, deaths, marriages) must be selected from church documentary materials according to its regulations. However

the Minister of Culture, in agreement with the Slovenian Bishops' Conference, determines the special conditions and the means for carrying out the archival activities of the Church.[24]

XII. Bibliography

Constitutional jurisprudence in the area of the freedom of religion and beliefs, XI the Conference of the European Constitutional Courts, Tribunal Konstytucyjny, Warsaw 2000, National report by the Constitutional Court of Slovenia, p. 677-718.

Andrej Graselli, Sporazum s Svetim sedežem (Agreement with the Holy See), Pravnik 55, 2000, 1-3, str. 94-106.

OdlUS: Decisions and Rulings of the Constitutional Court I-XII, Ljubljana 1992-2003:

Urša Prepeluh, Pravni položaj verskih skupnosti v Sloveniji (The legal status of religious communities in Slovenia), Ljubljana 1997. Website www.us-rs.si.

Anton Stres, Država in cerkev (State and Church), Ljubljana 1998.

Lovro Šturm (ed.), Cerkev in država. Pravna ureditev razmerja med državo in cerkvijo (Church and State. Legal regulation of the relationship between the state and the church), comparative survey, Ljubljana 2000, p. 1-360.

Lovro Šturm: The State and Church relationship in Slovenia, p. 157-196, in: The status of the states applying for membership to the European Union. *Francis Messner* (ed.). Milano 2002.

Lovro Šturm: The Legal Status of Religious Communities in the Republic of Slovenia at the Time of Its Inclusion in the Free Democratic Society of Modern Europe, p. 385-398, in *A. Šelih* (ed). State and Church. Selected historical and legal issues, Slovenian Academy of Sciences and Arts, Ljubljana 2002.

Lovro Šturm: (ed), Komentar Ustave Republike Slovenije (Commentary of the Constitution of the Republic of Slovenia, Ljubljana, 2002, p. 1-1247.

Lovro Šturm: Church and State in Slovenia, in: *Silvio Ferrari, W. Cole Durham* (eds.), Law and Religion in Post-Communist Europe, 2003.

---

24 The Act on Archival Materials and Archives, Art. 37.

Michaela Moravčíková
State and Church in the Slovak Republic

I. Social Facts

A visitor to the Slovak Republic today can buy in any bookshop a bulky book under the name Catholic Slovakia, and picture publications on Greek Catholics in Slovakia, or on the new evangelical churches. 14 years ago this was unthinkable. Even elementary religious literature had to be smuggled into Slovakia from Italy, Yugoslavia, Poland, or other countries. Before 1989 pilgrimages were mostly prohibited, and those that were held were strictly monitored by the State security service; nowadays even State representatives customarily attend these events.
Until 1989, when political upheaval occurred in the former Czechoslovak Socialist Republic, changing from a totalitarian regime[1] to a democracy, religion was, in the spirit of Marxist philosophy, considered an enemy of the developing socialist republic. There was no Census question on religious affiliation. A public declaration of a church or any religious group affiliation, or simply of religious belief, was an excuse for being monitored by the State security system, discrimination against a person's access to public positions and career promotion, or other forms of victimisation with no right of redress. Research in the field of religiosity could be carried out only at the institutes of scientific communism.
The most recent Census was taken in May 2001,[2] for the first time since the establishment of the independent Slovak Republic.
Census data on the religious denominations of the population were collected on a self-assessment method, separately from other demographic characteristics.[3] Each person was allowed (but was not

---

1 In the then valid Constitution of the Czechoslovak Socialist Republic (Act no. 100/1960 Zb.) clause 4 set out a leading role for the communist party in society.
2 According to Act no. 165/1998 Z.z. on census, count of houses and flats in 2001.
3 *Sčítanie obyvateľstva, domov a bytov 2001. Základné údaje. Náboženské vyznanie obyvateľstva. no. 600-0615/2001.* Bratislava: Štatistický úrad Slovenskej republiky, 2001. 240 p.

obliged) to declare freely their religious denomination. The religious denomination of children under 15 was entered by their parents.

Compared with the previous Census that was held on 3 March 1991, the most significant shifts can be seen in items characterising the whole population. The number of people professing an allegiance to a church or religious group increased from 72.8 % to 84.1 %, that is to say 11.3 %; in absolute terms the increase was from 3,840,949 to 4,521,549, an increase of 680,600 citizens. If 4.5 million of the total number of 5,379,445 inhabitants claim membership of a church or religious group, it must be said that not only is religion not losing its meaning, nor is it merely holding its own, but rather that its influence is increasing.

On the other hand, the number of those that did not claim membership of any church or religious community, that is to say are persons without confession, has increased. In 1991 it was 515,511 persons, representing 9.8 % of the resident population, while after the last Census it was 697,308 persons, representing 12.96 %; in absolute figures this means an increase of 181,797 persons, or 3.16 %.

The formation of religious views and of attitudes towards religion is occurring gradually, through a return to roots that were restrained or broken during the period before 1989. It can happen through personal decision: individuals joining a religious community on the basis of their individual life situation and judgment, through a quest for a spiritual environment that can change a person's life, or a definitive rift with a particular church or religious community in terms of personal commitment and declared in the Census.

Public discussion on the new model for financing the church, and the ensuing campaigns – especially of left-wingers – that preceded the census, and portrayed state contributions to registered churches as misspent, played an undoubtedly significant role.

Given that in 1991 917,835 inhabitants declined to declare their religious affiliation, there was an issue as to what the number would be in the next census. Today we can say that it has decreased to 757,238, that is to say that there are now only 160,598 inhabitants of Slovakia refusing to declare a religious affiliation.

There was an increase in the number of those that professed to belong to an 'other religious community or church' (other then registered). It is now 6,294 inhabitants compared with 3,625 in 1991. Newly established religious communities in Slovak society are responsible for this increase.

The increase in people claiming membership of particular churches and religious communities is because a large number of inhabitants professed non-established confessions in the year 1991. It must be related to the pastoral work of particular churches and an information campaign organised by the churches before the census itself, as well to a process of internal commitment or rejection by each inhabitant, recalling the confession of their ancestors, or changing their religious conviction.[4]

	Difference	Number in 2001	Number in 1991
Roman Catholic Church	+ 520,737 + 8.6 %	3,708,120 68.9 %	3,187,383 60.3 %
Greek Catholic Church	+ 41,098 + 0.69 %	219,831 4.1 %	178,733 3.41 %
Protestant Church of Augsburg Confession	+ 46,461 + 0.7 %	372,858 6.9 %	326,397 6.2 %
Reformed Christian Church	+ 27,190 + 0.4 %	109,735 2.0 %	82,545 1.6 %
Orthodox Church	+ 15,987 + 0.3 %	50,363 0.9 %	34,376 0.6 %
Protestant Methodist Church	+ 2,988	7,347	4,359
Religious community of Jehovah's Witnesses		20,630	
Brethren Unity of Baptists	+ 1,097	3,562	2,465
Brethren Church	+ 1,356	3,217	1,861
Church of Seventh Day Adventists	+ 1,708	3,429	1,721
Apostolic Church	+ 2,789	3,905	1,116
Jewish religious communities	+ 1,398	2,310	912
Old Catholic Church	+ 851	1,733	882
Christian congregations	+ 5,819	6,519	700
Czechoslovak Hussite Church	+ 1,071	1,696	625
Without denomination	+181,797 + 3.16 %	697,308, 12..96 %	515,511, 9.8 %
Affiliating to churches and religious communities	+680,600 + 11.3 %	4,521,549 84.1 %	3,840,949 72.8 %

---

4 Comp. *Moravčíková, M.; Cipár, M., Religiozita na Slovensku II.* Bratislava: Ústav pre vzťahy štátu a cirkví, 2002. p. 8 – 11 nn.

	Difference	Number in 2001	Number in 1991
Affiliating to other churches and religious communities	+ 2,669	6,294	3,625
No response	- 757,237 - 14.42 %	160,598 2.98 %	917,835 17.4 %

II. Historical Background

There is little credible or reliable report of pagan cults within the territory of the present Slovakia. No myths have been preserved, only various legends. The former Indo-European monotheistic confession of Slavs north of the Danube seems the prerequisite of the later relatively non-violent acceptance of Christianity.

The first Christian church was built on the territory of the present Slovakia in 828 A.D. in Nitra. Byzantine mission (together with missions from the west, from the Frankish Empire, Ireland and Scotland, and from the south, from Aquilia) played the most significant role. Rastislav, the ruler of the Great Moravian Empire, asked the Byzantine Emperor Michal III for church hierarchs and mentors. In 863 he sent brothers from Solun, Constantine (later he accepted a monastic name Cyril) and Methodius, to Great Moravia. Before their arrival Constantine compiled the Slav script – glagolica, the first Slav literary language – Old Church Slavonic, and translated the most useful religious and liturgical texts into it.[5] Both of them laid the foundations not only of the Christian faith but also of culture in general.

As a result of the collapse of the Great Moravian Empire at the beginning of the 10th century, Slovakia became part of multinational State formations for a very long time: the Hungarian state from 10th to 16th century, the Habsburg monarchy from the 16th century until 1867, and the Dual Monarchy of Austro-Hungary between 1867 and 1918.

According to Act no. 11/1918 Zb. and decrees on the establishment of the independent Czechoslovakian State, Austro-Hungarian legal regulations were incorporated into the newly established Czechoslovak Republic. This included ecclesiastical law: the churches' existing organisational and legal structure was also transferred.

---

5 Comp. *Papastathis, Ch., K., L'Œuvre législative de la Mission cyrillo-méthodienne en Grande Moravie.* Thessalonique: Association hellénique d'Études slaves, 1978, 142 p.

Issues of church and state separation, and allied issues as to the constitutional resolution of the church and state relationship were the most complex challenge facing the initial political and legal programme of the young State. In the result, neither the temporary constitution of 1918 nor its amendment of 1919 touched on the issue.

In 1928 a Modus Vivendi – the Agreement between Czechoslovakia and the Holy See – was accepted; it guaranteed mutual respect for the new contracting parties, but relations between church and State did not change in principle from that of the previous period of the Austro-Hungarian Dual Monarchy.

The military Slovak State that was founded on 14 March 1939, defined itself as Christian in the preamble to its Constitution. Jozef Tiso, a Catholic clergyman, became President, and one-fifth of the deputies in the Parliament of the Slovak Republic were clergy.

After World War II a course was set towards the suppression of the church's natural influence in public life, and in February 1948 when power was taken by the communists, there began a tragic chapter in the history of the church in the Slovak territory. The previous course of state and church relations was interrupted, not to be recovered until after 1989. A priority objective of the communist regime was to get hold of churches for its purposes by proxy of their representatives. When it turned out that their endeavours were not producing the expected results, the communist power centred its anti-clerical activities on the minimisation of the churches' influence and the establishment of strict state supervision.

Act no. 217/1949 Zb. created the State Office of Church Affairs as the central body of state administration. Act no. 218/1949 Zb. on financial provision for churches and religious communities by the State was adopted, enabling a state-differentiated approach towards clergy. Churches and religious communities lost their identity as public legal entities and in economic affairs they became completely dependent on the State. The State controlled the liturgical, pastoral, social, charitable, educational, financial, and all other church activities; it established the obligatory registration of churches, and clergy were allowed to work only on the basis of the state approval that was dependant on a pledge of loyalty to the Republic.

The communist State never considered the separation of church and state. They presumed that the step would have enhanced church social influence, given the historical conditions. It would even have strengthened the control over the clergy of the church hierarchy which would be counter-productive for a power trying hard to corrode the churches from within. Strict totalitarian control of churches resulted in illegal activities by individual worshippers, clergy, and different groups that were outside State control, and which became the target of State security persecution.

After November 1989 when the so-called Velvet Revolution took place, the change in the position of church and religious communities was part of the general social and political changes. The churches regained their independent position, and at the same time opportunities opened up concerning their position in Slovak society. After the peaceful separation of the Czech and Slovak Republic into two independent entities the Slovak Republic was established on 1 January 2003.

III. Basic Structures

1. Legal Sources of Slovak Law on Religion

After the Czech and Slovak Federative Republic ceased to exist, the Slovak Republic succeeded to bilateral and multilateral international agreements to which the former entity had been the contracting party. The International Pact on Civil and Political Rights, the Optional Protocol to the International Pact on Civil and Political Rights and the Convention on the Protection of Human Rights and Basic Freedoms must be mentioned here.

Legal regulations that oblige the Slovak Republic to guarantee religious freedom, freedom of consciousness, and the elementary principles of the state and church relations are as follows:

The Constitution of the Slovak Republic no. 460/1992 Zb. as implemented in Constitutional Act no. 244/1998 Z.z., Constitutional Act no. 9/1999 Z.z., Constitutional Act no. 90/2001 Z.z, Constitutional Act no. 140/2004 Z.z. and Constitutional Act no. 323/2004 Z.z.

Constitutional Act no. 23/1991 Zb. introduces a Bill of basic rights and freedoms. The Bill contains legal regulations that are not found in the Constitution and vice versa.

Act no. 308/1991 Zb. as amended by Act no. 394/2000 Z.z. on the freedom of religious beliefs and the status of churches and religious communities.

Act no. 163/1990 Zb. on theological colleges.

Act no. 192/1992 Zb. on church and religious community registration, which regulates the conditions of church registration.

Property relations between Greek Catholic[6] and Orthodox churches were resolved on the basis of the legal measure of the Slovak National Council Chairmanship no. 211/1990 Zb. The arrangement was finalised in an Agreement between the Slovak Government, the Greek Catholic Church in SR and the Orthodox Church in SR on the final settlement of property questions between the Greek Catholic Church in SR and the Orthodox Church in SR of 20 December 2000.

The Slovak Republic was the first of the post-communist countries to resolve issues of church property in a consistent manner. This was done by means of Act no. 282/1993 Z.z. on the mitigation of some legal property injuries caused to churches and religious communities. The legal regulation set the method and conditions for a partial restitution of property of which churches had been deprived from 8 May 1945 – Jewish religious communities from 2 November 1938 – until January 1990.

The financing of churches is regulated by Act no. 218/1949 on the economic provision of churches and religious communities by the State. Clergy stipends are paid in full by the State in accordance with the Government Decree no. 578/1990 Zb. on the regulation of personal benefits provided to the clergy of churches and religious communities.[7] Act no. 16/1990 Zb. amended Act no. 218/1949 Zb., so ending State control of the churches was repealed.

On 30 November 2000 the National Council of SR adopted the Basic Agreement between the Slovak Republic and the Holy See no. 326/2001 Z.z. Its aim was to be a political international agreement of a presidential nature. As far its contents are concerned it comprehensively and in general terms regulates relations between SR and the Holy See. It was signed on 24 November 2000, and came

---

[6] A Uniate Church that suffered severe persecution during the years of the communist regime. In April 1950 Prešov "sobor" was held, which de facto meant the elimination of the Greek Catholic Church for the next 18 years. It concerned the so-called act of return of Greek Catholics into the Roman Catholic Church, arranged by the Central Committee of the Communist party of Slovakia on the basis of the resolution of 7 January 1950. Under the influence of the Prague Spring in 1968 that was to bring socialism with a human face, and brought some liberalisation into society, the Greek Catholic bishop Vasil Hopko requested Alexander Dubček, the then Secretary General of the Communist party, to rehabilitate and renew Greek Catholic Church activity. The government order no. 70/1968 Zb. of 13 June that was signed by the then deputy chairman of the Czechoslovak Socialist Republic Government, Gustáv Husák, permitted Greek Catholic Church activity once more.

[7] Amended by Government Order no. 691/2004 Z.z. from 1 December 2004. The salary scale of clergy have risen by 42 %, and their base pay could be augmented by 30 % in case of the quality performance (the constituent part of the salary which cannot be claimed).

into effect on the exchange of ratification documents in the Vatican on 18 December 2000. The Agreement confirmed that the contracting parties would conclude four partial Agreements. The first one on clergy service in the armed forces and armed corps no. 648/2002 Z.z. was ratified in the Vatican on 28 October 2002, the second one on the Catholic upbringing and education in the same place on 4 June 2004.

On 11 April 2002 the President signed the Agreement between the Slovak Republic and registered churches and religious communities in the Slovak Republic no. 250/2002 Z.z. It was consented to by the Government of SR and the National Council of SR. The Agreement, although it is of different nature (intrastate, not an international treaty), is almost identical with the Basic Agreement between the SR and the Holy See (their content is almost the same). Eleven registered churches and religious communities, through this Agreement, took advantage of the opportunity to conclude agreements with the State, which is given to all registered churches by Act no. 394/2000 Z.z.

According to the Opinion of the Constitutional Court of SR of 24 May 1995, the Constitutional Court did not uphold a judgment of the district military court that there was a discrepancy between the Act on civil service and the Constitution. The petitioner claimed a discrepancy in the case of conscripts changing their religious confession or religion to one that exempted them from military service after the period stipulated by the Act had elapsed, so that they could refuse to perform military service under the lex specialis of Section 25(2) of the Constitution of SR: *"No one can be made to execute military service if it shall contradict its conscience or religious confession. The details shall be regulated by the Act."*

Conscience, religious confession, thinking and religion are, according to the Constitutional Court decision, rights internal to a person, forum internum. Their essence lies in not being subject to any measure that aims to change a person's process and way of thinking, and further that no one can be made to change their thinking, religious confession or beliefs. These rights cannot be restricted by the law – they have an absolute character. Every external, externally identifiable, action of a person, motivated by their conscience, religious confession or beliefs, is treated as a right with external extent, forum externum, according to this decision of the Constitutional Court. These rights may be restricted by law, where measures essential for public order, health, morals, or the protection of the freedom of others in a democratic society are concerned (Constitution 24(4)). Section 9(1) and (2) of the Convention on the Protection of Human Rights and Basic Freedoms contains the same approach: while freedoms themselves cannot be restricted, their manifestations are subject to limits.

In this case the Constitutional Court established that the Slovak Republic respects the right to refuse to perform military service because of conscience or religious confession, but this is conditioned by adhering to the terms stipulated for each group of persons claiming this right, while the requirement of applying this inner standard in non-discriminatory way, that is in the same way to every person, must be fulfilled. The claim of a person to refuse to perform military service is to be considered valid only if it has been made within the period stipulated by the law. The reason for such a restriction is the need to maintain the SR Army's effective preparedness for war and readiness for action, and to avoid using the reason of conscience or religious confession as justifying a refusal to do military service, for example, immediately after the call-up/draft has been received, while on military service duty, or in a period of the state's military preparedness.

On 31 May 2001 the Constitutional Court ruled on a citizen's petition that his basic rights and freedoms had been infringed by the district and county courts. As far as the origin, contents, and termination of a legal relationship between a petitioner and the church headquarters were concerned, those courts accepted the rulings of the church authority according to church law, and did not examine them from the point of view of SR law.

The issue of the validity of the petitioner's removal from office was thus dealt with outside SR law. According to the Constitutional Court the general courts should consider every aspect of the legal relationship of the petitioner to the church relevant to their decisions according to SR law, and not, as had happened in the lower courts, prefer the internal church law to the SR law. Those courts had not ruled on the petitioner's rights according to the law valid in the SR, but had considered church law to be part of the applicable law and not as part of the facts of the case. As a result the petitioner's rights had not been respected: by accepting the rulings of the church authority on the legal, employment and financial issues in the dispute, the district and county courts had violated the petitioner's rights of access to the court and other legal protection guaranteed by the SR Constitution 46(1). That provision required that a person's case against the church be adjudicated upon by a general court according to SR law, or according to regulations that were to be applied under

SR law. The Constitutional Court held that the petitioner was, as a member of the clergy, discriminated against in the judicial application of his rights. At the same time, it held that the general courts did not inflict injury to the petitioner right because he applied his basic rights and freedoms. The Constitutional Court did not passed judgement on Church authorities' decision. It means that the Constitutional Court did not examine if the petitioner, applying his basic rights and freedoms, suffered detriment because of Church authorities' action.

2. Basic System Categories

Among European systems the Slovak approach to churches and religious communities may be seen as "a middle of the road approach" between strict separation and a State church system. It is a relationship of co-ordination and parity. None of the churches is a State Church with special privileges. Legislation deals with churches as a whole; churches as legal entities are subject to restrictions arising from rules that are generally binding.
The basic law declares that the Slovak Republic is a neutral state as far as religion and ideology are concerned.
In its preamble the SR Constitution acknowledges the Cyril-Methodius spiritual heritage, and the historical legacy of Great Moravia. In Section 1 it stipulates that the SR is not committed to any ideology or religion. Section 24 guarantees freedom of thinking, conscience, religious confession, and beliefs. Everyone has the right to have no religious confession. Everyone also has the right to manifest their religion or beliefs, either on their own or together with others, in private or in public, by means of worship, religious acts, services, and to receive religious education.
Churches and religious communities are self-governing: they establish their own institutions, appoint clergy, provide religious instruction, and found monastic and other church institutions independent of the State. These may, according to the Constitution, be restricted only by an Act, if measures necessary for protection of public order, health and morals or rights and freedoms, are involved.
According to Section 11 of the SR Constitution, international agreements on human rights and basic freedoms that the SR has ratified and which have been proclaimed in a way stipulated by law, take precedence over SR Acts if they secure a broader scope of basic rights and freedoms.

Act no. 308/1991 Zb., on the freedom of religious beliefs and the status of churches and religious communities, adopts and supplements the provisions of Section 24 of the Constitution. It stipulates that a confession of religious belief must not be a reason for restricting the rights and freedoms of citizens guaranteed by the Constitution, especially rights to education, job choice and performance, and access to information. Further it stipulates that believers have a right to celebrate festivals and services according to the requirements of their own religious belief, in accordance with generally binding legal rules.

At present the Slovak Republic has five national holidays, of which one has a religious basis – the feast day of Ss Cyril and Methodius (5 July). There are 11 work rest days, of which nine are religious: the Revelation of God, Good Friday, Easter Sunday, Easter Monday, Our Lady of Sorrows Day – patroness of Slovakia, All Saints Day, Christmas Eve, and the first and second days of Christmas. Remembrance days are 9 September – day of Holocaust victims and racial violence, 31 October – Reformation Day, and 30 December – declaration day for the independent church province of Slovakia.

In the Basic Agreement between the SR and the Holy See, the SR is committed to respecting Sundays as days of rest from work, 1 January (which is the national holiday marking the anniversary of the establishment of SR), Virgin Mary Mother of God, the Circumcision of Jesus, the feast-day of Basil the Great, and the holy days mentioned above.

Rights and freedoms stipulated by SR law may be invoked in the field of the general judiciary, including the administrative judiciary, or at the Constitutional Court. If these avenues have been exhausted it is possible to appeal to the European Court of Human Rights in Strasbourg.

The SR Ministry of Culture provides State administration in the area of churches and religious communities, in accordance with the Competence Act.

IV. *Legal Status of Religious Communities*

In its relations with the churches, the Slovak Republic proceeds from acknowledgement of their social and legal status as public and legal institutions sui generis, and co-operates with them according to the principles of partnership co-operation; this may be deduced from Government policy documents. It provides registered churches and religious communities with financial support in carrying out their charitable work, and guarantees their legal status and functions in public life. It considers them subjects with irreplaceable moral potential, which is why it expects their help in the moral recovery of society. It sees churches as a significant part of the cultural and social life of the State, and a crucial factor in the creation of a spiritual and moral consciousness in society. The SR and churches' relationship may be defined as one of parity and co-operation.

Churches and religious communities are special types of legal entity taking advantage of special status (according to Section 24 of the Constitution) and other rights awarded to legal entities by the Constitution. Among these rights are: privacy inviolability, property protection, the right to petition, the right to assembly, association, right to court and other legal protections.

The Act on freedom of religious beliefs and the status of churches and religious communities, no. 308/1991 Zb., considers a voluntary association of persons of the same religious belief, in an organisation with its own structure, bodies, internal regulations and services, to be a church or religious community. They are legal entities and they can band together. They may create communities, orders, associations and similar institutions.

The State acknowledges only churches and religious communities that are registered. According to Act no. 192/1992 Zb. on the registration of churches and religious communities, the registration body is the Ministry of Culture of the SR. A church or religious community may submit a proposal for registration if it can prove that its membership includes at least 20,000 adult persons domiciled within the territory of the SR. The acceptance or rejection of a church is conveyed by the Ministry of Culture within 10 days of its decision on registration or its cancellation, to the Statistics Office of the SR.

In addition to these requirements, the proposal for registration must contain a declaration that a church or a religious community will fully respect the law and generally binding legal rules, and will show respect for other churches and religious communities and persons without a confession. If the registration is rejected, the applicant body may submit an appeal against the decision to the Supreme Court of the SR within 60 days of the date of delivery of the decision.

According to the Act, the Ministry of Culture administers registration of churches and religious communities and legal entities that derive their legal personality from churches and religious communities, so long as they are not subject to the other registry or registration. If the church or religious community acts contrary to the Act or the conditions of its registration, the Ministry of Culture must take steps to cancel the registration. In this case there is also the opportunity for an appeal against the decision to the Supreme Court of the SR.

Most of the registered churches and religious communities do not fulfil the membership condition. They were registered under the provision of the Act that stipulates that churches and religious communities already pursuing their activities, either under the Act or on the basis of State consent, on the day that the Act came into force, are considered registered. Most of the churches and religious communities in the SR work on this basis of deemed registration.

Since the Act on freedom of religious belief and the status of churches and religious communities came into effect, only one religious community has been registered that satisfied the required membership criterion. It was the religious community of Jehovah's Witnesses, registered in the year 1993. The New Apostolic Church submitted relevant documents for state consent to the performance of its activities in the territory of the SR before the coming into effect of Act no. 308/1991 Zb. It was registered in September 2001, and therefore not included in the May 2001 Census.

As at 12 December 2003 the following churches were registered in the Slovak Republic:

- Apostolic Church in Slovakia
- Brethren Unity of Baptists in the Slovak Republic
- Church of Seventh Day Adventists, Slovak Association
- Brethren Church in the Slovak Republic
- Czechoslovak Hussite Church in Slovakia
- Protestant Church of the Augsburg Confession in Slovakia
- Protestant Methodist Church, Slovak Area
- Greek Catholic Church in the Slovak Republic
- Christian congregations in Slovakia
- Religious community of Jehovah's Witnesses
- New Apostolic Church in the Slovak Republic
- Orthodox Church in Slovakia
- Reformed Christian Church in Slovakia
- Roman Catholic Church in Slovakia
- Old Catholic Church
- Central union of Jewish religious communities in the Slovak Republic.

Apart from other functions, churches and religious communities may provide spiritual and material services, teach religion, teach and educate their clergy and secular workers in their own schools and other facilities at theological universities and colleges, organise assemblies without prior announcement, own movable and immovable property and have other property and intangible rights, establish and run dedicated facilities, operate press, publishing, and printing plants, establish and operate their own cultural institutions and facilities, establish and operate their own health and social service facilities, and take part in providing these services in national institutions in accordance with generally binding legal rules. They also have the right to send representatives abroad, and to receive representatives of churches and religious communities from abroad.

The Slovak Republic, through the Basic Agreement with the Holy See and in the Agreement with registered churches and religious communities, guarantees the inviolability of holy sites and cathedrals that are designated for the performance of religious offices on the basis of canon law and the internal directives of churches and religious communities. An exception to the rule of the inviolability of holy sites is allowed only in the case of impending danger to life, health or property.

Among other things worshippers have right to choose clerical or monastic status, and make decisions on life in communities, orders and similar institutions.

Slovak society is faced with a phenomenon of new and non-traditional religious movements, especially since 1989 when the collapse of the former regime and the opening up to the world brought greater interest in spiritual issues on the one hand, and on the other hand interest in Slovakia as new destination for missionaries and propagators of new spiritual movements. It can be estimated that more than 200 different new and non-traditional religious communities, movements and trends have appeared on the Slovak spiritual scene. Those that present themselves most markedly are: the Church of Jesus Christ of the Latter Day Saints (Mormons), Zazen International Slovakia, the Scientology Church, Slovak community for Krishna consciousness, and others based on Christianity, Buddhism, Hinduism and on esoteric principles. At present, reaching the required number of members seems to be a stumbling block for establishing themselves as religious communities acknowledged by the state.

V. Churches and Culture

Section 23 of the Constitution stipulates that churches and religious communities "provide religious education" and Act no. 308/1991 Zb. reads that worshippers have the right to be raised in a religious spirit, or to teach religion after fulfilling the conditions stipulated by internal directives of the churches and religious communities and by generally binding legal rules. The issue is regulated in more detail by the Basic Agreement between the SR and the Holy See and the Agreement between the SR and registered churches and religious communities, yet they both refer to future detailed regulation in separate agreements. The right to religious teaching is established by Act no. 29/1984 Zb. on the primary and secondary school system. Registered churches and religious communities are allowed to provide religious education in all schools and school facilities that are the part of the SR educational system. A teacher of religion has the same legal position as teachers of other subjects, but a necessary condition of their activity is authorisation by their own registered church or religious community. Parents or legal guardians decide on the religious education of children up to the age of 15.

Churches and religious communities have the right to found and administer primary schools, secondary schools, universities, and school facilities for the purpose of education in accordance with conditions stipulated by the law. Church schools and school facilities are in the same position as state schools and school facilities; they are a non-separable and equal part of the SR educational system. The Slovak Republic acknowledges the validity of certificates of graduation at these schools and facilities to the full extent of certificates of graduation of the same type, discipline or level at state schools. It considers them equivalent to State certificates; the same applies to certificates of academic degrees and ranks.

Church schools in Slovakia began to be founded immediately after 1989, but recently the number of new foundations seems to have slowed down. In terms of educational assessment they are in first place within the selected main subject quality survey. That is why there is a great interest in church primary schools and secondary grammar (high) schools. At present in Slovakia there is one Catholic university, 45 church grammar schools, 11 church secondary technical schools, five church secondary technical training schools, 103 church primary schools, and 18 church nursery schools. The state financial contribution per pupil is the same for church schools as for state schools.

Theological colleges form part of several state universities. There are Roman Catholic theological colleges, Protestant, Orthodox and Greek Catholic theological colleges. Theological institutes and ecclesiastical seminaries are also to be found. Missio canonica, or church commission, is a necessary prerequisite for teaching in these institutions. The internal directives of theological colleges and confessional universities are approved by an academic senate after the relevant church or religious community have submitted them. Act no. 131/2002 Z.z. stipulates which sections of the Act shall "proportionally" apply to confessional universities and theological colleges. 22 sections of the University Act are relevant. They concern academic rights and freedoms, the establishment of faculties, academic self-government and its competency, rectors, deans, entrance and disciplinary proceedings, students' and teachers' rights and duties, scientific and academic board, and public university administrative board competence.

In 2000 the Catholic Church established a Catholic University in Ružomberok.[8] The State contributes to its running costs. It was established by the Bishops Conference of Slovakia. The Catholic University has a Faculty of Arts, a Theological Faculty (in Košice), and a Faculty of Education.

Additionally, there are pastoral centres serving students in university towns. Their legal status is subject to the Catholic Church; other churches usually appoint student chaplains for pastoral duties with students.

Churches and religious communities have a right to broadcast on the public service media. About 3 % of broadcasting time is devoted to religious programmes on Slovak Television and Slovak Radio. Religious broadcasting must not be interrupted by commercial breaks. Religious programmes are produced by the religious broadcasting staff of Slovak Radio and by the Slovak Television spiritual life programme centre. The Catholic Church owns and runs Radio Lumen and the video studios *LUX Communication*. Churches and religious communities own publishing houses; the oldest are the Catholic publishing house of St Vojtech Fraternity and the Protestant publishing house Tranoscius. At present more than 100 different religious periodicals are on sale in Slovakia.

---

8 Founded on the basis of Act no. 167/2000 Z.z. on the establishment of the Catholic University in Ružomberok.

The Church owns about 23 % of real estate, and movable cultural treasures that are a significant part of Slovak cultural heritage.

On 20 January 2004 the National Council of the SR consented to the conclusion of the Agreement between the Slovak Republic and the Holy See on the Catholic upbringing and education (ratified on 4 June 2004, came into effect on 9 July 2004) and to the conclusion of the Agreement between the Slovak Republic and registered churches and religious communities on the religious upbringing and education (signed on 13 May 2004, on the same day as the Agreement on the Catholic upbringing and education).

The above mentioned documents introduce religious instruction as a compulsorily optional subject into the Slovak educational system, with ethics as an alternative. The minimum required number of pupils in a class for the purpose of religious instruction is twelve but registered churches and religious communities may, by prior arrangement, form classes by pupils of different age and religious belief. Nevertheless, if the class cannot be formed, the director of the school allows the teaching at the time of another confession's religious instruction, of the ethics instruction or when all classes end. The Slovak Republic committed itself to provide for religious instruction in the pre-school facilities by the agreement as well. The religious instruction curriculum is approved by the respective church after the SR Ministry of education has pronounced on it. The missio canonica or the church/the religious community permission is required for teaching in addition to the professional qualification. This appears also to the teachers of the theological disciplines at the universities and colleges.

Churches and religious communities have the right to establish and operate their own schools and school facilities of any type or discipline. The State guarantees not to demand from church schools to carry out such an upbringing and educational programs that do not accommodate the respective churches' upbringing and education. The churches undertake that the teaching of the general and vocational subjects will be equivalent to the teaching of the general and vocational subjects on the State schools of the same type or discipline. The church schools are to be given the same financial resources as any other schools. According to the agreement, churches can establish the pedagogical and catechetic centres to provide an expert and methodical conducting of the church schools as well as a professional training of the pedagogic and other staff of the church schools. The State undertakes to support theological faculties and not to hinder the establishment and activities of the pastoral centres serving students. Article 6 of the Agreement between the SR and registered churches and religious communities on religious upbringing and education says that the agreement is open to accession for the other registered churches and religious communities on the grounds of the consent of all participating churches and religious communities. In full compliance with the Slovak legislation, every registered church or religious community that is not a party of the agreement, may express its willingness to conclude a similar agreement with the Slovak Republic.

VI. Labour Law within the Church and Religious Communities

Registered churches and religious communities employ more than 4,700 clergy and over 600 other employees. A provision in the Employment Act[9] exempts churches and religious communities from the requirement to employ people with limited working ability or people who are severely mentally or physically disabled.
The Labour Code[10] stipulates that labour law relations between churches and religious communities and their employees performing ecclesiastical work must be in accordance with the Act unless an Act, a separate directive, an international agreement, an agreement between the SR and churches and religious communities, or internal directives of churches and religious communities provides otherwise. Section 52 of the Labour Code stipulates that the provisions of working time and collective labour law relations do not apply to employees of churches and religious communities performing ecclesiastical work.
The Basic Agreement between the SR and the Holy See gives the Holy See the exclusive right to fill church offices according to canon law, independently and exclusively to select candidates for bishoprics and to take decisions on their appointment, redeployment, retirement and recall. The Catholic Church also has the exclusive right to decide on the appointment, redeployment, retirement and recall of a person in connection with any other church office or assignment related to the apostolic mission of the church. The Agreement be-

---

9 Act no. 387/1996 Z.z. on employment as amended by later regulations.
10 Act no. 311/2001 Z.z. Labour Code as drafted in later regulations and amendments.

tween the SR and registered churches and religious communities establishes the right of churches and religious communities to fill church positions and church offices in accordance with their internal directives. According to their own internal directives they have the right to elect and appoint their members into church offices, place them, recall or terminate their service.

The full force of the Labour Code applies to churches and religious communities' employees who do not perform spiritual work, or whose work is not regulated by the above-mentioned directives, and to all other issues not separately regulated. Details are set out in the employment contracts with individual employees. Employers with legal personality derived from churches and religious communities on the basis of Act no. 308/1991 Zb. treat their employees as does any other employer.

VII. Churches and Matrimonial and Family Law

In the Slovak Republic matrimony is entered into by the declaration of a man and a woman before a State authority or an authority of a church or religious community that they enter the marriage publicly, solemnly, and in the presence of two witnesses. If it is a church ceremony, it must be solemnised by a person authorised to perform ecclesiastical functions or a minister of that religious community, and a church form of service must be used. According to the Act on the Family no. 94/1963 Zb., as implemented in later regulations, the church authority must deliver a certificate of the marriage to a body authorised to administer registration in the district where the wedding was held.

Issues of marriage according to canon law are regulated by Section 10 of the Basic Agreement between the SR and the Holy See. If a marriage fulfils the conditions stipulated in SR law, it has the same legal status and effects as a civil marriage taking place within the territory of the Slovak Republic. The same provision is found in Section 10 of the Agreement between the SR and registered churches and religious communities.

VIII. Financing of the Churches

After 1989 new legislation enabled churches and religious communities to have full internal self-government, but it did not eliminate their direct financial dependence on the state.
Act no. 218/1949 Zb. on financial provision for churches and religious communities, as much amended, eliminated a discriminatory approach and state control over the churches, but still maintains a paternalistic approach to the churches in the field of finance. By means of the Act the communist state imposed a unified form of direct state subsidy on churches and religious communities. The subsidy should have superseded the whole spectrum of individually differentiated traditional sources of income. In the period between 25 February 1948 and 1 November 1949 when the Act no. 218/1949 Zb. came into force, a crucial part of the churches' productive property was nationalised without redress, particularly by means of a unilateral implementation of the Acts on land and agrarian reforms. Restitution of church property is one of the processes enabling churches to start working towards economic independence.
On the basis of Federal Act no. 298/1990 Zb. on the regulation of some property relations of monastic orders and congregations and the Olomouc archbishopric as spelt out in Act no. 338/1991 Zb., some property of monastic orders and congregations was returned. In the territory of the Slovak Republic, 95 monasteries were involved.
Act no. 282/1993 Z.z. on the mitigation of some of the legal injustices to property caused to churches and religious communities enabled some ownership rights to be restored. This related to movable and immovable things of which churches and religious communities were dispossessed on the basis of decisions of state bodies, civil law and administrative Acts issued in the period between 8 May 1945 – 2 November 1938 in the case of Jewish communities – and 1 January 1990. The Act stipulated that proceedings relating to the surrender of immovable things be exempt from administrative and court fees, and compensation for costs connected with the geographical location of surrendered real estate must be provided by the State. Act no. 97/2002 Z.z. amending Act no. 282/1993 Z.z., added to the property to be restored lands that are the part of the forest land in national parks.
At present, on the basis of Act no. 218/1949 Zb. and its amendment by Act no. 522/1992 Zb., the State must provide churches and religious communities with funds for payment of their clergy stipends

(including contributions to social and health care funds and the employment fund), if churches and religious communities so request. Churches and religious communities that were provided with personal benefits for their clergy up to 31 December 1989 are not obliged to do this. Four[11] of the total of 16 registered churches and religious communities do not exercise their claim for contributions. The classification and levels of clergy stipends are regulated by SR Government decree.[12]

The State contributes to the operation of the headquarters of registered churches and religious communities. The Ministry of Culture SR is the administrator of the financial support assigned in the national budget by the National Council SR for churches and religious communities. Through the church department it remits assigned funds to each church headquarters on a monthly basis. The national budget sets contributions to the Slovak Catholic Charity and evangelical Diakonia. The State may make financial contributions of up to 80 % of the purchase price for the installation of electronic security devices designed to protect sacred cultural treasures.

All proceeds of church collections, income for church activities, and regular contributions of registered churches' and religious communities' members are tax exempt. The value of gifts provided for humanitarian, charitable and religious purposes of the churches and religious communities registered by the State may be deducted from the taxable income of natural persons and legal entities to the amount stipulated by the Act. Lands forming one functional unit with a building or part of a building which is used for the performance of religious ceremonies, and with the whole or part of a building which serves as offices for persons commissioned for church administration, are exempt from land tax. Lands where cemeteries are founded are also exempt from land tax. Buildings and those parts of them used exclusively for the performance of religious ceremonies or as the offices of church administrators are exempt from the tax on buildings. Legacies and gifts earmarked for the development of registered churches and religious communities[13] are exempt from inheritance tax. Under conditions stipulated by Ordinance no. 17/1994

---

11 The Religious Community of Jehovah's Witnesses, Christian congregations, Seventh Day Adventist Church, New Apostolic Church.
12 Government Order SR no. 578/1990 Zb. as amended by Government Order no. 187/1997 Z.z.
13 Act no. 366/1999 Z.z. on taxes on earnings, Act no. 317/1992 Zb. on real estate tax, Act no. 318/1992 Zb. on inheritance tax, donation tax and transfer tax and real estate transfer.

Z.z., religious objects and gifts for churches and religious communities are exempt from import duty.

On the basis of Section 48 of Act no. 366/1999 Z.z. on tax on earnings, as amended by later regulations, each taxpayer is entitled to remit, through the tax administrator, a sum of money equivalent to 1 % of his or her income tax to one of the specified legal entities[14] among which are agencies of churches and religious communities. In addition to this, churches and religious communities as well as entities with legal personality derived from them, may apply for various grants and subsidies. Churches may apply for grants towards the preservation and recovery of cultural landmarks that are in their ownership as well as for social, charitable, educational and cultural projects.

Since 2000, work has been in progress towards the goal of a new model of financial provision for churches and religious communities. In 2001 the Ministry of Culture submitted a Bill on financial provision for churches and religious communities. The Bill preserves the principle of the existing model, but with the difference that financial provision takes into account the number of members of each church and religious community and specific conditions of their activity in relation to their size. The Bill passed through the legislative process up to being discussed by the National Council SR plenary. However, it was removed from the agenda on the proposal of one of the deputies, and up to now it has not been put back. A broad consensus of churches and religious communities, political parties, and other involved society constituents, seems to have foundered again.

IX. *Religious Assistance in Public Institutions*

According to Section 9 of Act no. 308/1991 Zb. on the freedom of religious belief and the status of churches and religious communities, persons performing spiritual work have the right to enter public social care, health and children's home institutions. They have the right to enter military bases, and places where custody, custodial sentence,

---

14 Apart from the facilities of registered churches and religious communities, these include civic associations, foundations, non-investment funds, non-profitable organisations providing generally beneficial services, organisations with an international element, and the Slovak Red Cross.

protective care or protective upbringing are carried out. In such institutions and organisations each person has the right to be provided with spiritual service, usually by a minister of their own choice, especially in life-threatening situations. Furthermore, each person has the right to possess religious and spiritual literature of their own choice.

Act no. 370/1997 Z.z. on military service enables soldiers to take part in religious ceremonies in military bases out of duty hours. Military chaplains have been active in the SR Army since 1994. In 1995 on the basis of an order of the Minister of Defence, the Office of Military Chaplains of the Ministry of Defence SR was established. The office reports directly to the Minister of Defence. It is the highest specialist body on spiritual and religious matters in the organisation of the Ministry of Defence and the main conception, standard-bearing and executive body of the military and spiritual service. The Military Deanery of the SR Army General Headquarters is the main specialist responsible body charged with meeting the needs and development of spiritual and religious care for SR Army members. Details of spiritual and religious activities, their organisation and implementation, and logistics provision in the army corps, at military schools, and the duties of the chaplains, are regulated by an internal directive of the Ministry of Defence SR. Spiritual service is performed by military chaplains of religious denominations that have the most members in the armed forces and armed bodies, that is especially the Catholic and Augsburg Confession Churches.

The Office of Police Chaplains was established in 2002, headed by a director who reports directly to the Minister of the Interior. The office provides policemen as well as their families with individual and collective spiritual care and liturgical services.

The Agreement between the Slovak Republic and the Holy See on spiritual service for Catholic worshippers in the armed forces and armed corps of the Slovak Republic no. 648/2002 Z.z. came into effect on 27 November 2002.[15] On the basis of the Agreement the Ordinariate for the armed forces and armed corps SR has been established at diocesan level, and an Ordinary has been appointed at the level of bishop.[16] The Agreement regulates spiritual service for Catholics in the Armed Forces SR, Police Corps, Prison and Judicial

---

15 The President of the Slovak Republic ratified the Agreement on 11 October 2002 and ratification charters were exchanged on 28 October 2002.
16 The Ordinariat has canonical and state legal personality. The Ordinary is appointed by the Holy See, he is a member of Bishops' Conference of Slovakia, and incorporated in the SR armed forces.

Guard, Railway Police, and for persons deprived of their freedom by the State. A similar agreement has been prepared by registered non-Catholic churches and religious communities.

Churches and religious communities have the right to establish and operate health and social service institutions, and to take part in the provision of services in public institutions. The Act on freedom of religious belief and the status of churches and religious communities establishes the right of persons performing spiritual activities to enter public health and social care institutions, and children's homes. The issues are regulated by the Basic Agreement between the SR and the Holy See, and the Agreement between the SR and registered churches and religious communities. The above-mentioned Agreements broaden the access of clergy to facilities for persons with mandatory institutional rehabilitation, and State institutions for the treatment and rehabilitation of drug addicts and other addicted persons. The conditions governing clergy activities in the above-mentioned institutions are governed by generally binding legal rules and the particularities of each specific institution; they therefore depend on individual agreements.

X. *Criminal Law and Religion*

Offences or criminal acts directly or indirectly concerning religion and its manifestations are covered by Criminal Act no. 140/1961 Zb. The Criminal Act provides that a person who by violence, threat of violence, or threat of other detriment forces another person to take part in a religious act, hinders other person without permission in such participation, or hinders other person in the use of the freedom of confession in any other way shall be liable to imprisonment for up to two years or a fine. A religious act is considered to be any act or ceremony that relates to a confession of a church or religious community belief, such as divine service, confession, Eucharist, and so on. Another example of obstructing the freedom of religion can be found in the damage or destruction of items needed for the performance of religious ceremonies. The Criminal Act refers to the motive for violence against a group of citizens or an individual in terms of their denomination, or the fact that they are undenominational. Denomination implies an active or passive relationship to a particular religion, an ideology or world-view presented by a particular church or religious community. Violence can arise if a person is threatened to breaking point, or when groups of people get together to commit a criminal act. The crime of defamation of religious opinion is based on public defamation – vituperation, belittlement of groups of citizens because of their denomination or because they are undenominational.

The Act on imprisonment forbids a sentenced person from acquiring or owning a printing press or any item promoting religious intolerance; it also enables church organisations to obtain compensation in the criminal process. The Act on imprisonment confirms the right of an accused person to the provision of spiritual service. However, the purpose of the imprisonment must be taken into consideration, and spiritual provision may be subject to the approval of the relevant body acting in the criminal proceedings, except in cases of danger to life or health.

XI. The Legal Status of Clergy

Neither administrative nor civil law give any special status to the clergy; their status in administrative or civil proceedings is the same as that of the laity. If a minister acts on behalf of a church legal entity, he or she will have the status of agent of a private law entity. This is also the case in the field of criminal law, with the exception of the issue of confessional secrets.

According to Section 8 of Act no. 308/1991 Zb. the State acknowledges a pledge to secrecy of persons commissioned to perform spiritual work. The Criminal Act provision as to the duty of each citizen with knowledge of a criminal act does not apply to a person who would violate the confidentiality of the confessional, or to information that has been confided to them orally or on paper under conditions of secrecy. Criminal Rule no. 141/1961 Zb. enables clergy called as witnesses to refuse to testify for the same reason.

The inviolability of the confessional and the right to refuse to give evidence before State bodies is guaranteed by the Basic Agreement between the Slovak Republic and the Holy See, and the Agreement between the Slovak Republic and registered churches and religious communities in the Slovak Republic, in addition to the Criminal Rule.

Act no. 308/1991 Zb. on the freedom of religious belief and the status of churches and religious communities lays down that persons performing spiritual work must be authorised by those churches and religious communities according to their internal directives and generally binding legal rules. Churches and religious communities must deploy clergy and others according to their qualifications. In accordance with their internal directives, churches appoint persons performing spiritual work and teachers of religion to a specific position, or a particular territorial district.

The Agreement between the Slovak Republic and the Holy See on spiritual service for Catholic worshippers in the armed forces and armed corps of the Slovak Republic guarantees clergy the right to perform national service in the form of spiritual service. Clergy in the armed forces and armed corps are given a salary on the scale for army officers or police officers according to their rank and length of service. Social benefits for armed forces members also apply to clergy.

XII. Particular Issues of Civil Ecclesiastical Law Development

Issues of relations between the Slovak Republic and churches, and church involvement in public life often arise on the Slovak political scene. Following the acceptance of agreements with the Holy See, registered churches engage in discussion on the national budget or the Act on induced termination of pregnancy or abortion. Liberal and left wing parties most often call for a full separation between Church and State.

In the near future two further Agreements between the SR and the Holy See should be concluded. These are on the exercise of conscience, and issues of finance. The Agreement on the exercise of conscience is at present being debated; the Agreement on finance issues is the subject of discussions about whether it is to follow or precede amendment of the legislation concerning financial provision for churches and religious communities. Other registered churches and religious communities are to make similar agreements with the Slovak Republic.

Issues of legal conditions for acquiring the status of a registered church or religious community have arisen in connection with the relationship of the State to the new and non-traditional religious movements. More are showing an interest in registration, but they do not fulfil the legal condition as to membership numbers. It seems that issues of conditions for church registration will soon attract the interest of authorised bodies.

XIII. Bibliography

Cipár, Marián; Moravčíková, Michaela. Cirkvi a náboženské spoločnosti v zjednocujúcej sa Európe. In: *Vznik a perspektívy politickej vedy na Slovensku.* Trnava: Fakulta humanistiky Trnavskej univerzity v Trnave, 2002, p. 52-57, ISBN 80-89074-33-2.

Jozefčiaková, Silvia. Cirkvi a náboženské spoločnosti v Slovenskej republike. Bratislava: Ústav pre vzťahy štátu a cirkví, 2002, 93 p., ISBN 80-968559-7-2.

Moravčíková, Michaela, Cipár, Marián. Religiozita na Slovensku. In: *Ročenka ústavu pre vzťahy štátu a cirkví 1997,* Bratislava: Ústav pre vzťahy štátu a cirkví, 1998, p. 124-139, ISBN 80-968072-5-0.

Moravčíková, Michaela, Cipár, Marián. Religiozita na Slovensku II. Bratislava: Ústav pre vzťahy štátu a cirkví, 2003, 110 p., ISBN 80-89096-05-0.

Moravčíková, Michaela, Procedure of Declaration of Consent by the National Council of the Slovak Republic with the Principal Treaty between the Slovak Republic and the Holy See. In: Šmid, Marek, Vasiľ, Cyril (a cura) *Relazioni internationali giuridiche bilaterali tra la Santa Sede e gli stati: esperienze e prospettive.* Città del Vaticano: Libreria Editrice Vaticana, 2003, p. 271-278, ISBN 88-209-7431-2.

Moravčíková, Michaela; Cipár, Marián. Cisárovi cisárovo. Ekonomické zabezpečenie cirkví a náboženských spoločností. Bratislava: Ústav pre vzťahy štátu a cirkví, 2001, 277 p., ISBN 80-968559-0-5.

Papastathis, Charalambos, K. L'Œuvre législative de la Mission cyrillo-méthodienne en Grande Moravie. Thessalonique: Association hellénique d'Études slaves, 1978. 142 p.

Potz, Richard; Schwarz, Karl; Synek, Eva Maria; Wieshaider, Wolfgang. Recht und Religion in Mittel- und Osteuropa. Band 1 Slowakei. Koordinatoren *Mulík, Peter, Wieshaider, Wolfgang.* Wien: WUV/Universitätverlag, 2001. 150 p. ISBN 3-85114-461-9.

Sčítanie obyvateľstva domov a bytov 2001. Základné údaje. Náboženské vyznanie obyvateľstva. Č. 600-0615/2001. Bratislava: Štatistický úrad Slovenskej republiky, 2001. 240 p.

Šmid, Marek. Svätá stolica ako osobitný subjekt medzinárodného práva: zmluvné vzťahy so štátmi. Štúdie a materiály. Zošit IX. Bratislava: Slovenská spoločnosť pre medzinárodné právo pri Slovenskej akadémii vied, 2003. 53 p.

Markku Heikkilä, Jyrki Knuutila, Martin Scheinin[1]
State and Church in Finland

I. Social Facts

The criteria for belonging to a religious denomination vary to some extent according to the traditions of each denomination. In Finland, the membership criterion for most Christian churches is baptism. Most churches recognize a baptism carried out in another church. Thus, the transfer of membership from one church to another requires only the person's own declaration and participation in the teaching offered by the new religious community. The minority denominations that do not accept infant baptism (e.g., Baptists and several Pentecostal churches) require adult baptism, conditional upon a personal religious confession, from their members. The number of Muslims multiplied in Finland during the 1990s. To begin with, only few of them organized themselves into registered religious groups. However, their registrations have clearly increased in the early 21st century (2000: 1,199 and 2001: 2,104).
Finnish membership of registered religious denominations in 2000 was as follows:

Population by religious affiliation at the end of 2000[2]

	2000	%
Total population	5,181,115	100.0
Evangelical Lutheran Church	4,408,381	85.1
Other Lutheran Churches	2,228	0.0
Greek Orthodox Church of Finland	55,692	1.1
Other Orthodox Churches	1,088	0.0
Jehovah's Witnesses	18,492	0.4
Free Church in Finland	13,474	0.3

---

1 Sections 1-2, 5, 7, 9, 11-12 written by *Markku Heikkilä* and *Jyrki Knuutila*, sections 3, 4, 6, 8, 10 by *Martin Scheinin*.
2 Statistical Yearbook of Finland 2002, p. 117.

Seventh Day Adventists	4,316	0.1
Roman Catholic Church	7,247	0.1
Church of Jesus Christ of Latter-day Saints	3,307	0.1
Baptist Congregations	2,395	0.0
Methodist Churches	1,260	0.0
Jewish congregations	1,157	0.0
Islamic congregations	1,199	0.0
Others	920	0.0
Persons not belonging to any religious community	650,979	12.7

Between 1980 and 2000 the membership of the Lutheran Church increased slightly; however, due to the increase in total population, its relative share has decreased (1980: 90.2 % and 2000: 85.1 %). The Orthodox church, Jehovah's Witnesses and the Free Church of Finland are among those whose membership has grown. The number of members of the Catholic church has more than doubled (1980: 3,051 and 2000: 7,227), yet it is still a relatively small community. The membership of the Pentecostal congregations is at approximately the same level as the Orthodox church; however, the Pentecostals are not registered as a religious community. Because of this, its members appear in the statistics with those who do not belong to any religious community. Its total number has almost doubled (1980: 372,640 and 2000: 659,979).

II. Historical Background

Most parts of Finland were incorporated into Sweden during the 12th and 13th centuries and so came under the influence of Western Christianity. Only a part of Karelia remained in the Orthodox Church. In the Middle Ages the Church wielded both economic and political power, in Finland as elsewhere. The Church was independent of – even supreme over – the secular powers, and the Bishop of Turku was among the country's most prominent people.

The Reformation, which lasted from 1530 to 1593, severely impaired the Church's economic and political power in Sweden and the Church was made subordinate to the State authorities. The King became head of the Church instead of the Pope, and the Protestant Church the only Church in the kingdom. Cathedral chapters were made into royal offices and the Church's assets were transferred to the royal family. The Bishop became an official of the realm, appointed by the King.

In the 17th century, when Sweden was a major power, the Church became a State Church, religious activities being safeguarded by the secular powers. Church teaching had to serve the social equilibrium and support the ideological bases of a world power. The State-Church relationship remained unchanged in the 18th century, until Sweden finally lost its position as a major political power.

The Church Code, which applied to all the subjects of the kingdom, was adopted in 1686 by the authorities of the realm and enacted by the king, as were various Acts concerning the clergy and their activity. In the 18th century the clergy became one of the four estates of the realm, which gave them certain privileges.

The relationship between ruler and Church, as well as the Church Code from the time of Swedish rule, was maintained when Finland became part of Russia in 1809. The established (Lutheran) church remained unchanged under the rule of the Orthodox Grand Dukes. In fact, it was due to the Lutheran concept and doctrine of authority that the transfer of Finland to Russian rule took place peacefully – compared with the situation in Poland.

Liberalism and new theological movements contributed to a loosening of the extremely close link between church and society in the 19th century. The 1869 Church Code (for the Lutheran Church of Finland) concerned solely the members of the Lutheran denomination. The Church Code of 1869 was a particularly large collection of legal texts. An attempt was made to block all possible openings for the Russian Grand Duke to issue decrees affecting the internal organization of the church. It was not yet possible to make the proposed freedom of religion a reality since, because of the situation regarding religious politics in the Russian Grand Duchy, Orthodox Christians could not yet be granted the right to renounce the church. Church law continued to be passed by the Regent – the Russian Grand Duke – on the proposal of Parliament.

The Church Synod alone held the right of initiative in matters of Church law. The secular authorities were not allowed to influence the content of the legislation. Their role was merely to accept or reject any proposed law. The Law on Dissenters of 1889 legalised the first Protestant minority churches.

The denominational neutrality of the State and the freedom of religion were enshrined in the Constitution Act of independent Finland in 1919. The principles of religious freedom were set out more precisely in the Law on Religious Freedom which was passed in 1922. At the same time, the Lutheran and the Orthodox Churches were granted a particular status in public law, in contrast to the other religious communities. This preferential position was based on the fact that the majority of the population belonged to these national churches.

The role of the Church as a moral supporter of the nation became increasingly important during the Second World War. The amendment to the Church Code of 1963 was concerned only with codification, but parallel discussions of church politics led to an adjustment of the church administrative structure to make it compatible with the principles of a democratic society.

In the field of politics as well as in the Church, there is now greater independence of the Church on the one hand and the State on the other. For this reason, in 1993 Lutheran Church law was divided into two parts. A Church Code passed by the State authority regulates the relations between Church and State, while a Church Ordinance passed by the Church regulates the Church itself – its doctrines as well as its life.

With the majority of the Finnish population belonging to the Evangelical Lutheran Church of Finland, the Church formerly took care of the main population register in Finland. Since 1998, the main population register of all citizens of Finland has been taken care of by the State. Now, the Evangelical Lutheran Church of Finland oversees its own population register. It can, for example, conduct a civil marriage and issue a marriage certificate to church members.

Relations between the State and the Evangelical Lutheran Church of Finland went through a degree of change during the years 1997 to 2000. During this time, new relationships between State, bishops and cathedral chapters have been put into place. This has brought to an end the old tradition dating from the 16th century. The status of bishops has been transformed from state official to church servant. As a sign of this, elected bishops are not now nominated by the Head of State, the President of Finland. Instead, bishops are elected and receive a formal letter of appointment to the bishopric from the cathedral chapter. In addition, the stipends of bishops and the funding of cathedral chapters are now the responsibility of the Church, not the State.

The new Constitution of Finland was passed in 1999. In this Constitution, the freedom of the individual has been emphasized. Because of this, the Law on Religious Freedom has been updated; a new Law on Religious Freedom was passed in 2003. This Act deals with various issues relating to state and church. The new Law will make all Christian churches and other religious communities more equal in society. The dominant status of the Evangelical Lutheran Church of Finland has decreased. A sign of this is that exemption from Lutheran religious education does no longer require a request by the family of pupils who are not members of the Evangelical Lutheran Church of Finland. Instead they are automatically exempt unless the family wishes to sign up for education in the Lutheran religion. In addition, teachers belonging to other religions are now permitted to teach Lutheran religious education. Another sign of the equality of all Christian churches and other religious communities is that seceding from a church or religious community has been made easier.

III. Basic Structure

1. Legal Sources

a) Constitutional provisions

After revision of the fundamental rights chapter in 1995 within the framework of the 1919 Constitution Act, and a subsequent total reform of the Constitution which was completed in 2000 by the entry into force of the 1999 Constitution, freedom of religion is now enshrined in Section 11 of the new Constitution of Finland:[3]

> Section 11 – Freedom of religion and conscience
> Everyone has the freedom of religion and conscience.
> Freedom of religion and conscience entails the right to profess and practise a religion, the right to express one's convictions and the right to be a member of or decline to be a member of a religious community. No one is under the obligation, against his or her conscience, to participate in the practice of a religion.

Supplementing Section 11, the general clause on equality and non-discrimination in Section 6 includes a prohibition against discrimination on account of religion, conviction or opinion.

---

[3] Act 731 of 1999. English, French, German and Spanish translations by the Ministry of Justice are available at http://www.om.fi/74.htm.

In the course of the total reform of the Constitution, four separate instruments, each with constitutional status, were replaced by a single Constitution. Partly as a result of this structural change but partly also reflecting changes in society, the constitutional recognition of the special status of the Lutheran Church is less prominent in the framework of the Constitution than formerly. Nevertheless, both the traditional special status and the constitutionally protected autonomy of this Church are still reflected in Section 76 of the new Constitution, which reads:

> Section 76 – The Church Act
> Provisions on the organisation and administration of the Evangelic Lutheran Church are laid down in the Church Act.

The legislative procedure for the enactment of the Church Act (or Church Code) and the right to submit legislative proposals relating to the Church Act are governed by specific provisions in that Act.
As in the old constitutional framework, this clause in the Constitution includes a restriction on the sovereignty of the legislator, to the effect that the procedure for amendment of the Church Act is prescribed by the Church Act itself.
Section 127(2) of the Constitution guarantees the right of conscientious objection to military service:

> Provisions on the right to exemption, on grounds of conscience, from participation in military national defence are laid down by an Act.

The right in question is implemented by the Alternative Civilian Service Act.[4]
The Constitution of 1999 no longer prescribes that the President of the Republic appoints the bishops of the Lutheran Church.[5] This change reflects a general trend towards gradually dissociating State and Church from each other.

b) Other Acts of Parliament

The Church Act[6] is the "Constitution" of the Lutheran Church. According to Chapter 2, Section 2 only the General Assembly of the Lutheran Church may propose amendments to the Church Act, and

---

4 Act 1723 of 1991.
5 Compare Section 87 of the 1919 Constitution Act.
6 Act 1054 of 1993.

the role of the President and of Parliament is limited to either approval or disapproval of proposals submitted by the Assembly.

There is also a separate Act of Parliament dealing with the Orthodox Church.[7] Section 1 of this Act expresses the confession of the Church. According to Section 9, the Government of Finland is to be the highest authority within the Orthodox Church.

The new Freedom of Religion Act,[8] enacted to implement the new Constitution in the field of freedom of religion, enshrined in Section 11 of the Constitution. It gives further protection for the freedom of religion and establishes a legal framework for the foundation and operation of religious communities other than the Lutheran Church and the Orthodox Church which have their legal basis in the separate laws mentioned above.[9] A religious community may be founded by a group of at least 20 persons, and the National Board of Patents and Registration has the task of keeping a register of such communities.[10]

The Freedom of Religion Act regulates the right to join and renounce a religious community,[11] whereas the right of non-members to be exempted from religious instruction in school is nowadays regulated in the legislation concerning educational institutions. The 1922 Freedom of Religion Act provided that confessional religious education corresponding to the religious affiliation of the majority of pupils was to be a part of the curriculum of public schools, with the right of exemptions for those who were not members of the majority religion.[12] However, the starting point of the new legislation is that religious education is to be non-confessional. Nevertheless, the education provided is to be in the religion followed by the majority of pupils; non-members will be exempted and, provided that there are at least three of them, they may opt for separate education in their own religion.[13] Pupils who do not belong to any religious community who opt out of education in the majority religion may be taught ethics. As with the situation under the old legislation, the reference to the relig-

---

7   Act 521 of 1969.
8   Act 453 of 2003.
9   Chapters 1 and 3 of the Freedom of Religion Act are nevertheless applicable to the two Churches.
10 See Chapter 2 of the Freedom of Religion Act (Sections 7 to 27).
11 Sections 3 and 4.
12 Section 8 of Act 267 of 1922.
13 Section 13 of the Act on Comprehensive Education (Act 628 of 1998), as amended by Act 454 of 2003; Section 9 of the Upper Secondary School Act (Act 629 of 1998), as amended by Act 455 of 2003. The situation of pupils belonging to the Orthodox Church is somewhat different as the provision of separate education in their religion only requires that there are at least three pupils belonging to this Church and not participating in the education in the majority religion. In other words, no request for arranging such education is required.

ion of the majority of pupils means in practice that all public schools include in their curriculum teaching of the Lutheran religion.

c) International guarantees

Finland is a party to several international human rights treaties which are of relevance for the protection of religious freedom, notably the European Convention of Human Rights, the International Covenant on Civil and Political Rights, the International Covenant on Economic, Social and Cultural Rights, the Convention on the Rights of the Child and the Convention for the Elimination of Discrimination against Women. As a rule, these treaties also form part of applicable domestic law as they have been incorporated into Finnish Law through a treaty-specific Act of Parliament.[14] Finland has also subordinated itself to all existing international control mechanisms under the treaties in question.

2. System Approach

The Finnish State is neither nondenominational nor denominational. There are close institutional and legislative links between the State and the Lutheran Church, and the public school system which is run primarily by the municipalities and partly financed by the State, makes nondenominational religious instruction on the majority religion a part of the curriculum.[15] Additionally, the Orthodox Church has a special institutional status, while the Constitution and secular laws secure the freedom of religion and the rights of religious and non-religious minorities. Members of minority religions and persons not belonging to any religious community have a constitutional right to be exempt from participation in religion. Within the school system this means separate education in the minority religion concerned, or education on ethics, or total exemption.

The Church Act of the Lutheran Church is an Act of Parliament despite the fact that neither the President nor Parliament are allowed to change the wording agreed by the General Assembly of the Church.

---

14 Of the treaties mentioned in the text, the International Covenant on Economic, Social and Cultural Rights is an exception, as it was incorporated not through an Act of Parliament but through a President's Ordinance after Parliament gave consent for its ratification.
15 The formulation used in the relevant laws is neutral: it speaks of the denomination of the majority of the pupils in any particular school. In practice, all Finnish schools have a Lutheran majority, except for some separate religious schools.

The Church Act includes provisions with a clear denominational character.[16] The confession and structure of the Orthodox Church is also regulated through an Act of Parliament. Therefore, one may conclude that there still are two State Churches in Finland despite a gradual process towards fewer constitutional or other official links between the State and the two Churches.

IV. Legal Status of Religious Bodies

The Lutheran Church and the Orthodox Church are self-governing public law entities. Their internal structure and relationships with the state are determined by specific Acts of Parliament. The autonomy of the Lutheran Church is "strong" in the sense that the only the Church itself may propose amendments to the Church Act. The public law nature of the two State Churches is manifested in the fact that both Churches have their own internal court system.[17]

Other religious communities are private law subjects operating under the Freedom of Religion Act. They have, after registration by the National Board of Patents and Registration (previously the Ministry of Education), full legal capacity as autonomous juridical persons,[18] and individual members are not personally responsible for their communities' debts.[19] Earlier restrictions on the right of religious communities to own real property were abolished with the adoption of the 2003 Freedom of Religion Act. According to the new Act, the purpose of a religious community must not be the generation of economic profit or the running of predominantly economic activities.[20]

The Freedom of Religion Act includes relatively detailed provisions on the requirements for registering a religious community.[21] These requirements are mostly of a technical nature and do not interfere with the autonomy of religious communities to determine their confession and the forms for manifesting a religion. However, the law

---

16 See, in particular, Chapter 1 which includes a short formulation of the confession of the Lutheran Church.
17 See Chapters 19, 23 and 24 of the Church Act, and Chapter 6 of the Act on the Orthodox Church.
18 Section 17 of the Freedom of Religion Act.
19 Section 17(2).
20 Section 7(3).
21 Sections 9, 10 and 18.

includes a requirement that all religious communities must respect constitutional and human rights in their operation.[22] This provision complements the prohibition on generating economic profit and a general clause stipulating that the aim of a religious community must be to organise and support the manifestation and practice of a religion.[23]

In case a religious community operates in a way that is essentially contrary to the law or to its registered aim, secular courts are competent to suspend the activities of the community or to order its dissolution, on the basis of a lawsuit initiated by the Ministry of Education, a prosecutor, or a member of the community in question.[24]

There are no obstacles to clergy participating in political life. The electoral system gives special status to entities registered as political parties, which are entitled to nominate candidates. Religious communities do not possess such status but it is possible to collect signatures of voters for the nomination of independent candidates.[25]

V. Church and Culture

The communal system of comprehensive schools carries the main responsibility for providing compulsory education in Finland. Compared with the total number of schools, the proportion of licensed private schools is small. The English school in Helsinki is a Catholic foundation. Licences have also been granted for a few comprehensive schools which are based on religious confessions.

According to the current law, every child under school-age has a right to day care arranged by the municipality. Religious and ethical teaching is a statutory part of the day care. In order to enable the participation of as many children as possible, religious education is broadly Christian in scope. As the variety of children's nationalities and cultures increases, there are more and more children in day care whose religious and cultural background differs from the Finnish tradition. This creates further challenges for religious education in day care.

---

22 Section 7(2).
23 Section 7(1).
24 Sections 25 and 26.
25 Act on Elections, Act 714 of 1998.

Based on the law of religious freedom and the current school laws, every student in comprehensive and upper comprehensive schools has a right to religious teaching according to his or her own confession. The communal school system is responsible for its organisation and funding. Students who do not belong to a church or religious community participate in world view studies (ethics). In the matriculation examination, it is possible to take either a test of one's own religion or of world view studies. The increasing number of the students representing different cultures has created a need to train teachers for Muslim religious education.

All Finnish universities are government-run. They include three theological faculties: the faculty within Helsinki University deriving its origin from the establishment of the old Academy of Turku in 1640, the Swedish-speaking faculty founded in "new" Åbo Akademi in 1924, and the faculty established in Joensuu University in 2002. The last mentioned includes departments of western theology and of orthodox theology which is responsible for the education of priests and cantors for the Orthodox Church. The theological research and teaching in these universities is non-confessional, according to the Nordic tradition.

More than 20 commune- or foundation-based vocational high schools and polytechnics have been established in Finland during the last decade. The state covers most of their expenses. These institutions include the Diaconia Polytechnic which is involved in networks with several training centres in the fields of diaconia and youth leadership studies.

Under their current contracts, the communications centre of the Lutheran Church co-ordinates the supply of religious programmes on the TV and radio channels of the national broadcasting company. Live programmes of services and hours of devotion are mainly broadcast on TV2 and the Yle Suomi radio channel. Services and hours of devotion of minority denominations are broadcast according to a jointly agreed programme. Occasional religion-related programmes may be broadcast on any TV and radio channels of the national broadcasting company. The Porvoo Diocesan Council co-ordinates the broadcasting of Swedish-speaking services and religious documentaries together with Finland's Svenska Television.

Congregations and religious communities may buy air time from regional and local TV and radio channels. Several Christian associations have been involved in radio broadcasting since the 1990s. The only Christian local radio station in Finland, Radio Dei, was founded in 1997. Since its inception it has had more than 30 partners, for instance, the capital area Lutheran parishes and associations, the Pentecostal Saalem congregation and the Christian Centre. In 1999 the Council of State permitted Radio Dei to extend its activities to several other localities.

VI. Labour Law within the Churches

Some Lutheran Church and the Orthodox Church personnel are considered as public officials. In addition, these public law entities may make private law employment contracts. Persons employed by other religious communities work under a private law employment contract, the conditions of which are regulated by labour law.
Part II (Chapters 5 and 6) of the Church Code includes detailed provisions on the public law and private law employment relations within the Lutheran Church. For both categories of personnel, there is a system for negotiation and collective agreements.
The regulation concerning the Orthodox Church is based on the same essential classifications but the concrete rules are not as modern and complete.[26]
The State Church nature of both the Lutheran and the Orthodox Church was previously reflected in the fact that the President of the Republic appointed the bishops of both Churches. However, this arrangement was discontinued in 2000.[27]

VII. Matrimonial and Family Law

On the subject of matrimonial and family law, the interests of Church and society have always been widely disparate in Finnish history.
Only under Swedish rule did the Finnish Church obtain the right to conduct marriages for its members (with effect under secular law as constituting a marriage) by the Swedish Law of 1734. Church mar-

---

26 See, the Act on the Orthodox Church and the Ordinance on the Orthodox Church (No. 179 of 1970).
27 See Act 201 of 2000, amending Chapter 18(4) of the Church Act and Ordinance 880 of 2000, amending Section 153 of the Ordinance on the Orthodox Church.

riage, which was the norm for all classes of society, had until then been understood legally merely as a church blessing of an already existing marriage, despite of the fact that the church had always endeavoured to obtain the right to conduct the marriages of its members. This law also reflected other Church opinions on matrimony and the family. Because of the close connection between the kingdom and the church, the church wedding became in practice the only official form of marriage. This situation continued under Russian rule until the beginning of the twentieth century. Orthodox marriage was seen as an exception (the Orthodox Church was also granted an official right to perform marriages). The new ideologies at the turn of the century – atheist ideologies, for instance – as well as the growth of other Christian communities were the impetus for discussions on the possibility of civil marriage in a register office.

After the independence of Finland in 1917 the register office wedding became an alternative to the church wedding through the Laws on Civil Marriage of 1917, on the Freedom of Religion of 1922 and on Marriage of 1929. The State also granted several church and religious communities, which had been given equal standing by the Law on the Freedom of Religion, the right to conduct marriages for their adherents. According to these laws, marriage by a church or religious community represents a more natural form of marriage, whereas civil marriage was an alternative for certain special cases. These are where the bride and bridegroom are not members of a church or religious community; bride, bridegroom or both belong to a religious community which does not have the right to conduct the marriages of its members; or bride and bridegroom simply prefer to have a register office wedding. In addition to this the various churches and religious communities have their own preconditions for church marriages.

In the twentieth century, marriage by the Lutheran Church, the largest religious community with the right of marriage, was the most popular form of marriage. Every member of a religious community who has had a civil wedding may if he or she so desires obtain a church blessing on the marriage. A bride and bridegroom belonging to two different communities are married (constituting the legal marriage) in the Church in which the banns have been called, then the other Church – for instance the Roman Catholic Church which regards marriage as a sacrament – blesses the marriage according to its own practice.

The Law on Marriage of 1929 also governs the preconditions of marriage (e.g. capacity to marry, the banns), the legal position of family members, and divorce which has been possible in Finland since the end of the 16th century. These rules clearly reflect a Christian point of view. In spite of the changes in matrimonial law introduced in the twentieth century (the last important amendment being made in 1987) the basic principles have remained the same throughout the process of social development. All the amendments represent a retreat of traditional Christian concepts of marriage and family in favour of new concepts in society especially in the last decades of the twentieth century, for instance in the equality of man and woman and a more generous definition of the term 'family'.

Matrimonial and Family Law was the subject of lively discussion at the turn of the 21st century on two counts, both touching on relations between State and church.

Because cohabitation has become widespread, many new problems have become apparent. For example, cohabiting partners do not have the same right to inherit as do married partners. A working party has been set up by the Finnish Ministry of Justice to consider how the inheritance of cohabiting partners who are widowed should be remedied (compare the situation in Sweden). When the same legal right to inherit is given to cohabiting and married partners, society will be seen and understood to consider marriage and cohabitation as equal. This is not in accordance with the Lutheran doctrine of marriage: the Evangelical Lutheran Church of Finland does not, for example, sanction clergy cohabitation.

Cohabitation of persons of the same sex was agreed by the Finnish Parliament in 2001 to have the same legal status as marriage. In accordance with this law, persons of the same sex can formalize their relationship by contracting a civil marriage. This has given rise to much discussion especially in the Evangelical Lutheran Church of Finland as to the extent to which the Church can approve of this kind of partnership. Some bishops, pastors and laypersons would like to bless such a partnership. On other hand, some bishops, pastors and laypersons would deny this kind of blessing because they do not approve of homosexuality and homosexual partnerships at all.

VIII. Financing of Churches

The Lutheran and the Orthodox Church are both entitled to levy taxes from their members.[28] These taxes are collected by the general tax authorities together with state and municipal taxes and, if necessary, enforced by state authorities. Except for religious communities, juridical persons – including companies and associations – are obliged to participate in the funding of Lutheran or Orthodox Churches through their general income tax; a certain proportion of which is directed to the two Churches.[29] There is no system of exemption for companies or other juridical persons whose shareholders or members belong to minority religions.
The Lutheran Church, the Orthodox Church and religious communities are exempted from State Income Tax.[30] Cemeteries are exempted from Real Property Tax.[31]

IX. Religious Assistance in Public Institutions

Ecclesiastical activity within the armed forces consists of the activities of the Lutheran and Orthodox churches among conscripts, staff, reservists, and peace-keepers. The activities are led by a state-financed Lutheran Chaplain General who has 25 full-time, 13 part-time, and five fee-paid army chaplains as his subordinates. All full-time army chaplains are Lutheran. The needs of the Orthodox and minority religious communities are met by part-time officials. Additionally, religious activity involves priests and theology undergraduates serving as conscripts.

---

28 The Church Act, Chapter 15(2); The Act on Official Buildings and Funds of Evangelical-Lutheran Parishes (Act 106 of 1966); The Act on the Orthodox Church, Sections 11, 30 and 31.
29 See Sections 1 and 124 of the Income Tax Act (No. 1535 of 1992). The income tax rate of juridical persons is currently 29 per cent of taxable income. According to Section 12 of the Act 532 of 1998, regulating the distribution of tax revenues and as amended by Act 1003 of 2003, the Lutheran Church receives 1.79856% and the Orthodox Church 0.00144% of the income tax collected from juridical persons.
30 Income Tax Act, Section 21(2), as amended by Act 1343 of 1999. Parishes of Churches and other religious communities may be obliged to pay income tax to the municipality.
31 Real Property Tax Act (No. 654 of 1992), Section 3(2).

Most of the spiritual work carried out in prisons is State-funded. In 1999, there were 17 full-time priests working in prisons. One of them was Orthodox. Their commissions come from their own churches but salaries from the state. Additionally, there are working in the prisons deacons, paid by the Lutheran church, as well as volunteers who represent various denominations.

Most hospital counsellors are supported by congregations or parish unions. In 1999, there were 112 full-time and 12 part-time positions. The aim is that those appointed to these positions participate in the training and work supervision offered by the Church Education Centre to supplement their basic degrees.

X. *Criminal Law and Religion*

Chapter 17 of the Criminal Code[32] includes several provisions that protect religious entities and the free exercise of religion through criminalization. After long discussions Chapter 17, Section 10 on breach of the sanctity of religion retained a recognition of the special status of Christianity by referring specifically to "God" in addition to neutral formulations of "what is otherwise held to be sacred by a church or religious community" and "religious proceedings or a funeral".

Section 11 of the same Chapter criminalises the prevention of worship, and Section 12 establishes a penalty for a breach of the sanctity of the grave.

Furthermore, Chapter 11, Section 8[33] makes it a criminal offence of ethnic agitation or public agitation where a religious group is threatened, defamed or insulted. Similarly, Section 9 of the same Chapter criminalises, as discrimination, discrimination on account of a person's religion.

---

32 As amended by Act 563 of 1998.
33 As amended by Act 578 of 1995.

XI. The Legal Status of Clergy

1. Criminal and Civil Procedure; Confessional Confidentiality

In the Evangelical Lutheran Church of Finland, clergy are subject to both civil and ecclesiastical law. A pastor may be tried for offences in office or for matters of discipline. If he or she is charged for an offence in office, for example, action against an official duty or against the common criminal code, the case is heard in the Court of Justice. If a pastor is accused of a disciplinary offence, for example, dereliction of duty, the case is heard by the cathedral chapter. If another church worker, such as a deacon, is accused of a disciplinary offence, the case is heard by the Church Council or Parish Board in the parish where he or she is working.

In the cathedral chapter, and church council or parish board, a special disciplinary advocate acts as the prosecuting authority. Every diocese should have such a person. He or she should have a legal degree and be familiar with church activities and administration.
In accordance with the Church Code and Church Ordinance of the Evangelical Lutheran Church of Finland, any matter disclosed during a personal confession to a pastor is a confessional secret. It should not be disclosed to a third party. The same rule applies to the name of the person who has confessed his or her sins to the pastor. This regulation is enshrined in the common code of legal proceedings (Oikeudenkäyntikaari 17:23,2). In accordance with this, a pastor should not disclose secrets of the confessional to a court of law. However, a pastor should declare all that he or she knows about the case at issue.

XII. Particular Questions of Civil Ecclesiastical Law, and Recent Developments

The Freedom of Religion Act of 2003 will be a very important influence on the future development of relations between state and church in Finland. It seems inevitable that the bond between state and church will become progressively looser. This development will not necessarily be obvious. Old traditions will probably remain. Thus, the President of Finland and other representatives of government will continue to take part in the hour of devotion on Finnish Independence Day and in the opening ceremonies of new sessions of Parliament. However, the guidelines concerning content of those four intercession days will not any more by State but the Finnish Ecumenical Council.

However, there is ongoing reform of the taxes paid by companies and associations. This reform will change to some degree the financial situation of the Evangelical Lutheran Church of Finland. An attempt is being made to ameliorate these changes by the establishment of new foundations in a number of parishes.

XIII. Bibliography

Kirkon tilastollinen vuosikirja 2002, Statistik årsbok för kyrkan 2002, Suomen evankelis-luterilainen kirkko, kirkkohallitus. Evangelisk-lutherska kyrkan i Finland, kyrkostyrelsen. Helsingfors 2003, p. 245.

Kirkko uudelle vuosituhannelle, Suomen evankelis-luterilainen kirkko vuosina 1996-1999. Kirkon tutkimuskeskus 2000. Jyväskylä 2000, p. 336.

Hannu Juntunen, Oikeuden ideaa teologiset perusteet. Oikeusteologian hahmottelua oikeusjärjestyksen teologisena kritiikkinä. Helsinki 2000, p. 291.

Pekka Leino, Kirkko ja perusoikeudet. Suomalaisen lakimiesyhdistyksen julkaisuja E-sarja N:o 6. Saarijärvi 2003, p. 369.

Pekka Leino, Kirkkolaki vai laki kirkosta. Suomalaisen lakimiesyhdistyksen julkaisuja A-sarja N:o 231. Vammala 2002, p. 376.

Juha Seppo, Uskonnonvapaus 2000-luvun Suomessa. Helsinki. 2003, p. 251.

Suomen tilastollinen vuosikirja 2002, Statistisk årsbok för Finland 2002, Statistical Yearbook of Finland 2002, Tilastokeskus, Statistikcentralen, Statistics Finland. Helsinki 2002, p. 703.

Lars Friedner
State and Church in Sweden

I. Social Facts

The majority of the Swedish population belongs to the Evangelical-Lutheran Church of Sweden (80,8 % 2002).[1] The second biggest religious group in Sweden is the Roman Catholic Church (just over 1 %).[2] Roughly the same size are the Swedish Mission Convenant Church and the Pentecostal Movement as well as Muslim groups, in several different denominations. There are also quite a few Jews, Methodists, Buddhists and Hindus in Sweden.

The Christian churches and associations mostly count their members using the criterion of baptism: either persons that have been baptised within their own church or persons that have been baptised within another church. However, until 1996 the Church of Sweden – then still the state church – could legally acquire members through a person's parent or parents having membership of that church. Because of this, there are still members of the Church of Sweden who have not been baptised.

Within the Muslim groups there is no formal membership. The number of Muslims in Sweden is monitored by the Swedish Commission for State Grants to Religious Communities.[3]

Most Swedish citizens belong to a church or another faith group. Some Swedes are legally non-believers. The Swedish Humanist Association[4], though, numbers only a few hundred members. However, there is a gradual increase in the number of inhabitants that are not members of any church or denomination.

A large total membership is not a reflection of religious activity. Only a minority of members regularly attends services. This applies especially to the Church of Sweden. Within the other churches and denominations, the activity level is higher. Whether a lower or higher

---

1 Nyckeln till Svenska kyrkan – verksamhet och ekonomi 2002.
2 www.sst.a.se.
3 Sw. *Samarbetsnämnden för statsbidrag till trossamfund.*
4 Sw. *Humanisterna.*

degree of church activity reflects a difference in the beliefs of members is a matter for debate.

II. Historical Background

Sweden became a Christian country in about the year 1000. The first Swedish king to be a Christian was Olof Skötkonung, who is said to have reigned at this time. Christianity, in its Roman Catholic form, became the state religion.

The Lutheran Reformation came to Sweden in 1527. Gustav Vasa had become King in the year 1523. In 1527, the Swedish Parliament, on a proposal of the King, decided that the "surplus estate" of the Church should be transferred to the State and confirmed the interventions made somewhat earlier against bishops and monasteries. The matter of doctrine was mostly left on one side for the time being.

During the reign of the sons of Gustav Vasa, the religious situation changed. The grandson of Gustav Vasa, Sigismund, was also king of Poland (and a Catholic). He was deposed by his uncle, later king Karl IX, who was a Lutheran. In 1593, Karl IX convened the Uppsala meeting, where the Augsburg Confession was adopted by the Swedish church. This decision marked the foundation of the Swedish Evangelical-Lutheran Church.

During the following century, the Evangelical-Lutheran Church was the only church that was permitted in Sweden. From the middle of the 18th century the situation gradually changed. Foreign citizens, living in Sweden, were permitted to belong to other Christian churches. The same freedom was granted to Jews.

In 1860 Swedish citizens were given the right to leave the Church of Sweden, if they declared that they were going to join another accepted church or denomination. This was the starting point for the establishment of other Christian churches in Sweden. From 1951 full religious freedom was granted to the Swedes. At that time they were given the freedom to leave the Church of Sweden without stating any reason.

A short time after Parliament's decision on religious freedom, discussion began on the abolition of the State Church system. In 1958, the Government appointed a committee which had the task of analysing the problems and suggesting possible solutions. After ten years, the committee presented four different proposals: one retaining the existing system, while the other three involved greater changes. The proposals were handed over to a new committee, now under the chairmanship of the Social-democratic church minister. This committee proposed a new state-church relationship which effectively meant an end to the State Church system. During the 1973 election campaign, however, the Government – somewhat under pressure – declared that the State Church system should remain.

In 1979, a liberal government made a proposal for new state-church relations, again with the aim of getting rid of the existing system. At this time, changes in church law were still subject to the approval of the General Synod. And the synod rejected the proposals.

A further committee, appointed in 1992, came up with its proposals in 1994. These were in favour of a new relationship between state and church in Sweden, including an end to the State Church system. In 1995, the General Synod (at this time still a State body) approved by an overwhelming majority a governmental proposal for new state-church relations. Later the same year, the proposal was also approved by Parliament.

After that, there began a period of planning for the reform. The new relationship was worked out in detail, and several Acts, including amendments to the Constitution, were passed by both General Synod and Parliament. On 1 January 2000, the new state-church system came into effect.

III. Basic Structure

1. Legal Sources

The state-church system in Sweden is reflected in the 1973 constitution, as well as in the old constitution of 1809, the relevant part of which is still in force. The constitutional Act on Succession to the Throne (1810) also contains some church provisions. The 1973 Constitution (amended in 2000) states that provisions relating to the Church of Sweden as well as other churches or denominations should be made by Acts of Parliament.[5] It also states that the Parliament may only amend or abolish such acts *either* by double, identical decisions, where there has been a general election between those decisions, *or* a

---

5 8:6 regeringsformen.

single decision by Parliament with a 75% majority. The provision relating to the King and the heir to the throne states that they shall confess the "pure evangelical doctrine, as it is approved and explained in the unaltered confession of Augsburg and the decision of the Uppsala meeting in 1593".

The Constitution also grants religious freedom to Swedish citizens. This right is expressed as "the freedom to practise their religion, alone or together with others".[6] According to the Constitution the citizens are, in relation to the State and other authorities, also protected from the obligation to state his or her religious opinions. Every citizen is also protected from the obligation to belong to any denomination.[7] Since Sweden is a party to the European Convention of Protection of Human Rights and Basic Freedoms, the right of religious freedom is also granted to Swedish residents (or visitors) who are not Swedish citizens. The Convention is, through an Act of Parliament,[8] valid as Swedish law.[9]

The Swedish legal system consists of Constitutional Acts, Acts of Parliament, and Statutes. A further tier is that of directions, given by central or regional authorities on behalf of the Government.

The two central Acts of Parliament in the field of religion are the Act on Denominations[10] and the Church of Sweden Act.[11] Both are part of the new state-church relations in Sweden. The Act on Denominations states that the Church of Sweden is a registered denomination; it also gives the opportunity to other churches and denominations to become registered denominations as well. Through registration, a church or denomination acquires a legal personality *as a denomination*. Registration is, however, not compulsory. A church or a denomination can act in another legal form, as either an association or a foundation. Apart from the legal entity, registration gives no special advantages to a church or denomination. However, only registered denominations may use the taxation system for levies from members, have the right to solemnise marriages, and receive contributions from the State. About 40 churches and other denominations are so registered.

---

6 2:1 regeringsformen.
7 2:2 regeringsformen.
8 Lagen (1994:1219) om den europeiska konventionen angående skydd för de mänskliga rättigheterna och de grundläggande friheterna.
9 Before Sweden became a member of the European Union, the Swedish legal point of view was that an international convention had to be adopted through Swedish legislation in order to become directly applicable within Sweden.
10 Lagen (1998:1593) om trossamfund.
11 Lagen (1998:1591) om Svenska kyrkan.

The Church of Sweden Act provides for the Church of Sweden to be the Evangelical-Lutheran, open church of the whole nation, which – in a partnership between a democratic organisation and the ministry of the church – pursues activities that cover the whole country.[12] These provisions express the identity of the Church of Sweden. It may seem unexpected that the identity of a Church, which is no longer the State Church, is given through an Act of Parliament. This is, however, because the State has accepted that, through the Act, it guarantees the continuation of the identity of the church. The Church of Sweden Act also contains provisions concerning the internal organisation of the Church. The aim of these provisions is to guarantee the continuation of the basic organisation of the Church.

In the preparation of the new relationship between State and church, Parliament also passed an Act on Introducing the Church of Sweden.[13] This Act consists of provisions, mostly concerning the church estates. Through this Act, the majority of the estates were handed over to the Church or its parishes. Only parts of the estates, those that were originally granted as an allowance for the priest,[14] still remain as distinct legal entities. However, the Church of Sweden Act provides that these estates are held in trust by the Church of Sweden.

Another Act of importance for the religious situation in Sweden is the Funeral Act,[15] which stipulates that funerals in Sweden continue to be carried out mainly by Church of Sweden parishes (in two Swedish towns, though, the communities are responsible). Church of Sweden parishes are also, through the Act, obliged to provide burial-grounds for those inhabitants who are not members of the Church. There is no obligation for the Church to open its church buildings to other than its members.

Members of the Church of Sweden pay for funerals through the church levy.[16] Swedish inhabitants who are not members of the Church pay through a special annual funeral tax,[17] which is proportional to income and collected by the tax authorities together with other income taxes. The level of funeral tax varies across the country, depending on local costs, but is determined by the State authorities.

---

12 1-2 §§.
13 Lagen (1998:1592) om införande av lagen om Svenska kyrkan.
14 Sw. *prästlönetillgångar*.
15 Begravningslagen (1990:1144).
16 Sw. *kyrkoavgift*.
17 Sw. *begravningsavgift*.

The Cultural Heritage Act[18] contains express provisions in respect of cultural church heritage. Church buildings that belong to the Church of Sweden and were built before 1940 (and items belonging to such church buildings) may be altered only with the approval of the cultural heritage authorities. On the other hand, the Church of Sweden is granted a state contribution towards the maintenance of its church buildings. There is also an agreement between the Swedish State (through the Government) and the Church of Sweden concerning co-operation in this field.

The Church of Sweden may opt to use the State taxation system for collecting church levies. The Government also makes this available to other churches and denominations (Act on Levies to Registered Denominations[19]). Apart from the Church of Sweden, seven churches and denominations use the taxation system for collecting their levies.

The Act on Contributions to Denominations[20] allows for contributions from the State to the churches and other denominations. A church or denomination that has chosen to use the taxation system for collecting levies (and has governmental approval for this), will have their financial contributions reduced. The Church of Sweden does not receive financial contributions from the State under this Act but only the right to use the taxation system.

The Government has granted to most churches and other denominations in Sweden the right to solemnise marriages (Act on Officiating of Marriages within other Denominations than the Church of Sweden[21]). Priests of the Church of Sweden have this right through the Matrimony Act.[22]

Besides the provisions mentioned, there are no rights granted to the churches and denominations in Sweden that are not applicable to Swedish society as a whole. There have, for example, been discussions on the issue of religious slaughter, that is the need for some groups of Muslims and Jews to have the slaughter of cattle conducted in way that does not comply with the Act on Prevention of Cruelty to Animals.[23] So far, no amendment of that Act has been proposed.

---

18 Lagen (1988:950) om kulturminnen m.m.
19 Lagen (1999:291) om avgift till registrerat trossamfund.
20 Lagen (1999:932) om stöd till trossamfund.
21 Lagen (1993:305) om rätt att förrätta vigsel inom andra trossamfund än Svenska kyrkan.
22 Äktenskapsbalken.
23 Djurskyddslagen (1988:534).

2. State-Church System

The state-church decisions in Sweden which came into effect in the year 2000 are often described as a separation of State and Church in Sweden. As is obvious from what is mentioned in the section *Legal Sources*, this is not the whole truth. There are still several links between the Swedish State and the Church of Sweden. The changes have also, somewhat unexpectedly, led to closer relations between the state and the other churches and denominations.

One of the cornerstones of the new state-church relations in Sweden is that the different churches and denominations shall be regarded as equal. Though this is true from a theoretical point of view, the reality is different. Of course, the Church of Sweden with its size, economic strength, and history is difficult to compare with other churches and denominations in Sweden. On the other hand, members of the other churches are much more active than those in the Church of Sweden. The proportion of active worshippers within these churches is much higher.

Legally, the Church of Sweden is treated in a special way, through the Church of Sweden Act. This Act could be regarded as a special privilege, granted to the Church of Sweden. But the Act contains, as mentioned, provisions as to the identity of the Church and its organisation. Thus, another way of regarding the Act is that it restricts the Church of Sweden in essential matters. There are, then, good reasons to ask why the State has wanted to apply such restrictions to the Church of Sweden, but not to the other churches and denominations. And the answer is that the Church of Sweden, through its Synod – at that time still a State body – requested these restrictions. The likely reason for this request was the desire of several different groups within the Church that, when it ceased to be a State Church, the Church should remain unchanged in its identity and organisation.

As also mentioned above, the Church of Sweden has a special position in the Swedish funeral system, and with regard to its old church buildings. The reason for Church of Sweden responsibility in the area of funerals is mainly historical – the burial-grounds have been, ever since Sweden became Christian, a task for the State Church. When the new relations between State and Church were created, only the Church of Sweden was ready to take this responsibility. No one – neither churches nor denominations nor other organisations in Swedish society – had any criticism of the Church of Sweden's handling of burial-grounds. So this task remains with the Church of Sweden. The Church has a special responsibility to act respectfully towards those inhabitants who are not its members. The Church of Sweden is also obliged to arrange for special burial-grounds for those who do not wish to be buried in a Christian burial-ground.

The care of Sweden's cultural heritage, represented by its old church buildings, is a task for the Church of Sweden, with financial support from the State. The Cultural Heritage Act applies exclusively to the Church of Sweden. The reason for this is that there are no really old church buildings belonging to any other churches in Sweden. As mentioned in an earlier section, there were practically no other churches working in Sweden before the 19th century.

The new state-church relations in Sweden enabled the Church of Sweden, together with other churches and denominations, to receive legal status as registered denominations. The possibility of becoming legal personae also applied to different parts of each church or denomination (e.g. diocese, district, or parish). The churches and denominations are treated equally in this respect. Such equality also applies to the opportunity of receiving financial support from the State or using the taxation system for collecting member levies and solemnising marriages. Public burial-grounds are maintained by the Church of Sweden, but every church and denomination is given the option of establishing private burial-grounds.

IV. Legal Status of Religious Bodies

As already mentioned, the new state-church relationship in Sweden enables churches and other denominations to appear as legal personae – registered denominations. For the Church of Sweden this is a big change, as the Church per se – as a part of the state – did not formerly have a legal persona. The Church of Sweden achieved the status of a registered denomination through legislation, whereas the other churches and denominations have to register in order to achieve this status.

Today, about 40 different churches and faith groups are "registered denominations". This includes the Roman Catholic Church as well as different Muslim organisations. Even a denomination devoted to old Nordic heathen gods has registered. The questions of registration are handled by the Legal, Financial, and Administrative Services

Agency.[24] The decisions of the Agency do not involve an assessment of a denomination's doctrine. For registration the only criteria are that the church or denomination has divine service as its purpose, and that it has reached a considerable numerical strength. This strength may be proved either through membership records or that the church or denomination belongs to a worldwide community. The Swedish Humanist Association has been denied the right to register, due to the fact that its purpose is not divine service. On the other hand, the expression "divine service" is interpreted quite widely, as Buddhist organisations – where the element of direct worship is rather limited – have been accepted for registration. The Agency does not ask for proof that divine service is carried out within the applicant church or denomination: a statement from the church or denomination is normally sufficient. Thus, the Scientology Church has become a registered denomination in Sweden.

Registration is not compulsory for a church or denomination that wants to be active in Swedish society. Although practically all churches and denominations in Sweden have now registered, those who choose not to register are free to take other legal forms.

As already mentioned, registration itself does not grant any special rights. However, registration is necessary to obtain the right to use the taxation system for collecting membership fees, the right to receive financial contributions from the state, and the right to solemnise marriages. However, churches and denominations that had the right to officiate at marriages before the year 2000 have not lost this right as a side-effect of the state-church reforms.

As also mentioned earlier, a registered church or denomination may have its own burial-grounds.

There are no other special rights granted to churches or denominations in Sweden. A church or denomination may start a school – and some churches do – but under the same provisions as other organisations in Swedish society. A church or denomination may run a hospital or home for abusers or elderly people – and some churches do – but also under the same provisions as other organisations in Swedish society. The Swedish systems for schools and health-care are closely linked to the financial contributions to these systems from the State community and social security funds. In fact, it is practically impossible for a church or a denomination in Sweden to run a school or a hospital without public financial support. Thus, the question of the "right" of a church to carry on such activities is of little interest in

---

24 Sw. *Kammarkollegiet.*

Sweden. Instead, the question of the "right to public contributions" is much more discussed.

And there is no direct right to contributions. The granting of contributions is decided locally or regionally, and often against a background of political opinion and the level of support by public authorities for alternative schools or hospitals. Thus, religious schools and church-maintained health care are quite rare in Sweden, though in recent years there has been some progress with regard to schools.

There are no special provisions regarding church contact with the political system. Clergy are not prohibited from political engagement; on the other hand there are no special religious movements in the political system. Sweden has a Christian Democratic Party, which holds about 10 per cent of the seats in Parliament. The party is not, however, linked with any particular church or denomination in Sweden.

V. Church and Culture

As already mentioned, there are in Sweden no specific rights for churches or other denominations to run schools. On the other hand, there *are* schools run by religious organisations, but under the general law.

The Church of Sweden, as well as certain other churches, has its own educational institutions for clergy and for other parish workers. These sometimes receive financial contributions from the State. This is the case when the education is organised as a people's university,[25] which is a special Nordic form of high-school education, run mostly by religious, political or other ideological organisations. For the training of priests, though, there are no state subsidies, either to the Church of Sweden or to other churches.

Education in state schools is non-confessional. The subject of religion is compulsory in both primary and secondary schools.

State universities are also non-confessional. Church of Sweden priests are normally supposed to pass an examination in theology at such a university before starting the ordination training provided by the Church. The other Swedish churches that train ministers do not normally require university education as a prerequisite.

---

25 Sw. *Folkhögskola*.

There are no special provisions concerning the churches and the media. The churches are not granted special rights regarding state licensed broadcasting companies. In fact, the main radio and television channels cover the religious field quite broadly: this is part of their task as public-service broadcasters. Every Sunday, services are broadcast on both radio and television, alternating between the Church of Sweden and the other churches.

The churches have no representation in media companies.

VI. Labour Law

Sweden has no special labour law provisions concerning the churches and denominations. Thus, the same labour law applies to them as to all other legal bodies in Sweden. During its last years as the State Church, this became rather a problem for the Church of Sweden. The employment of priests in the Church had to be according to general labour law, so if a priest had broken his or her ordination vows this was a question of labour law, not a question for the Church. Under its new relationship with the State, the Church of Sweden has been able to change the system, so that the ordination of a priest is no longer a part of his or her employment contract (which remains under labour law).

The whole of the Swedish labour market is covered by collective agreements. So the churches and other denominations are mostly members of different employers' associations; the Church of Sweden has its own, The Church of Sweden Parishes' Association.[26] The employees of churches are also often members of various trades unions. Priests (and some other groups of employees) of the Church of Sweden have formed the Association of Church of Sweden Employees.[27]

---

26 Sw. *Svenska kyrkans församlingsförbund*.
27 Sw. *Kyrkans Akademikerförbund*.

VII. Matrimonial and Family Law

The matrimonial and family law of Sweden is part of Swedish State law. But, as mentioned, most churches and denominations have been granted the right to officiate at marriages. Divorce or separation is legally not a matter for the churches or denominations.

VIII. Finances of the Churches

As already mentioned, the new relationship between State and Church in Sweden from the year 2000 includes a provision for certain churches and denominations to use the taxation system for collecting their membership levies. The Church of Sweden is granted the right to this through legislation. The State makes grants to the other churches and denominations amounting to 50 Million SEK (Swedish Krona) annually. A church which has the right to use the taxation system has a corresponding reduction in its grants.

Through the new arrangements, the Church of Sweden has also been granted State allowances to maintain the church cultural heritage of Sweden. Parliament has undertaken to make these grants up to the year 2010.

Several churches and denominations count returns from property as part of their income. The Church of Sweden received the existing church property as part of the 2000 agreement.

There has been an ongoing legal discussion in Sweden as to whether this church property is legally to be regarded as State property or something different, for example, trusts. Since 2000 it has become clear that the majority of church property, endowments for clergy stipends,[28] should now be legally regarded as a form of trust. The Church of Sweden has been appointed by law as administrator of these trusts. The trust property consists by and large of forests, worth about 10 billion SEK. Other church property has been legally handed over to the Church of Sweden, its dioceses and its parishes. As a matter of fact the Act on Introducing the Church of Sweden contains a provision granting anyone who can prove a right to any part of this property financial compensation from the state. Up till now, no one

---

28 Sw. *Prästlönetillgångar*.

has claimed such a right. One of the reasons for this provision was the protection of the right of ownership under the European Convention.

Churches and denominations that are part of international churches (or denominations) may also receive grants from abroad.

IX. Religious Assistance in Public Institutions

For religious assistance within the Swedish armed forces, there is an agreement between the armed forces and the Church of Sweden. The agreement obliges the Church to make payments to the armed forces, mainly for the services of a Military Dean. He is a member of the staff of the commander-in-chief. The Military Dean is appointed by the armed forces in consultation with the Church of Sweden.

In the peace-time military organisation, part-time employed chaplains provide religious assistance in the various military units. The Military Dean supervises these chaplains. A chaplain can be either a priest in the Church of Sweden or from any other Christian church. The military authorities – in consultation with the local church, where the chaplain is mainly employed – appoint the chaplain. So far, no Islamic or Jewish chaplains have been appointed.

In wartime, the Swedish armed forces rely on compulsory military service for every man. This includes priests and pastors, who are often placed as chaplains.

Religious services and cure of souls for prisoners are organised by the Swedish Christian Council on behalf of the National Prison and Probation Administration. The Council is a joint association of almost all the Christian churches and denominations in Sweden. The Council maintains close relations with the Islamic and Jewish organisations in Sweden. Every prison is supposed to have two chaplains, one from the Church of Sweden and one from any of the other Christian churches and denominations. The chaplains are responsible for inter-faith contacts. If, for example, the visit of an Imam or a Buddhist monk is needed, it is the chaplain who makes the arrangements.

Religious assistance, through priests, deacons and other people, is offered in almost every institution for health care in Sweden. The task is organised ecumenically through the Church of Sweden together with the other Christian churches and denominations in Sweden. Within the Church of Sweden, the local parish in which the hospital or other health-care institution is situated is responsible. When needed, the hospital chaplains call for representatives from other religions. Due to the structure of the Swedish social security system, there are practically no private hospitals in Sweden. Virtually all hospitals in Sweden are public, mostly run by the regions.

The churches and denominations in Sweden have no particular right to religious assistance in schools or by the police. There is, of course, contact and co-operation between schools and police authorities and the churches (most often the Church of Sweden). Some churches and denominations run their own schools, but under the same provisions as do other non-public school enterprises.

X. Criminal Law and Religion

Swedish criminal legislation does not contain any provisions that apply particularly to religious contexts. As in most countries, though, discrimination against special groups of people, because of their race or faith, is a criminal offence. Recently actions have been brought against people publicly using Nazi greetings or symbols.[29] There are no exemptions on religious grounds from the application of the criminal law.

XI. Legal Status of the Clergy

In criminal and civil procedure in the Swedish courts, a priest (or a person who has a position similar to a priest) cannot be heard as a witness about what he or she has come to know under confession or individual cure of souls.[30] This provision was much discussed by the Swedish public, when the Svea Appeal Court[31] was criticised by the Ombudsman for Public Affairs.[32] The Court had heard a priest as a

---

29 Supreme Court (Sw. *Högsta Domstolen*) 1996 p. 577.
30 36:5 rättegångsbalken.
31 Sw. *Svea Hovrätt*.
32 Sw. *Justitieombudsmannen*.

witness, because of a request from the defendant who had confessed to a priest and wanted to use this as evidence. But, according to the Ombudsman, this was not fair, as a priest's obligation to observe secrecy has to be regarded as "absolute". The Court had no choice whatsoever, but to have respect for this obligation.[33]
Aside from the aforementioned provision of the Act on Procedure,[34] there are no particular legal rules applying to priests or other religious leaders in Sweden.

XII. Bibliography

Doe (ed.), The portrayal of religion in Europe: the media and the arts (Leuven 2004).

Dübeck & Overgaard (ed.), Social Welfare, Religious Organizations, and the State (Milano 2003).

Edqvist, Friedner, Lundqvist-Norling & Tibbling, Kyrkoordning för Svenska kyrkan – med kommentarer och angränsande lagstiftning (Stockholm 2003).

Ekström, Makten över kyrkan – om Svenska kyrkan, folket och staten (Stockholm 2003).

Ekström, Svenska kyrkan – historia, identitet, verksamhet och organisation (Stockholm 2004).

Göransson, Svensk kyrkorätt – en översikt (Stockholm 1993).

---

33 Decision of the Ombudsman June 16, 1993.
34 Sw. *Rättegångsbalken*.

David McClean
State and Church in the United Kingdom

The United Kingdom is a composite State, made up of three distinct countries each with its own legal system: England and Wales, Scotland, and Northern Ireland. English and Scottish law have quite different histories, and in some respects Scots law is quite distinct from the common law developed in England. Modern legislation is often made separately for each country, and in 1999 a Scottish Parliament was restored after an interval of 292 years. Certain matters are reserved to the United Kingdom Parliament, including those aspects of the (unwritten) constitution dealing with the Crown and the Union of England and Scotland[1] and this is thought effectively to reserve constitutional questions affecting Church and State. Northern Ireland law is based on English law, but at various times since 1920 there has been a separate, subordinate, legislature in Northern Ireland.[2] A Welsh Assembly was created in 1999, but it does not have power to enact primary legislation.

In the field of Church and State the complications are even greater. There is an Established Church in England (the Church of England) of which the Queen is Supreme Governor. But the Anglican churches in Wales[3] and Northern Ireland[4] have been disestablished, and that in Scotland[5] is small by comparison with the (Established) Church of Scotland. The Queen, Supreme Governor of an episcopal church in the southern part of her kingdom, is a member of a reformed, presbyterian, church in the north.[6]

Because of this complexity, the reader must be aware that some statements made below will apply to the whole United Kingdom, but many only to England, or England and Wales, or Scotland. Some

---

1   Scotland Act 1998, s. 30, Sched.5, para 1(a)(b).
2   The Northern Ireland Act 1998 re-established a Northern Ireland Assembly, which has from time to time been suspended owing to continuing political difficulties in Northern Ireland.
3   The Church in Wales, created in 1920 from the Welsh dioceses of the Church of England.
4   The Church of Ireland, whose dioceses cover the whole of Ireland and not just Northern Ireland.
5   The Episcopal Church of Scotland.
6   The Church of England has a special status in the Isle of Man (where the Bishop of Sodor and Man has a seat in the legislature) and in the two Bailiwicks of Guernsey and Jersey, but none of those territories is part of the United Kingdom.

aspects of the situation in Northern Ireland reflect the history of Ireland as a whole.

I. Social Facts

The Census conducted in 2001 asked a (voluntary) question on religion, the first time this had been done for 150 years. The Census question offered the choices as set out in Table 1 below, and in Scotland there were additional questions seeking information about allegiance to the major Christian denominations.

Table 1: Religious Allegiance in Great Britain, 2001
(percentages of total population)

	England	Wales	Scotland	Total for Great Britain
Christianity	71.74	71.90	65.08	71.16
Islam	3.10	0.75	0.84	2.78
Hinduism	1.11	0.19	0.11	0.98
Sikhism	0.67	0.07	0.13	0.59
Judaism	0.52	0.08	0.13	0.47
Buddhism	0.28	0.19	0.13	0.26
Other	0.29	0.24	0.53	0.31
No religion	14.59	18.53	27.55	15.94
None stated	7.69	8.07	5.49	7.51

So far as the overall picture is concerned, the proportion regarding themselves as Christian (71.16 % for Great Britain as a whole) was greeted with some surprise, as many commentators had expected a lower figure. Religious allegiance seems lowest in Scotland (with a third answering 'no religion' or refusing to reply), and the non-Christian faiths are largely concentrated in England.
The non-Christians are, as expected, principally from immigrant communities. The Census results contain an analysis of ethnic groups by religion. For example, almost 80 % of Muslims identified themselves as of Asian or African descent; and the district with the high-

est proportion of Muslims in its population (Tower Hamlets, in Greater London) has a very large immigrant population. The long-established Jewish community has its greatest concentration in North London. Only Buddhism presents a rather different picture, with almost 40 % of its adherents classifying themselves as White.

Information about the relative strengths of the various Christian denominations is notoriously difficult to obtain and interpret. Table 2 is based on the statistics collected from the various churches by a respected organisation, Christian Research, and published in *Religious Trends 4* (2003). The information about congregations (usually represented by a building) and ministers is more reliable than the membership figures which often reflect a particular legal status. For example, the Church of England figures are only of those who register themselves on the church electoral rolls, and some other churches distinguish between the formal 'membership' and the much larger 'community'. Even the ministerial data can be misleading: Methodism, for example, as a strong tradition of lay 'Local Preachers', whose numbers are not included in the Table which includes only ordained ministers.

Table 2: Christian Denominations in Britain, 2001

	Membership	Congregations	Ministers
ENGLAND			
Church of England	1,372,000	16,220	12,587
Roman Catholic Church	930,000	3,351	5,144
Methodist churches	308,300	5,906	2,200
Pentecostal churches	225,700	2,414	3,805
Orthodox churches	225,500	253	217
Baptist churches	164,800	2,586	2,382
Salvation Army	43,600	657	1,253
Other trinitarian denominations	314,800	4,963	3,420
WALES			
Church in Wales (Anglican)	80,900	1,510	653
Presbyterian/Reformed churches	44,300	974	139
Roman Catholic Church	39,500	231	253
Methodist churches	15,300	402	98
Other trinitarian denominations	70,300	1,000	452

	Membership	Congregations	Ministers
SCOTLAND			
Church of Scotland	587,700	1,543	1,090
Roman Catholic Church	212,500	461	851
Episcopal Church of Scotland	48,000	310	158
Other Presbyterian churches	31,000	99	218
Methodist churches	5,700	75	35
Other trinitarian denominations	79,300	911	689

There is a sharp contrast between the membership figures in Table 2 and the picture obtained, for the same year, in the Census. The churches report a total membership of some 4.8 million but 40.6 million declared themselves 'Christian' in the 2001 Census. The extra information in the Census for Scotland illustrates the same phenomenon: it found 2,146,251 persons who regarded themselves as Church of Scotland, and 803,732 Roman Catholics. In each case the Census figure is almost 4 times that reported by the churches. All this points to a large number of nominal, or inactive, or lapsed members who still identify themselves not just with Christianity but with a particular expression of it: as is sometimes said, they know which church it is they do not attend.

For completeness, it may be noted that there are a number of adherents of non-trinitarian churches in Britain, including some 177,000 Mormons, and 125,000 Jehovah's Witnesses.

The trend in church attendance is clearly downward. According to Christian Research, 11 % of the population of Great Britain attended church on an average Sunday in 1980 but only 7.7 % in 2000. Research by the Church of England suggests that there is a smaller drop in the number of 'church-goers' but they tend to attend less frequently.

Although Northern Ireland forms part of the United Kingdom, the churches operate on an All-Ireland basis, and the history of at least the Catholic and Anglican churches is best considered in that context. Table 3 is based on the Census data (even more detailed than in Scotland) and church returns on the same basis as those given above for Great Britain.

Table 3: Major Christian Churches in Northern Ireland, 2001

	Allegiance in Census return	Church membership	Number of ministers
Roman Catholic Church	678,462	522,000	547
Presbyterian Church in Ireland	348,742	189,000	370
Church of Ireland (Anglican)	257,788	160,700	300
Methodist Church in Ireland	59,173	14,300	93

Of the main Christian churches, the Catholic and Anglican both have a diocesan structure. There are 44 dioceses in the Church of England,[7] forming two Provinces, those of Canterbury and York. There are six dioceses in the Church in Wales and seven in the Episcopal Church of Scotland. The Church of Ireland has 12 dioceses covering the whole of Ireland in two Provinces, those of Armagh and Dublin. In the Roman Catholic Church, there are five archdioceses and 17 dioceses in England and Wales, two archdioceses and six dioceses in Scotland, and four archdioceses and twenty-three dioceses in Ireland.

II. Historical Background

The pre-Reformation Church in England, *Ecclesia Anglicana*, had a certain independence from Rome. Canon law in England was modified by provincial 'constitutions' and there were assemblies of bishops and clergy in the Convocations of Canterbury and York (which still exist as part of the General Synod, the Church of England's governing body). Under King Henry VIII, Papal authority was abrogated and royal supremacy over the Church of England asserted in the Act of Supremacy 1534. The Convocations were obliged to obtain royal authority for their acts by the Submission of the Clergy Act of the same year.

This first stage in the English Reformation was political rather than doctrinal, but notably under Edward VI (1547-1533) the Church adopted a more Protestant position. The Roman jurisdiction was restored on Queen Mary I's accession in 1553 but Anglican independ-

---

7 Including the Diocese in Europe (technically, 'of Gibraltar in Europe') for the Anglican chaplaincies on the mainland of Europe.

ence and a classical Anglican theology which was 'both Catholic and Reformed' was put in place in the Elizabethan settlement from 1558 onwards. In Wales the Anglican dioceses were disestablished in 1920 and formed a separate Church in Wales.

In Scotland, the Reformation dates from 1560. The Scottish Parliament guaranteed the liberties of the church and its presbyterian form of government in 1592; the latter was restored, after an episcopal interlude, in 1690. The episcopalians then formed the (Anglican) Episcopal Church of Scotland.

In Ireland, English domination saw the creation of the (Anglican) Church of Ireland, finally disestablished in 1871 but retaining the ancient cathedrals and parish churches. It was always a minority church, the majority of the Irish remaining Roman Catholic in allegiance. The presence of large numbers of Scottish settlers in the north contributed not only to the present political difficulties but to the growth of the Presbyterian Church of Ireland which is centred in Ulster.

III. Basic Structure

There are three quite distinct bodies of law applying to the churches.

For most of the churches, all but the Church of England and the Church of Scotland, the applicable legal principles are those of the general law of charities and especially of charitable trusts. The non-Established churches are essentially organised as voluntary associations, and their property is held by trustees (which may be registered companies) under the ordinary secular law. They have no special status.

So far as the Established churches are concerned, the position is very different north and south of the border between England and Scotland.

In Scotland, the General Assembly Act 1592 remains the statutory foundation of the Presbyterian character of the reformed Church of Scotland, a church often called simply 'the Kirk'. At the time of the Union between England and Scotland, the Scottish Parliament passed the Protestant Religion and Presbyterian Church Act 1706 ('the Act of Security'), requiring that its terms be expressly declared to be a fundamental and essential condition of the Treaty of Union in all time to come.[8] The Scottish Act giving effect to the actual Union declared that it was 'reasonable and necessary that the true Protestant religion as presently professed within this kingdom with the worship discipline and government of this Church should be effectually and unalterably secured'; Presbyterian government was to be 'the only government of the Church within the kingdom of Scotland'.

The nineteenth century saw a number of disputes within the Kirk, some of the most acute concerning the right of the State to intervene in church affairs to disallow church decisions and legislation. A number of separate churches came into being, most of which were re-united in 1921. To facilitate the reunion, Parliament passed the Church of Scotland Act 1921 which declares lawful the Articles Declaratory of the Constitution of the Church of Scotland in Matters Spiritual agreed in the negotiations between the Kirk and the United Free Church of Scotland, which are set out in a Schedule to the Act. The Articles contain a statement of the separate jurisdiction of the Church in matters spiritual and give the church very considerable freedom in its government. The key provision is Article IV:

> IV. This Church, as part of the Universal Church wherein the Lord Jesus Christ has appointed a government in the hands of Church office-bearers, receives from Him, its Divine King and Head, and from Him alone, the right and power subject to no civil authority to legislate, and to adjudicate finally, in all matters of doctrine, worship, government, and discipline in the Church, including the right to determine all questions concerning membership and office in the Church, the constitution and membership of its Courts, and the mode of election of its office-bearers, and to define the boundaries of the spheres of labour of its ministers and other office-bearers. Recognition by civil authority of the separate and independent government and jurisdiction of this Church in matters spiritual, in whatever manner such recognition be expressed, does not in any way affect the character of this government and jurisdiction as derived from the Divine Head of the Church alone, or give to the civil authority any right of interference with the proceedings or judgments of the Church within the sphere of its spiritual government and jurisdiction.

The Act is relied on by the authorities of the Church of Scotland to resist any court action concerning its affairs.[9] In one of the most re-

---

8 An English Act of 1706, sometimes known as the Maintenance of the Church of England Act, made equivalent provision for the position of the Church of England.
9 Ballantyne v Presbytery of Wigtown [1936] SC 625 (a dispute about the union of two parishes); Logan v Presbytery of Dumbarton, 1995 SLT 1228 (a clergy discipline case); Percy v Church of Scotland Board of National Mission, 2001 SLT 497 (another discipline case, with allegations of sex discrimination).

cent cases, it was even suggested in a lower court[10] that the 1921 Act protected the Church of Scotland from legislation giving effect to European Community Directives, but the point was not determined by the higher court.

The position of the Church of Scotland is highly anomalous in terms of the traditional categorisation of churches. It is clearly an Established Church, yet the Church of Scotland Act 1921 gives it such a high degree of autonomy as almost to separate Church and State.

In England, the Establishment of the Church of England has a very different effect. The Church is closely bound up with the business of the State, many senior church appointments involving Crown patronage and a number of bishops sitting as of right in the House of Lords (though continuing debates as to the further reform of the House of Lords may lead to their removal). There can be no 'concordat' or treaty-like relationship between Church and State. The ecclesiastical law relating to the Church of England (including its Canon law) is regarded as an integral part of the law of England. Its continuity with the pre-Reformation church is recognised in the principle that a rule of pre-Reformation ecclesiastical law can be relied upon if it is proved to have been recognised, continued and acted upon in England since the Reformation; if that test is met, the rule is treated as part of the ecclesiastical common law of England.[11] From the 16th to the early 20th century, much legislation affecting the Church was passed in the usual way by Parliament.

The power to make changes in this body of law is now vested in the General Synod.[12] The Synod consists of three Houses, a House of Bishops (which has special powers in matters of doctrine), a House of Clergy[13] and a House of Laity, the two latter each comprising some 250 elected members. All three Houses must assent to any proposal; which means that the representatives of the laity have a full part in the making of Canon Law.

The Synod has power to pass Measures on any matter affecting the Church of England, and a Measure has the same effect as an Act of Parliament and can amend or repeal existing Acts. In effect, the Synod enjoys some of the powers otherwise reserved exclusively to

---

10 Percy v Church of Scotland Board of National Mission, 1995 SLT 1228 (in the Employment Appeal Tribunal).
11 See Lord Westbury in Bishop of Exeter v Marshall (1868) LR 3 HL 17.
12 Church of England Assembly (Powers) Act 1919; Synodical Government Measure 1969. The General Synod is the successor body to the Church Assembly created by the 1919 Act.
13 The House of Bishops and the House of Clergy are technically formed by the union of the Upper and Lower Houses of the ancient Convocations of Canterbury and York, which now meet separately only occasionally.

Parliament. Parliament retains some control: a Measure passed by the Synod can only be presented for the Royal Assent required to make it law if each House of Parliament resolves that this should be done; but while Parliament may (but very seldom does) reject a Measure it has no power to amend the text of a Measure. It is now recognised as a constitutional convention that legislation affecting the Church should be introduced into the General Synod and not into either House of Parliament.

The Canon Law of the Church of England is made by the Synod without reference to Parliament, though the formal promulgation of a new Canon requires the Royal Assent and Licence, a formal act expressing the Queen's position as Supreme Governor of the Church of England. The legal significance of this is that the Queen will not be advised to assent to a Canon if it would conflict with English law in a wider sense. It is often necessary, therefore, for the Synod to pass two types of legislation on the same topic: a Measure which removes any legal obstacle to the making of a proposed Canon, and then the Canon itself making the desired change.

No other Church in England (or, with the exception of the Church of Scotland, elsewhere in the United Kingdom) has anything which the State would recognise as 'ecclesiastical law'.

In the absence of a written Constitution there can no formal constitutional guarantees of religious freedom. However, the United Kingdom was one of the first signatories of the European Convention on Human Rights and effect was eventually given to that Convention as part of the domestic law of England by the Human Rights Act 1998. The effect of the 1998 Act was that the freedoms guaranteed by the Convention, including the freedom of thought, conscience and religion in Article 9, can be relied upon in the English courts which can make 'declarations of incompatibility', that a provision in primary legislation is incompatible with the Convention.[14] If such a declaration is made, corrective action can be taken by an order of a Government minister, but if the primary legislation in question is a Measure of the General Synod only the Synod can take the necessary action.

There is little doubt that even before the European Convention, there was a recognised right to religious freedom. One encyclopaedic work on the Law of England[15] asserts as follows:

---

14 Human Rights Act 1998, ss. 4, 21(1).
15 Halsbury's Laws of England, vol 14, para 339.

The civil power, while exercising complete control over all estates and degrees, whether ecclesiastical or temporal, and affording all necessary protection from wrongful acts, refrains from exercising any purely spiritual functions, and, save insofar as positive law may otherwise provide,[16] recognises and has always recognised the right of all to follow the dictates of their consciences in the religious opinion they hold.

IV. Legal Status of Religious Bodies

Another way of making that same point is to observe that the other churches, the Roman Catholic Church as well as the Protestant denominations, and other faiths, enjoy in general no greater rights than those enjoyed by any other form of voluntary organisation. Their Canon Law (if they use this term; most do not) has the status of a contract between their members. Property matters are generally managed through the 'trust', that ubiquitous device of English property law; but, especially in the larger churches where some complex division of functions is required as between national and local organs of the church, this may be supplemented by a private Act of Parliament.[17]

For the same sort of reason, there is no formal listing of churches 'recognised' as such by the State. Places of worship may be registered for a variety of purposes, mainly the solemnisation of marriages.[18] Nor has English law a fully-developed notion of public law status or rights; the notion of a church as a 'corporation under public law' is meaningless to the English lawyer.

There can, of course, be problems in determining whether a particular body does constitute a church. The Church of Scientology wished to register a building as a place of worship, but the Court of Appeal held that this involved the assembly of persons to worship God or to do reverence to a supreme being or deity; instruction in a secular philosophy was not sufficient.[19] A humanist body, the South Place Ethi-

---

16 A necessary qualification, given the absence of an over-riding Constitution.
17 A private Act is one promoted in Parliament by private petition; it is not printed in the annual collection of statutes.
18 Places of Worship Registration Act 1855.
19 R v Registrar-General, ex parte Segerdal [1970] 2 QB 697. Lord Denning recognised that Buddhism might be an exception; it was undoubtedly a religion, but whether or not its beliefs involved a Supreme Being was unclear; on that point see also Barralet v Attorney-General [1980] 3 All ER 918.

cal Society, was held for similar reasons not to be entitled to charitable status; it did not exist for the advancement of religion.[20] The Mormon church (the Church of Jesus Christ of Latter-Day Saints) would seem to qualify as a church, but its temple in England, which is only open to Mormons 'in good standing' especially recommended for the purpose, was held not to be a place of *public* religious worship for rating (local tax) purposes.[21]

The general position, therefore, is that the churches have the same rights as any other voluntary association to enter into contracts and hold property, to discipline their officers and members (using internal tribunals if they so wish), and to operate social welfare or other charitable (or indeed commercial) enterprises. There are some special provisions affecting all churches, noted in the material that follows; but paradoxically the privileged position of the Church of England as an Established Church compromises its autonomy in a number of respects.

One aspect of that has already been referred to, the existence of Parliamentary control over the exercise by the General Synod of its special powers of legislating on church matters. The Church obtained its special powers over legislation when the 'Life and Liberty Movement' persuaded the government of the day to pass the Church of England Assembly (Powers) Act 1919, commonly called the Enabling Act.

The scope of this Act was closely examined in the course of the legislation to allow women to be ordained to the priesthood passed by the General Synod in 1992. Opponents of women priests challenged the validity of the proposed legislation, seeking judicial review in the High Court on the ground that the Enabling Act did not in fact enable the Synod to do what it had done. The 1919 Act allows the Synod to make provision by Measure for any matter relating to the Church of England but it was argued that this must be interpreted to exclude any change in custom, practice or doctrine that could be regarded as 'fundamental'. The High Court refused to restrict the plain language of the 1919 Act in this way. As Mr Justice Tuckey put it, in passing the 1919 Act, Parliament had intended that the church should have the right to debate matters such as the ordination of women, legislate

---

20 Barralet v Attorney-General [1980] 3 All ER 918. Reforms in the law of charities, under consideration in 2003, may place greater emphasis on the need to prove actual benefit to the public, even in the case of religious and educational charities.
21 Church of Jesus Christ of Latter-Day Saints v Henning (Valuation Officer) [1963] 2 All ER 733 (HL).

its own affairs, and place them before Parliament for it either to approve or reject.[22]

A more controversial limitation on the freedom of the Church is the right of the Crown, the Queen acting on the advice of the Prime Minister, to appoint the archbishops and diocesan bishops of the Church of England. This power is now qualified by the agreement between the leaders of the Church and the then government in 1977 to restrict the field from which the Crown's choice could be made to those nominated by the Church.

The system is operated by a Crown Nominations Commission consisting of 14 people, the two archbishops, 3 clergy and 3 lay people elected by and from the General Synod and 6 people elected by the diocese concerned. Two officers, the Archbishops' Appointments Secretary and the Prime Minister's Appointments Secretary, serve as secretaries and conduct soundings in the diocese to complement the diocese's own statement of needs. The Commission sends two names to the Prime Minister and may indicate an order of preference. The Prime Minister decides which name to present to the Queen; he may not submit any other name, though he can chose either and can ask for more names, for example if one or both of the original nominees declines appointment. The role of the Prime Minister in this process is the subject of frequent criticism, and the introduction of an appointing commission for members of the House of Lords (the Prime Minister being bound by its recommendations) has led to fresh calls for reform. An idea often advanced is that the advice to the Crown as to the appointment of bishops should come not from the Prime Minister but from the archbishops, each of whom is ex officio a Privy Councillor.

V. Church and Culture

1. Schools

In England[23] schools are either 'maintained' (i.e. State) schools or independent (confusingly, they are often called 'Public Schools'). The

---

22 R v Ecclesiastical Committee of the Houses of Parliament, ex parte the Church Society, Queen's Bench Divisional Court, 28 October 1993.
23 Space prevents an account of the position in other parts of the United Kingdom.

churches were the main provider of education for many centuries, and many schools continue to have a church affiliation: within the category of maintained schools they are 'voluntary controlled' or 'voluntary aided' schools. In the latter group, the Church accepts responsibility for 15 per cent of the cost of any building works and has in return a stronger position on the school's board of managers.

In every maintained school the 'basic curriculum' includes religious education for all pupils[24] and a National Curriculum comprising a range of other subjects; religious education thus enjoys a special status. England has since 1870 had non-denominational religious education in its State schools. The construction of local 'agreed syllabuses' is governed by a complex procedure first introduced in 1944. A conference is convened made up of four committees, each of which must consent to the syllabus. The committees represent:

(a) the Church of England (except in relation to an area in Wales);
(b) such Christian and other religions as reflect the principal religious traditions of the area;
(c) teachers' associations;
(d) the local educational authority.[25]

This procedure gives the Church of England representatives the right of veto, but they cannot insist on any element in the syllabus unacceptable to the other groups, and cannot obtain anything approaching 'confessional' religious teaching. Every agreed syllabus must reflect the fact that the religious traditions in Great Britain are in the main Christian whilst taking account of the teaching and practices of the other principal religions represented in Great Britain.[26]

The School Standards and Framework Act 1998 contains provisions concerning the appointment of 'reserved teachers'. Where a voluntary (i.e. church) school has more than two teachers, the school must have at least one teacher appointed as competent to give religious education in accordance with the tenets of the church concerned; the numbers change with that of the total staff complement.[27] In non-denominational schools, however, it is expressly provided that religious opinions or attendance or non-attendance at religious worship may not affect appointment, salary or promotion as a teacher.[28] In

---

24 Education Act 2002, s. 80(1).
25 Education Act 1996, Sched. 31.
26 Education Act 1996, s. 375(3).
27 School Standards and Framework Act 1998, s. 58.
28 Ibid., s. 59.

appointing the head teacher of a voluntary or foundation school having 'a religious character' regard may be had to the appointee's 'ability and fitness to preserve and develop the religious character of the school'.[29] In voluntary aided schools, the appointment of any teacher may take into account religious opinions, observance and willingness to give religious education in accordance with the tenets of the church; and conduct incompatible with those tenets may be a ground for dismissal.[30]

The School Standards and Framework Act 1998 also contains provisions as to religious worship in maintained schools. All pupils must take part in an act of collective worship on each school day.[31] It must be 'of a broadly Christian character', but not distinctive of any particular Christian denomination. Not every act of worship need be Christian, as the social circumstances of some areas mean that a majority of pupils may be from other faiths; but a majority of acts of worship in any term must be.[32]

Churches are of course free to establish their own independent schools, and can use denominational forms of worship and conduct religious education in accordance with their own requirements. The churches have also made a major contribution to the training of teachers through church Colleges of Education. These are now reduced in number by a process of amalgamation (sometimes with non-Church colleges) but offer a range of higher education courses often in association with a university, and some have gained power to award their own degrees.

2. Universities

There are now no religious tests for entry into any University. There are however a number of posts in certain Theology Faculties, notably in Oxford and Durham, which are held with canonries of a Church of England cathedral church[33] and so are effectively restricted to Anglican priests. In other universities, the staff of theological faculties or departments are appointed under the usual university procedures with

---

29 Ibid., s. 60(4).
30 Ibid., s. 60(5).
31 Ibid, s. 70.
32 Ibid, Sched. 20, para. 3.
33 In Oxford the cathedral actually stands within a college of the University and serves as the college chapel; in Durham the ancient cathedral is in the physical heart of the University area.

no Church involvement; and indeed no religious allegiance is required.
Theological colleges provide ministerial training and, in some cases, other theological education (for example, distance learning programmes for lay students). Typically, a theological college is owned by a trust, but is subject to inspection by the church authorities which decide at which colleges clergy training may take place and the number of places to be taken up in this way. Increasingly, colleges are entering into relationships with local universities. The colleges remain independent (and most of the students receive no grant from State funds) but the relevant University may admit college students to its degree courses.

3. The Media

The British Broadcasting Corporation, the main public service broadcaster, has long taken a major interest in religious broadcasting. For example, a daily service is broadcast each weekday morning and there are regular periods of religious programming on television (as there are in the other television channels). Radio and television stations, national and local, have religious advisory committees on which the major churches in the relevant area will have representation. This is all a matter of practice, as is the involvement of the major cathedrals in local tourist agencies.
So far as licences for other radio, television and teletext operations are concerned, the Communications Act 2003 prohibits a body whose objects are wholly or mainly of a religious nature from being given certain types of licence (e.g., those for national sound broadcasting and public teletext services) and to allow such bodies to hold other licences only with the permission of the Office of Communications ('OFCOM') established by the Act. OFCOM is to produce guidelines indicating the criteria it will apply, but none have yet appeared.

VI. Labour Law within the Churches

Under English law, as in the legislation of the European Community, not all workers are employees; some are self-employed or in the category of 'office-holders'. To be an employee, the individual must be employed under a contract of employment; in the case-law, an employment situation is discerned by examining a whole series of factors, including method of recruitment, method of payment, and the way in which such matters as the provision of clothing or tools necessary for the work are arranged. Some office holders may well not be regarded as employed, and will therefore fall outside much employment law.[34]

Although some church personnel may be employees, parish clergy, of all churches, are regarded as 'office-holders' and not employees.[35] In particular circumstances the effect of classifying someone as an office-holder may be to give greater security of tenure because of the special requirements to be met before the office-holder can be removed from office. This can be illustrated by the position of many Anglican clergy, whose removal from office is very difficult to bring about. This is largely because the vicar of a parish holds 'the benefice', a legal concept which includes rights to the office and its stipend and to the house provided for its holder; this is regarded as a piece of property to which the vicar has freehold title and of which he cannot be deprived without due process of law, usually involving resort to the disciplinary procedures now set out in the Clergy Discipline Measure 2003. By way of contrast, those Anglican clergy who do not possess the freehold have much less security, a matter which has led to litigation,[36] and even a resolution of the European Parliament of 7 November 2001 calling on the Church of England to review the position. In other churches, the freehold concept does not exist, and there is more need to invoke the protection of the secular

---

[34] See Barthorpe v Exeter Diocesan Board of Finance [1979] I.C.R. 900 (Employment Appeal Tribunal).

[35] Re National Insurance Act 1911; re Employment of Church of England Curates [1912] 2 Ch 563; President of the Methodist Conference v Parfitt [1984] Q B 368 (CA); Davies v Presbyterian Church of Wales [1986] 1 WLR 323; Coker v Diocese of Southwark [1998] ICR 140 (CA). See P Petchey 'Ministers of Religion and Employment Rights: an Examination of the Issues' (2003) 7 Ecc.L.J. 157.

[36] See the well-known case of the Reverend Raymond Owen: in the English courts, R v Bishop of Stafford ex parte Owen High Court, QBD, unreported, 5 April 2000; Court of Appeal, unreported, 14 August 2000; and in the European Court of Human Rights: Owen v United Kingdom (app 37983/97), held inadmissible, 28 August 2001.

law and the issue as to employment of office-holding is more commonly raised in those churches.³⁷There have been similar decisions involving non-Christian bodies, one involving the *granthi* of a Sikh temple,³⁸ the other a rabbi.³⁹

Section 23 of the Employment Relations Act 1999 gave power to the Secretary of State for Trade and Industry to extend certain employment rights to 'atypical' workers, which includes ministers of religion. The rights concerned include defined leave entitlements, procedural safeguards such as a written statement of terms of service and of pay, access to dispute resolution procedures, and – most significantly – access to Employment Tribunals to claim unfair dismissal or breach of the other guaranteed rights. This power has not yet been exercised, but the churches were consulted during 2002; most argued that this was a matter for self-regulation. The Archbishops' Council of the Church of England acknowledged that, for some clergy, the Church's present arrangements did not provide sufficient safeguards against possible injustice, and that there was a need to review the balance between clergy rights and responsibilities, with possible implications for the freehold. The relevant law is now under review.

The churches at present enjoy certain exemptions from the scope of the legislation on sex discrimination. So, the Sex Discrimination Act 1975 (which also deals with gender reassignment cases) does not apply to employment 'for purposes of an organised religion where the employment is limited to one sex so as to comply with the doctrines of the religion or avoid offending the religious susceptibilities of a significant number of its followers'.⁴⁰ The scope of this exemption is being reviewed in the light of the amendments made to Council Directive 76/207/EEC on the implementation of the principle of equal treatment by European Parliament and Council Directive 2002/73/EC of 23 September 2002. Similar provisions apply in respect of discrimination on grounds of sexual orientation.⁴¹ It is not clear that these latter provisions are a correct application of Council Directive 2000/78/EC of 27 November 2000 establishing a general framework for equal treatment in employment.

One issue which has aroused some interest concerns the effect on employment of the religious obligations of individuals. It has been

---

37 President of the Methodist Conference v Parfitt [1984] QB 368 (CA); Davies v Presbyterian Church of Wales [1986] 1 WLR 323 (HL).
38 Santokh Singh v Guru Nanak Gurdwara [1990] ICR 309.
39 R v Jacobovits, ex parte Wachman, The Times, 8 January 1991.
40 Sex Discrimination Act 1975, s.19.
41 Employment Equality (Sexual Orientation) Regulations 2003, S.I. 2003 No. 1661, reg. 7(3).

held in a number of cases that it is not necessarily unfair to dismiss an employee whose religious obligations prevent his attendance when required by the terms of his contract. In a case involving a Muslim school teacher who absented himself for part of Friday to attend prayers in the mosque, it was held by a majority in the Court of Appeal that he had no right to such time off without loss of pay, as his employer's need to have him present at all times in the school day took precedence.[42] This type of case would now require consideration of the Employment Equality (Religion or Belief) Regulations 2003.[43]

VII. Matrimonial and Family Law

Throughout the United Kingdom, parties wishing to marry may do so either by a religious ceremony or by a secular ceremony conducted by a State-appointed registrar of marriages at a register office or some other location (such as a hotel) licensed for the purpose. In the case of weddings in the Church of England and the Church in Wales, the whole procedure including the preliminaries as to notices and licences, is carried out by the church. In other cases a religious ceremony requires certain civil preliminaries, usually the grant of a 'superintendent registrar's certificate' after notice has been given 21 days beforehand. In England (but not in Scotland where different rules apply) a non-Anglican religious ceremony must be held in a registered building (or, for historical reasons, a synagogue or a Meeting House of the Society of Friends) and registered either by the minister if he is authorised for the purpose or by a registrar of marriages. Government proposals may lead to radical reforms of English law, ensuring that in every case the preliminaries to marriage (advance notice, now often given by 'the calling of banns', announcements in the parish church on three Sundays) will be civil in nature, and possibly moving from the English practice of registered buildings to the Scottish model of approved officiants.

Although the Roman Catholic Church maintains its system of diocesan tribunals to hear nullity of marriage cases, the decisions of those tribunals have no legal status in United Kingdom law. The Anglican Consistory courts, which are part of the English legal system, have

---

42 Ahmad v Inner London Education Authority [1978] QB 36.
43 S.I. 2003 No. 1660 implementing Council Directive 2000/78/EC of 27 November 2000.

had no matrimonial jurisdiction since 1857 when the secular courts assumed this function. There is a matrimonial jurisdiction, equally denied direct recognition by English law, in the rabbinical courts. Provision was made to deal with some of the consequences of the existence of this jurisdiction in the Divorce (Religious Marriages) Act 2002. This sought to remedy the plight of some Jewish women who may have their marriages ended by a divorce in the civil courts but who find themselves in grave difficulty because the other spouse refuses to enter into the religious divorce procedure of a *get* from the rabbinical court. The Act enables the courts to issue an order that the civil divorce decree shall not be made absolute until both parties certify that the required religious procedures have been complied with.[44]
The churches, and especially the Church of England, are regularly consulted on family law matters. Any change in marriage law (for example relaxations in 1986 in the law as to affinity) is preceded by close consultation; in that case a Church report was prepared for and published by the Archbishop of Canterbury before the State acted.

VIII. Finances of the Churches

State financial support for the churches in the United Kingdom is extremely limited. They enjoy certain advantages in common with other charities, in respect of certain tax exemptions (but not, for example, from Value Added Tax) and by an arrangement under which certain gifts by individuals to the charity also transfer to the charity the income tax paid by the donor in respect of the sum given. However, there are no payments by the State in respect of clergy stipends or pensions or of the operating costs of the churches. Although the law requires Church of England clergy to conduct weddings and funerals and a fee is fixed by law, the payment of that fee is a matter for the parties and not the State.
The only State finance is in respect of the maintenance of historic buildings. This is a particular issue for the Church of England: some 13,000 of its 16,000 parish churches are 'listed' under the planning legislation, and 4,000 are in the highest grade, Grade I. In the case of redundant churches, grants may be made by the State to the Churches

---

44 Matrimonial Causes Act 1973, s.10A as inserted by the Divorce (Religious Marriages) Act 2002, s.1(1).

Conservation Trust under the Redundant Churches and Other Religious Buildings Act 1969. In recent years, the State grant has amounted to 70 % of the total funding. Since 1978, the State has, through an agency called English Heritage, made grants towards the repair of churches (and, recently, cathedrals) in use, and the funds available reached £30million for 2003-2004. The Government announced in 2002 that it hoped to reduce Value Added tax on repairs to listed churches from 17.5 % to 5 %. Although this was disallowed by the European authorities, the same effect has been achieved by making grants equivalent to the proposed saving. The amount of State money remains small compared with that from Church funds. In 1999 the parishes of the Church of England spent over £86million on major repairs to churches, and another £13million on major work to church halls and related buildings. Routine repairs cost another £20million.

IX. Religious Assistance to Public Institutions

The Armed Forces, the National Health Service, and the Prison Service all employ chaplains. They are recruited from the ordained clergy of the various denominations, and in the two latter cases most are part-time. Stipends for full-time chaplains (and fees in respect of part-time chaplains) are paid by the employing service; the churches have of course paid the costs of the initial training of the clergy and provide, in various forms, pastoral oversight of their work.

X. Criminal Law and Religion

It is a criminal offence to publish blasphemous material. That is material which attacks, without observing the decencies of controversy, the truth of the Christian religion or the existence of God. Prosecutions are rare, and controversial. In 1979, in the first case for 60 years, *Whitehouse v Gay News Ltd and Lemon*[45] it was held that

---

45 [1979] AC 617 (HL).

while the defendant had to intend to publish the material, he need not be shown to have intended to attack Christianity or to insult believers. Proposals for the abolition of the offence, and the substitution of an offence involving insulting language in places of worship, have been made by the Law Commission[46] but not acted upon. The pressure for reform increased after the decision of the Divisional Court in 1991 that blasphemy protected only Christianity and not other religions.[47]

In the context of terrorism, the Government proposed in 2001 to create an offence of incitement to religious hatred, but this was opposed in Parliament and did not appear in the eventual Anti-Terrorism, Crime and Security Act 2001. Similar proposals were made in a separate Bill in the House of Lords and that House established a Select Committee on Religious Offences which reported in April 2003. The report came to no clear recommendations, but having noted the important place of religion ('the United Kingdom is not a secular state') the Committee merely recorded its view that there should be a degree of protection of faith, equally available to all faiths, through both the civil and the criminal law.

XI. Legal Status of Clergy

It was formerly the case that certain of the clergy were unable to seek election to the House of Commons. The origins of this rule lay in the representation of the clergy in the Convocations of Canterbury and York rather than in Parliament, but after the union with Scotland it was put on a statutory basis. The House of Commons (Clergy Disqualification) Act 1801 barred 'persons having been ordained to the office of priest or deacon, or being a minister of the Church of Scotland'. This excluded not only the clergy of the Churches of England and of Scotland but also of other Anglican churches[48] and of the Roman Catholic Church.[49] After full consultation with the churches, the

---

46 Law Com. No. 79 1981.
47 R v Chief Metropolitan Magistrate, ex p Choudhury [1991] 1 All ER 306. The case involved The Satanic Verses by Salman Rushdie; the House of Lords refused leave to appeal.
48 Re MacManaway [1951] AC 161, concerning a priest of the Church of Ireland.
49 The exclusion of Roman Catholic clergy was expressly preserved by section 9 of the Roman Catholic Relief Act 1829 which removed the disqualification of Catholic laity to allow Daniel O'Connell to serve as the elected member for Co. Clare in Ireland.

Government secured the enactment of the House of Commons (Removal of Clergy Disqualification) Act 2001 which applied to the Parliament at Westminster the position which had already been accepted in respect of the Welsh Assembly and the Scottish Parliament.[50] All clergy are now eligible for election save the 'Lords Spiritual', the Anglican bishops who are members of the House of Lords. Those bishops cannot vote in elections for the House of Commons.

The clergy appear to enjoy no special privilege in respect of confessional secrets. This statement rests on very limited authority beyond obiter dicta and statements of writers, and is open to challenge in that the (Anglican) Canon Law, which is seen as part of the law of the land, contains a provision, the only part of the Canons adopted in 1603 still unrepealed, forbidding disclosure of such secrets 'except they be such crimes as by the laws of this realm his own life may be called into question for concealing the same', an exception which since the abolition of capital punishment for treason has no meaning.[51] It has been suggested that evidence of a confession to a priest might be excluded in a criminal trial as 'unfair' and in civil cases on account of the still-developing law as to confidentiality.[52]

Some disputes about the religious status of individuals may be held 'non-justiciable' as the courts are unwilling to enter into doctrinal disputes, whether arising in a Christian context[53] or that of another faith.[54] It is possible that the quality of the Canon Law of the Church of England as part of the law of the land may require different treatment of issues concerning that church.[55]

XII. Other Special Problems

There remain in England certain constitutional rules directed against Roman Catholics and designed to secure the Protestant succession to the Throne. The Sovereign is required to join in communion with the

---

50 Government of Wales Act 1998, s. 13(1)(b); Scotland Act 1998, s. 16(1)(b).
51 See *R Bursell*, 'The Seal of the Confessional' (1990) 2 Ecc LJ 84.
52 See *M Hill*, Ecclesiastical law (2nd ed., 2001), para 5.61.
53 Blake v Associated Newspapers Ltd [2003] EWHC 1960 (defamation action turning on validity of the plaintiff's consecration as a bishop).
54 R v Chief Rabbi ex p Wachmann [1992] 1 WLR 1036; Ali v Iman of Bury Park Jame Masjid, Luton (CA, The Times, 20 May 1993).
55 See the discussion in *M. Hill*, 'Judicial Approaches to Religious Disputes' in Law and Religion (ed *R O'Dair* and *A Lewis*), OUP 2001.

Church of England of which she is Supreme Governor, and anyone who becomes or who marries a Roman Catholic is excluded from succession to the Throne. These rules reflect historical events (and some residual popular prejudice) but do not hinder the close working relationship between the Catholic Church and the other churches, or between that Church and the State. A Papal Pro-Nuncio is accredited as part of the diplomatic corps, a situation which would have been unacceptable in past decades.

XIII. Bibliography

In recent years there has been a notable increase in the available literature. Books include:

R. H. Bursell, *Liturgy, Order and the Law* (Oxford University Press, 1996);
N. Doe, The Legal Framework of the Church of England, Oxford University Press, 1996;
N. Doe, *Canon Law in the Anglican Communion*, Oxford University Press, 1998;
M. Hill, *Ecclesiastical Law* (2nd ed), Oxford University Press, 2001;
L. Leeder, *Ecclesiastical Law Handbook*, Sweet and Maxwell, 1997;
E. G. Moore, *Introduction to English Canon Law* (ed T Briden and B J T Hanson), 3rd edn, Mowbray 1992;
English Canon Law: Essays in Honour of Bishop Eric Kemp (ed N Doe, M Hill and R Ombres), University of Wales Press, Cardiff, 1998;
Essays in Canon Law: a Study of the Law of the Church in Wales (ed N Doe), University of Wales Press, Cardiff, 1992;
Law and Religion (Current Legal Issues volume 4) (ed R O'Dair and A Lewis), Oxford University Press, 2001;
Legal Opinions Concerning the Church of England, Church House Publishing, 1994; new edition pending;

and valuable material is to be found in the dissertations submitted by candidates for the degree in Canon Law offered by Cardiff University and in the *Ecclesiastical Law Journal*, published since 1989 by the Ecclesiastical Law Society.

Gerhard Robbers
State and Church in the European Union

I. *Social and Historical Background*

There are few other areas of law in which historic experience, emotional ties and basic convictions have as direct an influence as in civil ecclesiastical law (the law as to Church and State). The diversity of the civil ecclesiastical law systems in the European Union mirrors the diversity of the national cultures and identities. New Member States add specific experiences and needs concerning religion. This being the case for all of these new Member States it is of special relevance in respect of former communist countries. State interference in and against religion, the role of religion in the transition process, and questions of restitution not only of property but also of public positions enrich the stock of historic experience.

On the other hand the different systems have common roots in the basic experiences of shared history. All the systems are based on the common background of Christianity. As can be said of European law in general, civil ecclesiastical law particularly is rooted in Christianity. At the same time, however, the contribution made by Islam and Judaism to European culture must not be forgotten. Both religions also are important factors of today in most of the Member States of the European Union to which civil ecclesiastical law must give adequate consideration. And finally there is a multitude of small religious communities, often linked with larger communities in other parts of the world, which forms a social factor in the structure of civil ecclesiastical law.

Statistical data in the Member States of the European Union differ strongly according to the basis of the inquiry and the social background; generally speaking there exist little more than plausible estimates. Thus in Germany the most important sources are the statistics on baptism and withdrawal from Church membership, in other States only those on baptism or the self-assessment of those questioned.

The following table will give a more or less adequate view of the situation:

Catholics	55,40 %
Protestants	13,40 %
Anglicans	6,70 %
Orthodox Christians	3,10 %
Muslims	2,90 %
Jews	0,30 %
other denominations and persons not belonging to a denomination	18,25 %

The differences between the civil ecclesiastical law systems go back mainly to the varying results of the Reformation and the ensuing Wars of Religion of the 16th and 17th centuries. Whereas some States, for instance Spain and Portugal, remained largely untouched by these events, the Reformation prevailed almost completely in other countries and sometimes established a system limited strictly to the existence of a State Church. The results were different again, though of no less consequence, in those countries where the different denominations co-existed and were of approximately equal strength, particularly in Germany and the Netherlands.

The continental European States have for the most part the common experience of absolutist State Church sovereignty in the 17th and 18th centuries. A number of the Member States of the European Union took part to various degrees and with differing consequences in the *Kulturkampf* at the end of the 19th century; its results are particularly evident in France today. Recent Muslim immigration raises new questions as to the law on religion throughout Europe

II. Types of Systems

In the European Union it is possible to differentiate between three basic types of civil ecclesiastical law systems. The first basic type is characterised by the existence of a State Church or predominant religion. In this system there are close links between State power and the existence of the Church. The systems of England, Denmark and Greece, Malta and Finland belong to this basic category. On the other hand there are systems founded on the idea of a strict separation of State and Church, for instance in France with the exception of the three eastern *départements*, and also in the Netherlands. There is to a great extent a legal separation in Ireland also. The third type features the basic separation of State and Church while simultaneously recognising a multitude of common tasks, in the fulfilment of which State and Church activity are linked: Belgium, Poland, Spain and Italy, Hungary, Austria, the Baltic States and Portugal belong to this group. In some of these states, agreements between state and religious communities play an important role, and therefore some speak of states with a covenantal system of state-church relations. However, the impact of such agreements must not be overestimated, important as they certainly are; it seems that they mirror a system of cooperation rather than they would establish it.

This classification according to legal and theoretical considerations is instantly overlaid and rendered questionable by social circumstances which suggest different groupings. The religious influence on the State in mainly Catholic Ireland is probably stronger and more direct than the wording of the constitutional provisions suggests. In the same way there would be a closer similarity in the social relevance of religion as between Greece, Spain and Italy than would be revealed in a comparison of Greece with Denmark or the United Kingdom.

Despite all the differences between the systems there does, however, seem to be a measure of convergence. In some countries the earlier anti-Church and anticlerical attitudes faded as the centuries passed and their legal consequences are being gradually reduced. Religious communities are given space for action and allowed greater freedom. Religion is acknowledged as an important element of social life; and, further, the conditions for meeting religious needs are created by the State. Often this follows from a more comprehensive understanding of the function of fundamental and human rights, according to which it is the task of the community positively to create the preconditions for human rights, and human rights are no longer held to be mere protective rights against State infringement. Finally it is generally acknowledged that, given a comprehensive support by the State of social activities, the religious communities may not be excluded from such support and so discriminated against.

On the other hand there are clear moves towards the disestablishment of the established churches. This may be exemplified by the power of decision which is increasingly being granted the General Synod of the Church of England. Sweden has to a very large extent cut the close ties between the State and the Lutheran Church.

There also is a general tendency towards acknowledging the right of self-determination of religious communities. Even if in some systems still strongly influenced by the tradition of a State Church the power of making final decisions on some genuinely religious questions remains with State bodies, those who do not wish to be subject to such a decision appear to be completely free to form their own independent communities. Religious freedom as an individual right is generally and completely recognised. Nowhere are there legal provisions as to what the individual must or must not believe.

Significant differences in the legal mode of existence of religious communities are immediately apparent. While in some systems the religious communities themselves, their associations and subdivisions are legal entities, other systems do without any legal classification of religious communities as such. Everywhere, however, legal instruments are provided to allow the religious communities to act in the legal system, even if only indirectly by way of *associations cultuelles* or *diocesaines* or trustees.

A Church right to self-determination in a stricter sense is also commonly found. A number of Constitutions expressly mention this right. However the extent to which this right is granted differs greatly. The right of self-determination may be accorded to all institutions which are quite remotely connected with the term "church" in the stricter sense of an official Church or synodical structures of government. It can on the other hand be limited to the official Church itself or similar institutions.

However, there seems to be a predominant tendency to recognise the relevance of special religious aspects in an adequate way. This is certainly true in cases falling within the principle, created for enterprises of a certain ideological leaning, under which the ideological tendency of an institution, be it political, social or religious, has special consequences for the employees' obligation of loyalty and the internal organisational structure of the institution. The incorporation of such needs is present in a more fundamental way in the idea of religious freedom, which expresses the special needs of churches and religious communities more directly and precisely.

III. Law on Religion in the European Union

1. Features of Development

Civil ecclesiastical law is enjoying growing attention by the law of the European Union. Whereas primary Community law completely excluded this area for a long time, new developments show striking awareness of the religious factor in the life of the Union. Former reluctance may be explained by the history of European unification, which was at first conceived and executed as a primarily economic process. From the start, however, it was intended to anchor European legal ideas in a common European culture and in the cultures of the Member States. The economic unification of Europe is now far advanced; important new impulses are hardly to be expected from it anymore. The draft Constitution for Europe and the European Charta of Human Rights to be included in the new Constitution give evidence of this new level of European integration.

Since the signing of the Treaty on European Union of 7 February 1992, the extended scope of unification and its intensification through cultural and social components had become evident. Its scope now extends to areas which directly concern the churches. Art. 2 EC states that the amelioration of the quality of life is a task of the European Community. It is also to take action towards developing cultural life in the Member States and contributes toward general and professional education of a high standard. This wording clarifies for civil ecclesiastical law also what had gone largely unnoticed for a long time: the competence of the European Union in matters of education and culture, in economic and labour law, in tax and social law today directly or indirectly concern the churches, as well. Even though the Charter of Fundamental Rights of the European Union has not yet gained complete legally binding force its provisions do have legal impact. No legal act in European Union Law can pass by its guarantees in fact.

2. Basic Structures

Basic structures of a European law on religion are now evident. It finds its basis, first of all, in religious freedom as an element of Community law. Further structural principles are the obligation of the Union to remain neutral in questions of religion and philosophy, to show tolerance towards different religions and philosophies, to grant equal treatment to religious communities. The safeguard of the cultures of the Member States and their national identity according to Art. 6 sec. 3 EU requires special respect towards traditionally developed institutions of civil ecclesiastical law in the Member States. The principle of Community loyalty in the form of respect for the constitutional structure of Member States prohibits unilateral assimilation of the law where these matters are concerned. Finally the principle of subsidiarity according to Art. 5 EC requires a reticence on the part of the EU with regard to questions of the law on religion.

Secondary Community law also respects religious needs. Apart from the Statute on Community Officials, there are attempts to approach the problem in the Television Directive. According to this, transmissions of Church services or religious programmes of a scheduled duration of transmission of less than thirty minutes must not be interrupted by advertising spots (Art. 11 sect 5). Television advertising must not injure religious feelings (Art. 12 c).[1] Of major impact on the churches' right of self determination is Art. 4 of the directive concerning equal treatment in employment and occupation.[2]

3. Case Law

The European Court of Justice had first acknowledged the fundamental right to religious freedom at least in its core in the decision of *Prais v. Council* of 1976,[3] providing for basic respect of religious needs.

---

1 Dir 89/552/EEC.
2 Council Directive 2000/78/EC of 27 November 2000 establishing a general framework for equal treatment in employment and occupation. Art. 4 provides:
Occupational requirements
1. ...
2. Member States may maintain national legislation in force at the date of adoption of this Directive or provide for future legislation incorporating national practices existing at the date of adoption of this Directive pursuant to which, in the case of occupational activities within churches and other public or private organisations the ethos of which is based on religion or belief, a difference of treatment based on a person's religion or belief shall not constitute discrimination where, by reason of the nature of these activities or of the context in which they are carried out, a person's religion or belief constitute a genuine, legitimate and justified occupational requirement, having regard to the organisation's ethos. This difference of treatment shall be implemented taking account of Member States' constitutional provisions and principles, as well as the general principles of Community law, and should not justify discrimination on another ground.
Provided that its provisions are otherwise complied with, this Directive shall thus not prejudice the right of churches and other public or private organisations, the ethos of which is based on religion or belief, acting in conformity with national constitutions and laws, to require individuals working for them to act in good faith and with loyalty to the organisation's ethos.
3 Case 130/75, [1976] ECR, p. 1589, compare *Alexander Hollerbach*, Europa und das Staatskirchenrecht, ZevkR 35 (1990), p. 263; *Ingolf Pernice*, Religionsrechtliche Aspekte im Europäischen Gemeinschaftsrecht, JZ 1977, p. 777.

In other contexts the European Court of Justice has also had the opportunity of making decisions relevant to the churches. The *Baghwan* case[4] of 1988 states that remunerated labour and services in the context of the economic activity of the religious community can form part of economic life within the meaning of the EC.

The difficulties Community law has had in dealing with the special characteristics of Church existence became particularly clear in the case of *van Rosmaalen v. Bestuir van de Betrijfsvereinigingen.*[5] Van Rosmaalen, a Premonstratensian priest and missionary in Zaire, had for some decades been maintained by the members of his missionary community rather than by his order, and the European Court of Justice therefore held the priest to be self-employed in the sense intended by Community law, so that he received a pension according to the laws of the Member State. This decision had provided particularly clearly that the categories of Community law for a long time were hardly able to deal adequately with Church circumstances, even if the European Court of Justice reached an appropriate decision in the particular case. It has at the same time, however, underlined the need for explicit provisions on religion within the framework of Community Law thus supporting the cause for an open and conscious approach towards the religious sphere.

4. Underlying Structures

The Churches' right to self-determination finds a first means of support in religious freedom. The European Court of Justice has acknowledged it. According to Art. 6 sec. 2 EU the Union respects the fundamental rights as they are guaranteed by the ECHR and as they may be derived from the common constitutional tradition of the Member States as a general principle of Community law.

Art. 9 ECHR protects the freedom of religion as a right of the individual and of communities. Churches and religious communities have a right of complaint in their own right before the bodies of the ECHR which are charged with giving legal redress if they can claim to be injured in their rights under Art. 9 ECHR.

A restriction on the action of Community law in matters of the law of religion in the Member States of the European Union is formed in particular by the principle of subsidiarity. Art. 5 EC provides that the

---

4 Case 196/87 [1988] ECR p. 6159.
5 Case 300/84 [1986] ECR p. 3097.

Community, according to the principle of subsidiarity, takes action only if and insofar as the goals of the intended measures cannot adequately be achieved at the level of the Member States and so because of their scale or their effects may be achieved better at Community level. In the area of religious matters a better achievement of goals usually means that the needs of historically developed religious beliefs determined by national and regional circumstances, emotional ties and historic experience must be given space. In consequence, the realisation of goals in these matters may be achieved at the level of the Member States and their subdivisions, not however at Community level.

Art. 6 sec. 3 EU obliges the Union to respect the national identity of its Member States. The variety of the religious circumstances and their legal treatment in the Member States of the European Union shows how great the formative influence of the churches on the national identity of the Member States is. History, culture and tradition of the Member States are always influenced by the system of civil ecclesiastical law.

The idea of common constitutional traditions of the Member States still forms a basis for the development of religious law structures in Community law in other matters apart from those of human rights. The contributions in this book clearly show that such common Constitutional traditions exist to a great extent. Everywhere religious freedom is recognised, everywhere the churches possess institutional independence. That is true even where the system includes a State Church, at least for those religious communities in the Member State which are not State churches. It is clear that for instance in labour law the churches' religious conception of themselves as an employer must be taken into consideration. Art. 151 EC confers responsibility for the protection of cultural variety upon the Community. The law of State and Church is indeed a part of this culture. According to Art. 151 EC the Community itself contributes to the development of the cultures of the Member States while safeguarding their national and regional diversity. In this, the common cultural heritage of Europe is emphasised. This also and especially points to the religious roots and traditions of Europe. Art. 151 EC is however based on a restricted understanding of culture. Cultural competences refer to research and education, to general and professional education, to artistic and literary creation, to the protection of historic monuments, literature, architecture and the mass media. Competences of the Community may be derived from Art. 149 EC for the area of professional and general education. In this way all Church educational in-

stitutions such as private schools, theological faculties and Church academies and not least religious education classes benefit from support according to Community law. Art. 149 EC at the same time strictly excludes any harmonisation of legal or administrative provisions of the Member States. The Community promotes and recommends, supports and complements the activity and co-operation of the Member States, as far as this is necessary.
According to Art. 307 EC the rights and obligations created by treaties concluded between a Member State and a third State before the Treaty came into force are not affected by the Treaty. Insofar as the agreements are not compatible with the EC the Member States are obliged to remedy these incompatibilities, if necessary by re-negotiation. According to Art. 300 EC the European Community can conclude treaties with other States. According to the *ratio legis*, this also applies to the Holy See as a subject of international law. Because of the Community law principle of equal treatment of all religious communities, similar contractual relationships may be entered into with other religious communities. Because of their lack of legal status in international law, this does not result directly from Art. 300 EC, but from Art. 308 EC in connection with Art. 300, 282 EC as well as the general principle of equality. The clearer the implications of Community law for the position of the religious communities become, the more it becomes reasonable to take this possibility of contractual regulation into consideration.

IV. *The Constitution for Europe*

The draft Constitution for Europe is fully facing the question of religion. The reference in the preamble to the religious inheritance is not directly linked to the question of state church relations. However, in indicating that Europe will continue on the path of civilisation directly after the reference to the religious inheritance the constitution implicitly refers to the important function of religious communities within this kind of civilisation.
In broadly acknowledging fundamental rights in Art. I-7 the constitution refers also to religiously relevant fundamental rights within the Charta of Fundamental Rights, the European Convention of Human Rights, and as they stand as common constitutional traditions of the Member States.

Of particular relevance is Art. I-52 concerning the status of churches and religious communities. It reads:

> 1. The Union respects and does not prejudice the status under national law of churches and religious associations or communities in the Member States.
>
> 2. The Union equally respects the status of philosophical and non-confessional organisations.
>
> 3. Recognising their identity and their specific contribution, the Union shall maintain an open, transparent and regular dialogue with these churches and organisations.

Art. I-52 sec. 1 and 2 originates from the Declaration No. 11 of the Final Act of the Treaty of Amsterdam. The question of the legal relevance of this declaration is thus solved; it becomes directly binding constitutional law. Art. I-52 is an expression of the existing neutrality of the European Union in religious and philosophical matters. This neutrality according to the wording of the provision relates to the Member States' law on religion; indirectly this neutrality also relates to churches, religious and philosophical communities.

The provision acknowledges churches as factors within community law. It respects the competence of the Member States in the field of religion. Whenever the European institutions exercise their competences they must respect and not prejudice the Member States' law on religion within the scope of European Union law. Because of the principle of unity of the European Constitution the institutions are bound also by the other provisions of European constitutional law. This gives an impact of e.g. freedom of religion, equality, non-discrimination and democracy in this field.

Art. I-52 does not perpetuate state church relations within the Member States. They are completely free in developing these relations. It is the status of churches and religious communities as it stands at the respective time that has to be respected.

Art. I-52 sec. 3 provides for a dialogue between the European Union and all of its institutions with those churches and religious communities. The dialogue will have to be developed in full respect of the identities, special needs and relevance of the religious entities. This includes the possibility of concluding agreements with them. The dialogue must be open, transparent and regular. In acknowledging the special contribution of those churches and communities the constitution does in fact acknowledge their spiritual, social, and cultural contribution. However, it also acknowledges openly the impact of Christianity on the existing European Constitution without disregarding the contributions of other religions and philosophies. By explicitly using the term churches special reference is being made to Christianity, this term being an exclusively Christian term. The intense public debate about an explicit reference to Christianity in the preamble thus seems to have been somewhat overexcited. Art. I-52 carries interesting parallels and differences in relation to Art. I-47. The latter provision relates to an open, transparent and regular dialogue with the representative institutions of the civil society. The dialogue with churches, religious and philosophical communities is based on similar principles as is the dialogue with institutions of the civil society. Churches and similar communities must not be placed in a worse position. By giving them a special place in the constitution the Union recognises that churches, religious and philosophical communities are not a mere part of civil society. On the contrary, the constitution acknowledges the special contribution and the specific identities of these churches, religious and philosophical communities.

Churches, religious and philosophical communities are relevant and suitable partners for hearings according to Art. I-47 sec. 3, and a relevant number of citizens of the Union can initiate a referendum also in religiously relevant matters according to Art. I-47 sec. 4.

The Charta of Fundamental Rights guarantees freedom of religion in Art. II-70 in the same wording and basically the same meaning as does Art. 9 ECHR. Since the provision on restrictions to fundamental rights according to Art. II-112 are somewhat stricter than Art. 9 sec. 2 ECHR Art. II-112 sec. 3 is of particular relevance: restrictions to freedom of religion according to Art. II-70 can be based on Art. 9 sec. 2 ECHR only, further limitations do not apply.

Art. II-81 prohibits discriminations on grounds of religion or belief. The Union respects the multitude of cultures, religions and languages according to Art. II-82.

European unification in its very existence must depend on the churches if it wishes to give the necessary anchoring in culture, in tradition and history a secure long-term future. Such culture is based on autonomy and self-determination. Community law must not monopolise the religious communities, it must not eradicate the differences between them. Anything else would provoke the opposition of the churches, would endanger European unification, because internal disagreements would create fronts the destructive energy of which the otherwise mainly economic unity would not be able to counteract with anything substantial.[6]

V. Bibliography

Jean Baubérot (ed.), Religions et Laïcité dans l'Europe des Douze, 1994.
Consortio Europeo di Ricerca Sui Rapporti tra Stati e Confessioni Religiose (ed.), Stati e confessioni religiose in Europa, modelli di finanziamento publico, scuola e fattore religioso, 1992.
Consortium européen pour l'étude des relations Eglises-Etat (ed.), Le statut des confessions religieuses des Etats candidats à L'Union européenne, 2002.
Consortio Europeo di Ricerca Sui Rapporti tra Stati e Confessioni Religiose (ed.),Cittadini e fideli nei Paesi dell'Unione Europea, 1998.
Cole W. Durham/Silvio Ferrari (ed.), Laws on Religion and the State in Post-Communist Europe, 2004.
Norman Doe (ed.), The Portrayal of Religion in Europe: the Media and the Arts, 2004.
European Consortium for Church and State Research (ed.), Churches and Labour Law in the EC Countries, 1993.
European Consortium for Church and State Research (ed.), The Legal Status of Religious Minorities in the Countries of the European Union, 1994.
European Consortium for Church and State Research (ed.), Religions in European Union Law, 1996.
Silvio Ferrari/Iván C. Ibán, Diritto e religione in Europa occidentale, 1997.
Silvio Ferrari/Cole W. Durham (ed.), Law and Religion in Post Communist Europe, 2004.
Alexander Hollerbach, Europa und das Staatskirchenrecht, in: Zeitschrift für evangelisches Kirchenrecht 35 (1990), p. 263.
Stefan Mückl, Religions- und Weltanschauungsfreiheit im Europarecht, Schriften der philosophisch-historischen Klasse der Heidelberger Akademie der Wissenschaften, vol. 24, 2002.
Peter-Christian Müller-Graff/Heinrich Schneider (ed.), Kirchen und Religionsgemeinschaften in der Europäischen Union, 1. ed., 2003.
Richard Potz/Wolfgang Wieshaider (ed.), Islam and the European Union, 2004.

---

6 See *Gerhard Robbers*, Die Fortentwicklung des Europarechts und seine Auswirkungen auf die Beziehungen zwischen Staat und Kirche in der Bundesrepublik Deutschland, in: Essener Gespräche zum Thema Staat und Kirche (27), ed. by *Heribert Heinemann and Heiner Marré*, Münster 1993, p. 81.

Gerhard Robbers, Die Fortentwicklung des Europarechts und seine Auswirkungen auf die Beziehungen zwischen Staat und Kirche in der Bundesrepublik Deutschland, in: Essener Gespräche zum Thema Staat und Kirche (27), *Heribert Heinemann* und *Heiner Marré* (ed.), 1993.

Gerhard Robbers, Europarecht und Kirchen, in: *Joseph Listl/Dietrich Pirson* (ed.), Handbuch des Staatskirchenrechts der Bundesrepublik Deutschland, 2. Aufl. 1994, p. 315.

Gerhard Robbers (ed.), Religion-Related Norms in European Union Law, Institut für europäisches Verfassungsrecht, Trier 2001 (as of: 2003).

Gerhard Robbers, Community Law on Religion. Cases, Sources and Trends, in: European Journal for Church-State Research 2001 (Vol. 8).

Michał Rynkowski, Status prwany kościołów I związków wyznaniowych w Unii Europejskiej, 2004.

Marco Ventura, La Laicità dell'Unione Europea. Diritti, Mercato, Religione, Collana di studi di diritto canonico ed ecclesiastico, 2001.